WHAT LAWYERS DO

UNDERSTANDING THE MANY AMERICAN LEGAL PRACTICES

■ ■ ■

Catherine L. Fisk
Barbara Nachtrieb Armstrong Professor of Law
University of California, Berkeley

Ann Southworth
Professor of Law & Founding Faculty Member
University of California, Irvine, School of Law

AMERICAN CASEBOOK SERIES®

WEST ACADEMIC PUBLISHING

444 Cedar Street, Suite 700
St. Paul, MN 55101
1-877-888-1330

Printed in the United States of America

ISBN: 978-1-64242-611-3

For my family.

CLF

For John, Amy, and Ben.

AS

ACKNOWLEDGMENTS

This book draws inspiration from other scholars and teachers too numerous to mention by name. It is an outgrowth of a rich and continuing conversation about what universities should do to educate students to become knowledgeable and reflective about the legal profession. Our students, our colleagues, and the many lawyers and scholars who participated in our course over the past ten years, have helped us immeasurably as we have worked to translate an abstract proposition about the interconnectedness of professional identity, legal institutions, and the varied forms of legal practice, into a set of teaching materials.

We are grateful to the many authors and publishers who have given us permission to reprint their copyrighted work. UC Irvine's law librarians, especially Dianna Sahar, and several of our students, Sasha Nichols, Aaron Benmark, Dion Diederich, and Quiyarra McCahey, provided superb research assistance. Rick Abel, Sameer Ashar, Swethaa Ballakrishnen, Susan Carle, Scott Cummings, Bryant Garth, Robert Gordon, Clare Pastore, Cassandra Burke Robertson, Carole Silver, Beatrice Tice, and Benjamin van Rooij, as well as anonymous reviewers of earlier versions of this manuscript, gave us many excellent suggestions. Nicola McCoy and Pedro Aguilar devoted countless hours to a multitude of tasks required to prepare this manuscript for publication.

In editing excerpts of articles, books, and cases, we have omitted some textual material without ellipses, and we have omitted most footnotes and citations without notation, in order to manage the book's length and promote its readability.

SUMMARY OF CONTENTS

PART II. A SURVEY OF PRACTICE SETTINGS/TYPES

SUBPART A. CRIMINAL PRACTICE

SUBPART B. LARGE ORGANIZATIONAL CLIENTS

TABLE OF CONTENTS

SUBPART B. LARGE ORGANIZATIONAL CLIENTS

SUBPART D. LAWYERS AND THE PRACTICE OF DISPUTE RESOLUTION

SUBPART E. PUBLIC INTEREST PRACTICE

TABLE OF CASES

What Lawyers Do

UNDERSTANDING THE MANY AMERICAN LEGAL PRACTICES

PART I

AN INTRODUCTION TO THE AMERICAN LEGAL PROFESSION

■ ■ ■

This book is designed to introduce you to the variety of practice settings in which lawyers work and the professional opportunities and challenges of each. It will also teach you about the enormous legal, cultural, and economic forces that are reshaping the legal profession.

This book is divided into three units. Part I introduces the concept of a profession, the legal profession's history and demographics, competing conceptions of the lawyer's role, diversity in the profession, and whether and how personal identity does or should influence a lawyer's professional life. Part II explores the many different types of practice settings in which lawyers work and issues of professionalism as they arise in those types of practice. Part III addresses issues facing the entire profession, including access to justice, the profession's relationship to the market for legal services, competition for regulatory control, technology's influence on practice, globalization, legal education, bar admission and discipline, lawyer satisfaction and well-being, and the legal profession's future.

A. THE ROLE OF THE LAWYER AND THE LEGAL PROFESSION

Students typically arrive at law school with some ideas about what they might want to do with a law degree. Perhaps there are causes they would like to advance, or maybe they think instead in terms of providing excellent service to particular types of clients. All students come with a set of values, attributes, and political commitments that comprise their personal identity—perhaps tied in some way to where they come from, social background, parents' expectations, prior experiences, religion, race, ethnicity, gender, and/or sexual orientation. At the same time, students are entering a profession with its own history and a set of institutions and practices that may be relevant to the search for an attractive future within it. In addition, one's conduct as a lawyer will be constrained by various sources of law and regulation and by work-related pressures that lawyers need to navigate. One of new lawyers' challenges lies in finding ways to reconcile their sense of justice and personal identity with professional aspirations, legal duties, workplace norms, and the expectations of clients and other participants in the legal system.

Nothing in law itself will tell lawyers how to accomplish that. Indeed, the law will not answer many of the most critical questions that aspiring lawyers confront as they seek a satisfying career in the legal profession—including what practice areas to pursue and what types of clients to represent, how to resolve tensions and sometimes outright conflicts between the pressures of practice and one's moral compass, and when and how to express personal identity in professional life. One of the purposes of this book is to provide some of the information and tools that new lawyers need to navigate a professional life that is consistent with their values and sense of self.

This Part introduces those issues and offers some perspectives on how one might address them. Chapter 1 introduces the role of the lawyer as a professional and considers why lawyers generally believe they should be bound by ethical rules that differ from those that govern the conduct of nonlawyers. Chapter 2 provides an overview of the profession's history, demographics and institutions, and explores what people mean when they refer to lawyers as a profession and to certain types of lawyer conduct as "professional" or "unprofessional." Chapter 3 examines and evaluates different conceptions of lawyers' roles—their responsibilities to clients, third parties, and the public. Chapter 4 addresses diversity in the profession, and Chapter 5 considers whether and how a lawyer's background, experience, political values, and identity traits do or should influence a lawyer's professional life.

CHAPTER 1

THE ROLE OF THE LAWYER

■ ■ ■

A. INTRODUCTION TO THE ROLE OF THE LAWYER

Most lawyers share a fundamental belief that their role as lawyers legally and ethically obligates them to engage in some behavior that might not be permissible if they were acting in a capacity other than as a lawyer. That belief underlies a great deal of the law governing lawyers. More significant, many lawyers are guided in their daily work by the notion that a lawyer's role requires or prohibits certain types of behavior. The notion is reflected not just in the law governing lawyers (such as formal rules of legal ethics) but in the ways that lawyers relate to their clients and to third parties and in the implicit norms governing law offices. In this chapter we begin to consider the lawyer's role. In particular, we focus on the question of whether and how the legal and moral responsibilities of lawyers differ from those of non-lawyers. We begin with a problem based on a classic case about whether a lawyer's duties to her client compel her to keep confidential information that she would almost certainly feel morally obligated to disclose if she were acting in a capacity other than as a lawyer. We then read an excerpt of an influential article by a legal philosopher explaining and critiquing the idea that the lawyer's role allows lawyers to behave under different ethical norms than should govern non-lawyers.

B. ARE LEGAL ETHICS DIFFERENT FROM OTHER ETHICS?

Why do lawyers believe they owe special duties to their clients that do not conform with ordinary ethics? Besides the rules of professional responsibility, what norms, market pressures, and other sources of guidance influence how lawyers behave in their role as lawyers? If you found yourself in the situation confronting each of the lawyers and clients in the case below, what would you do?

PROBLEM 1-1: THE CASE OF SPAULDING V. ZIMMERMAN, *263 MINN. 346 (MINNESOTA SUPREME COURT 1962)*[1]

David Spaulding, age 20, was injured in an automobile accident in 1956. The accident involved two cars at a rural crossroads late in the day. David was riding to the county fair with five others in a car driven by Florian Ledermann, age 15, who was driving on a farm permit. Florian's sister, Elaine, was killed in the accident, and many others, including David, were seriously injured. In the other car, John Zimmerman, age 19, was driving himself and four friends and family members home from their jobs at the Zimmerman family's small business. Passengers in that car also died and were seriously injured. Because children of both the Ledermann and the Zimmerman families were injured and killed, the families were both plaintiffs and defendants in the litigation.

After the accident, David was examined by his family physician, Dr. James Cain, who diagnosed a severe chest injury with multiple rib and clavicle fractures and a concussion and hemorrhages of the brain. At Dr. Cain's suggestion, David was examined by Dr. John Pohl, an orthopedic specialist, who took X-rays of his chest. Dr. Pohl made a detailed report which stated, among other things: "The lung fields are clear. The heart and aorta are normal." The report did not indicate that David was suffering an aortic aneurysm, although in fact he was. At the suggestion of Dr. Pohl, David received a neurological examination by Dr. Paul Blake, who also did not find the aortic aneurysm.

In the meantime, at defendants' request, David was examined by Dr. Hewitt Hannah, a neurologist. It is customary in civil litigation involving claims for a plaintiff's personal injury for defendants to retain their own doctor to examine the plaintiff to assess the nature and extent of the injury. Dr. Hannah reported to attorneys for defendant Zimmerman that:

> "The one feature of the case which bothers me more than any other part of the case is the fact that this boy of 20 years of age has an aneurysm, which means a dilatation of the aorta and the arch of the aorta. Whether this came out of this accident I cannot say with any degree of certainty. Of course an aneurysm or dilatation of the aorta in a boy of this age is a serious matter as far as his life. This aneurysm may dilate further and it might rupture with further dilatation and this would cause his death.
>
> "It would be interesting also to know whether the X-ray of his lungs, taken immediately following the accident, shows this dilatation or not. If it was not present immediately following the accident and is now present, then we could be sure that it came out of the accident."

---

[1] The facts stated here and in the notes following Problem 1-1 are drawn from the Minnesota Supreme Court's opinion and from an article about the case written by two law professors who interviewed the surviving participants. Roger C. Cramton & Lori P. Knowles, *Professional Secrecy and Its Exceptions:* Spaulding v. Zimmerman *Revisited,* 83 MINN. L. REV. 63 (1998). *See also* Roger Cramton, Spaulding v. Zimmerman: *Confidentiality and its Exceptions,* in LEGAL ETHICS: LAW STORIES (Deborah L. Rhode & David Luban, eds., 2006).

Neither David nor his father was aware that David had the aortic aneurysm. They believed that he was recovering from the injuries sustained in the accident. After the medical examinations, lawyers for David and for the defendants agreed that for $6,500 David and his father would settle all claims arising out of the accident.

After the parties agreed to settle the case, David's lawyer presented to the court a petition for approval of the settlement. The petition, which included affidavits from David's doctors, described David's injuries as found by Dr. Cain. The defendants did not present any evidence and, based on David's petition, the court approved the settlement and dismissed the case.

Two years later, David was examined again by Dr. Cain as part of a checkup required by the Army reserve. This time, Dr. Cain discovered the aortic aneurysm. He re-examined the X-rays which had been taken shortly after the accident and at this time discovered that they disclosed the beginning of the process which produced the aneurysm. He promptly sent David to another doctor who confirmed the finding of the aortic aneurysm and immediately performed surgery to repair it. The surgery saved David's life, but it caused him to lose the ability to speak.

Shortly thereafter, David filed a suit seeking to vacate the settlement and to reopen the case. David alleged that the aortic aneurysm was caused by the accident and, therefore, that his damages were greater than he had believed at the time the suit was settled.

The trial court vacated the settlement and the Minnesota Supreme Court affirmed. Their reasoning rested on three crucial points. First, the courts emphasized that the mistake concerning the existence of the aneurysm and, therefore, the extent of David's injuries was not mutual. For unknown reasons, David's lawyer failed to use the procedures available in civil litigation that enable each party to discover the facts known to the other party before the case goes to trial or is settled.

Second, the Minnesota Supreme Court said: "That defendants' counsel concealed the knowledge they had is not disputed. The issue is the character of the concealment. Was it done under circumstances that defendants must be charged with knowledge that plaintiff did not know of the injury? If so, an enriching advantage was gained for defendants at plaintiff's expense. There is no doubt of the good faith of both defendants' counsel. There is no doubt that during the course of the negotiations, when the parties were in an adversary relationship, no rule required or duty rested upon defendants or their representatives to disclose this knowledge."

Third, although the Minnesota Supreme Court determined that the defendants had no obligation to reveal their medical evidence to the plaintiffs in the absence of a request through the mechanisms of pretrial discovery, the court stated, "once the agreement to settle was reached, it is difficult to characterize the parties' relationship as adverse. At this point all parties were interested in securing court approval." The court then said that "to hold that the concealment was not of such character as to result in an unconscionable advantage over plaintiff's ignorance or mistake, would be to penalize innocence and incompetence and reward less than full performance of an officer of the court's duty to make full disclosure to the court when applying for approval in minor settlement proceedings." Yet the court also stated: "While no canon of ethics or legal obligation may have required them to inform plaintiff or his counsel with respect [to their medical evidence], or to advise the court therein, it did become obvious to them at the time, that the settlement then made did not contemplate or take into consideration the disability described."

NOTES ON SPAULDING V. ZIMMERMAN

1. ***What Would You Do?*** If you knew someone was suffering a life-threatening condition and you knew that he did not know, would you consider yourself morally obligated to tell him to enable him to get medical care that might save his life? If you believe you would have a moral obligation to tell him, why (if at all) should a lawyer not have the same obligation? The most important question the *Spaulding* case asks you to consider is what aspects of the lawyer's role prompted the defendants' lawyers to say nothing to David Spaulding about his condition if, as non-lawyers, they would certainly have told him.

2. ***What Did David's Lawyer Do Wrong?*** David Spaulding's lawyer owed David competent representation. Ordinarily, it would seem to be incompetent to settle a personal injury case without first obtaining the defense evidence about the extent of the plaintiff's injuries, and Dr. Hannah's report was available to David through a routine discovery request. David's lawyer was young and inexperienced, which may partly explain why he did not request a copy of Dr. Hannah's report. But the lawyer may also have feared that if he requested the defense doctor's report, the defense would request the reports of David's physicians, one of which recommended waiting to settle the case until the full extent of David's injuries became known. Apparently both families wanted to settle the case quickly, so David's lawyer may have feared that a court would not approve a settlement if David's doctor recommended waiting. If David's lawyer made a strategic calculation rather than an ignorant blunder in failing to request Dr. Hannah's report, would your decision about whether to allow David to reopen the case change? Why should clients be bound by the strategic (or simply stupid) choices of their lawyers?

3. ***What Is Sound Advice?*** Did counsel for the defendants serve their clients well? The two lawyers representing the Zimmerman defendants never informed their clients about David's aneurysm; they apparently made the decision not to disclose without consulting either the Zimmermans or the insurance company that was paying them. Although the duty of confidentiality prohibited them from disclosing David's injury without a discovery request or client consent, nothing in the rule would have discouraged them from seeking consent to disclose or counseling the Zimmermans and the insurance company about the full range of options. Indeed, the rules of ethics encourage lawyers to keep clients informed and to consult with clients in making important

decisions. Why do you imagine the lawyers did not discuss disclosure of the aneurysm with their clients?

Some empirical literature suggests that lawyers wrongly tend to assume their clients are governed only by selfish concerns and prefer their own financial interests over the interests of others. But clients often want a helpful counselor and may be more concerned about the welfare of others than lawyers tend to think.[2]

4. ***Who Was the Client of the Defense Counsel?*** In accident cases like *Spaulding v. Zimmerman,* it is common for the defendant to be represented by a lawyer who is chosen and paid by the insurance company. The lawyer typically represents both the defendant-insured and the insurance company, and their interests are not always aligned. The Zimmermans, for example, might have wanted David to learn of the aneurysm, both because they cared about saving his life and because the damages would be paid by the insurance company and not by them personally. The insurance company's interests are perhaps more complex to determine. If one thinks of the company solely as an entity interested in minimizing its immediate financial liabilities, one can imagine it preferring that David not know. If one thinks of its reputation in the community, or of the wishes of the company's executives, employees and shareholders as people, one might imagine the insurance company would prefer that its lawyers tell David. If you can imagine why the insurance company would have preferred that David not learn about the aneurysm, can you imagine any reason why the Zimmerman family would wish him not to know? If the wishes of the Zimmermans and the insurance company conflict about whether to disclose, how should the lawyer act? At the time this case was decided, insurance defense counsel tended to view the liability insurer as the client in cases likely to settle within the policy limits. Since then, the law has been clarified in most jurisdictions to emphasize that a lawyer chosen and paid by the insurance company nevertheless owes a primary duty to the insured. There are ethics rules in every state designed to address these and many other types of situations in which there is reason to worry that the lawyer's own interests or the lawyer's obligations to others might jeopardize the lawyer's ability to provide loyal client service. These rules, called conflict of interest rules, are designed to ensure that lawyers serve clients loyally.

5. ***Duty of Confidentiality.*** A rule of legal ethics in effect in Minnesota at the time these events occurred prohibited the defendants' lawyers from revealing David's condition to David or his counsel without either a discovery request or the defendants' consent. That is, without a discovery request or the consent of their clients, the defense lawyers were prohibited from disclosing David's injuries to him even if they thought it was necessary to save his life. Today, the role governing the duty of confidentiality that lawyers owe to their clients in most jurisdictions has an exception that might allow the defendants' lawyers to disclose the aneurysm to David even if their clients did not consent.

---

[2] *See* Marvin Mindes, *Trickster, Hero, Helper: A Report on the Lawyer Image,* 1982 AM. B. FOUND. RES. J. 177.

The rule in most states today permits a lawyer to disclose confidential information obtained in the course of representing a client when the lawyer "reasonably believes" disclosure is necessary "to prevent reasonably certain death or substantial bodily harm." Model Rule 1.6(b)(1).

6. ***Would You Argue the Defense Side?*** The young lawyer, Richard Pemberton, who argued the case for the Zimmermans in the Minnesota Supreme Court, later said he received the opportunity to argue it because one of the more senior lawyers in his firm found the case unpleasant. A supreme court argument is ordinarily a fun and prestigious assignment that a senior lawyer would not pass up. But many would find it difficult to defend the proposition that a lawyer may not disclose confidential information even to save someone's life. If you had been Richard Pemberton and had been assigned the case because a senior lawyer found it distasteful, would you take the case even if you found your client's position morally wrong? What would be the professional and personal advantages and disadvantages for the junior lawyer to handle the matter or to refuse to handle it?

7. ***Protecting Clients from Wrongful Lawyer Conduct.*** In very rare cases, a lawyer may conclude that her conscience compels her to do something that the law of professional responsibility prohibits, or vice versa. Some violations of legal rules, even if motivated by conscientious objection, can have grave consequences for the lawyer, including in some cases disbarment and criminal prosecution, and can harm clients. If the defense counsel had disclosed the aneurysm over the objection of their clients, should they be subject to professional discipline? Would your answer depend on whether you think the disclosure harmed their clients? Would it depend on whether the clients have other ways of protecting themselves from whatever harm their lawyers did to them, such as suing the lawyer for malpractice or firing the lawyer?

Powerful clients (like the insurance company in a case like *Spaulding*) sometimes sway lawyers to act in what the client perceives to be its interests by the implicit or explicit threat to fire the lawyer or to withhold future business. The defense counsel's failure to consult with the Zimmermans about whether to inform David may have been motivated less by the lawyers' sense of what the rules of professional responsibility required than by what they believed the insurance company would want and by their unwillingness even to raise a delicate issue that might alienate a valuable client.

C. JUSTIFICATIONS FOR A DISTINCT FORM OF LEGAL ETHICS

As *Spaulding v. Zimmerman* illustrates, lawyers sometimes believe that their duties to their client may permit or require them to do things that they would not do except in their capacities as lawyers. Legal philosopher Richard Wasserstrom wrote the classic article exploring the philosophical justifications for role differentiation. As you see,

Wasserstrom is critical of the idea that the professional role of lawyers permits or justifies behavior that would be considered unethical if engaged in by non-lawyers.

LAWYERS AS PROFESSIONALS: SOME MORAL ISSUES

Richard Wasserstrom
5 Human Rights 1 (1975)

[This paper examines a moral criticism of lawyers which, Wasserstrom notes, tends to be made by non-lawyers and to be rejected by lawyers.] The criticism is that the lawyer-client relationship renders the lawyer at best systematically amoral and at worst more than occasionally immoral in his or her dealings with the rest of mankind.

[T]he issue I propose to examine concerns the ways the professional-client relationship affects the professional's stance toward the world at large. The primary question that is presented is whether there is adequate justification for the kind of moral universe that comes to be inhabited by the lawyer as he or she goes through professional life. For at best the lawyer's world is a simplified moral world; often it is an amoral one; and more than occasionally, perhaps, an overtly immoral one.

[O]ne central feature of the professions in general and of law in particular is that there is a special, complicated relationship between the professional, and the client or patient. For each of the parties in this relationship, but especially for the professional, the behavior that is involved, is to a very significant degree, what I call role-differentiated behavior. And this is significant because it is the nature of role-differentiated behavior that it often makes it both appropriate and desirable for the person in a particular role to put to one side considerations of various sorts—and especially various moral considerations—that would otherwise be relevant if not decisive.

Being a parent is, in probably every human culture, to be involved in role-differentiated behavior. In our own culture, and once again in most, if not all, human cultures, as a parent one is entitled, if not obligated, to prefer the interests of one's own children over those of children generally. That is to say, it is regarded as appropriate for a parent to allocate excessive goods to his or her own children, even though other children may have substantially more pressing and genuine needs for these same items. If one were trying to decide what the right way was to distribute assets among a group of children all of whom were strangers to oneself, the relevant moral considerations would be very different from those that would be thought to obtain once one's own children were in the picture. In short, the role-differentiated character of the situation alters the relevant moral point of view enormously.

A similar situation is presented by the case of the scientist. For a number of years there has been debate and controversy within the scientific community over the question of whether scientists should participate in the development and elaboration of atomic theory, especially as those theoretical advances could then be translated into development of atomic weapons that would become a part of the arsenal of existing nation states. The dominant view, although it was not the unanimous one, in the scientific community was that the role of the scientist was to expand the limits of human knowledge. Atomic power was a force which had previously not been utilizable by human beings. The job of the scientist was, among other things, to develop ways and means by which that could now be done. And it was simply no part of one's role as a scientist to forego inquiry, or divert one's scientific explorations because of the fact that the fruits of the investigation could be or would be put to improper, immoral, or even catastrophic uses. The moral issues concerning whether and when to develop and use nuclear weapons were to be decided by others; by citizens and statesmen; they were not the concern of the scientist qua scientist.

In both of these cases it is, of course, conceivable that plausible and even thoroughly convincing arguments exist for the desirability of the role-differentiated behavior and its attendant neglect of what would otherwise be morally relevant considerations. Nonetheless, in the absence of special reasons why parents ought to prefer the interests of their children over those of children in general, the moral point of view surely requires that the claims and needs of all children receive equal consideration.

All of this is significant just because to be a professional is to be enmeshed in role-differentiated behavior of precisely this sort.

Consider, more specifically, the role-differentiated behavior of the lawyer. Conventional wisdom has it that where the attorney client relationship exists, the point of view of the attorney is properly different—and appreciably so—from that which would be appropriate in the absence of the attorney-client relationship. For where the attorney-client relationship exists, it is often appropriate and many times even obligatory for the attorney to do things that, all other things being equal, an ordinary person need not, and should not do. What is characteristic of this role of a lawyer is the lawyer's required indifference to a wide variety of ends and consequences that in other contexts would be of undeniable moral significance. Once a lawyer represents a client, the lawyer has a duty to make his or her expertise fully available in the realization of the end sought by the client, irrespective, for the most part, of the moral worth to which the end will be put or the character of the client who seeks to utilize it. Provided that the end sought is not illegal, the lawyer is, in essence, an amoral technician whose peculiar skills and knowledge in respect to the law are available to those with whom the relationship of client is established. The question, as I have indicated, is whether this particular and pervasive feature of professionalism is itself justifiable. At a minimum, I do not think any of the typical, simple answers will suffice.

One such answer focuses upon and generalizes from the criminal defense lawyer. For what is probably the most familiar aspect of this role-differentiated character of the lawyer's activity is that of the defense of a client charged with a crime. The received view within the profession (and to a lesser degree within the society at large) is that having once agreed to represent the client, the lawyer is under an obligation to do his or her best to defend that person at trial, irrespective, for instance, even of the lawyer's belief in the client's innocence. There are limits, of course, to what constitutes a defense: a lawyer cannot bribe or intimidate witnesses to increase the likelihood of securing an acquittal. And there are legitimate questions, in close cases, about how those limits are to be delineated. But, however these matters get resolved, it is at least clear that it is thought both appropriate and obligatory for the attorney to put on as vigorous and persuasive a defense of a client believed to be guilty as would have been mounted by the lawyer thoroughly convinced of the client's innocence. I suspect that many persons find this an attractive and admirable feature of the life of a legal professional. I know that often I do. The justifications are varied and, as I shall argue below, probably convincing.

Nor, it is important to point out, is this peculiar, strikingly amoral behavior limited to the lawyer involved with the workings of the criminal law. Most clients come to lawyers to get the lawyers to help them do things that they could not easily do without the assistance provided by the lawyer's special competence. They wish, for instance, to dispose of their property in a certain way at death. They wish to contract for the purchase or sale of a house or a business. They wish to set up a corporation which will manufacture and market a new product. They wish to minimize their income taxes. And so on. In each case, they need the assistance of the professional, the lawyer, for he or she alone has the special skill which will make it possible for the client to achieve the desired result.

And in each case, the role-differentiated character of the lawyer's way of being tends to render irrelevant what would otherwise be morally relevant considerations. Suppose that a client desires to make a will disinheriting her children because they opposed the war in Vietnam. Should the lawyer refuse to draft the will because the lawyer thinks this a bad reason to disinherit one's children? Suppose a client can avoid the payment of taxes through a loophole only available to a few wealthy taxpayers. Should the lawyer refuse to tell the client of a loophole because the lawyer thinks it an unfair advantage for the rich? Suppose a client wants to start a corporation that will manufacture, distribute and promote a harmful but not illegal substance, e.g., cigarettes. Should the lawyer refuse to prepare the articles of incorporation for the corporation? In each case, the accepted view within the profession is that these matters are just of no concern to the lawyer qua lawyer. The lawyer need not of course agree to represent the client (and that is equally true for the unpopular client accused of a heinous crime), but there is nothing wrong with representing a client whose aims and purposes are quite immoral. And having agreed to do so, the lawyer is required to provide the best possible assistance, without regard to his or her disapproval of the objective that is sought.

The lesson, on this view, is clear. The job of the lawyer, so the argument typically concludes, is not to approve or disapprove of the character of his or her client, the cause for which the client seeks the lawyer's assistance, or the avenues provided by the law to achieve that which the client wants to accomplish. The lawyer's task is, instead, to provide that competence which the client lacks and the lawyer, as professional, possesses. In this way, the lawyer as professional comes to inhabit a simplified universe which is strikingly amoral-which regards as morally irrelevant any number of factors which nonprofessional citizens might take to be important, if not decisive, in their everyday lives. And the difficulty I have with all of this is that the arguments for such a way of life seem to be not quite as convincing to me as they do to many lawyers.

Is it right that the lawyer should be able so easily to put to one side otherwise difficult problems with the answer: but these are not and cannot be my concern as a lawyer? What do we gain and what do we lose from having a social universe in which there are professionals such as lawyers, who, as such, inhabit a universe of the sort I have been trying to describe?

One difficulty in even thinking about all of this is that lawyers may not be very objective or detached in their attempts to work the problem through. For one feature of this simplified, intellectual world is that it is often a very comfortable one to inhabit.

To be sure, on occasion, a lawyer may find it uncomfortable to represent an extremely unpopular client. On occasion, too, a lawyer may feel ill at ease invoking a rule of law or practice which he or she thinks to be an unfair or undesirable one. Nonetheless, for most lawyers, most of the time, pursuing the interests of one's clients is an attractive and satisfying way to live in part just because the moral world of the lawyer is a simpler, less complicated, and less ambiguous world than the moral world of ordinary life. There is, I think, something quite seductive about being able to turn aside so many ostensibly difficult moral dilemmas and decisions with the reply: but that is not my concern; my job as a lawyer is not to judge the rights and wrong of the client or the cause; it is to defend as best I can my client's interests. Role-differentiated behavior is enticing and reassuring precisely because it does constrain and delimit an otherwise often intractable and confusing moral world.

But there is also an argument which seeks to demonstrate that it is good and not merely comfortable for lawyers to behave this way. It is good, so the argument goes, that the lawyer's behavior and concomitant point of view are role-differentiated because the lawyer qua lawyer participates in a complex institution which functions well only if the individuals adhere to their institutional roles.

For example, when there is a conflict between individuals, or between the state and an individual, there is a well-established institutional mechanism by which to get that dispute resolved. That mechanism is the trial in which each side is represented by a lawyer whose job it is both to present his or her client's case in the most attractive, forceful light and to seek to expose the weaknesses and defects in the case of the opponent.

When an individual is charged with having committed a crime, the trial is the mechanism by which we determine in our society whether or not the person is in fact guilty. Just imagine what would happen if lawyers were to refuse, for instance, to represent persons whom they thought to be guilty. In a case where the guilt of a person seemed clear, it might turn out that some individuals would be deprived completely of the opportunity to have the system determine whether or not they are in fact guilty. The private judgment of individual lawyers would in effect be substituted for the public, institutional judgment of the judge and jury. The amorality of lawyers helps to guarantee that every criminal defendant will have his or her day in court.

In addition, of course, appearances can be deceiving. Persons who appear before trial to be clearly guilty do sometimes turn out to be innocent. The adversary system, so this argument continues, is simply a better method than any other that has been established by which to determine the legally relevant facts in any given case. It is certainly a better method than the exercise of private judgment by any particular individual. And the adversary system only works if each party to the controversy has a lawyer, a person whose institutional role it is to argue, plead and present the merits of his or her case and the demerits of the opponent's. Thus if the adversary system is to work, it is necessary that there be lawyers who will play their appropriate, professional, institutional role of representative of the client's cause.

Nor is the amorality of the institutional role of the lawyer restricted to the defense of those accused of crimes. [W]hen the lawyer functions in his most usual role, he or she functions as a counselor, as a professional whose task it is to help people realize those objectives and ends that the law permits them to obtain and which cannot be obtained without the attorney's special competence in the law. The attorney may think it wrong to disinherit one's children because of their views about the Vietnam war, but here the attorney's complaint is really with the laws of inheritance and not with his or her client. The attorney may think the tax provision an unfair, unjustifiable loophole, but once more the complaint is really with the Internal Revenue Code and not with the client who seeks to take advantage of it. And these matters, too, lie beyond the ambit of the lawyer's moral point of view as institutional counselor and facilitator. If lawyers were to substitute their own private views of what ought to be legally permissible and impermissible for those of the legislature, this would constitute a surreptitious and undesirable shift from a democracy to an oligarchy of lawyers. For given the fact that lawyers are needed to effectuate the wishes of clients, the lawyer ought to make his or her skills available to those who seek them without regard for the particular objectives of the client.

These arguments are neither specious nor without force. Nonetheless, it seems to me that one dilemma which emerges is that if this line of argument is sound, it also appears to follow that the behavior of the lawyers involved in Watergate was simply another less happy illustration of lawyers playing their accustomed institutional role. I am not, let me hasten to make clear, talking about the easy cases—about the behavior of the lawyers that was manifestly illegal. For someone quite properly might reply that it was no more appropriate for the lawyer who worked in the White House to obstruct justice or otherwise violate the criminal law than it would be for a criminal defense lawyer to shoot the prosecution witness to prevent adverse testimony or bribe a defense witness in order to procure favorable testimony. What I am interested in is all of the Watergate behavior engaged in by the Watergate lawyers that was not illegal, but that was, nonetheless, behavior of which we quite properly disapprove. I mean lying to the public; dissembling; stonewalling; tape-recording conversations; playing dirty tricks. Were not these just effective lawyer-like activities pursued by lawyers who viewed Richard Nixon as they would a client and who sought, therefore, the advancement and protection of his interests—personal and political?

It might immediately be responded that the analogy is not apt. For the lawyers who were involved in Watergate were hardly participants in an adversary proceeding. They were certainly not participants in that institutional setting, litigation, in which the amorality of the lawyer makes the most sense. It might even be objected that the amorality of the lawyer qua counselor is clearly distinguishable from the behavior of the Watergate lawyers. Nixon as President was not a client; they, as officials in the executive branch, were functioning as governmental officials and not as lawyers at all.

While not wholly convinced by a response such as the above, I am prepared to accept it because the issue at hand seems to me to be a deeper one.

As I indicated earlier, I do believe that the amoral behavior of the criminal defense lawyer is justifiable. But I think that justification depends at least as much upon the special needs of an accused as upon any more general defense of a lawyer's role-differentiated behavior. As a matter of fact I think it likely that many persons such as me have been misled by the special features of the criminal case. Because a deprivation of liberty is so serious, because the prosecutorial resources of the state are so vast, and because, perhaps, of a serious skepticism about the rightness of punishment even where wrongdoing has occurred, it is easy to accept the view that it makes sense to charge the defense counsel with the job of making the best possible case for the accused—without regard, so to speak, for the merits. This coupled with the fact that it is an adversarial proceeding succeeds, I think, in justifying the amorality of the criminal defense counsel. But this does not, however, justify a comparable perspective on the part of lawyers generally. Once we leave the peculiar situation of the criminal defense lawyer, I think it quite likely that the role-differentiated amorality of the lawyer is almost certainly excessive and at times inappropriate. That is to say, this special case to one side, I am inclined to think that we might all be better served if lawyers were to see themselves less as subject to role-differentiated behavior and more as subject to the demands of the moral point of view. In this sense it may be that we need a good deal less rather than more professionalism in our society generally and among lawyers in particular.

Moreover, even if I am wrong about all this, four things do seem to me to be true and important. First, all of the arguments that support the role-differentiated amorality of the lawyer on institutional grounds can succeed only if the enormous degree of trust and confidence in the institutions themselves is itself justified. If the institutions work well and fairly, there may be good sense to deferring important moral concerns and criticisms to another time and place, to the level of institutional criticism and assessment. But the less certain we are entitled to be of either the rightness or the self-corrective nature of the larger institutions of which the professional is a part, the less apparent it is that we should encourage the professional to avoid direct engagement with the moral issues as they arise. And we are, today, I believe, certainly entitled to be quite skeptical both of the fairness and of the capacity for self-correction of our larger institutional mechanisms, including the legal system. To the degree to which the institutional rules and practices are unjust, unwise or undesirable, to that same degree is the case for the role-differentiated behavior of the lawyer weakened if not destroyed.

Second, it is clear that there are definite character traits that the professional such as the lawyer must take on if the system is to work. What is less clear is that they are admirable ones. Even if the role-differentiated amorality of the professional lawyer is justified by the virtues of the adversary system, this also means that the lawyer qua lawyer will be encouraged to be competitive rather than cooperative; aggressive rather than accommodating; ruthless rather than compassionate; and pragmatic rather than principled. This is, I think, part of the logic of the role-differentiated behavior of lawyers in particular, and to a lesser degree of professionals in general. It is surely neither accidental nor unimportant that these are the same character traits that are emphasized and valued by the capitalist ethic—and on precisely analogous grounds. Because the ideals of professionalism and capitalism are the dominant ones within our culture, it is harder than most of us suspect even to take seriously the suggestion that radically different styles of living, kinds of occupational outlooks, and types of social institutions might be possible, let alone preferable.

Third, there is a special feature of the role-differentiated behavior of the lawyer that distinguishes it from the comparable behavior of other professionals. Why is it that it seems far less plausible to talk critically about the amorality of the doctor, for instance, who treats all patients irrespective of their moral character than it does to talk critically about the comparable amorality of the lawyer? Why is it that it seems so obviously sensible, simple and right for the doctor's behavior to be narrowly and rigidly role differentiated, i.e., just to try to cure those who are ill? And why is it that at the very least it seems so complicated, uncertain, and troublesome to decide whether it is right for the lawyer's behavior to be similarly role-differentiated?

The answer, I think, is twofold. To begin with (and this I think is the less interesting point) it is, so to speak, intrinsically good to try to cure disease, but in no comparable way is it intrinsically good to try to win every lawsuit or help every client realize his or her objective. In addition (and this I take to be the truly interesting point), the lawyer's behavior is different in kind from the doctor's. The lawyer—and especially the lawyer as advocate—directly says and affirms things. The lawyer makes the case for the client. He or she tries to explain, persuade and convince others that the client's cause should prevail. The lawyer lives with and within a dilemma that is not shared by other professionals. If the lawyer actually believes everything that he or she asserts on behalf of the client, then it appears to be proper to regard the lawyer as in fact embracing and endorsing the points of view that he or she articulates. If the lawyer does not in fact believe what is urged by way of argument, if the lawyer is only playing a role, then it appears to be proper to tax the lawyer with hypocrisy and insincerity. To be sure, actors in a play take on roles and say things that the characters, not the actors, believe. But we know it is a play and that they are actors. The law courts are not, however, theaters, and the lawyers both talk about justice and they genuinely seek to persuade. The fact that the lawyer's words, thoughts, and convictions are, apparently, for sale and at the service of the client helps us, I think, to understand the peculiar hostility which is more than occasionally uniquely directed by lay persons toward lawyers. The verbal, role-differentiated behavior of the lawyer qua advocate puts the lawyer's integrity into question in a way that distinguishes the lawyer from the other professionals.

Fourth, and related closely to the three points just discussed, even if on balance the role differentiated character of the lawyer's way of thinking and acting is ultimately deemed to be justifiable within the system on systemic instrumental grounds, it still remains the case that we do pay a social price for that way of thought and action. For to become and to be a professional, such as a lawyer, is to incorporate within oneself ways of behaving and ways of thinking that shape the whole person. It is especially hard, if not impossible, because of the nature of the professions, for one's professional way of thinking not to dominate one's entire adult life. Thus, even if the lawyers who were involved in Watergate were not, strictly speaking, then and there functioning as lawyers, their behavior was, I believe, the likely if not inevitable consequence of their legal acculturation. Having been taught to embrace and practice the lawyer's institutional role, it was natural, if not unavoidable, that they would continue to play that role even when they were somewhat removed from the specific institutional milieu in which that way of thinking and acting is arguably fitting and appropriate. The nature of the professions—the lengthy educational preparation, the prestige and economic rewards, and the concomitant enhanced sense of self—makes the role of professional a difficult one to shed even in those obvious situations in which that role is neither required nor appropriate. In important respects, one's professional role becomes and is one's dominant role, so that for many persons at least they become their professional being. This is at a minimum a heavy price to pay for the professions as we know them in our culture, and especially so for lawyers. Whether it is an inevitable price is, I think, an open question, largely because the problem has not begun to be fully perceived as such by the professionals in general, the legal profession in particular, or by the educational institutions that train professionals.

NOTES ON WASSERSTROM

1. ***How Do Lawyers Conceive Their Role?*** How does Wasserstrom describe the "conventional wisdom" about the lawyer's proper role? Based on what you know so far about lawyers, do you think his description is accurate? What kinds of lawyers do you think are likely to adopt this perspective on how they should behave, and what kinds of lawyers might be more likely to view their role differently?

2. ***What Is the Appeal of Role Differentiation?*** Wasserstrom suggests that lawyers embrace role differentiation because it spares them from struggling with difficult ethical issues. Does the "simplified universe" that Wasserstrom associates with role differentiated morality actually make lawyers comfortable?

3. ***Criticisms of Role Differentiation.*** What is Wasserstrom's critique of role differentiated behavior by lawyers? Do you agree with his argument? Is role differentiated behavior more justifiable in some circumstances than others? If so, what are the circumstances when role differentiated behavior is justified and when is it not?

D. SUMMARY

This chapter introduced the concept of role differentiation: the idea that the role of the lawyer permits or requires certain behavior that is not permitted or required for non-lawyers. It considered a particular example of role differentiation involving a duty to keep confidential information that one might think a non-lawyer would be ethically obligated to reveal. The chapter explored reasons why lawyers believe their role demands different ethical judgments than are expected of non-lawyers and offered critiques of the concept of role differentiation as applied to lawyers. The chapter also introduced the many forces shaping lawyers' behavior that are as significant as the rules of professional responsibility. Among those forces are lawyers' assumptions about client preferences, the way lawyers handle conflicting interests when they represent multiple clients in the same matter, the pressures lawyers feel to get and keep valuable clients, and the social norms within their law office, their sector of law practice, and the community in which they live and work. Most important, we emphasized the importance for every lawyer of reflecting upon the lawyer's personal values and goals.

CHAPTER 2

THE AMERICAN LEGAL PROFESSION: AN OVERVIEW

■ ■ ■

A. INTRODUCTION

This chapter considers several related questions that set the stage for all other topics addressed in this course. What is a profession and how is a profession different, if at all, from a "mere" occupation or business? Is it accurate to call American lawyers a profession, and, if so, why? How has the American legal profession developed and changed since its earliest days? Who are the over one million lawyers in the profession today—what are their characteristics, where do they practice, and how much do they have in common with one another? How are American lawyers regulated, and what other sources of authority influence their norms and behavior? What do lawyers mean when they talk about "professionalism"?

The chapter begins by examining one commonly-cited definition of a profession and what critics say about the notion that professions hold distinctive expertise and ethical ideals. It briefly traces the history of the American legal profession and describes several major studies of the contemporary bar. It then identifies the primary sources of law governing lawyers' conduct. Finally, this chapter explores what people mean by the term "professionalism."

B. WHAT IS A PROFESSION?

The sociologist Talcott Parsons argued that professions serve a critical function in advanced societies through their commitment to specialized knowledge and their distinctive ethical ideals, which subordinate the members' own interests to the interests of others. According to this view, professions are different from business and other occupations and independent of both the market and the state; they mediate between the interests of individuals and private organizations, on the one hand, and the social demands and norms of society, on the other.[1] Because of the special knowledge required of professionals, advocates of this perspective

[1] *See* Talcott Parsons, *A Sociologist Looks at the Legal Profession, in* ESSAYS IN SOCIOLOGICAL THEORY 370–85 (Talcott Parsons ed. 1954).

generally argue that regulation of professions should be handled primarily by others trained and immersed in the same activity.[2]

One commonly cited definition of a profession describes it as "an occupation whose members have special privileges, such as exclusive licensing, that are justified by the following assumptions":

1. That its practice requires substantial intellectual training and the use of complex judgments.
2. That since clients cannot adequately evaluate the quality of the service they must trust those they consult.
3. That the client's trust presupposes that the practitioner's self-interest is overbalanced by devotion to serving both the client's interests and the public good, and
4. That the occupation is self-regulating—that is, organized in such a way as to assure the public and the courts that its members are competent, do not violate their client's trust, and transcend their own self-interest.[3]

Critics, from both the political left and the right, argue that that the legal profession's claims to distinctive expertise and ethical ideals tend to disguise self-interested concerns about controlling entry and stifling competition for the benefit of lawyers, or at least some lawyers. They argue that the notion that the legal profession subordinates self-interest to the needs of others helps lawyers justify exclusionary policies and exercise unilateral power to govern their own behavior at the expense of the public interest. Critics of the legal profession assert that claims of distinctive knowledge and ethical commitments have served primarily to enable lawyers to maintain market control over a range of services that are not particularly arcane and to pursue their own narrow advantages to the detriment of competitors and the larger public.[4]

As you read the following materials, try to decide whether and to what extent the American legal profession measures up to the description offered by Parsons and other defenders of professions and to what extent it is vulnerable to the charges posed by critics.

---

[2] *See* Eliot Freidson, *The Changing Nature of Professional Control*, 10 ANN. REV. SOC. 1–20 (1984).

[3] Eliot Freidson, *quoted in In the Spirit of Public Service: A Blueprint for the Rekindling of Lawyer Professionalism*, ABA COMMISSION ON PROFESSIONALISM, 112 F.R.D. 243, 261–62 (1986).

[4] *See, e.g.*, Richard L. Abel, *United States: The Contradiction of Professionalism*, in LAWYERS IN SOCIETY: THE COMMON LAW WORLD 186–243 (Richard L. Abel & Philip S.C. Lewis eds., 1988).

C. HISTORICAL PERSPECTIVES ON THE AMERICAN LEGAL PROFESSION

The two excerpts below very briefly describe the history of the American legal profession. The first covers the period up through the Civil War, and the second covers the period since then.

A HISTORY OF AMERICAN LAW

Lawrence M. Friedman (3d ed. 2005)

At various points in history, the lawyer has been labeled a Tory, parasite, usurer, land speculator, corrupter of the legislature, note shaver, panderer to corporations, tool of the trusts, shyster, ambulance chaser, and loan shark. Some of the lawyer's bad odor is due to the role of the lawyer as a hired gun. Rich and powerful people need lawyers and have the money to hire them. Also, lawyers in the United States were upwardly mobile men, seizers of opportunities. The American lawyer was never primarily a learned doctor of laws; he was a man of action and cunning. He played a useful role, sometimes admired, but rarely loved.

Under the conditions of American society, it would have been surprising if a narrow, elitist profession grew up—a small, exclusive guild. No such profession developed. There were tendencies in this direction during the colonial period; but after the Revolution the dam burst, and the number of lawyers grew fantastically. It has never stopped growing.

In England, there were distinctions between different grades and types of lawyer: between attorneys, counselors, barristers, and sergeants. The idea did not catch on in the United States. The established bar did struggle to keep their guild small and elite. Success eluded them. By the early nineteenth century, the bar was, formally speaking, an undifferentiated mass. There were rich and poor lawyers, high ones and low; but all were members of one vast sprawling profession. The bar was very loose, very open. Nobody controlled it at the top, or from within. Requirements for admission to the bar were lax.

The number of lawyers grew very rapidly after the Revolution. In the last half of the [19th] century, there was even greater increase. The transformation of the American economy after the Civil War profoundly affected the demand for lawyers, and hence the supply. By 1880, there were perhaps 60,000 lawyers; by 1900, about 114,000.

The law itself was changing. Life and the economy were more complicated; there was more, then, to be done, in the business world especially; and the lawyers proved able to do it. There was nothing inevitable in the process. It did not happen, for example, in Japan. The legal profession might have become smaller and narrower; lawyers might have become highly specialized, like the English barrister, or confined themselves, like the brain surgeon, to a few rare, complex, and lucrative tasks. Automation and technological change were challenges for lawyers, just as they were challenges to other occupations. Social invention constantly threatened to displace lawyers from some of their functions. It was adapt or die. Lawyers in the first half of the century made money searching titles. After the Civil War, title companies and trust companies were efficient competitors. By 1900, well-organized companies nibbled away at other staples of the practice, too: debt collection and estate work, for example.

Still, lawyers prospered. The profession was exceedingly nimble at finding new kinds of work and new ways to do it. Its nimbleness was no doubt due to the character of the bar: open-ended, unrestricted, uninhibited, and attractive to sharp, ambitious men. In so amorphous a profession, lawyers drifted in and out; many went into business or politics because they could not earn a living at their trade. Others reached out for new sorts of practice. At any rate, the profession did not shrink to (or rise to) the status of a small, exclusive elite. Even in 1860, the profession was bigger, wider, more diverse than it had been in years gone by.

THE AMERICAN LEGAL PROFESSION, 1870–2000

Robert W. Gordon
The Cambridge History of Law in America Vol. III
(Michael Grossberg & Christopher Tomlins eds. 2008)[5]

The Organized Bar and Its Professional Projects: 1870–1970. Lawyers' jobs and lives in 1870 were not very different from what they had been at mid-century. Lawyers' numbers (ca. 40,000 in 1870) in proportion to population were about the same. Only fifteen states required any formal preparation for admission to the bar, such as a cursory oral examination or three years of apprenticeship. Only about 1,600 lawyers, or 3 percent of the bar, had attended a law school, usually for one or two years at most. Nearly all lawyers were in private practice, and they usually practiced alone or in two- to three-person partnerships. The profession was highly stratified and its incomes widely dispersed. At the top, lawyers grew wealthy from retainers from merchants, manufacturers, banks, insurance companies, and especially from railroads. But even elite lawyers were rarely specialists; they still made their public reputations as trial lawyers, representing prominent clients in divorce, will, and libel contests and acting for murderers in criminal cases and for tort plaintiffs in civil suits against businesses. As they had since 1800, a small corps of elite lawyers virtually monopolized practice before the highest state and federal courts. Lawyers also dominated high elective and appointive office; two-thirds of U.S. presidents, senators, governors, and top executive appointments; and of course the entire judiciary above petty misdemeanor and probate courts

[5] Reprinted with the permission of Cambridge University Press.

were lawyers. At the bottom of the profession lawyers could not make a living at law alone; they scraped by on a practice of miscellaneous small pickings from individual clients—debt collection, real estate deals and disputes, writing and probating wills, criminal cases—combined with non-legal business on the side.

The first bar associations were little more than social clubs of "the best men." By 1916 there were more than 600 bar associations, and they had developed a fairly consistent and uniform agenda. The central aim was to restrict entry to the legal profession, first by requiring passage of a bar examination and later by raising educational standards to graduation from law school and at least a high-school degree before that. These were high barriers: only 2 percent of Americans had a high-school degree in 1870 and only 8.6 percent in 1910; as late as 1940 only 6 percent had a college degree. The bar associations also sought to close down alternative routes to practice, such as apprenticeship, the diploma privilege (the admission of graduates of a state's law schools without examination), and especially the part-time night law schools proliferating in the cities. The night schools were the quickest route into practice for immigrant lawyers; by 1915 they turned out almost half the total number of new lawyers.

[Those who sought to restrict entry to the legal profession] partly succeeded and partly failed. In the long run they won the battle for the bar exam and formal educational credentials. They gradually drove out admission through the diploma privilege and apprenticeship in almost every state; introduced written bar exams; and, in states with large cities and immigrant populations, reduced bar pass rates. But the elites failed to close down the part-time night schools, which flourished and multiplied to the point of graduating over half of all new lawyers until the Depression killed most of them off. And the nativist project to cleanse the bar of what Henry S. Drinker, a prominent legal ethicist, called "Russian Jew boys . . . up out of the gutter . . . following the methods their fathers had been using in selling shoe-strings and other merchandise," failed completely. New Jewish and Catholic immigrant lawyers flooded into the profession.

The bar in 1900 was exclusively white and male with token exceptions: There were about 730 African American lawyers in the entire country and about 1,000 women lawyers. The ABA refused to admit African Americans to membership until 1943; they formed their own professional organization, the National Bar Association, in 1925. No Southern school after Redemption—with the prominent exception of Howard University Law School in Washington, D.C.—would admit African Americans before 1935; several states later opened all-black law schools simply to forestall integration orders.

Women fought their own long battle for admission to practice. In the most famous challenge to state laws excluding women from practice, Myra

Bradwell of Illinois argued that such laws abridged the privileges and immunities of citizens to choose their professions. The Supreme Court rejected the claim in 1873, upholding discriminatory licensing laws as a valid exercise of the police power. Justice Joseph Bradley in a concurring opinion said that the "paramount destiny and mission of women are to fulfill the noble and benign offices of wife and mother" and they were thus "unfit for many of the occupations of civil life." Some state courts disagreed, however, and between 1869 and 1899, thirty-five states and territories, often under pressure from lawsuits, admitted women to practice even though in most of the women could not vote or hold office. All but Delaware and Rhode Island admitted women by 1918.

Legal barriers to admission turned out to be the least of obstacles in the path of women to practice. Many schools refused to admit women as students. Harvard held out until 1950. Male lawyers viewed women as intruders on a masculine preserve, especially in the courtroom. Judges and lawyers treated women with undisguised hostility.

Even when young Jewish men, and much more rarely, occasional women and African Americans, made their way onto the first rungs of the meritocratic ladder—elite law schools, law review, and high class standing—almost none of them, until the 1970s, were ever hired at major law firms. The stories are legendary—the future Supreme Court justices Ruth Bader Ginsburg and Sandra Day O'Connor, the African American lawyers Raymond Pace Alexander and William T. Coleman, Jr., all stars of their respective law school classes, were turned away from every law firm in the cities where they first applied. Between 1890 and 1920, all African American lawyers admitted to the Philadelphia bar practiced alone or in all-black firms or worked for the government.

Blocked from the conventional pathway to success—big-firm transactional practice on behalf of corporate clients—what did marginal lawyers do to advance in their profession? The usual choice of occupation was litigation representing the other side from the elite bar's corporate clients. This was often simply routine personal injury work—tort plaintiffs' suits against railroads and streetcar companies or worker's compensation claims—but could also be fairly complex litigation, such as derivative suits or proxy fights against corporations. Labor law was often a Jewish specialty as well, attracting lawyers from immigrant socialist families to the workers' cause. Women were steered away from the courtroom: a survey of 1920 found that most women thought their best opportunities were in office practices, such as trusts and estates, domestic relations, real estate, and social welfare law. In fact, they were mostly confined to general office practice. Jewish, African American, and women lawyers also dominated what we now call public interest and cause lawyering.

Ethics and Discipline. Prominent among the historical ambitions of the newly organized profession was the development of ethical standards and disciplinary machinery to improve the ethics of lawyers and judges and to police or expel the deviants. Bar association speakers and writers on ethics delivered hundreds of jeremiads between 1890 and 1920 lamenting the increasing commercialization of the bar and its growing dependence on corporate clienteles; they continued to hold out the ideal of the lawyer as an independent objective advisor. As a practical matter, however, the new grievance committees of the elite bar associations focused their crusades almost entirely on lower tier attorneys, the personal injury plaintiffs' bar. High-end lawyers almost entirely escaped the notice of disciplinary committees.

Expansion and Upheaval: 1970–2000. A century after the founding of its major modern institutions, the legal profession began to undergo momentous changes in virtually all sectors of practice.

The bar's project to limit admissions by raising pre-legal and legal educational requirements and lowering bar exam pass rates—combined with the collapse of part-time night schools in the Depression—had kept the proportion of lawyers to the population reasonably stable since 1900. But after 1970 the volume of new entrants soared. The total number of lawyers rose from 355,000 in 1970 to 542,000 in 1980 and by the end of the century had doubled again to over a million.

Beginning in the late 1960s, anti-discrimination laws and affirmative action combined to produce a substantial increase in African American enrollments in law schools, from 2,000 in 1969 to 6,000 in 1985. Thereafter, however, there was a slight decline; and African American lawyers remained strikingly underrepresented in law firms, making up 3.3 percent of associates in 1996 and only 1.7 percent of partners. In 2000 4.2 percent of all lawyers were African American. The biggest change was in the profession's acceptance of women. Between 1967 and 1983, enrollment of women at ABA-approved law schools rose 1,650 percent, from 4.5 to 37.7 percent of the total; at the end of the century it had stabilized at almost 50 percent. In 1980 only 8 percent of lawyers were women; by 2000, 27 percent were women. However, some combination of continuing discrimination and the brutal time demands of corporate practice continued to keep law firm partner ranks predominantly male—around 85 percent or more in most firms. By 2000 women were much better represented (around 25 percent) in prosecutors, government, and house counsel offices and among law teachers; they were often the majority in legal aid offices and public interest firms. Hispanic-Americans in the profession rose slightly from 2.5 percent in 1980 to 3.4 percent in 2000, Asian Americans from 1.4 to 2 .2 percent.

The most explosive transformations were in the corporate practice sector. The demand for corporate lawyers multiplied with client demands for lawyers to staff an exploding increase in transactions, government regulations, and litigation. The most visible effect of these demands for more lawyers was a sharp rise in the number, size, and geographic reach of law firms. In 1900, a "large firm"—so large that contemporaries called it a "law factory"—was eleven lawyers. Around 1960 only thirty-eight firms had more than fifty lawyers; half of them were in New York City. By 2005, 17 firms had over 1,000 lawyers. In the 1980s and 90s, firms extended their reach by opening both domestic and foreign branch offices. As they expanded, firms transformed the nature of legal practice by competing aggressively with one another to attract clients and hire senior lawyers and associates. Confronted with escalating legal costs, companies tried to keep these costs down by severing long-term ties with outside firms and bringing substantial pieces of legal work in-house. The job of in-house general counsel to a business, once a resting place for lawyers who had failed to make partner in law firms, became newly prestigious and powerful. The general counsel's job was purchasing and managing all the legal services for his or her company, auctioning off fragments of specialized work to many different outside firms. The result was a whole new style of corporate practice—ruthlessly competitive [and] powered pretty nearly exclusively by the drive for profits. The old stable institutional order of law firm practice dissolved. Lawyers no longer expected a lifetime career in a single firm.

The profession's individual practice sector also experienced seismic shocks. In 1900 solo and small-firm lawyers serving individual business encompassed the entire profession save for a few big-city big-business firms. In 2000 individual practice was still numerically the largest segment of the private bar, but accounted for a rapidly diminishing share, relative to corporate practice, of total lawyers' efforts and earnings. The most dramatic development in the individual practice sector was the rise of a mass-tort class action specialty within the personal injury bar.

By the 1960s, the professional ideal—and the attendant privileges and authority—were under attack from the right, the left, and within the profession's own ranks. Left-wing cultural critics attacked the professions as elitist conspiracies to exclude, dominate, exploit, and paternalistically control social inferiors by mystifying professional knowledge. Right-wing critics and economists attacked them as cartels designed to restrict entry and fix prices. Valid or not, the critiques had a corrosive effect on attempts to defend professional values, good as well as bad, in terms of civic virtue or social trusteeship.

NOTES ON THE PROFESSION'S HISTORY

1. ***Continuity and Change.*** What are the consistent threads running through these accounts of the American legal profession's history? What are the most significant changes in the profession over the past 100 years?

2. ***Entry Standards.*** Both Friedman and Gordon identify a tension between openness and elitism as an important phenomenon in the history of the American legal profession. How did easy admission to the practice of law allow lawyers to survive or thrive? How did restrictions on entry and efforts to ensure that lawyers were highly competent, as measured by elite standards? What is better for the public?

D. EMPIRICAL RESEARCH ON THE CONTEMPORARY BAR

Social scientists have studied American lawyers for the purpose of shedding light on the profession's membership, the institutions in which lawyers practice, and lawyers' behavior and values. This section describes several major pieces of research on the profession.

All of the research described in this section is empirical, meaning that it relies on methods involving data collection or direct observation by researchers. Empirical research is time and labor intensive, but it is also generally more reliable than anecdotal accounts. This section reports on three of the most ambitious empirical studies of the legal profession ever undertaken. The first two studies focus on Chicago, but the findings may be more broadly relevant for lawyers working in major U.S. cities. The third study, designed to explore lawyers' careers, examines the experience of a geographically diverse set of law school graduates admitted to the bar in 2000.

We will consider other empirical research on the American legal profession elsewhere in the book, wherever the studies' topics are most relevant. But you should be aware that there are many interesting and important issues as to which there is little available empirical evidence. For example, attorney-client interactions are notoriously difficult to study because the presence of third parties (such as researchers) sacrifices confidentiality and therefore eliminates the privilege that communications between lawyers and clients otherwise enjoy. Similarly, it is challenging to gain lawyers' cooperation in studies of lawyer misconduct because lawyers generally do not wish to expose their own misdeeds, and their reports of misbehavior of other lawyers may be unreliable. Sensitive issues regarding the internal operations of law firms and law departments in corporations and government agencies are challenging to study for similar reasons. There has been little recent systematic research on lawyers who work in small towns and rural areas, perhaps because it is logistically difficult and expensive for researchers to gather such data. All of this means that for many questions you might have about the profession, the only available answer is, "So sorry; we just do not know!" Where no empirical research is available, we sometimes offer anecdotal accounts that we believe may be revealing even if they are not methodologically rigorous.

Chicago Lawyers I. The first of the empirical studies highlighted in this chapter examined the characteristics of, and differences among, lawyers in one major American city, based on surveys of 777 randomly selected lawyers working in Chicago in 1975. The study found that the Chicago bar was divided into two broad sectors, or "hemispheres"—one serving primarily large organizations and the other serving individuals and small businesses.

CHICAGO LAWYERS: THE SOCIAL STRUCTURE OF THE BAR

John P. Heinz & Edward O. Laumann (1982)

[M]uch of the differentiation within the legal profession is secondary to one fundamental distinction—the distinction between lawyers who represent large organizations (corporations, labor unions, or government) and those who represent individuals. The two kinds of law practice are the two hemispheres of the profession. Most lawyers reside exclusively in one hemisphere or the other and seldom, if ever, cross the equator.

Lawyers who serve major corporations and other large organizations differ systematically from those who work for individuals and small businesses whether we look at the social origins of the lawyers, the prestige of the law schools they attended, their career histories and mobility, their social or political values, their networks of friends and professional associates, or several other social variables. Though there certainly are distinctions among lawyers that cut across the line between the two broad classes of clients, this fundamental difference in the nature of the client served appears to be the principal factor that structures the social differentiation of the profession. . . . Though the two principal parts of the Chicago bar are not exactly equal in size, the total amounts of effort devoted to each and the total numbers of lawyers practicing in them are roughly comparable. There is substantial overlap in these categories, but a solid majority of the practicing lawyers worked exclusively in one hemisphere or the other. The two hemispheres thus tend to be largely separate, to be populated by different lawyers. Relatively few lawyers do substantial amounts of work in both.

The types of clients represented, the mechanisms by which lawyers obtain business, the sorts of tasks performed, the organizational setting of the practice, the type of law school attended, and the religion of the practitioners appear to create an overall structure that is strongly associated with the extent to which Chicago lawyers perceive that each of the fields has a claim to deference [based on prestige] within the profession.

We believe that our findings provide strong support for the inference that the prestige accorded by the legal profession to the fields of law is determined in large measure by the types of clients served by the fields. Fields that serve corporate, wealthier, more "establishment" clients are accorded more deference within the profession than are those that serve individual, poorer clients. This suggests the thesis that prestige within law is acquired by association, that it is "reflected glory" derived from the power possessed by the lawyers' clients.

NOTES ON HEINZ & LAUMANN'S CHICAGO LAWYERS I

1. ***Implications for Self-Regulation.*** What are the implications of the "two hemispheres" thesis for the bar's ability to regulate itself? Is a bar that is fundamentally divided by the types of clients represented, types of work performed, organizational settings, and social backgrounds of the lawyers likely to be able to agree on a rigorous set of standards by which lawyers' behavior should be judged? For example, do you think that lawyers who serve corporations are likely to be able to agree with lawyers who specialize in bringing products liability class actions against corporations about whether lawyer advertising is a problem, and, if so, what should be done about it? If some lawyers are paid by the hour and others on a contingency basis (as a percentage of plaintiffs' recovery), might they have different perspectives on what types of fee arrangements are appropriate and reasonable? If some types of lawyers earn much larger incomes than others, might those differences influence whether they favor mandatory pro bono service?

2. ***Prestige of Practice Fields.*** Heinz and Laumann's assessment of the prestige of various fields of practice relied on ratings provided by the lawyers in their study. In other words, those measures of prestige are derived empirically, based on what the lawyers in the study reported about the prestige they associated with different types of work. How might one explain the study's finding that prestige within the legal profession is linked with the types of clients served, and that lawyers who served big business were perceived as more prestigious than those who served individuals? Do you think that greater prestige *should* be accorded to lawyers who serve large organizational clients than to those who serve individuals and small businesses?

* * *

Chicago Lawyers II. Subsequent research tested Heinz and Laumann's "two hemispheres" thesis by comparing data from the first Chicago lawyers study with data compiled in 1995. Between 1975 and 1995, the profession had almost doubled in size, and women had entered the profession in large numbers. There had also been substantial changes in the demand for various types of legal services. The researchers investigated whether these changes had affected the organization of lawyers' work and separation between the two hemispheres of practice.

THE CHANGING CHARACTER OF LAWYERS' WORK: CHICAGO IN 1975 AND 1995

John P. Heinz, Edward O. Laumann, Robert L. Nelson & Ethan Michelson
32 Law & Society Review 751 (1998)

Overall, [since 1975] the corporate client fields have grown much more rapidly than the personal client fields, and the "hemispheres" are now even more unequal in size. In the 1975 data, the estimate is that 53% of lawyers' time was allocated to the corporate fields (including work for nonbusiness organizations such as unions and governmental entities), while 40% was devoted to the personal client fields and another 7% was not clearly assignable or was spread across a variety of small fields. By 1995, the disparity between the two sectors had increased considerably. [T]he corporate sector consumed more than twice the amount of Chicago lawyers' time devoted to personal and small business client work in 1995 (64% vs. 29%). The "large corporate" cluster of fields increased most—from 18% of the total in 1975 to 32% in 1995—while the "personal business" and "personal plight" [a category including criminal defense, divorce, family, plaintiff's side personal injury, and civil rights] clusters both declined.

The growth of the corporate sector of practice and the decline in the percentage of personal and small business legal work has been paralleled by a corresponding realignment of the organizational contexts within which law is practiced. In the 1975 survey, 23% of the respondents were in private law firms with 2 to 10 lawyers; in 1995, only 14% worked in firms of that size. At the same time, the percentage of lawyers working in firms with more than 30 lawyers nearly doubled—from 15.7% in 1975 to 29.3% in 1995. The average number of lawyers in the private law firms represented in the 1975 sample was 27; by 1995, the average number per firm had grown to 141. The percentage of lawyers practicing alone has been declining for as long as data are available.

Even in the personal and small business sector of practice, legal work is increasingly concentrated in larger organizations. Some routine, high-volume matters—such as divorce, simple wills, and consumer bankruptcies—are now handled by franchise legal service companies and group legal service plans such as Jacoby & Meyers and Hyatt Legal Plans, which employ lawyers at relatively low wages.

Other organizational contexts in which lawyers work have had similar patterns of growth. The average size of "house counsel" offices (i.e., lawyers employed within corporations and other private organizations) in the 1975 sample was 17, while by 1995 the average number of lawyers in each such office had grown to 55. Government law offices averaged 64 lawyers each in 1975, but the average increased to 399 in 1995.

Although demand for legal services to corporations and other large organizations has grown far more rapidly than demand for services to individuals and small businesses, entry into the market is easier in the latter types of practice. Any lawyer can hang up a shingle and seek clients in auto accident or refrigerator repossession cases, but it is difficult for lawyers to obtain access to the venues where corporate legal services are delivered. Therefore, since demand was expanding in the types of practice where entry is difficult but growing only much more slowly in the areas where entry is easy, lawyers in the former tended to prosper while those in the latter languished. From 1972 to 1982 the real incomes of lawyers in solo practice decreased by 46%. Thus, the increasing gap between rich and much less rich within the bar has also accentuated the differences among the types of practice.

There are, then, several reasons to suppose that Chicago lawyers might be less cohesive in the 1990s than they were in the 1970s, and urban lawyers may now have become subdivided into smaller clusters. But the division between the two classes of clients—between large organizations, on the one hand, and individuals and small businesses, on the other—endures.

Is the legal profession still divided into hemispheres? Well, "hemi" means "half," and it is now hard to argue that the two parts are of approximately equal size, at least in Chicago (and probably in other large cities). Work for corporate clients is a much larger part of the profession than is work for individuals or small businesses. The amount of Chicago lawyers' time devoted to corporate fields and to fields serving other large organizations is more than twice that devoted to personal client fields. Within each of the broad parts, the fields are now more distinct than they were 20 years ago. Specialization has increased markedly in most fields. We think it unlikely that the present organizational structures provide enough interchange among the specialties to produce a bar that functions as a community of shared fate and common purpose.

NOTES ON CHICAGO LAWYERS II

1. ***Broader Patterns Among Urban Lawyers.*** The trends identified in the research on the Chicago bar are widely believed to reflect larger changes in the American legal profession as a whole, at least in urban areas. For example, the size of the organizations in which lawyers practice has increased dramatically. The largest firm identified in Heinz & Laumann's second study employed 1800 lawyers. (Recall from Gordon's excerpt that only thirty-eight U.S. firms had more than fifty lawyers in 1960.) In 2018, the largest U.S.-based firm, Baker & McKenzie, had over 4,700 lawyers worldwide. Between 1997 and 2006, the 200 largest law departments in U.S. corporations increased the number of their in-house counsel from a total of 19,400 to 27,700—an average of 4.8% per year.[6] Even in the individual client hemisphere, large organizations

[6] *Analysis of the Legal Profession and Law Firms*, HARV. L. SCH. PROGRAM ON LEGAL PROF., http://www.law.harvard.edu/programs/plp/pages/statistics.php#wlw.

have become more prevalent, as franchise law firms and group legal services plans have consolidated and rationalized legal work for middle-class individuals. Hyatt legal plans employ more than 14,000 lawyers nationwide.[7] The increased specialization documented by Heinz et al. in the Chicago bar is generally true elsewhere; very few lawyers today consider themselves generalists. Likewise, the income disparities between the most prosperous and most marginal lawyers in the U.S. are enormous; some partners in major firms make millions per year, while many lawyers in the individual client sector are barely scraping by. Overall, the bar is more highly stratified by types of clients served, practice specialty, and income than ever before in its history.

2. ***Implications for Self-Regulation.*** In a refrain from the first Chicago lawyers study, the authors of the second study ask whether a bar so divided can "function[ ] as a community of shared fate and common purpose." Do you think they are right to doubt whether the bar can speak with one voice about important policy matters? What are the implications of your answer for the bar's ability to articulate shared norms of practice and rules governing lawyers' conduct?

3. ***One Profession or Many?*** Does it make any sense to talk of "the American legal profession" at all today? Would it make more sense to speak of multiple legal professions?

* * *

After the JD. In the late 1990s, a consortium of organizations launched a major longitudinal study (meaning that it followed research subjects over time) of lawyers' careers. The *After the JD* ("AJD") study was designed to track a nationally representative group of lawyers admitted to the bar in the year 2000. Key purposes of the study were to understand how lawyers launch careers, what kinds of work environments and skills help them reach their goals, and how the experiences and opportunities of lawyers vary by their characteristics, especially race, ethnicity, and gender. The sample included lawyers from 18 legal markets, including the four largest markets (New York, the District of Columbia, Chicago, and Los Angeles).

The first wave of the study ("Wave 1") gathered survey data from 4,538 lawyers, augmented by an oversampling of minorities. The first report, published in 2004, documented the demographic characteristics of the AJD lawyers and examined their experiences in the first two to three years of law practice. It offered initial findings on a variety of topics, including these new lawyers' practice settings, work lives, income, satisfaction, mobility, law school debt, and the transition from law school to practice, and it is packed with fascinating data. It showed, for example, that the median number of hours worked per week was 50, as compared with a median of 40 hours for all full-time workers in the U.S. Twenty percent of all new

---

[7] *History & Timeline*, HYATT LEGAL PLANS, https://www.legalplans.com/history/.

attorneys reported working 60 or more hours per week, and those who did were mostly in the largest firms. The median income of the full-time lawyers in the study was $73,000, but that number masked substantial differences within the sample; about 25% reported incomes of more than $110,000, while 25% reported incomes below $50,000. AJD respondents reported relatively high levels of satisfaction with their decisions to become lawyers and with their legal practices; 80% said that they were "moderately" or "extremely" satisfied with their decision to become a lawyer. More than a third of the respondents in the AJD data had already changed jobs at least once. Women were almost equally represented with men in the AJD sample, but evidence of divergence in their careers was already evident even though they were only two to three years into their careers. There were also variations in geographic location and practice settings among the racial and ethnic groups represented in the sample. Respondents reported a median undergraduate and law school debt upon graduation of $60,000. (Excluding the 15% of respondents who graduated with no educational debt, the median educational debt was $70,000.)[8]

The second report (AJD II or Wave 2) assessed the progress of the same cohort of lawyers through seven years of practice, drawing from additional data collected in 2007–2008.[9] The report showed that the median work week for AJD lawyers remained the same—50 hours, but more than 41% of attorneys in mega-firms reported working 60+ hour weeks (up from 32% in Wave 1). The median income for lawyers in the AJD II sample was $98,000, a 40% increase from 2003, adjusted for inflation. The top quartile earned $145,000 or more (up from $100,000 in 2003), and the bottom quartile topped out at $70,000. Lawyers from the highest ranked law schools worked disproportionately in the most well-paid job settings. Fifty-four percent of AJD attorneys said that they considered themselves specialists, and 86% reported that they spent at least 50% of their work time in only one of 20 possible areas of practice. More than two-fifths of AJD lawyers reported that they had performed some kind of pro bono service in the previous year, with an average of 28 hours per attorney in the sample.

Three-quarters of respondents in Wave 2 indicated that they were moderately or extremely satisfied with their decision to become a lawyer. Overall levels of satisfaction were similar across practice settings, but the particular sources of satisfaction varied by practice setting. Black and Hispanic respondents reported the highest levels of overall career satisfaction of all members of the sample.

---

8 AFTER THE J.D.: FIRST RESULTS OF A NATIONAL STUDY OF LEGAL CAREERS (2004). The full report is available at http://www.americanbarfoundation.org/uploads/cms/documents/ajd.pdf.

9 AFTER THE JD II: RESULTS FROM A NATIONAL STUDY OF LEGAL CAREERS (2009), The 4,160 completed surveys included 70.4% of the AJD1 respondents and an additional 26.9% of those not surveyed in Wave 1.

There was a gender disparity in the rates of partnership in private firms, and men earned higher incomes than women in every setting except legal service/public defender and nonprofits. Women were also more likely than men to have delayed marriage and childbearing; 17.9 percent of women had not married as compared to 15.2 percent of men, and 54 percent of women had one or more children as compared to 59 percent of men. Yet 74.1 percent of women reported being extremely to moderately satisfied with their decision to become a lawyer, as compared to 78.4 percent of men.

AJD lawyers in Wave 2 of the study had moved in large numbers out of private law firms into other practice settings, but the patterns varied by race and ethnicity. A greater proportion of non-white respondents left large and mega firms compared to white respondents, while non-white respondents were more likely to remain in government positions than their white counterparts. Slightly more than half of attorneys in the survey had changed jobs at least once.

Results from the third wave of data collection (Wave 3 or AJD III) showed that the median number of hours worked per week by AJD III lawyers was 47. Lawyers in private practice worked longer hours on average than lawyers in government, legal services, public defense, or public interest law, and lawyers in the largest firms worked the longest hours, with a median of 53 hours per week. The share of AJD lawyers working more than 60 hours per week had declined across all employment settings as these lawyers entered mid-career. Median earnings were up 8% unadjusted for inflation, with half of AJD III respondents (working full time) earning more than $106,000 and half earning less.

By Wave 3, the median educational debt was about $50,000. The percentage of AJD III lawyers with more than $100,000 of educational debt remaining had declined to 5.4% by Wave 3. The overall percentages of respondents with zero debt increased from 16.3% at Wave 1 to 36.1% at Wave 2 to almost half (47.4%) at Wave 3. But Hispanic and Black respondents were least likely to report zero educational debt at Wave 3; only 23.3% of Blacks reported zero debt compared with 30.4% of Hispanics, 60.1% of Asians, and 48% of Whites.

There remained significant gender disparities in rates of pay, partnership, and life events outside of work. By Wave 3, female respondents working full-time earned 80 percent of the pay of their male counterparts. Only 52.3 percent of female respondents working in law firms were partners in 2012, compared with 68.8 percent of male respondents working in law firms. Ten percent of women had never married as compared to 8 percent of men, and 35 percent of women had no children as compared to 27.8 percent of men. Women were significantly more likely to indicate that they were working part time (15 percent) or not working (9 percent) in order to care for children, while 96 percent of the men worked full time.

Overall rates of satisfaction with career choice remained high; 12 years into their careers, most lawyers (76%) reported they were moderately or extremely satisfied with their decision to become a lawyer, a proportion virtually unchanged from prior waves of the survey. Overall rates of satisfaction were almost identical for men and women (76.1 percent v. 76.2 percent), but there were gender differences within practice sectors. Women were more likely than men to report being moderately or extremely satisfied with their decision become a lawyer if they worked in solo practice, firms of 250+ lawyers, legal services, or public interest practice.

Movement away from private practice had continued; the percentage of respondents in private practice after twelve years decreased from 68.6 percent in 2003 to 44.1 percent in 2012. About two-thirds of the AJD III lawyers identified themselves as specialists, and about three quarters of attorneys reported working at least half their time in a single area of law.[10]

We will explore additional key findings from the *After the JD* study in our survey of practice settings in Part II.

NOTES ON THE AFTER THE JD STUDY

1. ***Consistency Between Chicago Bar Research and After the JD.*** To the extent that there is overlap between the studies of the Chicago bar and the AJD study, are the findings consistent?

2. ***Lawyer Satisfaction.*** Are you surprised by the data on lawyer satisfaction from the *After the JD* study? Based on what you may have read in the popular press before attending law school, you might well believe that most lawyers are dissatisfied with their careers. However, much of the best available research contradicts this common view. We will return to this issue in Part III.

3. ***What Other Implications?*** What might these data from the *AJD* study suggest about current opportunities and challenges for the American legal profession? We take up some of those broad issues in Part III.

* * *

Lawyer Demographics. The following data provide a snapshot of the American Legal Profession.

NUMBER OF LICENSED LAWYERS—2017

1,335,963

Source: American Bar Association's National Lawyer Population Survey

---

[10] AFTER THE JD III: THIRD RESULTS FROM A NATIONAL STUDY OF LEGAL CAREERS (2014).

GENDER

	1980	1991	2000	2010	2018
Male	92%	80%	73%	69%	64%
Female	8%	20%	27%	31%	36%

Sources: for 1980–2000, *The Lawyer Statistical Report*, American Bar Foundation, 1985, 1994, 2004, 2012 editions; for 2010–2018, ABA National Lawyer Population Survey

RACE/ETHNICITY

	2008	2018
African-American	4%	5%
Asian	2%	3%
Caucasian/White	89%	85%
Hawaiian/Pacific Islander	1%	0%
Hispanic	3%	5%
Native American	1%	1%

Source: ABA National Lawyer Population Survey

LAW STUDENTS

Academic Year	2009–2010	2017–2018
	145,239	110,156
Gender		
Male	53%	49.7%
Female	47%	50.3%

Source: ABA Section of Legal Education & Admissions to the Bar

PRACTICE SETTING

% of lawyers in...	1980	1991	2000	2005
Private Practice	68%	73%	74%	75%
Government	9%	8%	8%	8%
Private Industry	10%	9%	8%	8%
Retired/Inactive	5%	5%	5%	4%
Judiciary	4%	3%	3%	3%
Education	1%	1%	1%	1%
Legal Aid/Public Defender	2%	1%	1%	1%
Private Association	1%	1%	1%	1%

Sources: *The Lawyer Statistical Report*, American Bar Foundation, 1985,1994, 2004, 2012 editions

PRIVATE PRACTITIONERS

% of private practitioners...	1980	1991	2000	2005
Solo	49%	45%	48%	49%
2–5 lawyers	22%	15%	15%	14%
6–10 lawyers	9%	7%	7%	6%
11–20 lawyers	7%	7%	6%	6%
21–50 lawyers	6%	8%	6%	6%
51-100 lawyers	7%	5%	4%	4%
101+ lawyers	*	13%	14%	16%

Sources: The Lawyer Statistical Report, American Bar Foundation, 1985,1994, 2004, 2012 editions

* Largest firm size for 1980 data was 51+ lawyers

E. THE RULES OF PROFESSIONAL RESPONSIBILITY AND OTHER SOURCES OF LAWYER REGULATION

All jurisdictions have rules governing the behavior of lawyers. The overwhelming majority of states have adopted some version of the Model Rules of Professional Conduct—a set of rules drafted, and periodically revised, by the American Bar Association ("ABA"). The effect of these rules on lawyers' obligations depends entirely on their adoption by a jurisdiction's courts. The ABA also occasionally publishes ethics opinions designed to provide additional guidance on the interpretation of the Model Rules.

Disciplinary agencies acting under the supervision of state supreme courts hold primary responsibility for enforcing the rules of professional conduct. For lawyers practicing in federal courts, the situation is more complicated. Most federal district courts adopt the rules of the state in which the district court is located, but that practice is not uniform. Many federal agencies have adopted special rules governing the conduct of lawyers who practice before them.

There has been a gradual evolution in the format and content of bar-issued standards of conduct—from broad aspirational standards to enforceable black-letter law.[11] The first widely adopted standards were the Canons of Ethics, adopted by the ABA in 1908. These brief, general guidelines drew complaints about their failure to provide adequate guidance to lawyers confronted with particular questions. In 1969, the ABA adopted a new Model Code of Professional Responsibility, which combined broad principles, aspirational standards (called "ethical considerations"), and disciplinary rules. Less than a decade after the Code's adoption, dissatisfaction with a variety of problems with the Code, including

---

[11] *See* David Luban & Michael Millemann, *Good Judgment: Ethics Teaching in Dark Times*, 9 GEO. J. LEGAL ETHICS 31 (1995).

confusion created by the disparity between some of the ethical considerations and the disciplinary rules, led to the appointment of a new commission to evaluate professional standards. In 1983, the ABA adopted the new set of rules, the Model Rules of Professional Conduct. The Model Rules departed significantly from the Code by largely abandoning any effort to articulate aspirational standards, focusing instead almost exclusively on disciplinary rules.

As a practical matter, the bar controls the process by which states adopt and enforce rules of professional conduct. Nonlawyers have played almost no role in the commissions that have drafted the Model Rules and their revisions, and the state supreme courts that ultimately adopt or modify the rules rely heavily on bar associations' recommendations. Roughly half of the states have disciplinary agencies that are nominally independent of the bar, but they are staffed primarily by lawyers. The profession has argued that regulatory autonomy is justified in order to ensure that the profession remains independent and able to challenge government abuses.

The rules of professional conduct, cases and ethics opinions interpreting them, and the disciplinary processes that enforce the rules of conduct, are not the only sources of authority over lawyers. Courts and agencies have long claimed authority to regulate the lawyers who practice before them, and they frequently are in a position to observe misconduct and to respond immediately. The Federal Rules of Civil Procedure, for example, authorize judges to punish lawyers who engage in certain types of misconduct in litigation. In criminal cases, lawyer misconduct sometimes can be a basis for overturning a conviction. Lawyers who practice before federal agencies, such as the Securities Exchange Commission, Internal Revenue Service, Office of Thrift Supervision, and Patent and Trademark Office, must comply with special rules adopted by those agencies, and they are subject to discipline, including loss of the right to practice before those agencies, if they fail to comply. Injured clients, and, less commonly, third parties harmed by lawyers' misdeeds, sometimes sue lawyers for legal malpractice and other types of common law and statutory violations. Even when the bar finds that lawyers have violated their professional duties to clients and third parties, the sanctions imposed are limited to suspension of the lawyer's license, disbarment, and various forms of reprimand and warning; the bar disciplinary processes typically provide no remedies for clients or third parties harmed by lawyer misconduct. But malpractice actions, which are claims against lawyers for harm caused by a lawyer's departure from standards of ordinary care, sometimes enable clients to obtain monetary compensation. In recent years, malpractice insurance providers have taken an increasingly active role in monitoring lawyers' behavior and educating them about sources of potential liability. In addition, lawyers' peers, including other lawyers in the same workplace and colleagues in the same practice area, establish and reinforce norms of acceptable practice.[12] Some practice specialties, such as family law and tax, have issued their own more demanding rules of conduct to supplement the general rules of professional conduct applicable to all lawyers within a jurisdiction.

NOTES ON SOURCES OF LAWYER REGULATION

1. ***Aspirational Standards v. Enforceable Rules.*** Do you think there might be any costs associated with the evolution of the bar's standards of conduct from broad aspirational guidelines to enforceable minimum rules? If so, what are they?

2. ***Lowest Common Denominator?*** Some have argued that the bar's size, diversity, and specialization are in significant tension with the goal of articulating rigorous, ethically demanding rules of conduct. The result, these critics say, is a set of rules that appeal to the lowest common denominator and/or are phrased too abstractly to hold any real bite.

3. ***A Need for More Contextually Appropriate Ethics Rules?*** Some have argued that we should have more contextualized ethics rules for lawyers engaged in different types of practice. The Model Rules already distinguish between litigation and counseling; they require lawyers who serve as counselors to exercise independent professional judgment and to render candid advice. However, the rules otherwise generally assume that the lawyer's role is to maximize the client's interests through loyal and diligent advocacy.[13]

4. ***External Sources of Regulation.*** Recall that the definition of a profession included at the beginning of this chapter provides that professions are occupations that are "self-regulating." Does the increased incidence of other sources of regulation indicate that American lawyers' status as a profession is eroding? Do you think that non-lawyers should play a larger or smaller role in regulating lawyers' conduct than they currently do?

F. GLOBALIZATION AND THE LEGAL PROFESSION

Although this book is primarily about the American legal profession, it is impossible to cover that topic without paying some attention to globalization. Until recently, the operation and regulation of the practice

[12] For a more detailed discussion of each of these sources of control over lawyers' conduct, see David B. Wilkins, *Who Should Regulate Lawyers?*, 105 HARV. L. REV. 799 (1992).

[13] For examples of arguments in favor of more contextualized standards, reflecting the many roles lawyers play and the many types of clients they serve, see David B. Wilkins, *Making Context Count: Regulating Lawyers After Kaye Scholer,* 66 S. CAL. L. REV. 1145 (1993); Eli Wald, *Resizing the Rules of Professional Conduct,* 27 GEO. J. LEGAL ETHICS 227 (2014). For arguments focusing especially on the inadequacy of the ethics rules in non-adversary settings, see Carrie Menkel-Meadow, *The Limits of Adversary Ethics,* in ETHICS IN PRACTICE: LAWYERS' ROLES, RESPONSIBILITIES, AND REGULATION (Deborah L. Rhode Ed. 2000); Carrie Menkel-Meadow, *The Evolving Complexity of Ethics in Dispute Resolution,* 30 GEO. J. LEGAL ETHICS 389 (2017).

of law has been local and regional. But the globalization of economic activity and the rise of information technology are dramatically reshaping the delivery of legal services. International trade agreements increasingly exert influence over how lawyers work and are regulated.

The effects of globalization have been especially apparent in the sector of the profession that serves large international business entities.[14] Multinational corporations move products, services, and personnel around the globe, and they expect lawyers who serve them to easily navigate national and regulatory boundaries. There are now forty-seven global law firms with more than 1,000 lawyers. The largest of these, Dentons, has almost 7500 lawyers in 55 countries.[15] Global law firms also compete with other professional service providers, including the Big Four accounting firms. The Big Four and their affiliated law firms offer a model of "globally integrated business solutions" including not only accounting and tax-related advisory services but also legal services in a broad variety of fields, including compliance, finance, mergers and acquisitions, and employment law. They aggressively promote this model in emerging economies in the Asia-Pacific, Latin America, Africa and the Middle East.[16]

Globalization is shaping other sectors of practice as well. Lawyers who serve individuals and small businesses deal with ethnically diverse clients, including immigrants, foreign nationals, and citizens. Many of these clients have economic and family ties abroad and require lawyers who can assist them with problems and opportunities that cross national borders. Prosecutors and criminal defense lawyers also regularly interact with their counterparts in foreign legal systems.

The growing importance of cross-border practice has led some American law schools to revamp their curricula to provide international perspectives and legal training designed to equip new lawyers to interact with foreign legal systems and to practice in a world in which information technology and the flow of goods and services have made political borders less relevant. There has been a huge growth in international LLM programs and in the enrollment of international students in U.S. JD programs in the past decade.[17] Moreover, international students have

---

[14] *See* James Faulconbridge and Daniel Muzio, *Organizational Professionalism in Globalizing Law Firms*, 22 WORK, EMPLOYMENT & SOC'Y 7 (2008).

[15] *The Global 100 2017: The World's Top Law Firms Ranked by Lawyer Headcount*, LEGAL WEEK, Sept. 25, 2017.

[16] David B. Wilkins and Maria Jose Esteban, *The Reemergence of the Big Four in Law*, THE PRACTICE, Jan. 2016.

[17] Carole Silver and Swethaa Ballakrishnen, *Sticky Floors, Springboards, Stairways and Slow Escalators: Mobility Pathways and Preferences of International Students in U.S. Law Schools*, 3 UC IRVINE J. INT'L, TRANSNAT'L & COMP. L. 39 (2018).

become a more significant part of the overall diversity of the law student population at many law schools.[18]

G. WHAT IS PROFESSIONALISM?

Professor Michael Kelly has observed that "practicing lawyers are never opposed to professionalism. Professionalism is the law's apple pie and motherhood."[19] Kelly is undoubtedly right that it would be hard to find many American lawyers who oppose professionalism. But getting American lawyers to agree on exactly what professionalism is, or even to rally behind a particular set of values, is more difficult. The term is sometimes used to refer to issues of dignity and reputation, sometimes to refer to competence and craft, sometimes to mean independence from improper client demands, and sometimes to refer to lawyers' roles in making the legal system more accessible and just. Moreover, when lawyers and bar leaders speak of unprofessional conduct, they may have in mind categories of conduct that are more prevalent in some types of practice than others, and lawyers tend to most strongly repudiate behaviors associated with *other* practice areas—not their own. Thus, advertising and solicitation have historically drawn opposition from the elite bar, which generally has avoided these practices (at least until recently) and condemned them on the ground that they are undignified and thus unprofessional. Lawyers in small economically marginal firms may be more likely to neglect clients, miss filing deadlines, or to cut corners on research when the demands of high-volume practices become overwhelming, and those types of misconduct violate notions of professionalism grounded in commitment to competence and excellent client service. Complaints about high billing rates and complicity in corporate misconduct are much more commonly leveled against lawyers in large law firms than those in small firms. Those behaviors also are called unprofessional, but the emphasis there is on excessive commercialism, lack of personal integrity, and undue deference to clients' unreasonable expectations. Lawyers who serve clients of modest means and those who perform large amounts of pro bono work tend to view lawyers who serve only wealthy and powerful clients as failing to live up to a vision of professionalism that emphasizes access to justice. In other words, what the term professionalism *means* in particular contexts may vary according to the perspective of the person using the term.

Over the years, bar groups have examined the meaning of professionalism and what role the organized bar should play in promoting fundamental values of the American legal profession. A 1986 report by the ABA Commission on Professionalism noted that "the public views lawyers,

---

[18] Swethaa Ballakrishnen and Carole Silver, *A New Minority? International JD Students in U.S. Law Schools,* LAW & SOCIAL INQUIRY (forthcoming 2019).

[19] MICHAEL J. KELLY, LIVES OF LAWYERS: JOURNEYS IN THE ORGANIZATIONS OF PRACTICE (LAW, MEANING, AND VIOLENCE) 14 (1994).

at best, as being of uneven character and quality" and that many judges believed that lawyer professionalism was declining. The commission observed that the American legal profession had become more diverse and specialized than ever before, and that those changes made it difficult to articulate a common conception of professionalism; it noted that " 'Professionalism' is an elastic concept the meaning and application of which are hard to pin down." Nevertheless, the commission cited with approval a broad definition offered by former Harvard Law School Dean, Roscoe Pound:

> The term refers to a group . . . pursuing a learned art as a common calling in the spirit of public service—no less a public service because it may incidentally be a means of livelihood. Pursuit of the learned art in the spirit of a public service is the primary purpose.

The 1986 report included a series of recommendations, including that all segments of the bar should: (1) preserve and develop within the profession integrity, competence, fairness, independence, courage and a devotion to the public interest; (2) resolve to abide by higher standards of conduct than the minimum required by the Code of Professional Responsibility and the Model Rules of Professional Conduct; (3) increase the participation of lawyers in *pro bono* activities and help lawyers recognize their obligation to participate; (4) resist the temptation to make the acquisition of wealth a primary goal of law practice; (5) encourage innovative methods which simplify and make less expensive the rendering of legal services; (6) educate the public about legal processes and the legal system; (7) resolve to employ all the organizational resources necessary in order to assure that the legal profession is effectively self-regulating.[20]

In 2009, the ABA Standing Committee on Professionalism again examined the meaning of professionalism and how the ABA might "promot[e] the fundamental traditions and core values of the legal profession in the 21st Century." It noted that the public perception of lawyers remained "overwhelmingly negative" and that the situation had "not been helped by recent headlines showing lawyers involved in Ponzi schemes [and other fraudulent conduct]." The Commission concluded that "[a]lthough we can never eliminate wrongdoers from our midst, we can try harder, as a profession, to make the legal system more efficient, the day-to-day interactions between lawyers and clients more meaningful, and the professional lives of our colleagues more fulfilling." It proposed a new five-part professionalism initiative called "SERVE"—an acronym summarizing the following broad goals:

---

[20] ABA COMMISSION ON PROFESSIONALISM, ". . . IN THE SPIRIT OF PUBLIC SERVICE:" A BLUEPRINT FOR THE REKINDLING OF LAWYER PROFESSIONALISM (1986).

> **S—Support** the Legal **System**; **E—Exemplify** professionalism through enhanced teaching, technology and training; **R—Reaffirm** access to the Legal System, promoting justice through a dispute resolution system that is available to all; **V—Value** our place in society, integrating our core values of professionalism in each representation to provide our clients with real value while ensuring that we and our associates maintain professional values and act with integrity; **E—Embrace** professional **Excellence** while establishing balance and **Equilibrium** in lawyers' lives.[21]

One prominent legal ethics scholar has explored how the bar's statements about professionalism, such as those contained in the 1986 and 2009 reports, relate to increased competition in the market for legal services:

> [M]any lawyers express concern about the "decline of professionalism." That phrase captures a range of more specific complaints, such as increasing commercialism and competition and decreasing civility and collegiality. The perception of law as a craft and calling is under siege, and the consequence is an eroding sense of public service and cultural authority. Practitioners feel adrift. To borrow one bar association's description, it is as if lawyers are "looking for their lost wigs."[22]

Sociologist Eliot Freidson, whose definition of a profession we considered earlier in this chapter, describes professionalism as a set of "claims, values, and ideas" that professions offer to justify their relatively privileged position in terms of their monopoly on the provision of service and their authority to regulate themselves:

> The ideology of professionalism asserts above all else devotion to the use of disciplined knowledge and skill for the public good. Individual disciplines are concerned with different aspects of that good, in some cases the immediate good of individual patients, students, or clients, in others of firms and groups, and in others the general good. But such service must always be judged and balanced against a still larger public good, sometimes one anticipated in the future. Practitioners and their associations have the duty to appraise what they do in light of that larger good.[23]

---

[21] ABA Standing Committee on Professionalism, Reviving a Tradition of Service: Redefining Lawyer Professionalism in the 21st Century (2009).

[22] Deborah L. Rhode, *The Professionalism Problem*, 39 WM. & MARY L. REV. 283 (1998).

[23] ELIOT FREIDSON, PROFESSIONALISM: THE THIRD LOGIC (ON THE PRACTICE OF KNOWLEDGE) 217 (2001).

Notice that Freidson is not using the term "ideology" pejoratively here; the phrase "ideology of professionalism" simply refers to a vision of ideal lawyering and the lawyering role.

The bar's official statements about professionalism are not the only important expressions of professional values. Law students also find explicit or implicit assertions about what professionalism means in law school, where professors and law school administrators introduce students to legal culture and expectations of lawyers. Understandings of professionalism are also forged in lawyers' workplaces, where mentors and colleagues say or signal to young lawyers what types of behaviors are proper. In fact, some scholars have argued that lawyers' workplaces, practice specialties, and relationships with clients play a larger role than the bar's rules and proclamations in shaping lawyers' ideas about professionalism, and that this fact spells trouble for the bar's ability to regulate itself:

> [T]he vision of a unitary set of professional values invoked by leaders of the bar is a fiction. Workplace contexts develop widely varying and often mutually contradictory "local versions" of professionalism. At least some of these are inconsistent with the professional ideal projected in the bar's official rhetoric. One of the implications of the diversity in professional vision one observes among lawyers at work is that the task of professional self-regulation is significantly more complex than most observers would allow. In a world of widely shared professional values, it is plausible to think that ethical canons can be interpreted, taught, and enforced in the ways envisioned by the traditional model of self-regulation. But this model breaks down when lawyers develop very different conceptions of professionalism based on the particular circumstances of their practices.[24]

We do not attempt to offer our own definition of either the concept of a profession or professionalism—either in this chapter or elsewhere in the book. Nor do we expect you to adopt such definitions yourself. But you should become attuned to the ways that different lawyers, and types of lawyers, use the terms and the assumptions and expectations that underlie those uses.

NOTES ON PROFESSIONALISM

1. ***Do We Have a Coherent Definition?*** Can you derive any precise or concrete notion of professionalism from either of the reports issued by the ABA Commission on Professionalism? Even if not, do the reports nevertheless

[24] Robert L. Nelson & David M. Trubek, *Arenas of Professionalism: The Professional Ideologies of Lawyers in Context*, *in* LAWYERS' IDEALS/LAWYERS' PRACTICES 198–99 (Robert L. Nelson, David M. Trubek & Rayman L. Solomon eds., 1992).

suggest some elements of competing understandings of professionalism? Notice some of the particular priorities contained in the professionalism initiative outlined in the 2009 report: 1) providing excellent and efficient service to clients, 2) adhering to standards of civility in interactions with adversaries, 3) obeying ethical rules, 4) promoting justice and access to the legal system, 5) resisting unreasonable client demands, 6) engaging in public service, and 7) achieving work-life balance. Are any of these concepts inconsistent, or in tension with one another? If so, how?

2. ***Is Agreement About the Meaning of Professionalism Possible?*** The ABA Commission on Professionalism acknowledged that the great diversity of the American legal profession has made it difficult to articulate a coherent vision of professionalism, but it nevertheless asserted that "more unites than separates us." Is that right? If so, are the sources that unite the profession primarily ideas about the meaning of professionalism or something else? One critic has argued that an appearance of consensus is essential to the bar's monopoly and regulatory independence but that the profession has become too diverse and specialized to articulate and enforce "any unifying vision of professional ideals."[25] Do you agree?

3. ***Implications for Self-Regulation.*** If the organized bar has been unwilling or unable to articulate a unifying vision of professionalism, might that help explain why other regulators—courts, agencies, legislators, malpractice insurance providers, and leaders of practice organizations—have increasingly stepped in to state and enforce standards to govern law practice?

H. SUMMARY

This chapter introduced the concept of a profession, the history of the American legal profession, and its current demographic composition. It described several major empirical studies of the American legal profession and their primary findings. The chapter also identified various sources of law governing lawyers' conduct and other types of influence over lawyer behavior. It noted that globalization is shaping how legal services are delivered. Finally, it considered what we mean by "professionalism" and how various competing understandings of professionalism relate to diversity and specialization within the bar and to prospects for effective self-regulation.

---

[25] Deborah L. Rhode, *The Professionalism Problem*, 39 WM. & MARY L. REV. 283 (1998).

CHAPTER 3

THE LAWYER'S ROLE: THE AMORAL CONCEPTION AND ITS CRITICS

■ ■ ■

A. INTRODUCTION

Recall the first chapter of this book and particularly Richard Wasserstom's troubling assertion that "the lawyer-client relationship renders the lawyer at best systematically amoral and at worst more than occasionally immoral in his or her dealings with the rest of mankind." No issue regarding lawyers has commanded more attention from the public and academic commentators than the question of whether lawyers as a whole do more to contribute to justice or subvert it. As to the behavior of particular lawyers, the question becomes, when, if ever, is it morally permissible to do something as a lawyer that would be wrong to do if one were not a lawyer?

This chapter begins by considering one common view about lawyers' roles—a view that is sometimes called the "amoral" conception, and we explore problems with this conception of the lawyer's role. We also consider various alternatives to the amoral conception.

This chapter also addresses the related question of whether lawyers should be morally accountable for the clients and causes they choose to represent. In particular, we analyze when lawyers should represent unpopular clients, whether it matters why the client is unpopular, and the kinds of factors lawyers and law firms might use in deciding what types of clients to represent.

B. THE AMORAL CONCEPTION

One conception of the lawyer's role maintains that the lawyer must—or at least may—pursue any goal of the client through any arguably legal means and assert any non-frivolous legal claim. This view is sometimes called the "amoral" conception, because it suggests that the lawyer's role stands apart from morality. It is also sometimes referred to as the "standard" conception, because it corresponds with a view of role endorsed by many practicing lawyers. That understanding, as described by one of its critics, consists of two principles that guide the lawyer's actions and a third that informs how the lawyer and the public should evaluate that conduct.

1. *Principle of Partisanship.* The lawyer should seek to advance the interests of her client within the bounds of the law.
2. *Principle of Neutrality.* The lawyer should not consider the morality of the client's ends, nor the morality of particular actions taken to advance the client's ends, as long as they are lawful.
3. *Principle of Nonaccountability.* If a lawyer complies with the first two principles, neither third-party observers nor the lawyer herself should regard the lawyer as morally culpable.[1]

Several of the attractions of this view—its simplicity and consistency with the demands of clients—are captured in the attitude of the protagonist in a novel, a young associate trying to make his way toward partnership in a major law firm.

IN THE SHADOW OF THE LAW

Kermit Roosevelt (2005)

On the whole, Ryan very much liked being a lawyer. The lifestyle was not quite what he'd expected, not quite what television and movies had promised. There were fewer beautiful clients, mysteriously troubled, to collapse weeping into his arms, and more documents to be sorted and stamped and placed in various files. There was less pacing around the courtroom, wheeling to fire unexpected questions at cowering witnesses, and more solitary research and tedious memo-writing. But there was one thing that television and movies hadn't even hinted at: there was certainty.

As a lawyer, Ryan was realizing, as a litigator, you had a license to say anything. You're not responsible. In a way it was like being crazy, being given a free pass for whatever came out of your mouth, but it was better, because people didn't try to pretend you weren't in the room or lock you away in an attic. Instead they praised you for zealous advocacy, for doing your duty to the client. Duty to the client made things wonderfully clear. . . . You never have to admit that you're wrong, and if other people think you are, they also have to concede that you're supposed to be wrong—supposed to be a zealous advocate. . . Law is the license to be always in the right, Ryan thought; law means never having to say you're sorry.

1 William Simon, *The Ideology of Advocacy: Procedural Justice and Professional Ethics*, 1978 WIS. L. REV. 29 (1978).

NOTES ON ROOSEVELT

1. ***A Justifiable View?*** Is this view of the lawyer's role defensible? If so, on what grounds?

2. ***Within the Bounds of the Law.*** Does this associate place sufficient emphasis on the "as long as they are lawful" limitation in the principle of neutrality?

* * *

The following exchange explores those questions. Stephen Pepper, who offers perhaps the best defense of the amoral conception of the lawyer's role in the excerpt below, uses another term to describe this conception; he calls it the "first-class citizenship model."

THE LAWYER'S AMORAL ETHICAL ROLE: A DEFENSE, A PROBLEM, AND SOME POSSIBILITIES

Stephen L. Pepper
1986 American Bar Foundation Research Journal 613

[In 1975] Richard Wasserstrom published a provocative paper focusing attention on the moral dimension of the lawyer-client relationship. Much of Wasserstrom's exposition concerned the role-differentiated morality of the lawyer-client relationship, what he referred to as the amoral professional role. Wasserstrom was critical, but "undecided," about the value of that role. This essay is a defense of the lawyer's amoral role.

The role of all professionals, observed Wasserstrom, "is to prefer . . . the interests of client or patient" over those of other individuals. "[W]here the attorney-client relationship exists, it is often appropriate and many times even obligatory for the attorney to do things that, all other things being equal, an ordinary person need not, and should not do." Once a lawyer has entered into the professional relationship with a client, the notion is that conduct by the lawyer in service to the client is judged by a different moral standard than the same conduct by a layperson. The traditional view is that if such conduct by the lawyer is lawful, then it is morally justifiable, even if the same conduct by a layperson is morally unacceptable and even if the client's goals or means are morally unacceptable. As long as what lawyer and client do is lawful, it is the client who is morally accountable, not the lawyer.

The First Class Citizenship Model. The premise with which we begin is that law is a public good available to all. Society, through its "lawmakers"—legislatures, courts, administrative agencies, and so forth—has created various mechanisms to ease and enable the private attainment of individual or group goals. The corporate form of enterprise, the contract, the trust, the will, and access to civil court to gain the use of public force for the settlement of private grievance are all vehicles of empowerment for the individual or group; all are "law" created by the collectivity to be generally available for private use. In addition to these structuring mechanisms are vast amounts of law, knowledge of which is intended to be generally available and is empowering: landlord/tenant law, labor law, OSHA, Social Security—the list can be vastly extended. Access to both forms of law increases one's ability to successfully attain goals.

The second premise is a societal commitment to the principle of individual autonomy. This premise is founded on the belief that liberty and autonomy are a moral good, that free choice is better than constraint, that each of us wishes, to the extent possible, to make our own choices rather than to have them made for us. This belief is incorporated into our legal system, which accommodates individual autonomy by leaving as much room as possible for liberty and diversity. Leaving regulatory law aside for the moment, our law is designed (1) to allow the private structuring of affairs (contracts, corporations, wills, trusts, etc.) and (2) to define conduct that is intolerable. The latter sets a floor below which one cannot go, but leaves as much room as possible above that floor for individual decision making.

The third step is that in a highly legalized society such as ours, autonomy is often dependent upon access to the law. And while access to law—to the creation and use of a corporation, to knowledge of how much overtime one has to pay or is entitled to receive—is formally available to all, in reality it is available only through a lawyer. Our law is usually not simple, usually not self-executing. For most people most of the time, meaningful access to the law requires the assistance of a lawyer. If the conduct which the lawyer facilitates is above the floor of the intolerable—is not unlawful—then this line of thought suggests that what the lawyer does is a social good.

For the lawyer to have moral responsibility for each act he or she facilitates, for the lawyer to have a moral obligation to refuse to facilitate that which the lawyer believes to be immoral, is to substitute lawyers' beliefs for individual autonomy and diversity. Such a screening submits each to the prior restraint of the judge/facilitator and to rule by an oligarchy of lawyers. If the conduct is sufficiently "bad," it would seem that it ought to be made explicitly unlawful. If it is not that bad, why subject the citizenry to the happenstance of the moral judgment of the particular lawyer to whom each has access? If making the conduct unlawful is too onerous because the law would be too vague, or it is too difficult to identify the conduct in advance, or there is not sufficient social or political concern, do we intend to delegate to the individual lawyer the authority for case-by-case legislation and policing?

A final significant value supporting the first-class citizenship model is that of equality. If law is a public good, access to which increases autonomy, then equality of access is important. For access to the law to be filtered unequally through the disparate moral views of each individual's lawyer does not appear to be justifiable. Even given the current and perhaps permanent fact of unequal access to the law, it does not make sense to compound that inequality with another. If access to a lawyer is achieved (through private allocation of one's means, public provision, or the lawyer's or profession's choice to provide it), should the extent of that access depend upon individual lawyer conscience? One of the unpleasant concomitants of the view that a lawyer should be morally responsible for all that she does is the resulting inequality: unfiltered access to the law is then available only to those who are legally sophisticated or to those able to educate themselves sufficiently for access to the law, while those less sophisticated—usually those less educated—are left with no access or with access that subjects their use of the law to the moral judgment and veto of the lawyer.

The Adversary System. Much writing on the amoral role of the lawyer has dealt with the layperson's common conception of what lawyers do: criminal defense. The amoral role is justified by the need of the "man in trouble" for a champion familiar with the law to aid him in facing the vast resources of the state bearing down on him, attempting to seize his most basic liberties and put him in jail. In this context, however, there is another champion, the prosecutor, with greater resources, opposing and balancing the lawyer's amorality. More important, there are a neutral judge and a jury whose roles are significantly less amoral than the advocate's. Critics of the lawyer's role have had a field day distinguishing this situation from civil litigation and from nonlitigation (what most lawyers are working on most of the time). The critics suggest that a role justified by the rather unusual context of the criminal justice system simply is not justified in the far more common lawyer roles. Where there is no judge responsible for applying the law from a neutral stance, where there is no lawyer protecting those who may be victimized or exploited by another person's use of "the law"—in these situations the critics of the amoral role argue that the lawyer must take on the neutral judge's role and screen access to and use of the law. Their point is that a role modeled on Perry Mason does not fit the lawyer working for Sears drafting form consumer contracts.

It is therefore significant that the justification for the lawyer's amoral role sketched above has not once mentioned the adversary system, has not been based on any premise involving an opposing lawyer or a neutral judge or jury.

Before moving on from the adversary system criticism, it is appropriate to note that the adversary system image of the lawyer as the champion against a hostile world—the hired gun—is not the proper image for the general role of the lawyer presented here (although it may be the proper image for the criminal defense lawyer). Rather, the image more concordant with the first-class citizenship model is that of the individual facing and needing to use a very large and very complicated machine (with lots of whirring gears and spinning data tapes) that he can't get to work. This is "the law" that confronts the individual in our society. It is theoretically there for his use, but he can't use it for his purposes without the aid of someone who has the correct wrenches, meters, and more esoteric tools, and knows how and where to use them. Or the image is that of someone who stands frustrated before a photocopier that won't copy (or someone whose car won't go) and needs a technician (or mechanic) to make it go. It is ordinarily not the technician's or mechanic's moral concern whether the content of what is about to be copied is morally good or bad, or for what purpose the customer intends to use the car.

The Problem of Legal Realism. Up to this point in the discussion, access to the law as the primary justification for the amoral professional role has been presented with relatively little focus on what "the law" refers to. The implication has been that the law is existent and determinable, that there is "something there" for the lawyer to find (or know) and communicate to the client. The "thereness" of the law is also the assumption underlying the commonly understood limit on the amoral role: the lawyer can only assist the client "within the bounds of the law." This accords with the usual understanding of the law from the lay or client point of view, but not from the lawyer's point of view. The dominant view of law inculcated in the law schools, which will be identified here as "legal realism," approaches law without conceiving of it as objectively "out there" to be discovered and applied. A relatively little explored problem is the dynamic between the amoral professional role and a skeptical attitude toward law.

By "legal realism" I mean a view of law which stresses its open-textured, vague nature over its precision; its manipulability over its certainty; and its instrumental possibilities over its normative content. What is the interaction between this view of the law and the view of the lawyer as an amoral servant of the client whose assistance is limited only by "the law"?

The apt image is that of Holmes's "bad man." The modern lawyer is taught to look at the law as the "bad man" would, "who cares only for the material consequences." The lawyer discovers and conveys "the law" to his client from this perspective and then is told to limit his own assistance to the client based upon this same view of "the law." The modern view of contract law, for example, deemphasizes the normative obligation of promises and views breach of contract as a "right" that is subject to the "cost" of damages. Breach of contract is not criminal and, normally, fulfillment of a contractual obligation is not forced on a party (not "specifically enforced," in contract law terminology). The client who comes in with a more normative view of the obligation of contracts will be educated by the competent lawyer as to the "breach as cost" view of "the law." Similarly, modern tort law has emphasized allocation of the "costs" of accidents, as opposed to the more normative view of 19th- and early 20th-century negligence law. Thus, negligence law can be characterized as establishing a right to a nonconsensual taking from the injured party on the part of the tortfeasor, subject once again to the "cost" of damages. An industrial concern assessing and planning conduct which poses risks of personal injury or death to third parties will be guided by a lawyer following this view away from perceiving the imposition of unreasonable risk as a "wrong" and toward perceiving it as a potential cost.

From the perspective of fully informed access to the law, this modification of the client's view is good because it accords with the generally accepted understanding of the law among those who are closest to its use and administration—lawyers and judges. It is accurate; it is useful to the client. From the perspective of the ethical relationship between lawyer and client, it is far more problematic. If one combines the dominant "legal realism" understanding of law with the traditional amoral role of the lawyer, there is no moral input or constraint in the present model of the lawyer-client relationship. The client who consults a lawyer will be guided to maximize his autonomy through the tools of the law—tools designed and used to maximize freedom, not to provide a guide to good behavior. If one cannot rely on the client or an alternative social institution to provide that guide, to suggest a moral restraint on that which is legally available, then what the lawyer does may be evil: lawyers in the aggregate may consistently guide clients away from moral conduct and restraint.

Assume client consults lawyer concerning discharge of polluted water from a rural plant. Client wants to know what the law requires, respects "the law," and intends to comply. Removing ammonia from the plant's effluent is very expensive. The EPA limit is .050 grams of ammonia per liter of effluent, and the EPA has widely publicized this standard to relevant industries. In addition to this information, however, lawyer informs client that inspection in rural areas of the state is rare and that enforcement officials always issue a warning (give a second chance) prior to applying sanctions unless the violation is extreme. Moreover, lawyer also informs client that it is known informally that violations of .075 grams per liter or less are ignored because of a limited enforcement budget. In such a situation, lay ignorance of legal technicalities and the realities of enforcement would seem to lead toward more obedience of "the law" (the .050-gram limit). Access to an amoral, "legal realist" lawyer leads toward violation of "the law."

Potential Answers to the Problem of Legal Realism. [Pepper offers several ideas about how to ameliorate the dilemma sketched above, including the possibility of wide-ranging communication and moral dialogue with the client and, in extreme cases, conscientious objection.]

Conclusion: The Moral Autonomy of the Lawyer. Given this essay's stress on autonomy, it is fair to ask: Where in the amoral role is there a place for the lawyer's moral autonomy?

Part of the answer lies in the principle of professionalism sketched at the beginning of [this essay]. Because of the large advantages over the client built into the lawyer's professional role, and because of the disadvantages and vulnerability built into the client's role, the professional must subordinate his interest to the client's when there is a conflict.

The rest of the answer can be found in those limited areas in which the moral autonomy of the lawyer can function compatibly with the amoral professional ethic. Initially, the lawyer has the choice of whether or not to be a lawyer. Second, the lawyer has the choice of whether or not to accept a person as a client. Third, a large degree of moral autonomy can be exercised through the lawyer-client moral dialogue. Fourth, conscientious objection is an ever present option within the realm of the lawyer's moral autonomy. These four areas combined create a meaningful field for the exercise of the lawyer's moral autonomy.

The result, I believe is that the good lawyer can be a good person; not comfortable, but good.

NOTES ON PEPPER

1. ***Are Clients Entitled to Lawyers' Assistance for All Goals and Means That Are Not Illegal?*** Are you persuaded by Pepper's argument that, if conduct is sufficiently bad, it ought to be made explicitly unlawful, and that if it's not that bad, or if "making that conduct unlawful is too onerous," clients are entitled to legal assistance with their projects?

2. ***An Oligarchy of Lawyers?*** What do you think of Pepper's argument that encouraging lawyers to refuse to facilitate that which they believe to be immoral would subject clients to rule by an "oligarchy of lawyers"? Are lawyers likely to agree among themselves as to what projects are objectionable on moral grounds?

3. ***What Types of Clients Does Pepper Envision?*** Pepper paints a picture of the attorney-client relationship in which clients lack access to the machinery of law without help from lawyers and are therefore vulnerable to lawyers who would deny clients access to law based on the lawyers' moral objections. He also refers to "the disadvantages and vulnerability built into the client's role." What types of clients do you think Pepper envisions when he says that clients are vulnerable to lawyers in this way?

C. CRITIQUES OF THE AMORAL CONCEPTION

Moral philosopher and Professor David Luban rejects the amoral conception of the lawyer's role. He argues that lawyers are just as morally accountable for the choices they make as lawyers as they would be as ordinary citizens.

THE LYSISTRATIAN PREROGATIVE: A RESPONSE TO STEPHEN PEPPER

David Luban

1987 American Bar Foundation Research Journal 637

Abraham Lincoln once said to a client in his Springfield law practice:

> Yes, we can doubtless gain your case for you; we can set a whole neighborhood at loggerheads; we can distress a widowed mother and her six fatherless children and thereby get you six hundred dollars to which you seem to have a legal claim, but which rightfully belongs, it appears to me, as much to the woman and her children as it does to you. You must remember that some things legally right are not morally right. We shall not take your case, but will give you a little advice for which we will charge you nothing. You seem to be a sprightly, energetic man; we would advise you to try your hand at making six hundred dollars in some other way.

Lincoln seems to have taken "some things legally right are not morally right" to be an important truth. It shows that exercising one's legal rights is not always morally acceptable. Lincoln evidently concluded that helping someone exercise their legal rights is not always morally acceptable. And so, Lincoln rejected the lawyer's amoral ethical role.

Pepper disagrees with this line of thinking, arguing instead that "[t]he lawyer is a good person in that he provides access to the law." But some things legally right are not morally right, and so in any such argument we must ask how the rabbit of moral justification manages to come out of the hat. And the answer, I believe, is the one we all expected: rabbits don't come out of hats unless they have been put in the hats to begin with. Pepper, I believe, assumes that the morality is already in the law, that in an important sense anything legally right is morally right. That, however, cannot be.

The argument for the amoral role goes as follows: *First premise*: "law is intended to be a public good which increases autonomy." *Second Premise*: "autonomy [is] preferred over 'right' or 'good' conduct;" "increasing individual autonomy is morally good." *Third premise*: "in a highly legalized society such as ours, . . . access to the law . . . in reality . . . is available only through a lawyer." *Conclusion*: "what the lawyer does is a social good." "The lawyer is a good person in that he provides access to the law."

I deny the second premise, that individual autonomy is preferred over right or good conduct: it is the point at which the rabbit gets into the hat.

Pepper appears to have blurred the crucial distinction between the desirability of people acting autonomously and the desirability of their autonomous act. It is good, desirable, for me to make my own decisions about whether to lie to you; it is bad, undesirable, for me to lie to you. It is good that people act autonomously, that they make their own choices about what to do; what they choose to do, however, need not be good. Pepper's second premise is plausible only when we focus exclusively on the first of each of these pairs of propositions; it loses its plausibility when we turn our attention to the second. Other things being equal, Pepper is right that "increasing individual autonomy is morally good," but when the exercise of autonomy results in an immoral action, other things aren't equal. You must remember that some things autonomously done are not morally right.

Pepper's subsequent argument is that since exercising autonomy is good, helping people exercise autonomy is good. Though this is true, it too is only half the story. The other half is that since doing bad things is bad, helping people do bad things is bad. The two factors must be weighed against each other, and this Pepper does not do.

Compare this case: The automobile, by making it easier to get around, increases human autonomy; hence, other things being equal, it is morally good to repair the car of someone who is unable by himself to get it to run. But such considerations can hardly be invoked to defend the morality of fixing the getaway car of an armed robber, assuming that you know in advance what the purpose of the car is. The moral wrong of assisting the robber outweighs the abstract moral goodness of augmenting the robber's autonomy.

Pepper admits that it "may be morally wrong to manufacture or distribute cigarettes or alcohol, or to disinherit one's children for marrying outside the faith, but the generality of such decisions are left in the private realm." That is true, but that doesn't imply that such exercises of autonomy are morally acceptable. On the contrary, it concedes that they are immoral. And this is simply to return to the distinction between the desirability of exercising autonomy and the undesirability of exercising it wrongly.

To make his argument work, he distinguishes between (merely) immoral conduct and intolerable conduct, and says that intolerable conduct "ought to be made explicitly unlawful"; at one point, indeed, he equates "not unlawful" conduct with conduct "above the floor of the intolerable." Using this distinction, he argues in effect that unlawful conduct is conduct the immorality of which does not outweigh the value of autonomous decision-making. If we didn't want people to make up their own minds about such conduct, we would make it illegal, and thus the fact that we haven't shows that we do not disapprove of it sufficiently to take the decision out of people's own hands.

The conclusion does not follow, however. There are many reasons for not prohibiting conduct besides the reason that we don't think it's bad enough to take it out of people's hands. We should not put into effect prohibitions that are unenforceable, or that are enforceable only at enormous cost, or through unacceptably or disproportionately invasive means. We should not prohibit immoral conduct if it would be too difficult to specify the conduct, or if the laws would of necessity be vague or either over or underinclusive, or if enforcement would destroy our liberties. All these are familiar and good reasons for refraining from prohibiting conduct that have nothing whatever to do with the intensity of our disapprobation of the conduct.

Pepper acknowledges this too, but resists its implication by posing this rhetorical question: "If making the conduct unlawful is too onerous because the law would be too vague, or it is too difficult to identify the conduct in advance, or there is not sufficient social or political concern, do we intend to delegate to the individual lawyer the authority for case-by-case legislation and policing?" I do not treat this question as rhetorical; I answer it "yes." The reason goes, I think, to the heart of my disagreement with Pepper.

What bothers Pepper the most, I believe, is the idea that lawyers should interpose themselves and their moral concerns as "filters" of what legally permissible projects clients should be able to undertake. His concern, in turn, appears to have two aspects to it, one specific to lawyers, the other more general: "Such a screening submits each to . . . rule by oligarchy of lawyers." More generally, it appears to me that Pepper objects to anyone, lawyer or not, interposing his or her scruples to filter the legally permissible projects of autonomous agents.

The first of these worries is illusory, for there is no oligarchy of lawyers, actual or potential, to worry about. An oligarchy is a group of people ruling in concert, whereas lawyers who refuse to execute projects to which they object on moral grounds will do so as individuals, without deliberating collectively with other lawyers.

The second worry is more interesting. Unlike Pepper, I am not troubled by the existence of informal filters of people's legally permissible projects. Far from seeing these as a threat to the rule of law, I regard them as essential to its very existence. We—people, that is—are tempted to a vast array of reprehensible conduct. Some of it can be and is tolerated; some of it we do not engage in because of our scruples; and some of it the law proscribes. But the law cannot proscribe all intolerable conduct, for human society would then be crushed flat by a monstrous, incomprehensible mass of law. And scruples—conscience, morality—will not take up all the slack. Instead, we rely to a vast extent on informal social pressure to keep us in check. When conscience is too faint, people worry about what other people will say, think, and do, and guide their behavior accordingly.

Imagine now what would happen if we could no longer count on this sort of motivation, so that we would have to enforce desirable behavior legally. When we begin to reflect on the sheer magnitude of altruistic behavior we take for granted in day-to-day life, we realize that society could not exist without the dense network of informal filters provided by other people.

Among those filters is noncooperation. Many nefarious schemes are aborted because an agent's associates or partners or friends or family or financial backers or employees will have nothing to do with them. Far from this being an objectionable state of affairs, neither society nor law could survive without such filters.

I do not see why a lawyer's decision not to assist a client in a scheme that the lawyer finds nefarious is any different from these other instances of social control through private noncooperation. It is no more an affront to the client's autonomy for the lawyer to refuse to assist in the scheme than it is for the client's wife to threaten to move out if he goes ahead with it. Indeed, the lawyer's autonomy allows him to exercise the "the "Lysistratian prerogative"—to withhold services from those of whose projects he disapproves, to decide not to go to bed with clients who want to "set a whole neighborhood at loggerheads."

Pepper wants to allow the lawyer's autonomy a narrower scope: to refrain from being a lawyer, to engage in moral dialogue with clients, to decline to represent a client, and in extreme cases to engage in conscientious objection against odious professional obligations. The last two of these together add up to the Lysistratian prerogative, except for Pepper's limitation of conscientious objection to extreme cases. He includes this limitation because he thinks that only extremely objectionable actions outweigh the value of enhancing client autonomy. I believe, however, that in almost every case of significant client immorality the good of helping the client realize his autonomy will be outweighed by the bad of the immoral action the client proposes.

The morally pernicious effect of "legal realism" is a splendid discovery of Pepper's. As we have seen, Pepper's defense assumes that the law itself reflects a society's moral beliefs and the relative intensities of its moral judgments. The legal realist, on the other hand, is a moral skeptic about the law, who has bathed its clauses in cynical acid until all encrustations of morality have been dissolved. The result, as Pepper notes, is that "there is no moral input or constraint in the present model of the lawyer-client relationship."

There are two versions of "legal realism": one, which I will call High Realism, is an important philosophy of law; the other, which I will call Low

Realism, amounts to skepticism about law, and is no more a philosophy of law than "what's right is whatever you can get away with" is a philosophy of ethics. Low Realism is the claim that law is "a prediction of what human officials will do." High Realism is the claim that law is a prediction of what human officials will do *in their good faith efforts to interpret and enforce authoritative rules*. According to Low Realism, as long as the relevant officials will not sanction you, you have *by definition* committed no infraction of the law. Low Realism drains law of its normative content.

When we realize this, we realize that while the problem Pepper raises is of enormous practical importance, it arises only because Low Realism has come to be believed and lived by many lawyers.

I cannot, however, resist pointing out that the amoral ethical role Pepper defends contributes to the prevalence of Low Realism. When getting the client whatever he or she wants is conceived of as the lawyer's preponderant professional obligation, it is psychologically natural to reduce the dissonance between that obligation and legality by understanding the law as *whatever I can get officials to give my client*. Take the normative content out of the lawyer's role and the lawyer will feel impelled to take the normative content out of law as well and define it as victor's spoils pure and simple.

NOTES ON LUBAN'S CRITIQUE OF PEPPER

1. ***Lawyers as Informal Filters.*** Is Luban right that there is nothing wrong with lawyers serving as an "informal filter" on people pursuing legally permissible projects? Does your answer depend at all on the type of client or the particular circumstances of the matter at hand?

2. ***High Realism v. Low Realism.*** Which type of Realism do you think is taught in law school—the High version or the Low?

D. ALTERNATIVES TO THE AMORAL CONCEPTION

If one finds the amoral conception of the lawyer's role unsatisfactory, what other possibilities are available? This section canvasses various alternatives.

Moral Activism. The strongest version of the argument against the amoral conception comes from David Luban, author of the critique of Pepper excerpted above. He argues that lawyers should be guided and judged by the same types of moral considerations that apply to ordinary citizens. He makes a single exception for criminal defense work, because he believes that aggressive, client-centric advocacy is necessary to protect the constitutional rights of defendants and to guard against abuses of governmental power.[2]

Deborah Rhode similarly argues that "[a]ttorneys should make decisions as advocates in the same way that morally reflective individuals make any ethical decision." Under her approach, lawyers "could not simply retreat into some fixed conception of role that denies personal accountability for public consequences or that unduly privileges clients' and lawyers' own interests":

> Client trust and confidentiality are entitled to weight, but they must be balanced against other equally important concerns. Lawyers also have responsibilities to prevent unnecessary harm to third parties, to promote a just and effective legal system, and to respect core values such as honesty, fairness, and good faith on which that system depends.[3]

Contextual Approaches. William Simon has argued for what he calls the "Contextual View," according to which "Lawyers should take those actions that, considering the relevant circumstances of the particular case, seem likely to promote justice."[4] He carefully distinguishes his notion of justice from "ordinary morality":

> "Justice" here connotes the basic values of the legal system. Decisions about justice are not assertions of personal preferences, nor are they applications of ordinary morality. They are legal judgments grounded in the methods and sources of authority of the professional culture. I use "justice" interchangeably with "legal merit."

Simon's approach requires consideration of the totality of circumstances, but it also directs the lawyer's attention to several types of recurring tensions at the heart of our legal system. One is the tension between substance and procedure. As a general rule, lawyers may reasonably assume that judges, juries, and officials overseeing administrative procedures are better positioned than individual lawyers to make reliable determinations about the merits of cases. However, where lawyers have reason to believe that the relevant procedures are defective, they must take greater responsibility for ensuring a just outcome:

> Perhaps an adverse party or official lacks information or resources needed to initiate, pursue, or determine a claim. Or perhaps an official is corrupt, or politically intimidated, or incompetent. Or perhaps the relevant procedures are ill designed to resolve the matter. The basic response of the Contextual View is this: the

---

2 DAVID LUBAN, LAWYERS AND JUSTICE: AN ETHICAL STUDY (1988).

3 DEBORAH L. RHODE, IN THE INTERESTS OF JUSTICE 67 (2000).

4 WILLIAM H. SIMON, THE PRACTICE OF JUSTICE 138–39 (1998).

> more reliable the relevant procedures and institutions, the less direct responsibility the lawyer need assume for the substantive justice of the resolution; the less reliable the procedures and institutions, the more direct responsibility she needs to assume for substantive justice.

This attention to procedural context suggests that in situations where the checks and balances of adversary processes are not present, including, for example, in counseling private clients about legal compliance or government agencies about their conduct, the lawyer has a greater responsibility to ensure that outcomes are just than in situations where processes are reliable.

Another type of tension noted by Simon is that between the form and purpose of rules. Simon argues that lawyers should take responsibility for ensuring that the rules they invoke are applied in a manner that takes into account their purposes: the clearer and more fundamental the relevant purposes, the more the lawyer should consider herself bound by them; the less clear and more problematic the relevant purposes, the more justified the lawyer is in treating the relevant norms formally [by which he means "understanding them to permit any client goal not plainly precluded by their language."]

The Citizen Lawyer. Robert Gordon has argued that lawyers should strive to be "citizen lawyers" who not only seek to avoid subverting justice in their daily practices but also attempt to serve the public and to improve the operation of law and its administration. The following excerpt sketches some attributes of this ideal type, which he concedes "has lately fallen out of favor."

THE CITIZEN LAWYER—A BRIEF INFORMAL HISTORY OF A MYTH WITH SOME BASIS IN REALITY

Robert W. Gordon
50 William & Mary Law Review 1169 (2009)

In advising clients contemplating litigation, the citizen lawyer takes into account the merits or justice of the claim. She seeks to dissuade plaintiffs from pursuing plainly meritless claims, and encourages defendants towards fair settlements and away from invalid defenses of just claims.

When involved in litigation, the citizen lawyer regards herself as an "officer of the court," that is, a trustee for the integrity and fair operation of the basic procedures of the adversary system, the rules of the game, and their underlying purposes. She fights aggressively for her client, but in ways respectful of the fair and effective operation of this framework. In discovery, she frames requests intended to elicit useful information rather than to harass and inflict costs, and responds to reasonable requests rather than obstructing or delaying. She claims privilege or work product protection only when she thinks a fair-minded judge would be likely to independently support the claim. In deciding how ferociously to attack the credibility of a witness on cross-examination, she tries to assess and take into account the likely truthfulness of the witness and the underlying merits of the case.

In advising clients outside litigation, the citizen lawyer is the "wise counselor," who sees her job as guiding the client to comply with the underlying spirit or purpose as well as the letter of laws and regulations to desist from unlawful conduct, and if needed, to do so with strong advice backed by the threat of withdrawal, and in extreme cases, of disclosure. If the client needs her help to resist or change unfavorable law, she makes the challenge public and transparent, to facilitate its authoritative resolution.

To generalize more broadly, the citizen lawyer identifies broadly with the institutions, goals, and procedures of the legal system, even though she may (and if she is conscientious, probably does) also think that aspects of the existing system are inefficient, oppressive, or fundamentally unjust. She feels a sense of proprietorship, or ownership in common, of the legal framework—that the law, considered aspirationally as well as conservatively, as a set of norms and principles rather than a collection of particular rules, is in her profession's special stewardship, to preserve and cultivate and reform so it can serve its best purposes. In some instances, it may be that unjust laws or bad interpretations of them are so entrenched in conventional legal practice that a lawyer could not deprive a client of the unjust advantages they confer without committing malpractice. In that case, the citizen lawyer works with law reform commissions, bar committees and task forces, legislative committees, and administrative agencies to reform laws to make them more just and efficient, regardless of whether the reforms would help or hurt their clienteles.

* * *

Fidelity to Law. Bradley Wendel rejects the notion that lawyers' conduct should be guided by ordinary morality. He also denies that lawyers should take responsibility for serving the public interest or achieving justice. Legality, rather than morality, justice, or the public good, is his touchstone. He views lawyers as part of a scheme of political institutions and practices whose goal is the governance of the community. Wendel advocates for an approach that is similar to the amoral conception (which he calls the "Standard Conception") but places much greater emphasis on what he calls "fidelity to law." Many types of lawyer conduct that Pepper says are permitted to facilitate "first-class citizenship" are unavailable under Wendel's approach because they are inconsistent with the lawyer's obligation to uphold the law.

LAWYERS AND FIDELITY TO LAW

W. Bradley Wendel (2010)

[T]he first aspect of a conception of legal ethics centered on fidelity to law [is] that the legal entitlements of clients, not client interests, ordinary moral considerations or abstract legal norms such as justice, should be the object of lawyers' concerns when acting in a representative capacity. When representing clients, lawyers must respect the scheme of rights and duties established by the law, and not seek to work around the law because either they or their clients believe the law to be unjust, inefficient, stupid, or simply inconvenient. The obligation of respect means that lawyers must treat the law as a reason for action as such, not merely a possible downside to be taken into account, planned around, or nullified in some way. This obligation applies even if it would be very much in the client's interests to obtain a result that is not supported by a plausible claim to a legal entitlement.

The ideal of partisanship, properly understood, represents a commitment to the value of legality. Legality may be seen as narrower than morality in general, but as I will argue, it also represents a distinctive way for citizens to live together and treat each other with respect, as equals. Thus, rather than inhabiting a "simplified moral world," lawyers actually inhabit a world of demanding ethical obligations of fidelity to law. The Standard Conception, therefore, should be modified so that the Principle of Partisanship is understood as requiring lawyers representing clients to protect the legal entitlements of their clients, not merely to seek to advance their interests. Talking about obligations such as loyalty and partisanship is unobjectionable, as long as it is understood that the object of the lawyer's commitment is not obtaining whatever the client wants, but what the client is legally permitted to have. In this modification of the Standard Conception, which is grounded on the fidelity to law, lawyers still have obligations of loyalty and partisanship which run to clients, but which are constituted by the legal entitlements of clients. Legal ethics is therefore not primarily an excuse for immoral behavior but a higher duty incumbent upon occupants of a professional role.

Lawyers who represent clients act to protect legal entitlements by asserting them in litigated disputes or negotiations, counsel their clients on what the law permits, and structure their clients' affairs with reference to the law. As this term will be used here, a legal entitlement is a substantive or procedural right, created by the law, which establishes claim-rights (implying duties upon others), privileges to do things without interference, and powers to change the legal situation of others (e.g., by imposing contractual obligations). Entitlements may be created by courts, legislatures, administrative agencies, or by citizens themselves, using legal tools for private ordering, such as wills, trusts, contract, partnerships, and corporations. Whatever lawyers do for their clients must be justified on the basis of their clients' lawful rights, permissions, and obligations.

This approach to legal ethics depends to a great extent on the determinacy of law. Clients and lawyers sometimes talk as though the law can be made to mean pretty much anything a clever lawyer wants it to mean. I am not really worried about this caricatured version of legal realism here. A more serious objection is that there is a range of reasonable interpretations that the law might bear, and it is an important aspect of legal ethics to determine what a lawyer should do within that zone of reasonableness.

There is a difference between trying to figure out what the law actually is, and acting in accordance with what one believes the law ought to be. Where the law is unclear, citizens and lawyers may be aiming at a moving target, they may see only through a glass darkly, or some other metaphor may better capture the idea that legal judgments are not always capable of being made with a great deal of precision. Nevertheless, it is possible to distinguish aiming at the law from trying to get around it (which requires, ironically, that one have the law fairly clearly in view, to know how to evade it).* It is permissible, of course, to make arguments about what one believes the law ought to be, but these are formally different from statements about what the law actually permits or requires. This observation about this formal difference leads to a point about the institutional structure of litigation and non-litigation representation. Lawyers representing clients in litigated matters must have some leeway to assert arguable legal interpretations, leaving it up to opposing counsel to challenge these positions, and to the court to make a decision about the best interpretation of the law. However, litigation is a special case, in which lawyers share responsibility for other institutional actors for getting the law right. In counseling and transactional representation, by contrast, the lawyer is frequently the only actor who has any power to render a judgment about what the law permits. That is not to deny that there is a range of meanings that the law can reasonably be understood to bear—within that range, there is nothing wrong with the lawyer adopting a view that is consistent with her client's interests. At the same time, however, lawyers are not permitted to adopt positions outside the range of reasonable interpretations, simply because it would be advantageous to their clients if they did so.

* [Eds.: This footnote is Wendel's.] Compare Harry Frankfurt's distinction between lies and bullshit, in HARRY G. FRANKFURT, ON BULLSHIT (2005). Lying is necessarily parasitic upon belief in the existence and knowability of the truth. A liar seeks to persuade others of something that the liar believes not to be true. Bullshit, by contrast, is indifference to the truth. The lawyers who structured the transactions underlying the Enron collapse and the [U.S. Department of Justice Office of Legal Counsel (OLC)] lawyers who drafted the torture memos were engaged in lying, because they knew what the law was and sought to evade it. Those who claim that the law is radically indeterminate, including some defenders of the Enron and OLC lawyers, are bullshitting.

* * *

Client Power. Susan Carle argues that lawyers should calibrate the zealousness of their representation in inverse relationship to their clients' power relative to other interests affected by the representation:

> Lawyers for clients with substantially greater power relative to that of other interests affected by the representation should strive to temper the zealousness of their client advocacy with an eye to protecting consideration of less powerful interests. In contrast, lawyers for clients with substantially less power—in other words, lawyers representing "underdogs" vis a vis powerful interests—should be guided by the ethical principle of zealous. . . representation. In the middle range of cases, involving representations of clients with substantially equivalent power, or power relationships that are sufficiently complex or multifaceted as to produce indeterminate results under a power-based test, consideration of relative client power should not come into play in guiding lawyers' ethical judgments.

Carle asserts that one justification for this approach is that it pushes against the temptations of lawyer self-interest, which vary with the relative power of lawyers' clients. In the context of representing powerful clients, lawyers' incentive is to "do too much for their clients," while in the context of representing clients with fewer resources, lawyers' incentive is to "do too little."[5]

NOTES ON ALTERNATIVES TO AMORAL ADVOCACY

1. ***Strengths and Weaknesses of the Alternatives.*** What are the strengths and weaknesses of these alternatives to amoral advocacy? Do you find any (or all) of them preferable to the amoral conception of the lawyer's role? If so, why?

2. ***What Factors Might Matter?*** Under Simon's "Contextual View," what kinds of factors might a lawyer consider in deciding how to respond to particular dilemmas? Might a partial list include the procedural context (litigation, counseling, transactional work, internal investigations, writing opinion letters, etc.), the interests of other affected parties, whether other affected interests are well represented, access to relevant information, and the purposes of the relevant laws and rules?

3. ***Good Citizenship as a Business Asset.*** There are obvious benefits for the legal system in lawyers' adherence to Gordon's conception of the citizen lawyer. Are there circumstances in which a lawyer's reputation for good

[5] Susan D. Carle, *Power as a Factor in Lawyers' Ethical Deliberations*, 35 HOFSTRA L. REV. 115 (2006).

citizenship might enhance her ability to attract clients? What types of clients might want to hire citizen lawyers?

4. ***Plausible and Reasonable Interpretations of Law.*** What is the significance of Wendel's use of the term "plausible" in the last sentence of the first paragraph and "reasonable" in the last sentence of the final paragraph?

5. ***Client Power and Lawyer Self-Interest.*** Carle suggests that taking client power into account in deciding how zealously to represent clients might help to address the moral hazards of lawyer self-interest. Is Carle correct to suggest that a client's ability to pay for superior legal services and to deliver repeat business might tend to lead a lawyer for a powerful client to provide overly-aggressive representation, and that a client's inability to provide those rewards might lead a lawyer for a poor or disadvantaged client to skimp on the quality of representation or devotion to the client?

6. ***Simplicity and Ease of Application.*** Are any of the alternative models as easy to apply as the amoral view? Are some more difficult to follow than others? To the extent that these alternative models require lawyers to engage in more reflection than the amoral advocacy model, is that a strength or weakness of the alternatives?

Luban and Wendell characterize one common objection to alternatives to amoral advocacy in this way:

> You simply cannot lead a professional life in a constant state of moral arousal, any more than a physician can practice emergency room medicine in a constant state of sympathetic anguish for the patients. The traits of character the moralists call for are not functional, realistic, or desirable. They would make a lawyer a misfit in the teamwork-based setting of a law firm, and constant moral evaluation of client ends and means assumes cognitive capacities and moral virtue at an unrealistic level.[6]

Do you agree with this critique? Is the analogy between law practice and emergency room medicine a good one? Is it more relevant for some types of practice than others?

E. IS CRIMINAL DEFENSE DIFFERENT?

One common feature of many alternatives to the amoral conception is that they tend to carve out criminal defense work for special treatment. For example, David Luban, who takes a hard line against amoral advocacy in all other contexts, makes an exception for criminal defense work because he thinks aggressive advocacy is justified in order to protect individuals against a powerful institution—the state.[7] Simon rejects the idea that

---

[6] David Luban & W. Bradley Wendel, *Philosophical Legal Ethics: An Affectionate History*, 30 GEO. J. LEGAL ETHICS 337, 25 (2017).

[7] David Luban, *Partisanship, Betrayal and Autonomy in the Lawyer-Client Relationship: A Reply to Stephen Ellmann*, 90 COLUM. L. REV. 1004, 1027–29 (1990).

critics of amoral advocacy should make a special exception for criminal defense, but he would allow aggressive tactics in particular cases involving procedural breakdowns that would lead to legal injustice or excessive or arbitrary punishment of the defendant.[8] Wendel's approach, emphasizing fidelity to law, would allow the use of some tactics in criminal defense work that would be unjustified in most other practice settings. He argues that aggressive advocacy is permissible in criminal defense work because the defendant has a procedural legal entitlement to have the case against him proven beyond a reasonable doubt. Outside of the criminal defense context, he argues that deceptive tactics are much more difficult to defend, especially in counseling and transactional contexts, where there is no adversary process and no neutral adjudicator.[9]

NOTES ON CRIMINAL DEFENSE AS A SPECIAL CASE

1. ***Is Criminal Defense Special?*** Are you persuaded by arguments that criminal defense presents a special case that generally permits criminal defense lawyers to engage in tactics that would be immoral for other lawyers, or do you find Simon's critique of that view more compelling?

2. ***Must One Choose?*** If you're finding it difficult to choose among these conceptions of role, you are in good company. Many thoughtful observers (including your casebook authors) find it easy to reject the amoral conception as articulated by Pepper but more difficult to settle on an alternative that seems entirely satisfactory in every situation. Perhaps it's unnecessary to embrace any particular approach for all purposes.

F. THE CHOICE OF CLIENTS AND CAUSES

As a matter of aspirational ideals, the American legal profession has long acknowledged that lawyers should assist in meeting the profession's duty to make legal services broadly available. In practice lawyers are generally free to pick and choose their clients and causes and to decline matters for weighty moral reasons or for the most pedestrian reasons, including the most common reason of all—the client's inability to pay. Accordingly, many commentators think it appropriate to hold lawyers accountable for their decisions about whom to serve. According to this view, lawyers' freedom to decline to represent a client for moral reasons necessarily entails moral accountability for the clients that lawyers *do* choose to represent. An essay on the decision of a black lawyer affiliated with the ACLU to represent the Ku Klux Klan in resisting the state of

---

8 WILLIAM H. SIMON, THE PRACTICE OF JUSTICE 170–194 (1998).

9 W. BRADLEY WENDEL, LAWYERS AND FIDELITY TO LAW 191–93 (2010).

Texas's attempt to subpoena the Klan's membership list endorses this logic:

> Once we accept [that a lawyer should not be compelled to represent a client because of his moral disagreement with that individual's views or objectives], it is no longer possible to contend that lawyers bear no moral responsibility for their decision to represent particular clients. If a lawyer has the moral right to refuse to accept a case, then the decision not to exercise this option—in other words, to agree to take the case—also carries moral significance.[10]

Monroe Freedman, a strong advocate for the amoral conception ("that the client is entitled to make the important decisions about the client's goals and the lawful means used to pursue those goals"), also insisted that the lawyer's broad discretion to accept or reject a particular client means that it is a decision for which lawyers are properly held accountable.

Concluding that lawyers are morally accountable for their choice of clients, however, is not the same as saying that it is wrong to represent disreputable clients. Criminal defense lawyers, for example, do not necessarily approve of their clients or the conduct that is the basis for their clients' prosecution; instead, they typically justify their roles in terms of defending constitutional rights, checking police and prosecutorial power, and protecting defendants from unjustifiably harsh punishment. Similarly, civil libertarians sometimes represent clients they find abhorrent in order to advance principles they hold dear.

In assessing lawyers' accountability for representing unpopular clients, should it matter *why* the client is unpopular? Suppose the source of the unpopularity is that the client has engaged or is engaging in anti-social behavior that escapes law enforcement—e.g., promoting racial violence, bribing government officials, producing unreasonably dangerous products, defrauding consumers, polluting the environment, or disregarding safety regulations designed to protect workers. Should it matter whether the representation relates to past conduct or future projects? Should it matter whether the representation is paid or pro bono, or whether the lawyer is "the last lawyer in town"?

Lawyers sometimes assert that it should be sufficient justification for representing an unpopular client that everyone deserves representation. Is that right—is that sufficient justification when there is no reason to believe that the client cannot find other counsel? David Wilkins has argued that "[t]he claim that 'this person deserves legal representation' is fundamentally different from the argument that 'I should provide that service.' " William Kunstler drew the same distinction in explaining why

---

[10] David B. Wilkins, *Race, Ethics, and the First Amendment: Should a Black Lawyer Represent the Ku Klux Klan?*, 63 GEO. WASH. L. REV. 1030 (1995).

he would defend the World Trade Center bombers but not the Ku Klux Klan; "Everyone has a right to a lawyer, that's true. But they don't have a right to me."[11]

Questions about the morality of lawyers' representation of unpopular clients sometimes arise as to whole classes of clients, such as when people ask how criminal defense lawyers can represent defendants they know are guilty, or when people ask corporate litigators to explain how they justify representing tobacco companies and gun manufacturers. In 2007, Charles Stimson, Deputy Assistant Secretary of State for Detainee Affairs, considered such a question about the representation of Guantanamo detainees:

> Somebody asked, "Who are the lawyers around this country representing detainees down there?" And you know what, it's shocking. The major firms in this country are out there representing detainees, and I think quite honestly, when corporate CEOs see that these firms are representing the very terrorists who hit their bottom line back in 2001, these CEOs are going to make those law firms choose between representing terrorists or representing reputable firms.[12]

Such questions also arise as to lawyers' representation of particular clients in particular matters, as revealed in the following examples:

Bernard Madoff. Lawyer Ira Lee Sorkin represented Bernard L. Madoff, who pled guilty in 2009 to having operated a massive Ponzi scheme that defrauded investors of billions of dollars. According to a *New York Times* story at the time, Sorkin received many angry messages about his willingness to represent Madoff, including one so threatening that he referred it to the F.B.I. Sorkin explained that he understood the anger but that "to preserve a system that can protect the people who didn't do bad things, you have to represent people who did do bad things. That's the role we play."[13]

Philip Morris. During her years in private practice at the law firm of Davis Polk, Kirsten Rutnik, now U.S. Senator (N.Y.) Kirsten Gillibrand, represented tobacco giant Philip Morris in connection with the Department of Justice's efforts to obtain the company's research on the health effects of cigarette smoking and the connection between smoking and cancer. The Justice Department sought to obtain documentation of that research to prove that tobacco industry executives had lied about the dangers of smoking. A *New York Times* article on the matter asserted that Gillibrand

---

[11] DEBORAH L. RHODE, IN THE INTERESTS OF JUSTICE 79 (2000).

[12] David Luban, *Lawfare and Legal Ethics in Guantanamo,* 60 STAN. L. REV. 1981 (2008) (quoting Stimson).

[13] Diana B. Henriques, *Madoff Lawyer Absorbs Part of the Rage,* N.Y. TIMES, Mar. 11, 2009, at B1.

"was involved in some of the most sensitive matters related to the defense of [Philip Morris]," including efforts to shield damaging company documents from public disclosure.[14]

John Demjanjuk. In 1993, Hofstra Law Professor Monroe Freedman published an article in the *Legal Times* critical of lawyer Michael Tigar's decision to represent John Demjanjuk, the man the Justice Department accused of being Ivan the Terrible of Treblinka, accessory to the murder of 850,000 Jews. Freedman argued that all lawyers should bear a "burden of justification" for the work they undertake and that Tigar should ask himself these questions: "Is John Demjanjuk the kind of client to whom you want to dedicate your training, your knowledge, your extraordinary skills? Did you go to law school to help a client who has committed mass murder of other human beings with poisonous gases? Of course, someone should, and will, represent him. But why you?" In a subsequent interview, Tigar called Freedman's notion that lawyers should bear a burden of justification for the clients they choose to represent a "pernicious" ethical standard. He explained that in representing Demjanjuk, he was seeking to hold the U.S. government to its own principles, a fitting way to honor victims of the Holocaust.[15]

The Defense of Marriage Act Case. In 2011, Republicans in the House of Representatives hired the law firm of King & Spalding to defend the constitutionality of the Defense of Marriage Act (DOMA), which prohibited federal recognition of same-sex marriages, after Attorney General Eric Holder announced that the Obama Administration would no longer defend the statute. Gay rights groups criticized King & Spalding, as did lawyers within the firm who objected on moral grounds to the position the client was taking and believed that the firm's handling of this matter would interfere with its ability to recruit and retain gay lawyers. The firm eventually withdrew from the representation in June of 2011. A statement issued by the firm's chairman explained that the firm's process for vetting the matter prior to accepting it had been inadequate. Perhaps noteworthy in this respect, the contract between the law firm and the House contained a provision that prohibited any of the firm's lawyers and other employees from engaging in any kind of advocacy "to alter or amend" DOMA.

When the firm decided to withdraw, Paul Clement, the former U.S. Solicitor General and King & Spalding partner who was handling the case, resigned the firm in protest. In explaining the move, Clement wrote: "I resign out of the firmly held belief that a representation should not be abandoned because the client's legal position is extremely unpopular in certain quarters. Defending unpopular clients is what lawyers do." Gay

---

[14] Raymond Hernandez & David Kocieniewski, *As New Lawyer, Senator Was Active in Tobacco's Defense*, N.Y. TIMES, Mar. 27, 2009, at A1.

[15] David Margolick, *At the Bar; The Demjanjuk Episode, Two Old Friends and Debate from Long Ago*, N.Y. TIMES, Oct. 15, 1993, at B18.

rights advocates responded strongly against Clement's suggestion that his representation of the G.O.P House members in this matter was analogous to the representation of indigents, political dissenters, or downtrodden criminal defendants. One observer argued, "No serious case can be made that an institution as powerful as Congress has a right to the services of the biggest law firms and the most credentialed lawyers. The Defense of Marriage Act is not unpopular, and while Congress may be indebted, it is not indigent."[16] The spokesman for a gay rights group said, "Mr. Clement's statement misses the point entirely. While it is sometimes appropriate for lawyers to represent unpopular clients when an important principle is at issue, here the only principle he wishes to defend is discrimination and second-class citizenship for gay Americans."[17] However, Attorney General Eric Holder defended Clement, saying that "[i]n taking on the representation—representing Congress in connection with DOMA, I think he is doing that which lawyers do when we're at our best."

Some observers thought while King & Spalding had no obligation to take the case, it should have continued to serve the client after having accepted the matter. Both the *New York Times* and the *Washington Post* published editorials condemning King & Spalding's withdrawal.[18]

Which side do you think had the better of the argument about the propriety of the firm's decision to represent the House in this matter and its subsequent decision to withdraw?

The Supreme Court found the Defense of Marriage Act unconstitutional. *United States v. Windsor,* 570 U.S. 744 (2013).

Viktor Yanukovych. Special Counsel Robert Mueller's investigation into Russian interference in the 2016 election uncovered details about the role of a prominent New York law firm in efforts to improve the public image of Viktor Yanukovych, the Russia-aligned president of Ukraine. In 2012, President Trump's former campaign manager, Paul Manafort, hired Skadden, Arps, Slate, Meagher & Flom, on behalf of Yanukovych to write a report justifying the jailing of Yanukovych's chief political rival, Yulia Tymoshenko. The purpose of the report was to address suspicions that the Ukrainian government brought the prosecution against Tymoshenko for political reasons and without sufficient evidence. Skadden's report concluded that Tymoshenko's conviction was supported by the evidence.[19] Former U.S. ambassador to Ukraine John Herbst called the report "a nasty

---

[16] Dale Carpenter, *How the Law Accepted Gays,* N.Y. TIMES, Apr. 29, 2011, at A27.

[17] Michael D. Shear & John Schwartz, *Law Firm Won't Defend Marriage Act,* N.Y. TIMES, Apr. 26, 2011, at A1.

[18] *See The Duty of Counsel,* N.Y. TIMES, Apr. 28, 2011 at A24; *A Law Firm Caves to the Left's Hypocrisy,* WASH. POST, Apr. 28, 2011 at A24.

[19] Debra Cassens Weiss, *Manafort Pleads Guilty in Cooperation Deal: Skadden Report an Issue in Charging Document,* ABA JOURNAL, Sept. 14, 2018.

piece of work" and said that Skadden "should have been ashamed of it."[20] Representing foreign authoritarian governments has become a lucrative business for Washington lawyers, lobbyists and public relations consultants.

Harvey Weinstein. In January 2019, Ronald S. Sullivan, Jr., director of Harvard Law School's Criminal Justice Institute, joined a team of lawyers representing Hollywood producer Harvey Weinstein, who had been charged with rape and sexual assault. Sullivan's decision to represent Weinstein led to student protests and calls for him to resign from his position as the first black dean of one of Harvard's undergraduate residential colleges. Some students argued that Sullivan's representation of Weinstein jeopardized his ability to serve as an effective residential dean with responsibility for overseeing a comfortable social climate at the college. Sullivan said of his decision to represent Weinstein, "Lawyers are not an extension of their client. Lawyers do law work, not the work of ideology. When I'm in my lawyer capacity, representing a client, even one publicly vilified, it doesn't mean I'm supporting anything my client may have done."[21] Many of Sullivan's colleagues defended him. One wrote that "[t]hose calling for Sullivan's resignation or dismissal as a faculty dean solely because he is serving as Harvey Weinstein's lawyer in a rape prosecution are displaying an array of disturbingly widespread tendencies . . . [including] impatience with drawing essential distinctions such as that between a lawyer and his client."[22] A journalist criticized this line of argument:

> Sullivan isn't a public defender who's simply taking the clients assigned to him. He's not even a full-time criminal defense lawyer who just takes whichever clients happen to come through his door. . . . While it's obviously true that all criminal defendants have a right to an attorney, it's equally obvious that criminal defendants don't have a particular right to Ronald Sullivan's services. It would be genuinely outrageous to condemn a public defender for catching some heinous clients in the course of pursuing an honorable vocation. But as Sullivan is obviously picking and choosing his clients—and, in Weinstein's case, getting well paid

---

[20] Kenneth P. Vogel and Andrew E. Kramer, *Skadden, Big New York Law Firm, Faces Questions on Work with Manafort*, N.Y. TIMES, Sept. 21, 2017.

[21] Jan Ransom and Michael Gold, *'Whose Side Are You On?': Harvard Dean Representing Weinstein Is Hit With Graffiti and Protests*, N.Y. TIMES, Mar. 4, 2019, https://www.nytimes.com/2019/03/04/nyregion/harvard-dean-harvey-weinstein.html?searchResultPosition=1.

[22] *Id.* (quoting Harvard Law Professor Randall Kennedy's column in *The Chronicle of Higher Education*).

for his time—it doesn't seem unreasonable to draw some inferences based on his choices.[23]

In May 2019, Harvard announced that Sullivan would no longer serve as a faculty dean of the residential college. Sullivan thereafter withdrew from Weinstein's defense team.[24]

Setting aside whether it was appropriate for Harvard not to allow Sullivan to continue to serve as residential dean, which side do you think has the better of the argument about whether Sullivan's willingness to represent Weinstein supports some legitimate "inferences"? If you think that some inferences based on his choices might be reasonable, what might such inferences be? Could one reasonably infer that his representation of Weinstein reveals something about his attitudes regarding sexual assault, the #MeToo movement, the #MeToo backlash, something else, or none of the above?

NOTES ON THE CHOICE OF CLIENTS AND CAUSES

1. ***What Would You Do?*** Would you have been willing to represent Bernie Madoff in his fraud prosecution, Phillip Morris in tobacco cases, John Demjanjuk in connection with charges that he was an accessory to murder of many thousands, the House of Representatives in the DOMA case, an authoritarian-kleptocratic regime in its efforts to improve its political image in the U.S., or Harvey Weinstein in his trial for rape and sexual assault?

2. ***Fair to Judge?*** A *New York Times* article on Kirstin Gillibrand's role in the tobacco litigation quotes University of Chicago law professor Todd Henderson saying that it is unfair to assess lawyers by whom they represent: "Nobody would want to live in a world in which lawyers are judged by the clients they take." Do you agree?

3. ***Factors Relevant for an Individual Lawyer's Choice of Clients?*** If you were practicing on your own, what factors would you take into account in deciding what clients to serve? Would your answer depend on what particular projects and/or positions the clients wanted you to take on their behalf? How might financial considerations affect your decisions?

4. ***Criteria and Processes for Law Firms.*** If you were working as an associate in a private firm, what criteria and processes would you want your firm's management to use in choosing clients? If you were a senior partner in the same firm, do you think you would give the same answers? What arguments would you anticipate from those who disagree with you?

---

[23] Matthew Yglesias, *The Raging Controversy Over Ronald Sullivan, Harvey Weinstein, and Harvard, Explained,* VOX, May 17, 2019, https://www.vox.com/2019/5/17/18626716/ronald-sullivan-winthrop-house-harvard-law-school.

[24] Yohana Desta, *Ex-Harvard Dean Dismissed for Repping Harvey Weinstein Says He Did "Nothing Wrong,"* VANITY FAIR, June 25, 2019, https://www.vanityfair.com/hollywood/2019/06/harvey-weinstein-ronald-sullivan-jr-lawyer.

G. SUMMARY

This chapter considered whether lawyers are sometimes permitted, or required, to do on behalf of clients things that would otherwise be wrong to do. We analyzed one role conception that many lawyers seem to adopt: the "amoral" conception, which says that lawyers are unaccountable for anything they do on behalf of clients so long as it is not illegal, and we considered why many lawyers find that model attractive. This chapter explored criticisms of the amoral conception of the lawyer's role and examined various alternatives. We also considered the related issue of lawyers' accountability for their decisions about what clients and causes to serve. We examined the propriety of representing unpopular clients and the kinds of factors that might be relevant to individuals and firm leaders who make decisions about whether to handle controversial clients and matters.

CHAPTER 4

DIVERSITY OF THE LEGAL PROFESSION

■ ■ ■

A. THE DIVERSITY OF THE LEGAL PROFESSION

Although the American legal profession today includes people of almost every identity group or demographic characteristic in the national adult population, for much of American history the organized bar excluded all but white, Protestant, native-born men from the practice of law. While explicit exclusionary practices are now illegal, the profession remains less diverse than the general population. According to the ABA, in 2018, among the 1.34 million lawyers in America, 64% identified as male and 36% as female, 85% identified as non-Hispanic white, 5% as non-Hispanic black, 5% as Hispanic, 3% as non-Hispanic Asian-Pacific American, 1% as Native American, and 1% as multi-racial. The percentage of lawyers who identify as other than white and male has increased steadily, and may continue to do so. According to the ABA, law students nationally are more diverse than the bar, as about 29% identify as nonwhite and about 49% as female. In the 2010 Census, 72% of the population identified as white (by race), 83% identified as non-Hispanic (by ethnicity), and 50.8% as female.[1] After surveying the data on the demographic composition of the legal profession with respect to race, ethnicity, gender, sexual orientation, and disabilities, this chapter considers why some groups are over- and under-represented generally, and within various practice settings, and whether diversity is beneficial for lawyers, clients, and the public.

1. RACE AND ETHNICITY

A 2017 report on demographics of law firms of all sizes based on self-reported data from 1,064 offices nationwide made the following significant findings about the diversity of law firms:

- In 2017, racial and ethnic minorities accounted for 8.42% of partners in the nation's major firms, and women accounted for 22.70% of the partners in these firms, up from 8.05% and 22.13%, respectively, in 2016. The change has been small since 1993, when minorities accounted for 2.55% of partners and women accounted for 12.27% of partners. In 2017

[1] *See* https://www.americanbar.org/content/dam/aba/administrative/market_research/national-lawyer-population-10-year-demographics-revised.authcheckdam.pdf; http://www.census.gov/prod/cen2010/briefs/c2010br-03.pdf.

minority women were still the most underrepresented group among all law firm partners (2.90% of partners at all firms and 3.31% at firms with more than 700 lawyers). Minority men accounted for 5.52% of partners in 2017.

- Most of the increase in minority representation among partners since 2009 reflects an increase of Asian and Hispanic male partners. Representation of Black/African-Americans among partners has not significantly changed: 1.83% in 2017, and 1.71% in 2009.[2]

The report found that women and people of color are a more substantial share of the ranks of associates. But there is variation among them:

- Representation of minority associates increased from 19.53% in 2010 to 23.32% in 2017. The representation of women increased steadily from 38.99% in 1993 to its peak of 45.66% in 2009 and since has been essentially unchanged. In 2017, women were 45.48% of associates.
- Representation of minority women among associates increased from about 11% (2009–2012) to 12.86% in 2017.
- Asian associates now make up 11.4% of all associates, up from 9.28% in 2009.
- Hispanic associate representation rose from 2.81% in 2009 to 4.57% in 2017.
- The percentage of Black/African-American associates fell every year from 2010 to 2015, but increased slightly in both 2016 and 2017; 4.28% of associates are Black/African-American, which is less than the 2009 level of 4.66%.[3]

Data from many sources show differences among racial and ethnic groups in the sectors of practice in which they are most likely to work. African-Americans are the most likely among nonwhite groups to enter the not-for-profit sector, especially government and academia, and are the best represented nonwhite group among judges. Latinx lawyers are more likely than any group except African-Americans or whites to work in government practice and as judges. Asian-Americans are the most likely minority group to work in the for-profit sector, the best represented minority group among law firm associates, and the least represented in the judiciary.[4] (Some of

[2] https://www.nalp.org/uploads/2017NALPReportonDiversityinUSLawFirms.pdf.

[3] *Id.*

[4] After the JD III: Third Results of a National Study of Legal Careers (American Bar Foundation 72 (2014), www.americanbarfoundation.org/uploads/cms/documents/ajd3report_final_for_distribution.pdf; Tracey E. George & Albert H. Yoon, The Gavel Gap: Who Sits in Judgment on State Courts? (American Constitution Society 2016), http://gavelgap.org/pdf/gavel-gap-report.pdf.

the studies from which these data are drawn did not separately report on numerically small minority groups such as Native Americans and Pacific Islanders.) A survey of Asian American lawyers found only 4.7% of respondents said that one of their top three motivations for attending law school was to gain a pathway into government or politics; the AJD study found that 14% of Asian-Americans considered politics as an alternative career to law, compared to 34% of whites, 32% of blacks, and 27% of Latinx.[5] A study of Latinx lawyers in Los Angeles in 2000 found a smaller percentage of Latinx lawyers in solo practice in Los Angeles (35%) than the percentage of lawyers in solo practice statewide (53% of all private practitioners) or nationwide (47%), but that the percentage of Los Angeles Latinx in firms of 2–5 lawyers or 6–10 lawyers was roughly similar to that of lawyers nationwide and statewide.[6]

NOTES ON RACIAL AND ETHNIC DEMOGRAPHICS OF THE PROFESSION

1. ***Is There a Pattern?*** To the extent that the data reported above show patterns in the representation of racial and ethnic groups in the profession, what might account for them?

2. ***Selection Bias.*** Data on race and ethnicity usually rely on self-identification by survey respondents. The NALP Report, like another commonly cited source, the *American Lawyer* "Diversity Scorecard," is compiled from responses by law firms, which may in turn depend on what the person who fills out the form surmises about the racial or ethnic identity of lawyers in the firm.

3. ***Gaps in Data.*** Available data do not report every racial or ethnic group that might be of interest, and they do not reveal variations among geographic areas. For example, they do not report information on some ethnicities or national origin groups, such as Arabs or Africans, and they do not disaggregate some racial, ethnic, or national origin groups (such as southeast Asians, or people with origins in the Indian subcontinent, or European or Middle-Eastern minority groups such as Armenians). What information do you wish these surveys provided?

2. GENDER

Women constituted only 3 percent of law school classes in 1947 and in 1972, but they began entering law school in significant numbers in the mid-1970s. Women reached parity with men for the first time in the class that entered law school in 1993. Women have earned approximately 50 percent

---

[5] Eric Chang, *et al.*, A Portrait of Asian Americans in the Law (Yale Law School, National Asian Pacific American Bar Association 2017).

[6] Cruz Reynoso, *A Survey of Latino Lawyers in Los Angeles County—Their Professional Lives and Opinions*, 38 UC DAVIS L. REV. 1563, 1593 (2005).

of JDs since the early 2000s.[7] Yet, women are more likely to leave law practice.[8] Women are underrepresented in positions of power and elite compensation, including in equity partnerships in large law firms, as general counsel of Fortune 500 companies, and in top positions in government. For example, although women have constituted somewhere between 40% and 45% of first-year associates at large law firms since the 1990s, they are only 22.70% of partners in law firms in the NALP Directory of Legal Employers, 16% of equity partners and 6% of managing partners.[9]

These gendered career patterns continue with younger lawyers. As shown in the first wave of the AJD study, which surveyed a nationwide sample of nearly 4000 lawyers who first joined the bar in 2000 about their experience two or three years into practice, women were much better represented in government and public interest jobs than in private practice.[10] By the third wave (twelve years out of law school), a greater percentage of women than men had left private practice and women were more likely than men to be in government or public interest employment.[11]

All three waves of the AJD study also found that women are paid less than their male peers in all legal labor markets for all jobs across the country. The first wave of the AJD study found that after only two or three years in practice, the average full-time woman lawyer earned 5.2% less than the average full-time man. After seven years of practice, the difference increased to approximately 13% for full-time lawyers.[12] The third wave found the pay gap had grown even more. Female respondents working full time earned 80 percent of the pay reported by their male counterparts. The most dramatic gap occurred between women and men working in business in a capacity other than as a lawyer; women made 67 percent of the pay reported by men.[13] Scholars who analyzed the AJD data determined that only 15% of the salary gap could be explained by different work experience, work settings, or other endowments of the lawyers; the scholars attributed

7 Joyce S. Sterling & Nancy Reichman, *Navigating the Gap: Reflections on 20 Years Researching Gender Disparities in the Legal Profession*, 8 FLA. INT'L L. REV. 515 (2013).

8 Id. at 516.

9 https://www.nalp.org/uploads/2017NALPReportonDiversityinUSLawFirms.pdf.

10 Gita Z. Wilder, *Women in the Profession: Findings from the First Wave of the After the JD Study* (NALP 2007); AFTER THE JD III: THIRD RESULTS FROM A NATIONAL STUDY OF LEGAL CAREERS (2014).

11 RONIT DINOVITZER, ET AL., AFTER THE JD III, THIRD RESULTS FROM A NATIONAL STUDY OF LEGAL CAREERS TABLE 8.1.

12 RONIT DINOVITZER, BRYANT GARTH, RICHARD SANDER, JOYCE STERLING & GITA WILDER, AFTER THE JD: THE FIRST RESULTS OF A NATIONAL STUDY OF LEGAL CAREERS (2004) (After the JD Wave I); RONIT DINOVITZER, ROBERT L. NELSON, GABRIELLE PLICKERT, REBECCA SANDEFUR & JOYCE STERLING, AFTER THE JD: SECOND RESULTS FROM A NATIONAL STUDY OF LEGAL CAREERS 67 (2009) (After the JD Wave II); Ronit Dinovitzer, Nancy Reichman & Joyce Sterling, *The Differential Valuation of Women's Work: A New Look at the Gender Gap in Lawyer's Incomes*, 88 SOC. FORCES 819 (2009).

13 "10 Interesting Stats from the After the JD Survey," ABA News Archives, available at https://www.americanbar.org/news/abanews/aba-news-archives/2014/02/10_interesting_stats.html.

75% of the gap to women being rewarded less than men for their endowments, although the reasons for the different valuation were unexplained.[14]

WOMEN IN THE LEGAL PROFESSION

Fiona Kay & Elizabeth Gorman
4 American Review of Law & Social Science 299 (2008)[15]

Numerous studies suggest that in recent years overt discrimination has receded, while more subtle and structural discrimination persists (1995, 1996). However, some research finds pregnant female litigators still face overt discrimination (2001), and women are often excluded from mentorship (2005) and opportunities to work on challenging files (1995; 2003, 2005; 2006; 1995).

In addition, sexual harassment continues (2001, 1998, 2001). 26% of male lawyers in private practice reported observing sexual harassment of female lawyers, while 66% of female lawyers reported observing sexual harassment of female colleagues (1998). Furthermore, nearly 50% of the female lawyers working in corporate or public agency settings reported having experienced or observed one or more of five types of sexual harassment by male superiors, colleagues, or clients during the two years prior to the survey (1998).

What explains women's generally lower rates of attaining high-ranking legal positions? [W]omen's law school performance is similar to or better than that of men. Moreover, among Chicago lawyers who entered practice after 1970, neither class rank nor law school prestige influenced the probability of holding a senior position in either a firm or nonfirm setting, net of years of experience (2000), so neither factor could explain the gender gap. Some studies find that women work fewer hours than men (2000, 2001, 1999), but others find no gender difference in working hours (1998, 2005). The impact of hours worked on promotion prospects is also unclear. In the Chicago sample, hours worked per week were positively associated with being a law firm partner (2000). However, hours worked were negatively associated with senior positions in nonfirm settings. Women are more likely to take parental leaves (1998, 2004). However, because the number of fathers who take parental leaves is too small to produce meaningful results, it is impossible to disentangle the human capital effects of parental leaves from their likely reinforcement of decision-makers' gender biases.

---

[14] Dinovitzer, Reichman & Sterling, *Differential Valuation of Women's Work*, 88 SOC. FORCES at 836.

[15] This article is a survey of the literature. We have omitted the author names in the citations in parentheses, but have retained the dates so that readers may consider whether the passage of time since the publication of the cited works may affect whether similar findings would be made if the studies were conducted today.

An alternative possibility is that women lack the social networks and cultural dispositions that are crucial for forming and maintaining relationships with clients and other lawyers. Indeed, Kay & Hagan (1998) found, in a 1990 survey, that women scored lower than men on measures of both social capital (professional activities, association memberships, client origination, and representation of corporate clients) and cultural capital (disposition to share firm values versus valuing goals outside the firm). Inclusion of the social and cultural capital measures explained approximately one-third of the impact of gender on lawyers' partnership promotion chances, net of marital and parental status, hours and weeks worked, leaves taken, and urban location; a significant gender gap remained.

[R]esearch suggests that firms hold men and women to different standards in evaluating their skills, social networks, and cultural dispositions. Thus, among University of Michigan graduates, Noonan & Corcoran (2004) observed a stronger positive effect of law school grades on promotion for women than for men. Similarly, hours worked per week, disposition toward firm culture, number of professional activities, and client origination improved women's partnership prospects but had no effects for men (1998). This did not mean that women were better rewarded than men; men with low scores on social and cultural attributes still had better partnership chances than did women with exceptionally high scores. Thus, Kay & Hagan's results suggest that women had to demonstrate their affinity with firm culture and their ability to form valuable social ties, whereas men's capacities in these areas were taken for granted. In addition, children have a positive impact on men's promotion chances but none on women's (2000, 1998, 2004), suggesting that firms interpret parenthood as signaling stability and work commitment for men but not for women.

Studies suggest that gender bias plays a lesser role when firm decision-makers are female, when they are influenced by female clients, and when they have worked in environments where female leadership is institutionalized. Thus, Gorman's (2006) study of 1450 promotion events in 503 large firms showed that firms are more likely to promote women when they already have a larger proportion of women among existing partners. Beckman & Phillips (2005), who analyzed longitudinal data on 200 large law firms, observed that the number of female partners grew faster in firms that represent corporate clients with women in leadership positions. In a longitudinal study of Silicon Valley firms, Phillips (2005) found that new firms were quicker to select a first female partner when their founders had left parent firms with more female partners or where women had served as partners for longer periods of time.

[M]ost studies reveal that women and men are surprisingly similar in their levels of job satisfaction (1989; 2007; 1999, 2005; 1999; 1996). Several explanations have been offered for the paradox of why women have equal job satisfaction despite inferior jobs in terms of pay, levels of authority, and mobility prospects. The most common explanation centers on differential values. The argument is that women and men have different values and therefore care about different things in their jobs; women's work satisfaction is determined more by subjective, or intrinsic, work characteristics, for example, perceived autonomy and variety, than by objective, or extrinsic, features such as salary and promotions. Women may use different reference groups in assessing their satisfaction, comparing themselves only with other women or with women who stay at home. As a result, women may approach their work lives with lower expectations or a lower sense of personal entitlement, making satisfaction easier to achieve.

The assumption of reduced career commitment among women lawyers who are also parents has been challenged empirically. Wallace (2004) analyzed interview data with lawyers who were mothers and a large-scale survey of lawyers in Calgary, Alberta. Wallace found that women lawyers who are mothers exhibited higher levels of career commitment than other women practicing law, controlling for hours worked, alternative work arrangements, leaves taken, law experience, earnings, and work settings. Wallace suggested a selection process may be at work whereby less-committed women may have left law to raise their family or pursue other career avenues.

Research reveals that women are overrepresented in the exodus from law (1989, 1989a, 1992).

NOTES ON GENDER AND THE PROFESSION

1. ***Attrition.*** Kay and Gorman cited studies from 1989 and 1992 showing that women are overrepresented among those who leave the practice of law. Studies based on more recent data on the attrition of women from law practice also found that women were more likely than men to leave law practice at all career stages, and to leave law firms to practice in nonprofits, small firms, and businesses. For example, 40% of women who graduated from law school in the early 1980s had left law by the early 2000s, primarily to begin new careers in business or nonprofits. One study noted that the youngest women lawyers in the sample had generally not left law practice to raise children full-time, but had instead left large firms to move to different types of law practice settings.[16]

2. ***What Has Changed?*** Which of the gender differences in the legal profession identified by Kay and Gorman do you think persist today and which do you think have changed or will change shortly? A 2016 study of gender inequality in private practice that attempted to determine whether there had been a change the phenomena identified by Kay and Gorman found persistence

[16] These studies are summarized in Sterling & Reichman, *Navigating the Gap*, 8 FLA. INT'L L. REV. at 13.

of many of the same problems. The authors attributed the glacial pace of change to the effects of the Great Recession and to the continuing challenge of integrating family with the demands of law firm practice.[17]

3. ***What Is the Outsider Experience?*** In contrast to racial and ethnic minorities, white women may be more likely to have close connections to people of wealth and power. Yet the rates of attrition from large law firms remain comparably high for white women and for people of color. What causes attrition?

4. ***#MeToo and the Law?*** As hundreds of women came forward in 2017 and 2018 to report on sexual harassment by powerful men in media, government, and other industries, there were relatively few allegations of harassment by high profile lawyers. (Allegations did, however, end the judicial career of a federal appeals court judge, and prompt federal courts to institute policies and procedures for addressing harassment.) Why do you suppose that law firms have not (yet) had their high-profile #MeToo moment?

5. ***Pay Equity.*** A 2016 study of partner compensation at large law firms nationwide found a 44 percent difference between male and female partners. The survey asked 2,100 partners nationwide to explain the factors underlying compensation, and it appeared that males were better than females both at bringing business to the firm and at getting credit for bringing in business. The gender pay disparity among law firm partners was 47 percent in 2014.[18] What would you recommend to a law firm about whether or how to address pay disparities in partner compensation?

3. SEXUAL IDENTITY

Few aspects of the legal profession have changed as rapidly and recently as the treatment of lawyers who are openly lesbian, gay, bisexual transgender, or queer. Employment discrimination on the basis of gender identity or sexual orientation remains legal in most states, however. Change in employment policies of legal employers appears to be due to evolving social norms, not legal requirement.

The NALP Report on Diversity for 2017 found that 2.64% of lawyers in law firms identified as LGBTQ, up from 2.48% in 2016. That reflected a small increase in the number of LGBTQ partners and a larger increase in the number of LGBTQ associates. NALP found that openly LGBTQ associates are better represented at large law firms. There is significant geographic variation in the number of lawyers who publicly identify themselves as LGBTQ; about 56% of openly LGBTQ lawyers are in New York, Washington, DC, Los Angeles, and San Francisco, four cities that

---

[17] Joyce Sterling & Nancy Reichman, *Overlooked and Undervalued: Women in Private Law Practice*, 12 ANN. REV. OF L. & SOC. SCI. (2016).

[18] Elizabeth Olson, *Men v. Women in Law: A Pay Divide of 44%*, N.Y. TIMES, Oct. 14, 2016, at B3.

together account for about 39% of the total number of lawyers in the NALP study.

NOTES ON THE DEMOGRAPHICS OF LGBTQ LAWYERS

1. ***What Accounts for the Patterns?*** The studies reported above identify growth and geographic variation in the number of LGBTQ lawyers. There are no studies of attrition comparable to the well-documented attrition of women and racial minorities. What do you think are the major issues with respect to equality for LGBTQ lawyers?

2. ***Disaggregating the Group.*** Legal and policy discussions with respect to identity traits tend to identify categories (e.g., Black, LGBTQ, Jewish) and treat them as monolithic, overlooking the variations within the group and the intersections among different identities. The failure to disaggregate may be especially significant in thinking about trans and gender-fluid lawyers. To what extent do you think the experiences of lawyers vary within these groups and when one considers intersections among them?

4. LAWYERS WITH DISABILITIES

In contrast to the abundant data on the experiences of racial and ethnic minorities in the legal profession, much less is known about the experiences of people with disabilities.[19] We do not even know precisely how many people with disabilities are lawyers or law students. Persons with disabilities have been estimated to constitute from four to seven percent of lawyers (according to the ABA), 2.6% of lawyers (according to the Bureau of Labor Statistics), or less than one percent (according to the 2017 NALP Report on Diversity).[20]

Even less is known about the types of disabilities that lawyers have, or whether there is a pattern in where lawyers with disabilities work. According to NALP, the number of lawyers who are reported as having disabilities does not seem to vary in any systematic way either by firm size or by associate/partner status, but NALP did not report data showing the types of disabilities. Although some data suggest that lawyers with disabilities are more likely to work in government, public interest, and small firm settings, anecdotal evidence suggests they work in a broad range of jobs in the profession.[21]

---

[19] A helpful resource is Adeen Postar, *Selective Bibliography Relating to Law Students and Lawyers With Disabilities*, 19 AM. U. J. GENDER SOC. POL'Y & L. 1237 (2011).

[20] ABA Commission on Disability Rights, Goal III Report 7 (ABA 2012). The report did not indicate why the number of lawyers reported having a disability abruptly fell by a third in one year. Because this is a survey of ABA members (not lawyers generally), and the survey methodology is not reported, it is difficult to assess the reliability of the data.

[21] *See, e.g.*, Second National Conference on the Employment of Lawyers With Disabilities (ABA 2009); John F. Stanton, *Breaking the Sound Barrier: How the Americans with Disabilities Act and Technology Have Enabled Deaf Lawyers to Succeed*, 45 VAL. U. L. REV. 1185 (2011).

NOTES ON THE DEMOGRAPHICS OF LAWYERS WITH DISABILITIES

1. ***Are Disabilities Under-Reported?*** The NALP study found a very small number of summer associates reported having disabilities, far less than one would predict given the number of people with reported disabilities in the profession and in law schools. Why do you suppose law students are so hesitant to reveal they have disabilities during a summer job?

2. ***Definitions of Disability.*** Although disability is a technical term of art in any statute that regulates the rights of people with disabilities, in colloquial usage its meaning may have changed as some conditions (e.g., mood disorders, autism-spectrum conditions) have become better understood, more common, or more culturally salient. To what extent does the absence of a consensus definition affect both the data about lawyers with disabilities and policies that might address their underrepresentation in the profession?

B. UNDERSTANDING THE REASONS FOR THE DEMOGRAPHICS

This section explores the literature and other sources analyzing the reasons why the legal profession does not represent the diversity of identity groups in American society.

Fiona Kay and Elizabeth Gorman conducted an analysis of 2006 NALP law firm data to determine whether formal practices regarding mentoring and training, early opportunities for significant responsibility, a longer time to partnership, and a cultural commitment to professional development were correlated with larger numbers of African-Americans, Latinx, and Asian-Americans making partner. Their findings included:

- The proportion of minorities among associates had a strong positive effect on minority presence among partners, and minority representation was greater in the West and South than in the Northeast.
- Minority presence among partners was positively associated with a higher ratio of nonpartners to partners and with status as a branch office, but a two-tier partnership structure had no effect.
- Neither formal training nor a formal mentoring program was significantly associated with minority presence among partners.
- Longer partnership tracks reduced minority representation in the partnership, as did a cultural value of fostering

professional development and a cultural norm of encouraging early responsibility.[22]

EXPERIENCING DISCRIMINATION: RACE AND RETENTION IN AMERICA'S LARGEST LAW FIRMS

Monique R. Payne-Pikus, John Hagan, & Robert L. Nelson
44 Law & Society Review 553 (2010)

Even though women and minorities now enter America's largest law firms in growing numbers, neither women nor minorities are well integrated into America's largest and most elite law firms. We know more about the slightly longer-term experiences of women than about the more recent experiences of minorities, but the experiences in large law firms of women and minorities bear notable similarities and can help us understand the fate of both groups as institutionally predictable.

Becker's human capital theory is an important academic account of resistance to both women and minority lawyers.* The emphasis of Becker's theory is on the efficient development of human capital. His gender theory [assumes] women [are] less committed to their legal careers because they also invest heavily in their families.

[As applied to racial and ethnic minorities, who like women have lower levels of advancement to partnership relative to entry], Beckerian human capital theory substitutes an emphasis on racial differences in legal learning for the emphasis on gender differences in family/work specialization. Thus in this human capital race theory of law firms, hiring preferences linked to affirmative action and resulting lowered requirements of academic achievement replace personal family preferences as the root causal force.

Partner contact and mentoring is increasingly recognized as a key process and source of dissatisfaction and departures from law firms, especially for African American lawyers. In contrast with human capital theory, an institutional discrimination theory suggests that disparity in social contacts with partners and mentoring experiences with partners, rather than disparities in merit and performance, can explain the "paradox" of high rates of minority lawyers' dissatisfaction and departures after being hired into large law firms. If demonstrated to occur, this discrimination in partner contact and mentoring net of merit and performance would make racial/ethnic differences in attrition easily understandable. [I]t would simply be institutionally predictable rather

[22] Fiona M. Kay & Elizabeth H. Gorman, *Developmental Practices, Organizational Culture, and Minority Representation in Organizational Leadership: The Case of Partners in Large U.S. Law Firms*, ANNALS OF THE AM. ACADEMY OF POL. AND SOC. SCI. (2011), available at http://ann.sagepub.com/content/639/1/91.

* [Eds.: *See* GARY S. BECKER, HUMAN CAPITAL (1964), and Gary S. Becker, *Human Capital, Effort, and the Sexual Division of Labor*, 3 J. LAB. ECON. 533–58 (1985).]

than paradoxical for these minority associates to leave firms in search of better career opportunities.

Wilkins and Gulati (1996) conducted an in-depth qualitative study of African American associates in large law firms. They maintain that racial/ethnic differences in treatment may be systemic within large law firms. They argue that while the "superstar" associates of any ethnicity will receive mentoring and training, racial/ethnic differences emerge when the "average" associate, the bulk of the cohort, is considered. They maintain that "average" whites are more likely to be mentored then "average" African Americans. Once African Americans realize they are not receiving the training needed to become partner, they decide to leave earlier in the process, while they still have some market value.

In contrast, Sander (2006) argues that African American associates are less likely to be mentored because of their differences in human capital. If Sander's human capital-based argument is accurate, then one would expect mentoring and training to matter less in explaining disparities in retention outcomes once "merit" is controlled for. If Wilkins and Gulati (1996) and institutional discrimination theory [are] correct, one would expect mentoring to continue to impact attrition even when "merit" is controlled for.

It is this debate between stereotype and institutional discrimination that we address in our analyses. We find, using the same data Sander considered, that institutional discrimination is a better predictor of minority attrition.

Cross-tabulations of the race/ethnicity of associates with key variables indicate that white associates consistently differ from minority group associates in large firms. Thus the reports of law school grade point averages (GPA) confirm the influence of affirmative action based racial/ethnic hiring preferences emphasized in the human capital merit performance theory. While approximately half of white associates (49.1 percent) in large firms report average marks between 3.5 and 4.0, about one fourth of African American (23.3 percent) and less than one-third (28.6 percent) of Hispanic associates report receiving these top-tier grades. This difference is especially noteworthy given the finding that minorities are more likely to attend top 20 law schools (60.0 percent of African Americans and 57.1 percent of Hispanics vs. 38.5 percent of whites), which on average give higher grades. However, it is still unclear what role these law school credentials play in lawyer retention and satisfaction.

More than half of the white associates in large firms report joining partners for meals (54.4 percent), while just more than one-quarter of African American (26.7 percent) but more than half of the Hispanic associates (57.1 percent) do so. Once more, less than half of the white associates (47.3 percent) desire more and/or better mentoring by partners, compared to more than two-thirds of African American (70.0 percent) and Hispanic (71.4 percent) associates. Both theories predict resulting disparities in outcomes such as plans to leave the firms and work satisfaction. So it is perhaps unsurprising that about one-fourth of white associates (23.0 percent) plan to leave in the next year, while in contrast half of African American (50.0 percent) and Hispanic (53.6 percent) associates are so inclined.

Several measures of in-firm merit and performance reveal much smaller differences than are reflected in law school grades between groups. White associates in large firms score slightly higher than African American associates and about the same as Hispanic associates on a four-level measure of taking leadership on legal matters versus doing routine legal work. Of course, this could reflect differences in work assignments rather than initiative. Meanwhile, African American (41.688) and Hispanic (42.825) associates score slightly higher than white associates (40.796) in hours billed per week. This could, in part, be due to the large number of minority lawyers in the four major cities, where lawyers work more hours on average. There is a notable difference in perceptions of discrimination in these large firms, with African Americans and Hispanics [reporting more discrimination and] whites [reporting the least]. Finally, African American associates score lowest on a 17-item scale of work satisfaction, while Hispanic associates report higher satisfaction than African American associates but lower satisfaction than white associates.

While the burden of effort to integrate American law firms has focused on recruitment of new associates into large firms, our research suggests that problems are not confined to recruitment policies but rather extend to the practices of partners with regard to minority lawyers once they are employed. Affirmative action mandates with regard to partner contact and mentoring of minority associates may be essential to achieve an effective racial integration of the upper reaches of the legal profession.

NOTES ON PAYNE-PIKUS, HAGAN, & NELSON

1. ***What Explains Attrition?*** What are the various factors that are suggested to account for the attrition of minority lawyers from law firms and other practice settings? Which seem most plausible to you and why? To what extent are the experiences of some races and ethnicities likely to be different from those of others?

2. ***The Racial Paradox Hypothesis.*** As the authors note, studies of the experiences of racial minorities in the legal profession conducted by Professor Richard Sander concluded that the affirmative action by law schools and law firms actually hurts minorities by recruiting them into environments in which they do not thrive. This is the racial paradox hypothesis: affirmative

action paradoxically winds up hurting the very people it is intended to help.[23] In particular, Sander argued that affirmative action in law school admissions hurts minority students by placing them in academic competition with students who are more likely to succeed than they are, which results in minority students getting lower grades than they would have received if they had gone to a less selective law school, which in turn harms their chances to thrive in the profession. He further argued that the deleterious effects of affirmative action continue in law firms as senior lawyers believe that minority lawyers are less qualified and therefore invest less effort in mentoring them. Sander's research prompted a large number of studies and articles in response; most of the responses, including the one excerpted above, focused on the core questions in Sander's research: whether affirmative action is good for minorities and what accounts for the underrepresentation of minorities in large law firms.

* * *

Both anecdotal reports and research data indicate that women are more likely to leave the practice of law than are men.[24] Many surmise that this difference is attributable to gendered patterns in family responsibility. Moreover, women lawyers are less likely than their nonlawyer age peers to be married and to have children. In this section we explore these phenomena. In the process, we consider both the larger issue of norms about working time in the legal profession (and in elite occupations more generally) and the narrow question whether time norms explain the attrition of women lawyers. We also examine the question whether issues about working time, part-time work and work-life balance *should* be considered a gender issue.

THE PART-TIME PARADOX: TIME NORMS, PROFESSIONAL LIVES, FAMILY, AND GENDER

Cynthia Fuchs Epstein, Carroll Seron, Bonnie Olensky, & Robert Sauté (Routledge 1999)

Professional work typically entails workdays and workweeks that spill over into what others might regard as personal or "after-hours" time. In the course of professional socialization, doctors and lawyers usually acquire motivation for hard and demanding work, and become embedded in a professional environment where devotion to task is rewarded by upward

---

[23] Richard H. Sander, *A Systemic Analysis of Affirmative Action in American Law Schools*, 57 STAN. L. REV. 367–483 (2004); Richard H. Sander, *The Racial Paradox of the Corporate Law Firm*, 54 N. C. L. REV. 1755–822 (2006).

[24] Fiona M. Kay, *et al.*, *Undermining Gender Equality: Female Attrition from Private Law Practice*, 50 LAW & SOC'Y REV. 766 (2016) (based on survey of 1,270 law graduates, finding that both men and women leave law firms in large numbers before partnership, but women leave private practice at higher rates after partnership.).

mobility while ordinary effort is punished with stagnation, diminished rank, or lesser remuneration.

In law, where work may be evaluated both objectively (measured by cases won and value of deals closed), or subjectively (assessment of a person's "ideas"), hours worked serve as both objective and subjective evaluations, translating into a proxy for dedication and excellence.

Lawyers' human capital is the coin of their professional success. Their reputation for service and quality is a key component, along with training and experience in practicing law—skill, craft, and shrewdness; a passion for winning; and an attractive personal style. A reputation for availability is also part of the attorney's "symbolic capital." [R]ound-the-clock availability is no longer regarded as a gesture made only in cases of last-minute deadlines or emergencies—a theoretical promise of being "on duty" all the time. High-profile clients expect immediate and constant responsiveness.

When people work and *where* they work are also noticed and provide an overall cast to the social perception of a lawyer's time at work. [W]ork at home may have multiple consequences for lawyers; it permits flexibility, but it also removes the lawyer from visibility.

Law, as well as other occupational communities, is bound by mystiques about the distinctive and unique feats performed by its members. In law, part of the mystique is communicated by stories about arduous and long hours on cases, tales that bolster a sense of professional community.

No matter where they work, most of the lawyers we studied who work fewer hours than their peers are *de facto* deviants from established guidelines for work time. In the invidious comparison with full-time lawyers, the part-timer is often seen as less dedicated and less professional—a "time deviant." We use the term "stigma" here in its sociological sense to convey the way in which "otherness" is determined by social definition. Stigma, as Erving Goffman (1963) pointed out, has to do with relationships, not attributes. Stigma serves to place a boundary around the "normal." What is at issue is deviation from the norm.

Describing this study, the author asked [a law professor who was also a consultant for a major New York law firm] about the feasibility of part-time work in the New York firm. "Impossible," he asserted without hesitation. "But don't you work part-time for the firm?" she asked. "That's different," he said. "I provide expertise they need." "But couldn't a woman who wanted to limit her hours also provide expertise on a part-time basis as you do?" "I don't think we are getting anywhere with this conversation," the professor snapped.

Mobility is a good indicator of the regard with which lawyers are held and of their integration within the profession. About 60 percent of a nationally representative sample of attorneys surveyed by the American Bar Association believed that reduced-hour or part-time employment limited opportunities for advancement including partnership. [A] part-time associate [said], "I'm not sure I have a career. I have a job. A career has a future and a path. I'm not sure I have a path." [P]art-time attorneys face ambivalence about how much responsibility they wish to have. On the one hand, many express a desire to be assigned to meaty cases—the interesting ones with high visibility. At the same time they know that taking them may cause them to work beyond their desired schedule and may not lead to increased recognition or status.

Despite the obstacles, some structural and cultural conditions and strategic choices support mobility. Searching for patterns in the careers of part-time lawyers who attained some type of mobility we found these: Firms that are innovative in other spheres seem more receptive to reduced hours. For example, in California's Silicon Valley, five successful women partners in high-tech law firms of more than 100 attorneys [had worked part time]. (Part-time meant 8 a.m. to 6 p.m. five days a week). Firms that do not have constant quick-turnaround pressures also are more receptive to part-timers' advancement. The cultivation of legal specialties creates a pathway to lateral and upward mobility, providing an extra element of human capital that enhances the value of part-timers and cancels some of the stigma attached to reduced hours.

NOTES ON THE PART-TIME PARADOX

1. ***Time and Devotion.*** Could you envision the legal profession altering the norms of devotion to client and craft, at least as measured by time? Which aspects of the norms of devotion to client and craft do you find admirable and which do you think are undesirable, or at least dispensable?

2. ***The Billable Hour.*** Do you think that the reliance of many law firms, especially big firms, on hourly billing might help explain why private practice tends to demand time commitment? Critics of hourly billing say that it discourages efficiency and leads lawyers to measure each other's contributions to the firm in terms of the numbers of hours they bill and, in the case of partners, in terms of junior lawyers' hours for which partners claim billing credit.

Some firms have abandoned hourly fees in favor of flat fees and various types of "value-based" fee arrangements that take into account the quality of the work and/or outcomes for clients. These firms assert that their reliance on alternative billing methods reduces pressure to bill long hours and enables them to attract talented lawyers who want to avoid the billable hour rat-race.[25]

[25] *See* STEVEN J. HARPER, THE LAWYER BUBBLE: A PROFESSION IN CRISIS 77–79, 171–75, 191–92 (2013).

3. ***Are Norms About Working Time a Gender Issue?*** In what ways is part-time work a gender issue? In what ways is it not? Does considering part-time work as an issue of gender equality make the reforms you would like to see on that point more or less likely to occur?

4. ***The Having It All Debate.*** In the legal profession as in many other elite jobs, women lag behind men in almost every measure of professional attainment. A lively and sometimes acrimonious debate has raged for at least a generation about whether the gender gap is due to women choosing less demanding jobs in order to balance work and family and, if so, whether those choices are cause for concern. One articulation of the problem is that women need to "lean in" and challenge themselves to lead and to show others that women can be leaders.[26] Another is that women "can't have it all," except for those who are wealthy, powerful, and/or have partners who are willing to sacrifice their own professional advancement to care for family.[27] Another framing of the problem challenges the notion that women's choices to prefer family over career explain the gender gap and insists that framing the issue as one of choice is wrong.[28] What do you think?

* * *

In contrast to race and gender, which have been extensively studied to understand the reasons for different career paths and higher rates of attrition from law firms, less is known about whether, when, and why people with disabilities experience difficulties navigating a rewarding career as lawyers. As noted above, it appears that people with disabilities are underrepresented in law compared to the general population, but the reasons are unclear. One reason may be that some people with particularly severe disabilities are underrepresented among the population of persons who possess the educational prerequisites to become a lawyer. Cornell University's Employment and Disability Institute—using data from the American Community Survey (ACS), an annual survey that is sent to about 3 million households—reports that 12.2% of working-age persons with disabilities hold a bachelor's degree or higher, compared to 30.8% of non-disabled persons. Yet the percentage of lawyers with disabilities is small even compared to the population of persons with disabilities who are highly educated. A second factor—one which distinguishes the bar's treatment of race and gender from its treatment of disabilities—is that many state bars until very recently explicitly excluded people with some disabilities from the practice of law, and many make it more difficult for them to obtain a license by requiring them to explain as part of the bar admission process

---

[26] SHERYL SANDBERG, LEAN IN: WOMEN, WORK, AND THE WILL TO LEAD (2013).

[27] *See* Anne-Marie Slaughter, *Why Women Still Can't Have It All*, THE ATLANTIC (June 13, 2012) (Princeton professor who left a high-level government job to spend more time with her children explains that women cannot "have it all at the same time" because of "the way America's economy and society are currently structured").

[28] *See* Nicole Buonocore Porter, *The Blame Game: How the Rhetoric of Choice Blames the Achievement Gap on Women*, 8 FLA. INT'L U. L. REV. 447 (2013).

that their disability will not prevent them from performing the essential functions of the job of lawyer.

A third factor, reported anecdotally by many lawyers, is explicit or implicit bias and the lack of encouragement or mentoring. Some disabled lawyers report having been discouraged from pursuing a career in law. One small national qualitative study of lawyers with disabilities reported a number of common experiences.[29] Aspiring lawyers with disabilities were ignored, treated as fragile, or discouraged from pursuing the rigors of a career at a large law firm. Others reported the difficulty of managing other people's reactions to and stereotypes about disability,[30] or difficulty in convincing colleagues that they were capable of doing the work. A blind lawyer, for example, described the difficulty of persuading partners to staff him on their cases because they did not realize that technology would enable him to do the work as well as a lawyer with sight.[31] Anecdotal evidence drawn from news accounts suggests that gradual changes in attitudes about lawyers with disabilities have occurred as lawyers in powerful positions became effective advocates for the abilities of lawyers with disabilities and for the need to accommodate the differently abled.[32]

NOTES ON UNDERSTANDING THE UNDERREPRESENTATION OF LAWYERS WITH DISABILITIES

1. ***Diversity Within the Group.*** Some disabilities are easily perceived by other people and others are not. To what extent are both demographic data and the experiences of lawyers with disabilities affected by the choice not to reveal a disability?

2. ***Understanding Institutional Behavior.*** Some lawyers with disabilities, like lawyers with other "outsider" statuses, note that although their law firm maintains a formal antidiscrimination policy, success in the firm is dictated not by the policy but by the power of individual partners. The blind lawyer who, as noted, said it was challenging to persuade partners to staff him on their cases, described his large firm as "a federation of mini law firms." What light does that shed on the nature of discrimination and on why firms that assert they are equal opportunity employers nevertheless have a persistent underrepresentation of some people?

---

[29] Carrie Griffin Basas, *The New Boys: Women With Disabilities in the Legal Profession*, 25 BERKELEY J. GENDER L. & JUSTICE 32 (2010).

[30] *Id.* at 57.

[31] Remarks of Kareem A. Dale, Second National Conference on the Employment of Lawyers With Disabilities (ABA 2009).

[32] Terry Carter, *The Biggest Hurdle for Lawyers With Disabilities: Preconceptions,* ABA J. (June 2015), 55.

C. EVALUATING THE ARGUMENTS FOR DIVERSITY

Underlying the debate over the reasons for the underrepresentation of some groups in certain segments of society is a significant disagreement over whether or to what extent we as a society *should* aspire to having a world in which the demographics of any particular institution reflect the demographics of the general population. Here we focus on one part of that larger debate: to what extent does diversity of the legal profession matter? What are the arguments for and against efforts to remedy the underrepresentation of certain groups in certain sectors of law practice? The article excerpted below addresses that issue in the context of whether diversity is good for large law firms and their clients (as opposed to whether it is good or bad for lawyers or the public generally).

GOOD BUSINESS: A MARKET-BASED ARGUMENT FOR LAW FIRM DIVERSITY

Douglas E. Brayley & Eric S. Nguyen
34 Journal of the Legal Profession 1 (2009)

This article relies on data reported for 2007 from *The American Lawyer* for the 200 highest-grossing law firms, the so-called AmLaw 200. [We] compare highly diverse firms with the rest of the AmLaw 200. [T]he phrase "highly diverse firms" refers to the 50 most diverse firms in the AmLaw 200. Highly diverse firms have anywhere from 22 to 294 minority attorneys, representing between 15 percent and 25 percent of their attorneys.

[O]n average, firms in the top quartile of diversity scores have higher profits per partner (PPP) and generate more revenue per lawyer (RPL) than the rest of the AmLaw 200. As with the relationship between diversity and firm size, this analysis does not show a necessary link between diversity and financial success: the firms with the lowest and highest PPP and RPL in the AmLaw 200 are not in the top quartile of diversity scores. Diverse firms may perform better simply because they have more lawyers working longer hours in bigger cities. [The authors then attempt to isolate the effect of diversity by controlling for hours worked and a firm's size and location.]

As expected, firms with an office in a major market and attorneys who work a higher number of hours each week are likely to generate greater revenue per lawyer. City and hours worked also matter. Even controlling for these factors, the AmLaw diversity rank had a strongly significant effect on a firm's revenue per lawyer. In other words, for two firms in the same city, working the same number of hours, with the same number of lawyers, differences in diversity are significantly correlated with differences in financial performance.

The models assume that causation runs in only one direction: greater diversity allows firms to generate higher revenue. In reality, the causation may also run in the opposite direction: higher revenue allows firms to make themselves more diverse. As a result, it is difficult to conclude that diversity itself causes higher revenue.

There are at least three possible explanations for the correlation between firm diversity and financial performance. First, diverse firms may perform better because large corporate clients have begun to send their business to firms with better representation of racial minorities and women. Second, diverse firms may be more productive, especially because they can recruit and retain top legal talent. Third, causation may run in the opposite direction, with financially successful firms able to devote greater resources to diversity programs.

Client demand may drive part of the diversity-profitability relationship. As corporate clients demand that their matters be staffed with a diverse set of attorneys, firms with a demonstrable commitment to diversity are more successful in bringing in new business and retaining existing clients. Strong anecdotal evidence supports this theory. A number of major American companies have begun to demand publicly that law firms pay more attention to issues of diversity. In 2004, Sara Lee general counsel Roderick Palmore issued "A Call to Action: Diversity in the Legal Profession," in which signatory companies promised "to end or limit . . . relationships with firms whose performance consistently evidences a lack of meaningful interest in being diverse." Since the Call was issued, about 90 companies have signed on.

Of the five firms with the most Call to Action signatory clients, four [are] in the top quartile of diversity. Of the top 11 firms, seven [are in the top quartile of] diversity and all but one are above the median. Of the top 20 firms, nine are in the top diversity quartile and 16 have above-median diversity scores. This ranking thus suggests that the Call to Action signatories are indeed using some of their market power to choose firms with good diversity records.

A second possible explanation for the correlation is that diverse law firms produce legal services at higher quality or more efficiently. Two specific mechanisms may be at work. First, associates may be more satisfied with their work when they are surrounded by a more heterogeneous group of coworkers. Satisfaction in turn increases the ability to retain good lawyers, helping the firm both keep a productive worker and avoid the expense of recruiting a replacement. The data provide only weak support for this theory. Second, diverse firms may be able to recruit better talent if students at highly ranked law schools consider firm demographics and diversity efforts when deciding on a place to work. The data we analyzed, however, do not provide support for this theory. If diversity pushes revenue and profits, it is likely because clients—not young lawyers—demand it.

NOTES ON THE ARGUMENTS FOR DIVERSITY

1. ***The Call to Action.*** The Brayley & Nguyen article refers to the "Call to Action," a high-profile 2005 effort of corporate in-house counsel to persuade law firms to hire more lawyers of color. Similar efforts have been made since. In 2010, for example, general counsel of a number of large corporations pledged to direct $30 million in legal work to law firms owned by minorities and women.[33] In 2016, the ABA House of Delegates passed a resolution calling on corporate legal departments to use their decisions about hiring outside counsel to increase opportunities for minority and underrepresented attorneys, and in 2017, HP announced a "diversity holdback mandate" that allows the company to withhold up to 10% of fees from law firms that fail to meet or exceed minimum requirements for diverse staffing on HP matters.[34] (Diverse is defined as including race, ethnicity, gender, LGBTQ, and disability.) Why do corporate counsel care about the race, gender, and ethnicity of the lawyers in the law firms they hire?

2. ***Debating the Business Case for Affirmative Action.*** Brayley and Nguyen's argument that diversity is beneficial to law firms and clients from a business standpoint echoes a long-term debate over the strategic costs and benefits of defending affirmative action policies by appealing to the instrumental benefits of diversity for institutions rather than the intrinsic justice of equal representation or the benefits or harms to those affected by affirmative action policies. One scholar summarized the debate, as applied to law firms, this way:

> [T]he advancement of the "business case for diversity," while well-reasoned and well-intended, has backfired, ending up weakening and eroding the meaning of diversity. Meant to enhance the normative case for diversity with utilitarian grounds, and motivate large law firms and other legal employers to pursue diversity vigorously, it led to debates over the instrumental value of diversity, increasingly overlooking other compelling grounds for it. [A]dvocates of the "business case for diversity" likely did not mean to weaken diversity by undermining its normative justifications, but opponents of diversity initiatives have seized the opportunity to reframe and focus attention on the (admittedly often questionable) instrumental grounds for diversity.[35]

---

[33] Zach Lowe, *Major Companies Pledge $30 Million to Minority and Women Owned Law Firms*, AM. LAW. (Mar. 5, 2010).

[34] Liane Jackson, *HP Mandates Diversity*, ABA J. (May 2017), 14.

[35] Eli Wald, *A Primer on Diversity, Discrimination, and Equality in the Legal Profession or Who Is Responsible for Pursuing Diversity and Why*, 24 GEO. J. LEGAL ETHICS 1079, 1081–82 (2011).

If one were not persuaded by Brayley and Nguyen's data and analysis on the benefits of diversity for large law firms and their clients, would their normative claims be undermined, in your judgment? Is there is a better case to be made for or against law firm efforts to promote diversity?

3. ***Satisfaction as a Measure of Business Success?*** Brayley and Nguyen find little evidence to support the common argument that diversity benefits law firms because associates at diverse firms are more satisfied with their work lives and therefore diverse firms are more able to recruit and retain talent than less diverse firms. Chapter 24 addresses the lively scholarly debate about how properly to measure lawyer satisfaction; many frequently cited measures of lawyer satisfaction lack social science rigor and may be unreliable. Why might lawyer satisfaction be correlated, or not, with diversity? Is the satisfaction of large law firm associates a good justification for the efforts of such firms to promote diversity?

4. ***Implicit and Institutional Bias.*** A growing literature examines the extent and nature of the underrepresentation of women and various minorities in private practice, especially in large law firms, and, to a lesser extent, in government and small firm practice. An empirical study of 2000 lawyers has found that women of color are more likely than others to perceive unfair treatment based on race, gender, and age and that this perception contributes to lower career satisfaction for female attorneys of color than for others.[36] Even firms that have adopted policies aimed at prohibiting intentional discrimination have failed to eradicate practices that may operate to the disadvantage of outsider groups. On this analysis, promotional practices that valorize certain measures of individual achievement obscure the ways that structural constraints rather than individual ability and hard work disproportionately influence who succeeds in the law firm.[37]

D. SUMMARY

This chapter surveyed data on the demographics of the legal profession with respect to race and ethnicity, gender, gender identity and sexual orientation, and disability. It explored hypotheses explaining the demographics, and examined the effect of identities on career patterns, norms about devotion to work, and the relationship between sexual or gender identity and notions of professionalism. The chapter then considered different perspectives on whether diversity in law offices is intrinsically or instrumentally beneficial for lawyers, clients, and society at large.

---

[36] Todd Collins, et al., *Intersecting Disadvantages: Race, Gender, and Age Discrimination Among Attorneys*, 98 SOC. SCI. Q. 1642 (2017).

[37] Russell Pearce, Eli Wald & Swethaa Ballakrishnen, *Difference Blindness vs. Bias Awareness: Why Law Firms With the Best of Intentions Have Failed to Create Diverse Partnerships*, 83 FORDHAM L. REV. 2407 (2015).

CHAPTER 5

EXPRESSIONS OF SELF IN LAWYERING

■ ■ ■

A. INTRODUCTION

How should one's background, experience, political values, and identity traits influence a lawyer's professional life? Is it desirable, or is it inevitable, that elements of "self" should inform the kinds of careers one pursues as a lawyer, the types of clients and causes one represents, and how one goes about one's work?

There is a vast academic and legal press literature about the experiences of various social groups in the legal profession. Some of that literature, with particular emphasis on the demographics of the profession and institutional and other factors that explain the underrepresentation of some social groups, is examined in Chapter 4. In this chapter, we focus on a specific topic: whether or how personal identity does or should influence a lawyer's professional behavior and conception of role. In the context of considering these issues, we also introduce some of the rich literature on the salience of particular identities—such as race, gender, religion, and sexual orientation.

B. SHOULD PERSONAL IDENTITY INFLUENCE PROFESSIONAL IDENTITY?

BEYOND "BLEACHED OUT" PROFESSIONALISM: DEFINING PROFESSIONAL RESPONSIBILITY FOR REAL PROFESSIONALS

David B. Wilkins in Ethics in Practice: Lawyers' Roles, Responsibilities, and Regulation (Deborah Rhode ed., 2000)[1]

In the standard view, becoming a professional involves more than simply performing a specific job or assuming a certain social standing. Instead, it involves becoming a particular kind of person; a person who both sees the world and acts according to normative standards and conventions that are distinct from those that govern nonprofessionals. Through a complex process involving self-selection, professional education, collegial socialization, and the threat of professional discipline, individuals who enter into professions are presumed to adopt a new professional identity

---

[1] © 2000 Oxford University Press, Inc. By permission of Oxford University Press, USA.

based on the unique norms and practices of their craft. This "professional self," in turn, subsumes all other aspects of a professional's identity—gender, race, ethnicity, religion—and becomes the sole legitimate basis for actions undertaken within the confines of his or her professional role. Bleached out professionalism, as I will refer to this standard account, is central to the dominant model of American legal ethics.

It is not surprising that bleached out professionalism has become a core professional ideal. Norms such as neutrality, objectivity, and predictability are central to American legal culture. Lawyers are the gatekeepers through which citizens gain access to these important legal goods. If the law is to treat individuals equally, the argument goes, then lawyers must not allow their nonprofessional commitments to interfere with their professional obligation to give their clients unfettered access to all that the law has to offer. A professional ideology that treats a lawyer's nonprofessional identity as relevant to her professional conduct appears to threaten this important role.

In addition to the benefits that bleached out professionalism offers to the consumers of legal services, it also appears to safeguard the interests of the women and men who become lawyers. The universalizing claims made on behalf of the professional self suggest that differences among those who become lawyers that might matter outside of the professional sphere are irrelevant when evaluating these individuals' professional practices. This "professional" status is particularly important for the profession's new entrants—Jews, women, blacks, and other racial and religious minorities. These traditional outsiders have a powerful stake in being viewed as lawyers simpliciter, freed by their professional status from the pervasive weight of negative identity-specific stereotypes.

Finally, bleached out professionalism appears to uphold the legal system's core commitment to the fundamental equality of persons. Thus, the idea that a lawyer's gender, race, or religion is irrelevant to her professional role seems to flow directly from the broader claim that the legal rules and procedures that lawyers interpret and implement should also be unaffected by identity. The claim that "our constitution"—and, indeed, justice itself—is colorblind" (or "gender blind") is a bedrock principle of our legal order, and indeed of our public morality. Lawyers who either explicitly or implicitly call attention to issues involving race or gender—including their own racial or gender identity—seemingly undermine this ideal.

Like every normative system, the current understanding of professional role was created at a particular time and a particular place. [A] handful of relatively homogeneous elite New York lawyers wielded considerable influence over the creation of the modern professional ideal. Moreover, these founders acted in an era in which various forms of identity-based discrimination were an accepted part of the legal and moral landscape.

Acknowledging a greater role for identity-specific professional commitments can help the legal profession fulfill its fundamental mandate of promoting social justice. Consider, for example, the evolving role that black lawyers have played in the struggle for racial justice in the United States. The legal campaign to end "separate but equal" was spearheaded by Charles Hamilton Houston, Thurgood Marshall, and an elite core of black lawyers. As vice dean of Howard Law School in the 1930s, Houston expressly taught his students that they had an obligation to use their legal talents to improve the status of the black community. Although this stance did not prevent Houston and his protégé Thurgood Marshall from forming valuable and enduring relationships with white lawyers, it was a direct call on black attorneys to carry their racial identity into their professional role.

Today, many of the brightest and best-educated black lawyers spend some or all of their careers working in large corporate law firms, in corporate legal departments, or otherwise servicing the needs of large corporations. At first blush, it appears that these lawyers will have little to do with helping African Americans achieve social justice. There is, however, another way to look at the connection between black corporate lawyers and the social justice concerns of the African American community. Although these women and men may never be as directly involved in the struggle for racial justice as their forbearers in the civil rights movement, they nevertheless have important opportunities to contribute to this cause. These contributions include challenging stereotypes about black intellectual inferiority; acting as "role models" for other African Americans; helping to open up additional opportunities for blacks in law and elsewhere; directing their own resources and the resources of their employers toward projects that will benefit the black community; using corporate practice as a springboard to gain political influence to assist black causes; and persuading their powerful clients to act in ways that are less harmful (and perhaps even beneficial) to the interests of the black community.

For many blacks, having a strong sense of connections to the black community is an important source of strength and well-being in an otherwise hostile world. Bleached out professionalism suggests that these feelings must be confined to the "private" realm.

Connecting one's self-worth to the "recognition" of one's identity as a black (or as a woman, or as a Jew, or as a gay man) can be an essential step toward being treated as a whole human being, but it can also produce "scripts" about the proper way to be black (or a woman, or Jewish, or gay) that deny our individual humanity. And caring about the welfare and advancement of group members can either help to produce a more equitable society or contribute to the oppression of one group over another.

[I]t is apparent that certain kinds of identity consciousness, based on certain kinds of identity, are more likely than others to produce either positive or negative effects. Thus, the first kind of identity consciousness—noticing how identity affects you and the world—is, in our contemporary era, both the least problematic and the most applicable to all forms of identity. One can see the benefits of this first form of identity consciousness by comparing [Los Angeles District Attorney] Gil Garcetti's actions in the [high-profile murder trial of O.J. Simpson, a noted African-American athlete and movie actor who was charged with killing his wife and her friend] with [New York] Governor Pataki's in the Johnson case. [The Johnson case involved Robert Johnson, an elected black district attorney representing the Bronx. Johnson announced that he would refuse to seek the state's newly enacted death penalty in a highly publicized case involving three minority youths accused of shooting a white police officer, in part because he believed it would inevitably be applied in a racially discriminatory manner].

Garcetti took concerted steps to ensure that Simpson would be prosecuted in a jurisdiction where there were likely to be black jurors, by a prosecution team that included at least one prominent black lawyer. It is important to note that Garcetti would not have been able to take these important steps unless he had first "noticed" the manner in which race was likely to play an important role in the case. Although Garcetti, like virtually all of the other participants in the case, initially took the position that race was not an issue in the Simpson prosecution, this standard bleached out view was clearly false. Long before racism [of some LA police officers] or the racial composition of the jury surfaced as issues in the case, the simple fact that a black man was accused of murdering his white ex-wife and her handsome white friend ensured that race was likely to play an important role in how many participants in the process viewed the case. By coming to terms with this reality, Garcetti helped to produce a proceeding that would protect Simpson from unfair inferences based on the color of his skin.

Pataki's decision to replace Robert Johnson with a white attorney who was a committed death penalty hawk had the opposite effect. But by not "noticing" how race affects capital punishment cases, Pataki's actions arguably further entrenched existing racial divisions about the administration of capital punishment For reasons that have been well documented, black citizens have reason to believe that equal justice under law is often not achieved in practice. This is particularly true in cases involving the death penalty. There is substantial evidence that race does play an important role in whether prosecutors seek the death penalty and whether juries are likely to impose this punishment. Replacing a black district attorney who has expressly attempted to take this reality into account with a white lawyer who is a known death penalty hawk sends a powerful message to the black constituents of this district that their concerns about the discriminatory nature of capital punishment will not be heard.

By carefully examining the moral claims underlying various calls for identity consciousness, we can begin to separate those moves away from bleached out professionalism that are likely to promote fundamental fairness and those that are likely to detract from this goal.

NOTES ON WILKINS

1. ***Possible Benefits of Identity Consciousness?*** According to Wilkins, awareness of a lawyer's various identity traits plays a positive role for clients, lawyers, and the legal system. In what ways? In Wilkins' terms, which "moves away from bleached out professionalism are likely to promote fundamental fairness" and which will not?

2. ***Will Identity Traits Influence Your Career?*** Are you persuaded by his account? How, if at all, do you imagine your identity traits will play a role in your career?

3. ***Professional Norms and Identity Performance.*** To the extent that professional norms demand particular gendered or culturally specific behavior or attire, should lawyers be expected to abandon nonconformist aspects of their identity performance? Law students receive explicit or implicit messages from friends, mentors, administrators, or faculty regarding appropriate professional behavior. That advice sometimes includes guidance about how to dress for a job interview or for work on behalf of clients and how to respond to questions or to behave in various social or business situations. And that guidance often explicitly or implicitly encourages adherence to gendered and culturally specific expectations. It may be in suggestions about business attire, such as clothes, jewelry, or hairstyle, or it may be in terms of describing one's personal life and situation. Some lawyers insist that lawyers have a duty to their clients to behave in whatever way is necessary (within reason) to be effective in representation, and that can include adherence to gendered norms about professional attire. Others believe employment discrimination laws do (or should) prohibit legal employers from demanding adherence to some gendered or culturally specific norms of grooming and attire. What do you think?

C. HOW DOES PERSONAL IDENTITY INFLUENCE PROFESSIONAL ROLE?

Professor Wilkins asserts that "[e]mpirical and anecdotal research confirms that contingent features of a person's identity exert a strong influence over how that person perceives and is perceived by others." While few dispute some aspects of this claim and many find it obvious to describe how a person's race or gender influences how others perceive one in some circumstances, there is less consensus about whether or precisely how race, gender, national origin, religion, sexual orientation, disability, social class, or other traits or features of lawyers influence how they perform their professional role.[2]

In the late 1970s and early 1980s, lawyers and scholars contemplated whether the entry of a significant number of women into the legal profession would transform the practice of law. Many hoped that women would not merely assimilate into the practice of law, but rather that their entry would transform the profession and the legal system. The challenge—and it proved to be a huge challenge—was exploring the intuition that women might differ from men in how they approached being a lawyer in a way that avoided oversimplification or gender binaries or assuming that all women are one way and all men are another.

A particularly influential school of thought on the question whether women would perform the role of lawyer differently than men do was inspired by Harvard educational psychologist Carol Gilligan, who published a 1982 book, *In A Different Voice: Psychological Theory and Women's Development*, which said that male and female children learned to use different forms of moral reasoning. The male model of reasoning, according to Gilligan, used abstracted, universalistic principles applied to problematic situations to create an "ethic of justice." The female model of moral reasoning, which Gilligan termed an "ethic of care," was more relational, connected, and contextual and focused on people and the substance of a problem, rather than on rules. Gilligan's work inspired some legal scholars to suggest that the differences Gilligan found in male and female moral reasoning also manifested in differences in male and female styles of lawyering, and that women as lawyers were more likely to focus on relationships and men on rights and rules.[3]

Some doubted whether the research supported essentialist categories of male and female that correlated with different styles of moral reasoning. Professor Naomi Cahn explained: "Many men and most women actually combine aspects of each orientation in their thought processes." In Gilligan's study, many participants employed both styles of reasoning. Of those who employed only one style, one third of the female respondents focused on justice, and one third focused on care. In contrast, all but one of the men chose the justice perspective. Cahn advised against generalizing "that the different voice we have identified is feminine—that is, it describes many women, some men, and possibly the views of some members of other

[2] *See* KENNETH W. MACK, REPRESENTING THE RACE: THE CREATION OF THE CIVIL RIGHTS LAWYER (Harvard University Press, 2012).

[3] *See, e.g.*, Carrie Menkel-Meadow, *Portia in a Different Voice: Speculations on a Women's Lawyering Process*, 1 BERKELEY WOMEN'S L.J. 39 (1985); Carrie Menkel-Meadow, *Portia Redux: Another Look at Gender, Feminism, and Legal Ethics*, 2 VA. J. OF SOC. POL. & L. 75 (1994).

socially subordinate groups."[4] "Feminist theory helps us critique existing lawyering methods, and develop and appreciate alternative methods of being a lawyer, but does not require us to label these new developments by gender."[5]

One systematic exploration of feminist methods of being a lawyer is the following. Note that Professor Bartlett attempts to avoid the essentialism problem by referring to feminist lawyers rather than female lawyers.

FEMINIST LEGAL METHODS

Katharine T. Bartlett
103 Harvard Law Review 829 (1990)

When feminists "do law," they do what other lawyers do: they examine the facts of a legal issue or dispute, they identify the essential features of those facts, they determine what legal principles should guide the resolution of the dispute, and they apply those principles to the facts. This process unfolds not in a linear, sequential, or strictly logical manner, but rather in a pragmatic, interactive manner. Facts determine which rules are appropriate, and rules determine which facts are relevant. In doing law, feminists like other lawyers use a full range of methods of legal reasoning—deduction, induction, analogy, and use of hypotheticals, policy, and other general principles.

In addition to these conventional methods of doing law, however, feminists use other methods. These methods, though not all unique to feminists, attempt to reveal features of a legal issue which more traditional methods tend to overlook or suppress:

Asking the Woman Question. Feminists across many disciplines regularly ask a question—a set of questions, really—known as "the woman question," which is designed to identify the gender implications of rules and practices which might otherwise appear to be neutral or objective. [H]ave women been left out of consideration? If so, in what way; how might that omission be corrected? What difference would it make to do so? In law, asking the woman question means examining how the law fails to take into account the experiences and values that seem more typical of women than of men, for whatever reason, or how existing legal standards and concepts might disadvantage women. The question assumes that some features of the law may be not only nonneutral in a general sense, but also "male" in a specific sense. The purpose of the woman question is to expose those features and how they operate, and to suggest how they might be corrected.

---

4 Naomi R. Cahn, *Styles of Lawyering*, 43 HASTINGS L.J. 1039, 1052 (1992).

5 *Id.* at 1068–1069.

Feminist Practical Reasoning. [Many] feminists have argued that individualized factfinding is often superior to the application of bright-line rules, and that reasoning from context allows a greater respect for difference and for the perspectives of the powerless. Practical reasoning approaches problems not as dichotomized conflicts, but as dilemmas with multiple perspectives, contradictions, and inconsistencies. These dilemmas, ideally, do not call for the choice of one principle over another, but rather "imaginative integrations and reconciliations," which require attention to particular context. Practical reasoning sees particular details not as annoying inconsistencies or irrelevant nuisances which impede the smooth logical application of fixed rules. Nor does it see particular facts as the *objects* of legal analysis, the inert material to which to apply the living law. Instead, new facts present opportunities for improved understandings and "integrations."

Consciousness Raising. Another feminist method for expanding perceptions is consciousness-raising. Consciousness-raising is an interactive and collaborative process of articulating one's experiences and making meaning of them with others who also articulate their experiences. Feminist consciousness-raising creates knowledge by exploring common experiences and patterns that emerge from shared tellings of life events. What were experienced as personal hurts individually suffered reveal themselves as a collective experience of oppression.

Consciousness-raising is a method of trial and error. When revealing an experience to others, a participant in consciousness-raising does not know whether others will recognize it. The process values risk-taking and vulnerability over caution and detachment. Honesty is valued above consistency, teamwork over self-sufficiency, and personal narrative over abstract analysis. The goal is individual and collective empowerment, not personal attack or conquest.

NOTES ON BARTLETT

1. ***Women and the Transformation of the Legal Profession.*** In what ways and to what extent do you believe that the entry of large numbers of women into the legal profession has changed the profession's structures and norms? What changes, if any, do you think are yet to come?

2. ***Gender, Legal Ethics, and the Role of the Lawyer.*** If one does not consider gender as a binary, in what way (if any) does it make sense to think of men and women as having different styles of being lawyers or of approaching ethical dilemmas? If the distinction is not, in your view, between men and women, but instead between masculine and feminine styles, what are those styles?

3. ***Are There Feminist Legal Methods?*** In what respects, if any, do the three feminist legal methods discussed by Bartlett allow for the integration

of personal identity into professional role? If they acknowledge the possibility of expression of self in a professional role, are they limited to gender identity, or are they applicable to any aspect of identity?

D. PERSONAL IDENTITY AS A SOURCE OF INSPIRATION IN PROFESSIONAL LIFE

Thus far in this chapter, we have considered whether personal identity should or does influence how lawyers perform their professional role. We now consider another aspect of those two questions: how might personal identity be a source of inspiration or guidance to lawyers?

Many aspects of one's personal experience or identity might be a source of inspiration. One obvious source of inspiration is religion.

RELIGIOUS LAWYERING IN A LIBERAL DEMOCRACY: A CHALLENGE AND AN INVITATION

Russell G. Pearce & Amelia J. Uelmen
55 Case Western Reserve Law Review 127 (2004)

Although one of us prays as a Jew and one of us prays as a Christian, our prayers express who we are and who we want to be. We aspire to weave God's law into our professional lives, and to discover God's own hand at work, sanctifying our world and our lives.

In one sense, the religious lawyering movement builds upon and strengthens these long-standing commitments. For example, it would be interesting to trace the extent to which efforts to integrate religious values into professional life have contributed to the growth of faith-based pro bono legal services to the poor. Religious lawyering may also strengthen lawyers in their resolve to set aside the necessary time for religious observance, even in the midst of the profession's pressing demands on their time.

But we posit that the religious lawyering project which has been germinating over the past decade asks for more—and presents a much deeper challenge for the legal profession. Unlike many previous "law and religion" discussions, the religious lawyering movement focuses less on the conceptual relationships and tensions between law and religion and how these play out in a democracy, and more on ways in which religious values and perspectives may provide a completely different structural framework for an approach to professional life.

As anthropologist Clifford Geertz has described, the core of religious perspective is "the conviction that the values one holds are grounded in the inherent structure of reality, that between the way one ought to live and the way things really are there is an unbreakable inner connection." Religious lawyering draws out the "unbreakable inner connection" between "the way things really are" and "the way one ought to live"—not only in a private "non-work" sphere, but also in professional life. On this basis religious lawyering insists that there should be room in the profession for such convictions about the "inherent structure of reality," and for lawyers then to integrate this perspective and to apply its substantive critiques and contributions to the issues which arise not just at the margins, but in the heart of ordinary day-to-day legal practice.

Religion offers religious lawyers a constructive framework within which they can respond to a host of questions that the professionalism rhetoric leaves unanswered. It not only offers answers to the more practical question of how to be a good lawyer and a good person, but also responds to deeper and more existential questions such as why try to be a good person in the first place. For many religious people, this larger overarching framework provides a moral anchor that enables them not only to resist temptations of greed and abuse of power, but also to situate their legal work within a sense of responsibility and service to the larger community.

Religion also offers religious lawyers a way to transcend the dichotomy between the noble professional and the selfish business person. The notion of a calling or vocation, common to many religions, can make all work meaningful. As Martin Luther King, Jr. taught: "If it falls your lot to be a street sweeper, sweep streets like Michelangelo painted pictures, like Shakespeare wrote poetry, like Beethoven composed music; sweep streets so well that all the host of Heaven and earth will have to pause and say, "Here lived a great street sweeper, who swept his job well." What is true of street sweepers is equally true of lawyers.

Religious lawyering provides a robust framework for lawyers to explain why they are morally accountable for their service as the governing class and why they must incorporate personal integrity and consideration of the public good into client representation.

Despite these benefits, religious lawyering faces three types of objections related to its effectiveness, fairness, and compatibility with liberal democracy.

1) Does religious lawyering really make a difference?

Our claim is not that religious people are inherently more moral. Rather, we argue that religious lawyering offers lawyers a reason to behave ethically at a time when persuasive reasons to accept moral accountability are hard to find. While no guarantee, it does offer religious lawyers a way to draw a substantial and consistent connection between their religious values and their professional decisions.

2) Is religious lawyering unfair to clients?

This brings to mind an incident in which an American Airlines pilot asked Christian passengers to raise their hands and suggested that the other passengers might want to speak to the Christians about their faith during the flight. Many thought that it was extremely unfair for the pilot to proselytize his captive passengers.

Is a religious lawyer like that American Airlines pilot? Model Rule 2.1 provides that "in rendering advice, a lawyer may refer not only to law but to other considerations, such as moral, economic, social and political factors, that may be relevant to the client's situation." The Comment to the rule makes clear that "it is proper for a lawyer to refer to relevant moral and ethical considerations in giving advice." If the religious lawyer explains to the client the full range of options, including the moral implications of each, that seems to fall squarely within the rule and not to present a problem.

Even while permitted, discussion of religion with clients is often inappropriate. What is most bothersome about the American Airlines example is the pilot's abuse of his power in imposing his views on a literally captive audience of buckled-in passengers. While perhaps not captive to the same degree, in many practice contexts clients are often more vulnerable than their trusted lawyers. Like those American Airlines passengers who felt that the pilot was disrespectful, clients who wish to avoid proselytizing of any kind in their professional relationships should be able to do so.

3) Is religious lawyering dangerous for democracy?

These fears appear to arise from two sources. First, in a country that is more than 75% Christian, Jews, Muslims, and people of other minority religions might very well worry that they will suffer unequal and unfair treatment if actors in our legal system make decisions based on religious identity. Moreover, non-believers may have an even greater fear of discrimination given that close to 87% of Americans identify themselves as believers. A second and related worry is that allowing more room for religion in the public square will inevitably lead to divisiveness and intolerance, adding further fuel to the fires of polarizing culture wars.

Despite these fears, religious lawyering does not offend our system of liberal democracy. Whether and how to express religious convictions in the public square, especially when one serves a public role, is of course the subject of intense controversy. But even assuming the disputed point that the lawyer-client relationship is part of the public square, this debate implicates how religious lawyers discuss their religion with their clients, not whether they can appropriately ground their approach to lawyering in their religion.

If a lawyer's religious approaches to lawyering generate discrimination and intolerance, the lawyer's conduct should be subject to professional and social critique, and discipline where appropriate, just as any other approach that is less than respectful of others. To the extent that religious approaches and perspectives are difficult for others to understand, religious lawyers should work harder to make themselves understood—as would be reasonable to ask of any attorney who fails to communicate her views effectively.

At a time when many believe that law is no longer a noble profession, many lawyers see no reason to devote time and energy to promoting the public good. Religious lawyering may offer a powerful antidote: a robust framework for lawyers to integrate into their professional lives their most deeply rooted values, perspectives and critiques, and persuasive reasons to improve the quality of justice and work for the common good. At its best, religious lawyering echoes Martin Luther King's advice to the street sweeper. How wonderful it would be, indeed, if we practiced law so well that the host of heaven and earth would pause to say, here lived great lawyers who did their job well.

NOTES ON PEARCE & UELMEN

1. ***Does Personal Identity Enrich the Lawyer's Conception of Professional Role?*** Do you agree with Pearce and Uelmen that the rhetoric of professionalism does not answer a host of important questions that lawyers may have about their work lives—that the legal profession has "fail[ed] to offer lawyers a satisfactory way to understand their role and responsibilities"?

2. ***Does Emphasis on Personal Identity Create Tension in a Pluralist Society?*** To what extent might the desire of a deeply religious lawyer to find an expression of self in professional role create tension with other actors in a secular legal system on issues as to which religious and secular values differ? Do Pearce and Uelmen adequately answer such concerns? Is drawing inspiration from religion in a professional role more or less likely to create tension with other actors in a legal system than is expressing other aspects of one's identity in professional role? Is religion different from race or national origin or other aspects of oneself with respect to how it inspires or guides lawyers?

3. ***An Ethical Poverty in the Relationship Between Lawyer and Client?*** Pearce and Uelmen's argument draws on views expressed by Thomas Shaffer, who rejects amoral advocacy on the ground that it promotes a morally defective relationship between the lawyer and client. He argues that lawyers are obliged to counsel clients about their obligations to community and not just their interests and rights.[6]

* * *

The following two brief excerpts illuminate some of the ways in which lawyers find inspiration even as they grapple with the difficulties of their personal and professional lives.

---

[6] Thomas L. Shaffer, *The Unique, Novel, and Unsound Adversary Ethic*, 41 VAND. L. REV. 697 (1988).

BE PROFESSIONAL!

Dean Spade

33 Harvard Journal of Law & Gender 71 (2010)

What does it mean to be invited in? To be included, to be the first (or to appear to be the first)? What are the terms of that inclusion, its costs, its motives?

[Professor Spade describes various instances in which he found it challenging to be the only trans person in his work environment as a lawyer and law professor. He then discusses the significance of his experiences for thinking about how lawyers' identity performance affects their work.] What are these stories? They are the moments of identity management and discord that are the specific burden of those with tenuous relationships to the purportedly neutral, meritocratic, multicultural, inclusive terrain of white, straight, hetero, cisgender, bourgeois male legal academic culture. My experiences of being trans and my experiences of having a welfare class background emerge sometimes in different moments, sometimes simultaneously, but always require this management. At the same time, however, I am acutely aware that getting to be the "only one" is really a testament to my privilege.

[Those of us with outsider identities] are called into reform projects. We can join more committees, provide more support, expose more contradictions. We are aware that our students are frozen with fear over their debt, that they work so many hours outside school to get by that their school participation is harmed, that many live in fear of their own or a family member's deportation, that the standards by which we evaluate them (just like those by which we ourselves are evaluated) reproduce race, gender, and class hierarchies. There is so much to do to intervene on all this. I feel this call, I join this call.

[On the other hand,] [t]he pressures of being illegible, unspeakable, constantly misread, and constantly managing projected interpretations wears thin.

This is the location in which I find myself, ambivalent and insecure in my new position, trying to resist and survive various disciplining forces and to support and to make space for others to do the same. Perhaps, as we outsiders inside navigate the daily decisions about what to keep and what to let go of in the wind tunnel of professionalization, we can offer one another moments of respite and shared experience.

FROM THE CLOSET TO THE COURTROOM

Carlos Ball (Beacon Press 2010)

[This chapter describes the early career of Bill Rubenstein, who was a gay rights lawyer at the ACLU in the 1980s before becoming a law professor.]

While Rubenstein was taking small yet determined steps to come out of the closet [in law school in the early 1980s], AIDS was transforming itself from a relatively rare illness into a national epidemic of frightening proportions. The stigma that accompanied the spread of AIDS pushed some gay men back (or further) into the closet. But for Rubenstein, as for many LGBT people of his generation, AIDS had the opposite effect. As it became clear that the epidemic would soon have a devastating impact on thousands of gay men across the country, Rubenstein started feeling a growing sense of solidarity both with those who were becoming ill and with the partners and friends who were caring for them.

By the middle of the 1980s, the AIDS epidemic had become the leading cause of death among twenty-five- to forty-four-year-olds in the United States. Surrounded by so much death and dying, Rubenstein came to assume that the disease would kill him before he reached the age of thirty. With a perceived life expectancy of less than five years, he decided in 1987 to dedicate his professional life as a lawyer to doing whatever he could to help people with AIDS. As a result, he got a job with the ACLU's Lesbian and Gay Rights Project (as well as its recently created AIDS Project).

In his first year at the ACLU, Rubenstein represented a woman with AIDS quarantined by public health officials in South Carolina. The young lawyer filed a habeas corpus petition in federal court in Charleston, demanding that the government justify the continued detention of his client. The case was assigned to district court (now U.S. Court of Appeals) judge Karen Henderson, a Reagan appointee. When Rubenstein showed up in Judge Henderson's courtroom to argue the petition, he noticed that the furniture had been rearranged so that the quarantined woman and her lawyer would have to sit in the back of the courtroom. It seemed that the judge, apparently fearing that she might contract HIV from the mere presence of Rubenstein's client in the courtroom, wanted her as far away from the bench as possible. Rubenstein was forced to make his legal arguments from the back of the room, practically shouting in order to be heard. Perhaps not surprisingly, Judge Henderson denied the habeas corpus petition. Rubenstein then went across the street to the state courthouse and, with the assistance of a local lawyer, convinced a judge there to issue an order releasing his client from confinement.

In another instance, Rubenstein threatened to sue the state of Alabama when it refused to use Medicaid money to pay for AZT prescribed to individuals with AIDS. When confronted with the possibility of a lawsuit brought by the ACLU, the state relented and agreed to pay for the medication. The evening after state officials announced their change in policy, a group of Alabamians with AIDS gathered at a Birmingham apartment to celebrate the good news. From there, one of them called Rubenstein at his New York office to thank him for his help with the case. As Rubenstein spoke to the caller, and as he heard the celebratory din in the background, he felt pleased that he had been able to help his clients in a tangible way; as a direct result of his advocacy, after all, the state government had agreed to pay for their AIDS treatment. But he also suspected, as in fact would turn out to be the case, that every person with AIDS present in that Birmingham apartment that evening would be dead in a few years.

Rubenstein found some solace in the fact that the legal work he was doing was challenging and fascinating. There had never before in the United States been an epidemic quite like this one; the disease tested not only political and medical institutions but also legal ones. Although Rubenstein was aware that there were limits to what the law could accomplish, he also knew that it could be deployed in certain instances to benefit people with AIDS in tangible ways. There was also a creativeness to the AIDS activism of the late 1980s that motivated Rubenstein to keep fighting for his clients. In the end, Rubenstein felt proud to be manning the barricades, so to speak, with individuals, most of whom were quite young, who were committed to fighting until their last breaths to pressure, cajole, and embarrass those in power to treat the epidemic with the seriousness that it demanded. There was a dignity and pride in this perseverance that, despite the relentlessness of the disease, was inspiring.

NOTES ON SPADE AND RUBENSTEIN

1. ***Can You Choose an Identity or Does It Choose You?*** Bill Rubenstein, who enjoyed a successful career as a civil rights lawyer specializing in LGBTQ issues before becoming a law professor, noted the significance of his gay identity to his career choices. He also said the following about one of his faculty colleagues: "Professor Halley identifies herself as a member of the LGBT community in the law professors' directory—the first full member of the Harvard faculty to do so. Professor Halley's work, however, challenges the identity-based nature of social movements, investigating whether identity is not, ultimately, as imprisoning as it is liberating. In a unique demonstration that the personal is political, Professor Halley refers to herself as a 'gay man.'" Rubenstein remarked that twenty years after he graduated, Harvard Law School "finally has a faculty member willing to

identify publicly as a gay man—and he's a woman."[7] What does Rubenstein mean by saying that a woman can choose to be a gay man?

2. ***Liberation or Constraint?*** In what respects might finding expressions of self in one's legal work be liberating? In what respects might it be constraining?

3. ***There Are Limits on What Lawyers Can Do.*** A classic article reflecting on a lawyer's experience representing activists engaged in civil disobedience described the rewards of using legal skill to advance a social justice movement to which the lawyer felt deeply, personally committed. It also described two sets of conflicts between the lawyer's role and the clients':

> The first set of conflicts occurs because, as an attorney, I have legitimacy within the legal system that my clients, as lawbreakers, lack. I must behave in a manner consistent with a lawyer's designated role, even if this distinguishes, and therefore distances, me from my clients. Additionally, to be an effective advocate, I need to capitalize upon my relationships with those in positions of authority, such as judges, prosecutors, and police. My ability to sustain these relationships, however, depends precisely upon the differences between me and my clients—I am the lawyer, and they are the lawbreakers; I am an insider, and they are outsiders. Finally, I recognize that some of my clients have had experiences with lawyers who used their legitimacy within the legal community to emphasize their distance from clients and that as a result of their experiences, these clients may not treat me as a trusted comrade.
>
> The second set of conflicts I experience occurs because I believe that a good lawyer must be a client-centered counselor who does not make decisions for her clients. If my clients feel as connected to me as I feel to them, they may want me to make decisions that I feel are theirs to make. My resistance, often followed by their insistence, can open a gulf between us. On the other hand, I am perhaps most profoundly troubled when my clients make choices with which I disagree. Although all lawyers have had this experience, the impact of such disagreement is minimized when the lawyer understands that the client must have the final say about his or her life. Yet my persistent sense that these activists represent me as much as I represent them inspires my wish for us to have common values and priorities.[8]

4. ***Professional Identity as a Different Constraint.*** Another way of thinking about the constraints of professional identity focuses on the notion that a lawyer is someone who should not object to working long hours at low

---

[7] William B. Rubenstein, *My Harvard Law School*, 39 Harv. C.R.-C.L. L. Rev. 317 (2004). *See also* JANET HALLEY, SPLIT DECISIONS: HOW AND WHY TO TAKE A BREAK FROM FEMINISM (2006).

[8] Nancy D. Polikoff, *Am I My Client? The Role Confusion of a Lawyer Activist*, 31 HARV. CIV. RTS.—CIV. LIBS. L. REV. 443, 446–47 (1996).

pay. Transformations in the market for legal services and in technology have spawned businesses that hire lawyers as temporary staff to do relatively menial tasks that formerly were done by junior lawyers who would then move on to more interesting work. Some of these temp lawyers have tried to unionize in order to negotiate collectively for higher pay and better working conditions. One person who studied this effort said that attachment to the idea of professionalism was a major obstacle to organizing for better pay: "they have to disavow the professional nature of what they do in order to avail themselves of the federal law" requiring premium pay for overtime work.[9]

E. SUMMARY

In this chapter we have considered three sets of questions about the role that personal identity traits play in a lawyer's role as a professional. We began with normative questions: Should lawyers aspire to express aspects of their personal identity in their work as lawyers? If so, when and why? If not, why not? Second, we considered descriptive questions: in what ways does personal identity influence how lawyers go about their work? Do aspects of one's identity lead one to approach ethical problems, or client relations, or legal reasoning, or any other aspect of a lawyer's work differently than others who do not share those identity traits? Third, we examined a mix of descriptive and normative issues on the particular question of whether lawyers find aspects of their personal lives to be a source of inspiration and meaning in their work, and whether the inspiration that some find in expressing their self in their work is alienating to others. We also raised questions about whether or to what extent identity traits define how people think of themselves and are perceived by others, either as a defining factor (e.g., women are different from men, or people generally think women are different from men) or as a tendency on a spectrum (e.g., gender identities as masculine and feminine tend to be associated with different behaviors, but there are wide variations in the way that people perform their identities and in the ways in which others perceive them).

As the context for our study of these three sets of questions, we considered examples of several of the most salient identity traits in contemporary American society: race, gender, religion, sexual orientation, and class. Other aspects of your sense of self may be more important to you than these, and we encourage you to reflect on whether that is so and why. Which identity traits will matter to you and to others who work with you? As you consider the notion that professional role is influenced by identity traits, consider the significance in your life of those that you choose, those that are ascribed by others, those that are more or less mutable, and those that may not be as salient to others as they are to you.

---

[9] Lydia DePillis, *The Lawyers Who Are Fighting for the Same Rights As Janitors*, WASH. POST, Feb. 29, 2016.

PART II

A SURVEY OF PRACTICE SETTINGS/TYPES

■ ■ ■

INTRODUCTION

We devote this Part to a survey of the many different types of practice settings in which lawyers work. We first consider lawyers who work as either prosecutors or defense lawyers in the criminal process. We then examine attorneys who serve large organizational clients while working at large firms, in corporations, and in government. Next, we consider lawyers who serve primarily individual and small business clients from solo practices and small firms. Boutique firms, which straddle the two hemispheres of practice, also appear in this survey. We then study lawyers who work as mediators and arbitrators, as well as those who work in legal aid programs and public interest organizations. For each of these practice types, we draw on materials from a variety of disciplines that lend useful perspectives on how these practices operate and the forces that tend to shape lawyers' behavior in each setting.

SUBPART A

CRIMINAL PRACTICE

■ ■ ■

The criminal justice system offers a rich array of issues regarding the role of the lawyer. Many of the most acute ethical dilemmas lawyers face occur in criminal defense or criminal prosecution. Many of the proudest achievements of the American bar and American law are reflected in the role of criminal lawyers. Many of their most abject failures are found here too. In this segment, we consider many big issues about lawyers' conduct in criminal justice, an aspect of the American legal system in which lawyers play a central role.

We begin in Chapter 6 by examining the lawyer's role in criminal defense. Chapter 6 considers the rewards and challenges of criminal defense practice. The chapter focuses especially on the difficulties faced by lawyers and clients in the vast segment of criminal practice in which lawyers represent clients who are too poor to pay their own lawyer. It explores the consequences for indigent clients of the systemic underfunding of indigent criminal defense and the relationship between poor funding and the law governing the constitutional right to effective assistance of counsel in criminal cases.

In Chapter 7, we study the work and unique responsibilities of the criminal prosecutor, who serves a dual role as an advocate seeking conviction and as an officer of justice. This chapter considers the vast power and the vast discretion of prosecutors, the tension between their dual roles as advocates and ministers of justice, and some of the law regarding the exercise of their discretion and the disclosure of exculpatory information to the defense.

CHAPTER 6

CRIMINAL DEFENSE PRACTICE

■ ■ ■

A. INTRODUCTION

Criminal defense practice is not one practice setting but many varied ones. But there are characteristics of criminal defense practice that are common to all. Most criminal defense lawyers spend most of their time prior to trial, investigating the facts, litigating over which evidence may properly be considered proof of guilt, and negotiating the terms on which clients would be willing to enter a plea to a criminal charge. While all criminal defense lawyers occasionally try cases and some do so frequently, the popular perception that the criminal defense lawyer is always and only a well-resourced and clever courtroom tactician is a misconception. Some lawyers spend significant time and money investigating a case prior to trial; others have relatively little time or money to investigate a case prior to negotiating a plea agreement or trying the case. Only a small segment of the criminal defense bar has the resources to conduct the most thorough investigation and to mount the cleverest defense.

The arena in which a lawyer practices is a powerful influence on her conception of her role, her working relationships with clients, other lawyers, and third parties, and her approach to legal and ethical problems. Criminal defense practice varies radically, depending on the resources available to the lawyer and client, and the rewards and challenges of the practice vary accordingly. Some public defenders represent large numbers of impoverished persons in a high-volume practice that involves negotiating guilty pleas and seeking social services for clients and their families. Some, on the other hand, have manageable caseloads and bring a great deal of expertise to the craft of lawyering and their work with very vulnerable clients. Many corporate or white-collar criminal defense lawyers in large firms devote substantial resources to the pre-indictment investigation of a single, complex case but rarely go to trial. The various kinds of criminal defense work have different kinds of rewards and satisfactions, and different kinds of ethical issues.

The overwhelming majority of people charged with crimes are poor. By one estimate, 82 percent of felony defendants in state courts are indigent, as are 66 percent of federal felony defendants.[1] Ninety-five percent of criminal defendants are charged in state courts. Because the vast majority of criminal defendants are too poor to hire their own lawyers, they are represented by lawyers whom they neither choose nor pay for. The representation they receive from appointed counsel is in some cases superb. In others, it is abysmal. Criminal defendants without much personal wealth but who are not poor enough to qualify for representation by the public defender or court-appointed counsel typically hire lawyers in solo practice and small firms; lawyers in such practices handle criminal defense matters ranging from misdemeanors to the most serious felonies.

At the other end of the spectrum, a segment of lawyers in private practice, in both large and small firms, specialize in criminal defense for wealthy individuals and companies suspected or accused of crimes. Lawyers in that specialty, known as white-collar criminal defense because the crimes often involve business wrongdoing, typically spend a great deal of time and money during the investigative stage before criminal charges are filed. They advise clients about whether or how proposed transactions may risk criminal investigation and they attempt to persuade the law enforcement agency and prosecutors that no crime was committed or that criminal prosecution is unwarranted for some other reason. As one leading study of white-collar criminal defense practice observed, the white collar criminal defense attorney "is usually called in by the client to conduct a defense before the government investigation is completed and in some cases even before it begins." White collar criminal defense firms typically employ experts in accounting and finance, and may have more resources than the prosecutor. White collar defense attorneys, in contrast to attorneys handling street crime, have opportunities to argue the innocence of their clients before the government makes a decision to seek an indictment and, importantly, to keep potential evidence out of government reach by controlling access to information.[2]

The same ethical rules apply to all lawyers. The Model Rules promulgated by the ABA have been adopted by most states as ethical rules governing the practice of law in that state. Among the fundamental rules governing all lawyers is Model Rule 1.1, which requires all lawyers to "provide competent representation to a client." Competent representation "requires the legal knowledge, skill, thoroughness and preparation reasonably necessary for the representation." Model Rule 1.3 requires a lawyer act with "reasonable diligence and promptness" in representing a client. For lawyers with reasonable caseloads and adequate resources, the requirements of competence and diligence present no problem. Although

---

[1] Caroline Wolf Harlow, *Bureau of Justice Statistics Special Report: Defense Counsel in Criminal Cases*, U.S. DEPT. OF JUSTICE, BUREAU OF JUSTICE STATISTICS (Nov. 2000), https://www.bjs.gov/content/pub/pdf/dccc.pdf.

[2] *See* KENNETH MANN, DEFENDING WHITE COLLAR CRIME: A PORTRAIT OF ATTORNEYS AT WORK 5 (1985).

lawyers in all practice settings occasionally fail to meet the minimum standards of competence and diligence, we address these two rules here because indigent criminal defense is poorly funded in some jurisdictions.

Critics charge that paltry pay, crushing caseloads, and scarce resources for investigators, forensic experts, and other services necessary to investigate a case and mount a defense lead some criminal defense lawyers to provide poor quality representation.[3] Competent representation for all lawyers is ensured first and foremost by workplace training and supervision. Senior lawyers in an office train junior lawyers about what is expected and how to perform the job well. A second important source of regulation of lawyer competence is the market: clients seek out skilled lawyers, as reflected in reputation and results in past cases. A third important source of regulation of lawyer competence is the threat of liability for malpractice. Most lawyers who can afford it purchase insurance policies to cover the threat of being sued by a client for malpractice. Malpractice insurers therefore also play a role in ensuring minimum lawyer competence by requiring certain office procedures (like a calendaring system), as a condition of issuing an insurance policy and by charging a price for insurance that reflects the experience of the lawyer. Finally, the organized bar attempts to regulate lawyer competence through the threat of discipline either by the state bar (which can suspend or revoke a lawyer's license to practice law) or by the tribunals in which lawyers appear (every court can suspend or revoke a lawyer's privilege to appear in that court).

When a lawyer has a huge caseload and few resources to conduct factual and legal research, however, it may be difficult to decide, as a matter of law or practical moral judgment, whether representation is reasonably competent and diligent. The Comments to the Model Rules do not acknowledge the problem of scarce resources. Competence "includes inquiry into and analysis of the factual and legal elements of the problem, and use of methods and procedures meeting the standards of competent practitioners. It also includes adequate preparation." Model Rule 1.1 Comment [5]. The Comment allows that the required preparation is determined "in part by what is at stake; major litigation and complex transactions ordinarily require more extensive treatment than matters of lesser complexity and consequence." In criminal defense when a client may face a long prison sentence, the matter is certainly of great consequence. How should an overworked lawyer manage? Comment [2] to Model Rule 1.3 insists that "A lawyer's work load must be controlled so that each matter can be handled competently." Yet the Comment does not indicate

---

[3] *See, e.g.*, Benjamin H. Barton & Stephan Bibas, *Triaging Appointed Counsel Funding and Pro Se Access to Justice*, 160 U. PENN. L. REV. 967 (2012); STANDING COMM. ON LEGAL AID & INDIGENT DEFENDANTS, AM. BAR ASS'N, GIDEON'S BROKEN PROMISE: AMERICA'S CONTINUING QUEST FOR EQUAL JUSTICE 9–10 (2004).

who will control that workload, and the shortage of lawyers available for indigent criminal defense in some jurisdictions make compliance with the rule difficult if not impossible.

Plea Bargains. A plea bargain is an agreement in which the defendant agrees to plead guilty to a crime, usually in exchange for a prosecutor's recommendation with regard to a more lenient sentence than is possible or sometimes in exchange for dropping some of the charges. Plea bargaining is extremely common; about 95 percent of criminal convictions are secured by a guilty plea. The negotiation of plea agreements is a major part of the job of every prosecutor and criminal defense lawyer. Prosecutors prepare their case and propose a plea deal. Defense lawyers present exculpating or mitigating evidence during the negotiations, and then decide whether to recommend that the client accept whatever deal the lawyer ultimately persuades the prosecutor to make. The role of defense counsel may be quite different depending on the case. Plea negotiation can be an elaborate and carefully managed process in cases, such as white-collar criminal matters, in which the defense has abundant resources and proof of the crime involves a great deal of complex documentary evidence and testimony. In some cases, however, where the evidence of guilt is clear and straightforward and the defendant does not have the money to pay a lawyer to conduct exhaustive negotiations over the plea, the plea negotiation may be a relatively short process in which the prosecutor offers to accept a plea to certain charges and to recommend a particular sentence and the defendant may accept it without much more than urging leniency based on assertions about the defendant's character or circumstances.

Although plea bargaining is common in the U.S., it is not without controversy. Defenders of the system see it as essential to conserve scarce resources and an unproblematic way to handle the vast majority of cases in which there is no serious doubt about the defendant's factual guilt. Critics believe it allows prosecutors to extort confessions from innocent defendants who are too risk averse (or whose lawyers are ill-prepared) to go to trial and risk a long sentence.

B. UNDERSTANDING INDIGENT CRIMINAL DEFENSE

The shortage of resources for the defense of indigent persons is a pervasive problem in many areas of the United States and raises significant and difficult questions for the legal profession about the quality of justice and the meaning of the constitutional right to effective assistance of counsel. In this section, we first read two of the leading empirical studies describing the job of the public defender in a major American city. Both are by sociologists who conducted extensive and in-depth interviews with lawyers in the public defender's office of Cook County, Illinois, located in

Chicago. While these studies reveal a great deal about the job of a state public defender in an urban area, and especially one in which funding may not be adequate to the demands of the caseload, not every finding of the study applies to the job of public defenders in smaller cities or in offices, including the federal defender service, where the funding is adequate.

REINTERPRETING THE ZEALOUS ADVOCATE: MULTIPLE INTERMEDIARY ROLES OF THE CRIMINAL DEFENSE ATTORNEY

Nicole Martorano Van Cleve
Lawyers in Practice: Ethical Decision Making in Context
(Leslie C. Levin & Lynn Mather, eds., University of Chicago Press 2012)[4]

The main Cook County Criminal Courthouse is the biggest and busiest felony courthouse in the United States. The 36 Criminal Division judges hear more than 28,000 felony cases [annually], half of which are nonviolent, drug-related charges. At any one time, these judges have about 275 pending cases on their dockets. The defendants awaiting trial are decidedly male, minority, and poor. The Cook County Public Defender's Office represents between 22,000 and 23,000 indigent defendants each year. These individuals are determined by a judge to be too poor to secure private defense counsel. The vast majority are pretrial detainees unable to make bond. Compounding these disadvantages, many inmates suffer from drug addiction, mental illness, or both.

Adjacent to the main criminal court is a jail complex that houses 10,000 criminally accused defendants. More than two-thirds of the jail population meets the criteria for drug dependency or abuse. In addition, the Cook County Jail holds so many inmates with serious mental illness that it is one of the largest providers of psychiatric care in the country.

Defense attorneys conceptualize their work as being structured by two central challenges: (1) defendant-based challenges fueled by addiction, poverty, and/or mental illness; and (2) system-based challenges that compromise the quality and character of justice. System-based challenges include limitations in treatment resources and cultural norms that stigmatize zealous advocacy within the courtroom workgroup. Regardless of the lawyers' inclination to be client-centered in their approach to decision making, defense attorneys are acutely aware that they are representing defendants with co-occurring problems like poverty, addiction, and mental illness and there may be more than just their client's freedom at stake. Many defendants stand to be deported, lose custody of their children, or forfeit their jobs or benefits because of the possibility of felony conviction. Yet, system-based challenges confound defense lawyers' obligations and

[4]

decisions. Defense attorneys describe a criminal justice system that is woefully underfunded. Treatment options are particularly limited.

Cook County criminal defense attorneys identify two distinct types of advocacy in criminal defense—"zealous trial advocacy" or "zealous treatment advocacy." Trial advocacy addresses the client's legal needs while treatment advocacy addresses the client's rehabilitative needs and social challenges.

For many defense attorneys, justice is not based on an acquittal or reduction of charge but on understanding and responding to the clients' needs—both legal and extralegal. For example, through his public defender, one defendant made an appeal to the judge to seek a longer intensive probation with drug treatment rather than a shorter term in the state penitentiary. As the defendant appealed in open court, "I need to change and be there for my six children. I want this longer sentence for the drug program. I need the structure in my life."

Criminal defense lawyers find themselves widening the scope of the practice of law into areas traditionally viewed as "social work." This is particularly true when the client is battling addiction or mental illness and the "word of the client" is not reliable. In these instances, like a social worker, the attorney must reach out to other resources, family networks, and specialists to investigate and piece together the best interest of the client and help define his rehabilitative and/or adjudicative goals.

Given the inadequacies of the system [of mental health and drug treatment for offenders] and the intolerance of prosecutors and some judges [to arguments that a defendant's criminal behavior was influenced by drug or mental health problems], defense attorneys are placed in a precarious ethical position when they advocate for treatment. While their client may desperately need social services and/or treatment, many attorneys try to "save" their clients from the system itself—hiding the client's mental health issues or addiction. The best they can do is minimize time for their client.

In advocating for their clients, defense attorneys must navigate and adjust to the court culture itself—anticipating how their strategies and tactics will be received by their prosecutor and judge. Cook County is characterized by a horizontal representation system in which public defenders and prosecutors are assigned to a single courtroom as consistent members of a courtroom workgroup. Over time, they become friends, and their biggest concern is to be sure not to hurt each other too much. In Cook County, public defenders described this organizational arrangement as exerting strong incentives to assume a cooperative posture—as well as harsh penalties for seeming adversarial. Some public defenders discussed a relative "power imbalance" between them and the prosecutor and judge.

Public defenders were careful "not to annoy them, or otherwise their clients would receive poor deals in the plea bargaining process."

Prosecutors often classified which defense attorneys were "good" or "bad" based on whether the attorney was able to "control" her client into pleading guilty. Defense attorneys who pursue "too many" motions and trials often find that their reputations suffer as a result. Some defense attorneys described a court culture of prosecutors and judges that often punished defendants for the zealous actions of their attorneys.

THE PUBLIC DEFENDER: THE PRACTICE OF LAW IN THE SHADOWS OF REPUTE

Lisa J. McIntyre (University of Chicago Press 1987)[5]

When I asked current public defenders what had surprised them about the job, almost all responded by saying that one of their biggest surprises (and disappointments) had been the lack of respect. Although some public defenders believe that many judges are prosecution minded, they seem to regard this as inevitable, if not entirely fair. What the lawyers find less easy to accept is that judges often treat them as second-class lawyers.

If something is going to hurt a client's case, the lawyers said, they must object. Over and over I was told that when a judge refuses to let you argue a motion that is important to your case, you must object; when the judge allows into evidence what you believe to be incompetent or improper material you must object: "There are times when you have got to say, 'Come on, judge.' You have to do that sometimes and of course it's scary. Now I have been scared, and I've backed down sometimes when I shouldn't have. But I go back in there the next day and start all over again, because I will have gone home that night and chewed myself out for backing down." But when a judge's treatment of a lawyer merely reflects a disregard of the lawyer's dignity, the lawyers feel that to fight back will hurt their client: "Everything you do is going to affect your client, you know? If I'm being a jerk, or if I'm taking myself too seriously, I've got a client who's going to suffer."

Ironically, it is the clients who tend to be among the most dismissive of the lawyers' claims to respect. Two-thirds of the former public defenders interviewed agreed with the statement, "My clients often seemed to doubt my ability as a lawyer just because I was a public defender."

The myth of competency embraces public defenders from the moment that they are appointed to the office. [P]ublic defenders work as a company of equals. Even when supervision or teaching and the like do occur, they are carefully done in a way that nurtures the myth and allows it to go unchallenged. Similarly, the lack of general policy identified by these lawyers suggests that, as far as they are concerned, the organization's hand rarely intrudes into their professional autonomy.

All of the current public defenders with whom I spoke and nearly all (93 percent) of the former assistants interviewed in my research agreed that people "constantly" ask public defenders, "How can you defend those people?" The overwhelming majority (97 percent) of former public defenders interviewed agreed that they had believed that they were putting their legal skills to good use by working as public defenders. Only five (8 percent) said that they would not join the office if they had it to do over again.

How can you defend people whom you know are guilty? Public defenders usually respond in a manner that is more weary than indignant: "Oh God, *that* question! How do you represent someone you know is guilty? So you go through all the things. You know, 'he's not guilty until he's proven guilty, until he's been proved guilty beyond a reasonable doubt.' I think everyone deserves the best possible defense, the most fair trial he can get. It's a guarantee of the Constitution, no more, no less."

Under some circumstances, mere empathy with the client's situation permits lawyers to feel justified when defending someone whom they know is factually guilty. "Look, kids get into trouble, some kids get into serious trouble. I can understand that. In juvenile court, our job isn't to punish, the result is supposed to be in the best interests of the minor. Here you've got to keep them with their family and give them all the services you can so they don't do this again."

But the alien character especially of the crimes that their clients are alleged to have committed often mean that "you have to care more about your clients' rights than you can usually care about your clients." On the surface, what a defense lawyer does is simply protect the client's rights. But many lawyers transform the nature of the battle. They are not fighting for the freedom of the client per se but to keep the system honest: "It doesn't mean that I want to get everybody off. It means that I try to make sure the state's attorneys meet up to their obligations, which means that the only way they can prove someone is guilty is beyond a reasonable doubt, with competent evidence. If they can't do that, then my client deserves to go home." They do not defend simply because their clients have rights but because they believe that those rights have been, are, or will be ignored by others in the criminal justice system.

Public defenders do feel as if they are often mugged—by the legal system. There is a lot of real and passionate anger: "Some people said I'd become cynical after a while. Well, I might be more cynical about some things, but I don't think I have really changed my attitude. If anything, I might have become a little more gung ho. You see that there really is an awful lot of injustice. It becomes very real and it's scary. I find myself becoming very angry in this job, all the time."

Public defenders are quick to admit that they usually do not ask their clients whether they are guilty or innocent. [When asked why, one responded:] "Because in the first place, it is irrelevant. It's not my role to decide whether they are guilty—in our sense of the term guilt. [I]t is my role to fashion a defense and to be creative. If the person says to me 'This is how I did it,' it's pretty hard for me to come around and try to do something for them. In general, I fence around with some of my questions. I ask them about an alibi or something like that. But the more I think they are guilty, the less I will ask."

Public defenders do not begin their relationship with a client by asking awkward questions because once the client admits guilt, it limits what the public defender can ethically do. Being honest, ethical and "scrupled" in a system that many of them believe is corrupt is very important to the lawyers with whom I spoke.

Public defenders try not to go into a trial with cases that cannot be won. Unfortunately, most of their cases are of this type—loser (or "dead-bang loser") cases, cut-and-dried situations in which the client was caught red-handed and "the state has everything but a videotape of the crime." In large part, being competent is being able to convince a client that it is not in his or her best interests to insist on a trial that cannot be won.

Ask any public defender "What was your worst case?" and chances are you will hear about a case that was a loser. Understanding the nature of a loser case is crucial, for embedded in the concept—and in the distinctions that lawyers make between losers and other sorts of cases—is the clue to what makes public defenders tick. "The worst case is where the state has an overwhelming amount of evidence and there is nothing you can do with it. It's a case where you get beat up in court. And that is just no fun."

The opposite of a loser case is not necessarily a winner. It is a fun case, which in turn must be distinguished from a boring case:

> I don't like armed robberies because they are boring. There are only one or two issues—either the guy did it or he didn't—and that doesn't make for very interesting work. The case I am trying right now is a murder that is really a lot of fun. Listen to me! "A murder is a lot of fun." How can I say that? But it's an interesting case because the facts are such that they [the state] don't really have much evidence in the case—a lot of people could have done it. It's all circumstantial evidence. That's fun.

Talcott Parsons once commented: "The fact that the case can be tried by a standard procedure relieves [the attorney] of some pressure of commitment to the case of his client. He can feel that, if he does his best then having assured his client's case of a fair trial, he is relieved of the responsibility for an unfavorable verdict." One of the attorneys with whom I spoke seemed to confirm Parsons's hypothesis: "There is a certain consolation of going to trial with a loser case. If I lose, what the hell. I gave it my best shot. If I lose, *it was a loser*. If I win, it's amazing."

Most of the attorneys, however, were not so sanguine and could not detach themselves from the outcomes of their cases so easily. Even losing a loser case, most of them said, is incredibly hard on the attorney. The attorneys are not much comforted by the fact that the client was guilty—or probably guilty, anyway. "There was a case, not too long ago, that I really came to believe that they had no evidence on my man, and I fought very hard for him. We lost, and I felt very bad about that. Afterward, he just fell apart, started screaming at me back in the lockup. We had this big fight. And I yelled at him, 'You know, I really put myself on the line, too, and I did everything I could for you, and what are you doing yelling at me? Cause I really believed, and I worked hard.' And then I misspoke myself, because I said, 'And I really believed that you didn't do this.' And he said, 'Would it make you feel any better if I told you that I did do it?' [Laugh] I said, 'I don't want to know; don't tell me!' I still don't want to know, and that's how it is."

The stress of being on trial and the pain of losing are compounded on those rare occasions when the lawyer believes the defendant is innocent. For this reason, although the lawyers will say, "I don't care if he's guilty or innocent," their claim to neutrality is often a lie. When they say, "I don't care if my client is guilty," what they usually mean is, "I prefer my clients to be guilty."

Losing is one of the costs of being an attorney; losing a lot (I was told) is one of the costs of being a public defender.

Perhaps the most important way in which they cope with losing is knowing that they do not always lose. When I asked one attorney "How do you keep going when you lose?" he said: "Always remembering that there is a flip side of that—you feel great when you win."

Failure is something with which every professional must cope. But implicit in the question, "How can you defend those people?" is the idea that public defenders ought to have trouble coping with winning. The lawyers are protected by the fact that they rarely win cases for clients who are horrible criminals. But however rarely it occurs, the possibility of winning big someday and then having your client kill again exists in the future of every defense lawyer. Often it seemed that one of the things that helps the lawyer not to feel too bad about winning is one of the things that makes it so hard to lose—that is, their relationship with the client. Most of the lawyers said that usually, especially when they go to trial, they end up liking their clients.

There is in any human being a soul you can reach. [Pause] Now I use language like this hesitantly, you know; people usually look at you like you're crazy when you talk like this. But if you are willing to take the risk and open up your heart and reach into their hearts, you will reach it.

You need to do that for yourself. You need to do that, too, because if you are going to try the case for either a judge or a jury, you have to make that person human. They are someone. And that is what costs. 'Cause every time you do that, you are giving something of yourself away. You get something, sure, but you give away a lot.

NOTES ON THE ROLE OF THE PUBLIC DEFENDER

1. ***Understanding the Role of the Public Defender.*** How do the lawyers in these two studies describe their role? What value do they perceive in their work? Which aspects of their descriptions of their job do you think would be generalizable to any lawyer appointed to represent an indigent person accused of a crime, and which do you think are a function of practice in a large city and/or in an office in which the resources are inadequate to manage the case load?

2. ***"How Can You Defend Those People?"*** Why do the lawyers in the McIntyre study seem "weary" rather than "indignant" about being asked to explain why they defend people who are (or may be) guilty of a crime? What value is there in defending people who have (or may have) committed crimes? To what extent do you think a lack of social consensus about the value of representing those accused of crime influences the respect for criminal defense lawyers and the funding for indigent criminal defense?

3. ***Scarce Resources.*** How does the scarcity of resources—for hiring enough lawyers and investigators, for drug or mental health treatment, or for operating the court system—affect the way that these public defenders see their role? What ethical dilemmas arise because of the scarcity of resources and the huge caseloads for judges, public defenders, and prosecutors? In public defender offices with adequate resources, such as the federal and some state public defender services such as the one described in the Ogletree excerpt below, lawyers describe the rewards and challenges of indigent criminal defense differently (and generally much more positively) than the lawyers in these two studies. And, in contrast to these two studies of Cook County, in many regions the office of the public defender attracts talented lawyers who relish the challenge of a fast-paced trial practice and the rewards of advocacy on behalf of those accused of crime.

4. ***Respect.*** Some of the public defenders in McIntyre's study identify lack of respect from clients, other lawyers, and judges as a major source of frustration in their job. What accounts for that lack of respect? What are the consequences—for public defenders, for the legal profession, and for the

criminal justice system—of the lack of respect (by some) for the work of indigent criminal defense lawyers? Do you think issues of respect are a product of lack of funding and heavy caseloads or do they stem from other causes? If so, what might lawyers and judges do to address the situation?

C. THE RIGHT TO EFFECTIVE ASSISTANCE OF COUNSEL

One of the most momentous U.S. Supreme Court decisions affecting the legal profession was *Gideon v. Wainwright*, 372 U.S. 335 (1963), which created a constitutional right to counsel for individuals charged with a crime that could result in imprisonment. Although the Court held that those too poor to afford a lawyer are entitled to have one appointed at government expense, the Court left it up to governments to fund the provision of lawyers. As we will see, there is wide variation among counties, states, and the federal government in how the *Gideon* obligation is funded and administered. In this section, we look first at the constitutional law governing appointed criminal defense lawyers. We then survey some of the challenges in implementing the right to counsel. Finally, we look at a body of constitutional law that has developed in large part because the quality of representation provided by some appointed criminal defense is sometimes very poor. That law attempts to decide when the criminal defendant has received such ineffective assistance of counsel as to violate the constitutional right to counsel.

1. THE CONSTITUTIONAL LAW GOVERNING APPOINTED CRIMINAL DEFENSE LAWYERS

Many aspects of the attorney-client relationship are worked out privately by agreement between the lawyer and the client. To the extent the relationship is governed by law, it is governed by the contract between the lawyer and client, by the rules of professional responsibility adopted by the state in which the lawyer practices, and by the tribunals in which the lawyer appears in the course of the representation. However, when an indigent individual is charged with a crime that could result in imprisonment or an indigent juvenile is charged with any crime, *Gideon* and later cases require an attorney to be provided at government expense. The source of the right to counsel in *Gideon* is the Sixth Amendment to the U.S. Constitution, which provides that "in all criminal prosecutions, the accused shall enjoy the right . . . to have the assistance of counsel for his defense." In that circumstance, because the government is choosing and paying for the lawyer, the Constitution regulates the relationship. As we will see, however, the level of competence demanded of indigent criminal defense lawyers by the Constitution as the courts have interpreted it is fairly minimal. (See below *Ineffective Assistance of Counsel*.)

2. THE CHALLENGES OF IMPLEMENTING *GIDEON*

All 50 states, the District of Columbia, and the federal government have created separate systems to comply with the Sixth Amendment right to counsel for indigent criminal defense. Jurisdictions have adopted one of two systems, or sometimes a combination of both, to discharge their responsibility under *Gideon*. The vast majority have established public defender offices as a government office staffed by lawyers and investigators who specialize in indigent criminal defense. Some rely on private lawyers appointed by the court to handle indigent criminal defense. Public defenders' offices are the counterpart of the prosecutors' offices in each jurisdiction. The federal government has created an Office of the Federal Defender in 91 of the 94 federal districts across the country to represent indigent persons accused of federal crimes. The Federal Defender handles 60 percent of federal indigent criminal defense cases nationwide. The other 40 percent are handled by private lawyers appointed by the court and paid a statutory rate set by the federal Criminal Justice Act (CJA). (Co-defendants cannot both be represented by lawyers in the same office because of conflicts of interest. That explains why the Federal Defender handles only 60 percent of federal cases involving indigent defendants.) In 2019, the CJA rate for appointed counsel is $148 per hour for most cases, and $190 for capital cases. The fees are capped at $10,900 for a felony, $7,800 for an appeal, and $3,100 for a misdemeanor.

States use a combination of public defenders and private lawyers. Some states pass on the responsibility for establishing and funding indigent criminal defense to county governments, most of which are limited in their ability to raise revenue through taxes. Some counties provide indigent defense cheaply by contracting with local lawyers who are paid a set amount to defend those in need of counsel. Such flat fee agreements create incentives for lawyers to spend as little time and money as possible working on a case. For example, a federal court overturned a death sentence in Texas on the grounds that the defense lawyer, who had been paid only $11 per hour (which was just over twice the legal minimum wage), had provided ineffective assistance and "the justice system got only what it paid for."[6]

The availability and quality of appointed counsel varies widely from state to state and even among counties in a single state. *Gideon* requires counsel be appointed, but the Court has no power to order governments to

---

[6] *Martinez-Macias v. Collins*, 979 F.2d 1067 (5th Cir. 1992); *see also* STANDING COMM. ON LEGAL AID & INDIGENT DEFENDANTS, AM. BAR ASS'N, GIDEON'S BROKEN PROMISE: AMERICA'S CONTINUING QUEST FOR EQUAL JUSTICE 9–10 (2004) (collecting examples of underpaid criminal defense lawyers in many jurisdictions). A leading expert on the administration of the death penalty in southern states reported that in one case a lawyer defending a capital case in Alabama was paid $4 per hour and another received $5 per hour, which at the time were only slightly above the legal minimum wage. Stephen B. Bright, *Counsel for the Poor: The Death Sentence Not for the Worst Crime But for the Worst Lawyer*, 103 YALE L.J. 1835 (1993) (collecting examples).

appropriate funds to pay for the enforcement of constitutional rights, and the money that states and counties spend varies. The Federal Defenders and some county public defenders offices are generally excellent, staffed with talented criminal defense lawyers and investigators who provide outstanding representation. The Public Defender Service in the District of Columbia, the only local defender funded by Congress, is widely considered to provide superb representation.[7] In the federal system and states with well-funded offices, the job of public defender is highly sought-after. In some areas, however, as noted in the excerpt below, the money the county spends for indigent criminal defense is grossly inadequate and the quality of the defense provided in some cases is very poor. Moreover, over a third of people charged with misdemeanors in state and federal courts are represented by no lawyer at all because the constitutional right to counsel applies only where the defendant faces incarceration.[8]

Many state legislatures have increased the number of crimes and the length of sentences but cut the budget for indigent criminal defense. As a result, public defenders must juggle ever-larger case loads. Although the National Advisory Commission on Criminal Justice Standards recommends that attorneys handle no more than 150 felony cases a year, according to one study, in the five years preceding 2009, the average public defender case load in Miami-Dade County jumped from 367 felonies per year in 2006 to 500 per year in 2009, even though the public defender's office budget was cut 12.6 percent.[9] The Florida Supreme Court held that the Miami-Dade county public defenders were justified in responding to the situation by refusing to take new cases because they could not competently represent so many clients.

Similar crises occurred in other states. In Louisiana, the state provides less than half the funding for indigent criminal defense, forcing the local public defender offices to rely on fluctuating sources of local revenue such as traffic tickets and court fees. A study conducted under the auspices of the ABA found that as of 2017, the state had enough indigent criminal defense lawyers to handle only 20 percent of the pending cases. In other words, every public defender would have to do the work of five full-time lawyers to adequately represent their clients.[10] Although New Orleans had

---

[7] Bob Kemper, *Gideon: Right to Counsel? Landmark Decision Falls Short of Promise,* WASH. LAW., Sept. 2009, at 25–26.

[8] Caroline Wolf Harlow, *Bureau of Justice Statistics Special Report: Defense Counsel in Criminal Cases,* U.S. DEPT. OF JUSTICE, BUREAU OF JUSTICE STATISTICS (Nov. 2000), https://www.bjs.gov/content/pub/pdf/dccc.pdf.

[9] THE CONSTITUTION PROJECT, JUSTICE DENIED: AMERICA'S CONTINUING NEGLECT OF OUR CONSTITUTIONAL RIGHT TO COUNSEL (Apr. 2009).

[10] AMERICAN BAR ASSOCIATION, THE LOUISIANA PROJECT: A STUDY OF THE LOUISIANA DEFENDER SYSTEM AND ATTORNEY WORKLOAD STANDARDS (February 2017), https://www.americanbar.org/content/dam/aba/administrative/legal_aid_indigent_defendants/ls_sclaid_louisiana_project_report.pdf. See also Richard A. Oppel, Jr. & Jugal K. Patel, *One Lawyer, 194 Felony Cases, and No Time,* N.Y. TIMES, Jan. 31, 2019.

an exemplary public defender office in 2010, the local revenues abruptly dried up when the number of traffic citations dropped. (A hotly contested election for local sheriff apparently prompted the drop.) In 2016 in 7 of Louisiana's 42 judicial districts, public defenders refused to take new cases after budget cuts forced drastic layoffs. As indigent defendants were put on wait lists for lawyers, judges in some parishes experimented with requiring every member of the bar to take a felony case pro bono, regardless of skills or experience. In others, defendants languished in jail for weeks awaiting the appointment of counsel so that the court could conduct a bail hearing and other pretrial proceedings.[11] The Southern Poverty Law Center and the ACLU filed lawsuits against Louisiana's public defender system, but attorneys for the plaintiffs conceded that the lawsuits alone "can't change anything. The political actors in Louisiana have to step up. The lawsuit can put pressure on them. It can point out that the system is unconstitutional. But if the state wants a better system, it has to fix it."[12]

The underfunding of indigent criminal defense became so acute in Missouri that the ACLU filed a class action suit in 2017 asserting that the quality of representation had fallen below the constitutional minimum. According to the suit, there were so few public defenders that each could spend only 8.7 hours on the most serious non-homicide felonies and, overall, were able to devote fewer than the ABA's recommended minimum hours in 97 percent of their cases.[13] In an effort to force a political solution, the chief public defender, invoking a Missouri statute authorizing him to assign a case to any member of the Missouri bar, assigned a case to the state governor. The state challenged the action, and a Missouri court eventually ruled that only courts have the power to appoint lawyers to represent litigants. The fracas did, however, bring national and local media attention to the systemic underfunding of indigent criminal defense.[14]

In these and other states, some attributed the underfunding to a mismatch between low tax revenues prompted by politically popular tax cuts and the continued need for public services. Is there a way to effectively guarantee a federal constitutional right to counsel without a state commitment to pay for it? The following excerpt addresses the challenge of implementing *Gideon*:

---

[11] Campbell Robertson, *In Louisiana the Poor Lack Legal Defense*, N.Y. TIMES, Mar. 19, 2016.

[12] Edwin Rios, *These Public Defenders Actually Want to Get Sued, Mother Jones*, Apr. 11, 2016; *See Allen v. Edwards*, Verified Petition for Class Certification and Declaratory and Injunctive Relief, available at https://www.splcenter.org/sites/default/files/2617indigentdefense lawsuitfiled.pdf (visited July 29, 2019).

[13] Matt Ford, *A Constitutional Crisis in Missouri*, THE ATLANTIC, Mar. 14, 2017.

[14] *Recent Case*—State v. Quehl: *Missouri Court Refuses Public Defender's Delegation of Indigent Legal Representation to Governor*, 130 HARV. L. REV. 1776 (2017).

THE RIGHT TO COUNSEL IN CRIMINAL CASES, A NATIONAL CRISIS

Mary Sue Backus & Paul Marcus
57 Hastings Law Journal 1031 (2005–2006)

In a case of mistaken identity, Henry Earl Clark of Dallas was charged with a drug offense in Tyler, Texas. After his arrest, it took six weeks in jail before he was assigned a lawyer, as he was too poor to afford one on his own. It took seven more weeks after the appointment of the lawyer, until the case was dismissed, for it to become obvious that the police had arrested the wrong man. While in jail, Clark asked for quick action, writing, "I [need to] get out of this godforsaken jail, get back to my job . . . I am not a drug user or dealer. I am a tax-paying American." During this time, he lost his job and his car, which was auctioned. After Clark was released, he spent several months in a homeless shelter.

Sixteen-year-old Denise Lockett was retarded and pregnant. Her baby died when she delivered it in a toilet in her home in a South Georgia housing project. Although an autopsy found no indication that the baby's death had been caused by any intentional act, the prosecutor charged Lockett with first-degree murder. Her appointed lawyer had a contract to handle all the county's criminal cases, about 300 cases in a year, for a flat fee. He performed this work on top of that required by his private practice with paying clients. The lawyer conducted no investigation of the facts, introduced no evidence of his client's mental retardation or of the autopsy findings, and told her to plead guilty to manslaughter. She was sentenced to twenty years in prison.

Tony Humphries was charged with jumping a subway turnstile in Atlanta to evade a $1.75 fare. He sat in jail for fifty-four days, far longer than the sentence he would have received if convicted, before a lawyer was appointed, at a cost to the taxpayers of $2330.

A mother in Louisiana recently addressed a state legislative committee:

> My son Corey is a defendant in Calcasieu Parish, facing adult charges. He has been incarcerated for three months with no contact from court-appointed counsel. Corey and I have tried for three months to get a name and phone number of the appointed attorney. No one in the system can tell us exactly who the court-appointed attorney is. The court told us his public defender will be the same one he had for a juvenile adjudication. The court-appointed counsel told me he does not represent my son. The court clerk's office cannot help me or my son. We are navigating the system alone.

> Eight weeks ago, we filed a motion for bond reduction. We have heard nothing—not even a letter of acknowledgement from the court that it received our motion.

The Chief Public Defender of Fairfax County, Virginia (metropolitan Washington, D.C.) resigned in July 2005, after just ten months in the position. She said that even with legislative reforms in Virginia her office had so many clients and so few lawyers that the attorneys simply could not adequately represent the defendants at trials and on appeal. [In 2004], the twenty lawyers in the office defended more than 8000 clients.

Although professional standards for defenders are clear, systemic deficiencies push defenders to compromise their efforts on behalf of clients. These questionable compromises undermine ethical standards and, in turn, contribute to the denigration of the legal profession and the criminal justice system. Judges, prosecutors, lawyer disciplinary bodies, and defenders themselves are loath to call attention to these ethical failings.

Ethically a lawyer is required to serve her clients with competence and diligence. The lawyer must be thorough, adequately prepared, and a zealous advocate on behalf of the client's interests. Regular communication is expected in order to keep the client reasonably informed and to respond to the client's reasonable requests for information. In addition, a lawyer is required to consult with the client regarding how the lawyer will pursue important objectives and to explain matters to clients so that they may make informed decisions.

In practice, the average lawyer working in an overburdened public defender office, or as an appointed or contract attorney whose compensation is so anemic that the hourly wage barely covers overhead expenses, may do none of these things. The problem arises, for instance, with a lawyer carrying a misdemeanor caseload three times the size of the national recommended standards, who meets a client for the first time just before court is called into session. That attorney simply does not have the time or the resources to investigate, prepare, or communicate adequately with the client so that the client can make an informed decision and the attorney can advocate zealously for his client's best interests. Even where the matters are not complex, sheer volume can preclude anything other than an assembly line approach, which falls far short of professional standards. Such is the case for the two contract defenders in Allen County, Indiana, who were assigned 2668 misdemeanor cases last year. Each attorney makes less than $2000 a month and maintains a private practice on the side. Not surprisingly, the overwhelming majority of defendants plead guilty; only twelve went to trial in a year.

Calling the practice unethical, chief public defenders in two jurisdictions, Broward County, Florida and St. Louis, Missouri, recently refused to continue the "meet 'em and greet 'em and plead 'em" approach.

In Broward County, public defenders will no longer be allowed to recommend plea agreements to clients at arraignments or first hearings unless the attorney has met with the defendant, established a relationship and has an opportunity to properly assess the case, the client and any plea offer. The change was made in acknowledgment that the prior practice of recommending a plea, often portrayed as a one-time offer that would worsen over time, at a lawyer's first encounter with a client with almost no information about the case fails to meet ethical standards. Such an approach makes it nearly impossible to determine whether a plea is in a defendant's best interest or to fulfill the duty to explain the matter sufficiently for the client to make an informed decision. For this reason, the ABA Criminal Justice Standards require independent investigation: "Under no circumstances should defense counsel recommend to a defendant acceptance of a plea unless appropriate investigation and study of the case has been completed, including an analysis of controlling law and the evidence likely to be introduced at trial." Similarly, in St. Louis the chief defender characterized representation of certain misdemeanor defendants as "unethical, unprofessional and unconstitutional." As a result, he instituted a policy of no longer automatically representing defendants the first time they appear in court after having been arrested on misdemeanor charges. The chief defender concluded that it was not possible to "render constitutional, ethical and professional assistance of counsel upon walking into court with no discovery, no opportunity for investigation and no opportunity to counsel the accused. Both of these jurisdictions have simply recognized that, despite caseload pressures, ethics rules require more of defense attorneys than encouraging their clients to accept the prosecution's plea offers.

Alaska explicitly acknowledged a "heightened concern for professional ethics violations." And, although the state expressed a willingness to defend its legal professionals against claims of such violations, the report candidly advised that "each attorney must weigh his/her ever increasing caseload and the demands from the public, against the potential of violating the professional code of ethics, resulting in disciplinary action." That is a rather stark and appalling warning that ethical violations may be inherent in the job of public defender.

The recent ABA report assessing the status of *Gideon's* mandate found that "defense lawyers throughout the country are violating these ethical rules by failing to provide competent, diligent, continuous, and conflict-free representation." As disturbing as it is to suggest that ethical violations are commonplace, it is even more alarming that courts and disciplinary authorities routinely overlook these breaches of professional rules of conduct. Most disciplinary agencies seem reluctant to bring charges against defenders whose conduct breaches ethical rules, perhaps because it seems unfair to blame an individual attorney when the failings are more a function of systemic inadequacies. The reluctance to sanction defenders of the indigent may also reflect the concern that sanctions could discourage other lawyers from accepting cases of indigent defendants. Such a result would exacerbate the problem of an already short supply of attorneys willing to take on this type of work.

Another possible enforcement mechanism, malpractice actions by defendants, is likely to be as unavailing as recourse to lawyer disciplinary bodies has been. Many states require that a plaintiff must first succeed in obtaining post-conviction relief for ineffective assistance of counsel before bringing a malpractice claim. [S]ome courts have held that the plaintiff must effectively demonstrate her actual innocence, not just that she would have been acquitted save for the attorney's negligence.

Prosecutors and judges must also bear some responsibility in maintaining ethical standards within the criminal justice system, and the roles of both warrant further exploration. The prosecutorial ideal of seeking to "do justice," rather than just pursuing conviction of those who are arrested, has long established roots in our legal tradition. Despite their duty to seek justice, some prosecutors are more likely to exploit defense incompetence than to take steps to guard against it. For example, there are prosecutors who encourage quick guilty pleas as a way of clearing their dockets and maintaining high conviction rates with low costs. Most authorities hold that prosecutorial intervention in the face of ethical violations by defense counsel is only required if there is a constitutional violation, not if the performance of defense counsel is simply lacking. There is a substantial concern that if the standards were too lax as to when a prosecutor could report a defense attorney for ethical violations, the procedure would become another litigation tactic.

The role of judges in both monitoring and correcting ethical abuses by defense counsel is also worthy of further attention. Although judges have strong incentives to encourage the quick resolution of cases and to sidestep the issue of the effectiveness of defense counsel in order to move the docket along, judges are uniquely situated to prevent ethical violations. In appointing counsel, monitoring pretrial activities and evaluating counsel's preparedness, observing courtroom performance and participating in plea bargaining negotiations, the judge must be cognizant that it is the judge, not counsel, who has the ultimate responsibility for the conduct of a fair and lawful trial.

[D]efense attorneys themselves have a strict ethical obligation to control their workload in order to ensure that they can deliver competent representation. The Eastern District of Pennsylvania has suggested that if a public defender is overburdened, he may at any time decline an appointment, and should decline to accept an appointment if the defender is not in a position to properly defend an action. Similarly, the California

Court of Appeal stated, "when a public defender reels under a staggering workload, he should proceed to place the situation before the judge, who upon a satisfactory showing can relieve him, and order the employment of private counsel at public expense. Courts have occasionally done just that. For example, the Florida District Court of Appeals has upheld a trial court order allowing a public defender to withdraw from representation in six felony cases because of an excessive caseload.

* * *

In the following excerpt, Professor Paul Butler argues that Backus' and Marcus' focus on improving the amount and quality of indigent criminal defense is misplaced, and may even legitimate what he sees as a massive racial and class-based injustice in the criminal system.

POOR PEOPLE LOSE: *GIDEON* AND THE CRITIQUE OF RIGHTS

Paul D. Butler
122 Yale Law Journal 2176 (2013)

The reason that prisons are filled with poor people, and that rich people rarely go to prison, is not because the rich have better lawyers than the poor. It is because prison is for the poor, and not the rich. In criminal cases, poor people lose most of the time, not because indigent defense is inadequately funded, although it is, and not because defense attorneys for poor people are ineffective, although some are. Prison is designed for them. This is the real crisis of indigent defense. *Gideon* obscures this reality, and in this sense stands in the way of the political mobilization that will be required to transform criminal justice.

Poor people lose, most of the time, because

(1) The spaces that poor people, especially poor African Americans, live in receive more law enforcement in the form of police stops and arrests.

(2) The criminal law deliberately ignores the social conditions that breed some forms of law-breaking.

(3) African Americans, who are disproportionately poor, are the target of explicit and implicit bias by key actors in the criminal justice system, including police, prosecutors, and judges.

(4) Once any person is arrested, she becomes part of a crime control system of criminal justice, in which guilt is presumed. Prosecutors, using the legal apparatus of expansive criminal liability, recidivist statutes, and mandatory minimums,

coerce guilty pleas by threatening defendants with vastly disproportionate punishment if they go to trial.

(5) Repeat the cycle. A criminal caste is created.

If *Gideon* was supposed to make the criminal justice system fairer for poor people and minorities, it has been a spectacular failure. Fifty years after *Gideon*, poor people have both the right to counsel and the most massive level of incarceration in the world. *Gideon* provides a legitimation of the status quo. [T]he poor—especially the poor and black—are incarcerated at exponentially greater levels now than when *Gideon* was decided. *Gideon* creates a formal equality between the rich and the poor because now they both have lawyers. The vast overrepresentation of the poor in America's prisons appears more like a narrative about personal responsibility than an indictment of criminal justice.

NOTES ON THE CONSTITUTIONAL RIGHT TO COUNSEL

1. ***Considering the Options.*** What options face an individual public defender who has too many cases to handle? What are the advantages and disadvantages of the strategies described by Backus and Marcus?

2. ***Why Are Resources Scarce?*** Why is the issue of too many cases and too few resources a problem in some jurisdictions? If it is such a significant problem, why do legislatures not simply solve it by appropriating more money to fund criminal defenders? Why has Congress yet to act on the many calls issued by scholars, judges, and the bar to provide funding to implement *Gideon*?[15]

3. ***Enforcing the Right to Competent Counsel.*** Why do you suppose judges have not been more insistent (or effective) in calling for improved representation for indigent criminal defendants?

4. **Gideon *and Mass Incarceration.*** Butler says that since *Gideon* was decided, the number of people in prison has skyrocketed, the racial imbalance in the prison population has grown worse, and lawyers may do a disservice to the cause of justice by imagining that the criminal system would be fairer if only there were more and better lawyers for poor people. Where *should* lawyers who are concerned about mass incarceration focus their energies? Are there ways in which *Gideon* has improved the way that lawyers think about their responsibility for ensuring justice in criminal justice, or do you agree with Butler that it has largely legitimated injustice?[16]

5. ***Should All Lawyers Step Up?*** In some parishes in Louisiana, judges resorted to appointing every member of the bar to represent an indigent

---

[15] *See* Will Isenberg & Tom Emswiler, *Federally Fund Public Defenders*, BOSTON GLOBE, June 19, 2016.

[16] *See* Sara Mayeux, *What* Gideon *Did*, 116 COLUM. L. REV. 15 (2016) (arguing that *Gideon* may have transformed the bar's sense of responsibility to ensure that justice is done in the criminal system).

criminal defendant. A lawyer in one Louisiana parish who ran a family business and had never practiced law was assigned to represent a defendant charged with a felony. So were a tax attorney who had never appeared in court and another lawyer whose practice was limited to representing insurance companies. All protested to the judge that they were not competent to handle the defense, but all three judges rejected the objection.[17] What should the lawyers do? If you were on the Louisiana Supreme Court, what would you do? Can you think of any advantages of the Louisiana all-hands approach to indigent defense?

6. ***Meet 'em, Greet 'em, Plead 'em: Has the Bar Failed Its Responsibility?*** Critics have complained for years about the widespread practice of courts accepting guilty pleas from indigent criminal defense before counsel has been appointed or, if a lawyer has been appointed, before the lawyer has had an opportunity to confer with the client or conduct even minimal investigation. The collateral consequences of a guilty plea, even to a minor offense, can be considerable, including rendering the defendant subject to deportation. Yet defendants face enormous pressure to enter an early plea in order to be released from jail and to get back to work and family. ABA Standard 4–6.1, adopted in 2015, provides that defense counsel "should not recommend to a client acceptance of a disposition offer unless and until appropriate investigation and study of the matter has been completed. Such study should include discussion with the client and an analysis of relevant law, the prosecution's evidence, and potential dispositions and relevant collateral consequences. Defense counsel should advise against a guilty plea at the first appearance, unless, after discussion with the client, a speedy disposition is clearly in the client's best interest." Should the ABA have taken a stronger stance in Standard 4–6.1 to condemn lawyers who counsel clients to plead at arraignment before the client has had meaningful legal representation based on adequate investigation?[18]

3. INEFFECTIVE ASSISTANCE OF COUNSEL

In a series of cases, the Supreme Court has interpreted the Sixth Amendment not simply to protect the right to have a lawyer but to provide the right to *effective* assistance of counsel. In *Strickland v. Washington*, 466 U.S. 668, 687, 695 (1984), the Court held that a defendant may have his conviction overturned and receive a new trial if he can prove (1) that his lawyer "made errors so serious that counsel was not functioning" as an any reasonable lawyer would and (2) that, but for the errors, "the fact finder would have a reasonable doubt respecting guilt." The Supreme Court extended the protections of the Sixth Amendment to the plea bargaining stage. *Padilla v. Kentucky*, 559 U.S. 356 (2010) (failure to inform client of

[17] *See* Eli Hager, *When Real Estate and Tax Lawyers Are Forced to Do a Public Defender's Job*, THE MARSHALL PROJECT, Sept. 8, 2016, www.themarshallproject.org; Oliver Laughland, *The Human Toll of America's Public Defender Crisis*, THE GUARDIAN, Sept. 7, 2016.

[18] *See* Steven Zeidman, *Eradicating Assembly-Line Justice: An Opportunity Lost By the Revised American Bar Association Criminal Justice Standards*, 46 HOFSTRA L. REV. 293 (2017).

the immigration consequences of pleading guilty to a crime is ineffective assistance); *Missouri v. Frye*, 566 U.S. 134 (2012) (failure to inform defendant that prosecution offered a plea agreement is ineffective assistance). The extension of the right to effective assistance at the plea bargaining stage is crucial because over 90 percent of convictions are the result of guilty pleas.[19]

Courts have made it difficult for defendants to set aside convictions on the ground of ineffective assistance of counsel. They have declined to find ineffective assistance when defense counsel was drunk, asleep, or absent from the courtroom during crucial parts of the prosecution's case. *See Tippens v. Walker*, 77 F.3d 682, 687 (2d Cir. 1996) (articulating a test for how much sleeping during trial renders counsel ineffective); *Burdine v. Johnson*, 262 F.3d 336 (5th Cir. 2001) (split en banc court rules that counsel's sleeping during portions of a death penalty trial is presumptively prejudicial to the defense). Courts have done so either because they have determined that the lawyer's failures did not fall below the prevailing standards of acceptable conduct or because, even if it did (as the dissent reasoned in the *Burdine* case involving the lawyer who slept through some portions of the trial), they found that counsel's errors did not prejudice the defense.

The Supreme Court has held that some total failures on counsel's part constituted ineffective assistance. Thus, in *Wiggins v. Smith*, 539 U.S. 510 (2003), the Court held that a lawyer's failure to investigate the existence of mitigating evidence in a death penalty case was ineffective assistance when an investigation would have revealed that the defendant suffered extreme childhood neglect and physical and sexual abuse which affected his mental and emotional capacity and health. Similarly, in *Rompilla v. Beard*, 545 U.S. 374 (2005), the Court set aside a death sentence after determining that the defendant's lawyers failed to conduct an investigation into the defendant's criminal record even after the prosecutor informed them that it intended to use the criminal record to prove the aggravating factors necessary to impose a death sentence.

Other total failures of counsel, however, have not been ineffective assistance. Defense counsel's complete failure to prepare a case for mitigation in a death penalty case was held to be a reasonable strategic decision, notwithstanding the fact that counsel knew of evidence suggesting the possibility that mitigating evidence might be available (in that case, that defendant had spent time in a state hospital for emotionally

---

[19] *See* Dept. of Justice, Bureau of Justice Statistics, *Sourcebook of Criminal Justice Statistics Online, Table 5.22.2009*, U. OF ALBANY, SOURCEBOOK OF CRIMINAL JUSTICE STATISTICS (May 22, 2009), http://www.albany.edu/sourcebook/pdf/t5222009.pdf; Sean Rosenmerkel, Matthew Durose, & Donald Farole, Jr., *Felony Sentences in State Courts, 2006—Statistical Tables*, DEPT. OF JUSTICE, BUREAU OF JUSTICE STATISTICS 1 (last updated Nov. 2010); *Padilla v. Kentucky*, 559 U.S. 356 (2010) (recognizing pleas account for nearly 95% of all criminal convictions).

handicapped children and a psychologist had recommended confining him in a mental institution). *Cullen v. Pinholster*, 563 U.S. 170 (2011).

The Sixth Amendment is not a solution to the problems of competent indigent criminal defense. The remedy for a violation of the defendant's Sixth Amendment right to effective assistance of counsel is not that the defendant will be acquitted. Rather, the most the defendant will get is a new trial, and not necessarily with an excellent lawyer. When the ineffective assistance prejudiced the defendant's decision whether to accept a plea bargain, the court must require the prosecution to re-offer the plea and the judge will have discretion whether to impose a new (and lighter) sentence based on the plea or to leave the sentence the same.

D. THE REWARDS AND CHALLENGES OF CRIMINAL DEFENSE PRACTICE

The bleak accounts offered by Van Cleve and McIntyre of the nature of work in the Cook County public defender's office and the chronic underfunding of indigent criminal defense in some jurisdictions may leave you wondering why anyone would want to be a criminal defense lawyer, especially a public defender. In many jurisdictions, the public defender's office is adequately staffed and funded and the job is highly sought after by elite lawyers. All criminal defense lawyers, however, sometimes are asked, especially by nonlawyers, "how can you represent someone whom you know is guilty of a horrible crime?" The following excerpt explores the way in which one young public defender (who later became a professor at Harvard Law School) found satisfaction in being a public defender and the role that working in the highly-regarded and well-resourced Public Defender Service of the District of Columbia played in his thinking.

BEYOND JUSTIFICATIONS: SEEKING MOTIVATIONS TO SUSTAIN PUBLIC DEFENDERS

Charles J. Ogletree, Jr.
106 Harvard Law Review 1239 (1993)

Often, in attaining a client's end—typically that of avoiding conviction—public defenders do many things that would commonly be considered immoral. Public defenders defend clients who they know are guilty, seek to suppress relevant evidence, fail to reveal incriminating facts, and make truthful witnesses appear to be liars. If defenders do their jobs well, their work undoubtedly achieves results in the courtroom that may or may not reflect the truth.

Theorists of the ethical dimension of lawyering have struggled to endow this form of representation with moral coherence. Some theorists conclude that, in her role as public defender, a lawyer is not implicated in the guilt or immorality of her clients. Provided that she acts within the bounds of the law, she bears no responsibility for the choices and actions of her clients [This justification can be called "role-morality."] In addition to "role-morality," two other theories have been advanced to justify zealous advocacy on the part of the public defender: "client-centered" and "systemic" justifications. Commentators who espouse "client-centered justifications" maintain that zealous advocacy is necessary to promote the social and moral good of the client. "Systemic justifications" focus not on the interests of the various actors within the adversary system, but on the adversary system itself. Systemic justifications of zealous advocacy are premised on the underlying structure of the adversary system. This structure requires an advocate for each of the parties, an impartial judge, and in the criminal context, the right to have a jury determine, after hearing all evidence, where the "truth" lies.

My goal in this Article, however, is to move beyond defending and attacking these justifications. Regardless of their theoretical or logical merits, these abstract justifications simply do not inspire or excite; and, for the public defender who has become disillusioned or dispirited, they do not offer a source of renewed vitality or commitment.

[Professor Ogletree describes how his faith in the justice of criminal defense was shaken when his beloved sister Barbara, a police officer, was stabbed to death in her living room by an unknown assailant.]

As a public defender, I firmly believed in the necessity of putting the state to the test at trial, and just as importantly, of severely constraining the behavior of police in pursuit of criminal suspects. I now saw only the harm that could result from constitutional restrictions on a police officer's ability to search for evidence and suspects. When it came to my sister's murder, I did not want any procedural safeguards for the criminal. I wanted the state to use all evidence, obtained by any means whatsoever, to convict her attacker. I wanted the satisfaction of knowing that the person responsible for her death would be brought to justice. I wanted retribution.

[Ogletree was asked to represent a man named Craig Strong, who had recently been paroled after serving a sentence for rape, and who was charged with the rape and murder of a young woman.]

I went to visit Strong. When I saw him in the cell block, it was clear to me that he was frightened. He did not know what would happen to him that day or thereafter. In telling me about his life, his family, and his fears, Strong revealed that his father had been murdered when Strong was young, and that he had no positive male role models as he grew up. He did not know whether anyone would represent him, or how his family would react to his arrest. As awful as his crime was, I could see that he wanted someone—anyone—to say, "I'm on your side."

Despite my sister's recent murder, I accepted the case. Though I had made my decision, I was concerned that my feelings about my sister's murder might interfere somehow with my ability to represent Strong, especially in light of the fact that her assailant had not been caught. Might I subconsciously harbor unacknowledged resentments that would lead me to be underzealous in Strong's defense? Might I over-identify with the victim's family, and therefore be unworthy of my client's trust? Nothing in [the rules of professional conduct] explicitly addressed potential internal conflicts of the sort I was confronting.

I decided to tell Strong about Barbara's murder. I described the potential conflict and explained that he had the right to seek new counsel if he doubted my ability to represent him. We went before the judge, who also knew of my sister's murder, and the judge offered Strong the opportunity to seek new counsel. Strong confirmed that he wanted me to represent him, and the judge expressed no misgivings about that decision.

[Professor Ogletree then describes his efforts to secure Strong's acquittal, first by unsuccessfully seeking to suppress physical evidence linking Strong to the crime because the police had failed to obtain a search warrant, and then, at trial, by careful preparation and vigorous cross-examination of witnesses. Professor Ogletree also describes his misgivings about the possibility that Strong might be acquitted and released from jail.] During this time, I visited him regularly in jail, talked to him on the phone almost every day, and took pains to keep him apprised of our efforts. I sent him letters and copies of all motions and briefs filed on his behalf. I also visited his family. Strong lived with his mother, his sister, a niece, and a nephew. His mother was a proud woman who tried to hide her pain upon hearing that her son had again been arrested. She wanted the best for her son, and she could not bring herself to believe that he had again been accused of rape, let alone that he may have killed his victim.

[Strong was convicted on all counts and faced a likely sentence of life in prison.]

One need not experience personally the pain of violent crime to need a sustaining motivation in order to continue working as a public defender. Virtually all public defenders fight a daily battle against burnout and the creeping erosion of confidence that inevitably accompany defending acts we cannot condone and protecting those who are the source of so much harm and grief. This slow, daily erosion differs from my own personal motivational crisis only in that mine was more sudden and sharp in its onslaught. Whether the process unfolds subtly or suddenly, all defenders must confront the disturbing consequences of their zealous representation of guilty clients.

The phenomenon of burnout is one of the most powerful and widely experienced forces that causes public defenders to lose interest in their work, or to abandon criminal defense practice altogether. Former public defenders typically attribute burnout to the psychological impact of confronting hundreds of crimes, victims, and criminals on a daily basis. Moreover, the better the defender is, the more frequently she must face the consequences of getting favorable results, even for guilty clients.

In looking back on my experience with Craig Strong, I believe that my empathy for Strong became one of the primary sustaining motivations for continuing zealously to defend him in spite of the pain of my sister's murder. I viewed Strong as a person and as a friend, and thus I was able to disassociate him from the person who had murdered my sister. I did not blame him, nor did I resent him because I had been victimized by crime. Instead, I viewed Strong as a victim as well. However, my sense of his victimization differed from traditional justifications for criminal defense practice in that it was not based on generalizations about criminals or pity for him. Instead, my empathy was based on my ability to relate to him as a person and to develop a friendship with him. I viewed Strong as a man whom the police had surprised in a warrantless arrest; someone from whom the police had seized incriminating evidence without a search warrant. I did not think about what he had done, nor did I feel responsible for what he might do if released. I knew that at that moment I was my client's only friend, and that my friend wanted to go home.

My view of empathy has significant implications for the character of the lawyer-client relationship. My relationships with clients were rarely limited to the provision of conventional legal services. I did not draw rigid lines between my professional practice and my private life. My relationship with my clients approximated a true friendship. I did for my clients all that I would do for a friend. I took phone calls at all hours, helped clients find jobs, and even interceded in domestic conflicts. I attended my clients' weddings and their funerals. When clients were sent to prison, I maintained contact with their families. Because I viewed my clients as friends, I did not merely feel justified in doing all I could for them; I felt a strong desire to do so.

I realize that empathy alone did not sustain me. I also felt various motivations that centered around how I envisioned myself and my task. I saw myself as a kind of "hero" of the oppressed, the one who fights against all odds, a sort of Robin Hood figure who can conquer what others cannot and who does not always have to conform to the moral rules society reserves for others. One element of this "hero" mentality, of course, is the thrill of winning. Certainly, many public defenders are driven in part by a desire to win; at PDS, for example, lawyers with excellent track records of acquittals were regarded with awe. For the public defender, there is glory in the "David versus Goliath" challenge of fighting the state, and the battle of wits that characterizes the courtroom drama only adds to the thrill of the trial. Even the phrase we commonly used to describe a successful defense—"stealing" the case from the prosecution—invoked the image of Robin Hood stealing from the rich and powerful to give to the helpless and weak. Indeed, some people become criminal defenders because they love the challenge, are competitive by nature, and have unusual personal curiosity. They like the idea of representing the underdog, where the scales are tipped against them, the prosecutor has all the resources, and they have virtually none.

The daily realities of the PDS office pose challenges to both empathy and heroism as motivations. Even the most empathetic public defender will find her commitment sorely challenged by the persistence of defendants who commit violent crimes repeatedly. Moreover, as an empathetic person, she may find that she has empathy for not just the defendant but also for the victim, and perhaps even for future victims whose safety would be threatened by the defendant's release. In the face of such feelings, empathy for one's client may prove difficult to sustain. Likewise, while the Robin Hood ideal will add a certain thrill to the job of public defender, the luster soon fades as the defender confronts the practical realities of the job—the daily drudgery of paperwork and the less-than-glamorous settings of the public defender's office, the criminal court, and the jail.

Empathy and heroism also may prove counterproductive when taken to the extreme. They may cause the public defender to lose sight of the external moral limitations on her conduct. Empathic feelings, for example, can result in over-identification with the client. Without the benefit of critical distance, a defender may be tempted to overstep ethical boundaries in her zeal to help her client. The same result can occur when a lawyer becomes overly enamored of the "heroic" role—the hero of the oppressed, after all, does not have to play by society's rules. For example, an overly empathetic or heroic attorney may be inclined to present a perjurious witness if this course of action is likely to win the case. Another potential danger of empathy is that it can lead to problematic allocation of resources. The empathic role I have described demands that the public defender devote substantial time and effort to every client. In a situation of extremely limited attorney resources, hours spent in the service of one client necessarily come at the expense of another equally needy criminal defendant.

The office at which I worked reminded defenders that most clients would be poor, uneducated, and from single-parent families, and that a family history of drug abuse would be common. We were taught to view the client as someone who had endured suffering and deprivation, and who would continue to suffer without our assistance. We were encouraged to immerse ourselves in the reality of each client's life, to get to know him, his background, his family and friends. The attorneys handle no more than 50 to 60 criminal cases or 40 juvenile cases at one time. The low caseloads allow PDS attorneys to devote a significant amount of time to each individual client. [Moreover,] [b]ecause they are working in an office that helps clients with employment, educational opportunities, and family support, PDS lawyers need not feel as though they are merely setting clients free to commit further criminal acts. Rather than focusing narrowly on the short-term goal of acquittal (although that certainly is the primary objective), the office helps clients in a comprehensive sense.

The culture at PDS also trumpeted heroism as a motivation for defenders. Attorneys developed reputations based on their success at trial. The entire office would join in the celebration of every acquittal won by a PDS attorney. Not only did PDS reward heroism, but it also worked to help lawyers realize the heroic ideal. [Through ongoing training, mentoring, and collaboration,] the office stressed the importance of attaining excellence in one's profession and of providing each client with the best possible defense.

NOTES ON THE REWARDS AND CHALLENGES OF INDIGENT CRIMINAL DEFENSE

1. ***What Are the Satisfactions of Criminal Defense Practice?*** We have examined in some detail the challenges of indigent criminal defense practice in a world of scarce resources. But the job also has many rewards. What are the common themes in the Van Cleve, McIntyre, and Ogletree descriptions of the ways that public defenders describe their role and the challenges and satisfactions of the job? What are the differences among them?

2. ***What Is the Relationship Between Money, Prestige, and the Intrinsic Rewards of Law Practice?*** The Public Defender Service of the District of Columbia, where Professor Ogletree worked, is one of the most prestigious indigent criminal defense offices in the country. It attracts young lawyers with sterling credentials, provides excellent training, and some of its alumni take jobs as law professors and in law practices in other elite settings. In addition, as noted above, the PDS receives funding directly from Congress and is comparatively better funded than many public defender's offices (perhaps in part because it does not have to rely on local tax revenues). How do the prestige of the PDS and the adequacy of its resources affect how PDS lawyers there regard their role? Is it reasonable to imagine that a massive infusion of resources into indigent criminal defense would address the problems identified in other readings in this chapter? Which problems would it not address?

3. ***What Should Motivate Lawyers?*** What do you find appealing, or problematic, in Ogletree's account of empathy and heroism as motivations for indigent criminal defense lawyers?

4. ***Another Reflection on Representing Those Accused of Crime.*** How would the Ogletree account differ, as a narrative or as an essay on the role of criminal defense counsel, if Strong had been acquitted and had later been accused of another rape? Would your willingness to accept an appointment to represent someone accused of a crime depend on whether you

believed the accused was innocent? Are there crimes for which you could not defend someone? Do your answers to those questions influence your views about the right to effective assistance of counsel in those cases?

E. SUMMARY

This chapter has studied criminal practice. Because the vast majority of people charged with crimes are poor, we focused on lawyers who represent the indigent and the rewards and challenges of that segment of criminal defense practice. Although there is a constitutional right to effective assistance of counsel in any criminal case in which the defendant faces a prison sentence, the funding to implement the constitutional right is inadequate in some jurisdictions, and some appointed criminal defense lawyers therefore struggle to provide adequate representation. Courts have been very reluctant to find that even serious lapses of competence violate the right to counsel, perhaps in part because courts lack meaningful ability to provide the funds to enable lawyers to do a better job and in part because of a belief that overturning a conviction is not an appropriate remedy for the problem.

CHAPTER 7

CRIMINAL PROSECUTION

■ ■ ■

A. INTRODUCTION

Federal, state, and local governments employ thousands of lawyers as criminal prosecutors. Criminal prosecutors are chosen in three ways. In the state criminal system, a District Attorney in each county is typically elected by the people. In addition, many state attorneys general are elected in statewide elections. In the federal system, the Attorney General of the United States and the U.S. Attorney in each federal district are appointed by the President and confirmed by the Senate. The thousands of prosecutors who work for the state attorneys general, county district attorneys, city attorneys, the U.S. Department of Justice in Washington, D.C., and the U.S. Attorneys in each federal district are hired under civil service rules, and thus typically do not serve just at the pleasure of one who is elected or who is appointed by the executive.

Work as a prosecutor is varied. Like most lawyers, they do the majority of their work out of court. Prosecutors supervise ongoing criminal investigations, working with police and other investigators to interview witnesses and to seek and review documentary and physical evidence. Once they have compiled evidence, prosecutors decide whom to charge with what crimes. Within each district attorney's or U.S. Attorney's office, there are procedures to enable more senior lawyers to oversee the investigations, charging decisions, trial work, plea bargaining, and the other work assigned to the more junior lawyers in order to ensure uniformity of policy. There is some independent review (either by the grand jury or by a judge) of the sufficiency of the evidence to support a charge, but the review is extremely deferential to the prosecutor. Prosecutors spend a great deal of time negotiating plea bargains with defense counsel, as the overwhelming majority of criminal cases are resolved by a guilty plea. Prosecutors appear in court in the pretrial process to litigate motions to suppress evidence or to deny bail. And, of course, prosecutors try cases and defend convictions on appeal.

Like most lawyers, prosecutors often specialize. Specialties include street crime like drug dealing, robberies, homicides, or gang-related violence; white collar crime, including financial, banking, or securities fraud; and crimes against children.

Prosecutors occupy a unique role with unique ethical responsibilities. Prosecutors exercise extraordinary power. They have access to all the investigatory resources of the government. They have the power, subject to some judicial oversight, to order people and their property to be searched, to order people arrested and held prior to trial, and to compel reluctant third parties to testify. Prosecutors have substantial power to determine what sentences people will serve because well over 90 percent of those charged plead guilty[1] and both federal and state criminal law have sentencing rules that limit or guide judges' discretion to depart from the sentence recommended in the statute. The crime charged determines the crime to which a defendant may plead and the sentence that will be imposed.

Prosecutors exercise significant discretion with little transparency. There is some accountability, although it is generally within the office rather than to the public in any meaningful sense, as it is rare for a president to ask for the resignation of a U.S. Attorney (except when the White House switches parties) or for the voters to turn an elected DA out of office. Prosecutors have judicially unreviewable discretion to decide whom to investigate, whom to charge, which crimes to charge, whom to call as a witness, whether to dismiss charges, and what sentence to recommend or to accept in exchange for a guilty plea.[2] Like most government lawyers, a prosecutor's client is the people or the government. The absence of a traditional client enables prosecutors to take a broad view of what justice requires in a particular case, but it also means that no one outside the bureaucracy of the federal or state Department of Justice or law enforcement community effectively constrains how prosecutors exercise their power.[3] As we will see in later chapters, prosecutors are not the only lawyers whose client is sufficiently amorphous to raise issues of accountability; most government lawyers, as well as lawyers who bring class actions, or who represent causes, movements, or loose organizations, also operate without strong client constraints.

While some standards do govern the exercise of discretion in the prosecutorial role, and office policies are often very detailed, there is little enforceable law that constrains prosecutors' discretion. Prosecutors are only rarely disciplined by the bar and are absolutely immune from civil liability for their exercise of prosecutorial judgment, even for egregious breaches of duty. Prosecutors are subject to judicial discipline, but judges rarely impose it. Criminal convictions may be overturned for prosecutorial misconduct, but courts are reluctant to do so.

---

[1] Ronald F. Wright, *Trial Distortion and the End of Innocence in Federal Criminal Justice*, 154 U. PA. L. REV. 79, 90 (2005).

[2] Bruce Green & Fred Zacharias, *Prosecutorial Neutrality*, 2004 WIS. L. REV. 837, 840–42.

[3] Fred C. Zacharias, *Structuring the Ethics of Prosecutorial Trial Practice: Can Prosecutors Do Justice?*, 44 VAND. L. REV. 45 (1991).

The prosecutor's duty to seek justice exists in some tension with the prosecutor's role as an adversary in the criminal justice system, which is one of the most adversarial sectors of the American legal system. Whatever one's views about the extent to which a criminal defense lawyer may ethically act as a zealous advocate, including by obtaining acquittal of a person whom the lawyer knows to be factually guilty, many believe a prosecutor's role as an advocate should be tempered by an obligation to ensure that only the guilty are convicted. The difficulty is in the details. Particularly in matters such as pretrial disclosure of evidence, which occurs without judicial supervision in both criminal and civil litigation, many lawyers (not only prosecutors) are tempted to slight their obligations to their adversary. Some prosecutors' failure to disclose exculpatory evidence, especially when combined with poor quality defense counsel, leads to wrongful convictions, although people disagree about the extent of the problem.

This chapter begins with an overview of the law governing the prosecutorial role. It then considers three of the most significant issues about the prosecutorial role. First is whether law and norms are effective in balancing justice and effectiveness in law enforcement in the context of the problem of wrongful convictions. The chapter next looks at prosecutorial power and discretion in charging crimes and in plea bargaining. Finally, we consider the prosecutor's responsibilities to disclose exculpatory information to the defense prior to trial.

B. THE LAW GOVERNING THE PROSECUTORIAL ROLE

Prosecutors serve a dual role as advocates seeking conviction and as officers of justice. The Supreme Court famously described the role of federal prosecutors in *Berger v. United States*, 295 U.S. 78 (1935):

> The United States Attorney is the representative not of an ordinary party to a controversy, but of a sovereignty whose obligation to govern impartially is as compelling as its obligation to govern at all; and whose interest, therefore, in a criminal prosecution is not that it shall win a case, but that justice shall be done. As such, he is in a peculiar and very definite sense the servant of the law, the twofold aim of which is that guilt shall not escape or innocence suffer.

The actions of prosecutors are governed by the United States Constitution and, in the case of state prosecutors, the constitution of the state. One principal federal constitutional provision regulating prosecutors' behavior is the Fifth Amendment, which provides that "No person shall be held to answer for a capital, or otherwise infamous crime, unless on a presentment or indictment of a Grand Jury" nor "shall be compelled in any criminal case to be a witness against himself, nor be deprived of life, liberty, or property, without due process of law." Another is the Sixth Amendment, which provides "In all criminal prosecutions, the accused shall enjoy the right to a speedy and public trial, by an impartial jury of the State and district wherein the crime shall have been committed," and the right "to be informed of the nature and cause of the accusation; to be confronted with the witnesses against him; to have compulsory process for obtaining witnesses in his favor, and to have the assistance of counsel for his defense." An elaborate body of law has developed under the Fifth and Sixth Amendments governing the criminal process; that law is typically covered in detail in law school courses on criminal procedure. A significant aspect of the constitutional role of prosecutors is the prosecutor's constitutional duty under the due process clause of the Fifth Amendment to disclose exculpatory information to the defense under *Brady v. Maryland*, 373 U.S. 83 (1963).

In addition to the ethical duties of all lawyers—such as diligence, competence, preparation, candor to the tribunal, and fairness to opposing counsel—prosecutors have specific obligations. The ABA ethics rule governing prosecutors provides that a prosecutor should prosecute only when there is probable cause, make reasonable efforts to ensure that the accused has been advised of the right to counsel and has been given a reasonable opportunity to obtain counsel, disclose exculpatory information to the defense, and take measures to overturn wrongful convictions.

Prosecutors are absolutely immune from civil liability for exercises of their prosecutorial judgment, regardless of their motives or the legality of their conduct, or even for their decisions in managing their office. For example, a prosecutor is absolutely immune from liability for damages even for an offense as egregious as knowingly using perjured witness testimony. What policies are supported by granting prosecutors absolute immunity from suit, both for their judgments as lawyers and for the management of their office?

Although discipline of prosecutors, either by courts or by the bar, is relatively rare, and prosecutors are generally immune from civil liability for their conduct, the most common form of penalty for prosecutorial misconduct is to suppress evidence, dismiss charges against the defendant, or overturn a conviction.

C. WRONGFUL CONVICTIONS

Nothing draws into sharper relief questions about the role of the prosecutor than the conviction of innocent people. If a prosecutor is imagined only as a zealous advocate for one side of an adversary proceeding, perhaps the prosecutor has no greater duty to avoid convicting the innocent than any other lawyer has to avoid winning a case that he should lose. But prosecutors have a duty to seek justice, and the difficult questions are how to reconcile a prosecutor's duty to seek justice with the prosecutor's role as an adversary in the most adversarial aspect of the American legal system.

Although it is difficult to determine precisely how frequently wrongful convictions occur, some believe the problem is serious. Between 1989 and 2019, 2,472 people have been exonerated.[4] Of course, these cases represent a tiny fraction of the tens of thousands of persons who are convicted of crimes; it is difficult to know whether wrongful conviction is an extreme rarity (as some believe) or is more common (as others believe). A study of forensic evidence in sexual assault convictions in Virginia between 1973 and 1987 found that the convicted offender could be ruled out as a source of evidence, suggesting exoneration, in 8 to 18 percent of cases.[5] Studies of wrongful convictions identify a number of reasons why innocent defendants are convicted, including mistaken eyewitness accounts (in 75 percent of cases in which the defendant is exonerated), false confessions induced after prolonged interrogation (16 percent of cases), perjured testimony by co-defendants or other criminal defendants who exchange testimony implicating the defendant for leniency in their own cases (21 percent of cases), and flawed forensic evidence (half of cases).[6] It is difficult to determine how often prosecutorial misconduct contributed to a wrongful conviction, although one study concluded that prosecutorial misconduct led to wrongful convictions in eighteen percent of the cases in which a defendant was exonerated.[7]

What responsibility should prosecutors bear to prevent wrongful convictions? If the prosecutor's role is to be a zealous advocate for conviction and if that conception of role imagines that it is the defense's job to prevent conviction, blame for the prevalence of false convictions may be laid primarily on inadequate defense counsel, inept or dishonest police, bungled handling of evidence, confused eyewitnesses, or jurors who are too easily swayed by argument rather than evidence. In this vision of the role, the honest prosecutor does justice by pressing as hard as the rules permit to seek convictions in every case in which there is sufficient evidence to convince the prosecutor of the defendant's guilt (more on this below), and

[4] The National Registry of Exonerations, a project of the University of California, Irvine, and the University of Michigan, maintains a database of exonerations. http://www.law.umich.edu/special/exoneration/Pages/about.aspx.

[5] JOHN ROMAN, POST-CONVICTION DNA TESTING AND WRONGFUL CONVICTION 506 (Urban Inst., June 2012).

[6] BRANDON GARRETT, CONVICTING THE INNOCENT (2011) (study based on files of first 250 DNA exonerations).

[7] EMILY M. WEST, COURT FINDINGS OF PROSECUTORIAL MISCONDUCT CLAIMS IN POST-CONVICTION APPEALS AND CIVIL SUITS AMONG THE FIRST 255 DNA EXONERATION CASES 1 (Innocence Project 2010) (reporting studies of cases alleging prosecutorial misconduct in which the defendant was later exonerated; finding that courts found prosecutorial misconduct led to 18 percent of convictions).

it is the job of the other players in the criminal justice and adversary system—judge, jury, defense attorneys, crime labs, witnesses, and police—to ensure that only the guilty are convicted.

If, however, the prosecutor's role is envisioned as a minister of justice who must seek justice, not merely convict, the prosecutor has an independent duty to ensure that only the guilty are convicted, even if she must step back from her role as an advocate. In this conception of role, the prosecutor cannot count on the adversary system to produce truth, but instead must ensure that truth is revealed regardless of whether witnesses, defense counsel, judge, and jury are doing their jobs.[8] Indeed, the more prosecutors suspect that defense counsel are not doing their job, the less appropriate it is for the prosecutor to serve as a zealous advocate for conviction.

Yet for lawyers trained to believe that the adversary system is the best vehicle for finding truth and that the criminal trial is the paragon of the adversary process, the question of when and how the prosecutor should temper her advocacy for conviction with affirmative steps to ensure that justice is done is a difficult one both in theory and in daily practice. The law and ethical norms governing prosecutors offer only general guidance.

Prosecutors vary in their approach to claims that persons in their jurisdiction may have been, or will be, convicted of crimes they did not commit. Some prosecutors recognize wrongful convictions as a problem and their offices have formal policies and procedures to prevent and correct wrongful convictions. Some earnestly believe that innocent people are never convicted in cases filed in their office and do not see any pressing need to examine the cases they have won or the processes in their office. Anecdotal evidence has shown that some prosecutors who have convicted innocent people have been reluctant to consider evidence strongly suggesting or proving that an innocent person was convicted.[9] An example of a prosecutor's reluctance to consider the possibility of wrongful conviction is the case of *Van de Kamp v. Goldstein*, 555 U.S. 335 (2009).

Thomas Goldstein was an engineering student when the Long Beach Police Department arrested him for the shooting of John McGinest, in 1979. Mr. Goldstein had no criminal record and no history of violence. There was no evidence that he owned a firearm or that he had ever had any contact with the victim. Several eyewitnesses described the possible perpetrator. Most descriptions bore no resemblance to Mr. Goldstein. Mr. Goldstein was a suspect because he lived near where the shooting occurred

---

[8] Bennett Gershman, *The Prosecutor's Duty to Truth*, 14 GEO. J. LEGAL ETHICS 309 (2001) (discussing the literature and arguments on whether the prosecutor has an independent duty to truth or can instead rely on adversary system to produce the truth, and concluding that the prosecutor has a duty to produce the truth).

[9] *See* Daniel S. Medwed, *The Zeal Deal: Prosecutorial Resistance to Post-Conviction Claims of Innocence,* 84 B.U. L. REV. 125 (2004).

and was at home the night of the murder. Police obtained one eyewitness identification after showing the man a photo of Goldstein and describing him as the perpetrator.

After Goldstein was in custody, the police placed a well-known jailhouse informant named Eddie Fink, a heroin addict and career felon, in Goldstein's cell. Fink had repeatedly testified to jailhouse confessions in return for favorable dispositions of his own criminal charges. After one night in Goldstein's cell, Fink reported to the police that Goldstein, a complete stranger to him, had confessed. Goldstein had told everyone else that he was innocent.

Fink testified to the confession at Goldstein's trial. Fink also swore that the Los Angeles District Attorney had not traded any benefits for his testimony against Goldstein and that he had never received any such benefits in the past. These were both lies. Fink had struck numerous deals over the course of a decade with the Long Beach Police and the Los Angeles District Attorney in exchange for his testimony. The District Attorney's Office had secured Fink's testimony against Mr. Goldstein with a promise to reduce Fink's sentence on a pending theft charge from 16 months to less than two months. Goldstein's trial counsel could not expose Fink as a liar because the prosecution did not disclose the deals. (This violated the prosecutor's constitutional obligation to disclose exculpatory evidence to the defense.) Goldstein was convicted and sentenced to life in prison.

A decade later, a Los Angeles County civil grand jury issued a report asserting that the Los Angeles District Attorney's Office and various police departments within its jurisdiction coached jailhouse informants to elicit (and sometimes fabricate) confessions from criminal defendants. After that, the eyewitness who had identified Goldstein recanted his testimony.

Although the only two pieces of evidence against Goldstein were discredited, the prosecution still refused to dismiss charges against him. Even after two courts determined that Goldstein was innocent and ordered him released, the government delayed his release for a few months while prosecutors considered whether there was a way to prove his guilt.[10]

* * *

Public attention to wrongful convictions due to prosecutorial misconduct has prompted a variety of strategies to reform prosecutors' offices.

One strategy is to create a division within the prosecutor's office to investigate possible wrongful convictions. A newly-elected district attorney in Dallas, Texas did exactly that. The unit, staffed by two prosecutors, an investigator and a paralegal, works with innocence projects in New York

[10] Henry Weinstein, *Man Wrongly Imprisoned for 24 Years Files Civil Rights Suit*, L.A. TIMES, Dec. 1, 2004; Henry Weinstein, *Justice Triumphs—Finally*, L.A. TIMES, Dec. 12, 2004.

and Texas as well as defense lawyers, and has helped exonerate over a dozen wrongfully convicted men. Similar divisions have been established in other prosecutors' offices. One prosecutor criticized the establishment of such divisions, insisting that his office ensures the integrity of convictions before filing any case and by scrutinizing the use of DNA evidence. Under what circumstances are the pretrial and trial process sufficient to ensure the integrity of convictions, as the prosecutor suggests? If the trial process alone is insufficient, what should be done? If independent conviction integrity divisions are established, how should they be structured and staffed in order to maximize their effectiveness?

Another strategy is for the state to establish a commission to examine prosecutorial (mis)conduct. In June 2018, the New York legislature enacted a bill that would create a Commission on Prosecutorial Conduct. It is modeled on state Commissions on Judicial Performance, which exist in many states. The Commission would be composed of members appointed by the state's chief judge, governor, and majority and minority leaders of the state senate and assembly. Some appointees would have to be judges, some prosecutors, and some public defenders. The Commission would have subpoena power and its decisions would be public. The state district attorneys' association opposed the measure, and the state criminal defense attorneys supported it. Why do you suppose advocates of greater oversight of prosecutors focused on creating a new commission rather than beefing up the grievance committees in the state's bar disciplinary committees? The New York bar disciplinary committees are overseen by the state's Appellate Division judges, who are elected to 14-year terms to serve on the state's trial courts and then are chosen by the governor from among the trial court bench to serve on the Appellate Division.

A third strategy has been tried by a few judges who despaired of state officials, the state bar, or elected prosecutors effectively addressing misconduct. This strategy was tried by a trial judge in Orange County, California. A public defender named Scott Sanders obtained district attorney office records on a jailhouse informant to whom Sanders' client, Scott Dekraai, allegedly had confessed details about a mass shooting. Sanders discovered the informant had provided information on a large number of inmates and had extensive correspondence with sheriffs to arrange contact between the informant and detainees. Sanders also discovered that the DA's office had not disclosed exculpatory information to defense counsel in the many cases in which the informant had been used.

Sanders asked Orange County Superior Court Judge Thomas Goethals to hold a hearing on the extent of the DA's and sheriff's use of jailhouse informants and the failure to disclose the information to the defense. After two extensive hearings over the course of a few years, Judge Goethals found that sheriffs and DAs had used jailhouse informants, failed to disclose the favorable treatment they granted in exchange for testimony, and lied about it in the hearings Goethals had conducted to uncover the problem. Among the innocent people who had been incarcerated based on the false testimony was a 14-year-old boy who spent two years in jail for a shooting he did not commit because the DA refused to believe the boy's proof of alibi. Both the DA's office and the sheriff's department denied they had done anything wrong, insisting that they were too busy to hand over all discovery material and that the constitutional violations were inadvertent.

Nevertheless, finding a widespread pattern of prosecutorial misconduct, Judge Goethals disqualified every lawyer in the Orange County DA's office from handling the mass shooting case in which the alleged misconduct had first come to light.[11] Judge Goethals assigned the case to the office of the California Attorney General for further proceedings. (The defendant eventually pleaded guilty and was sentenced to life in prison without the possibility of parole.)

After Judge Goethals began inquiring into misconduct in the DA's office in the Dekraai case, all assistant DAs who were assigned to try a case before Judge Goethals began to exercise their power under California law to strike the judge from presiding over a case. Although the Orange County Superior Court judges sought an appellate court determination that this was retaliation prohibited by California law, the California Court of Appeal ruled that California law gives lawyers a right to exercise a peremptory challenge on any basis. Thus, Judge Goethals found himself effectively removed from the criminal docket.[12]

NOTES ON WRONGFUL CONVICTIONS

1. ***Understanding How Prosecutors Think About Wrongful Convictions.*** What legitimate and illegitimate factors might influence some prosecutors to refuse to concede, or only very grudgingly concede, that they may be seeking to convict, or have convicted, the wrong person? How often do you think lawyers believe their case is shaky once they have spent substantial time on it? How often do you think lawyers believe that the result they obtained in a case was the wrong result?

2. ***Prosecutors and the Police.*** How skeptical of police should prosecutors to be? If a prosecutor suspects that the evidence presented by police officers is unreliable, or that the police have not provided exculpatory evidence to the prosecutor, what should the prosecutor do? What pressures might a prosecutor feel about challenging the reliability of police investigation, given that prosecutors routinely rely on and work with police officers?

3. ***Considering Incentives.*** When is an acquittal at trial or a decision to drop charges evidence that justice was done rather than that the prosecutor

---

[11] *People v. Dekraai*, 5 Cal. App. 5th 110 (2016) (upholding the disqualification).

[12] *People v. Superior Court*, 1 Cal. App. 5th 892 (2016).

made a mistake? In many settings, people tend to focus on what they can quantify, and it is particularly common to evaluate employees based on objective and easily quantifiable measures that serve as a proxy for harder to measure qualities of skill and diligence. If the common practice of counting and rewarding convictions based on verdicts or guilty pleas creates incentives for prosecutors to disregard evidence of innocence, what other measure of success would reward and incentivize skill and hard work? Are there other institutional reforms in prosecutors' offices that would make wrongful convictions less likely to occur?

4. ***Jail House Snitches and Other Forms of Unreliable Evidence.*** In the Goldstein case, the assistant DA apparently did not know that Fink was a well-known jailhouse snitch. Although Fink had provided testimony against several other cellmates in exchange for favorable treatment in his own many prior cases, there was no centralized record in the DA's office about witnesses and the deals they had previously struck in exchange for testimony. Moreover, there is no evidence that the assistant DA who tried the case knew that the police had gotten the eyewitness identification only by showing the witness a photograph of Goldstein and telling him that Goldstein was the perpetrator. Although, as we will see below in the discussion of prosecutors' duties to disclose exculpatory information to defense counsel, both the constitution and ethics rules hold prosecutors responsible for knowing and disclosing exculpatory information in the files of *all* law enforcement agencies, there are practical barriers to prosecutors knowing about evidence possessed by the police or other agencies. Thomas Goldstein filed civil litigation after being released from prison seeking to hold prosecutors responsible for negligence in failing to train deputy district attorneys or to maintain a system whereby prosecutors could learn about the deals witnesses had struck. The Supreme Court held that prosecutors' absolute immunity from suit covered the administrative management of the evidence, not just their prosecutorial decisions in filing charges or advocacy. *Van de Kamp v. Goldstein*, 555 U.S. 335 (2009).

5. ***How Do You Change Someone's Mind?*** What might explain the reluctance of new DAs to take a hard look at the case once informed about the possible or likely falsity of the evidence against Goldstein 20 years later? If all or most of the evidence and witnesses are no longer available, how is a prosecutor to evaluate the reliability of a conviction? The problems facing a prosecutor may differ when the exonerating evidence is based on DNA, although even there prosecutors may doubt the reliability of DNA evidence when other evidence pointed toward guilt. In some rape and murder cases, for example, once DNA evidence proved that the semen or biological material on or near the victim did not come from the defendant, prosecutors have nevertheless insisted that the conviction should stand because the defendant might have killed the victim and another man had sex with the victim. Defense counsel derisively call this the "unindicted co-ejaculator" theory.[13] Why does a

---

[13] Andrew Martin, *The Prosecution's Case Against DNA*, N. Y. TIMES, Nov. 25, 2011.

theory that seems patently ridiculous to some defense counsel seem plausible to some prosecutors?

6. ***Bar Discipline?*** Might the incentives and culture within prosecutors' offices change if bar disciplinary authorities increased their efforts to enforce the general duty of competence and the specific duties of prosecutors? What other strategies for the training, management, or oversight of prosecutors do you think would reduce the incidence of wrongful convictions?

7. ***Criminal Contempt?*** A former federal judge and a founder of the Innocence Project have proposed that judges should issue a standing order requiring prosecutors to disclose all exculpatory and mitigating evidence. If it later transpires that a prosecutor knowingly failed to disclose such evidence, the judge can find, after a hearing, that the prosecutor is guilty of criminal contempt. In a Texas case in which a judge had issued such an order, the prosecutor who failed to disclose exonerating evidence was sentenced to jail and lost his law license.[14] Why haven't all judges adopted such orders?

8. ***What if All Else Fails?*** Although one Orange County assistant district attorney resigned after Judge Goethals found he had committed misconduct and lied about it, it appears that no sheriff's deputy or assistant district attorney has been prosecuted or otherwise publicly disciplined for the misconduct in the use of jailhouse snitches and the cover-up about it.[15] What accounts for the cooperation between the DAs and the sheriff's deputies in the misconduct and for the apparent reluctance of the state attorney general, the state bar, or other entities to punish them for it? Why do you suppose the Superior Court judges were so alarmed that the DA's office was permitted to strike Judge Goethals from all criminal cases? What other mechanisms might exist to address such problems if judges risk retaliation for doing so?

D. PROSECUTORIAL DISCRETION IN CHARGING

Prosecutors have wide discretion that is not subject to judicial review in deciding which cases to investigate, which suspects to charge, what crimes to charge, and whether to offer a plea bargain and, if so, on what terms. Prosecutorial discretion is one of the most significant aspects of the lawyer's role. In this section, we examine the nature of prosecutorial discretion and three ethical and practical issues about charging: (1) the tension between allowing prosecutors and judges discretion to consider the specifics of context while ensuring consistency and uniformity; (2) how prosecutors should handle cases in which the evidence of guilt is less than overwhelming; and (3) how prosecutors should handle cases in which there may be reasons not to prosecute or to be lenient even where there is abundant evidence of guilt.

---

[14] Mark Godsey, *For the First Time Ever, a Prosecutor Will Go to Jail for Wrongfully Convicting an Innocent Man*, HUFFINGTON POST, Oct. 16, 2015.

[15] Jordan Smith, *Anatomy of a Snitch Scandal*, THE INTERCEPT, May 14, 2016.

PROSECUTORIAL DISCRETION IN THE POST-*BOOKER* WORLD

Norman C. Bay
37 McGeorge Law Review 549 (2006)

When a matter is referred to the prosecutor, she must first decide if it should be investigated. If the prosecutor chooses to decline prosecution, that declination is unreviewable. A prosecutor deciding to pursue the matter can often direct the investigation. Who should law enforcement agents interview? Which leads should be pursued? Should places be searched and evidence seized? If so, which places and what evidence? Is a warrant necessary, or is there an applicable exception to the warrant requirement? Would electronic surveillance be helpful? If so, can a warrant be obtained? What forensic analysis needs to be done?

At some point, the prosecutor may proceed to the grand jury. Absent a waiver by the defendant, the grand jury must indict all felony cases.* The prosecutor can determine what evidence the grand jury will hear and which witnesses should be subpoenaed to the grand jury. Once a witness is brought to the grand jury, counsel is excluded; nor is a judge present. The prosecutor can also ask the grand jury to issue subpoenas to compel the production of certain types of evidence, from documents to physical evidence. Thus, the prosecutor guides the grand jury's broad investigative powers.

If charges are warranted, the prosecutor now has the discretion to select the charges that the grand jury will be asked to consider. In the ordinary case, so long as the prosecutor has probable cause to believe that the accused committed an offense defined by statute, the decision whether or not to prosecute, and what charge to file or bring before a grand jury, generally rests entirely in her discretion.

Assuming the grand jury returns an indictment, the prosecutor now has the discretion to move for the defendant's pretrial detention if the defendant poses a danger to the community or a flight risk. Even if the defendant is not detained pretrial, the prosecutor can request that certain conditions of release be imposed.

If the parties enter into plea negotiations, the prosecutor wields the discretion to control the terms of an offer. The prosecutor also has the power to determine if she wishes to work with a potential cooperating defendant. Cooperation may be particularly important for defendants otherwise facing lengthy prison sentences, especially a mandatory minimum penalty under the drug laws. Once the cooperation is complete,

---

* [Eds.: In the federal system, a grand jury indictment is required unless it is waived by the defendant. Many states do not use the grand jury system and instead require prosecutors to file an "information" with the court showing that there is probable cause to prosecute the defendant for the crimes specified in the information.]

the prosecutor has the power to inform the court of the defendant's helpfulness. Obviously, an enthusiastic letter from the prosecutor may prove decisive to a sentencing judge.

If the case goes to trial, the prosecutor develops a theory of her case and the strategy for implementing it. She decides which witnesses to call and what evidence to present; she alone determines what the opening statement will be, as well as the closing argument and rebuttal.

Prosecutorial discretion arises again if the jury convicts the defendant. If the defendant was released pre-trial, the prosecutor may now move for his detention. At sentencing, the prosecutor may ask that a particular sentence be imposed. As part of that allocution, she may oppose the defendant's attempt to obtain a more lenient sentence and argue for a more severe sentence based upon the circumstances of the case.

Post-sentencing, the prosecutor still retains considerable discretion. Among other things, the prosecutor decides whether to appeal the sentence imposed by the court. She may also file a Rule 35 motion to reduce the sentence if the defendant cooperates post-sentencing and provides substantial assistance. While the Bureau of Prisons bears ultimate responsibility for the placement of prisoners, the prosecutor may advise the Bureau about where the defendant should be incarcerated. The prosecutor's views will be solicited at some later date if the defendant seeks executive clemency, such as a pardon or commutation of sentence.

1. THE TENSION BETWEEN UNIFORMITY AND DISCRETION

In the 1980s and 1990s, Congress and many state legislatures imposed mandatory minimum sentences to ensure that everyone convicted of the same crime received the same sentence. Such laws eliminated the discretion of judges in sentencing, but prosecutors retained discretion to charge crimes with greater or lesser sentences. In the same period, many legislatures enacted enhanced penalties for recidivists; some of these laws were enacted in the wake of horrible murders committed by men who had recently been released from prison and were intended to punish harshly those who had proven unable or unwilling to refrain from crime. Whatever the reasons for determinate sentencing laws and enhanced penalties for recidivists, they have had the perhaps unintended consequence of enhancing the power of prosecutors to decide what sentences defendants will serve by deciding what crime to charge. For example, a prosecutor could charge a person arrested with drugs and a gun with a relatively minor crime of drug possession, punishable by a year in prison or a fine, or major crimes including sale of drugs, and possession of drugs with the use of a weapon, punishable by many years in prison.

To the extent that determinate sentencing regimes are intended to treat like cases alike, they have failed in many jurisdictions because different prosecutors have different philosophies about which crimes to charge.

Studies have suggested that the exercise of discretion may be influenced by bias. In *McCleskey v. Kemp*, 481 U.S. 279 (1987), for example, the Supreme Court confronted evidence that in Georgia the death penalty was inflicted more often on black defendants and killers of white victims than on white defendants and killers of black victims. The Court rejected the contention that the racial disparity in death sentences violated the constitution. In the years since *McCleskey*, scholars have continued to compile evidence that criminal laws are enforced more often and more harshly against men of color than against whites.[16]

Under *McCleskey* and other cases, it is nearly impossible for any individual defendant to challenge his prosecution or sentence as the product of systemic or individual bias. What institutional mechanisms might be implemented to make prosecutors and police more attentive to the possibility that their individual or collective decisions about arrest, charging, and prosecution are having a disparate impact on the basis of race or other illegitimate factors? One scholar proposed the use of "racial impact studies" and criminal justice racial and ethnic task forces as a way to raise awareness of the existence of racial bias.[17] Studies of the results of many such initiatives in different states found that "they overlook the most glaring causes of disparity and the most promising measures to reduce them."[18] What would make state efforts to reduce racial disparities in criminal justice more effective?

One way to address disparities among prosecutors in charging decisions is by adopting a uniform policy that is applied to every prosecutor within the jurisdiction. At the state level, obtaining such uniformity would require some form of legislation, because district attorneys are typically elected at the county level and thus enjoy some autonomy in setting policy. The U.S. Attorney's Manual, which is issued by the U.S. Department of Justice and governs every U.S. Attorney's office in all 94 federal districts across the United States, in theory can produce national uniformity in federal charging. The U.S. Attorney's Manual under Attorney General John Ashcroft generated controversy with a new policy requiring all U.S.

---

16 Jeffrey Fagan & Mukul Bakhshi, *New Frameworks for Racial Equality in Criminal Law*, 39 COLUM. HUM. RTS. L. REV. 1 (2007) (surveying literature showing racial disparities in prosecution's request for death sentences and in imposition of death sentences when victim is white and defendant is black, and also racial disparities other crimes and sentences in many states).

17 Angela J. Davis, *Racial Fairness in the Criminal Justice System: the Role of the Prosecutor*, 39 COLUM. HUM. RTS. L. REV. 202 (2007).

18 Jesse J. Norris, *State Efforts to Reduce Racial Disparities in Criminal Justice: Empirical Analysis and Recommendations for Action*, 47 GONZ. L. REV. 493 (2012).

Attorneys to charge "the most serious offense that is consistent with the nature of the defendant's conduct, and that is likely to result in a sustainable conviction." The "most serious offense" was defined as the one likely to result in the longest sentence. In the Obama Administration, as controversy about mass incarceration gained public attention, Attorney General Eric Holder issued a memo instructing prosecutors to avoid charging non-violent drug offenders with crimes that would trigger long mandatory minimum sentences. Shortly after President Trump took office, Attorney General Jeff Sessions rescinded the Holder memo and instructed U.S. attorneys to pursue the maximum penalty in drug offenses.[19]

What are the arguments for and against requiring charging of the most serious readily provable offense? If uniformity is to be desired and yet you oppose choosing the most serious readily provable offense, what alternative would you propose?

What are the arguments for and against leaving charging and plea bargaining decisions to the discretion of individual prosecutors or to particular prosecutors' offices?

2. PROSECUTORIAL DISCRETION IN CHARGING DECISIONS BASED ON SOCIAL POLICY

What factors should a prosecutor consider in deciding whom to charge and for which crimes even when the prosecutor has evidence of guilt sufficient to convict? The ABA Standard governing prosecutors prohibits improper bias. What types of considerations are improper bias? How much social engineering should prosecutors attempt to do in their decisions about criminal prosecution? Is it appropriate for them to consider whether prosecution will achieve beneficial effects for the defendant or the community, or will harm a defendant's life prospects? How should prosecutors decide which social policy goals to pursue in charging? What relevance, if any, is there to the fact that elected prosecutors do not necessarily reflect the life experiences and values of the whole electorate or those who are likely to be charged with or victims of crime? (A 2015 study found that 95 percent of the 2,437 elected state and local prosecutors across the U.S. were white, and 79 percent were white men, while only 31 percent of the population are white males. Two thirds of states that elect prosecutors have no black elected prosecutors.[20])

One controversy associated with prosecutorial discretion concerns the relative scarcity of prosecutions of corporations and their officers for misconduct. Since 1990, there has been a substantial expansion of laws

---

[19] Sari Horwitz & Matt Zapotosky, *Sessions Issues Sweeping New Criminal Charging Policy*, WASH. POST, May 12, 2017.

[20] Nicolas Fandos, *A Study Documents the Paucity of Black Elected Prosecutors: Zero in Most States*, N.Y. TIMES, July 7, 2015.

criminalizing corporate fraud and other misconduct. The laws were enacted following news reports of widespread and egregious corporate crime. Yet relatively few prosecutions of corporations and their officers have occurred, and even fewer have resulted in punishment. Rather, corporations and their officers often reach so-called "deferred prosecution agreements" under which no crimes are prosecuted, or even sometimes charged, so long as the corporation agrees to implement reforms. Are these agreements a desirable exercise of discretion?[21]

As viewers of television crime dramas know, prosecutors sometimes charge low-level participants in a gang, a drug distribution network, or the Mafia with serious crimes in order to force them to cooperate in identifying and testifying against the high-level people in the criminal network. What are the problems with allowing prosecutors to threaten severe criminal penalties to induce cooperation? Is the answer to the objection that the legislature authorized severe penalties so the prosecutor bears no moral responsibility for using all the tools at her disposal? If you do not find that argument persuasive, is there any justification for the tactic?

E. PROSECUTORS AND PLEA BARGAINING

Plea bargaining is extremely common in both state and federal criminal systems. Over 90 percent of federal criminal convictions were secured by a guilty plea in 2009, as were 95 percent of state felony convictions in the nation's 75 largest counties in 2006.[22] Critics insist that the proliferation of long mandatory minimum sentences enables prosecutors to overcharge and to force innocent defendants to plead guilty to avoid extremely long sentences and/or incarceration in jails and prisons that cannot guarantee prisoners' safety.[23] On the other hand, some scholars argue that plea bargaining is not more likely than trial to convict innocent people, and may be less likely to do so. Yet even these scholars found evidence of innocent defendants pleading guilty; the debate is over the extent of the problem.[24] While prosecutors insist that plea bargaining saves resources when there is no serious doubt about guilt, critics insist that prosecutors tend to settle their weakest cases by guilty plea to boost their conviction rate and to avoid potentially embarrassing losses in some cases and also to manage a heavy caseload without adequate scrutiny of

---

[21] *See* BRANDON GARRETT, TOO BIG TO JAIL: HOW PROSECUTORS COMPROMISE WITH CORPORATIONS (2016); JESSE EISINGER, THE CHICKENSHIT CLUB: WHY THE JUSTICE DEPARTMENT FAILS TO PROSECUTE EXECUTIVES (2017).

[22] *Federal Justice Statistics, 2009*, BUREAU OF JUSTICE STATISTICS, U.S. DEP'T OF JUSTICE 12, Table 9 (2011), *available at* https://www.bjs.gov/content/pub/pdf/fjs09st.pdf; *Felony Defendants in Large Urban Counties, 2006*, BUREAU OF JUSTICE STATISTICS, U.S. DEP'T OF JUSTICE (2010), *available at* https://www.bjs.gov/content/pub/pdf/fdluc06.pdf.

[23] The literature on plea bargaining is vast. *See, e.g.*, Stephanos Bibas, *Plea Bargaining Outside the Shadow of Trial*, 117 HARV. L. REV. 2463 (2004) (surveying the literature and criticizing certain aspects of plea bargaining).

[24] Oren Gazal-Ayal & Avishalom Tor, *The Innocence Effect*, 62 DUKE L.J. 339 (2012).

the quality and accuracy of the police work that went into identifying and arresting the suspect.[25] The absence of trials makes the nature and extent of any problem of wrongful convictions based on guilty pleas invisible to the public and to the judiciary.[26]

Particular controversy surrounds plea bargaining in capital cases. Although many people find it hard to believe that a defendant would plead guilty to a murder he or she did not commit, a number of defendants have, in part because they lacked resources to mount a defense, their lawyer doubted their claims of innocence, and the prosecution offered to recommend a sentence other than death. As scholars have observed, police and prosecutors feel a particular pressure to solve murder cases, which compounds the risk of error at every stage of the investigation and trial.[27]

The Supreme Court has held that ineffective assistance of defense counsel during plea bargaining may be grounds to vacate the conviction and set aside the plea. *Padilla v. Kentucky*, 559 U.S. 356 (2010) (failure to inform client of the immigration consequences of pleading guilty to a crime is ineffective assistance); *Missouri v. Frye*, 566 U.S. 134 (2012) (failure to inform defendant that prosecution offered a plea agreement is ineffective assistance). Moreover, knowingly making a false statement of material fact or law violates a lawyer's ethical duties.

F. DISCLOSURE OBLIGATIONS

In *Brady v. Maryland*, 373 U.S. 83, 87 (1963), the Supreme Court established that prosecutors have a duty to disclose material exculpatory information to defense counsel upon request. The Court held "the suppression by the prosecution of evidence favorable to an accused upon request violates due process where the evidence is material either to guilt or to punishment, irrespective of the good faith or bad faith of the prosecution." In subsequent cases, the Court has expanded *Brady* obligations, providing the accused with greater access to evidence. In *United States v. Bagley*, 473 U.S. 667, 675–76 (1985), the Court held that prosecutors must disclose not only exculpatory evidence (that negates guilt, supports an affirmative defense such as self-defense or duress, or diminishes the severity of the crime or the sentence) but also impeaching evidence (that undermines the government's case). Prosecutors must disclose exculpatory evidence even if they do not find the information credible or have other contradictory information. Impeachment evidence

---

[25] Stephen J. Schulhofer, *A Wake-Up Call from the Plea-Bargaining Trenches*, 19 LAW & SOC. INQUIRY 135, 137 (1994).

[26] *See* John G. Douglass, *Fatal Attraction: The Uneasy Courtship of Brady and Plea Bargaining*, 20 EMORY L.J. 439, 489 (2001) (noting the controversy over the prevalence of pleas by innocent defendants).

[27] *See* Samuel R. Gross, *The Risks of Death: Why Erroneous Convictions are Common in Capital Cases*, 44 BUFF. L. REV. 469 (1996).

that must be disclosed includes evidence that might cast doubt on the credibility of government witnesses, including information regarding a witness's prior convictions, biases, or self-interest, such as inducements used to motivate a witness to testify on behalf of the government. Some states have adopted statutes that impose more expansive disclosure duties on prosecutors than the constitutional minimum. Several states require that prosecutors make timely disclosure to the defense of all evidence or information known to the prosecutor that tends to negate the guilt of the accused or mitigates the offense.

Other states and localities have adopted "open file" discovery policies, which generally require prosecutors to disclose all nonprivileged information gathered in a case to the defense "as early as possible." There are wide variations among them in which files they make available. Some invite defense counsel to view all information gathered in a case. Others give the defense substantial, but not total, access. In all open file systems, exceptions exist for witness safety or the protection of confidential informants.

Despite constitutional and statutory disclosure requirements, disclosure violations occur. Some believe prosecutorial failure to disclose is epidemic, while others contend disclosure violations are only episodic.[28] Studies conducted by academics and journalists offer conflicting assessments as to the frequency with which *Brady* violations occur. A 1998 analysis of 1,500 allegations of prosecutorial misconduct over the previous ten years found "hundreds" of instances in which prosecutors intentionally concealed exculpatory or impeachment evidence.[29] A 2011 survey of federal judges found that thirty percent of respondents had encountered at least one prosecutorial disclosure violation in the preceding five years.[30] The U.S. Department of Justice, however, found only fifteen disclosure violations between 2000 and 2009.[31]

Critics suggest *Brady* violations occur because prosecutors who commit them believe that they will not be caught (the defense rarely knows when evidence is withheld), and when they are caught they will not be punished, nor will a guilty verdict be overturned.[32] Indeed, prosecutors are

---

[28] Bennett L. Gershman, *Litigating Brady v. Maryland: Games Prosecutors Play*, 57 CASE WESTERN RESERVE L. REV. 531 (2007) (epidemic); Cynthia E. Jones, *A Reason to Doubt: The Suppression of Evidence and the Inference of Innocence*, 100 J. CRIM. L. & CRIMINOLOGY 415, 435–36 (2010) (episodic).

[29] Bill Moushey, *Discovery Violations Have Made Evidence-Gathering a Shell Game*, PITTSBURGH POST-GAZETTE, Nov. 24, 1998, at A1.

[30] Fed. Judicial Ctr., A Summary Of Responses To A National Survey Of Rule 16 Of The Federal Rules Of Criminal Procedure And Disclosure Practices In Criminal Cases 8 (2011).

[31] Mike Scarcela, *DOJ Outlines Changes after Stevens Case*, LEGAL TIMES, Oct. 19, 2009.

[32] *See* Alafair S. Burke, *Improving Prosecutorial Decision Making: Some Lessons of Cognitive Science*, 47 WM. & MARY L. REV. 1587 (2006); Alafair S. Burke, *Revisiting Prosecutorial Disclosure*, 84 IND. L.J. 481 (2009); Daniel S. Medwed, *Brady's Bunch of Flaws*, 67 WASH. & LEE L. REV. 1533, 1538–39, 1557 (2010).

rarely punished when disclosure violations are uncovered. A 1987 study of published compilations of state disciplinary decisions and surveys returned by professional disciplinary representatives in forty-one states since *Brady* was decided in 1963 found only nine cases "in which discipline was even considered."[33] Thirty-five states reported that no formal complaints had been filed for *Brady*-type misconduct. A follow-up study in 1997 found only seven bar disciplinary proceedings had been initiated against prosecutors for disclosure violations between 1987 and 1997; the prosecutors received discipline ranging from a reprimand to a six-month suspension.[34] A survey by the California Commission on the Fair Administration of Justice found 53 cases between 1997 and 2007 in which prosecutorial misconduct resulted in a reversal of the conviction; the California State Bar did not investigate or discipline any prosecutors.[35] A 2011 survey of federal trial judges reported that judges rarely hold prosecutors in contempt or report them to Department of Justice's Office of Professional Responsibility (OPR) or the state bar.[36] Instead, the two most frequently reported responses to disclosure violations were ordering immediate disclosure of the evidence and granting a continuance. One study found a reversal rate of less than twelve percent in cases with *Brady* violations.[37]

Brady violations also occur because some prosecutors find it difficult to fair-mindedly examine the evidence in their possession and determine what must be disclosed. An Assistant U.S. Attorney was charged in 2007 with illegally withholding evidence to secure convictions in a terrorism case in Detroit, but he was acquitted.[38] He may have believed so strongly in the guilt of the defendants and felt such pressure to convict suspected terrorists that he engaged in conduct that warranted charging him with a crime. In 2006, Durham, North Carolina District Attorney Michael Nifong withheld crime laboratory and other evidence in a case in which the public believed three Duke University athletes had raped an African-American woman. (Nifong was later disbarred for his misconduct, but he is one of the very few prosecutors ever to be disciplined for disclosure violations.)[39] A

---

[33] Richard A. Rosen, *Disciplinary Sanctions Against Prosecutors for Brady Violations: A Paper Tiger*, 65 N.C. L. REV. 693, 718–19, 731–32 (1987).

[34] Joseph R. Weeks, *No Wrong Without a Remedy: The Effective Enforcement of the Duty of Prosecutors to Disclose Exculpatory Evidence*, 22 OKLA. CITY U. L. REV. 833, 881 (1997).

[35] CALIFORNIA COMMISSION ON THE FAIR ADMINISTRATION OF JUSTICE, REPORT AND RECOMMENDATIONS ON REPORTING MISCONDUCT, at 3–5 (2007).

[36] Fed. Judicial Ctr., A Summary of Responses to a National Survey of Rule 16 of the Federal Rules of Criminal Procedure and Disclosure Practices in Criminal Cases, 29 (Feb. 2011). A study of state judges reached the same conclusion: judges are more likely to order disclosure and grant a continuance than to discipline prosecutors or overturn convictions. Ken Armstrong and Maurice Possle, *The Verdict: Dishonor*, CHI. TRIB., Jan. 10, 1999, at 1C.

[37] Burke, *Revisiting Prosecutorial Disclosure*, 84 IND. L.J. at 490 n.54.

[38] Mike Scarcella, *17 Prosecutors Behaving Badly*, NAT'L L.J., Dec. 21, 2009.

[39] Indeed, equally if not more egregious violations in two prior North Carolina cases in which defendants were sentenced to death and later exonerated resulted in no discipline of prosecutors in one case and only a reprimand in the other. Amir Efrati, *It's Rare for Prosecutors to Get the Book Thrown Back at Them*, WALL ST. J., Apr. 16, 2009, at A11; Robert P. Mosteller, *Exculpatory*

prosecutor does not violate *Brady* if exculpatory evidence is immaterial and, even if it is material, the failure to disclose it will not be the basis for overturning a verdict unless the defendant proves the failure to disclose changed the outcome of the proceeding. *United States v. Bagley*, 473 U.S. 667, 682 (1985). Such a standard requires prosecutors to assess pre-verdict what will change the result, and to overcome their own cognitive biases that lead them to forget the existence of or undervalue the significance of exculpatory evidence.

Brady and state ethics codes leave some uncertainty about the time at which exculpatory material must be disclosed. Although the *Brady* obligation theoretically spans the entire lifespan of the case, from arraignment onward, and state ethics rules require "timely disclosure," courts tend to be vague about exactly what "timely" means. Disclosure must be made in sufficient time to permit the defendant to make effective use of that evidence at trial. But since courts only have occasion to enforce the rule after it has been violated, they tend to frame violations in counterfactual terms as "the point at which a reasonable probability will exist that the outcome would have been different if an earlier disclosure had been made." *United States v. Coppa*, 267 F.3d 132 (2d Cir. 2001). Some states require disclosure a certain number of days after request by defense counsel or within a certain number of days before trial.[40] Prosecutors believe that early disclosure poses risks. A defendant who learns the names of witnesses may attempt to intimidate them, and even a defendant who would not dream of intimidating a witness may try to script the testimony of his or her own witnesses in response.

Under the Constitution, the Supreme Court ruled that *Brady* is not violated by the prosecution's failure to reveal impeachment evidence before a plea bargain. *United States v. Ruiz*, 536 U.S. 622, 631, 633 (2002). The Court reasoned that *Brady* is a trial right and that requiring the prosecution to reveal impeachment evidence would not advance the government's and the defendant's shared interests in efficient administration of justice and in facilitating guilty pleas from defendants who are factually guilty. The Court has not ruled on whether the Constitution compels disclosure of exculpatory (as opposed to impeachment) evidence in plea bargaining. What are the arguments for treating the two kinds of evidence the same or differently?

Open file discovery is not without flaws. Prosecutors fear it enables defendants to intimidate witnesses and fabricate their defense to rebut the evidence against them. Defense lawyers fear it enables prosecutors in

---

Evidence, Ethics, and the Road to the Disbarment of Mike Nifong: The Critical Importance of Full Open-File Discovery, 15 GEO. MASON L. REV. 257 (2008); *N.C. State Bar v. Brewer*, 644 S.E.2d 573 (N.C. Ct. App. 2007) (upholding the dismissal on statute of limitations grounds of disciplinary charges against prosecutors who hid exculpatory evidence in a capital case).

[40] Yaroshefsky, *Prosecutorial Disclosure Obligations*, 62 HASTINGS L.J. at 1337–1338.

complex cases to bury the defense in a mountain of inscrutable material. In the trial against former Enron executive Jeff Skilling, for example, prosecutors provided eighty million pages of documents to the defense.[41] A lower court in Skilling's case suggested that an attempt to bury exculpatory evidence in a mountain of irrelevant evidence may itself be a *Brady* violation.[42] The Supreme Court has not addressed whether overdisclosure is ever a *Brady* violation, but suggested in another case that it is not necessarily one. *Strickler v. Greene*, 527 U.S. 263, 283 n.23 (2004) ("We certainly do not criticize the prosecution's use of the open file policy").

Another difficulty with disclosure concerns evidence in the files of law enforcement agents other than the prosecutors. Prosecutors have a duty to learn of and disclose evidence known to all government agents, including the police. *Kyles v. Whitley*, 514 U.S. 419, 437 (1995). Yet, prosecutors may not know or have ready access to everything in every law enforcement agency file. Compulsory disclosure of evidence in police files may endanger witnesses or damage ongoing investigations. Generally, courts have held that a prosecutor does not violate *Brady* by not disclosing exculpatory evidence if the defense knew of the evidence and could have obtained it from a source other than the prosecutor.[43]

1. *BRADY* VIOLATIONS IN STREET CRIME CASES: *CONNICK V. THOMPSON*

The case of John Thompson, who spent eighteen years in prison (fourteen on death row) for a crime he did not commit, brought to light the problem of *Brady* violations in the run-of-the-mill street crime cases that dominate the dockets of local district attorneys. *Connick v. Thompson*, 563 U.S. 51 (2011). *See also State v. Thompson*, 825 So. 2d 552 (La. Ct. App. 2002). In 1985 the Orleans Parish District Attorney's Office charged Thompson with the murder of Raymond Liuzza, Jr. News coverage of the murder led three victims of an unrelated robbery to identify Thompson as their attacker.

> As part of the robbery investigation, a crime scene technician took from one of the [robbery] victims' pants a swatch of fabric stained with the robber's blood. Approximately one week before Thompson's armed robbery trial, the swatch was sent to the crime laboratory. Two days before the trial, assistant district attorney Bruce Whittaker received the crime lab's report, which stated that the perpetrator had blood type B. There is no evidence that the prosecutors ever had Thompson's blood tested or that they knew what his blood type was. Whittaker claimed he placed the report

---

[41] Medwed, *Brady's Bunch of Flaws*, 67 WASH. & LEE L. REV. at 1536–1537.

[42] *United States v. Skilling*, 554 F.3d 529, 576 (5th Cir. 2009); Joel Cohen & Danielle Alfonzo Walsman, *Ethics and Criminal Practice*, N.Y. L. J. Sept. 4, 2009.

[43] WAYNE R. LAFAVE, ET AL., CRIMINAL PROCEDURE § 24.3(b) (3d ed. 2011).

> on assistant district attorney James Williams' desk, but Williams denied seeing it. The report was never disclosed to Thompson's counsel. The prosecutors did not mention the swatch or the crime lab report at trial, and the jury convicted Thompson of attempted armed robbery. A few weeks later, Williams and special prosecutor Eric Dubelier tried Thompson for the Liuzza murder. Because of the armed robbery conviction, Thompson chose not to testify in his own defense. He was convicted and sentenced to death. In late April 1999, Thompson's private investigator discovered the crime lab report from the armed robbery investigation in the files of the New Orleans Police Crime Laboratory. Thompson was tested and found to have blood type O, proving that the blood on the swatch was not his. Thompson's attorneys presented this evidence to the district attorney's office, which, in turn, moved to stay the execution and vacate Thompson's armed robbery conviction. The Louisiana Court of Appeals then reversed Thompson's murder conviction, concluding that the armed robbery conviction unconstitutionally deprived Thompson of his right to testify in his own defense at the murder trial. In 2003, the district attorney's office retried Thompson for Liuzza's murder. The jury found him not guilty.

Connick, 563 U.S. at 55–56. Thompson sued the Orleans Parish District Attorney's Office and the DA, Harry Connick, alleging that the suppression of exculpatory evidence at his trial had been caused by Connick's deliberate indifference to an obvious need to train the prosecutors in his office. The trial court found Connick liable under 42 U.S.C. § 1983 for a violation of Thompson's constitutional rights. On appeal, the Fifth Circuit affirmed, but the Supreme Court reversed in 2011. *Connick v. Thompson*, 563 U.S. at 72.

NOTES ON CONNICK V. THOMPSON

1. ***Why Ignore Exculpatory Evidence?*** Why do you suppose the assistant DA Whittaker, who first received the crime lab report showing the blood type on the fabric swatch, did not ask to have Thompson's blood type tested? Why do you suppose he did not follow up with Williams to be sure that Williams received the report and handed it over to Thompson's lawyers? If Williams did indeed receive the report from Whittaker, why do you suppose he ignored it and did not provide it to the defense?

2. ***Institutional Reform.*** What institutional reforms would be effective in ensuring that exculpatory evidence is routinely provided to defense lawyers?

2. *BRADY* VIOLATIONS IN HIGH-PROFILE WHITE COLLAR CASES: *UNITED STATES V. STEVENS*

Beginning in early 2003, the U.S. Department of Justice and the Federal Bureau of Investigation ("FBI") began investigating Ted Stevens, a long-time Republican U.S. Senator from Alaska, for potential violations of Senate rules in failing to report gifts he received. The investigation focused on Stevens' relationship with Bill Allen, the chief executive and part owner of VECO, an Alaskan oil exploration and drilling company. In July 2008, a grand jury indicted Senator Stevens for failing to report gifts, concealing receipt of things of value, using his official position and his Senate office to benefit those who had given him gifts, and knowingly making false statements on Senate financial disclosure forms.[44]

After the trial had begun in Washington, Senator Stevens' defense team alleged that prosecutors withheld exculpatory evidence. The DOJ's Office of Professional Responsibility (OPR) launched an investigation into allegations of *Brady* violations before the trial had ended. After the jury convicted Senator Stevens on all counts but before he was sentenced, FBI Special Agent Chad Joy filed a whistleblower statement with the court alleging misconduct on behalf of several prosecutors and investigators involved in the case. Over the next several months, Judge Sullivan asked prosecutors for documents that Special Agent Joy claimed could exculpate Senator Stevens. As it became clearer to the DOJ that prosecutors involved in the case may have withheld exculpatory evidence, Attorney General Eric Holder dropped all charges against Stevens, and Judge Sullivan set aside the jury's verdict. Judge Sullivan initiated criminal contempt proceedings against several of the prosecutors and took the highly unusual step of appointing his own independent investigator, Henry Schuelke, to determine whether there was a basis to prosecute members of the prosecution team for violating court orders and obstructing justice.

In the wake of the Stevens trial, Attorney General Holder appointed a working group to propose changes in how federal prosecutors handle discovery. In January 2010, the group released three memoranda creating new procedures and a step-by-step guide for prosecutors working through the discovery process. Each U.S. Attorney's Office and the central DOJ must have a "discovery coordinator" to provide annual training to prosecutors and to serve as on-location advisors. Each office must establish

---

[44] This account of the Stevens matter is drawn from the following sources: Dept. of Justice, Office of Professional Responsibility, No. 08–231, Investigation of Allegations of Prosecutorial Misconduct in *United States v. Theodore F. Stevens* (2010); Report to Hon. Emmet G. Sullivan, *In re Special Proceedings* (2009) (Misc. No. 09–0198); Transcript of Motion Hearing, *United States. v. Stevens,* 2009 WL 6525926 (2009) (No. 08–231); Erika Bolstad, *Stevens Judge Orders Inquiry*, ANCHORAGE DAILY NEWS, Apr. 8, 2009, at A1; Evan Perez, *Judge Orders Probe of Prosecutors*, WALL ST.J., Apr. 8, 2009, at A4; Joe Palazzolo and Mike Scarcela, *Judge Dismisses Case Against Stevens*, LEGAL INTELLIGENCER, Apr. 8, 2009.

a discovery policy that reflects local, district, and national discovery requirements.[45]

In the spring of 2012, both OPR and Judge Sullivan's independent investigator, Schuelke, released their reports on the Stevens prosecutors. Joseph Bottini and James Goeke, Assistant U.S. Attorneys in Alaska, were found to have "engaged in professional misconduct by acting in reckless disregard of their disclosure obligations" and to have withheld and concealed significant exculpatory information. One was suspended without pay for 40 days and the other for 15 days. The OPR determined that supervising prosecutors involved in the Stevens prosecution did not violate any laws or rules, but did not properly supervise the investigation and prosecution. Schuelke decided not to pursue criminal charges against any of the DOJ attorneys involved in the investigation and prosecution.

In the wake of the reports, Schuelke, defense lawyers, and some members of Congress have pushed for changes to discovery rules. Congress considered, but has not enacted, "The Fairness in Disclosure of Evidence Act of 2012," which would require prosecutors to disclose evidence that "may reasonably appear to be favorable to the defendant . . . without delay after arraignment and before the entry of any guilty plea."[46] The DOJ, however, cautioned against adopting the proposed legislation because it "would upset the careful balance of interests at stake in criminal cases, cause significant harm to victims, witnesses, and law enforcement efforts, and generate substantial and unnecessary litigation that would divert scarce judicial and prosecutorial resources."[47]

The aftermath of the Stevens prosecution is a dismal story. Most of the lawyers avoided discipline and all avoided criminal prosecution, and the senior lawyers were able to remain prosecutors by transferring from the Washington, D.C. headquarters of the Department of Justice to U.S. Attorneys offices. But Nicholas Marsh, a young Justice Department lawyer who spent four years building the cases that resulted in convictions of several people involved in the Stevens incident, was not so lucky. As the internal investigation of misconduct dragged on for months and years, he was exiled to a position he considered the end of his career. Believing he had been scapegoated for the transgressions of his supervisors, Marsh

[45] Memorandum from David W. Ogden, Deputy Attorney General, Issuance of Guidance and Summary of Actions Taken in Response to the Report of the Department of Justice Criminal Discovery and Case Management Working Group (Jan. 4, 2010); Guidance for Prosecutors Regarding Criminal Discovery (Jan. 4, 2010); Requirement for Office Discovery Policies in Criminal Matters (Jan. 4, 2010).

[46] Fairness in Evidence Discovery Act of 2012, S. 2197, 112th Cong. (2012), §§ 2(a)(1) and 2(c)(1); *see also* Mike Scarcella, *Federal Discovery Reform Sought in Wake of Botched Stevens Case*, DAILY BUS. REV., Apr. 2, 2012; Mark A. Srere et al., *The Prosecutorial Misconduct Report in U.S. v. Stevens and the Fairness in Evidence Disclosure Act of 2012: Two Strong Steps Toward Open File Discovery*, U.S.L.W., May 8, 2012.

[47] Statement for the Record, Dept. of Justice, Comm. on the Judiciary, U.S. Senate, Hearing on the Special Counsel's report on the Prosecution of Senator Ted Stevens (Mar. 28, 2012), 1, 5.

became severely depressed and ultimately committed suicide. He was 37 years old.[48]

NOTES ON THE STEVENS *CASE*

1. ***Changing the Win-at-All Costs Mindset.*** If a win-at-all-costs mentality explains the prosecutors' failures in the Stevens case, what is the most effective strategy to address that problem?

2. ***What Would You Advise?*** Knowing what you know now, if Nicholas Marsh had been your friend, what advice would you have given him if he came to you and explained that he thought his team was not fully complying with its disclosure obligations but that he might jeopardize his own career if he rocked the boat? What if he was in charge of producing exculpatory and impeachment evidence to the defense and debated whether to provide more rather than less information?

3. ***The Politics of Political Cases.*** The Department of Justice (headed by an Attorney General appointed by a Democratic President) gave a high profile to its decision to dismiss the charges against Stevens, and some speculated it was an effort to convince the legal community that the Department was above politics and was determined to reform its ranks. Some believe DOJ's reputation was tarnished because it had become unduly politicized during the presidency of George W. Bush. Democratic Attorney General Holder may have been eager to prove that DOJ was once again above politics by pushing hard against prosecutors who had gone after a Republican Senator. It was too late to save Stevens' political career, of course, and Stevens had little time to feel vindicated; he died in a plane crash not long after.

Yet critics remain concerned that another case of an allegedly politicized prosecution of a Democrat did not get the scrutiny it deserved because it might be seen as Democrats going after Republicans for bringing corruption cases against Democrats. The Republican U.S. Attorney in Alabama appointed by George W. Bush, Laura Canary, initiated a prosecution of Don Siegelman, the Democratic governor of Alabama, asserting that campaign contributions were bribes. The investigation ultimately cost Siegelman re-election, and, although one jury verdict was overturned on the grounds of misconduct, he was eventually convicted of corruption. Some insisted that the prosecution was politically motivated because U.S. Attorney Laura Canary was married to a leading Republican political activist in Alabama and was closely connected to Karl Rove and to the man who eventually replaced Siegelman as Alabama's governor. The intrigue grew thicker in the wake of disclosures of improper contacts between the prosecutors and jurors in Siegelman's re-trial, conversations between Canary and Karl Rove suggesting Canary should "go after" Siegelman, and the failure of the DOJ to act on evidence of prosecutorial misconduct provided in 2007 by a whistleblower in the Alabama U.S. Attorney's office. The intrigue grew thicker still when it appeared that the DOJ

---

[48] Jeffrey Toobin, *Casualties of Justice*, NEW YORKER, Jan. 3, 2011, at 39.

had failed to investigate allegations of similar gifts made to leading Republican elected officials in Alabama, including Jeff Sessions (former Alabama Attorney General and U.S. Senator, now U.S. Attorney General).[49]

As revealed in both the Stevens and Siegelman cases, criminal prosecutions of elected officials for corruption pose challenges to prevent misconduct motivated either by a win-at-all-costs mentality or by a desire to target politicians of the opposing party. Is there reason to believe that investigations of prosecutorial misconduct are more or less immune to political pressure than are any other investigations? What should the Department of Justice and state prosecutors do to minimize the risk both that criminal investigations will be motivated by or influenced by political considerations and that investigations of prosecutorial misconduct will similarly be influenced by politics?[50]

3. THE DUTY TO DO JUSTICE

PROSECUTORIAL DISCRETION AT THE CORE: THE GOOD PROSECUTOR MEETS BRADY

Janet C. Hoeffel
109 Penn State Law Review 1133 (2005)

The professional codes are clear about one aspect of the [prosecutor's obligation] to do justice. It is the prosecutor's ethical duty to make timely disclosure to the defense all evidence or information known to the prosecutor that tends to negate the guilt of the accused or mitigates the offense. Therefore, the good "ethical" prosecutor discloses this evidence. A former prosecutor-turned-judge calls it the "ouch test": "If a prosecutor is looking at [his or her] case and says 'Ouch, that hurts,' that means it should be turned over to the defense. Basically, anything that hurts the prosecution's case is arguably favorable to the defense." Or, in the words of an Assistant United States Attorney, "when you are looking at [disclosure obligations under] *Brady*, if you have to think about whether it should be disclosed, it probably needs to be disclosed."

Scholars hope and expect most prosecutors will think and operate in accordance with these principles. This expectation is skewed by the fact that many of the legal scholars writing in the area of prosecutorial discretion are former Assistant United States Attorneys ("AUSA"s). It is enormously important to point out that neither an AUSA nor a former

---

[49] Adam Zagorin, *More Allegations of Misconduct in Alabama Governor Case,* TIME MAGAZINE, Nov. 14, 2008, *available at* http://www.time.com/time/nation/article/0,8599,1858991,00.html; Adam Zagorin, *Selective Justice in Alabama?* TIME MAGAZINE, Oct. 7, 2007, *available at* http://content.time.com/time/nation/article/0,8599,1668220,00.html.

[50] *See* Anthony S. Barkow & Beth George, *Prosecuting the Political Defendants,* 44 GEORGIA L. REV. 953 (2010) (proposing reforms to the way that DOJ handles prosecutions of political defendants); Richard E. Myers, II, *Who Watches the Watchers in Public Corruption Cases?* 2012 U. CHI. LEG. FORUM 13 (discussing the challenges of regulating the prosecution of public corruption).

AUSA-turned-academic is an average prosecutor. The typical AUSA has graduated from a good law school near the top of his class. Federal prosecutors are an elite group with enormous prestige. The young Assistant receives training, has a supervisor, and has an army of federal agents at his disposal. It does not take long for him to realize the incredible power of his position.

Hence, the federal prosecutor has a vested interest in seeing himself as just. Gifted with all of the prestige and power of the office, if forced to describe himself or his colleagues, he must say he is worthy of the power. He must show that the public can trust him, or he will be forced to cede his discretion.

The federal prosecutor may in fact be in a position to show some ethical restraint to his prosecutorial zeal. The run-of-the-mill federal case is a victimless drug or weapons charge that has been sealed up tightly by federal law enforcement before it reaches his desk. Most of the cases are slam-dunk convictions. He may need not stretch to the limit every exercise of discretion and every rule favorable to the prosecution in order to gain a conviction. Hence, it may be that some federal prosecutors occasionally serve the role of an "ethical" prosecutor, but this image, I submit, is far from reality.

I have a different vision of the good prosecutor because in my eight years as a criminal defense attorney, I met many prosecutors in different jurisdictions, and I never met the "ethical" prosecutor, in the sense envisioned by the ethics code.

Most crimes are handled by local prosecutors, who hail from a very different place than federal prosecutors. The typical state prosecution is much messier than a federal prosecution. The police work is sloppier, the resources are limited, and the caseloads are heavy. In many of the crimes, victims push for prosecution, the press follows every homicide or rape, and the boss needs a high record of convictions for re-election. The typical local prosecutor does not have the luxury, the time, or the inclination to draw his sense of power from exercising discretion in favor of the defendant. He will only be noticed, climb the career ladder, or become a member of elected office himself if he racks up the convictions.

The local prosecutor has plenty of power: power to pursue or dismiss charges, power to offer pleas and immunity, power of superior information, power of reputation, and power of lording it over the guilty, the pitiful, and the shamed. I never met a prosecutor who did not love the power he was able to cultivate. I have come to believe it is a matter of human nature rather than a despicable display: no rational human being can resist the temptation to enjoy and pursue this power. And it is not like the power of teacher over student, where the teacher may be inclined to show mercy toward the student. Rather, the prosecutor is placed in an adversarial process, in which he must pursue his side with adversarial zeal if the process is to work as designed. He has little problem mustering this zeal because he, the public, and the courts believe he wears the white hat. The combination of power and white hat justice form the intoxicating milieu of the prosecutor's office.

The prosecutor does not even think about "doing justice" in the sense the ethics professors envision. What prosecutor would not believe he is doing justice by fulfilling his concomitant duty to be a zealous advocate? Isn't the whole idea of becoming a prosecutor to put the bad guys behind bars and keep the public safe? And didn't the prosecutor sign up for an adversarial system of justice? Once the adversarial process has begun, we should fully expect the normal, human, and good prosecutor to have the single-minded goal of winning the case for the prosecution. That is the prosecutor our system of justice cultivates and encourages.

G. SUMMARY

Prosecutors occupy a unique and powerful role with unique responsibilities in the American legal system. They have access to all the investigatory resources of government, and they decide, with little judicial oversight, whom to investigate and charge with crime. State ethics rules and the federal constitution impose special duties on prosecutors, including a duty to ensure that adequate evidence supports any charges, to disclose exculpatory information to the defense, to ensure the accused has been given a right to counsel, and to rectify wrongful convictions. More generally, prosecutors have a duty to seek justice, not merely to seek convictions. Although bureaucratic policies, such as the U.S. Attorneys' Manual, constrain the exercise of their discretion, little external law is enforced against prosecutors, as they are absolutely immune from civil liability for their conduct as lawyers and are rarely subject to bar discipline.

The prosecutor's duty to seek justice exists in tension with the prosecutor's role as an adversary in the highly adversarial American criminal justice system. The tension in the prosecutor's role is particularly acute in the prosecutor's obligation under *Brady v. Maryland* and state ethics rules to disclose in a timely manner evidence known to the prosecutor or to other law enforcement agents to the defense before trial. Although timely disclosure of exculpatory, mitigating, and impeachment evidence is required, not all laws require disclosure of impeachment evidence before a plea bargain. Failure to disclose exculpatory evidence to the defense is a leading cause of wrongful convictions. No consensus exists about what institutional reforms within prosecutors' offices would most effectively address the problem of wrongful convictions, but state ethics rules in many states do impose upon prosecutors a duty to investigate and seek to rectify wrongful convictions.

SUBPART B

LARGE ORGANIZATIONAL CLIENTS

■ ■ ■

This unit focuses on lawyers who serve large organizational clients. Those lawyers work primarily in three practice settings: big law firms, in-house legal positions in corporations, and government. These practice areas share several distinctive features. First, lawyers who represent organizations face challenges that relate to the question of who speaks for the client. Second, lawyers in these work settings tend to work in teams; individual decision-making in these institutions is typically enmeshed in larger governance processes. Third, organizational clients typically are not vulnerable—or at least not in the same ways individual clients sometimes are.[1]

WHO IS THE CLIENT WHEN THE CLIENT IS AN ORGANIZATION?

Lawyers owe clients many duties, including the duty to communicate with the client, to exercise independent professional judgment and give candid advice, and to keep the client's confidences. But when a lawyer represents an entity rather than an individual, how does the lawyer fulfill those duties?

The ethics rule in most states provides that the lawyer represents the organization as a legal entity, acting through its "constituents," such as officers, directors, employees, shareholders, etc. ABA Model Rule 1.13. In circumstances when organizations are working well, it may not be particularly challenging for the lawyer to decide who has authority to speak for the client and with whom the lawyer should communicate. Ordinarily, the lawyer takes guidance from the person or persons designated by the organization's authority structure to interact with the lawyer.

Sometimes, however, the lines of authority within an organization are unclear, and then it becomes more difficult for the lawyer to determine how to interact with the organization's constituents. Moreover, internal disagreements sometimes arise within the client organization. When that happens, the interests and conduct of the constituents with whom the

---

1 For a fuller discussion of these and other assumptions underlying the ethics rules and their inconsistency with the conditions of modern law practice, see David B. Wilkins, *Everyday Practice is the Troubling Case: Confronting Context in Legal Ethics*, in EVERYDAY PRACTICES AND TROUBLE CASES 68 (Sarat et al., eds. 1998).

lawyer ordinarily interacts and the interests of the entity may diverge, and things then become tricky. It can be especially difficult for the lawyer to distinguish between the interests of the entity and those of its constituents when those constituents are the people with whom the lawyer interacts day-to-day and also the ones who hold the power to hire and fire the lawyer.

Another problem for the lawyer for an organization arises when constituents of the organization are violating their legal duties to the entity and/or engaging in illegal conduct that might be imputed to the organization. The ethics rule in most jurisdictions requires a lawyer in those circumstances to take action to protect the organization's interests. It further states that unless the lawyer reasonably believes that it is not necessary in the best interest of the organization to do so, the lawyer "shall refer the matter to higher authority in the organization, including, if warranted by the circumstances, to the highest authority that can act on behalf of the organization as determined by applicable law." ABA Model Rule 1.13. This obligation to take the matter up the organizational hierarchy is sometimes called the "up the ladder" reporting requirement.

LAWYERS' INDIVIDUAL RESPONSIBILITY WHILE WORKING IN LARGE ORGANIZATIONS

The ethics rules tend to emphasize lawyers' individual deliberation and decision-making. But decision-making can be complex when lawyers work in organizations. As David Luban has observed, "loyalties become tangled, and personal responsibility is diffused," "bucks are passed and guilty knowledge bypassed," and "[c]hains of command not only tie people's hands, they fetter their minds and consciences as well."[2] Particularly worrisome for a junior lawyer is the prospect that a boss might pressure the junior lawyer to engage in misconduct or that the junior lawyer will lose the ability to discern right from wrong.

State ethics rules generally provide that junior lawyers are bound by the ethics rules even when they act at the direction of another person, and the rules make senior lawyers responsible for junior lawyers' violations of the rules if the senior lawyers order or ratify the conduct or know of it at a time when its consequences can be avoided or mitigated and fail to take action. ABA Model Rules 5.1 and 5.2.

Although these rules establish certain duties of lawyers who work in organizations, they do not fully account for important sources of supervision, control, and influence on individual lawyer decision-making within organizations. While many of these sources of control and influence are entirely benign—and tend to reinforce individual lawyers' best instincts about how to behave—it is also true that lawyers who work in large organizations sometimes find it challenging to reconcile individual

---

[2] DAVID LUBAN, LEGAL ETHICS AND HUMAN DIGNITY 237 (2007).

conscience with their felt responsibilities and loyalties. The fragmentation of knowledge and accountability within large organizations sometimes adds to the complexity of exercising professional judgment and acting on it.

CLIENT VULNERABILITY

The image of an individual client vulnerable to the power of the state and his lawyer does not square well with the experiences of lawyers who represent organizational clients. These clients do not fit the paradigm of the criminal defendant whose freedom or even life might be taken away by the state. When the client is the government, the image of the lawyer as the champion of the individual against the state seems particularly inapt because the government lawyer's client *is* the state, or some subunit thereof—an agency, department or commission. Most corporations are highly sophisticated consumers of legal services, provided either in-house (by lawyers employed directly by the corporation) or by lawyers in an outside firm, and they are capable of discerning what services they need, shopping for competitive prices, and sanctioning lawyers who disappoint them by filing malpractice actions and withholding future business. Indeed, sometimes the experience of lawyers for organizational clients stands the image of client vulnerability on its head. Lawyers can find themselves susceptible to being drawn into grave trouble through misconduct by the organization's constituents, and they may feel vulnerable to the power of clients to punish their lawyers for refusing to go along.

CHAPTER 8

LARGE LAW FIRMS

■ ■ ■

A. INTRODUCTION

The following materials explore the large firm practice setting: how large law firms have changed over the past several decades, the current practices and cultures of these institutions, and their implications for lawyers, clients, and the public. Although many more lawyers work in solo and small firm settings than in large firms, the number of lawyers in large firms is still substantial. Lawyers in firms of 51 or more lawyers comprise roughly 20 percent of all American lawyers in private practice today.[1] The largest 500 U.S.-based firms collectively employ over 163,000 lawyers, with an average lawyer count per firm of 327.[2] Moreover, large law firms have enormous influence within the legal profession, American society, and the global economy. Understanding the history of these institutions, their operations, and the dramatic changes they have undergone over the past few decades, is important for understanding the American legal profession as a whole.

This chapter considers the origins and structure of large law firms, how they have changed over time, their internal labor markets, and the experience of large firm associates. It also examines the values of large firm lawyers, their relationships with clients, several scandals involving large firm lawyers, and the future of large firms.

B. THE LARGE LAW FIRM: ORIGINS, STRUCTURE, AND CHANGE

Large law firms serve primarily corporate clients, offering transactional, counseling, and litigation services and a broad range of legal expertise. Big firms typically are divided into departments—e.g., litigation, real estate, securities, banking, tax, etc.—and their lawyers' expertise is highly specialized. The firms are hierarchical, composed of working groups containing junior and senior lawyers. Many large firms include two tiers of partners: equity partners, who share in the firm's profits, and non-equity

---

[1] American Bar Foundation, The Lawyer Statistical Report (2012).

[2] *The NLJ 500: Our Annual Survey of the Nation's Largest Law Firms*, NAT'L L. J., June 26, 2017, https://www.law.com/nationallawjournal/almID/1202791138736/The-NLJ-500-Our-Annual-Survey-of-the-Nations-Largest-Law-Firms/.

partners, who are primarily salaried employees. Firms also employ a variety of other lawyers, including associates and lawyers who are "of counsel" to the firm. The latter title applies to lawyers with a variety of statuses, including permanent associates, lawyers with secure part-time arrangements, and retired partners who nevertheless remain available for consultation by the firm and its clients.

The large law firm and its distinctive practice style emerged around the turn of the twentieth century. The New York firm of Cravath, Swaine & Moore is widely credited with having pioneered the model, which is still the basic template for big private firms. Under the "Cravath system," firms hired lawyers directly out of prestigious law schools, and senior lawyers then supervised and reviewed these new lawyers during a prolonged apprenticeship of six to ten years. The firm then either promoted these associates to partnership or shepherded them into legal jobs outside the firm.

The Golden Age. A so-called "Golden Age" for large law firms was the 1950s and 1960s, as described in the following excerpt:

THE TRANSFORMATION OF THE BIG LAW FIRM

Marc Galanter & Thomas Palay
Lawyers' Ideals/Lawyers' Practices: Transformations in the American Legal Profession 31–62 (R. Nelson, D. Trubek & R. Solomon, eds., 1992)[3]

Before the Second World War the big firm had become the dominant kind of law practice. It was the kind of lawyering consumed by the major economic actors. It commanded the highest prestige. It attracted many of the most highly talented entrants to the profession. It was regarded as the "state of the art," embodying the highest technical standards. In the postwar years this dominance was solidified.

This golden age of the big firm, the late 1950s and the early 1960s, was a time of stable relations with clients, of steady but manageable growth, of comfortable assurance that an equally bright future lay ahead—which is not to say that its inhabitants did not look back fondly to an earlier time when professionalism was unalloyed.

New York firms loom disproportionately large in studies of the golden age. New York City was home to a much larger share of big-firm practice then than it is now. In the early 1960s, there were twenty-one firms in New York with fifty or more lawyers and only seventeen firms of that size in the rest of the country. A few years earlier, the largest firm in New York (and the country) was Shearman & Sterling & Wright with thirty-five partners and ninety associates. Three other Wall Street firms had over a hundred lawyers. The twentieth-largest firm in New York had fifty lawyers.

Firms were built by "promotion to partnership." Lateral hiring was almost unheard of, and big firms did not hire from one another. Partners might leave and firms might split up, but it didn't happen very often.

Hiring of top law graduates soon after their graduation was one of the building blocks of the big firm. Most hiring was from a handful of law schools, and walk-in interviews during the Christmas break were the norm. Starting salaries at the largest New York firms were uniform—$4000 in 1953, rising to $7500 in 1963. The "going rate" was fixed at a luncheon, attended by managing partners of prominent firms, held annually for this purpose.

Historically, the big firms had confined hiring to white Christian males. Few African-Americans and women had the educational admission tickets to contend for these jobs. But there were numerous Jews who did and, with a few exceptions, they too were excluded. This exclusion began to break down slowly after the Second World War. Jewish associates were hired, and some moved up the ladder to partner. The lowering of barriers to Jews was part of a general lessening of social exclusiveness. In 1957, 28 percent of the partners in the eighteen firms studied by Erwin Smigel were listed in the Social Register. [The Social Register is a directory of names and addresses of prominent American families who form the social elite; listing in it has historically been limited to members of "polite society," or those with "old money."] By 1968, the percentage had dropped to 20 percent. But African-Americans and other minorities of color were still hardly visible in the world of big law firms. In 1956 there were approximately eighteen women working in large New York firms—something less than one percent of the total complement of lawyers.

Only a small minority of those hired as associates achieved partnership. Of 454 associates hired by the Cravath firm between 1906 and 1948, only 36 (just under 8 percent) were made partners. Cravath may have been the most selective but it was not that different from other firms.

The time it took to become a partner varied from firm to firm and associate to associate. For the New York lawyers becoming partners around 1960 the average time seems to have been just under ten years. Outside New York the time to partnership was closer to seven years. Throughout the 1960s the time to partnership dropped.

One of the basic elements of the structure of the big firm is the up or out rule that prescribes that after a probationary period, the young lawyer will either be admitted to the partnership or will leave the firm. Many firms had an explicit up or out rule, but there was at work a competing and powerful norm that it was not nice to fire a lawyer. Termination tended to be drawn out and disguised. For associates who did not make partner, firms undertook outplacement, recommending them for jobs with client corporations and with smaller firms. Ties might be maintained as the firm referred legal work to them or they served as outside counsel to the corporation.

Partners were chosen by proficiency, hard work, and ability to relate to clients. In many cases there was some consideration of the candidate's ability to attract business. Achieving partnership, the "strongest reward," meant not only status but security and assurance of further advancement. There was certainly pressure to keep up with one's peers, but competition between partners was restrained.

The work of the big firm was primarily office work in corporate law, securities, banking, and tax with some estate work for wealthy clients. Divorces, automobile accidents, and minor real estate matters would be farmed out or referred to other lawyers. Litigation was not prestigious, and it was not seen as a money-maker. Where big firms were involved in litigation, it was typically on the side of the defendant. Big firms usually represented dominant actors who could structure transactions to get what they wanted; it was the other side that had to seek the help of courts to disturb the status quo. Disdain of litigation reflected the prevailing attitude among the corporate establishment that it was not quite nice to sue. Relations with clients tended to be enduring. Corporations had strong ties to "their" law firms.

Large firms elsewhere were constructed along the same "promotion to partnership" lines, but tended to operate a bit differently. Firms outside New York tended to be more recently founded. There was also less departmentalization, specialization, and supervision. The organization was less formal, with fewer rules about meetings, training, conflicts of interest, and so on. The turnover of associates was lower, and there was less up or out pressure. Partnership was also easier to attain and came earlier. Outside New York, firms were less highly leveraged. [Leverage is the ratio of associates to partners.]

For big firms, circa 1960 was a time of prosperity, stable relations with clients, steady but manageable growth, and a comfortable assumption that this kind of law practice was a permanent fixture of American life. Big law firms enjoyed an enviable autonomy. They were relatively independent vis-à-vis their clients; they exercised considerable control over how they did their work; and they were infused with a sense of being in control.

NOTES ON GALANTER & PALAY

1. ***Golden? For Whom?*** In what sense were the 1950s and 1960s a "golden age" for big law firms? What were the attractive and unattractive features of this era? For whom?

2. ***Relations with Clients.*** What were the most notable aspects of large law firms' relationships with clients during this period?

3. ***Hiring and Promotion.*** What were the most notable features of large law firms' hiring and promotion practices for attorneys during this period?

* * *

Changes Since the 1950s. Large law firms have changed significantly since the so-called "Golden Age." Perhaps the most striking changes relate to their increased size and geographic reach. In the 1950s, there were 38 law firms in the United States with more than 50 lawyers, most of them in New York City.[4] In 2016, there were 47 firms worldwide with over 1,000 lawyers.[5] In 1960, big firms were clearly identified with particular localities; it was unusual for a firm to have a branch office.[6] Today, over 10 percent of lawyers in the 250 largest U.S. firms work in overseas offices.[7] Large U.S. law firms increasingly compete with large global law firms and other professional service providers based in other countries.

Large firms have also changed markedly in their relationships with clients and in-house counsel and their hiring and promotion practices. The following excerpt summarizes some of the most notable of these changes in the legal services industry from the 1970s to 1990:

> Starting in the 1970s, lateral movement became more frequent, soon developing into a systematic means of enlarging the specialties and localities a firm could service and acquiring rainmakers who might bring with them or attract new clients. Eventually the flow of lateral movement widened out from individual lawyers, to whole departments and groups within firms, and finally to whole firms. Mass defections and mergers became common, enabling firms in one stroke to add new departments and expand to new locations.
>
> As firms get larger, the task of maintaining an adequate flow of business becomes more precarious, and firms become more prone to splitting up or failing. Firms are more vulnerable to defections by valued clients or by the lawyers to whom those clients are attached. Size multiplies the possibility of conflicts of interests, and the resulting tension between partners who tend old clients and those who propose new ones can often lead to a

---

4 ERWIN O. SMIGEL, THE WALL STREET LAWYER 58 (1964).

5 *The Global 100: Firms Ranked by Headcount*, AM. LAW., Sept. 25, 2017, https://www.law.com/americanlawyer/2017/09/25/the-global-100-firms-ranked-by-head-count/..

6 ERWIN O. SMIGEL, THE WALL STREET LAWYER 207 (1964).

7 *Analysis of the Legal Profession and Law Firms* (as of 2007), Harv. L. Sch. Program on Legal Prof., http://www.law.harvard.edu/programs/plp/pages/statistics.php#wlw.

breakaway. Surrounded by other firms attempting to grow by attracting partners with special skills or desirable clients, firms are vulnerable to the loss of crucial assets.

Contemporaneous with the growth of big law firms, in-house corporate law departments grew in size, budget, functions, authority, and aggressiveness. This change has resulted in a marked increase in the portion of the corporation's routine legal work conducted in-house. The relation of corporate law departments to outside counsel has shifted from comprehensive and enduring retainer relationships toward less exclusive and more task-specific ad hoc engagements. In their relationship with outside law firms, today's enlarged corporate legal departments impose budgetary restraints, exert more control over cases, demand periodic reports, and engage in comparison shopping among firms.

At the same time that business clients retracted much routine work into their corporate law departments, they experienced a great surge of litigation and other risk-prone, high-stakes transactions. Suddenly, the corporate work of large outside firms shifted from its historic emphasis on office practice back toward the litigation from which the large firm had turned away in its infancy. The new aggressiveness of in-house counsel, the breakdown of retainer relationships, and the shift to discrete transactions have made conditions more competitive. The practice of law has become more openly commercial and profit-oriented, "more like a business." Firms rationalize their operations and engage professional managers and consultants; firm leaders worry about billable hours, profit centers, and marketing strategies. "Eat what you kill" compensation formulas emphasize rewards for productivity and business-getting over "equal shares" or seniority.

The need to find new business leads to aggressive marketing. Some firms take on marketing directors, a position unknown even in 1980. Others place increased emphasis on "rainmaking" by more of the firm's lawyers, providing those lawyers responsible for bringing in business with a new ascendency over their colleagues. [T]he time required for promotion to partner has lengthened, firms have become more highly leveraged—that is, the ratio of associates to partners has risen, and the chances of becoming a partner are perceived to have decreased.[8]

---

[8] Marc S. Galanter & Thomas Palay, *Why the Big Get Bigger: The Promotion-to-Partner Tournament and the Growth of Large Law Firms*, 76 VA. L. REV. 747 (1990).

The following excerpt addresses how changes in the corporate legal services industry since the Golden Age have affected trust and loyalty among lawyers, as well as lifestyle concerns, within those institutions.

THE CHANGE AGENDA: TOURNAMENT WITHOUT END

Marc S. Galanter & William D. Henderson
American Lawyer, Dec. 1, 2008

Several key economic conditions of the so-called Golden Age no longer prevail. The bite of group opinion weakens with increased size, dispersion, and diversity; the power to sanction is undercut by mobility. A larger professional and public arena gives greater scope and incentive to express professional eminence in a monetary metric. As a result, large corporate law firms operate in an atmosphere of internal and external competition that has no historical antecedent. [There has been] a wide-scale adaptation to major structural changes in the marketplace, including the globalization of corporate clients, the bureaucratization of corporate legal departments, the lower cost and greater availability of information, and erosion of cohesive firm culture due to sheer size and geographic dispersion. But it is an adaptation that confers disproportionate power on the most single-minded pursuers of the bottom line.

This sea change is evident in the harried workplace endured by equity partners, who already hold the proverbial brass ring. [M]any of these partners would gladly trade a portion of their earnings for a shorter workweek, greater job security, more interesting work, the opportunity to mentor (or be mentored), do more pro bono work, or take a long, uninterrupted vacation. Yet, these aspirations are virtually impossible to negotiate when rainmaking partners located in multiple offices through the world are free to exit at any time with clients in tow. This outcome is dictated not by an absence of professional ideals but a widening and intractable collective action problem that undermines the requisite conditions for the embodiment of those ideals.

For the vast majority of modern large law firms, economics rather than culture are the glue that holds the firm together. Indeed, the distinguishing feature of the [prevailing culture of large law firms] is a constant focus on the real or imagined marginal product of each lawyer in the firm—associates, of counsel, sundry off-track attorneys, and equity and non-equity partners. Although this system is remarkably effective at maximizing the financial return on (at least some) human capital, it simultaneously undermines or hinders other values cherished by the profession.

The contemporary market for corporate legal services bears little resemblance to the comfortable regional guilds of the 1950s, 1960s, and 1970s. For example, law firms often expand geographically so that important clients have the benefit of "one-stop shopping." Yet, staffing a financially self-sufficient branch office often relies upon the recruitment of lateral partners.

Geographic expansion carries cultural costs that most law firm managers have tended to underestimate. When a partnership encompasses several hundred lawyers in a dozen widely spaced offices pieced together by mergers and lateral hires, it is very difficult to sustain (much less create from whole cloth) an organizational ethos in which partners are willing to make sacrifices for the long-term welfare of the firm. Too few lawyers trust that they will be around (or kept around) to reap the larger rewards.

How does a geographically dispersed law firm with 300 partners and 500 associates (most of whom avidly read the Above the Law blog) negotiate a more sustainable business model [and a more attractive lifestyle for lawyers working within large firms]? The economic power within the firm lies with potentially mobile rainmaking partners who are loath to subsidize the lifestyles of lower-earning colleagues whom they barely know.

NOTES ON CHANGES IN LARGE LAW FIRMS SINCE THE GOLDEN AGE

1. ***What Changed and Why?*** How have large law firms changed since the 1950s? What have been the major drivers of change?

2. ***Who Cares?*** Why should anyone other than the lawyers employed by large firms care about the more competitive atmosphere in these institutions? Are there any possible benefits or adverse consequences of those changes for clients? For the public?

3. ***Diversity.*** One of the major changes in large firms not captured in these excerpts is their increased diversity since the 1960s—the large influx into this sector by Jews, Catholics, women, and racial and ethnic minorities. The hiring practices that excluded these categories of lawyers have been abandoned. That is not to say, however, that the composition of lawyers in large law firms reflects the demographics of the profession as a whole. We explore some aspects of how women and racial, ethnic, and religious minorities have fared in large law firms in the next section.

* * *

Changed Hiring and Promotion Practices. In other parts of the Galanter and Henderson article excerpted above, the authors explain how the structure of firms has changed in recent years, from the inverted funnel shape of early firms (with large numbers of associates channeled through to the partnership decision, after which partners remained until they died or retired), to a "core and mantle" structure, in which a core of owner-partners ("equity partners") is surrounded by a much larger mantle of employed lawyers. The mantle includes not only associates who aspire to become partners, but also non-equity partners, who do not share in the firm's profits, and other salaried lawyers:

> There is a now an inner core of equity partners swathed in an outer mantle made up of senior nonpartners under an array of titles, such as nonequity partner, of counsel, special counsel, staff attorney, senior attorney, and permanent associate. In recent years, the mantle appears to be growing much faster than the core.
>
> The core and mantle model accommodates heavy lateral traffic between competing law firms. In a complete turnabout from the mid-century "Golden Age," lateral movement between firms is now routine.
>
> Within the firm, lawyers work longer to make equity partner; thereafter, they work in the shadow of possible de-equitization.* Thus, the key feature of the core and mantle model is perpetual competition within the law firm to achieve, enlarge, and maintain one's equity status. In other words, the promotion-to-partnership tournament has been transformed into a perpetual tournament. The only finish line is retirement or death.[9]

NOTES ON CHANGED STRUCTURE AND PERSONNEL PRACTICES

1. ***Core and Mantle.*** What changes in the structure of large law firms do Galanter & Henderson describe? What are the changes in personnel practices that correspond with a shift in large firm structure over the past three decades from an inverted funnel to a core and mantle?

2. ***Implications for Lawyers' Careers?*** If Galanter and Henderson have accurately described the structure of today's large firms, what are the implications of that structure for the careers of large firm lawyers?

3. ***Firm Culture.*** If Galanter & Henderson are right that "perpetual competition" is the "key feature of the core and mantle model," how would you expect that unending competition to affect the internal culture of large firms?

---

* [Eds.: De-equitization is a process by which an equity partner, who is a part owner of the equity of the law firm, is involuntarily divested of his/her ownership interest and becomes instead an employee of the firm.]

[9] Marc S. Galanter and William D. Henderson, *The Change Agenda: Tournament Without End,* AM. LAW., Dec. 1, 2008.

C. THE EXPERIENCE OF LARGE FIRM ASSOCIATES

The following article explores the experiences and expectations of young lawyers in large firms and the characteristics of those who stay long enough to be considered for partnership.

EXPLORING INEQUALITY IN THE CORPORATE LAW FIRM APPRENTICESHIP: DOING THE TIME, FINDING THE LOVE

Bryant G. Garth & Joyce Sterling
22 Georgetown Journal of Legal Ethics 1361 (2009)

This article began as an investigation into the reasons that women and minorities seem disproportionately not to "fit" in large law firm settings and stay on to become partners. Drawing on more than sixty-six interviews with lawyers in their third to sixth years of private practice, our particular aim was to see what factors contribute to the persistence of the inequalities that commentators expected to disappear long ago. On the basis of the interviews, we can indeed point to a number of examples demonstrating a lack of fit from the perspective of lawyers beginning their careers. The story suggested by the interviews, however, is more complex.

Our findings and approach in this article can be introduced through the career of a lawyer who at the time of the interview was five years into the partnership track of a leading Washington, D.C. litigation firm. Now, according to his firm's web site, he is a partner. Although the first in his family to attend college, and with a capacity for hard work that may have stemmed from that social position, he came from a solid middle class background and attended elite post-secondary schools capped by a federal clerkship. He began his career as a practitioner at the firm, and he reported three years ago that "I never thought I would be a big firm lawyer." He had expected instead to "burn out quickly." He liked the people in the firm, however—"the best part of the job is the people I work with." He also found strong mentors who advised and helped him, for example, to "try a case in [a particular] area." He did flirt with the law teaching market but did not find a suitable position. In short, he was not at all wedded to the large law firm or particularly focused on partnership. The main reason he was still there, he reported, was that, "nothing has driven me away." He had no children at the time of the interview, and his wife was a governmental attorney well acquainted with the work regime of a large law firm. He carefully noted, in addition, that he and his wife made sure that they were not "locked into" the big firm lifestyle of the high roller. Nevertheless, he stayed at the firm. From his perspective, he did not participate and compete in a seven or eight year "tournament of lawyers" seeking partnership. Instead, he did his apprenticeship and almost by accident ended up as a partner.

The story provides support for two complementary but also potentially competing narratives about the path of associates in large law firms. The relationship between the narratives is complex. One is the narrative of the path from associates to partners. From the perspective of the example just given, the accident that favored the partnership move depended on a number of factors that are not randomly distributed in the lawyer population. These factors, not surprisingly, tend to favor men over women, whites over minorities, and elite graduates over non-elite graduates. Minorities and women are not likely to survive the attrition process so essential to the corporate law firm partnership system.

This narrative recognizes that lawyers starting careers in corporate law firms need to find ways to put in very long hours for a substantial period of years. There are two key elements of that survival. One element is "finding the love" or support necessary to successfully fulfill the obligations of the apprenticeship. Put simply, they are more likely to be able to continue the work if they get support from others inside and outside of the firm—including junior and senior associates and partners. The other aspect of "finding the love" emerges from supportive spouses, family, and peers. One problem with the situation of minorities and women in large law firms is that these firms were built by and for white males with wives at home. Those who do not blend in terms of ethnicity, race, and gender face one set of obstacles; those without home support face another. Success comes most easily to those who feel welcome and comfortable at work and have a warm and supportive home outside of work.

The second element necessary to a successful corporate apprenticeship is "doing the time." Lawyers starting their careers in corporate law firms need to find ways to put in very long hours for a substantial period of time. "Doing the time" requires the patience and commitment to put in the time necessary to compete for and attain partnership. "Doing the time" may require lawyers to work weekends, spend late nights, and travel on assignments. In an earlier article, one of the current authors suggested that the law firm as currently organized fits Lewis Coser's definition of a "greedy institution." A greedy institution makes total claims on its members. Large corporate law firms command total loyalty and commitment and implicitly assume that lawyers will have someone at home to care for the personal aspects of life.

The second narrative is about the reproduction of the legal elite and more generally social class in the United States. Historically, the lawyers who gained the prestigious partnership positions were from the most elite law schools, which historically and currently draw mainly from relatively advantaged social groups. Individuals who gained entry into the leading law schools would join the ranks of the associates at the large corporate law firms, and out of that pool would come a new generation of partners. Those who did not become partners would be placed at boutique firms or would become in-house counsel of businesses with strong relationships with the particular corporate firms. In this manner a network of lawyers from similar backgrounds and schools secured the leading legal positions in the corporate law firms and the businesses with which they dealt. The status of the positions was reinforced partly by relatively high salaries, but also by the fact that they were occupied by individuals validated with degrees from the most prestigious schools.

Our interviews, we shall see, suggest a potential disconnect in the story of the reproduction of the elite dominated by the most prestigious law schools. The corporate law firms now hire associates from a much wider pool of law schools than in the past. A disproportionately large portion of the associates come from the most prestigious schools, but many other schools with students from relatively less advantaged backgrounds are also represented. One might posit that those who become partner will naturally tend to come from the most elite schools, partly because of the relative numbers, partly because they presumably have more talent as represented by their undergraduate grades and LSATs, and partly because they will be likely to fit in with the existing partners with similar backgrounds.

We will suggest, however, that the corporate law firm apprenticeship is increasingly becoming disconnected from the competition for partnership. In particular, the preliminary evidence suggests that the most elite law graduates will translate the prestige that comes from three or so years at a corporate law firm into a highly valued position *elsewhere* in the legal profession or business world. They will not stay around to build the bonds that might pull them into the partnership ranks.

This second narrative, therefore, co-exists unevenly with the first one. Women and minorities who were long excluded from the elite partnership positions at the corporate law firms continue to be unlikely to stay and make their way to a partnership position. But those who used to dominate the corporate law firm partnerships may also be unlikely to stay. It is certainly possible that existing partners could find some way to recruit a new generation from among the most prestigious schools—at least, as our example suggests, from those who are among the hungrier graduates at those schools. But it also appears that the emerging pattern for the most prestigious law graduates is to leave before playing the game for partnership. Our data suggest that those from the less prestigious schools and the less advantaged social backgrounds may take a disproportionate number of the corporate law partnerships.

To compare the two narratives, the corporate law firm apprenticeship may reproduce privilege *in the legal profession* as those who go through it move into prestigious and powerful positions that are mostly outside the corporate law firms, but the corporate law firms themselves may be losing some of their ability to reproduce the elite credentials of their traditional partnership stock. This outcome may not be a problem, and indeed it may be a welcome development. The problem, or more precisely the contradiction, is that the corporate law firms have historically used the prestige value of their partners' law degrees as a key aspect of their credibility as leaders of the profession and the provision of professional services.

The Large Law Firm Apprenticeship. Many beginning lawyers experience their work in a corporate law firm as an apprenticeship expected to last three years or so. Law students in elite settings are socialized to believe that the appropriate way to begin their careers as lawyers is to work very hard for a decent period of time at a large law firm. One self-assured lawyer contemplating moving into the government stated, for example, that he was "looking" for a new position since he had "done the three year thing at a firm." Another lawyer noted specifically that, "Being an associate is like being a resident. You do it for five years and then you think about your life." An Hispanic lawyer with South American roots working in a major Chicago firm stated simply, "OK well you know . . . let's take a stab at [the corporate law firm]," but not with the "goal of I'm going to be a partner." It is, in the words of another, "a stamp on the early portion of your career."

It is of course hard work, but, according to a lawyer who departed a top New York City firm after doing the apprenticeship, it is something that ought to be done at this stage of the career. Even though he "worked all those hours . . . for the first three years," he suggested, "you know three years is not a long time in your life." As many others, he was prepared to give up those years.

The process of socialization toward the apprenticeship in corporate law firms has been traced in studies of law schools, including popular works and works by social scientists. Sometimes the findings are presented as if there is some concerted effort within the law schools to move idealistic legal talent toward the service of large corporations, but it is more accurate to say that law students learn by many routes that there are hierarchies in the legal profession just as there are hierarchies in law schools, and that the "right" way to continue on the fast track is to start at a large corporate law firm.

This period of at least the first two or three years tends not to promote much planning or reflection among the lawyers. It is striking how many of the new corporate lawyers asked about their plans for the future made remarks that suggested a relative lack of planning. A lawyer five years into a large D.C. firm says, "I haven't" any plans. Another at a prestigious L.A. law firm says simply that he is "not very goal-oriented." A lawyer at a major Chicago firm said that he is "not a big goal setter or planner." A woman at a large firm also in L.A. said about her short term goals: "I have no clue."

She planned to be an associate for four or five years, not do anything "wrong" to preclude partnership, but also certainly not focus on partnership. A male associate at one of the most prestigious D.C. firms said about his future: "[I have] some vague ideas, but I wouldn't say any concrete goals."

Instead of planning for the future, these lawyers tend to take on faith that what they are doing will serve them well in whatever they do. Relatively few of the interviewees even commented on the importance of their apprenticeship in the corporate law firm. Those who commented certainly understood that the apprenticeship was part of what most considered the fast-track for legal careers. One lawyer without elite credentials who found a spot at a large Chicago firm did see what she had achieved: "everything I can learn here helps me here and would also help [me] anywhere else." Another referred to future "avenues of employment" opened by the corporate law firm apprenticeship. As stated by an Asian graduate in San Francisco, "they always tell you in law school, go to the highest point and then you can always go down." A lawyer from a non-elite school who found himself in a position a year into practice at a small firm taken over by a major national firm, decided to move and was able to secure a position at a top New York firm. He reported that he made his choice of firms because, "I figured it would be a good, gold star to have on my resume for a few years."

That faith in the utility of the apprenticeship allows lawyers to work very hard, doing work that is often drudgery. An elite law graduate at one of the most prestigious Wall Street firms noted that he worked until 8:30 or 9:00 most nights, but he also might work until midnight in a particular week in addition to a typical four or five hours on Sunday. He stated that he was, "willing to make the sacrifices to [his] personal life" and that the associates all built a norm of strenuous work. He said that the "associates know who's working hard and who's not working hard," and that he did not want to be a "slacker." A similar but more upbeat characterization of the hours by a Wall Street associate was, "when I was single it was just like, it was kind of fun." According to an Asian woman from a large urban law school working at a large San Francisco firm, "I kind of know my job is to make life easy for partners," and "because I'm a younger associate I want to get in as many hours as I can . . . to prove myself." An associate racking up prodigious hours for a leading D.C. firm said, "It's up to you to make it interesting perhaps or to perhaps work harder at it."

It took an Arab-American with a top law degree a while to recognize the reality and adapt: "My first year I hated it a lot," he reported, and "I never knew what time I could go home." He came "to appreciate that it's part of the job" stating, "Oh, yeah, okay, so this is my job, so deal with it." A woman doing real estate at an elite Los Angeles firm stated simply, "My job is a lowly job of sifting documents around and reviewing them," but she characterized the work as "fun." Associates in litigation similarly celebrate very small achievements. For example, a Chicago lawyer stated that, "overall I've been extremely happy here . . . learning to litigate," referring to participation in client contact depositions and relatively simple hearings in some smaller cases that the firm had. A less sanguine interpretation of an early litigation apprenticeship by a woman in the Silicon Valley was that she "basically spent a year reviewing documents" and writing some research memos.

Among those in the corporate law firms, in short, we find a very common identity and perspective. It is found in essential respects across the board among the different racial and ethnic groups and among men and women. They are putting in the time, building their resume, and learning some skills along with a large dose of drudgery. Few expect to stay and become partner. The general attitude toward partnership, however, is more complex than a simple plan and expectation to leave. Statements from respondents suggest a vague openness to partnership, such as the tentative expression by a woman at a large Chicago firm that she "thinks" she could go for partner. A lawyer at a prestigious D.C. firm admits likewise that his "assessment of partnership prospects" is relevant to his decision whether to leave the firm. The lawyer discussed in the beginning of this article, we discovered through a computer search, had indeed made partner. It may be recalled that he had expected to "burn out quickly," but apparently, he had enough openness to accept the partnership when it was offered. A recently named partner of a national firm in its New York City office intimated when we interviewed him that partnership would be a nice accomplishment, but he also talked of moving to a smaller firm closer to where he lived because, "It's not worth it if I miss my kid growing up." Apparently he has also been caught up by the lure of "the brass ring."

The Mutual Support Structure for Associates. We have seen how associates enact the role that they picked up in law school. They put in the time and do the work to get through the corporate law firm apprenticeship. There are factors that emerge from the interviews that help that survival process.

One key aspect of support for the corporate law firm apprenticeship is simply the fact of classmates and friends working in the same situation. When an entire cohort is in the same situation, it makes more sense to the participants. A woman with a degree from an elite law school working in a large L.A. firm stated, for example, "most of my friends work as hard as I do." An African American at a large Chicago firm stated similarly that "all your friends are working too." A woman working in New York City whose husband was also a lawyer said, "I would meet my friends for drinks or dinner at ten" and that her "husband did the same thing." This peer impact could also occur within a firm, for example, the D.C. lawyer who reported five to seven close friends within his peer group at the firm, and a New

York City lawyer who has "three or four" associates "that spend a lot of time talking about these issues" of careers.

There is a natural progression that leads to the almost inevitable departure of associates after three years or so. They sense that they have served their apprenticeship. They are both reminded and encouraged to move by the steady departures they witness among their cohort at the firm, their classmates, and their friends. These departures also shrink the support that helped to sustain them through the long hours and late evenings that are typical of associates' lives. The expected time horizon ends and much of the support structure collapses. The question then becomes which of the lawyers socialized to do the large law firm apprenticeship and move on will be the "outliers" who stay for the partnership tournament.

Those who stay around past three or four years tend to go against what seems to be the normal pattern of attrition. We see that the partnership tournament in some form may then engulf those who remain. But the "tournament" looks very different if we ask the most important question, which is who in these firms will be in a position to be one of the few survivors that turns his or her attention to partnership.

We have presented the self-reinforcing process that leads so many talented law graduates both to enter corporate practice and to move out prior to serious consideration for partnership. We know from the results of the process that women and minorities tend not to be there at the time of that serious consideration. They are disproportionately underrepresented in the partnership ranks despite what are often relatively positive numbers in the ranks of the beginning associates. Surveys from American Lawyer Media and NALP constantly reinforce the fact that women are hired as associates in the top firms, with 250 people and over, in equal proportions to their male counterparts. However, the proportion of partners that are women or minorities has remained stagnant for almost two decades.

Reproducing Elite? A Post-Script. We noted at the outset that corporate law firms were not only white male and protestant organizations, but they also were dominated by graduates of the most elite schools. Graduates of the most elite schools still start their careers at large law firms, especially the most prominent and profitable ones, in higher percentages than do graduates of other schools. Graduates of elite schools, in addition, are more likely to come from privileged backgrounds than are graduates from schools lower in the law school pecking order.

It is more difficult from our interviews to see how the relatively privileged fare in terms of attrition. Will the law firms, we asked earlier, find ways to ensure that enough of the graduates of the most elite schools will stay around for the partnership competition to ensure that they will keep what they might believe is a critical mass of such graduates and the symbolic value that comes from that presence? If so, does that mean both that the most elite graduates and those with the most privileged backgrounds who tend to graduate from those schools will disproportionately stay through the apprenticeship and beyond? It could be that more of their friends sustain them for longer, for example, or that they more easily form the kinds of relationships—marrying the firm—conducive to partnership.

Our qualitative data are inconclusive, but there are some hints that large law firm success in terms of partnership may not favor the privileged. Those from privilege may not feel the attraction of staying on the path to potential partnership, especially as the time to partnership continues to grow, and they also have a sense that they will land on their feet if they change positions. They are likely to be less hungry perhaps than those who fought their way into the corporate law firms. The partnership is also less attractive since it no longer is a ticket to a somewhat less-pressured elite status. Any impact from this unwillingness to stay in the apprenticeship would be compounded by the fact that the most elite law graduates are likely to work initially at the firms with the lowest partnership rates and accordingly the most demanding and stressful working conditions.

There is some evidence that the associates in our interview pool who stay late in their apprenticeship and potentially could become partners are those from relatively less privileged backgrounds and typically not the most elite schools. Those who are hungriest and who fought their way into large law firms are perhaps more averse to leaving and more willing to do what it takes to position themselves for the prestige and economic reward that goes with partnership. They may also have spouses or family that share that hunger. [Our interviews provide] some support for the idea that those who come up through the ranks will not only be disproportionately male and white, but also disproportionately from among the relatively less privileged among those law graduates able to enter these firms.

NOTES ON GARTH & STERLING

1. ***Who Stays and Leaves?*** What does this research suggest about the characteristics of those who drop out and those who stay to compete in the competition to become partners in large law firms?

2. ***Founder and Client Dynamics.*** Recall Garth & Sterling's observation that large law firms were "built by and for white males with wives at home." A study of Silicon Valley law firms found that lawyers who establish new law firms tend to transfer gender hierarchies from their former firms to the new firms. Law firms founded by lawyers who previously worked in firms with few women in prominent positions were less likely to view women as legitimate candidates for promotion to partnership positions, while founders who came from firms with women in leadership positions were more likely to create firms that promoted women into prominent positions because they had

experience working alongside women in high status positions.[10] Similarly, research has shown that large law firms with corporate clients in which women hold key leadership positions (general counsel, chief executive officer, or board director) have higher rates of growth in the promotion of women to partnership.[11] And a study of high status professional service firms in India found that gendered expectations by clients made it difficult for women to succeed in traditional litigation practice but worked to the advantage of women in new and elite law firms doing global transactional work for Western clients.[12] What does this research suggest about some of the mechanisms and power dynamics that influence law firm diversity?

3. ***The Large Firm Apprenticeship.*** According to Garth & Sterling's account, what do associates believe they gain through an apprenticeship in a large law firm? Why, according to this account, do many associates with elite credentials leave before being considered for promotion to partnership? Why would associates who seem well-positioned to achieve partnership decide to leave after just a few years?

4. ***Implications for Large Law Firm Recruiting.*** The authors note that large law firms currently sit "at the top of the professional hierarchy." If large firms lose their ability to attract elite law graduates, are they likely to remain at the top of the profession's prestige hierarchy? Do you think they already have begun to lose ground?

D. WHO IS THE CLIENT OF A CORPORATE LAWYER?

The following excerpt explores how "who is the client?" questions arise for lawyers who represent corporations—the client type most common for lawyers in large law firms. It explores why corporate lawyers sometimes may find it difficult to act on the knowledge that the corporation, rather than any of its constituents, is the lawyer's client.

WHO IS THE CLIENT? THE CORPORATE LAWYER'S DILEMMA

Ralph Jonas
39 Hastings Law Journal 617 (1988)

It is axiomatic that a corporation is a distinct, discrete legal entity that exists separate and apart from its officers, agents, directors, and shareholders. It is almost equally axiomatic that a lawyer who is retained

[10] Damon Phillips, *Organizational Genealogies and the Persistence of Gender Inequality: The Case of Silicon Valley Law Firms*, 50 ADMIN. SCI. Q. 440 (2005).

[11] Christine Beckman & Damon Phillips, *Interorganizational Determinants of Promotion: Client Leadership and the Attainment of Women Attorneys*, 70 AM. SOC. REV. 678 (2005).

[12] Swethaa Ballakrishnen, *She Gets the Job Done: Entrenched Gender Meanings and the New Returns to Essentialism in India's Elite Professional Firms*, 4 J. PROF. & ORG. 324 (2017).

to represent a corporation owes his allegiance solely to that legal entity, and not to the corporation's officers, directors, and shareholders.

These simple predicates, however, mask a morass. A corporation is a legal fiction. Its independent existence has been created out of statutory "whole cloth." Only by reason of legislative fiat has this "entity" been separated from its owners and its managers.

Therefore, we have the perverse situation in which the lawyer who represents a publicly held corporation is selected and retained by, and reports to and may be fired by, the principal officers and directors of the corporation—*who are not his clients*. Moreover, the shareholders of a corporation, who, collectively, are the owners of the mythical beast, typically do not participate in the process by which the lawyer is selected, retained, or fired.

In the corporate arena, the lawyer lives in an "Alice in Wonderland" world. The client to which he owes undivided loyalty, fealty, and allegiance cannot speak to him except through voices that may have interests adverse to his client. He is hired and may be fired by people who may or may not have interests diametrically opposed to those of his client. And finally, his client is itself an illusion—a fictional "person" that exists or expires at the whim of its shareholders, whom the lawyer does not represent.

It is not surprising, therefore, that to a great extent lawyers simply do not concern themselves with these ethical considerations, or if they do, become so frustrated in their application that they throw up their hands in despair.

NOTES ON JONAS

1. ***What's So Hard About Representing Corporations?*** One of the ABA ethics rules is designed to address the problem identified by Jonas here. It defines the corporation as the client of the corporate lawyer and specifies when and how the lawyer should respond to evidence that corporate constituencies are engaging in conduct that is likely to harm the corporation. Does this excerpt suggest reasons why corporate lawyers may find this rule challenging to implement and why they may sometimes be reluctant to follow its requirements?

2. ***What's Corporate Scandal Got to Do with It?*** Jonas describes an essential difficulty with important ethical implications for lawyers who represent corporations. The client is a legal fiction with no ability to communicate or make decisions except through the acts of its officers, directors, employees, and shareholders; the people with whom the corporate lawyers must interact every day in order to serve the client organization are not the client. Indeed, the interests of those individuals with whom the lawyer regularly communicates sometimes conflict with the client's interests. Nevertheless, those very people make decisions about which lawyers to hire

and fire. Does this "Alice in Wonderland" world that the corporate lawyer inhabits help explain some situations in which lawyers become embroiled in corporate wrongdoing?

E. LARGE FIRM LAWYERS' VALUES AND RELATIONSHIPS WITH CLIENTS

Here we examine the attitudes and values of lawyers who practice in large law firms. How do they view their relationships with clients? Do they seek to influence their corporate clients' positions on important issues affecting the public or third parties? How often do they disagree with what the client wants to accomplish or the means the client wishes to use to achieve its ends? When those situations arise, how do they respond?

This section surveys some of the available research on those questions.

IDEOLOGY, PRACTICE, AND PROFESSIONAL AUTONOMY: SOCIAL VALUES AND CLIENT RELATIONSHIPS IN THE LARGE LAW FIRM

Robert L. Nelson
37 Stanford Law Review 503 (1985)

My central thesis is that lawyers in large firms adhere to an ideology of autonomy in their perceptions of both the role of legal institutions in society and the role of lawyers vis-à-vis clients, but that this ideology has little bearing on their practice. In the realm of practice, these lawyers enthusiastically attempt to maximize the interests of clients and rarely experience serious disagreement with the broader implications of a client's proposed course of conduct. The dominance of client interests in the practical activities of lawyers contradicts the view that large-firm lawyers serve a mediating function in the legal system. The lawyers of elite firms may well take progressive stands on certain issues within the profession, may lead efforts at legal rationalization, and may exhibit a liberal orientation on general political questions, but the direction of their law reform activities and their approach to the issues that arise in ordinary practice ultimately are determined by the positions of their clients.

The principal database for the present analysis consists of structured interviews with a random sample of 224 lawyers [from four Chicago firms]. In addition, in-depth interviews were conducted with 61 "elites" who sat on their respective firms' governing committees or who were recognized leaders of a workgroup or department.

I chose to ask three questions about the relationships of lawyers to clients. First, I sought to measure the respondent's perception of the breadth of the lawyer's role. A commonly mentioned concern is that specialization in large firms has narrowed the lawyer's view of her normative role, that she may no longer see it as her responsibility to gain an overview of her client's affairs or to give clients more than technical legal advice. A second and related question dealt with lawyers' opportunities to give nonlegal advice. And third, I asked whether the lawyers had "ever refused an assignment or potential work because it was contrary to your personal values." This construction was intended to include matters that violated the code of professional ethics, as well as other values not codified.

Large-firm lawyers adhere to a broad conception of their role vis-à-vis clients. More than three-quarters of the sample (76%) responded that it was appropriate to act as the conscience of a client when the opportunity presented itself. Virtually the same majority (75%) responded that they had the opportunity to give nonlegal advice to clients, but there are significant differences by field and partnership status. Litigation presents practitioners with fewer opportunities for giving nonlegal advice.

By far the leading reason for giving nonlegal advice (mentioned by 43.8% of respondents) is that a business decision is involved. The majority of other responses have a pragmatic ring as well: that the client asked for advice (14.2%), that the field of law required it as part of the practice (24.9%), that matters required personal investment decisions (11.2%), or that the client needed personal advice (19.5%). Very few of the responses suggest broader moral or social concerns.

[H]ow often do they have conflicts with clients over the propriety or morality of client positions? Only 16.22% of the sample ever refused an assignment or potential work, and one-third of these 36 respondents had done so twice. [H]alf of the coded refusals were in response to violations of professional ethics, such as ongoing criminal conduct by clients, conflicts of interest, and the use of the law to harass other parties. [R]oughly one-half of the other refusals implicated personal values, with several respondents refusing to defend clients against certain types of accusations. Reflecting their seniority, partners were more than twice as likely as associates (28% to 11%) to have refused an assignment.

What can we infer from the finding that less than a quarter of the practitioners in this sample have encountered a conflict with personal values, and that half of the situations where lawyers refused work did not involve the subtleties of the public interest but were instead rather obvious violations of professional rules? Three broad explanations can be offered for this pattern. First, the vast majority of tasks that lawyers in these firms perform turn on technical matters involving parties of roughly equal status and resources. In preparing a securities offering, in arranging a leveraged leasing transaction, or in planning an estate, lawyers are not called on to deal with questions of good and evil (beyond considerations of simple honesty). Even in hotly contested matters, such as the hostile acquisition of a corporation or antitrust litigation, the contest is not between "good guys" and "bad guys." During the course of pretesting the values questions, one associate chuckled at the moral tone of the items. His comment was something like: "Are you kidding? My work [big case litigation] doesn't raise questions of conscience, it's just a fight over which big corporation is going to get a bigger chunk of the pie." The social questions of our time simply do not come up frequently in large-firm practice.

Second, even though the social values of my sample may be somewhat more liberal than those of business elites, the attitudes of lawyers and clients are not widely divergent. Operating with the same basic values as their clients, these lawyers will often interpret the social implications of a course of action in much the same way that their clients do. The similarity of values between lawyer and client is reinforced by the career choices of lawyers. Clearly there are some types of practice that involve rather explicit choices about which side a lawyer will take, for instance, between labor and management in labor relations, and between plaintiffs and defendants in several areas of litigation. Most of these choices are made when a lawyer chooses the law firm or other setting in which she will practice. Once this choice is made, lawyers are left with a limited set of case-by-case, client-by-client judgments about refusing assignments.

Third, it may be that professional training and experience teach lawyers to transform potentially troubling questions of values into matters of technique and strategy. [Norwegian sociologist Vilhelm] Aubert suggests that this is one of the primary functions of lawyers and that it may contribute to the resolution of disputes between embittered adversaries. But this tendency also may undercut the ability and inclination of lawyers to mediate conflicts or act as normative agents.

THE ELASTIC TOURNAMENT: A SECOND TRANSFORMATION OF THE BIG LAW FIRM

Marc Galanter & William Henderson
60 Stanford Law Review 1867 (2008)

Throughout the twentieth century, the elite corporate bar has perpetuated the lore that its organizations and individual members adhere to strict standards of professionalism rather than the morals of the marketplace. This image is reinforced within the popular culture by the tort reform movement, which casts plaintiffs' lawyers as greedy and unprincipled. Solo and small firm lawyers are also perennially overrepresented in state bar disciplinary proceedings because of higher levels of client complaints and alleged ethics violations. Conversely, as observed by Lisa Lerman, "[s]ome of the wealthiest American lawyers—partners in large firms—have enjoyed a widespread assumption that their ethical standards are impeccable."

In a seminal study on lawyer ethics conducted during the early 1960s, lawyer and sociologist Jerome Carlin provided compelling empirical evidence that large firm lawyers were much more likely to comport with the bar's formal and informal ethics regime. One of the major findings of Carlin's study was that large firm lawyers were much more likely to conform to, and internalize, the bar's formal and informal code of ethics.

Yet, as Carlin unpacked his findings, he observed that the different rates of ethical violation and conformity were not the product of firm size per se, but [varied] with the presence or absence of ethical stressors that were strongly correlated with different clientele and practice settings. In general, lawyers in the largest New York City firms enjoyed the largest incomes, the most stable base of clients, the fewest appearances in state courts (which were the most rife with corruption), less pressure from clients to violate the law, and the time and resources to participate in elite bar associations. Thus, inspecting all the data, Carlin concluded, "[l]arge-firm lawyers . . . have low rates of violation because they are largely insulated from client and court-agency pressures, while small-firm lawyers and individual practitioners have high rates of violation because they are most exposed to these situational inducements to violate."

A lot has changed in the forty years since Carlin published his study. The large firm lawyers studied by Carlin enjoyed enduring client relationships. According to a 1959 Conference Board survey of 286 manufacturing companies, "three fourths of them retain outside counsel on a continuing basis. . . . Companies more frequently report that 'present outside counsel have been with us for many, many years,' or that 'we are satisfied with the performance of our outside counsel and have never given any thought to hiring another.' " Only a few years after the publication of Carlin's study, another commentator on Wall Street law firms observed that the large commercial and investment banks were the "epitome of the locked-in client" because of the vast specialized knowledge that had accumulated within by the firms' large banking departments. One Wall Street partner estimated that client turnover during the 1960s, in dollar volume, was "5 per cent a year, mostly in one-shot litigation."

Ironically, Carlin's descriptions of the pressures surrounding small firm lawyers in the 1960s seem to apply aptly to today's large law firm marketplace.

> The lower the status of the lawyer's clientele, the more precarious and insecure his practice. Lawyers with low-status clients tend to have an unstable clientele; that is, they have a higher rate of [client] turnover . . . The small businessman is more likely than a large corporation to shop around and switch attorneys: he may be on the lookout for a less expensive, sharper, and more compatible lawyer. This type of client is also more likely to divide his legal

> business among several lawyers . . . Lawyers with low-status clients also report more competition from other lawyers in obtaining clients, and that they have been hurt by such competition.

John Conley and Scott Baker recently observed, "the Wall Street elite now occupy that circle of hell that Carlin had reserved for the most desperate of solo practitioners."

In [a] recent qualitative empirical study of ten large law firms, many factors contributed to the climate of insecurity.[85] Partners reported that "firms no longer 'own' the work they do because" a competitor is always working to lure the client away. Because the firm can no longer predictably hand off clients as older partners retire, younger lawyers are less likely to develop strong loyalties to the firm, which further undermines the project of developing firm-specific capital. Firm management evaluates the profitability of partners and practice groups by focusing on hours billed and fee collection (i.e., "realization"), which, in turn, fosters competition within the firm for marketing expenditures, equity partnership seats, and new hires. Similarly, the conflict of interest checks are a frequent source of tension because individual lawyers or practice groups could be forced to turn away lucrative business. Even if an individual partner manages to cement a strong business relationship with a corporate general counsel, that security could be disrupted by higher firm-imposed billing rates that the client is unwilling to pay. Further, the specter of de-equitization hangs over all lawyers who are slow to adapt.

Several commentators have argued that market power is a necessary precondition of professional values, including adherence to the formal ethical norms of the bar. According to Erwin Smigel's sociological account of large Wall Street law firms of the 1960s, large law firms flourished economically because their clients were paying a premium for expert and autonomous advice. "Independent legal opinion is perhaps the commodity they offer, and the primary commodity for which they are paid." Even if Smigel accurately described the client-firm relationship of the late 1950s and early 1960s, now there is broad consensus that the vast majority of corporate clients hire outside counsel to obtain a specific, cost-effective result. Not surprisingly, as extensive qualitative field work has revealed, the ethical norm that is most widely embraced by large firm lawyers is the very one that reduces the strains in the lawyer-client relationship: zealous advocacy.

Under the elastic tournament's regime of mobility, the structural implications for outside counsel are virtually impossible to ignore. In the pages of *The American Lawyer*, one large firm partner, who temporarily

---

[85] *See* Kimberly Kirkland, *Ethics in Large Law Firms: The Principle of Pragmatism*, 35 U. MEM. L. REV. 631 (2005).

served as a client's in-house counsel, offered two golden rules to solidify their client relationships: "[m]ake inside counsel's lives easier" and "[m]ake inside counsel look good in front of their clients, colleagues, superiors, and subordinates." In some instances, the outside lawyer is hired to reinforce to company executives the position staked out by the general counsel, and if he or she wants to be hired again, "it behoove[s] him [or her] not to offer a contrary opinion." In this highly atomized economic climate, it is likely that ethical gray zones will get resolved in the client's favor, and insecure lawyers will be less likely to acknowledge any black or white.

In our discussions with lawyers, we have run across examples of large law firms that continue to share risk and inspire investment in the collective enterprise of the firm. Ethical lapses were regarded as threats to a hallowed firm reputation and the trust of longtime colleagues. But this ethos becomes harder to maintain (and virtually impossible to create or restore) in larger, geographically dispersed firms that are perpetually competing for clients and entry-level associates.

NOTES ON NELSON AND GALANTER & HENDERSON

1. ***How Do These Lawyers Define Professionalism?*** If the descriptions of large firm lawyers' values and practices in the Nelson and the Galanter & Henderson excerpts are correct, how would you describe the prevailing conception(s) of professionalism held by lawyers in large law firms?

2. ***Implications of These Trends for Lawyer Independence.*** How do the trends described by Galanter & Henderson contribute to an environment in which individual lawyers within large firms are likely to find it difficult to follow professional and ethical principles that are "at odds with the client's objectives"?

3. ***Implications for Self-Regulation.*** To the extent that lawyers come to see their work for corporate clients simply as a series of self-interest-maximizing market transactions that tend to go more easily if the lawyer does not attempt to offer independent advice and instead focuses primarily on making inside counsel and executives look good, should the public value the work of lawyers? Should it respect the notion that the legal profession should be allowed to regulate itself without outside interference?

4. ***"Padding Hours."*** The study by Lisa Lerman noted in the Galanter & Henderson excerpt examined billing fraud by prominent lawyers in large elite law firms. The practice she examined involves "padding hours"—exaggerating the amount of time spent on projects and thereby cheating clients.

Lerman's research turned up no such cases involving large firm lawyers prior to 1989 and thirty-six such cases thereafter—a pattern she attributes to the "rising dominance of income generation as the central goal" of large firm practice. She also noted that most of the law firms at which the lawyers involved in these billing scandals worked billed clients by the hour, set high annual targets for billable hours, and used the number of hours billed per year as a primary criterion for evaluating and compensating lawyers. She suggested that these policies invite misconduct:

> As long as lawyers are making records of how long they work on particular matters, and the time recorded translates into dollars billed, there is an incentive to record more time than was actually worked, and/or to do unnecessary work in order to bill for it. Many lawyers, of course, would not inflate their hours or their work, but those whose moral compass is less focused will do so. By setting annual billable hour targets for lawyers, law firms may invite—perhaps almost require—dishonest recordation of time. The incentive to overbill already present as a result of hourly billing and as a result of the annual targets is intensified by [the practice of using the number of hours billed per year as a primary criterion to evaluate and compensate lawyers].[13]

Does Lerman underestimate the possibility that lawyers can work very hard without engaging in deception? Does she place too much blame on law firms' policies and too little on the individuals who engage in overbilling?

Additional factors that contribute to bill padding in large firms include firms' failures to monitor billing practices. In fact, in several high profile incidents, lawyers who have reported billing fraud within their firms have been either ignored or penalized.[14] Moreover, in some types of matters, such as bankruptcy, neither the lawyers nor clients have an incentive to keep fees under control because those costs are ultimately borne by others. In bankruptcy proceedings, creditors foot the bill for lawyers' fees.[15]

F. LARGE FIRMS AND CORPORATE MISCONDUCT

We now explore some of the pressures that may contribute to misconduct in this realm of practice. In a wave of scandals of the past several decades, lawyers in large firms appear to have facilitated wrongdoing by their corporate and banking clients. As you contemplate the following three such episodes, try to imagine why the lawyers behaved as they did and what they might have done differently.

Kaye, Scholer and the Lincoln Savings and Loan Debacle. In the 1980s and 1990s, long before the financial crisis relating to the housing

---

[13] Lisa G. Lerman, *Blue-Chip Bilking: Regulation of Billing and Expense Fraud By Lawyers*, 12 GEO. J. LEGAL ETHICS 205, 294–95 (1999).

[14] *See Bohatch v. Butler & Binion*, 977 S.W.2d 543 (1998) (a lawyer who reported what she believed was billing fraud by one of her partners was dismissed from the partnership); *see also* Nathan Koppel, *Lawyer Charge Opens Window on Bill Padding*, WALL ST. J., Aug. 30, 2006 (reporting on an incident in which a junior partner at Holland & Knight LLP believed that the partner in charge of billing had inflated the junior partner's hours; the junior partner reported the incident and thereafter left the firm because he was dissatisfied that the firm had not taken action against the billing partner).

[15] *See* Andy Peters, *Eight Firms to Share $30M in Delta Bankruptcy Legal Fees*, DAILY REPORT, June 7, 2006.

bubble, there was a crisis in the savings and loan ("thrift" or "S&L") industry; over one thousand savings and loan associations failed during that period. The bailout from that debacle cost American taxpayers hundreds of billions of dollars. S&Ls lent money to homeowners with long pay-back periods (usually 30 years) but acquired the money used to make those loans from short-term depositors to whom they paid interest. Deposits in S&Ls were federally insured, meaning that if the S&L lacked sufficient assets to pay depositors who wished to withdraw their funds, the depositor could collect from the government's Federal Deposit Insurance Corporation (FDIC). In return for FDIC protection, S&Ls were subject to extensive regulations and regular examinations designed to ensure that they did not take excessive risks that would ultimately be borne by the American taxpayer. When interest rates increased during the 1970s, the S&Ls were caught in a squeeze. Partial deregulation of S&Ls allowed thrifts to make riskier investments, and some engaged in fraudulent deals to stay above water.

Lincoln Savings and Loan, based in Irvine, California, was one of the most notorious institutions involved in the savings and loan crisis of the 1980s. Its owner/operator, Charles Keating, was known for his aggressive management of Lincoln and his political influence acquired through large campaign contributions. (The "Keating Five" lobbying scandal involved five U.S. Senators who received major campaign contributions from Keating and intervened on his behalf to ward off regulators and ease regulations that had made it difficult for Lincoln to continue making risky investments with taxpayer-insured dollars.) Lincoln engaged in a series of prohibited risky investments and fraudulent transactions to remain solvent and hide its true financial condition from regulators. The Office of Thrift Supervision (OTS), the agency charged with periodically examining S&L books to ensure their compliance with thrift regulations, sought access to Lincoln's records as part of its oversight responsibilities. Lincoln hired Jones Day, and later (when Jones Day was not sufficiently aggressive in fending off OTS inquiries) Kaye Scholer to represent it in connection with its interactions with bank examiners.

Kaye Scholer lawyers treated the matter like adverse litigation rather than a bank examination. That is, they conceived their role as defending their client against having to share information rather than as helping their client comply with the law by cooperating with the government investigators. The firm directed examiners—who were legally entitled to full access to the thrift's records—to channel all inquiries through the firm and not to communicate directly with Lincoln personnel. In its dealing with the regulators, Kaye Scholer also made a series of statements about Lincoln's underwriting practices and transactions that directly contradicted statements contained in Kaye Scholer's own memos. Those memos became available to the government when Lincoln finally collapsed and was taken over by the Resolution Trust Corporation (a governmental organization) as receiver.

In 1992, the Resolution Trust Corporation, charged with paying depositors from taxpayer funds and from proceeds from settlements made with those who allegedly assisted Lincoln in its schemes, brought charges against Kaye Scholer and three of its partners. It sought restitution of losses of at least $275 million. The agency also issued a "freeze" order designed to prevent the law firm's assets from being dissipated. Within a week, the firm settled the matter for $41 million without contesting the charges or admitting or denying the allegations.[16]

Enron. The collapse of the huge Houston-based energy company, Enron Corporation, in 2001 involved one of the largest corporate frauds of modern times. It resulted in many criminal prosecutions against Enron's officers and suits by shareholders against secondary actors, including several prominent law firms. The fraudulent scheme at issue was Enron's use of "special purpose entities" (SPEs) to hide losses and make the company look more profitable than it was. These SPEs were nominally independent of Enron but were in fact created for the purpose of hiding losses. Enron's in-house counsel and at least two outside firms played important roles in structuring and documenting the transactions. A report issued by the court-appointed bankruptcy examiner found that Enron's counsel were centrally involved in structuring the SPEs and reviewing company disclosures concerning them.[17] In some instances, the report attributed the lawyers' failure to prevent or disclose the fraud to their lack of understanding of the transactions involved, while in other instances the report called it willful blindness.

A report of the New York City Bar Association concluded that Enron's lawyers, including lawyers in its primary outside law firm, Vinson & Elkins, were in a position to have questioned various aspects of management's conduct and that, while some did so, none brought their concerns to Enron's board of directors.[18] The report emphasized the obligations of outside counsel to ask whatever questions were necessary to ensure that their services were not being used to improperly remove debt from the company's financial reports, as well as their duty to candidly advise the client on legal and other risks posed by a transaction or disclosure.[19] In trying to explain why lawyers failed to fulfill those duties, the report noted the trend toward "limited, piecemeal representations by

---

[16] For a fuller discussion of this matter, see In the *Matter of Kaye, Scholer, Fierman, Hays & Handler: A Symposium on Government Regulation, Lawyers' Ethics, and the Rule of Law*, 66 S. CAL. L. REV. 977 (1993).

[17] In re Enron Corp., Final Report of Neal Batson, Court-Appointed Examiner, Appendix C.

[18] As noted in the introduction to Part VA, Rule 1.13's up-the-ladder reporting provisions have become much more stringent since the time of the Enron debacle.

[19] New York City Bar, Report of the Task Force on the Lawyer's Role in Corporate Governance 25–26, 114–118 (2006).

outside firms," which means that no one outside firm has a complete understanding of a client's business and the general context of the transactions that he or she is structuring and documenting. It also noted that "[t]here is an increased risk, in this legal environment, that lawyers may unwittingly facilitate a client's misconduct, or lose the opportunity to counsel against it," and that this risk is magnified by the increasingly competitive nature of the profession:

> Both partners and clients are less tied to a given firm than was typical until roughly the 1980s. Today a partner's compensation may importantly depend on retaining a significant client, and a firm's profitability may depend on its ability to retain its partners with "portable business." At the same time, most public companies are no longer tied to a single law firm, a relationship that gave the firm a sturdy platform from which to render unwelcome advice. Today, public companies unhappy with the advice or service of one firm can and do readily switch their business to other firms. This competitive environment creates pressures on outside counsel to avoid confronting clients about questionable transactions or accounting treatments in order to maintain the client relationship.[20]

It may also be worth noting that Enron was Vinson & Elkins's largest client at the time of the events that led to the criminal prosecutions and civil suits.

Refco. In 2007, Joseph Collins, a partner in the large law firm of Mayer Brown, was charged with helping to hide the debts of his client, Refco, a futures and commodities broker that went public and collapsed in 2005. At the time, it was the fifth largest bankruptcy in U.S. history. Collins was accused of helping Refco's executives manipulate its balance sheet by drafting loan agreements that temporarily transferred Refco's losses from its books at the year's end to a related party controlled by the company's chairman and CEO, thereby creating the impression that Refco was a profitable company and defrauding shareholders. According to the indictment, Collins and other Mayer Brown lawyers played an indispensable role in facilitating the fraudulent scheme to hide $2.4 billion of debt from auditors and investors by preparing the documents that concealed the company's debt. In 2009, a jury convicted Collins on five securities fraud counts, and he was sentenced to seven years in prison. In January of 2012, the U.S. Court of Appeals for the Second Circuit overturned his conviction and ruled that he was entitled to a new trial because the judge had improper discussions with a juror outside the presence of Mr. Collins's lawyers.[21] However, on November 16, 2012, he

---

[20] *Id.* at 112–14.

[21] *See* Peter Lattman, *Conviction Overturned for an Ex-Refco Lawyer*, N.Y. TIMES, January 10, 2012.

was again convicted—of conspiracy, securities fraud, and wire fraud, and in July 2013 he was sentenced to a year in prison.[22]

During the trial, Collins testified that he was a victim of the Refco fraud, that Refco officials had lied to him, and that he was unaware that his client was engaging in fraud. He said that he relied on the numbers the client gave him, delegated the drafting of the documents to a Mayer Brown associate who worked for him, and spent little time on the transactions: "I didn't personally spend a lot of time. I delegated them . . . I didn't structure them. I didn't negotiate them. I didn't talk to customers about them. They just didn't require much of my time." He added, "I do many transactions for many clients and I can't possibly keep in mind everything" that happens. "I don't have that information. I can't compile it and I can't remember it." He also testified that his client lied to him about the purpose of the loans.[23]

It's hard to know exactly what Collins knew about the Refco fraud. One reading of the evidence suggests that he unknowingly facilitated the perpetuation of a massive fraud. But why didn't Collins and the associates who worked with him ask questions that would have uncovered the scandal? After all, his client had a history of unlawful activity. Since 1983, regulators had cited Refco more than 140 times for various misdeeds, including siphoning money from client accounts.[24]

As we ponder this question, it may be worth noting that Refco was Collins's biggest client; according to the indictment, his work for Refco generated $40 million in fees from 1997 to 2005[25] and accounted for more than half his time on matters for the firm.[26] Collins had a clean reputation at Mayer Brown; one of his former partners described him as "the Richie Cunningham of Mayer Brown."[27] But not all of his former partners accepted the notion that he had no reason to know that his client was engaging in fraud. One said that Collins should have been asking more questions: "It's hard for me to understand how anyone could work on loan documents and not ask, 'what is the purpose behind this loan?' When you're doing a financing, knowing the use of proceeds is important to understand whether the loan is illegal." One journalist speculated that "Mayer Brown's

---

[22] Mark Hamblett, *Ex-Mayer Brown Partner Convicted at Retrial*, N.Y. L. J., Nov. 19, 2012; Patricia Hurtado, *Ex-Refco Lawyer Gets Year for Aiding $2.4 Billion Fraud*, BLOOMBERG.COM, July 15, 2013.

[23] Mark Hamblett, *Collins Takes the Stand to Defend His Role as Attorney for Refco*, N.Y. L. J., June 19, 2009, p. 1.

[24] Susan Beck, *Target Practice*, AM. LAW, Nov. 1, 2008, p. 84, 87; *see also* Sung Hui Kim, *Naked Self-Interest? Why the Legal Profession Resists Gatekeeping*, 63 FLA. L. REV. 129, 130 (2011) ("Collins's claim that he just didn't know [about the fraud] remains troubling in light of Refco's long rap sheet of rogue transactions and prior criminal prosecutions.").

[25] *United States v. Collins*, 07–01170 (S.D. N.Y.), Indictment p. 2.

[26] Hamblett, N.Y.L.J., June 19, 2009.

[27] Richie Cunningham was the exceedingly wholesome character played by Ron Howard in the television sitcom Happy Days, 1974–1984.

eat-what-you-kill culture arguably led to lapses in judgment that that, in the end, hurt the clients and the firm." (Three civil suits relating the Refco's collapse were also filed against Mayer Brown.)[28] The judge who sentenced Collins after his first trial said, "I don't believe that Mr. Collins committed these crimes for greed or money because he would have been paid through his firm; I think this is a case of excessive loyalty to his client."[29]

NOTES ON THE CASE STUDIES

1. ***Why Did These Episodes Occur?*** What do you think might explain the lawyers' conduct in each of these incidents? What might the lawyers in each of these situations have done differently?

2. ***The Lawyer's Role?*** Some have argued that lawyers' conceptions of role should vary by the procedural context in which they operate. How should the lawyer for a client engaged in a bank examination view his role? Kaye Scholer and its defenders asserted that Kaye Scholer's tactics were justified by the firm's role as litigation counsel for Lincoln. But most commentators took the view that Kaye Scholer lawyers were not justified in behaving as aggressive advocates in a context in which the client had affirmative disclosure obligations as an insured, regulated thrift. OTS argued that Kaye Scholer acquired its client's disclosure duties by virtue of having taken control of the examination process and "interposing" itself between its client and the regulators. OTS further argued that Kaye Scholer violated its professional duties under the ethics rules by making misrepresentations about Lincoln's investments and underwriting standards, knowingly transmitting misleading material prepared by Lincoln to OTS, and doctoring files to obscure underwriting failures. Most commentators agreed that Kaye Scholer could not intentionally deceive regulators without violating its obligation under the ethics rules to avoid assisting the client in fraudulent conduct.[30]

3. ***Common Features.*** Notice some of the similarities between the Vinson &Elkins/Enron and Collins/Refco matters. In both, the client was the lawyers' major client, in both cases the lawyers insisted they didn't know that they were facilitating fraud, and in both the lawyers were documenting transactions whose purposes they later said they did not understand.

4. ***Who Is the Client (Yet Again)?*** Regarding the lawyers' conduct in Enron, consider the remark by one Vinson & Elkins lawyer: "When clients ask us [if they can do something] our job is to . . . figure out if there is a legally appropriate way to do it. That's what we do. And so does every other law firm in America."[31] Is the job of the lawyer to "figure out if there is a legally appropriate way to do" whatever the client asks? What does "legally

---

[28] Susan Beck, *Target Practice*, AM. LAW., Nov. 1, 2008, p. 84.

[29] Mark Hamblet, *Ex-Mayer Partner Gets 7 Years Over Refco*, N.Y. L. J., Jan. 15, 2010.

[30] *See From the Trenches and Towers*, 23 LAW & SOC. INQUIRY 243–271 (1998).

[31] Patty Waldmeir, *Inside Track: Don't Blame the Lawyers for Enron*, FINANCIAL TIMES, Feb. 21, 2002.

appropriate" mean? Who does this Vinson & Elkins lawyer appear to view as his client?

William Simon offered this comment on the above quote by the Vinson & Elkins lawyer: "That V&E could see its participation in the Enron deceptions as a matter of loyalty to its client bespeaks deep confusion that seems to arise from a failure to treat seriously the meaning of organizational representation."[32] Do you agree? What factors other than deep confusion might explain the role of outside lawyers in these corporate scandals?

5. ***Willful Blindness.*** Can lawyers avoid responsibility for client fraud by avoiding knowledge about their clients' business? How should lawyers handle clients that deliberately keep them in the dark? Should lawyers refuse to work for clients who do not give them sufficient information to ensure that they are not facilitating fraud?

Although the ethics rules sometimes require actual knowledge of client misconduct to trigger lawyers' responsibilities, such knowledge can be inferred from the circumstances. Lawyers who fail to investigate when they suspect that their clients are engaging in misconduct not only jeopardize their own reputations but also risk bar discipline and criminal and civil liability for facilitating the deception.

G. THE FUTURE OF THE LARGE FIRM

Is the big firm model sustainable? What does the future hold for large law firms and the lawyers who work for them?

In 2010, Professor Larry Ribstein published an article entitled "The Death of Big Law," in which he argued that the large firm business model is unworkable.[33] Noting that many large firms had recently dissolved, gone bankrupt, or significantly downsized, he asserted that these events indicated that the basic business model of the large U.S. firm is defective and requires fundamental restructuring. According to Ribstein, client demand for cheaper and more sophisticated legal services, and intensified competition in the global legal services market, threaten the large law firm's stability. He predicted that the dominant role that major law firms have enjoyed in the legal services market will end and that "big law" will devolve into smaller and less hierarchical firms.

The following commentary on the same topic offers a slightly less dire prediction.

---

[32] William H. Simon, *After Confidentiality: Rethinking the Professional Responsibilities of the Business Lawyer*, 75 FORDHAM L. REV. 1453, 1464, 1467 (2006).

[33] Larry E. Ribstein, *The Death of Big Law*, 2010 WIS. L. REV. 749 (2010).

BIG BUT BRITTLE: ECONOMIC PERSPECTIVES ON THE FUTURE OF THE LAW FIRM IN THE NEW ECONOMY

Bernard A. Burk & David McGowan
2011 Columbia Business Law Review 1

As Yogi Berra (or was it Neils Bohr?) said, predictions are hard, especially about the future. With all appropriate trepidation and humility, then, we offer the following [predictions about what we can expect in the market for corporate legal services].

Disaggregation of legal services, and the price competition that causes and results from it, will accelerate. Corporate clients are not going to become any less sophisticated, and will in increasing numbers scour their legal work for tasks that can be routinized, commoditized, and conveniently handed to low-cost providers or handled more economically in-house. Technology will continue to lower the cost of coordinating with economically-priced, appropriately skilled workers wherever in the world they may be found. Downsourcing, insourcing, and outsourcing will become more prevalent as clients insist on them, and elite law firms do what is necessary to remain competitive.

The number of highly compensated, partnership-track associate positions at large firms will fall. Legal process and similar routinized and commodified work will less and less support elite-firm associates' rates. As such work is pushed down and out at large firms, fewer conventional partnership-track associates will be needed to staff it.

The number of well-compensated, indefinite-term nonpartnership positions at large law firms will increase. These positions will increasingly be offered in lieu of partnership to highly qualified technical specialists, former "service partners," and other skilled and experienced practitioners who are useful in supporting the firm's practice.

The number of staff and spot-contract positions at large law firms, compensated at levels comparable to nonattorney staff and limited to legal process and other routine work, will increase (to the extent they are not replaced by technological substitutes). Their work will be limited to routinized and commodified work such as legal process, and possibly the kinds of routine legal work large companies (and some law firms) are increasingly outsourcing abroad.

Equity partnerships will grow more slowly, and be more rigorously limited to those demonstrating success in business generation and control. Because the highly leveraged work that tends to provide law firms the greatest profit margins will be under continuing cost and price pressure, margins will erode and higher-margin work will become more scarce. Relentless pruning of partnerships through de-equitizations and dismissals will continue, further focusing profits and power in an increasingly narrow equity "core" reached only through control of substantial amounts of profitable law business.

Lateral mobility will remain a significant force and BigLaw will remain brittle. Partnerships will continue to try and increase profits per partner (and the returns from their internal referral networks) by seeking new partners with relational capital, leading to profitability greater than the partnership's current mean. They will tend to splinter off partners with lower margins and profitability. Partners whose current practice environment is less complementary to their relational capital, or who otherwise perceive a better environment elsewhere, will also move.

Segmentation between a small cadre of "super-elite" firms and a larger group of "semi-elite" firms will become more pronounced. Because some practice specialties generally tend to be more profitable than others, these trends suggest increasing concentration in a more limited array of practices, at least nearer the top of the profitability scale.

High-margin specialty boutiques will remain a significant part of the competitive landscape. As technology allows small firms to enjoy scale economies, some may be able to achieve margins that approach the margins of large firms in similar market segments. Boutiques will remain a recognizable part of high-margin practice in the future as some portion of elite-firm lawyers leave profitable large firms to trade some amount of money for smaller scale, lower overhead, greater intimacy, and a more direct hand on the tiller.

One thing this discussion should make clear is that the large American law firm is not dying. The basic conditions that have driven increasing demand for sophisticated legal services for many decades remain in place. The legalized nature of society, business, and wealth-creation in this country has not materially changed, and governmental intervention in any number of areas (including the healthcare, energy, and financial services industries, among others) suggests more of the same for years to come. The same forces that drew elite lawyers together into larger and larger aggregations also remain in place, and while such phenomena as the erosion of firm-specific capital will continue to impart a certain brittleness to the form, there is no reason to believe that centripetal forces will not, on balance, remain paramount at least up to sizes at least as large as some of the larger firms today.

By the same token, however, the large law firm is evolving. Important changes are emerging as a result, the course of some of which we guess at above. But none of them should spawn revolutionary rather than evolutionary development in the way that complex and sophisticated legal services are produced and delivered.

NOTES ON BURK & MCGOWAN

1. ***The Forces of Change.*** What forces do Burk & McGowan identify as important features of the changed landscape in which large law firms now compete for business? How are those forces affecting how large law firms operate? What further consequences do the authors predict? Are the authors' predictions plausible?

2. ***Dewey & LeBoeuf's Collapse.*** In 2012, Dewey & LeBoeuf LLP, a global law firm headquartered in New York City, declared bankruptcy. At the time of the bankruptcy filing, the firm employed over 1000 lawyers in 26 offices around the world. Many factors likely contributed to the firm's collapse, including a weak economy, large debts, excessive multi-year compensation guarantees for some partners, and mistakes committed by the firm's senior managers. When rumors began to surface about the firm's financial difficulties, the partnership unraveled quickly, as lawyers headed for the doors to pursue lateral opportunities in other law firms.[34] The rapid disintegration of Dewey & LeBoeuf illustrates Burk & McGowan's observation that mega-firms are "brittle"—vulnerable to splinting apart suddenly when the firm's only major assets, its lawyers, begin to leave in significant numbers.

3. ***What's to Like and Dislike?*** Based on all you have learned thus far about large law firms, what do you find attractive and unattractive about this practice setting? Do you think that the future of practice in these institutions is likely to be more or less attractive than the present? Why?

H. SUMMARY

This chapter has examined the history of large law firms and enormous changes they have undergone since the 1950s. Those changes include huge increases in firm size, greater diversity in the lawyers hired by large firms, less stable relationships with corporate clients, more lateral movement by lawyers between firms, and ongoing struggle by lawyers within firms to maintain their status within the firm hierarchy. We also examined large law firms' hiring and promotion practices and how recent changes in the structure of large firms have affected the careers and experiences of large firm lawyers, including young associates. We next explored the professional autonomy, values, and ethics of lawyers who work in large law firms. We considered how large firm lawyers tend to view their roles and responsibilities, and how current conditions in this practice realm might relate to patterns of lawyer misconduct. We examined several specific examples in which large firm lawyers have become embroiled in corporate scandals and what lessons might be learned from those episodes.

---

[34] *See* Peter Lattman, *Dewey & LeBoeuf Files for Bankruptcy*, N.Y. TIMES, May 28, 2012; James B. Stewart, *The Collapse: How a Top Legal Firm Destroyed Itself*, NEW YORKER, Oct. 13, 2013.

Finally, we speculated about what the future holds for large law firms and the lawyers they employ.

CHAPTER 9

COUNSELING

■ ■ ■

A. INTRODUCTION

This chapter focuses exclusively on the counseling role. In the materials that follow, we pay particular attention to counseling corporate and governmental clients, but the questions raised in these materials are broadly relevant to lawyers' advising other types of clients.

Litigators' behavior receives a reasonable amount of scrutiny from opposing counsel, judges, and the press, and the publicity surrounding high-profile litigation makes it accessible and reasonably well-understood by the public. Lawyers' work in the counseling and regulatory compliance realm occurs largely behind closed doors, without external oversight or judicial scrutiny, and this activity is much less well-understood by the public. But lawyers' counseling may be at least as consequential as the work of litigators because it shapes clients' decisions about future behavior in important ways. For individual clients, counseling sometimes affects how clients treat relatives, employees, neighbors, business partners, and affected strangers. In the context of corporate counseling, lawyers influence how clients deal with regulators, competitors, accountants and other service providers, employees, and consumers. In government practice, advice to officials can have profound political and policy consequences. In all types of practices, lawyers in their counseling roles often affect whether and to what extent clients comply with the law.

The ethics rules require lawyers to exercise independent professional judgment and give clients candid advice. In giving advice, a lawyer may refer not only to law but to other considerations such as moral, economic, social and political factors that may be relevant to the client's situation. The rules prohibit lawyers from counseling a client to engage, or assisting a client, in conduct that the lawyer knows is criminal or fraudulent. They also provide that a lawyer retained by an organization represents the entity acting through its constituents, and that a lawyer who discovers that an officer or employee is engaged in activity that is a violation of a legal obligation to the organization, or a violation of law that might be imputed to the organization, and that is likely to result in substantial injury to the organization, must act in the best interest of the organization. That generally means that the lawyer must take the matter up the organizational hierarchy.

B. COUNSELING VERSUS ADVOCACY

How does counseling differ from advocacy, and why is the distinction important? The ethics rules do not address this question directly, but the following classic statement on the distinction and its significance is often cited:

PROFESSIONAL RESPONSIBILITY: REPORT OF THE JOINT CONFERENCE

Lon L. Fuller & John D. Randall
44 ABA Journal 1159 (1958)

The Lawyer's Role as Counselor. Vital as is the lawyer's role in adjudication, it should not be thought that it is only as an advocate pleading in open court that he contributes to the administration of the law. The most effective realization of the law's aims often takes place in the attorney's office, where litigation is forestalled by anticipating its outcome, where the lawyer's quiet counsel takes the place of public force. Contrary to popular belief, the compliance with the law thus brought about is not generally lip-serving and narrow, for by reminding him of its long-run costs the lawyer often deters his client from a course of conduct technically permissible under existing law, though inconsistent with its underlying spirit and purpose.

Although the lawyer serves the administration of justice indispensably both as advocate and as office counselor, the demands imposed on him by these two roles must be sharply distinguished. The man who has been called into court to answer for his own actions is entitled to a fair hearing. Partisan advocacy plays its essential part in such a hearing, and the lawyer pleading his client's case may properly present it in the most favorable light. A similar resolution of doubts in one direction becomes inappropriate when the lawyer acts as counselor. The reasons that justify and even require partisan advocacy in the trial of a cause do not grant any license to the lawyer to participate as legal adviser in a line of conduct that is immoral, unfair, or of doubtful legality. In saving himself from this unworthy involvement, the lawyer cannot he guided solely by an unreflective inner sense of good faith; he must be at pains to preserve a sufficient detachment from his client's interests so that he remains capable of a sound and objective appraisal of the propriety of what his client proposes to do.

NOTES ON FULLER & RANDALL

1. ***Counseling v. Litigating.*** How do lawyers' responsibilities in counseling differ from their responsibilities in litigation, according to Fuller and Randall? Do you agree with their view that the duties of lawyers in these two roles must be "sharply distinguished"?

2. ***Procedural Context.*** According to Fuller & Randall, how do differences in the duties of litigators and counselors relate to differences in the procedural context of their work?

C. CORPORATE COUNSELING

The last few decades have seen a spate of major corporate scandals in which lawyers have been implicated. The attention of the media and politicians has focused primarily on corporate officers and accounting firms, while the role of lawyers has received much less notice. But it is important to consider what role lawyers should play in averting the client's participation in such wrongdoing, especially when the lawyer's assistance is integral to its accomplishment. What steps should lawyers take to prevent the client from engaging in misconduct—or at least to ensure that lawyers play no part in assisting any such illegality?

The remaining materials in this section address that question.

A NEW ROLE FOR LAWYERS? THE CORPORATE COUNSELOR AFTER ENRON

Robert W. Gordon
35 Connecticut Law Review 1185 (2003)

Lawyers seem to have played a relatively minor part in the theater of deception and self-dealing that has led to the collapse of Enron Corp. ("Enron") and other corporate titans of the 1990s. [But] it is clear that the advice both in-house lawyers and outside law firms gave to the managers of Enron and other companies like it was instrumental in enabling those managers to cream off huge profits for themselves while bringing economic ruin to investors, employees, and the taxpaying public. Although the lawyers were not principally responsible for these acts of waste and fraud, their advice was a contributing (and often necessary) cause of those acts. Such fraud could not have been carried out without the lawyers' active approval, passive acquiescence, or failure to inquire and investigate.

How are we to understand why the lawyers acted as they did? Observers from outside the profession, and even some from within the profession, are tempted to say that the lawyers were simply weak and corrupt, or, for those who prefer to talk this way, that the lawyers were rational economic actors. They want the client's business, in an intensely competitive market, and so they will wish to approve anything senior management of the client firm asks, averting their eyes from signs of trouble and their noses from the smell of fish.

But this is the amoral rational calculator's perspective, and professionals in high-status jobs at respectable blue-chip institutions do not like to think of themselves as amoral maximizers. Like human beings everywhere who want to enjoy self-respect and the esteem of others, they tell stories about how what they do is all right, even admirable; however, some of the stories that the lawyers would like to tell were not available in this situation.

Law as the Enemy: Libertarian Antinomianism. In recent years many lawyers have taken on the values of and completely identified with their business clients, some of whom see law as an enemy or a pesky nuisance. I call this the viewpoint of the libertarian antinomian, because it rests on an express contempt for, and disapproval of, law and regulation. Tax law, products liability tort law, drug law, health and safety law, environmental law, employment discrimination law, toxic waste cleanup law, foreign corrupt payments law, SEC disclosure regulation, and the like are all shackles on risk-taking initiative. They interfere with maximizing profits, and anything that does that must be bad.

Law as Neutral Constraint: The Lawyer as Risk-Manager. This viewpoint is much like the first, but without the negative normative spin. Adverse legal consequences are not an evil, they are just a fact. In this view, law is simply a source of "risk" to the business firm; it is the lawyers' task to assess and, to the extent possible, reduce it. These lawyers do not feel a moral imperative, as libertarians do, to defy or undercut the law; but neither do they feel one to comply.

These two story-lines were not available in the case of Enron, for the obvious reasons that managers were looting the companies for their own benefit while concealing debts and losses from workers and investors. When the lawyers and accountants outwitted the pesky regulators—who, had they known what was happening, might have put a stop to it—they were not helping heroic outlaws add value to the economy and society by defying timid convention, but enabling, if not abetting, frauds and thieves. Nor were the professionals objectively, if amorally, assessing risks and weighing benefits against costs of efficient breach. It seems not to have occurred to them that outsiders might find out that the many-sided transactions with special entities were not actually earning any real returns, but merely concealing debts and losses, and that when that happened, Enron's stock price would tumble, and with it, all the houses of cards secured by that stock. The company they advised is now facing at least seventy-seven lawsuits as a result of its conduct. At best, the lawyers were closing their eyes to the risk of disaster; at worst, they were helping to bring it on.

The lawyers have been relying instead on different stories, somewhat in conflict with one another.

"We Din' Know Nothin' ": The Lawyer as Myopic or Limited-Function Bureaucrat. These are claims that the lawyers were not at fault because their role was limited: We didn't know, we weren't informed; the accountants said the numbers were okay; management made the decisions;

our representation was restricted to problems on the face of the documents or to information submitted to us.

Many of these claims of innocent ignorance now look pretty dubious. Some of the outside law firms in fact worked closely with Andersen accountants in structuring many of the transactions. Sometimes lawyers made notes that they needed further information or managers' or the board's approval to certify a deal, but signed opinions and proxy statements even if they never got it. Sometimes they expressed doubts about the deals. In the end, the doubting lawyers never pressed the issues.

Some of their claims of limited knowledge are plausible, however, because Enron never trusted any one set of lawyers with extensive information about its operations—it spread legal work out to over 100 law firms. If one firm balked at approving a deal, Enron managers would go across town to another, more compliant firm. It is this layering of authority, fragmentation of responsibility, and decentralization that has made it possible for the chairman, CEO and board of directors of Enron, as well as the lawyers, to claim that they did not know much about what was going on in their own company. One question for lawyers—as well as for senior managers and board members—is whether they can conscientiously and ethically do their jobs and exercise their functions as fiduciaries in organizations structured to diffuse responsibility and prevent their access to the big picture.

The Lawyer as Advocate. The classic defense of the corporate lawyer's role, both most often advanced and held in reserve if other defenses fail, is of course that we are advocates, whose duty is zealous representation of clients. We are not like auditors, who have duties to the public; our duties are only to our clients. Our job is to help them pursue their interests and put the best construction on their conduct that the law and facts will support without intolerable strain, so as to enable them to pursue any arguably-legal ends by any arguably-legal means. The paradigmatic exercise of the adversary-advocate's role is the criminal defense lawyer's; and the role is a noble role, both because it furthers the client's freedom of action and protects his rights against an overbearing state, and because it facilitates the proper determination of his claims and defenses.

Inadequacy of the Excuses. The Enron and similar scandals illustrate the limits of all these standard stories as adequate accounts of the corporate lawyer's proper role.

Despite their increasing popularity among practicing and some academic lawyers, the profession surely has to reject out of hand libertarian-antinomian and neutral-risk-assessment theories of its appropriate role and ethics. Both construe the client's interests and autonomously-chosen goals as supreme goods, and law as a set of obstacles that the lawyer helps to clear out of the way. The antinomian ranges the lawyer alongside his client as an opponent of law, someone who sees law as merely an imposition and a nuisance. The lawyer as risk-assessor also views legal norms, rules, institutions, and procedures in a wholly alienated fashion from the outside, as a source of opportunity and risk to his client.

Some might dispute whether even ordinary citizens of a liberal-democratic republic may, consistent with their enjoyment of its privileges and protections, legitimately adopt such a hostile or alienated attitude toward its laws. People who participate in self-rule through the representatives they elect—constrained by the constitutional limits their ancestors have adopted in conventions or by amendments—and whose lives are mostly benefited from the restraints law puts on private predation and public oppression, should generally internalize the norms and purposes of their legal system and voluntarily respect and obey even the laws they do not particularly like.

[U]nless people internalize the norms and respect the general obligation to obey the law, they will tend to violate it when they can get away with it. That is a recipe for anarchy, because all law depends on voluntary compliance, on my willingness to keep my hands off of your property even when nobody can see me stealing it, and to report my taxable income honestly even though I know only one percent of returns are audited. Societies whose leaders and institutions have conditioned their members into contempt for law and its norms and purposes are plagued by theft, fraud, crime, unenforceable contracts, uncollectible taxes, valueless currencies, and general civil strife. Evidently, this does not mean that society will fall apart unless everyone feels that they must obey every law all the time. In all societies, people obey some laws instinctually, some willingly, and others grudgingly; and they ignore or routinely violate others that they think do not matter all that much. But a general disposition in most people to respect the laws and the purposes behind them really does seem to be a precondition to peaceful, prosperous, cooperative, and orderly social life, which is why good societies put a lot of effort into socializing their citizens into dispositions of general law-abidingness.

However one comes out on this broader argument does not, it seems to me, really much affect the question at issue here: Whether lawyers representing *public corporations* may confront the legal system as alienated outsiders, determined to work around it and minimize its effects to the extent it gets in the way of the client's projects. To this the right answer ought to be, unequivocally, no.

People who defend corporations' taking a "bad man's" approach to law sometimes seem to suggest that business entities should have special privileges—more leeway than individual persons—to game and evade regulations they do not like, because, as engines of growth, job-creation, innovation, and shareholder wealth, they are heroic actors on the social scene, a breed of Nietzschean supermen, beyond good and evil. The taxes, regulations, and liabilities that government pygmies and plaintiffs' lawyers keep trying to impose on them, on the other hand, are often foolish and inefficient, the product of ignorant populism or envy or special-interest rent-seeking. This attitude plays well in boom periods, but it sounds a lot less convincing when defrauded and impoverished employees and investors are licking the wounds from their losses and looking to more, not less, regulation to protect them in the future. Anyway, it is basically an incoherent position. A strong state and effective legal system are preconditions, not obstructions, to successful capitalism, ones capable of legislating and enforcing an adequate infrastructure of ground-rules creating stable currencies, defining and enforcing property rights, contracts, and rules for the transparent and fair operation of markets, and deterring frauds, thefts, torts, discrimination, abuses of labor and harms to competition, health, safety, and the environment.

Of course, the laws in force are not always those businesses would prefer, nor are regulations anywhere near optimally efficient. But though businessmen running large public corporations love to grumble about the SEC, the EPA, and OSHA—and products-liability class-action suits—they are hardly in a position to claim that they are like Jim Crow southern blacks, or vagrants picked up and accused of crimes: powerless outcasts and victims. Big American business firms are not discrete and insular minorities. They have exceptional access to influence in legislatures, administrative agencies, and the courts through government advisory commissions, trade associations, lobbies, and lawyers.

Indeed, it is precisely because of their exceptional power to collectivize and command resources and employees, and to influence governments, that American legal tradition and popular opinion have usually concluded that corporations need to be more, and not less, constrained by law than ordinary citizens. If corporations cheat on or evade their taxes, the treasury loses billions; if corporations bribe politicians or officials, whole governments may be corrupted; and if corporations ignore environmental restraints, entire ecosystems may be wiped out. When it became clear that the financial statements of Enron, WorldCom, Tyco, Adelphia, and Global Crossing* could no longer be trusted, investors fled the markets en masse.

It may be that a natural person cannot be compelled to internalize the values promoted by law, or to feel an obligation to obey the law, without violating his or her dignity or freedom of conscience. But a company has no soul to coerce, dignity to offend, or natural freedom to restrain. Nor can it be schooled by parents, educators, and peers into a general disposition toward sociability or law-abidingness. It can only have the character that

* [Eds.: These were companies that appeared in the late 1990s to be quite profitable until they suddenly failed under circumstances suggesting that corporate officials had overstated their profitability and understated their liabilities.]

its managers, contracts, and organizational incentives and the legal system build into it. It is a creature of law made to serve limited social purposes. Since we are free to construct the character of these artificial persons, we should construct them for legal purposes as good citizens, persons who have internalized the public values expressed in law and the obligation to obey even laws they do not like, for the sake of the privileges of the law that generally benefits them as well as the rest of us.

Nothing in this conception prevents the good corporate citizen from challenging taxes and laws he thinks are unfairly or improperly applied to him; or trying to change them through political action. But it does foreclose the amoralist's argument, that the corporation should be free to ignore, subvert, or nullify the laws because the value it contributes to society justifies its obeying the higher-law imperatives of profit-seeking and shareholder-wealth-creation. If the artificial person is constructed as a good and law-abiding person, it follows that the manager who ignores or tries to nullify the valid objectives of law and regulation is not acting as a responsible or faithful agent of his principal, the good corporate citizen.

If the corporation should be constructed and presumed to have the interests of a good, law-respecting, citizen, so should its lawyers (even more so). Lawyers are not simply agents of clients—they are also licensed fiduciaries of the legal system, "part of a judicial system charged with upholding the law," to use the ABA's words. They do not have, as the dissenting citizen does, the option of taking up a position outside the legal order, rejecting the norms and public purposes of the legal system and limiting themselves to a grudging and alienated outward compliance with such of its rules as they think they cannot safely or profitably violate when their interest or inclination is to do so. The lawyer is, by vocation, committed to the law.

Now, of course, the "norms and purposes and public values" of law are not something fixed and definite and certain; rather, they are contested and dynamic and alterable—by, among other people, corporate clients and their lawyers. But there is a difference between trying to game and manipulate a system as a resistance movement or alienated outsider would, and to engage in a committed and good faith struggle within the system to influence it to fulfill what a good faith interpreter would construe as its best values and purposes.

Applying these general standards to many of the Enron transactions seems in some ways pretty simple. The purpose of the securities laws is to make public companies' financial condition transparent to investors. Agents of Enron had an interest in making their finances opaque, in order to boost the stock price of the company and with it their compensation in options, and to conceal the management fees they were paying themselves. They asked lawyers to manipulate the rules so that they would appear to be disclosing without actually disclosing. The lawyers obliged—and by so doing effectively thwarted the valid purposes of the laws.

How about the claims that the lawyers did not know the extent of the company's misrepresentations and frauds, relied on information given them by accountants or managers, saw only small pieces of the puzzle, and took on assignments validly narrowed and specialized in scope? I would make some general points about these claims.

One is that, although lawyers may take on an assignment that limits the scope of their representation or asks them to accept some facts as given, they may not agree to such limits as will preclude them from competent and ethical representation. They should not, for example, agree to write an opinion certifying the legality of a deal to third parties if they have some reason to be suspicious of the facts or numbers reported to them, without doing some digging to ensure that the facts are accurate. Nor should they give assurances that certain facts are true if they have no independent means of verifying them. If the client's agents are given unrestricted discretion to limit the scope of the lawyer's work, it becomes all too easy for them to use lawyers to paint a gloss of respectability (sprinkle holy water, as it were) on dubious transactions. Lawyers like to say that they have to assume and hope that their clients are not lying to them. But they should not passively cooperate in a corporate strategy to attach a respectable law firm's name to a scam, even if they are not dead certain that it is a scam.

More generally, the ways in which many corporations structure their legal services operate to prevent their receiving appropriately independent law-respecting advice. The practice of spreading fragments of business around to different outside firms, and different lawyers' offices within the company, makes it easy for managers to shop around for compliant lawyers, thus inducing races to the bottom, in which law firms or in-house counsel determined to give independent and conservative advice either lose out to their cross-town rivals or gradually acquiesce in the corrosion of their standards. It also eliminates responsibility, since no set of lawyers ever knows enough about the business decisions to know the likely purpose or effect of their advice, and how it fits into the company's plans as a whole. The lawyers could not sit down with managers and directly press them for information about the purposes and underlying facts of the transactions they were being asked to bless. And for the most part they did not try to do so.

The most important lessons of Enron, et al., for lawyers are the additional clouds of doubt they cast on the most common defense of the corporate lawyer's role, and the one most often invoked by the profession in the current debates over reform. That is the corporate lawyer as adversary-advocate.

This idea that the role of the corporate lawyer is really just like the role of the criminal defense lawyer has been criticized so often and so effectively that it always surprises me to see the idea still walking around, hale and hearty, as if nobody had ever laid a glove on it. I will quickly run through some of the strong objections to the analogy and then add another objection: The bar's standard construction of the corporate lawyer's role is deficient in part because it does not take the analogy seriously enough.

The most obvious objection is that legal advice given outside of adversary proceedings is not subject to any of the constraints of such proceedings. The reasons that the lawyer is given so much latitude to fight for his client in court is that the proceedings are open and public, effective mechanisms such as compelled discovery and testimony exist to bring to light suppressed inconvenient facts and make them known to adversaries and adjudicators, adversaries are present to challenge the advocate's arguments of law and his witnesses' and documents' view of facts, and there is an impartial umpire or judge to rule on their sufficiency and validity. Absent any of these bothersome conditions, lawyers can stretch the rules and facts very extravagantly in their clients' favor without risking contradiction by adversaries, or the annoyed reactions of judges or regulators to far-fetched positions.

In the trial setting, aggressive advocacy (at least in theory) supposedly operates to bring out the truth, by testing one-sided proof and argument against counter-proof and counter-argument. Ideally, it facilitates decisions of the legal validity of the parties' claims on the merits. Outside of such settings, one-sided advocacy is more likely to help parties overstep the line to violate the law, and to do so in such ways as are likely to evade detection and sanction, and thus frustrate the purposes of law and regulation.

The advocacy ideology regularly and persistently confuses the managers, who ask for lawyers' advice, with the lawyers' actual client, the corporate entity. Admittedly, much corporate-law doctrine makes this easy for them because it is excessively permissive in allowing lawyers to treat the incumbent managers who consult them as the entity. At least until the adoption of the Sarbanes-Oxley's Act's "up the ladder" reporting requirement, the bar's ethical rules also facilitated this conflation of the corporate client with management, by waffling over whether corporate counsel who becomes aware that a corporate agent has engaged in conduct that is a "violation of law" and is "likely to result in substantial injury to the organization" must report the misconduct up to or, if necessary, even beyond the board of directors. But the general principle is clear: A corporate agent acting unlawfully no longer represents the corporation, and the corporation's lawyer therefore owes him no loyalty, and no duty of zealous representation. On the contrary, if his illegal acts are harming the actual client, the lawyer should not help him out at all. And that, obviously, is a huge difference between representing a company and representing the criminally accused.

The point I want to add to these standard, but valuable, points is a simple one. Corporate lawyers could actually learn something useful from the role of the criminal defense lawyer. And that is that the adversary-advocate's role—like that of all lawyers—is in large part a public role, designed to fulfill public purposes: The ascertainment of truth and the doing of justice; the protection of the autonomy, dignity and rights of witnesses and especially of the accused; and the monitoring and disciplining of police and prosecutorial conduct. The defense lawyer is not merely or even mostly a private agent of his client, whose function is to zealously further the client's interest (which is usually to evade just punishment for his past conduct, or continue to engage in it in the future). He is assigned a specialized role in a public process in which his zealous advocacy is instrumental to the service of various public objectives. He is encouraged to make the best possible arguments for suppressing unlawfully seized evidence, not for the purpose of furthering his client's interest in freedom or getting away with crimes, but to protect third parties who are not his clients, i.e., other citizens whose freedom and security will be put at risk unless police misconduct is deterred. He is allowed to present a very one-sided, partial, and selective version of the evidence favoring the defense, in part because resourceful adversaries can poke holes in his story and present a counter-story, but even more to fulfill a public purpose—that of keeping prosecutors up to the mark, making sure they know that they have to put together a defense-proof case, deterring them from indicting where they do not have the evidence. Defense counsel's zeal is restricted precisely at the points where it might help the client at the risk of damage to the performance of his public functions and the integrity of the procedural framework that those functions are designed to serve. He may not, for example, lie to judges, suppress or manufacture real evidence, pose questions on cross-examination that he has no basis in fact for asking, or suborn or knowingly put on perjured testimony.

If you extend this analysis of the public functions of the defense bar to the corporate bar, what might you conclude? That, like the defense lawyer's, the corporate lawyer's role has to be constructed so that it serves and does not disserve its public functions as well as its private ones. I have explained the public benefits of allowing defense lawyers to suppress unlawfully seized evidence, or to refrain from volunteering inconvenient facts pointing to their clients' guilt. But what are the benefits of allowing lawyers to conceal—or hide in a maze of fine print—facts from regulators and investors that would be highly relevant to determining what the companies' real earnings were, or whether its tax shelters had some economic purpose beyond avoidance, or that managers were setting up side deals paying themselves and their cronies huge bonuses? What is the virtue of allowing lawyers to pull the wool over the eyes of the understaffed bureaucrats who monitor their transactions and try to enforce the laws? Even if all of these schemes should turn out to be (at least arguably) technically legal, what values of overall human happiness, individual self-fulfillment, or economic efficiency are served by helping clients promote them? The autonomy of clients generally is a good thing, to be sure; but there is no virtue per se in action, any old action, that is freely chosen, if it is likely to bring destruction in its wake—including, in these examples, harm to the real clients themselves, not their incumbent managements but the long-term corporate entities and their constituent stake-holders.

The real lesson from the defense lawyer's or advocate's role is simply that the lawyer is, in addition to being a private agent of his clients, a public agent of the legal system, whose job is to help clients steer their way through the maze of the law, to bring clients' conduct and behavior into conformity with the law—to get the client as much as possible of what the client wants without damaging the framework of the law. He may not act in furtherance of his client's interest in ways that ultimately frustrate, sabotage, or nullify the public purposes of the laws—or that injure the interests of clients, which are hypothetically constructed, as all public corporations should be, as good citizens who internalize legal norms and wish to act in furtherance of the public values they express.

NOTES ON GORDON

1. ***Evaluating Conceptions of the Corporate Counselor's Role.*** What are the various conceptions of the corporate counselor's role that Gordon identifies and rejects? Why does he find each of them defective? Do you agree with his critiques?

2. ***Corporations as Good Citizens?*** Do you agree with Gordon that lawyers who counsel corporations should construct the character of their clients for legal purposes as "good citizens who have internalized the public values expressed in law and the obligation to obey even laws they do not like"?

3. ***Can Lawyers Practice Competently and Ethically When Clients Leave Them in the Dark?*** Corporate clients sometimes keep lawyers involved in decision-making and in a position to detect misconduct and to influence the client toward legal compliance. But what happens when the client, such as Enron, disaggregates its work across many firms so that no one set of lawyers is entrusted with extensive information about the client's operations? Do you agree with Gordon that lawyers whose clients decline to give them the information they need to assess the legality of the client's objectives cannot practice competently and ethically and so should decline to represent such clients?

4. ***The Corporate Lawyer's Public Function.*** What public functions does a criminal defense lawyer serve? What public functions does a corporate

counselor serve? Does your answer to the latter question depend on how the lawyer conducts himself in that role?

* * *

The next two excerpts consider the consequences for corporate clients and lawyers when lawyers decline to offer independent advice to corporate management. Consider first William Allen's argument that professional independence is vital for serving corporate clients well and finding satisfaction in one's work as a business lawyer. The second excerpt, by David Wilkins, argues that excessive deference, which he calls the "agency model," leaves lawyers highly vulnerable to the misdeeds of powerful corporate clients.

CORPORATE GOVERNANCE AND A BUSINESS LAWYER'S DUTY OF INDEPENDENCE

William T. Allen
38 Suffolk University Law Review 1 (2004)

[W]hat arguments can support the happy thought that lawyers who subject their work for business clients to the discipline of their own independent review, will, if all other factors are held constant, tend to give more useful advice to their clients? Business clients are repeat players in most of the important contexts in which they have significant legal problems. They have ongoing relationships with government regulators, customers, suppliers, partners, joint-venturers, capital markets, etc. These relationships and the firm's reputation are valuable assets. Every action or dispute that affects the future of these relationships is likely to be optimally resolved only when appropriate weight is given to that fact. The zealous advocate can get in the way of a productive long-term relationship.

A legal counsel who views herself as an independent professional adds utility by helping her client see the reasonable limits of ambient legal ambiguity so that mutual satisfaction from important relationships can be achieved. An independent counselor never abandons a commitment to substantive legality. She will therefore ask what client action would most advantageously conform the client's activity to the principles underlying the relevant legal rule and protect future utility from the legal relationship at risk. The zealous advocate, on the other hand, asks whether there is any colorable argument that can be made to support an advantageous action. This approach—call it a litigator's stance—is shared, for example, by the accountant who invents abusive tax shelters, the lawyer who satisfies the aggressive opinion shopper, or the corporate lawyer who is willing to follow accounting technicality to call a loan a sale. This kind of advice may be an unavoidable stance in the one-shot litigation context, but it is dangerous to a business client in other settings.

In many instances, zealous advocacy attitudes will destroy or at least threaten states of mind that allow client firms to make relationship specific investments that produce value over time. To a substantial extent, large business corporations function on trust as well as on crisply defined legal rights. Trust is a valuable asset that emerges from a perception of shared norms of fair dealing, from patterns of prior fair practice, and from an expectation of future interactions. The diffusion of a zealous advocate mentality within a business firm, for example, would certainly erode trust and, in the long run, generate large increases in the costs of operating the firm. The detriments to the firm's relations with outside parties are not fundamentally different.

Think about what the zealous advocacy mentality might do in the context of a corporate crisis. In light of the Federal Organizational Sentencing Guidelines,* every large firm, from securities firms to chemical companies, must now be intensely concerned, not with stout resistance to law under every colorable theory clever counsel can imagine, but with compliance with regulatory law, with candor, and with voluntary remediation of violations. But corporate crises are not unique settings in which independent legal counseling will be valuable. In a business world in which all parties believed that their dealings were governed by the standards of zealous advocacy representation, sharply higher costs could be expected all over the place: in regulatory interactions, in commercial dispute resolution, and even in public product markets. Imagine, for example, the consequences of a zealous advocacy response to a product tampering scare.

Thus, except for the unfortunate pathologies that will arise in the one-shot litigation context, the world offers plenty of evidence that, for business clients, there is greater long-term value in legal services provided by lawyers whose zealous and loyal representation is constrained by a fundamental commitment to the finer ideals of the profession.

If the advice of talented lawyers with a developed sense of their own responsibilities as members of the bar will give more effective advice, why

* [Eds.: In 1991, the United States Sentencing Commission issued guidelines for federal judges imposing sentences on organizational defendants. These guidelines impose harsh penalties upon organizations whose employees or other agents commit federal crimes. The guidelines encourage organizations to develop "effective programs to prevent and detect violations of law," and identify seven "types of steps" that an effective program should include. Where organizations demonstrate an effort to implement the seven steps, judges impose lower sanctions. Revisions to the guidelines that took effect in 2004 contain new, heightened requirements for companies to try to detect and prevent violations of law and to establish an ethical culture. Those revisions require businesses to: ensure that the organization "has an effective compliance and ethics program"; "evaluate periodically the effectiveness of the organization's compliance and ethics program"; and "periodically assess the risk of criminal conduct and take appropriate steps to design, implement, or modify each requirement to reduce the risk of criminal conduct identified through this process." *See* United States Sentencing Commission, Organizational Guidelines, Chapter Eight—Sentencing of Organizations, https://www.ussc.gov/guidelines/2016-guidelines-manual/2016-chapter-8.]

do we observe great demand for zealous advocacy-inspired business advice? The problem lies largely in the "agency problem." The client of a corporate lawyer is the corporation, but the voice of the client is a human agent for the corporation. These officers inevitably have a shorter time horizon than the organization considered as a whole, and they have a set of incentives that are imperfectly matched with those of the firm. This disjunction in incentives is most obvious when we look at the incentive pay structures of senior management, but it is far more pervasive than that. Thus, while some business clients may sometimes appear to seek out lawyers without a commitment to independent professional judgment, not all corporations do, and it is plausible that those that seek aggressive or accommodating lawyers are not accurately expressing the best choice for the corporation.

Different and important reasons to keep alive the self-critical capacity that an independent attorney possesses concern the personal satisfactions drawn from our lives as lawyers.

Whether at the head of great Wall Street firms, or as trusted long-term advisors on Main Street, the role of independent counselor, not zealous advocate, is the role in which those who practice today are most likely to add value to their clients and to achieve the deeper satisfaction that seems absent from the lives of many lawyers.

Lawyers should be able to derive from their work in representing others some sense that they are contributing to the achievement of the deeper purposes of the justice system. We are too greatly invested in our professional lives to permit ourselves to merely be clever amoral agents. Certainly, we are not law enforcement officials; we serve a different role. But if we are to find our professional lives satisfying, our role as zealous advocates and loyal facilitators of legal transactions must be consistent with our role as independent professionals and moral actors dedicated to the achievement of the higher goals of the legal system. This role gives dignity and a sense of deeper meaning to our work as business lawyers.

NOTES ON ALLEN

1. ***Does Lawyer Independence Benefit Clients?*** According to Professor Allen, how do clients benefit when lawyers give them independent advice rather than telling them what they want to hear? In what ways does a "zealous advocacy mentality" harm corporate clients?

2. ***Reputation for Integrity as a Business Asset.*** Some commentators have observed that a lawyer's reputation for integrity may serve clients who wish to signal to outsiders the legality and respectability of the company's past or future conduct.[1] Does that claim seem plausible to you? Does

---

1 *See, e.g.*, Robert Gordon, *The Independence of Lawyers*, 68 B. U. L. REV. 1 (1988).

it also seem plausible that some corporate officers do not look for and reward such integrity in their lawyers?

3. ***The Agency Problem.*** In Allen's view, what is the "agency problem" that sometimes fuels demand for "zealous advocacy-inspired business advice"?

4. ***Benefits for Lawyers?*** According to Allen, how do business lawyers benefit in terms of personal satisfaction when they offer independent advice? Are there other types of potential benefits for lawyers?

TEAM OF RIVALS? TOWARD A NEW MODEL OF THE CORPORATE ATTORNEY-CLIENT RELATIONSHIP

David B. Wilkins
78 Fordham Law Review 2067 (2010)

There is arguably no more quoted, or in the minds of many lawyers beloved, understanding of the duties owed by an advocate to his or her client than Brougham's legendary speech in defense of Queen Caroline. Speaking on the floor of the House of Lords in 1820, Lord Brougham eloquently stated what many still believe to be the essence of the lawyer's role:

> An advocate, in the discharge of his duty, knows but one person in all the world, and that person is his client. To save that client by all means and expedients, and at all hazards and costs to other persons, and, amongst them, to himself, is his first and only duty; and in performing this duty he must not regard the alarm, the torments, the destruction which he may bring upon others. Separating the duty of a patriot from that of an advocate, he must go on reckless of the consequences, though it should be his unhappy fate to involve his country in confusion.*

For almost two centuries, these words have stood as the embodiment of the ideal of zealous advocacy that lawyers owe to their clients. But of late, there have also been many who have questioned whether such an extreme standard of partisanship—ignoring the "alarm," "torment," and "destruction" of others—is the proper standard for lawyers to take in all circumstances. [W]hatever the value of Brougham's conception in the context in which he made his famous claim—i.e., the representation of an individual criminal defendant facing the unchecked power of the King in circumstances where the defendant's head was quite literally on the line—this understanding has much less to recommend it when we consider how corporate lawyers ought to conceive of their duties, particularly in the area of regulatory compliance.

* [Eds.: Lord Brougham's speech occurred in his defense of Queen Caroline, estranged wife of King George IV, on charges of adultery and in connection with a bill aimed at dissolving the marriage and stripping Caroline of her royal title.]

[But] I want to suggest that the profession and those we purport to serve would do well to consider whether there is something more fundamentally wrong with applying Brougham's conception of the lawyer's role to the corporate context than the conflation of the standards of advocacy appropriate to the criminal context with those that should govern in civil or regulatory matters.

At the heart of Brougham's understanding of the lawyer's role stands a simple but powerful assumption: that the attorney-client relationship is essentially one of agency. Of course a lawyer "knows but one person in all the world" and is required to promote that person's interests "by all means and expedients and at all hazards and costs to other persons," even "to himself," Brougham would likely say. These are simply the duties that an agent owes to his or her principal. Lawyers are doing no more—and should be entitled to do no less—than others who are engaged by principals to protect their interests and pursue their goals

For all of its intuitive appeal, the agency model is no longer a helpful template for understanding the relationship between corporations and their outside firms.

A principal-agent model serves only to entrench the ability of powerful corporate-principals to impose their will on increasingly vulnerable lawyer-agents. Indeed, current market conditions have largely turned the traditional justification for the agency model on its head. By withholding information and manipulating incentives, sophisticated corporate clients now have the power to pressure their lawyers into taking risky or unethical actions that threaten to throw their law firms "into confusion" in the form of legal peril or financial ruin. "Innocent" lawyers who do not want to participate in such actions have no recourse other than to resign—or be fired.

Market conditions in the last decades of the 20th century made it increasingly difficult for lawyers to [stand up to client pressure to facilitate corporate misconduct].

[Wilkins then proceeds to spell out his idea for a set of reciprocal relations between lawyers and clients that would involve lawyers more directly in ensuring clients' legal compliance and would leave them less vulnerable to client wrongdoing. He argues that the relationship between large and sophisticated corporate clients and their increasingly large and sophisticated outside counsel is better conceptualized as a new kind of strategic alliance or partnership than as the typical agent-principal relationship envisioned by Brougham. He cites some examples of major corporations that have recently reduced the number of outside firms they use and involved those outside counsel much more extensively in the corporation's operation and ongoing efforts to promote legal compliance.]

NOTES ON WILKINS

1. ***Relations Between In-House Counsel and Outside Firms.*** Studies of large law firms (see Chapter 8) have found that corporations' in-house counsel have gained power since 1970 as they assumed greater control in hiring and firing outside law firms. Large law firms tend to be hired today for specific matters rather than to handle all of a corporation's legal work, and there is greater competition among law firms to be selected to handle corporate work. How might the decreased power of outside lawyers relative to in-house counsel have made lawyers in law firms less willing to offer independent advice to their clients?

2. ***Lawyer Vulnerability and Corporate Scandals.*** Is Professor Wilkins right to suggest that corporate lawyers' involvement in various corporate scandals over the past few decades is partly a consequence of their vulnerability to client demands under an agency conception of the attorney-client relationship? As you consider this question, you might review the facts of the O.P.M., Lincoln Savings/Kaye Scholer, Enron, and Refco scandals described in Chapter 8.

3. ***Internal Investigations.*** Similar issues of lawyer independence arise when a corporation or other organization hires a law firm to conduct an internal investigation of possible wrongdoing by or within the organization. Many corporate law firms now list investigations among the services they offer.[2] Lawyers who conduct such investigations must exercise independence and act reasonably and in the best interests of the client organization.

Lawyers who fail to meet those obligations sometimes find themselves in serious trouble. In *Kirschner v. K&L Gates, LLP,* 46 A.3d. 737 (Pa. Super. Ct. 2012), a firm hired by a company's board of directors to investigate concerns about CEO wrongdoing failed to find any evidence of fraud or malfeasance, when, in fact, the CEO had engaged in gross misconduct that led to the company's bankruptcy. The court concluded that the firm's failure to uncover the misconduct could constitute negligence, malpractice, and breach of fiduciary duty.

More recently, Skadden Arps Slate Meagher & Flom LLP became the subject of intense scrutiny over its handling of an investigation into and report on the prosecution of one of former Ukrainian president Victor Yanukovych's political rivals, Yulia Tymoshenko. Court filings by federal prosecutors allege that Skadden's report was not competent and independent but instead was a whitewash designed to lend false credence to the Ukrainian government's claim that its prosecution of Tymoshenko was conducted fairly and was not politically motivated.[3] The firm was paid more than $4 million for the report. Special counsel Robert Mueller, who uncovered evidence of the matter in

[2] Andrew Longstreth, *Double Agent: In the New Era of Internal Investigations, Defense Lawyers Have Become Deputy Prosecutors*, AM. LAWYER, 68–69 Feb. 2005.

[3] *See* Stephanie Baker, *Manafort Plea Delivers Yet Another Embarrassment for Skadden*, BLOOMBERG, Sept. 14, 2018, https://www.bloomberg.com/news/articles/2018-09-14/skadden-s-work-with-manafort-in-ukraine-extended-beyond-report.

connection with the investigation of Russian involvement in the 2016 presidential election, referred an investigation into the firm's work in the matter to the U.S. Attorney's Office for the Southern District of New York. The Skadden lawyers could face criminal liability if they knew that Paul Manafort would use their work in a lobbying effort on behalf of the Ukrainian government without registering with the United States government. They could also face bar sanctions for violating their ethical obligations. At issue are not only the duties of competence and independence in the preparation of the report, but also prohibitions on assisting a client in conduct that the lawyer knows is criminal or fraudulent, and engaging in conduct that is prejudicial to the administration of justice.[4]

D. COUNSELING GOVERNMENT CLIENTS

The distinction between advocacy and counseling also applies to lawyers who advise governmental clients. The following excerpt sets forth some of the relevant law and the generally accepted understanding of the professional duties of these lawyers in their advisory roles. It also addresses how government lawyers should respond if faced with pressure to approve unlawful policies and actions.

GOVERNMENT LAWYERS IN THE TRUMP ADMINISTRATION

W. Bradley Wendel
69 Hastings L. J. 275 (2017)

The President is entitled to have his policy positions respected and implemented by Executive Branch actors. Lawyers who advise the Executive Branch are obligated, by generally applicable agency law, rules of professional conduct, and longstanding traditions of professional ethics, to seek to further the client's lawful objectives. While any official "elected or appointed to an office of honor or profit in the civil service" must take an oath to support and defend the Constitution, lawyers have additional obligations. A lawyer may not "counsel a client to engage, or assist a client, in conduct that the lawyer knows is criminal or fraudulent." Depending on the nature of the client's proposed course of conduct and the lawyer's state of mind with respect to it, a lawyer may have at least the right, and possibly also the duty, to refuse to provide assistance. Lawyers also have duties of competence, communication, and independence.

The lawyers that are the primary concern of this analysis are serving as counselors; they provide advice to government actors on the legality of a proposed course of action. Because the client is receiving advice from only one side, it is essential that the lawyer provide a balanced treatment of the law and not just the type of partisan argument that would be appropriate

---

[4] See Rebecca Roiphe, *Paul Manafort's Lawyers May Have Broken the Law*, SLATE, Sept. 19, 2018.

in litigation. [P]roviding clear, candid, impartial legal analysis is one of a lawyer's core obligations, and that obligation in no way resembles the litigators' duty to zealously advocate for the client.

[T]he ethical analysis of lawyers in an advisory role should focus on whether the advice represents a reasonable application of relevant authority.

The assessment of legal interpretation requires engagement with the craft values that inform good lawyering. Criteria for excellent or even adequate performance are internal to the craft; they are given by the ends for which it is constituted. The lawyer's role as an advisor is to ensure the client has accurate information about what the law permits or requires. By implication, then, the reasonableness of a lawyer's application of relevant authority can be assessed by considering evidence tending to show either that the lawyer tried to get the law right, or not. This evidence will likely include facts about the lawyer's handling of adverse authority and counterarguments, consideration of the interpretive community's assessment of the argument, and the completeness of the set of information provided to the client about the applicable law.

NOTES ON ADVISING GOVERNMENT CLIENTS

1. ***Who Is the Client?*** We've already seen some of the special difficulties that lawyers encounter while representing corporations rather than flesh-and-blood individuals who can speak for themselves. The situation can be even more challenging for lawyers in government practice, where client identity and lines of authority can be even less clear than they are in the corporate representation. How do the challenges of identifying the client relate to the challenges of counseling government clients?

2. ***Another "Agency Problem."*** Recall that Allen identified an "agency problem" that sometimes fuels demand for "zealous advocacy-inspired business advice" in the context of corporate counseling. Wendel identifies a similar problem for lawyers in government counseling—that is "the potential divergence between the lawyer's view of the interests of the represented agency and the views of its incumbent agency head." Using the example of the White House Counsel's Office, he offers this explanation:

> Consider the White House Counsel's Office which, by tradition represents the office of the President, not necessarily the interests of the specific President currently serving in office. A lawyer serving in that office must be attentive to the long-range interests of the Presidency, and have the independence and fortitude to resist demands by the current President that may be contrary to these longer-term interests. Of course, the incumbent President may see this kind of resistance as disloyal. . . . This may be referred to as an *apparent* agency problem, because what the President perceives as disloyal may in fact be respect for the obligations of White House

> Counsel. The important point to see here is that this principle [of correctly identifying the client] is not formalistic, but supports an allocation of power to make decisions on behalf of the government, and ultimately on behalf of all citizens subject to the decisions of democratically elected officials. A government lawyer is the agent of the citizens of the nation, and stands in a co-agency relationship with the elected officials who may think of themselves (wrongly) as the client of the lawyer. [Like corporate lawyers who tend to conflate the interests of corporate management and the interests of the client organization], government lawyers engage in similarly fallacious reasoning when they defer to the interests of individual government officials, rather than acting in the best interests of the agency or the executive branch itself.[5]

If a government lawyer suspects that an official who is giving her instructions is acting in the interests of an individual government official rather than the agency or the executive branch itself, what are her options?

Donald McGahn, White House Counsel to President Trump, threatened to resign in June 2017 rather than follow an order to ask the Department of Justice to fire special counsel Robert Mueller. McGahn reportedly told senior White House officials that firing Mueller would have a catastrophic effect on Mr. Trump's presidency.[6] Why is a threat to resign sometimes an effective tactic for a high-profile government lawyer trying to influence a government official to change course? Would it also sometimes be an effective tactic for lawyers in private practice or in-house counsel positions who believe that a corporation's senior management plan to engage in risky or unethical conduct?

3. ***What Is at Stake?*** Why is it important for government lawyers to exercise independence in their counseling roles? Speaking of the responsibilities of lawyers who provide advice to presidents, former Justice Department attorney Harold Bruff offered this assessment of the stakes:

> The president's lawyers must translate the Delphic materials of the Constitution and the often opaque or conflicting statutes into real advice about the limits of law. This process is crucial to the operation of our government. In the realms of foreign policy and war, where the courts rarely intrude, the advice of the president's lawyers may well be final, in the sense that the executive action that implements it will not be reviewed by any court. Hence, whether the Constitution and statutes actually do bind the president is often a function of the relationship between the president and his or her lawyers. Accustomed as most Americans are to discovering what the law is from the pronouncements of the Supreme Court, it is unsettling to

---

[5] W. Bradley Wendel, *Government Lawyers in the Trump Administration,* 69 HASTINGS L. J. 275, 305 (2017).

[6] Michael S. Schmidt & Maggie Haberman, *Trump Ordered Mueller Fired, But Backed Off When White House Counsel Threatened to Quit,* N.Y. TIMES, Jan. 25, 2018.

> contemplate a law-deciding mechanism that exists mostly or wholly within the executive branch. Yet exist it does . . . .[7]

E. SUMMARY

This chapter considered the distinction between counseling and advocacy and why differences in the procedural context in which counseling and advocacy occurs might affect lawyers' responsibilities in these two types of work. We explored the special challenges and responsibilities of lawyers who advise corporate and governmental clients. Finally, we considered how independence in counseling relate to the interests of lawyers, clients, and society.

---

[7] Harold H. Bruff, BAD ADVICE: BUSH'S LAWYERS IN THE WAR ON TERROR 2 (2009).

CHAPTER 10

IN-HOUSE COUNSEL

■ ■ ■

A. INTRODUCTION

In-house lawyers (also called "inside counsel"), who are employed directly by their corporate clients, play an important role in the operation of major businesses. They generally hold responsibility for providing basic legal advice, selecting and monitoring outside attorneys, and preventing legal problems. Their duties have changed significantly since the 1960s, when in-house counsel were often viewed as inferior lawyers who could not make it in the competition for big firm partnerships. Beginning in the 1970s, corporations began to find it more efficient to handle routine and recurring matters in-house rather than to pay high fees for outside counsel. Corporations increasingly looked to outside firms to handle specialized matters only on a transaction-specific basis, meaning that they hired outside counsel to handle particular cases and transactions rather than whole categories of needs. Meanwhile, the general counsel (the most senior in-house lawyer) acquired new status as the manager of all of the corporation's legal services, with responsibility for hiring outside counsel, controlling the costs of legal services purchased from outside law firms and other legal services providers, and ensuring that the corporation complies with the law. The number of in-house lawyers in the U.S. has increased from about 40,000 in 1996 to over 100,000 in 2017.[1]

The chapter has four sections. The first examines the various functions of in-house counsel, in-house counsel's relationship with outside counsel, and the allocation of responsibilities between them. The second considers the question of professional independence—the extent to which in-house counsel can and should guide their clients toward legal compliance and how that occurs. The third section examines a series of scandals in which in-house lawyers have been involved and whether and how lawyers might have averted these disastrous episodes. The fourth section explores the roles of in-house counsel post-Enron.

[1] Hugh A. Simons and Gina Passarella, *The Rise (and Fall?) of In-House Counsel*, AM. LAWYER, Feb. 25, 2018.

B. WHAT DO IN-HOUSE COUNSEL DO?

In-house lawyers are called upon to handle a variety of law-related tasks within the corporation. Some, for example, may be primarily responsible for drafting contracts relating to the company's operations, while others are responsible for ensuring that the company complies with all relevant law relating to its hiring, firing, and ongoing relations with employees, environmental regulations, tax and regulatory filings, and technology licensing. In-house lawyers typically also handle the corporation's real estate matters. They often develop risk-management policies and educate other employees to avoid legal trouble. They are sometimes responsible for litigating basic matters, and they generally oversee higher stakes cases that the corporation farms out to law firms. Some in-house lawyers are generalists, while others specialize. The lead inside lawyer, the General Counsel, usually is part of the corporation's senior management team.

The first excerpt reports findings from a study based on 86 interviews with in-house counsel, legally trained executives, and non-lawyer managers in 46 large corporations and financial institutions in Northern California, Chicago, and New York. The authors found that in-house counsel played three primary roles: "cops" (also sometimes called "gatekeepers"), who ensure that the company complies with the law; "counsel," who advise the company; and "entrepreneurs," who market legal advice as a means of helping the company meet its financial goals. Lawyers might play each of these roles exclusively, or they might wear different hats depending on the circumstances.

COPS, COUNSEL, AND ENTREPRENEURS: CONSTRUCTING THE ROLE OF INSIDE COUNSEL IN LARGE CORPORATIONS

Robert L. Nelson & Laura Beth Nielsen
34 Law & Society Review 457 (2000)

Our analysis of the interviews suggested that lawyers played three ideal typical roles: some spoke of their role as narrowly legal, some spoke of mixing legal and business advice, and some emphasized entrepreneurial or profit-generating uses of law. Bearing in mind that the ways lawyers describe their tasks are complex and sometimes contested by others in the organization, we attempted to devise a conceptual scheme that would allow us to classify individual lawyers by role type [as cops, counsel, and entrepreneurs].

Cops. When corporate counsel are playing the "cop" role, they are primarily concerned with policing the conduct of their business clients. (In many interviews, the corporate counsel refer to various businesspeople and business units within their corporation as their "clients," even though technically both lawyers and the business personnel are employees of the same organization.) They interact with business people almost exclusively through legal gatekeeping functions, such as approving contracts, imposing and implementing compliance programs, and responding to legal questions. Cops are less willing [than in-house lawyers in other roles] to offer non-legal advice, even when they have the opportunity.

The vice president for legal affairs for a major chemical firm exemplified the role of lawyer as cop. He was hired for the position from outside the corporation after a distinguished career in government and private practice. He interpreted his hiring as an effort by the corporation to bring in someone who would be independent within the corporate environment.

> I think that the thought is when you get somebody who has an independent stature, apart from his or her position in the corporation, that the person is also more likely to be independent and give you that independent professional judgment that is so essential.

Even though he was a member of the corporation's Board of Directors and the corporation's Executive Committee, he characterized his work "principally as a lawyer." A theme that consistently emerged in this interview, despite some discussion of lawyers attempting to act as part of the management team in the various subsidiaries of the corporation, was the need for lawyers to say no.

> I mean there are [business] people who want to do something and they just simply can't do it, they can't understand why, and then I say, "Well, that's just the way the law is."

Counsel. The role that corporate lawyers most often play is the counsel. Counsel most often confine their advice to legal questions and legitimate their suggestions or demands based on legal knowledge. Yet the counsel role implies a broader relationship with business actors that affords counsel an opportunity to make suggestions based on business, ethical, and situational concerns.

Our exemplar of this type, a general counsel in a bank, described this mixture of legal and business functions.

> Forty percent of my time is spent managing the legal position, . . . 20% of my time is as the bank's chief compliance officer: dealing with regulators, overviewing the auditing process within the bank, [overseeing] training done by the legal division . . . Another 30% of my time is as consigliere of executive and senior management: I am the counselor; I am the guy who is asked to draft letters; to advise on particular issues, which can overlap with the first two primarily because it relates to the regulators . . . The remaining 10% of my time I practice law.

Our ideal typical counsel appears to be quite broadly involved in important managerial decisions; he draws on both legal and other forms of knowledge, and, according to his own account, he is highly influential.

Entrepreneurs. Although the ideal typical "counsel" is still primarily concerned with the legal aspects of business, entrepreneurs emphasize business values in their work. Entrepreneurial lawyers say law is not merely a necessary complement to corporate functions, law can itself be a source of profits, an instrument to be used aggressively in the marketplace, or the mechanism through which major transactions are executed. Our exemplar of the entrepreneur is the general counsel of a holding company, not yet 40 years old at the time of the interview, with a law degree from Harvard. He had been a securities specialist in a large corporate law firm before moving to his corporate employer, where he had worked his way up from being an inside transactional lawyer to general counsel of several subsidiaries, until reaching one of the top two law positions in the corporation. He became most animated in the interview when talking about the size of the "deals" he had put together, such as taking various subsidiaries public, the "phenomenal multiple" they had achieved in an especially large public offering, and the major acquisitions he had worked on for the corporation. His role, and that of many of the lawyers in the corporation, went well beyond giving legal advice.

Our entrepreneurial general counsel offered a telling contrast between his approach to his job and that of another general counsel in the corporation, a lawyer who was more senior than our informant, whom our informant had reported to prior to assuming a parallel position in the corporation. Our informant described why he thought he would eventually rise above his former superior.

[His comments suggested that his competitor was] a "cop" who was more influential in the corporation in an earlier era, when it "needed" a corporate conscience. According to our informant, the need for that role has diminished as the management of the corporation has become more professionalized. He attributes his own rise to influence to his ability to be a business counselor. Indeed, he expects to run the company some day in the future.

What is the motivating force in our informant's career?—his interest in making money and growing the company.

NOTES ON NELSON & NIELSEN

1. ***What Are the Roles?*** What exactly does a lawyer in each of these roles—cop, counsel, or entrepreneur—do for the corporation? Which of these role types is mostly likely to serve the corporation's interests? Does your answer depend upon the situation?

2. ***Playing Multiple Roles.*** Notice that Nelson & Nielsen are not claiming that individual in-house lawyers necessarily play just one of these roles. They might instead pursue different lawyering styles at different times, depending on the circumstances.

3. ***What Are the Personality Traits of Lawyers in These Positions?*** What characteristics would you expect to be most important for lawyers in each of these roles? Which of these roles would fit your own personality and aptitudes best?

* * *

Inside Counsel's Relationship with Outside Counsel. As noted in the materials on large firms, inside counsel have gained substantial power vis-à-vis outside counsel during the past three decades. Inside counsel once handled primarily routine and low-stakes work within the corporation, while outside counsel served as the corporation's true legal advisors. But inside counsel—and especially the lead in-house lawyer, the general counsel (GC)—now play much more powerful roles. The general counsel, not the senior partner in the law firm, is often the primary counselor for the CEO and the board on law, ethics, and risk.[2] In addition, inside counsel also decide what work will stay inside, what work will go to outside firms, and which firms will be hired to handle the outsourced work. That transformation in the role of inside counsel has gone hand-in-hand with their increased role in management. According to a recent study by Deloitte, the number of in-house attorneys who are members of the senior management/executive team rose from 47 percent in 2005 to 62 percent in 2010. The same study concluded that general counsel held a wider set of responsibilities than they did five years earlier and that they were more likely to be the first source of advice for senior management when serious legal or regulatory issues arise. Almost three-quarters of the 877 interviewed lawyers upon which the report was based said that the general counsel had greater influence in a business environment than a partner in a large law firm, compared with 35 percent who said that corporate counsel were more influential five years before.[3] One former general counsel of a major corporation has argued that these changes represent "a dramatic shift in power from outside private firms to inside law departments," which has contributed to a "dramatic[ ]" improvement in the quality of general counsel over the past two decades.[4]

Credentials and Identities. Just as the power of in-house counsel has increased vis-à-vis outside lawyers, there also has been an increase in the educational credentials and prior work experience of lawyers who work

---

[2] *See* Ben W. Heineman, Jr. *The Rise of the General Counsel*, HARV. BUS. REV., Sept. 27, 2012.

[3] DELOITTE GLOBAL CORPORATE COUNSEL REPORT 2011: HOW THE GAME IS CHANGING (2011).

[4] Ben W. Heineman, Jr., *The Rise of the General Counsel*, HARV. BUS. REV., Sept. 27, 2012.

in corporate legal departments. GCs now regularly come from the top ranks of law firm partners. Corporate legal departments rarely hire lawyers directly out of law school, but they are able to attract senior associates from premier law firms.

The demographic composition of corporate legal departments has also changed since the 1980s, when they began to attract significant numbers of female lawyers. Women now comprise 25 percent of the GCs of *Fortune 500* companies, which is considerably more than women's 19 percent share of equity partnerships in law firms.[5]

C. IN-HOUSE COUNSEL AND PROFESSIONAL INDEPENDENCE

One persistent question about in-house counsel has been whether they are able to exercise independent judgment. The traditional view has been that in-house counsel's economic and psychological dependence on her sole "client"—her employer—prevents her from monitoring her client's conduct and offering unwelcome advice. According to this view, pressure to perform as a "team player" undermines autonomy and interferes with the in-house lawyer's ability to protect the corporation from illegality.

The following excerpt focuses on the difficulty that in-house counsel sometimes face when they find themselves deprived of information they need to perform their jobs.

MORAL MAZES: THE WORLD OF CORPORATE MANAGERS

Robert Jackall
122–123 (Oxford University Press 1988)

Drawing lines when information is scarce becomes doubly ambiguous, a problem that often emerges in shaping relationships with one's colleagues. For instance, Black, a lawyer at Covenant Corporation, received a call from a chemical plant manager who had just been served with an order from the local fire department to build retaining dikes around several storage tanks for toxic chemicals so that firemen would not be in danger of being drenched with the substance should the tanks burst if there were a fire at the plant. The plant manager indicated that meeting the order would cause him to miss his numbers badly that year and he wondered aloud if the fire chief might, for a consideration, be persuaded to forget the whole thing. Black pointed out that he could not countenance even a discussion of bribery; the plant manager laughed and said that he was only joking and would think things over and get back to Black in a few weeks. Black never heard from the plant manager about this issue again; when they met on different occasions after that, the conversation was always framed around

5 David B. Wilkins, *The In-House Counsel Movement,* THE PRACTICE, May 2016.

other subjects. Black did inquire discreetly and found out that no dikes had been built; the plant manager had apparently gone shopping for a more flexible legal opinion. Should he, Black wondered, pursue the matter or in the absence of any firm evidence just let things drop, particularly since others, for their own purposes, could misconstrue the fact that he had not acted on his earlier marginal knowledge? Feeling that one is in the dark can be somewhat unnerving.

More unnerving, however, is the feeling that one is being kept in the dark. Reed, another lawyer at Covenant, was working on the legal issues of a chemical dumpsite that Alchemy Inc. [a subsidiary of Covenant] had sold. He suddenly received a call from a former employee who had been having trouble with the company on his pension payments; this man told Reed that unless things were straightened out in a hurry, he planned to talk to federal officials about all the pesticides buried in the site. This was alarming news. Reed had no documentation about pesticides in the site; if Alchemy had buried pesticides there, a whole new set of regulations might apply to the situation and to Covenant as the former owner. Reed went to the chemical company's director of personnel to get the former employee's file but was unable to obtain it. Reed's boss agreed to help, but still the director of personnel refused to release the file. After repeated calls, Reed was told that the file had been lost. Reed went back to his boss and inquired whether it might be prudent for Covenant to repurchase the site to keep it under control. This was deemed a good idea. However, the asking price for the site was now three times what Covenant had sold it for. Everyone, of course, got hesitant; another lawyer became involved and began working closely with Reed's boss on the issue. Gradually, Reed found himself excluded from discussions about the problem and unable to obtain information that he felt was important to his work. His anxiety was heightened because he felt he was involved in a matter of some legal gravity. But, like much else in the corporation, this problem disappeared in the night. Eventually, Reed was assigned to other cases and he knew that the doors to the issue were closed, locked, and bolted.

NOTE ON JACKALL

What Should Black and Reed Do? How would you respond in the situations facing Black and Reed? What are the personal and professional risks to these lawyers if they do nothing? What are the risks if they pursue the matters?

* * *

Consider the findings on lawyer independence in Nelson & Nielsen's study of inside counsel in the late 1990s:

COPS, COUNSEL, AND ENTREPRENEURS: CONSTRUCTING THE ROLE OF INSIDE COUNSEL IN LARGE CORPORATIONS

Robert L. Nelson & Laura Beth Nielsen
34 Law & Society Review 457 (2000)

The Gatekeeping Function: Pervasive but Circumscribed. When the corporate attorney acts as a gatekeeper, he or she monitors legal compliance and serves as a final hurdle or "gate" through which business ideas must pass prior to implementation. The ability to "trump" a business decision has been identified by researchers as a source of contention and confusion for both lawyers and their business clients from the earliest studies.

One lawyer put it this way:

> When individuals in the organization come to me and say, "will you help me execute my deal?" if I come across to them or the lawyers on my staff come across to them as cops, they are not going to come to us. They are . . . either going to go elsewhere or operate in the dark without lawyers.

This lawyer identifies two possible negative outcomes of behaving too much like a cop. The business people will simply go without legal advice, or they will engage in an intra-organizational version of "forum shopping," bringing their problems to the lawyer in the company who is least likely to challenge the business-person's project.

Lawyers and business executives recognize that without some level of autonomy, counsel would not be able to guard the corporation from unwise legal risks. The interviews have a somewhat schizophrenic character in this respect. Lawyers indicated that they have the autonomy required to act independently and to be "deal-stoppers," but several claimed that their companies are "very ethical." When they observed clear cases of legal problems, informants were sure that their company would do everything required to ensure legal compliance. When questioned, almost every attorney could imagine a situation in which he or she would go over the head of management to become a deal-stopper, but few could recall situations in which they had actually done so.

Yet some attorneys acknowledged that their autonomy is constrained by the need to "get the deal done." Although their "official" role is to advise on legal risks, the business-people would prefer it if the lawyers gave only business-friendly legal advice. One lawyer explained, "Every business manager says they want honesty. They don't mean it, none of them mean it." In fact, this lawyer said that in his corporation, "it's a no-no to say no."

Another general counsel indicated that to whom lawyers report was very significant to him. He said that

> Lawyers . . . report to the General Counsel, they do not report to business. That was a deliberate decision. I mean, that might even become, for me, a "resignation" kind of decision, but I don't think there's any prospect of it turning into that kind of issue. But I feel strongly about that—it's my job to protect their independence.

Apparently this general counsel would oppose decentralizing the legal function by placing lawyers under the authority of business units. Attorneys in centralized departments sometimes have difficulty learning what is happening throughout the corporation. An attorney who practiced in a centralized legal department complained that sometimes he had to "hunt down and chase and spy on [the business executives] in order to try to keep them in line."

Deploying lawyers in a decentralized structure, by housing them in functional units such as Human Resources or Engineering, allows lawyers to "stop [legally questionable] things earlier and know about those things earlier." Yet nesting attorneys in functional divisions exposes them to more intense pressure to agree with their business colleagues rather than offer objective legal advice.

No matter how much a lawyer may wish to be the moral compass of the organization and provide expert legal advice all the time, there are practical constraints on his or her ability to do so. The practical constraints most often mentioned by our respondents were lack of resources and profit pressures. One lawyer spoke of the bind between providing quality legal advice and keeping the costs associated with the legal department within a range that is acceptable to the businesspeople. She said,

> There simply aren't enough lawyers. There's enormous pressure to control costs and yet there's an inconsistent pressure . . . They have simultaneously said, "You've got to control expenses and you can't hire and in fact, you have to cut . . . " So you know that you're not doing the job all that well. You know you don't have enough people; you know you can't get any more.

Inside counsel, like their business peers, are under intense pressure to meet business objectives. The lawyers working in these conditions are, like the business professionals with whom they work, held responsible for the bottom line of their division. These constraints and pressures affect all three types of inside counsel. They render the gatekeeping functions, and indeed other advisory functions, more difficult to perform.

Obviously some of our respondents interpose legal opinions that frustrate the plans of the business executives. Even the attorneys who claim to have the power to be deal-stoppers admit that they must use this power judiciously, however. Half of the lawyers in our sample acknowledge that, most of the time, the businesspeople in the company make the final determination regarding whether to assume a legal risk. The lawyer's role is reduced to informing business executives about the legal risks associated with different actions.

The blending of law and business makes it sometimes difficult for one to establish exactly who is making final decisions regarding business matters. Who makes the final decision is a function of the nature of the issue at hand, the personalities of the people involved, and the complexity of the legal matter involved. One lawyer explained it this way:

> Our job is to assess risks, and it's the businessperson's job to make decisions about risks, what risks they are willing to assume. Now, having said that, I also think of it as my job to make sure that the decision about what risks to assume is being made at the appropriate level. So, if somebody was prepared to assume a risk which I felt was inappropriate, I would say, "I don't think this is a decision for you to make. I need to talk to your boss."

In these comments the lawyer reveals a recognition of the distinction between business decisions and legal decisions, a preference to make only "legal" decisions, and a desire for the businessperson to make the "business" decisions. Nonetheless, the lawyer retains the power to ensure that the business decisions are being handled appropriately.

Corporate counsel who participate in the top management of their companies are different in this respect, however. Ten of 11 respondents who were part of the corporate or divisional management (91%) indicated that they made the final decision about whether to incur a legal risk, whereas only 35% of other lawyers claimed to make the final decision about legal risk. If all questions of legal risk percolated to a legal officer in top management, lawyers would be making such judgments. The clear impression from the interviews, however, is that not all questions go up the legal chain of command. Moreover, corporate counsel in top management contain the same proportions of cops, counsel, and entrepreneurs as the entire sample. They appear, therefore, to confront the same tensions as other lawyers in balancing gatekeeping and entrepreneurial roles.

Views Across the Law/Business Divide: A Mixture of Suspicion and Appreciation. Lawyers' attitudes about the businesspeople in their organization may affect how these lawyers approach their work. Several informants reported altering the legal advice they provide according to how they think business executives view them, as well as how they assess business executives' knowledge of the law and business ethics. Inside counsel often noted the legal sophistication of higher levels of management.

Yet a substantial minority of informants criticized businesspeople for poor business judgment and for failing to understand basic legal principles. Less insidious, but no less problematic, a number of lawyers indicated that the businesspeople were simply ignorant regarding the importance of the law and lawyers within the organization.

Conversely, lawyers recognize that businesspeople do not always think highly of lawyers' roles within the company. Inside counsel report that businesspeople "do not really want to have them around," think of them as a "necessary evil," "don't associate lawyers with creative solutions," and do not view them as "team players."

Blending Law and Business. In a sense, all the lawyer roles we identify blend legal and business objectives. When a lawyer acts as a cop, he or she serves business by ensuring that the company meets its legal obligations. When a lawyer acts as a counsel, he or she tries to find legal means for doing business. When a lawyer acts as entrepreneur, his or her service to business is more obvious because the lawyer's goals and the businessperson's goals are the same—only the expertise is different.

[I]n order to ensure that business professionals will continue to consult them, lawyers try to make their advice more palatable to businesspeople. This marketing of the legal function is a response to a perceived threat.

As one lawyer-entrepreneur explained, "We need to make [the business executives] feel as though, by and large, our overall outlook is to try to help them accomplish the things they are trying to do, and, by and large, that's true and it's fine." Other general counsel related that they were trying to change how their departments were perceived in their respective corporations. [One] said,

> [A] significant part of our department was conceived, or seen, by the business people as a barrier to getting the job done, something to be gotten around, or past, or through, or whatever, and . . . we really needed to do some work to reestablish ourselves as counselors or partners.

Lawyers are now eager to be seen as part of the company, rather than as obstacles to getting things done. To do so, it appears that inside counsel are themselves interested in discounting their gatekeeping function in corporate affairs.

NOTES ON NELSON & NIELSEN

1. ***Are In-House Counsel Less Independent?*** As a general matter, are in-house lawyers likely to exercise more or less independence from clients than outside counsel? What factors, other than practice setting, are likely to influence corporate lawyers' ethical autonomy?

2. ***Can Team Players Be Independent?*** If, as Nelson & Nielsen suggest, many in-house counsel feel the need to prove themselves to be team players rather than nay-sayers, what are the implications for the in-house lawyer's professional independence? Is it possible to reconcile team participation and professional independence?

3. ***In-House Counsel and Corporate Scandal.*** Might there be some connection between the attitudes that Nelson & Nielsen describe and some of the corporate scandals noted in the chapter on large firm lawyers and the additional ones noted below?

D. CORPORATE SCANDALS AND THE ROLE OF IN-HOUSE COUNSEL

Here we consider a series of episodes in which in-house counsel were implicated in corporate scandals. In all of these incidents, there was plenty of blame to go around. We do not mean to suggest that the in-house counsel were the primary culprits. But in each of these incidents, in-house lawyers appear to have participated in, or failed to prevent, misbehavior that led to major damage to the company's earnings and/or reputation, as well as harm to the company's employees, stockholders, and others. As you read these stories, consider what in-house counsel might have done differently.

The Hewlett Packard Pretexting Scandal. On September 5, 2006, *Newsweek* revealed that Hewlett-Packard (HP), at the request of HP's chairwoman, Patricia Dunn, had hired a team of security experts to investigate board members and several journalists to identify the source of a leak of confidential information about HP's long-term business strategies. The security experts, in turn, used a spying technique known as pretexting, which involved using investigators impersonating HP board members and journalists in order to obtain their phone records. After the pretexting came to light, HP's general counsel, Ann Baskins, resigned, just hours before she was scheduled to appear as a witness before a U.S. House of Representatives committee that was investigating the spying scandal. The following article analyzes Baskins' role.

SAW NO EVIL

Sue Reisinger

Corporate Counsel (Online), Jan. 1, 2007[6]

Ann Baskins stood on September 28 before a congressional committee investigating the Hewlett-Packard Company spying scandal. Just hours earlier she had made the painful decision to resign as general counsel of the giant computer company. Standing before the committee, she held her right hand in the air and swore to tell the truth. Then, on the first question, Baskins exercised her Fifth Amendment right to remain silent and refused to tell anything.

While Baskins sat quietly, former HP chairwoman Patricia Dunn and CEO Mark Hurd told the committee that Baskins was to blame for the

[6] Reprinted with permission from the January 1, 2007 online version of Corporate Counsel.

mess. They said that she had given them bad legal advice, and that she knew about and permitted the use of "pretexting"—using false pretenses to obtain personal information about others.

Little has been written about Baskins's role in the spying efforts, but an in-depth analysis of more than 1,500 pages of documents, as well as interviews with people close to the investigation, offers insights into how she let the spying probe spin out of control. The records, which include HP e-mails and interviews conducted by lawyers at Palo Alto-based Wilson Sonsini as part of the company's internal investigation, were made public by the House committee.

In the end, the HP scandal comes down to this: The spying probe became a runaway train. And Ann Baskins was the person in the best position to recognize the danger and stop it. But she didn't. In fact, the records show that from June 2005 to April 2006, Baskins raised legal questions about the tactics at least six times. But she never pushed for a definitive answer about whether the methods used were, in fact, lawful. Or, more importantly, whether they were unwise and dangerous to the company.

The beginning of the end for Baskins, 51, came in February of 2005, when Dunn and her allies on the board forced out then-CEO and chairwoman Carleton "Carly" Fiorina. The directors chose Dunn to chair the board. On April 1 Hurd became CEO, but someone had leaked news of his appointment to the press a few days earlier. An irate Dunn hired a Boston-based private investigator named Ron DeLia to search for the leaker. (The California attorney general later accused Dunn of providing DeLia with the home, office, and cell phone numbers of various HP directors and managers.) Records show that Dunn initiated those first spying efforts—without Baskins's knowledge—on April 19. Dunn named the spy probe Project Kona because she was vacationing in Hawaii at the time.

Why did Dunn act on her own at first? Records suggest she may have done so because HP's internal corporate politics were roiling. Dunn suspected everyone, including Baskins, as a possible leaker. And Baskins noted in the Wilson Sonsini interviews that her working relationship with Dunn and the board was "strained" by all the distrust at that time.

Dunn brought Baskins into the loop two months later. On June 14, according to e-mails and congressional testimony, DeLia e-mailed a seven-page report to Dunn that discussed the phone record searches and used the word "pretexting." Dunn forwarded a copy to Baskins the same day.

Dunn told DeLia that Baskins would join them in a teleconference call the next day to discuss the report. During that June 15 call, DeLia told the two women that telephone records were obtained by ruse from a telecommunications carrier, and he explained the word "pretexting" to them, according to the complaint filed by the attorney general's office. Baskins made sketchy, handwritten notes referring to "pretexting."

According to an affidavit attached to the AG's complaint, "DeLia recalled that Baskins was curious about pretexting and concerned about its legality, and had asked DeLia whether it was lawful. DeLia replied that he was aware of no laws that made pretexting illegal, and was aware of no criminal prosecutions for such activities." Asked in later interviews why she didn't challenge the pretexting when she first learned it involved acts of deceit, Baskins said that Dunn hadn't asked for her opinion. Her relationship with Dunn was such, Baskins added, that "you answered what you were asked" and no more.

E-mails show that pretexting continued through August 2005. That's when Anthony "Tony" Gentilucci, the manager of HP Global Security investigations and a member of the spy team, reported that the probe still could not find the leaker. But his final report offered helpful suggestions for future spying efforts. He advised engaging "HP legal [department in order] to invoke the attorney-client privilege"; assigning an attorney to direct the investigation; and conducting all future briefings "verbally and keeping written work product to a minimum."

A new leak occurred in January 2006. A story on CNET Networks, Inc., a technology news service, reported confidential information about a potential HP acquisition. At Hurd's and Dunn's urging, Baskins quickly launched a new spy probe, dubbed Kona II. Baskins assigned Kevin Hunsaker, a six-year HP veteran and her senior counsel, to run it. On January 23, Hunsaker e-mailed HP security that he was heading the new leak probe, at Baskins's request, "in order to protect the attorney-client privilege in the event there is litigation or a government inquiry of some sort."

Baskins also asked Hunsaker to further explore the legality of pretexting. This was the second opportunity, after initially learning about the technique from DeLia six months earlier, that Baskins had to demand in-depth research by an expert in criminal law. But that didn't happen. Instead, on January 30 Hunsaker sent the now-infamous e-mail to Gentilucci, asking, "How does Ron [DeLia] get cell and home phone records? Is it all aboveboard?"

Gentilucci replied that ruses are common in investigations. He said pretexting has been used in a number of probes, and "has not been challenged," although phone company employees could be held liable. His e-mail concluded: "I think it's on the edge, but aboveboard."

In interviews with the Wilson Sonsini lawyers, Hunsaker explained how, at Baskins's urging, he researched the issue of pretexting. He said he did about an hour's worth of online reading. If he had looked at the Web sites of the Federal Trade Commission or Federal Communications

Commission—and there is no record that he did—Hunsaker would have seen that those agencies have a serious problem with pretexting and consider it illegal. In fact, the FTC at the time was investigating five private eye companies for pretexting. FTC lawyers sued the five companies for "unfair and deceptive practices" in May. In addition, more than ten states, as well as Congress, were considering specific legislation to outlaw pretexting. Several states have since made pretexting a crime.

Steeped in blissful ignorance, the HP spy team kept on pretexting until February 7, when the method faced its only real challenge. That's when two HP security employees, who were members of Hunsaker's spy team, saw some of the detailed phone records being collected. Former law enforcement officers, they went to their supervisor and questioned the legality and ethics of obtaining personal phone records. The supervisor confronted Hunsaker, who promised to relay their concerns to the "executives sponsoring this investigation" before proceeding or using the data. There is no record available of whether Hunsaker kept his promise.

Whether spurred by her own doubts or others', Baskins in early February ordered Hunsaker to undertake "a full process check" on the investigation, including the legality of its methods. This was yet another chance to ask the tough questions and to demand an outside counsel's opinion. Instead, she again turned to Hunsaker, who again merely asked DeLia to reassure them on the law.

To answer the question this time, DeLia, according to his Wilson Sonsini interview, turned to his outside attorney, John Kiernan, with whom he shared office space. Kiernan told DeLia that pretexting was not a crime. Kiernan said that neither HP nor DeLia had ever hired him to research the issue. He had based his quick comments to DeLia on a study done a year earlier by a law student who was clerking in his office.

But on the basis of Kiernan's snap opinion, DeLia e-mailed Hunsaker, saying that "right now" (February 2006) there were no state or federal laws prohibiting pretexting. DeLia's e-mail went on to say there "is a risk of litigation." And added: "Note: the Federal Trade Commission has jurisdiction."

There is no record available to show whether Hunsaker relayed this "risk of litigation" to Baskins, or whether he bothered to check with the FTC. Apparently satisfied with whatever Hunsaker did tell her, Baskins let the probe continue.

On March 10 Hunsaker sent an 18-page draft report to Dunn, Baskins, and Hurd. It connected board member George "Jay" Keyworth II to the leaks, and said the investigation was still ongoing. It did not mention the word "pretexting," but said on page three that "the investigation team obtained, reviewed, and analyzed HP and third-party phone records to identify calls made to or from reporters or other individuals of interest." A footnote added: "It should be noted that, with respect to non-HP phone records, the investigation team utilized a lawful investigative methodology commonly utilized by entities such as law firms and licensed security firms in the United States to obtain such records."

Shortly before Dunn and Baskins were to discuss the report with Hurd at a March 15 meeting in Los Angeles, Baskins apparently grew uneasy. She asked Hunsaker to talk with outside counsel about pretexting in case Hurd had questions. Again, Baskins had a chance to demand a written opinion from an outside criminal lawyer. But once more, she relied on Hunsaker, who asked Gentilucci to call DeLia's lawyer, Kiernan.

This time Kiernan had a paralegal respond to HP. The paralegal gave Gentilucci an "update in which she said she could not find additional lawsuits or criminal charges to indicate that pretexting was (had become) illegal." Hunsaker reported back to Baskins that he had confirmed the legality of pretexting with outside counsel.

On March 15 Baskins and Dunn told Hurd that the probe concluded that Keyworth, a noted physicist, was the leaker. Before they confronted Keyworth, the executives decided to consult Larry Sonsini, who would later tell Congress that he was asked in mid-April only to look at "the sufficiency of evidence." Sonsini said he wasn't asked for, and didn't offer, any opinion about pretexting at this time.

E-mails between Baskins, Dunn, and Hunsaker indicate that Baskins shared Sonsini's comments with them during an April 15 conference call. The records do not indicate what Sonsini said, but two incidents the following week suggest that Baskins was growing more cautious.

First, Hunsaker was moved out of HP's legal department to become director of ethics. In an e-mail to his spy team, Hunsaker says simply that he's "no longer a member of the HP legal department." His new title was "director of ethics and SBC [standards of business conduct] compliance," and he would report to a senior vice president in marketing.

In the other incident that hints at Baskins's fears, she asked Hunsaker once again to discuss the legality of pretexting, this time in a memo. On April 24 Hunsaker e-mailed a one-page copy of his note to Gentilucci and DeLia. [The note summarized the efforts made to confirm the legality of pretexting.] Hunsaker concludes: "As a result, the investigation team is confident that all phone records information . . . was obtained in a lawful manner."

After reading this memo, was Baskins as confident? If not, she could have tried to derail this runaway train a final time before the report went to the board. But she didn't.

At HP's May 18 board meeting, the directors were told that Keyworth was the leaker. When the board voted 6 to 3 to ask Keyworth to resign, director Thomas Perkins angrily quit in protest. Throughout June and July, Perkins, a high-profile Silicon Valley venture capitalist, challenged the legality of the investigation and demanded answers from Baskins and Sonsini. Sonsini replied with his now oft-quoted e-mail: "I am sure Ann Baskins looked into the legality of every step of the inquiry and was satisfied that it was conducted properly."

That wasn't enough for Perkins, who made the entire mess public in late July. He told the attorney general's office, the SEC, and others about the investigation, including the pretexting.

Now facing a public outcry, HP in August asked Sonsini's firm to conduct an internal "investigation of the investigation."

The Wilson Sonsini report on August 30 concluded that "all persons involved" acted in good faith, but that "certain errors in judgment were made." While the use of pretexting at the time "was not generally unlawful," the report said the subcontractors may have used Social Security numbers while pretexting, "which more likely than not violates federal law." The report did not fault Baskins or Hurd, who "reasonably relied" on Hunsaker's assurances.

But Baskins still wasn't off the hook. The scandal snowballed through September, and HP hired another outside law firm, Morgan Lewis, to do a second internal investigation. The company also filed a new document with the SEC, outlining the spy probe and admitting that it had spied on at least two HP employees, seven members of its board, nine reporters, and their relatives.

That's when the dominoes started falling. Morgan Lewis came up with undisclosed, and what Hurd called "disturbing," findings about the spying operation. Dunn immediately resigned. Gentilucci and Hunsaker were also forced out. Baskins offered her resignation, but Hurd at first refused it.

Then the law enforcers and regulators opened their investigations. And Congress got into the act by demanding that Baskins and others at HP appear before the House subcommittee. The subcommittee had introduced a bill making pretexting a federal crime in January, and used HP to make its point for passage on national TV.

Baskins flew to the hearing on an HP corporate jet, along with her attorney. [But Baskins decided to resign and to refuse to testify. She left HP with a $3.6 million severance package.]

One GC who has overseen investigations for his Fortune 500 media company says that beyond the legal and the ethical issues, Baskins failed to ask the crucial question: "How will all this affect the company if it shows up on page one of The New York Times?"

In Baskins's defense, [her attorney, K. Lee] Blalack argues that she was supervising more than 250 lawyers, and more than 600 employees globally. Under those circumstances, Blalack says, Baskins often had to rely on assurances from her subordinates. "Ms. Baskins asked for and received multiple assurances [from Hunsaker] that these investigative techniques were lawful," he insists.

In the end, Baskins's downfall came because of what she decided not to see. Susan Hackett, senior vice president and general counsel of the Association of Corporate Counsel, argues that it is unfair to expect GCs "to see around corners." But the unfortunate truth is, when it came to the legality of spying, Baskins had blinders on.

NOTES ON HP PRETEXTING SCANDAL

1. ***Ethical (v. Legal) Considerations.*** Bart Schwartz, a former federal prosecutor hired by HP to analyze HP's practices after the pretexting scandal broke, told a *New York Times* reporter that he was struck by the lack of consideration given to ethical considerations in the board's efforts to investigate press leaks: "Doing it legally should not be the test; that is a given," he said. "You have to ask what is appropriate and what is ethical."[7]

2. ***Discretion to Advise About Non-Legal Considerations.*** How might greater attention to ethics as well as law have informed how Baskins approached her responsibilities as HP's general counsel? Would she have served her client better if she had exercised more of the discretion that state ethics rules give lawyers to advise not just about law but also about related concerns?

3. ***A Junior Lawyer Takes the Fall.*** Notice that Hunsaker was forced out of HP, while Baskins left with a $3.6 million severance package. According to an in-house lawyer who practices in northern California (a friend of the authors of this textbook), the HP pretexting scandal generated a new term to describe situations in which a junior lawyer takes the blame for mistakes for which senior lawyers may also be responsible; it's sometimes called getting "Hunsakered."

* * *

Stock Options Backdating at Apple.[8] In 2001, Apple granted then-chief executive Steve Jobs and other members of the executive team,

---

[7] Damon Darlin, *Adviser Urges H.P. to Focus on Ethics Over Legalities*, N.Y. TIMES, Oct. 4, 2006.

[8] This case study is drawn from extensive journalist coverage and the pleadings, including these sources: Amended Complaint, Securities and Exchange Commission v. Nancy R. Heinen and Fred D. Anderson (2007) (No. C–07–2214 (JF)), 2007 WL 1908786; Steve Stecklow & Nick Wingfield, *U.S. Scrutinizes Grant to Jobs—Focus in Apple Case Is Cast on the Roles of 3 Ex-Officials*, WALL ST. J., Jan. 12, 2007, A3; Justin Scheck, *Apple Quietly Canned Lawyer Who Backdated*, LEGAL INTELLIGENCER, Jan. 9, 2007; Press Release, Apple, Apple's Special Committee Reports Findings of Stock Option Investigation (Oct. 4, 2006) (http://www.apple.com/pr/library/2006/10/04Apples-Special-Committee-Reports-Findings-of-Stock-Option-Investigation.html);

including Apple's then-General Counsel Nancy Heinen, options to purchase shares of Apple stock. Rather than set the strike price (the fixed price at which the owner of the option can purchase stock) at the closing price of the stock on the date of each grant, the options were backdated. Options backdating is the practice of altering the date a stock option was granted to an earlier date, usually a date when the price was lower. In the typical stock options backdating scenario, a company examines the company's historical stock market closing prices, picks a day when the company's stock price had dropped to a low or near-low point, and pretends that the options were awarded on that date. By setting the strike price below the market price, the company incurs a cost equal to the difference between the market price and the strike price, which also dilutes the values of the shares held by the public. To be legal, backdating must be clearly communicated to shareholders and properly reflected in earnings and tax calculations. The practice of backdating stock options without reporting and accounting for them properly had become widespread in the tech industry in the late 1990s.

Prior to 2002 and the enactment of the Sarbanes-Oxley Act, companies did not have to report the granting of stock options to the SEC until the end of the fiscal year. This lax reporting requirement meant that corporate boards could easily falsify dates on documents with little chance of being caught. (Changes in SEC reporting requirements under Sarbanes-Oxley require corporations to report stock option grants two business days after the options are granted, making backdating much more difficult.)[9] In March 2006, the *Wall Street Journal* and Professor Erik Lie of the University of Iowa analyzed stock options grants to top executives at several corporations between 1995 and 2002. They examined how much the stock price rose in the twenty days following the grant. Professor Lie hypothesized that a pattern of sharp stock appreciation after grant dates is an indication of backdating; by chance alone, grants ought to be followed by a mix of rises and declines in stock performance. They found instead a remarkable number of instances where companies granted stock options to executives immediately before a sharp increase in their stocks.[10]

In the wake of the *Wall Street Journal* report, the SEC and the Department of Justice ("DOJ") began investigating stock option grants before 2002, while companies affected by the options probe, including Apple and Broadcom, secured legal representation. Reports by the *New York*

John Markoff & Eric Dash, *Apple Panel on Options Backs Chief*, N.Y. TIMES, Dec. 30, 2006, at 1; Justin Scheck & Nick Wingfield, *Criminal Probe of Apple Options is Ended*, WALL ST. J., July 10, 2008, B3; Pamela A. MacLean, *Backdating Probes Lead to Changes*, NAT'L L.J., June 9, 2008; Order Granting Motion for Final Approval of Class Action Settlement; Granting Motion for Attorneys' Fees and Expenses; And Granting in Part Objector Pezzati's Motion for Attorneys' Fees and Incentive Award, *In re Apple Inc. Securities Litigation* (2011) (No. 5:06–CV–05208–JF), 2011 WL 1877988.

[9] 15 U.S.C § 78p(a)(2)(c) (2010).

[10] Charles Forelle & James Bandler, *The Perfect Payday*, WALL ST. J., Mar. 18, 2006.

Times and the *Wall Street Journal* indicate that by July 2006, at least sixty companies had been targeted for investigation by the SEC and DOJ for stock options violations. Apple conducted an internal investigation and eventually released a statement acknowledging "serious concerns regarding the actions of two former officers in connection with the accounting, recording and reporting of stock option grants." Apple admitted in its SEC filings for October 2006 "that stock option grants made on 15 dates between 1997 and 2002 appear to have grant dates that precede the approval of those grants." Apple restated its financial performance and reported an $84 million loss related to the backdating. Heinen abruptly left Apple shortly before the company admitted to improper handling of executive stock option dating.

Apple and its executives faced an array of lawsuits. In 2007, the SEC filed a civil lawsuit against Heinen and the former chief financial officer Fred Anderson for securities fraud. The SEC alleged that Heinen and Anderson participated in backdating the options and concealing the backdating. The complaint also alleged that Heinen personally benefitted by receiving options on 400,000 shares of Apple stock through one of the backdated grants. Anderson immediately settled with the SEC for $3.5 million, but Heinen denied all allegations of wrongdoing and fought the claims. (One of her criminal defense lawyers was Cristina Arguedas, who had previously represented Hewlett-Packard General Counsel Ann Baskins in connection with the pretexting scandal.) After a year of investigations and on the eve of testimony by Jobs, Heinen settled with the SEC for $2.2 million—the $1.6 million in "ill-gotten gains," $400,000 in interest on those gains, and a $200,000 fine. In the settlement agreement, Heinen agreed to a five-year ban against serving as an officer or director of any public company and a three-year suspension from practicing before the SEC. At roughly the same time Heinen settled with the SEC, the DOJ ended its criminal investigation without bringing charges against Heinen, Anderson, or anyone else involved in the assigning of options. Several months later, Apple executives, including Heinen, settled a class action lawsuit brought by shareholders.

NOTES ON BACKDATING AT APPLE

1. ***What Explains Heinen's Conduct?*** What do you think might explain Heinen's alleged role in the backdating of stock options at Apple as described in the government's complaint? Was it personal greed? Fear of her boss? A casual attitude about falsifying documents? Too little experience with corporate governance and securities law? A lack of appreciation for how backdating stock options related to the public policy underlying securities law—to provide investors with complete and truthful information about public corporations' finances?

2. ***GCs Take the Fall?*** Many Silicon Valley companies experienced high turnover in the general counsel ranks in the wake of the backdating scandal. A 2008 survey of 38 Silicon Valley companies that had to restate financial results because of backdating found that only three GCs at the 30 companies that had general counsel at the time of the scandal still remained in their positions. Fourteen GCs were direct casualties of the scandal; four were charged by the government, and ten either took the blame or resigned or were fired. Some observers suggested that technology companies unfairly blamed their GCs for the backdating mess and took swift action against them in order to appease the SEC.[11]

* * *

Bribery at Walmart.[12] On April 22, 2012, the *New York Times* broke a story about a vast bribery scheme by Walmart in Mexico and a subsequent "hush-up" by Walmart's Bentonville headquarters. While a deeper investigation of the facts will be necessary before firm conclusions can be drawn about what occurred and what the long-term consequences will be, this episode already provides telling examples of alternative courses of action that in-house counsel can take when confronted with alleged corporate wrong doing.

Walmart became an international retail presence when it opened its first store outside Mexico City in 1991. By 2012, Walmart, through its international division Walmart International, operated 5,651 stores and employed 780,000 people in 26 countries. Key to such rapid expansion was the work of attorneys at Walmart headquarters in Bentonville, Arkansas and attorneys at the various international subsidiaries of Walmart, such as Walmart de Mexico, also known as Walmex. These attorneys helped secure permits necessary to fuel the expansion. But these attorneys—especially the ones located in Bentonville—had to ensure that employees in the vast international operations conformed to business regulations, including the Foreign Corrupt Practices Act ("FCPA"), which prohibits bribing foreign government officials.[13] Through Walmart International, Walmart vastly expanded its presence in Mexico during the late 1990s and early 2000s. Eduardo Castro-Wright, who became chief executive of Walmex in 2002, played a large role in the growth of Walmex, setting

[11] Zusha Elinson, *GCs Get Optioned Out Over Backdating*, RECORDER, April 18, 2008.

[12] This account is based primarily on the following sources: David Barstow, *Vast Mexico Bribery Case Hushed Up by Wal-Mart After Top-Level Struggle*, N.Y. TIMES, Apr. 22, 2012; Peter J. Henning, *Weighing the Legal Ramifications of the Wal-Mart Bribery Case*, N.Y.TIMES, Apr. 23, 2012; Sue Reisinger, *Will Wal-Mart Regret Not Disclosing Its Bribery Investigation Sooner?*, CORP. COUNSEL, Apr. 24, 2012; Mark Tuohey et al., *An In-House Counsel Corporate Corruption Playbook*, CORP. COUNSEL, Apr. 26, 2012; Elizabeth Harris, *After Bribery Scandal, High-Level Departures at Walmart*, N.Y. TIMES, June 4, 2014.

[13] Foreign Corrupt Practices Act of 1977, Pub. L. No. 95–213, 91 Stat. 1494 (codified as amended at 15 USC §§ 78dd–1 to –3 (2000)).

aggressive growth goals and opening new stores quickly so that competitors would not have time to react.

According to the *New York Times,* bribes paid by Sergio Cicero Zapata, a Walmex attorney in charge of obtaining construction permits, also played a large role in Walmex's expansion. During his nearly 10-year tenure at Walmex, Cicero allegedly paid over $24 million in bribes to "gestors" who funneled bribes to government officials. Bribes paid by Cicero were used to change zoning laws and to make environmental objections disappear. In Walmex's effort to outpace its competition, the bribes quickened the pace at which Walmex could build new stores. Cicero explained in an interview with investigators that with the bribes "[w]hat we were buying was time."

Cicero told investigators that his orders to bribe officials came from the highest levels of Walmart de Mexico. Initially, Cicero paid two gestors—both attorneys—to funnel bribes to government officials. The gestors submitted invoices with brief, vaguely worded descriptions of their services. One code, for example, indicated a bribe to speed up a permit. Others described bribes to obtain confidential information or eliminate fines. At the end of each month, Castro-Wright and other executives at Walmex received a detailed report of all of such payments performed, and Walmex employees would then "purify" the payments in the company's records so that they appeared as simple legal fees. An internal audit reviewed by Walmart de Mexico executives in March 2004 raised red flags about the gestor payments. But rather than end the payments, Castro-Wright fired the auditor and instructed Jose Luis Rodriguezmacedo Rivera, Walmex's general counsel, to tell Cicero to diversify the list of gestors he used.

According to Cicero, he continued to bribe officials until he resigned in September 2004. Cicero said he was under orders to do whatever was necessary to obtain permits. But dealing with "greedy" bureaucrats and demanding corporate executives loaded Cicero with "pressure and stress." When the general counsel position for Walmex opened in 2004 and Cicero was passed over, Cicero was angry and bitter.

In September 2005, Cicero informed Maritza Munich, the general counsel of Walmart International, of " 'irregularities' authorized 'by the highest levels' at Walmart de Mexico." Munich was familiar with the corrupt practices of some business leaders and bureaucrats in Latin America. Before her brief tenure at Walmart, she served as general counsel in various departments with Procter & Gamble over a twelve-year period in Latin America. Once at Walmart she pushed the Walmart board to adopt a strict anticorruption policy. After receiving Cicero's email, Munich moved quickly to investigate. Within a few days, she hired a Harvard-trained lawyer based in Mexico City named Juan Francisco Torres-Linda to debrief Cicero. Later that fall, Munich compiled memos recounting what Cicero told Torres-Linda and sent them to executives at Walmart in Bentonville. Walmart executives, including the general counsel, Thomas A. Mars, initially turned to Willkie Farr & Gallagher to investigate the accusations. Willkie proposed a full investigation to scrutinize any payments to government officials and interviews with every person who might know about payoffs, including implicated members of WalMex's board.

Walmart executives opted for a more cursory inquiry—a "preliminary inquiry" conducted by the company's Corporate Investigations Unit ("CIU"). Munich objected to this approach, noting in an email that the investigation would be "at the direction of the same company officer who is the target of several of the allegations." Equally problematic in her view, CIU was understaffed and incapable of properly handling such an inquiry. Nevertheless, the CIU confirmed all of Cicero's allegations and noted that "[t]here is reasonable suspicion to believe that Mexican and USA laws have been violated."

Rather than pursue a deeper investigation recommended by the CIU, Walmart executives, including Mars, assigned responsibility for the investigation to Rodriguezmacedo, one of the executives under investigation.

Dissatisfied by the approach taken by Walmart executives, Munich communicated her reservations to Walmart executives and tendered her resignation. Her resignation letter stated her view that "Given the serious nature of the allegations, and the need to preserve the integrity of the investigation, it would seem more prudent to develop a follow-up plan of action, independent of Walmex management participation." She added that "The bribery of government officials is a criminal offense in Mexico."

Within a few weeks, Rodriguezmacedo completed his investigation. He concluded in a six-page report that "[t]here is no evidence or clear indication of bribes paid to Mexican government authorities with the purpose of wrongfully securing any licenses or permits." The CIU responded to Rodriguezmacedo's report by pointing out the numerous inconsistencies in the report and advising executives in writing that it was "lacking." Walmart executives nevertheless accepted the report and closed the investigation in May 2006.

In 2012, the Justice Department and SEC began investigating possible FCPA violations and cover-up of those practices by Walmart in Mexico[14] and later expanded the investigation to India, China, and Brazil.[15] Although the FCPA litigation had not settled as of summer 2018, negotiations had proceeded sufficiently to allow Walmart to estimate that it would pay $283 million—much less than the $600 million demanded by

[14] Stephanie Clifford & David Barstow, *Wal-Mart Inquiry Reflects Alarm on Corruption*, N.Y. TIMES, Nov. 15, 2012.

[15] *Wal-Mart's Foreign Bribery Investigation Expands to India*, N.Y.TIMES, Nov. 15, 2012.

federal negotiators at the end of President Obama's term.[16] Walmart has also spent over $800 million on legal representation and improvements in its compliance programs.[17]

* * *

Several days after the story about Walmart bribes in Mexico broke, Ben Heineman, former general counsel of GE, filed the following column:

WAL-MART BRIBERY CASE RAISES FUNDAMENTAL GOVERNANCE ISSUES

Benjamin W. Heineman, Jr.
Harv. L. Forum Corp. Gov. & Fin. Reg., April 28, 2012

Wal-Mart appeared to commit virtually every governance sin in its handling of the Mexican bribery case, if the long, carefully reported *New York Times story* is true.* The current Wal-Mart board of directors must get to the bottom of the bribery scheme in Mexico and the possible suppression by senior Wal-Mart leaders in Bentonville, Arkansas (the company's global headquarters) of a full investigation.

In addition, the board must also review—and fix as necessary—the numerous company internal governing systems, processes and procedures that appear to have been non-existent or to have failed.

Culture of Silence. Most corporate scandals are perpetuated by a culture of silence. Here there appears to have been no integrity hotline or whistleblower system that worked, because the alleged bribery scheme went on for years without anyone reporting it to an independent company ombudsperson (and some employees were clearly aware of it). Moreover, the Mexican business leaders hid the bribery scheme from the global Wal-Mart leadership in the U.S. And, as far as one can tell based on the allegations so far, the Wal-Mart leaders in the U.S., when they learned of the allegations in some detail, hid the matter from the Wal-Mart board of directors. Wal-Mart appears to have operated like a compartmentalized criminal enterprise rather than a lawful global company.

General Counsel and Key Finance Officials as Partners, Not Guardians. The general counsel and chief auditor in Mexico appear to have knuckled under to the demands of an ambitious country CEO with no legal and moral compass by helping to direct and hide the bribery scheme. Similarly, when the investigation was returned to Mexico by top Wal-Mart leaders in the U.S., the Mexican general counsel appears to have killed it

[16] Marc Butler, *FCPA Enforcement Getting Chopped at SEC?*, INTELLIGIZE, Nov. 30, 2017.

[17] *See* Amy Deen Westbrook, *Does the Buck Stop Here? Board Responsibility for FCPA Compliance*, 48 U. TOL. L. REV. 493, 494 (2017)(citing sources tracking Walmart disclosure of $820 million in FCPA and compliance related expenses since initial disclosure of FCPA issues).

* [Eds.: We use Walmart's current spelling in this text, but some sources, including Heineman's article, include the hyphen that appeared in the company's logo through 2008.]

with a false report after no further inquiry. Likewise, in the U.S., the Wal-Mart general counsel did not support the Wal-Mart international counsel—the heroine of the piece—who received the whistleblower's initial report and sought to have an independent, thorough investigation. The company's general counsel instead succumbed to the demands of top management in Bentonville who wanted to sweep the problem under the rug. The company's general counsel sent the investigative files back to the Mexican general counsel who had clearly been named as a central figure in the bribery scheme.

The hardest part of the GC and CFO jobs (and of inside legal and finance staffs) is to reconcile the tension between being partner to the business leaders and guardians of the corporation. This appears to be one of the most striking cases where top legal and finance officials were oblivious to their fundamental integrity role and "partnered" with business leaders who were complicit at worse and totally obtuse at best.

NOTE ON WALMART BRIBERY

Variations in the Behavior of Walmart Lawyers. Notice that Heineman concludes that there were important differences in the culpability of the various in-house lawyers at Walmart. He singles out one lawyer—"the heroine"—for praise because she voiced and acted on her concerns. He asserts that the other lawyers involved failed in their duties by succumbing to pressure to ignore, and, in some cases, by helping to hide, the bribery. Assuming that allegations summarized here are true, do you share Heineman's view that most of the Walmart lawyers involved in this episode fundamentally failed to fulfill their duties to the corporation? What explains why one lawyer spoke out and acted on her concerns while others did not? In retrospect, what might a corporate general counsel or senior executive do to create an environment in which lawyers take their legal and ethical obligations more seriously?

* * *

GM Ignition Switch Scandal. In 2015, the Justice Department identified criminal wrongdoing in General Motors' failure to disclose faulty ignition switches in some of its vehicles. The defect caused some GM models to lose engine power and deactivate air bags and has been tied to nearly 400 injuries and 124 deaths. The company eventually paid $900 million to settle a federal criminal investigation, and it set aside $594.5 million to compensate victims in switch-related crashes.[18] GM has acknowledged that some mid-level employees knew of the defect for many years before GM

---

[18] Bill Vlasic & Neal Boudette, *Shell of Old GM Surfaces in Court Fight Over Ignition Flaw*, N.Y. TIMES, Aug. 17, 2017.

issued a recall.[19] Federal law requires auto manufacturers to report any safety defects within five days.[20]

One of the issues under investigation was whether the company's lawyers played a role in delaying the recall and hiding information about the defects from regulators and families of crash victims.[21] GM's in-house lawyers reached a number of secret settlements of lawsuits over fatal accidents involving vehicles with defective ignitions before the recall on January 31, 2014.[22] In testimony at Senate hearings in April of 2014, GM's chief executive, Mary Barra, was asked to explain how GM lawyers could have known about the defects but failed to ensure that top management were aware of the problem. She testified that within GM "there were silos" and that information could be known by the legal team but not communicated to other parts of the business.[23] A report by former U.S. prosecutor Anton Valukas to the board of directors found that GM's legal department resisted investigating for fear of exposing GM to additional liability and that the lawyers with knowledge of the defect did not inform Michael Millikin, GM's General Counsel, about it.[24] If GM in-house lawyers knew of the ignition switch defect for a significant time period during which GM's top management were unaware of the problem, what would it suggest about how the lawyers viewed their responsibilities?

What should we make of the fact that that GM's General Counsel did not know about the defect? Did he have an obligation to know? The Valukas report to the board of directors found that GM's lawyers were allowed to settle lawsuits for up to $5 million without his approval. Millikin resigned soon after the recall.[25]

Volkswagen's Emissions Fraud. For years, millions of diesel cars sold by Volkswagen (VW) worldwide were equipped with software that was used to evade emissions tests. The company's "defeat device" software tricked the emissions tests and then disabled pollution controls when the diesel cars were on the road, allowing them to emit 40 times the legal pollution limit. VW admitted the scheme in 2015 only after being

---

[19] Bill Vlasic, *Inquiries at General Motors Are Said to Focus on Its Legal Unit,* N.Y. TIMES, May 17, 2014.

[20] 49 C.F.R. § 573.6.

[21] *See* Sue Reisinger, *GM In-House Lawyers Pulled Into Ignition Switch Probe,* CORP. COUNSEL, Apr. 7, 2014.

[22] Bill Vlasic, *Inquiries at General Motors Are Said to Focus on Its Legal Unit,* N.Y. TIMES, May 17, 2014.

[23] Sue Reisinger, *GM In-House Lawyers Pulled Into Ignition Switch Probe,* CORP. COUNSEL, Apr. 7, 2014.

[24] Anton R. Valukas, *Report to the Board of Directors of General Motors Company Regarding Ignition Switch Recalls,* May 29, 2014.

[25] *See* Nathan Bomer and Brent Snavely, *GM's Embattled Chief Lawyer to Retire,* DETROIT FREE PRESS, Oct. 17, 2014.

confronted with irrefutable evidence of its existence.[26] The Department of Justice's civil suit against VW settled for $14.7 billion, and VW has since set aside another $3 billion to cover additional costs of fixing its diesel engines.[27] In a separate criminal suit, VW has thus far pled guilty to three felonies. The plea agreement required the payment of $4.3 billion in criminal and civil penalties and the adoption of measures designed to prevent future violations. The federal investigation against individual VW employees continues, and at least one in-house lawyer has been implicated.[28]

In a column asking "where were the lawyers?" in connection with the Volkswagen scandal, one commentator asserted that "the real question" is whether the lawyers were "engaged enough in the business to know what was going on." To be truly effective in managing risk, he said, lawyers should spend more time "understanding the business and sources of risk":

> Skilled lawyers can combine the roles of a trusted problem solver with independent judgment *and* integrated understanding, working with the people making risk-based decisions. . . . In Volkswagen, not knowing was just as bad as knowing and acquiescing. Maybe we should start talking about a duty to know what's going on.[29]

Do you agree that in-house lawyers have a duty to "know what's going on"?

We may never know the extent of involvement or neglect by VW's in-house lawyers with respect to the emissions cheating scandal because some of the evidence is missing. The statement of facts attached to the plea agreement in the federal criminal case refers to one so-far-unidentified in-house lawyer whose instructions to VW employees may have induced them to delete thousands of documents in anticipation of a litigation hold.[30] Moreover, David Geanacopoulos, who was VW of America's general counsel at the time the scandal emerged, reported losing his cell phone on December 1, 2015, soon after the U.S. Environmental Protection Agency accused VW of cheating to bypass pollution tests. The head of VW's emissions-testing lab in California and 21 other executives also reported that their mobile devices were either lost or "wiped" (erased of data) in the

---

[26] *See* Jeff Plungis & Dana Hull, *VW's Emissions Cheating Found by Curious Clean-Air Group,* BLOOMBERG, Sept. 19, 2015, https://www.bloomberg.com/news/articles/2015-09-19/volkswagen-emissions-cheating-found-by-curious-clean-air-group.

[27] Jan Schwartz & Victoria Bryan, *VW's Dieselgate Bill Hits $30 Bln After Another Charge,* REUTERS, Sept. 27, 2017.

[28] Richard W. Blackburn & Jeffrey J. Binder, *Successful Partnering Between Inside and Outside Counsel,* COMPLIANCE § 47:37, May 2018 Update.

[29] Paul Lippe, *Volkswagen: Where Were the Lawyers?,* ABA J., Oct. 13, 2015, http://www.abajournal.com/legalrebels/article/volkswagen_where_were_the_lawyers/?icn=most_read (last visited July 3, 2018).

[30] Casey C. Sullivan, *Could Volkswagen's In-House Lawyers Be Prosecuted?,* IN HOUSE, Jan. 17, 2017.

months following the EPA's announcement of its investigation.[31] In a motion seeking to exclude references to the phones in a civil suit against VW filed in state court in Virginia, lawyers for VW asserted that "[n]o evidence exists that any of the phones were intentionally lost, reset or wiped."[32] The Federal Trade Commission has called the loss and wiping of 23 phones in the context of this scandal "a bright red flag."[33] If it could be proven that VW staff deliberately destroyed or disposed of their cell phones, they could be prosecuted for obstruction of justice or spoliation of evidence.

False Customer Accounts at Wells Fargo. Beginning in 2002, thousands of Wells Fargo employees falsified bank records, forged customer signatures, and opened more than 2 million false checking or savings accounts on behalf of customers in order to meet sales quotas, receive incentive compensation, and please their superiors. An internal report to the bank's board of directors blamed the misconduct on a decentralized theory of management that gave primary authority to business unit leaders and promoted a culture of silence at the expense of a uniform culture of legal compliance.

Where were the in-house lawyers? An internal investigation found that Wells Fargo's legal department, following the lead of the CEO, deferred to the business units and failed to confront the sales practice problems, highlight them, and solve them, despite numerous warnings.[34] According to the report, even after the Los Angeles City Attorney filed a lawsuit against Wells Fargo, alleging that the company set unrealistic sales goals, which pressured employees to engage in fraudulent tactics, and that Wells Fargo profited from these tactics through fees charged to customers, there continued to be "a lack of recognition within the Law Department" about the significance of the number of employee firings associated with "sales integrity" problems and the potential reputational consequences:

> The Law Department's focus was principally on quantifiable monetary costs—damages, fines, penalties, restitution. Confident those costs would be relatively modest, the Law Department did not appreciate that sales integrity issues reflected a systemic breakdown in Wells Fargo's culture and values and an ongoing

---

[31] Ryan Beene & Margaret Cronin Fisk, *Phones for VW Lawyer, Emissions Tester Were Lost or Wiped Clean,* BLOOMBERG, Aug. 31, 2017, https://www.bloomberg.com/news/articles/2017-08-31/phones-for-vw-lawyer-emissions-tester-were-lost-or-wiped-clean (last visited July 3, 2018).

[32] *Zelonis v. Volkswagen Group of American, Inc.*, CL–2015–13746, Circuit Court of Fairfax County, VA.

[33] FTC's Corrected Reply in Support of Its Motion for Additional Half-Day of 30(b)(6) Deposition Testimony, *In re Volkswagen "Clean Diesel" Marketing, Sales Practices and Product Liability Litigation,* Dec. 22, 2016. https://www.bloomberglaw.com/public/desktop/document/In_re_Volkswagen_Clean_Diesel_Marketing_Sales_Practices_and_Produ/27?1530035887.

[34] Ben Heineman, Wells Fargo Lessons: Will Leaders Ever Learn? Harvard Law School Forum on Corporate Governance and Financial Regulation, April 26, 2017, available at https://corpgov.law.harvard.edu/2017/04/26/wells-fargo-lessons-will-leaders-ever-learn/.

failure to correct the widespread breaches of trust in the misuse of customers' personal data and financial information.[35]

What does this account of the legal department's response suggest about the lawyers' understanding of their roles?

Enron. Recall the Enron scandal, briefly described in Chapter 8. The Court Appointed Examiner for Enron noted numerous situations in which Enron's in-house lawyers failed to analyze and advise Enron management or its board of directors about issues relating to the use of special purpose entities to hide debt and thus to make the company appear to be more profitable than it was. The Examiner noted that it "appeared that some of these attorneys considered officers to be their clients when, in fact, the attorneys owed duties to Enron." He further observed that "some of these attorneys saw their role in very narrow terms, as an implementer, not a counselor. That is, rather than conscientiously raising known issues for further analysis by a more senior officer or the Enron Board or refusing to participate in transactions that raised such issues, these lawyers seemed to focus only on how to address a narrow question or simply to implement a decision (or document a transaction)."[36]

Does the Examiner's account of the failings by Enron's in-house lawyers sound familiar? In what ways are the problematic behaviors identified by the Examiner for Enron similar to problematic conduct identified in the other more recent episodes described above?

NOTE ON THE SCANDALS

What Can We Learn? What general lessons can in-house counsel learn from these scandals? To what extent can we attribute disappointing behavior by in-house lawyers to a lack of moral courage, or to an excessively narrow view of their roles, or to insufficient involvement in establishing a culture, systems, and processes designed to prevent and detect the problems that led to these scandals? To what extent can we attribute such behavior to the difficulty of acting on the knowledge that the entity, rather than particular officers and managers, is the client? Consider William Simon's observation about the attitude of some of Enron's outside lawyers: "To suggest that a corporate lawyer's duty to her client requires her to do her best to effectuate a manager's request to find a lawful way to withhold information from the shareholders is to suggest that the manager is the client. Every corporate lawyer knows that the manager is not the client. Yet, most corporate lawyers think and talk much of the time as if the manager were the client. Moreover,

---

[35] Independent Directors of the Board of Wells Fargo & Company, Sales Practices Investigation Report, Apr. 10, 2017, available at https://www08.wellsfargomedia.com/assets/pdf/about/investor-relations/presentations/2017/board-report.pdf.

[36] *In re Enron Corp.*, Final Report of Neal Batson, Court-Appointed Examiner, at 115.

few corporate lawyers have a coherent idea of what a corporate client could be other than the manager."[37]

E. THE ROLE OF IN-HOUSE COUNSEL POST-ENRON

New regulatory controls and other reforms imposed in the wake of Enron and related scandals have given lawyers more responsibility and, perhaps, additional leverage to promote legal compliance by their corporate clients. This section examines those changes and considers their implications for the role of in-house counsel.

The Sarbanes-Oxley Act of 2002 set new requirements for U.S. public company boards, management, and accounting firms. Regulations adopted pursuant to Sarbanes-Oxley also impose an up-the-ladder reporting requirement on lawyers who advise clients in the preparation of documents that foreseeably might become part of submissions to the SEC.[38] One of those regulations requires an attorney who becomes aware of evidence of a material violation of securities law to report it to the chief legal officer, who must in turn investigate, make sure that the company responds appropriately, and report back to the attorney who made the initial report. If the lawyer who made the initial report does not receive a satisfactory response, she must take the issue up the ladder again and report the evidence to the company's board of directors.[39] Lawyers who violate the rule are subject to civil sanctions and penalties by the SEC.

The 2010 Dodd-Frank Wall Street Reform and Consumer Protection Act significantly increased the activity of audit committees and imposed new rules and governance along with many new regulatory requirements for corporate boards and the lawyers who advise them.

In response to these regulatory reforms, in-house lawyers have acquired greater authority within the corporation. There has been a trend in recent years toward making the general counsel part of the senior management team. A recent study of more than 50 GCs from a broad range of industries found that 90 percent of those GCs reported directly to the CEO.[40] Corporations are also making legal compliance a higher priority. For example, when a new general counsel took over Tyco following several ethics scandals that nearly destroyed the company, the legal team created

---

[37] William Simon, *After Confidentiality: Rethinking the Professional Responsibilities of the Business Lawyer*, 75 FORDHAM L. REV. 1453 (2006).

[38] *See* 17 C.F.R. § 205.2(e) (2009) (mandating up-the-ladder reporting if there is "credible evidence, based upon which it would be unreasonable . . . for a prudent and competent attorney not to conclude that it is reasonably likely that a material violation has occurred.")

[39] Alternatively, the company can set up a "Qualified Legal Compliance Committee" (QLCC) of independent board members, and the reporting attorney and chief legal officer can discharge their duties by reporting to the QLCC.

[40] David B. Wilkins, *The In-House Counsel Movement*, THE PRACTICE, May 2016.

a series of training programs designed to help employees and management appreciate the difference between what is legal and what is not and the importance of obtaining legal advice in close cases.[41] Walmart has significantly bolstered its compliance controls since the bribery scandal broke; it has reported spending over $141 million on global ethics and compliance systems since 2013.[42] (It is worth noting in this context that organizational sentencing guidelines adopted in 1991 reduce sentences for corporations found guilty of criminal conduct—sometimes by as much as 95 percent—if they can demonstrate that they had in place an effective compliance program.)

It remains to be seen whether such changes—in general counsel's stature within corporations and in companies' implementation of compliance protocols—is just window-dressing or will instead actually reduce corporate misconduct and the frequency of the kinds of major corporate scandals that have so routinely made headlines during the past few decades. It is also uncertain how those changes in the regulatory climate have affected in-house counsel's influence.

Recent Research on In-House Counsel's Role. Recall that Nelson & Nielsen's research on corporate counsel, based on interviews conducted in the 1990s, concluded that in-house counsel generally deferred to corporate management.[43] While all lawyers in that study claimed to have sufficient authority to stop illegal transactions from proceeding, they also said that it was generally the prerogative of management, not the lawyers, to determine whether the corporation should assume legal risk.

How might recent legislative initiatives designed to reform corporate governance and increase the transparency of corporate disclosures have influenced the power and authority of in-house lawyers? Might they have changed the in-house lawyer's role?

A pilot study based on interviews with ten general counsels of Fortune 1000 companies suggests a greater willingness by GCs to "assert jurisdiction over questions of legal risk" and to claim "broad gatekeeping duties" than did the lawyers in Nelson & Nielsen's research from the late 1990s.[44] The study found that most of the interviewed GCs reported directly to the Chief Executive Officer or Chair of the Board of Trustees. They believed that they occupied positions of power within the managerial hierarchy and played important roles in monitoring compliance. The

---

[41] David B. Wilkins, *Team of Rivals? Toward a New Model of the Corporate Attorney-Client Relationship*, 78 FORDHAM L. REV. 2067, 2118 (2010).

[42] Doug McMillon, *Reflecting on What We've Built: Walmart's Global Ethics and Compliance Program*, April 20, 2017, https://cdn.corporate.walmart.com/b0/91/87adea36485aa5e2054c46b84873/2017-global-ethics-compliance-program-report-layout-final-soraya.pdf.

[43] Robert L. Nelson & Laura Beth Nielsen, *Cops, Counsel, and Entrepreneurs: Constructing the Role of Inside Counsel in Large Corporations*, 34 LAW & SOC'Y REV. 457, 486–87 (2000).

[44] Tanina Rostain, *General Counsel in the Age of Compliance: Preliminary Findings and New Research Questions*, 21 GEO. J. LEGAL ETHICS 465 (2008).

enactment of the Organizational Sentencing Guidelines in 1991 had given corporations incentives to improve and disseminate compliance functions throughout the organization with respect to all types of corporate regulation. The guidelines also encouraged the adoption of codes of behavior, training programs, and the creation of procedures and controls to ensure compliance with legal mandates. The interviewed GCs claimed that they played significant roles in institutionalizing and monitoring compliance mechanisms.

Some of the lawyers in this pilot study also indicated that the Sarbanes-Oxley Act (commonly called SOX) had made directors and senior managers more reluctant to take legally aggressive positions and had strengthened the GCs' ability to influence board and managerial decisions relating to compliance. One GC, for example, said that:

> [Directors and senior managers] are afraid of going to jail. It is very effective in that way, in my view. . . Once you say compliance, you are very, very empowered. The thing about Sarbanes-Oxley that I don't like . . . I think it is overkill in a variety of areas, but the power . . . to mandate a culture of compliance is very strong.

The study's author found that "[a]lthough most general counsel initially claimed that SOX had not fundamentally changed board behavior at their companies, their responses suggest that the statute has had a subtle and widespread influence on directors' approach to serving on boards and serves as resource for general counsel to draw on to assert their authority within the corporation."[45]

NOTES ON THE ROLE OF IN-HOUSE COUNSEL POST-ENRON

1. ***Compare the Findings.*** The findings of this study are strikingly different from those of Nelson & Nielsen, who concluded that in-house counsel generally were "subservient to managerial prerogatives":

> We find that inside lawyers work hard to avoid conflicts with business executives; they typically leave the final call on acceptable levels of legal risk to the businesspersons involved; and managers can exercise control over which lawyers work on their matters and thus influence the very style of lawyering employed inside the corporation.
>
> In some sense this is an unsurprising, commonplace observation. Despite claims of professional autonomy, corporate lawyers—whether in law firms or in corporate counsel's offices—have been reported to be closely aligned with client interests throughout the twentieth century.
>
> In another sense our finding is significant because subordination to management continues in the contemporary period, despite profound

[45] *Id.*

> changes in the structural position of inside counsel, in the presence of law in the corporate environment and the ideology of management itself. Inside counsel have gained power relative to their peers in outside law firms, but this apparently has not resulted in a fundamentally different role within the corporation. Law almost certainly has become a more salient concern for American business as a result of increased exposure to litigation, the rise of regulatory structures, and the increasing reliance on legal expertise in corporate governance, financing, and transactions. It appears that lawyers are indeed involved in many corporate functions, yet they report similar sorts of pressure to conform to executives' preferences as the lawyers that [researchers] described from the 1960s and late 1970s. One significant reason may be the changed ideology of corporate management and a general corporate climate that devalues legal regulation. . . . Hence our lawyer informants have attempted to craft a new image within the corporation in which lawyers are team players, rather than cops. Inside counsel have not abandoned their roles as monitors of corporate legality and analysts of legal risk, but they have adopted the current idiom of corporate management as they play those roles. Corporate lawyers, like the management they serve, attempt to be lean and mean.[46]

Is it possible to reconcile the different findings of these two studies? If so, how?

2. ***Reasons for Caution?*** Do you think that this study's thesis—that SOX has strengthened in-house counsel's influence and their capacity to shape board and managerial decision making around compliance issues—is unduly optimistic? Do you think it might reflect the particular (perhaps biased or unrepresentative) perspectives of the general counsel who agreed to be interviewed? Remember that this article is based on interviews with just ten general counsel.

Notice that many of the scandals described in the previous section occurred very recently. Does that suggest that the influence of in-house counsel post-Enron may not have increased as much as this pilot study suggests? Alternatively, does it suggest that in-house lawyers may have been unwilling or disinclined to exercise their influence?

3. ***Inside Counsel as Lawyer-Statesman?*** Former GE general counsel Ben Heineman asserts that inside lawyers have risen in quality, responsibility, power and status in the past 25 years, but he insists that they should have done much more to prevent the corporate scandals of recent decades. He argues that inside counsel's job is to balance the client company's interest in "performance" (long-term profitability) with "integrity" and sound risk management. Performing this role successfully requires inside lawyers to resolve what Heineman calls the "most basic problem confronting inside

---

[46] Robert L. Nelson & Laura Beth Nielsen, *Cops, Counsel, and Entrepreneurs: Constructing the Role of Inside Counsel in Large Corporations*, 34 LAW & SOC'Y REV. 457, 486–87 (2000).

lawyers": "being a partner to the board of directors, the CEO, and business leaders but ultimately being guardian of the corporation."[47] He calls on inside counsel to function as "lawyer statesmen"—who serve as technical experts, wise counselors, and accountable leaders who assist the corporation attain the corporate mission of high performance with high integrity.

Some have expressed skepticism about the ability of in-house counsel to play the role that Heineman envisions for them. Professor Robert Gordon, for example, agrees with Heineman that corporate lawyers *should* counsel their clients to be good corporate citizens, but he questions the willingness of most in-house lawyers to play the lawyer-statesman role given the enormous pressure they face to conform to management demands. He observes that Heineman enjoyed exceptional stature as GE's general counsel, which gave him leverage to insist on legal compliance with little risk that he would be fired for doing so, while most in-house counsel today exercise much less influence.[48] Donald Langevoort, a prominent securities law scholar, has argued that in-house counsel should not be entrusted to oversee corporate compliance functions because lawyers tend to interpret legal constraints as barriers to be worked around, and because senior in-house lawyers usually "exemplify the characteristics and traits associated with zealous and aggressive promotion of the company's best interests, as those interests are construed by its board and CEO."[49] These observations cut against the expectation that in-house lawyers will serve as reliable guardians of good corporate citizenship.

* * *

Whistleblowing by In-House Lawyers. A whistleblower is an employee who reports a violation of law by her employer. Whistleblower protections, designed to protect whistleblowers from retaliation by employers, come from a variety of sources, including federal and state statutes and state common law. For example, Sarbanes-Oxley protects employees for disclosing violations of the Act. Similarly, regulations implemented pursuant to Dodd-Frank protect employees from being fired, demoted or harassed if they report legal violations to the SEC.

When an in-house lawyer's duty of confidentiality seems to conflict with whistleblower protections, which rules prevail? Can a lawyer ever gain protection from the whistleblower protections of Sarbanes-Oxley, Dodd-Frank, and other federal and state statutes in those circumstances? Courts have taken varying positions on the relationship between whistleblower protections and in-house lawyers' confidentiality duties. Some have held that the lawyer's duty of confidentiality trumps

---

[47] Ben W. Heineman, Jr., THE INSIDE COUNSEL REVOLUTION: RESOLVING THE PARTNER-GUARDIAN TENSION 4 (2016).

[48] Robert W. Gordon, *The Return of the Lawyer-Statesman*, 69 STAN. L. REV. 1731 (2017) (providing a lucid discussion of the attractions of Heineman's vision and questions about its feasibility).

[49] Donald C. Langevoort, *Getting (Too) Comfortable: In-House Lawyers, Enterprise Risk, and the Financial Crisis*, 2012 WIS. L. REV. 495 (2012).

whistleblower protections and therefore lawyers are not entitled to legal protection if they reveal confidential information when they blow the whistle on client misconduct. Other courts disagree and have granted some whistleblower protections to lawyers.

F. SUMMARY

This chapter explored the function of in-house counsel, relationships between in-house and outside lawyers, and the allocation of responsibility between them. It considered the extent to which in-house counsel can exercise independent judgment and ways in which the in-house lawyer's position as a full-time employee of the client can both facilitate and hinder the lawyer's ability to guide the client on legal compliance issues. It also examined the roles of in-house lawyers in several recent corporate scandals, and it invited you to contemplate what the lawyers involved in these episodes might have done to avert these outcomes. We also considered whether and how new corporate regulatory controls and other reforms introduced in the wake of Enron may have influenced the responsibility and authority of in-house lawyers and their ability and willingness to be effective guardians of corporate compliance and integrity.

CHAPTER 11

GOVERNMENT LAWYERS

■ ■ ■

A. INTRODUCTION

Approximately 8 percent of American lawyers work in government (excluding the judiciary): roughly one-third each in federal, state, and local government.[1] The work of government lawyers includes litigation, advising, and transactional work in a wide variety of substantive areas. We cover two types of government lawyer (public defenders and prosecutors) in Chapters 6 and 7. Here we focus on all other lawyers representing government. While we focus mainly on lawyers who are employed full-time as government employees, lawyers in private practice are retained by governments to handle transactions or litigation, just as law firms are retained by other organizational clients. In addition, some governments hire lawyers in private practice to act essentially as the government's in-house counsel and to advise on every aspect of the government's work in the same manner as would a lawyer elected or appointed to serve as a city or county attorney or as in-house counsel for an agency, commission, or department.

At the federal and state level, the government lawyer typically operates in a complex environment in which separation of powers principles coexist with hierarchy within the legislative and executive branches. Elected officials may rightfully believe that they have some sort of mandate to pursue the policy agendas on which they campaigned, but they also are constrained by various sources of law, including laws enacted or enforced by other branches of government pursuing different agendas. Government lawyers sometimes face challenging questions of accountability to the electorate and to the rule of law when advising on whether and how the elected and appointed officials can pursue their policy agendas consistent with existing law. The challenges are sometimes compounded for lawyers for local governments who represent multiple agencies and officials within the municipal entity simultaneously.

Government lawyers confront a broad range of practical and ethical challenges, but here we focus on variations of two questions we've considered in other practice contexts. First, who is the client of the

---

[1] AMERICAN BAR ASSOCIATION, LAWYER DEMOGRAPHICS (2012), *supra* Chapter 2; Harvard Law School Program on the Legal Profession, "Analysis of the Legal Profession and Law Firms (as of 2007)," http://www.law.harvard.edu/programs/plp/pages/statistics.php#wlw.

government lawyer? Second, how should the government lawyer approach her counseling duties?

B. WHO IS THE CLIENT OF THE GOVERNMENT LAWYER?

In Chapters 8 and 10 on lawyers in large law firms and in-house counsel positions, we noted that the client of the corporate lawyer is the corporation itself rather than any of the constituents. That abstract notion can be difficult to implement in practice, but at least there is some agreement in theory about who the client is. For some government lawyers, there is less agreement even in theory, in part because government typically does not have the kind of hierarchical and strictly defined authority structure that exists in most corporations. Our notion about who authoritatively speaks for the people on every issue is less clear than our notion of who speaks for a corporation. Who, then, is the client of the government lawyer? The answer to the question is important because it helps to define the government lawyer's obligations.

ABA Model Rule of Professional Conduct 1.13, the rule that guides lawyers who represent organizations as clients, does not attempt to identify the government lawyer's client except to note that "the duty defined in this Rule applies to governmental organizations." Although Rule 1.13 applies by its terms to all lawyers who serve organizational clients, it seems to contemplate its application to corporate clients more than governmental ones. The analogy to corporate representation is imperfect for many government lawyers because the lines of authority in government work are typically more complex than they are in corporate representation, the purposes of government more amorphous than the purposes of corporations, and the interests of the "ultimate" client of the government lawyer (citizens) are more diverse those of the ultimate client of the corporate lawyer (shareholders).[2]

There is surprisingly little consensus, or even discussion among commentators, about how the government lawyer should define the client. At the federal level, the most commonly expressed rule of thumb is that a lawyer working with the executive branch represents the United States in the form of that branch.[3] Lawyers who work for city governments, which typically are organized on something closer to a corporate model than separation of powers principles, are often understood to represent the municipal entity as a whole.

---

[2] GEOFFREY C. HAZARD, JR., SUSAN P. KONIAK, ROGER C. CRAMTON, GEORGE M. COHEN, W. BRADLEY WENDEL, THE LAW AND ETHICS OF LAWYERING 580 (5th ed. 2010).

[3] *See* HAZARD, KONIAK, CRAMTON, COHEN & WENDEL at 582; Michael S. Paulsen, *Who 'Owns' the Government Attorney's Attorney-Client Privilege?*, 83 MINN. L. REV. 473 (1998).

Government lawyers, like corporate lawyers, often face an "agency problem" in discerning whether the individuals who purport to speak for the client are acting in the best interests of the entity. Thus, the generally accepted understanding of the government lawyer's role accommodates several principles that are in tension with one another. On the one hand, it acknowledges that the lawyer serves an institution whose legitimacy depends on being responsive to democratic, political processes, and that the lawyer therefore should give considerable deference to elected officials and their appointees. On the other hand, it recognizes that the personal interests and political ambitions of individual government officials, as well as their short-sighted and narrow concerns, can interfere with their authority to speak for the public. Obviously, the government lawyer's client is not the individual agency head or elected official in his personal capacity, just as the corporate lawyer's client is not the individual who serves as the CEO. That is, the lawyer does not serve the personal interests of the person who happens to hold a government position.

Although the ultimate client of the government lawyer may be the public, it can be difficult for the government lawyer to act on that knowledge. One observer, while agreeing that the U.S. Attorney General ultimately represents the American people, has questioned what guidance that axiom gives to the government lawyer: "Can one meet with [the American people] on a Tuesday morning in a conference room? Can one get them on a conference call to determine their desired ends and their preferred means to achieve them?"[4]

Client identity questions can become especially vexing for government lawyers working at the state and local levels. These lawyers often are charged with responsibility for representing multiple agencies and officials that occasionally come into conflict with one another. Determining how to proceed in those circumstances can be challenging and politically fraught.

NOTES ON THE CLIENT OF THE GOVERNMENT LAWYER

1. ***Why Does It Matter for Government Lawyers to Identify Their Client?*** Every lawyer who represents a large organization must consider who her client is. Why might government lawyers face particular difficulty in identifying their client, and why is it particularly important that they do so?

2. ***Differences Among Government Clients.*** The structure of government and the lawyer's specific role within government may lead to a variety of answers to the question of who is the government lawyer's client. A lawyer who advises a state environmental protection agency, for example, may have a clear and stable sense that her client is the agency. A lawyer who handles appeals on behalf of all or many agencies may think his client is

[4] *See* William R. Dailey, *Who is the Attorney General's Client?*, 87 NOTRE DAME L. REV. 1113, 1121–22 (2012).

whichever agency is a litigant except when the position that one agency wishes the lawyer to take conflicts with the policy or position of another agency. But when a lawyer occupies a slightly more generalist position, such as the Office of Legal Counsel of the U.S. Department of Justice, the identity of the client may be more difficult to discern.

C. THE GOVERNMENT LAWYER AS COUNSELOR

As in other practice settings, much of the most consequential work of government lawyers takes the form of counseling rather than litigating. Government lawyers' advice to officials is often confidential and leads public officials to make decisions that never become public. Moreover, government lawyers' interpretations of law often are not tested in court. Even when government lawyers' interpretations of law reach the courts, judges sometimes decline to rule on them, because of separation of powers concerns, sovereign immunity, or because judges view the legal interpretations as political questions that deserve judicial deference. Thus, much of the legal advice that government lawyers provide has the practical effect of binding law.

Some of the most highly controversial recent incidents involving legal counseling by government lawyers have arisen in connection with the "war on terror." We focus here on the conduct of lawyers in the Office of Legal Counsel (OLC), the section of the United States Department of Justice charged with advising the President about the legality of proposed policies and action.

1. A CASE STUDY: THE TORTURE MEMOS

Shortly after 9/11, Assistant Attorney General Jay Bybee and his chief deputy John Yoo, on behalf of OLC, wrote a series of memoranda regarding the George W. Bush administration's use of tactics to combat terrorism and to deal with detainees. The most infamous of these memos, excerpted below, was written in 2002 but remained secret for almost two years, until it was anonymously leaked to the *Washington Post* in the summer of 2004, shortly after it was revealed that U.S. personnel guarding a prison in Abu Ghraib tortured, raped, and killed several Iraqi prisoners. The incidents at Abu Ghraib provoked a national and international outcry over American abuse of detainees. The OLC opinion memos argued that the United States was not limited by prohibitions on torture contained in international conventions and that the President was free to order what the administration referred to as "enhanced interrogation" (which critics deemed torture) of detainees. Administration officials relied on this and other related OLC memoranda to authorize the use of a variety of tactics, including waterboarding, sleep deprivation, stress positions, and cramped confinement. The OLC memos played an important role in paving the way for the use of these techniques because they had the effect of protecting officials from criminal liability. Jack Goldsmith, the head of OLC who succeeded Bybee and soon thereafter withdrew and repudiated several of the OLC opinions on the use of enhanced interrogation techniques, noted: "It is practically impossible to prosecute someone who relied in good faith on an OLC opinion."[5]

As you read the following excerpts of the most notorious of the OLC memos, try to imagine how the authors understood their roles and how they might have been influenced by the particular circumstances under which they were asked to provide an opinion.

MEMORANDUM FROM JAY S. BYBEE TO ALBERTO GONZALEZ

Office of Legal Counsel
U.S. Department of Justice, August 1, 2002

You have asked for our Office's views regarding the standards of conduct under the Convention Against Torture as implemented by Sections 2340–2340A of title 18 of the United States Code. We conclude that for an act to constitute torture as defined in Section 2340, it must inflict pain that is difficult to endure. Physical pain amounting to torture must be equivalent in intensity to the pain accompanying serious physical injury, such as organ failure, impairment of bodily function, or even death. For purely mental pain or suffering to amount to torture under Section 2340, it must result in significant psychological harm of significant duration, e.g., lasting for months or even years.

"Severe Pain or Suffering." The key statutory phrase in the definition of torture is the statement that acts amount to torture if they cause "severe physical or mental pain or suffering." Section 2340 makes plain that the infliction of pain or suffering per se, whether it is physical or mental, is insufficient to amount to torture. Instead, the text provides that pain or suffering must be "severe." The statute does not, however, define the term "severe." "In the absence of such a definition, we construe a statutory term in accordance with its ordinary or natural meaning." FDIC v. Meyer, 510 U.S. 471, 476 (1994). The dictionary defines "severe" as "[u]nsparing in exaction, punishment, or censure" or "[I]nflicting discomfort or pain hard to endure; sharp; afflictive; distressing; violent; extreme; as severe pain, anguish, torture." Thus, the adjective "severe" conveys that the pain or suffering must be of such a high level of intensity that the pain is difficult for the subject to endure.

Congress's use of the phrase "severe pain" elsewhere in the United States Code can shed more light on its meaning. See, e.g., West Va. Univ. Hosps., Inc. v. Casey, 499 U.S. 83, 100 (1991) ("[W]e construe [a statutory

[5] JACK GOLDSMITH, THE TERROR PRESIDENCY: LAW AND JUDGMENT INSIDE THE BUSH PRESIDENCY 96 (2007).

term] to contain that permissible meaning which fits most logically and comfortably into the body of both previously and subsequently enacted law."). Significantly, the phrase "severe pain" appears in statutes defining an emergency medical condition for the purpose of providing health benefits. These statutes define an emergency condition as one "manifesting itself by acute symptoms of sufficient severity (including severe pain) such that a prudent lay person, who possesses an average knowledge of health and medicine, could reasonably expect the absence of immediate medical attention to result in—placing the health of the individual . . . (i) in serious jeopardy, (ii) serious impairment to bodily functions, or (iii) serious dysfunction of any bodily organ or part." Id. § 1395w–22(d)(3)(B). Although these statutes address a substantially different subject from Section 2340, they are nonetheless helpful for understanding what constitutes severe physical pain. They treat severe pain as an indicator of ailments that are likely to result in permanent and serious physical damage in the absence of immediate medical treatment. Such damage must rise to the level of death, organ failure, or the permanent impairment of a significant body function. These statutes suggest that "severe pain," as used in Section 2340, must rise to a similarly high level—the level that would ordinarily be associated with a sufficiently serious physical condition or injury such as death, organ failure, or serious impairment of body functions—in order to constitute torture.

"Prolonged Mental Harm." As an initial matter, Section 2340(2) requires that the severe mental pain must be evidenced by "prolonged mental harm." To prolong is to "lengthen in time" or to "extend the duration of, to draw out." Webster's Third New International Dictionary 1815 (1988); Webster's New International Dictionary 1980 (2d ed. 1935). Accordingly, "prolong" adds a temporal dimension to the harm to the individual, namely, that the harm must be one that is endured over some period of time. Put another way, the acts giving rise to the harm must cause some lasting, though not necessarily permanent, damage. For example, the mental strain experienced by an individual during a lengthy and intense interrogation—such as one that state or local police might conduct upon a criminal suspect—would not violate Section 2340(2). On the other hand, the development of a mental disorder such as posttraumatic stress disorder, which can last months or even years, or even chronic depression, which also can last for a considerable period of time if untreated, might satisfy the prolonged harm requirement.

A defendant must specifically intend to cause prolonged mental harm for the defendant to have committed torture. It could be argued that a defendant needs to have specific intent only to commit the predicate acts that give rise to prolonged mental harm. Under that view, so long as the defendant specifically intended to, for example, threaten a victim with imminent death, he would have had sufficient mens rea for a conviction.

According to this view, it would be further necessary for a conviction to show only that the victim factually suffered prolonged mental harm, rather than that the defendant intended to cause it. We believe that this approach is contrary to the text of the statute. The statute requires that the defendant specifically intend to inflict severe mental pain or suffering.

The President's Commander-in-Chief Power. Even if an interrogation method arguably were to violate Section 2340A, the statute would be unconstitutional if it impermissibly encroached on the President's constitutional power to conduct a military campaign. As Commander-in-Chief, the President has the constitutional authority to order interrogations of enemy combatants to gain intelligence information concerning the military plans of the enemy. The demands of the Commander-in-Chief power are especially pronounced in the middle of a war in which the nation has already suffered a direct attack. In such a case, the information gained from interrogations may prevent future attacks by foreign enemies. Any effort to apply Section 2340A in a manner that interferes with the President's direction of such core war matters as the detention and interrogation of enemy combatants thus would be unconstitutional.

Defenses. In the foregoing parts of this memorandum, we have demonstrated that the ban on torture in Section 2340A is limited to only the most extreme forms of physical and mental harm. We have also demonstrated that Section 2340A, as applied to interrogations of enemy combatants ordered by the President pursuant to his Commander-in-Chief power would be unconstitutional. Even if an interrogation method, however, might arguably cross the line drawn in Section 2340, and application of the statute was not held to be an unconstitutional infringement of the President's Commander-in-Chief authority, we believe that under the current circumstances certain justification defenses might be available that would potentially eliminate criminal liability. Standard criminal law defenses of necessity and self-defense could justify interrogation methods needed to elicit information to prevent a direct and imminent threat to the United States and its citizens.

Necessity. We believe that a defense of necessity could be raised, under the current circumstances, to an allegation of a Section 2340A violation.

The necessity defense may prove especially relevant in the current circumstances. On September 11, 2001, al Qaeda launched a surprise covert attack on civilian targets in the United States that led to the deaths of thousands and losses in the billions of dollars. According to public and governmental reports, al Qaeda has other sleeper cells within the United States that may be planning similar attacks. Indeed, al Qaeda plans apparently include efforts to develop and deploy chemical, biological and nuclear weapons of mass destruction. Under these circumstances, a detainee may possess information that could enable the United States to prevent attacks that potentially could equal or surpass the September 11 attacks in their magnitude. Clearly, any harm that might occur during an interrogation would pale to insignificance compared to the harm avoided by preventing such an attack, which could take hundreds or thousands of lives.

Under this calculus, two factors will help indicate when the necessity defense could appropriately be invoked. First, the more certain that government officials are that a particular individual has information needed to prevent an attack, the more necessary interrogation will be. Second, the more likely it appears to be that a terrorist attack is likely to occur, and the greater the amount of damage expected from such an attack, the more that an interrogation to get information would become necessary. Of course, the strength of the necessity defense depends on the circumstances that prevail, and the knowledge of the government actors involved, when the interrogation is conducted. While every interrogation that might violate Section 2340A does not trigger a necessity defense, we can say that certain circumstances could support such a defense.

* * *

This opinion has been widely condemned on a variety of grounds.

Some critics argued that the lawyers had no business engaging in lawyerly analysis of whether the legal authorities permitted torture—that they should have immediately condemned the proposed techniques on moral grounds.

Other critics argued that the memo's failing was that it was incompetent and disingenuous—it misstated the law, failed to grapple with relevant precedent, and buried contrary authority in the appendix. These critics generally emphasized the distinction between advocacy and counseling and the lawyer's duty to give independent, candid advice in the latter role. Some of these critics also emphasized the special context in which OLC lawyers operate—that "advice" delivered by OLC is not *just* advice but also has the effect of law itself because OLC opinions provide a "golden shield" against criminal liability for those who rely on them. Thus, the effect of the opinion was to enable government actors to engage in criminal behavior without being accountable for their actions. One such critic, journalist Anthony Lewis, observed that "[t]he memo reads like the advice of a mob lawyer to a mafia don on how to skirt the law and stay out of prison. Avoiding prosecution is literally a theme of the memorandum."[6]

John Yoo has made very clear that he stands by the memos. He did not (and still does not) think it was his job "to provide moral answers"; it was, instead, "to interpret the law so that people who make policy know the rules

---

6 Anthony Lewis, *Making Torture Legal*, N.Y. REV. BOOKS, July 15, 2004.

of the game."[7] Jay Bybee has also defended his part in signing the memos, although he has expressed some misgivings about the quality of the analysis and explanations.[8]

NOTES ON THE TORTURE MEMOS

1. ***Should Government Lawyers Consider the Morality of Government Actions?*** Should the OLC lawyers who drafted this opinion have taken the morality of torture into account in the opinion? If so, how?

2. ***Should Government Lawyers Consider the Public Interest?*** Did the OLC lawyers have a special obligation to consider the public interest while advising the governmental client about the legality of the proposed interrogation techniques? If so, how would they go about discerning what is in the public interest in this case? How should the lawyer resolve the tension between national security and human rights?

3. ***What Is the Purpose of This Memo?*** Notice that much of the memo focuses on what is required to prove that "a defendant" engaged in criminal conduct, the necessary proof of mens rea (the intention or knowledge of wrongdoing that constitutes an element of a crime), and available defenses. What is the significance of the choice to refer to the government official conducting interrogation as a "defendant"? Does that raise questions about whether the primary purpose of the memo was to advise the government about whether certain interrogation techniques were legal or instead to assess whether individuals engaged in those techniques could be convicted of a crime?

4. ***Who Is the Client?*** Whose interests are served by the OLC memorandum of August 1, 2002? President George W. Bush? The Office of the President of the United States? The Department of Defense? The United States? Those conducting the interrogation? Should the lawyer's expectation about who will rely on an OLC opinion affect whom he regards as the client?

5. ***What Is Good Advice?*** Does the memo adequately consider arguments on the other side? Does it read like an advice memo, analyzing the issues in a thorough and fair-minded way, or more like a brief, arguing one side of the issue?

6. ***Should Context Matter?*** By many accounts, the atmosphere in Washington at the time OLC was asked to provide this opinion was extraordinarily tense. Many thought it likely that terrorists were planning another major attack. Vice President Cheney's lawyer, David Addington, is said to have declared that if the OLC lawyers did not approve the administration's counterterrorism measures, "the blood of the hundred

---

[7] "Frontline Interview with John Yoo," Oct. 18, 2005, available at http://www.pbs.org/wgbh/pages/frontline/torture/interviews/yoo.html.

[8] *See* Neil A. Lewis, *Official Defends Signing Interrogation Memo*, N.Y. TIMES, Apr. 29, 2009 (noting that he still believes that "the conclusions were legally correct" but that he would clarify and sharpen the analysis if he had it to do again).

thousand people who die[d] in the next attack [would be] on" their hands.[9] Should those circumstances have influenced the contents of OLC's opinion? How, or to what extent, should lawyers avoid such influence? Do their ethical duties require them to avoid it?

* * *

The next two excerpts reflect the debate about the legal and ethical merits of these memos. The first, a column by two University of Chicago law professors, supports Yoo's position; it challenges the notion that OLC lawyers should have tackled the moral as well as legal issues relating to the use of torture, and it rejects the claim that the opinion is incompetent. The second excerpt, by Bradley Wendel, agrees on the former point but disagrees with the latter.

A "TORTURE" MEMO AND ITS TORTUOUS CRITICS

Eric Posner & Adrian Vermeule
Wall Street Journal, July 6, 2004, A22

Recent weeks have seen a public furor over a Justice Department memorandum that attempted to define the legal term "torture," as used in federal statutes and treaties, and that pointed to constitutional questions that would arise if statutory prohibitions on torture conflict with the president's powers as commander in chief. An article in the *New York Times* quoted legal academics who criticized the memorandum's authors for professional incompetence, and for violating longstanding norms of professional practice and integrity in the Justice Department's Office of Legal Counsel (OLC). Neither charge is justified.

The academic critics have puffed up an intramural methodological disagreement among constitutional lawyers into a test of professional competence. Although we disagree with some of the memo's conclusions, its arguments fall squarely within the OLC's longstanding jurisprudence, stretching across many administrations of different parties, which emphasizes an expansive reading of presidential power.

[T]he memorandum's arguments are standard lawyerly fare, routine stuff. The definition of torture is narrow simply because, the memorandum claims, the relevant statutory texts and their drafting histories themselves build in a series of narrowing limitations, including a requirement of "specific intent." The academic critics disagree, but there is no foul play here.

As for the constitutional arguments, [e]veryone, including even the most strident of the academic critics, agrees that Congress may not, by statute, abrogate the president's commander-in-chief power, any more

[9] JACK GOLDSMITH, THE TERROR PRESIDENCY: LAW AND JUDGMENT INSIDE THE BUSH ADMINISTRATION 71 (2007).

than it could prohibit the president from issuing pardons. The only dispute is whether the choice of interrogation methods should be deemed within the president's power, as the memo concludes. That conclusion may be right or wrong—and we, too, would have preferred more analysis of this point—but it falls well within the bounds of professionally respectable argument.

The Justice Department memorandum came out of the OLC, whose jurisprudence has traditionally been highly pro-executive. Not everyone likes OLC's traditional jurisprudence, or its awkward role as both defender and adviser of the executive branch; but former officials who claim that the OLC's function is solely to supply "disinterested" advice, or that it serves as a "conscience" for the government, are providing a sentimental, distorted and self-serving picture of a complex reality.

Th[e] conventional view [of presidential power] has been challenged in recent years by a dynamic generation of younger scholars who argue for an expansive conception of presidential power over foreign affairs, relative to Congress. Among this rising generation are legal scholars who have recently held office in the Justice Department, including John Yoo at Berkeley. The memorandum thus focuses not on restrictive Supreme Court precedents, but on the constitutional text, the structure of foreign affairs powers and the history of presidential power in wartime. [T]he academic critics' complaints [about the memo] have intellectually partisan overtones.

The critics also argue that the Justice Department lawyers behaved immorally by justifying torture. Although it is true that they did not, in their memorandum, tell their political superiors that torture was immoral or foolish or politically unwise, they were not asked for moral or political advice; they were asked about the legal limits on interrogation. They provided reasonable legal advice and no more, trusting that their political superiors would make the right call. Legal ethics classes will debate for years to come whether Justice's lawyers had a moral duty to provide moral advice (which would surely have been ignored) or to resign in protest.

For our part, we find it hard to understand why people think that the legal technicians in the Justice Department are likely to have more insight into the morality of torture than their political superiors or even the man on the street. But whatever one's views on the use of torture on the battlefield, the memorandum is not "incompetent" or "abominable" or any more "one-sided" than anything else that the Justice Department has produced for its political masters.

LEGAL ETHICS AND THE SEPARATION OF LAW AND MORALS

W. Bradley Wendel
91 Cornell Law Review 67 (2005)

Spectacular scandals involving lawyers are certainly nothing new. Wrongdoing by lawyers brought about or exacerbated the Watergate crisis, the savings and loan collapse, the corporate accounting fiasco that brought the 1990s tech stock boom to a crashing halt, and innumerable less prominent harms. But for sheer audacity and shock value, it is hard to top the attempt by elite United States government lawyers to evade domestic and international legal prohibitions on torture. The Bush administration was faced with an urgent question regarding the limits to impose on the interrogation techniques used by military, FBI, CIA, and other government agents and civilian contractors. Officials in the Department of Defense (DOD) and advisers to the President naturally turned to lawyers to interpret and apply the domestic and international legal norms governing the treatment of prisoners.

[The August 1, 2002 OLC memo] is not legal analysis of which anyone could be proud. The overwhelming response by experts in criminal, international, constitutional, and military law was that the legal analysis in the government memos was so faulty that the lawyers' advice was incompetent. Indeed, after the news media disclosed the memos, the Bush administration immediately distanced itself from the analysis, disavowing the memos as "abstract," "over-broad," and even irrelevant, in some instances, to the policy decisions actually made by high government officials.

What accounts for the poor quality of legal reasoning displayed by the memos? It is difficult to credit the explanation that the authors themselves were incompetent, since they worked for agencies—such as the OLC—which traditionally employ some of the very best legal talent in the country. Rather, the explanation is that the process of providing legal advice was so badly flawed, and the lawyers working on the memos were so fixated on working around legal restrictions on the administration's actions, that the legal analysis became hopelessly distorted.

The story of the legal analysis of torture begins with the invasion of Afghanistan following the September 11th terrorist attacks, which resulted in the capture of numerous prisoners suspected of affiliation with the Taliban or al-Qaeda. [T]he capture of high-ranking al-Qaeda members such as Abu Zubaida, Mohamed al-Kahtani, and Khalid Sheikh Mohammed raised the possibility that American officials may have custody of individuals with extremely valuable "actionable intelligence," in the lingo of military intelligence officials.

Intelligence personnel naturally made it a high priority to get these detainees to talk. Because many suspected militants had proven to be skilled at resisting traditional, noncoercive interrogation techniques such as promises of leniency in exchange for cooperation, American officials sought advice to see whether it would be legally permissible to use certain coercive techniques on "high value" captives. Specifically, CIA officials wanted to know whether their field agents would be subject to criminal prosecution for using physically painful interrogation methods such as "waterboarding," in which a detainee is strapped to a board and submerged until he experiences a sensation of drowning. Alternatively, the Agency sought guidance on the legality of techniques that do not require direct physical contact, such as depriving prisoners of sleep, forcing them to stand for extended periods of time or to assume stressful positions, bombarding them with lights or sound (including, bizarrely, repeating the Meow Mix cat food jingle for hours on end), and leaving them shackled for hours.

It appears that the CIA was perfectly willing to take off the gloves, so to speak, but was concerned with protecting its agents from future prosecution. The administration had already signaled its willingness to get as tough as necessary in order to prevent terrorist attacks. White House Counsel Alberto Gonzales repeatedly instructed lawyers to try to be as "forward-leaning" as possible when considering how much latitude to give interrogators dealing with suspected terrorists. Officials at various detention centers in the far-flung Gulag archipelago created by the administration had also indicated their cavalier attitude toward restrictions on their treatment of prisoners. Although it is not the case that security officials were willing to do anything at all during interrogations—no one has suggested threatening the families of suspected terrorists, for instance—it is nevertheless apparent that some American officials in the field had a strong interest in pushing the boundaries of acceptable interrogation techniques.

Administration officials sought legal advice on the applicability of any other domestic and international legal norms that would restrict the questioning of detainees captured in Afghanistan. Most troublesome were the 1984 Convention Against Torture and the federal legislation implementing it. The Convention and the federal statute are both stated in terms of "torture," suggesting that they do not prohibit something coercive but less than torture, like inhuman or degrading conduct. Lawyers in the OLC therefore sought to construe the operative term, torture, as narrowly as possible. Torture is defined in the statute as an "act specifically intended to inflict severe physical or mental pain or suffering," and severe pain and suffering is further defined as the prolonged harm caused by one of several enumerated acts. By focusing on the specific-intent requirement and the element of severe pain or suffering, the lawyers created an implausibly restrictive definition of torture: "The victim must experience intense pain or suffering of the kind that is equivalent to the pain that would be associated with serious physical injury so severe that death, organ failure, or permanent damage resulting in a loss of significant body function will likely result." Despite the plain meaning of the statutory language to the contrary, burning detainees with cigarettes, administering electric shocks to their genitals, hanging them by the wrists, submerging them in water to simulate drowning, beating them, and sexually humiliating them would not be deemed "torture" under this definition.

The lawyers drew support for this narrow definition from an unlikely source, namely several federal statutes defining an "emergency condition" for the purpose of obtaining health care benefits. Not only do these statutes have nothing to do with torture, but the syntax of the statutory text shows that the OLC lawyers got the interpretation backwards. For example, one statute defines an emergency condition as one manifesting itself by acute symptoms of sufficient severity (including severe pain) such that a prudent layperson could reasonably expect the absence of immediate medical attention to result in serious impairment to bodily functions, or serious dysfunction of any bodily organ or part. The statute is plainly not setting out a definition of severe pain in terms of organ failure or dysfunction, but using severe pain as one symptom among many—including organ failure or dysfunction. The lawyers also downplayed cases arising under statutes in more closely analogous contexts, such as the Torture Victim Protection Act (TVPA). The TVPA also defines torture in terms of severe pain and suffering and has acquired a sizeable body of case law interpreting the severity standard. The memo did cite the TVPA, but labors to distinguish cases tending to show that severe pain can result from acts that do not necessarily threaten permanent organ failure or dysfunction. Other cases demonstrate that the courts are willing to treat individual acts as torture; the OLC lawyers, however, buried these cases in an appendix to the memo.

If anything, the OLC lawyers did an even worse job of analyzing the available defenses to a criminal prosecution for violating the federal statute implementing the Torture Convention. The memo's conclusion, that the standard criminal law defense of necessity could justify what would otherwise be prohibited torture, fails both by virtue of the specific principles of interpretation applicable in the area of international humanitarian law and by ordinary criminal law standards. For one thing, the Torture Convention itself contains a clear nonderogation provision, which provides that "no exceptional circumstances whatsoever, whether a state of war or any other public emergency, may be invoked as a justification of torture."

As for domestic criminal law on necessity, there is no acknowledgment anywhere in the memo of the extremely rare circumstances under which necessity can successfully be invoked as a defense. Dudley and Stevens were sentenced to death for killing and eating the cabin boy,* and a

* [Eds.: *Regina v. Dudley and Stephens* is an old English case (14 Q.B.D. 273 (Queen's Bench Division 1884)) in which Dudley and Stephens killed and ate a fellow young seaman (Parker) to

criminal law treatise cites numerous cases similarly rejecting the necessity defense. One could imagine, though, circumstances in which a court might apply the necessity defense to justify conduct that would otherwise be criminal. Suppose an Air Force commander was communicating with the pilot of an armed F-16 fighter, which had intercepted a civilian airliner that had gone seriously off course and failed to respond to repeated attempts to contact it by radio. If the commander knew with certainty that the plane was American Airlines Flight 11, with Mohammed Atta at the controls, bound for the North Tower of the World Trade Center, it would be difficult to envision a court not permitting the officer to assert the defense of necessity in response to prosecution for ordering the destruction of the airplane.

The memo's analysis is so vague and open-ended, however, that it is difficult to find the logical stopping point. The authors seem to have in mind a case like the Air Force commander, but they do not limit their analysis to that case. The fault in the reasoning lies in the careless extension of the ticking-bomb hypothetical to the far more mundane scenarios actually confronting investigators, in which there are no background facts to suggest a substantial likelihood that a given detainee is likely to have critical, time-sensitive information.

There is nothing necessarily wrong with advancing creative arguments as long as they are clearly identified as such, with weaknesses and counterarguments candidly noted. But an interpretation that one could not advance with some measure of pride and satisfaction in front of an impartial, respected lawyer or judge is an erroneous interpretation. A lawyer violates her obligation of fidelity toward the law by basing advice or structuring a transaction on the basis of such a reading of the law. In addition, a lawyer who does not flag creative and aggressive arguments as such violates her fiduciary duty to her client by providing purportedly neutral advice without the caveat that the lawyer's interpretation may not accurately represent the applicable law.

My argument is not that a lawyer must always offer the most conservative legal advice or, metaphorically, handle the law with kid gloves. There are many mechanisms within the law for pushing the boundaries or seeking change. In the context of litigation, lawyers are permitted to take aggressive stances toward the law, subject to the requirements that the position not be frivolous, that any contrary authority be disclosed, and that the lawyer make no misstatements of law or fact. Some measure of aggressiveness is permissible in litigation because of the checking mechanisms built into the adversary system, such as an impartial referee, rules of evidence and procedure, and, of course, a well-prepared adversary. Similarly, certain kinds of administrative proceedings are

save themselves from starvation while all three were marooned in a lifeboat after a shipwreck. They were found guilty of murder.]

accompanied by procedural checks to insure against the corrosive effect of excessive lawyer creativity. In transactional representation, however, these checks and balances are absent, and the lawyer in effect assumes the role of judge and legislator with respect to her client's legal entitlements. If a government lawyer says, for example, that the President has the authority as Commander-in-Chief to suspend the obligations of the United States under various international treaties, then for the purposes of that act, the lawyer's advice is the law. If the lawyer's advice is erroneous, the consequences for the government could be disastrous. Secrecy, combined with an aggressively "forward-leaning" stance toward the law, essentially creates an unaccountable legislature within the executive branch. Rather than assisting the client to comply with the law, the government lawyers in this case simply abandoned the ideal of compliance altogether in favor of their own, custom-built legal system.

At bottom, the vice of the torture memos is the ethical solipsism of lawyers who sincerely believed they were right, despite the weight of legal authority against their position. Academic defenders of the administration cite the works of "dynamic young constitutional scholars" whose views are better than those that have carried the day in the Supreme Court, Congress, and the forum of international treaty negotiation. No matter how brilliant these scholars are, their views are not the law. They have not been adopted by society, pursuant to fair procedures, as a resolution of the moral issue. Lawyers functioning in a representative capacity have no greater power to act on the basis of an all-things-considered moral judgment than do their clients. If clients are bound by the law, then lawyers are bound to advise them on the basis of the law, not on the basis of the lawyer's own judgment about what the best "forward-leaning" social policy would look like.

NOTES ON THE DEBATE OVER THE TORTURE MEMOS

1. ***"Standard Lawyerly Stuff" v. "Ethical Solipsism."*** What is the nature of the disagreement between Professors Posner and Vermeule, on the one hand, and Wendel, on the other? On what points do these commentators agree?

2. ***"Merely Plausible" v. "Honest Appraisal."*** In the fall of 2004, nineteen former OLC lawyers published *Principles to Guide the Office of Legal Counsel*, a document they described as their understanding of "the best practices of OLC" drawn from the longstanding practices of the Attorney General and the Office of Legal Counsel across time and administrations. The first of these principles was that:

> when providing legal advice to guide contemplated executive branch action, OLC should provide an accurate and honest appraisal of applicable law, even if that advice will constrain the administration's pursuit of desired policies. The advocacy model of lawyering, in which

> lawyers craft merely plausible legal arguments to support their clients' desired actions, inadequately promotes the President's constitutional obligation to ensure the legality of executive action.[10]

Would this principle be good policy?

3. ***Are Structural Changes Necessary to Ensure Independence?*** Can government lawyers realistically be expected to offer independent advice while under pressure from politically powerful superiors and embroiled in intense situations such as those that confronted the lawyers who drafted the torture memos? Norman Spaulding has argued that structural changes are needed to better ensure that OLC lawyers give independent advice. He proposes that formal opinions issued by the Office of Legal Counsel should be made public, subject to very narrow exceptions.[11] Would you favor that requirement?

4. ***Drone Strike Memos.*** OLC wrote nine memos in or since 2010 asserting that the United States government could target and kill American citizens and other nationals using unmanned aerial drones. The United States has used drone strikes to kill large numbers of suspected militants, some of whom were U.S. citizens, and a number of noncombatants have been killed as collateral damage. Although most of the memos have not been released to the public because the Obama Administration claimed they contain classified information, the Justice Department did prepare a white paper summarizing the legal arguments that it believed justified targeted killings, and the white paper was leaked to the public. The test summarized in the white paper for the targeted killing of an American citizen has been described as "marvelously abstract" and as being "like Swiss cheese" in its vagueness.[12] In response to court orders in lawsuits filed by the American Civil Liberties Union, the Obama administration in 2014 released a previously secret OLC memo outlining the legal justification for the 2011 killing of Anwar al-Awlaki,[13] and in 2016 it released a redacted version of a White House document that set out the government's policy framework for drone strikes.[14]

Scholars have disagreed about the legality of targeted killings by drone strikes, although debate about the legality was hampered by a lack of clarity as to how the program operated and what standards were used to determine

---

[10] *Guidelines for the President's Legal Advisors*, 81 IND. L. J. 1345 (2005).

[11] Norman W. Spaulding, *Professional Independence in the Office of the Attorney General*, 60 STAN. L. REV. 1931 (2008).

[12] Eugene R. Fidell, *Drones and Democracy: A Legal Question but Also One of Policy*, DER SPIEGEL ONLINE, Feb. 8, 2013.

[13] U.S. Department of Justice, Office of Legal Counsel, Memorandum for the Attorney General, Re: Applicability of Federal Criminal Laws and the Constitution to Contemplated Lethal Operations Against Shaykh Anwar al-Aulaqi, July 16, 2010, available at https://www.washingtonpost.com/r/2010-2019/WashingtonPost/2014/06/23/National-Security/Graphics/memodrones.pdf?tid=a_mcntx.

[14] Procedures for Approving Direct Action Against Terrorist Targets Located Outside the United States and Areas of Active Hostilities, May 22, 2013, available at https://www.aclu.org/sites/default/files/field_document/presidential_policy_guidance.pdf.

the permissibility of killing.[15] The secrecy surrounding the targeted killing program and the legal justifications for it drew criticism from members of Congress who were denied access to the memos, from former Obama Administration officials, and from former Bush Administration officials, including John Yoo.[16] If the legal standard was either unknown or very vague and if its application is entirely secret, did government lawyers do enough to ensure the legality of the government's policy? What is the appropriate mechanism to balance needs for secrecy while ensuring accountability of the government lawyers who authorize such uses of force and the officials who carry them out?

The Trump administration has ramped up the use of drone strikes and reportedly has relaxed the Obama-era rules governing their use, but it has not released the new standards or information about their content.[17]

5. ***Were the Torture Memos Professional Misconduct?*** The Department of Justice's Office of Professional Responsibility (OPR) investigated the conduct of John Yoo and Jay Bybee over a period of several years. It concluded that John Yoo had committed "intentional professional misconduct when he violated his duty to exercise independent legal judgment and render thorough, objective and candid legal advice," and that Jay Bybee had committed "professional misconduct when he acted in reckless disregard of his duty to exercise independent legal judgment and render thorough, objective, and candid legal advice."[18] But Associate Deputy Attorney General David Margolis rejected OPR's findings, concluding that while Yoo and Bybee had used "flawed" legal reasoning and "poor judgment," they were not guilty of professional misconduct. Under Department of Justice rules, poor judgment does not constitute professional misconduct and would not trigger a referral to state bar associations for disciplinary action. Margolis also rejected the harsher sanctions recommended by OPR.[19]

6. ***Torture Memos Back in the News.*** In May 2018, in hearings on Gina Haspel's nomination to become Director the CIA, she repeatedly emphasized that the harsh interrogation tactics used in 2002 at a secret detention site that she oversaw had been approved by the White House and

---

[15] Michael Hirsh & Kristin Roberts, *What's In the Secret Drone Memos*, NAT'L L. J., Feb. 22, 2013; Robert P. Barnidge, Jr., *A Qualified Defense of American Drone Attacks in Northwest Pakistan Under International Humanitarian Law*, 30 B.U. INT'L L.J. 409 (2012) (concluding attacks are legal).

[16] Scott Shane, *Ex-Lawyer in State Department Criticizes Drone Secrecy*, N.Y. TIMES, May 8, 2013; John Yoo, *The Real Problem With Obama's Drone Memo*, WALL. ST. J., Feb. 9, 2013.

[17] Greg Jaffe, *White House Ignores Executive Order Requiring Count of Civilian Casualties in Counterterrorism Strikes*, WASH. POST, May 1, 2018, https://www.washingtonpost.com/world/national-security/white-house-ignores-executive-order-requiring-count-of-civilian-casualties-in-counterterrorism-strikes/2018/05/01/2268fe40-4d4f-11e8-af46-b1d6dc0d9bfe_story.html?utm_term=.2349eef6fd8a.

[18] Department of Justice, Office of Professional Responsibility Report, July 29, 2009, at 260.

[19] Memorandum for the Attorney General/Deputy Attorney General, from David Margolis, Associate Deputy Attorney General, January 5, 2010.

deemed legal by the Department of Justice.[20] Nevertheless, Haspel vowed at the hearings never to start another detention and interrogation program. She added, "I would not allow the CIA to undertake activity that I thought was immoral, even it was technically legal."[21]

7. ***Whistleblowing.*** When, if ever, may a government lawyer who discovers illegal conduct while counseling a client blow the whistle on illegal conduct? Although there are several whistleblower statutes covering federal government employees,[22] they are designed to remedy particular types of waste, fraud, and abuse and are not a general license to reveal confidential government information. Moreover, these statutes generally do not preempt state rules of professional conduct. Therefore, a lawyer who reveals confidential information of a government client where the state ethics rule does not permit it does so at her peril.

2. A CASE STUDY: THE "MUSLIM BAN" ORDER AND THE FIRING OF SALLY YATES

During his presidential campaign, Donald Trump repeatedly promised to enact a ban on entry into the U.S. by Muslims and people from regions with a history of supporting terrorism. He also suggested during the campaign that he intended to establish a database or registry to track Muslims in the U.S. Once in office, he continued to proclaim his support for a ban or registry on entry of Muslims into the U.S. One of Trump's advisors, Rudy Giuliani, stated during an interview that Trump had asked him how to lawfully implement a Muslim ban.

During his first week in office, President Trump issued an executive order (EO) immediately blocking the entry into the United States of all refugees and all citizens of seven majority-Muslim countries.[23]

On January 30, 2017, Acting Attorney Sally Yates, who was Barack Obama's Deputy Attorney General and was serving as Attorney General pending Jeff Sessions' confirmation, refused to defend the executive order. She wrote the following letter to senior Justice Department officials:

> On January 27, 2017, the President signed an Executive Order regarding immigrants and refugees from certain Muslim-majority countries. The order has now been challenged in a number of

[20] Charlie Savage, *Gina Haspel's Testimony About CIA Torture Raises New Questions*, N.Y. TIMES, MAY 10, 2018, A1.

[21] *Haspel Vows Not to Restart Interrogation Program, Inside Politics*, CNN Video, CNN.com, May 9, 2018, https://www.cnn.com/videos/tv/2018/05/09/ip-haspel-hearing.cnn.

[22] *See, e.g.*, the Whistleblower Protection Act of 1989, Pub. L. No. 101–12, 103 Stat. 16 (codified as amended in various sections of 5 U.S.C.); Dodd-Frank Wall Street Reform and Consumer Protection Act, Pub. L. No. 111–203, 124 Stat. 1376 (2010)(codified as amended at 15 U.S.C. § 78u–6 (2012); Securities Whistleblower Incentives and Protections, 17 C.F.R. § 240.21F–4(b)(4)(iv) (2011).

[23] This synopsis of events leading up to the Yates firing draws from Bradley Wendel's account and critique, summarized below.

jurisdictions. As the Acting Attorney General, it is my ultimate responsibility to determine the position of the Department of Justice in these actions.

My role is different from that of the Office of Legal Counsel (OLC), which, through administrations of both parties, has reviewed Executive Orders for form and legality before they are issued. OLC's review is limited to the narrow question of whether, in OLC's view, a proposed Executive Order is lawful on its face and properly drafted. Its review does not take account of statements made by an administration or it [sic] surrogates close in time to the issuance of an Executive Order that may bear on the order's purpose. And importantly, it does not address whether any policy choice embodied in an Executive Order is wise or just.

Similarly, in litigation, DOJ Civil Division lawyers are charged with advancing reasonable legal arguments that can be made supporting an Executive Order. But my role as leader of this institution is different and broader. My responsibility is to ensure that the position of the Department of Justice is not only legally defensible, but is informed by our best view of what the law is after consideration of all the facts. In addition, I am responsible for ensuring that the positions we take in court remain consistent with this institution's solemn obligation to always seek justice and stand for what is right. At present, I am not convinced that the defense of the Executive Order is consistent with these responsibilities nor am I convinced that the Executive Order is lawful.

Consequently, for as long as I am the Acting Attorney General, the Department of Justice will not present arguments in defense of the Executive Order, unless and until I become convinced that it is appropriate to do so.

Upon learning that Yates would not defend his executive order on immigration, President Trump promptly fired her.

Many commentators lauded Sally Yates's refusal to defend the executive order, calling it evidence of her willingness to stand up against proposed unlawful action by the president.[24] But others reacted less favorably. Consider the following critiques by Jack Goldsmith and Bradley Wendel, whose views on the torture memos you've already encountered:

---

[24] *See, e.g.*, Brian Fallow, *Why Trump's Firing of Sally Yates Should Worry You*, POLITICO, Jan. 31, 2017; Marty Lederman, *Sally Yates Did the Right Thing*, JUST SECURITY, Jan. 31, 2017, available at https://www.justsecurity.org/37029/sally-yates/.

QUICK THOUGHTS ON SALLY YATES' UNPERSUASIVE STATEMENT

Jack Goldsmith
LawFare, Jan. 30, 2017

I have not yet examined the EO with sufficient care to determine for myself its legality. The EO was obviously issued in haste, without the usual procedural or substantive review within the Executive branch, and without thinking through its consequences. At a minimum, and entirely independent of its legality, the issuance of the EO was deeply imprudent. I know that many people who find the Trump EO abhorrent are cheering wildly for Yates. Nonetheless, the reasons that Yates gave in her carefully worded letter for not defending the EO in court are extraordinarily weak, in my opinion.

The Constitution vests the "executive Power" in the President, and states that "he shall take care that the laws be faithfully executed." These are the main constitutional provisions from which the president's authority over legal interpretation and legal superintendence of the Executive branch flow.

The Attorney General serves as the "head of the Department of Justice." The Attorney General's core responsibilities include supervising DOJ, providing legal advice to the rest of the Executive Branch, and "[r]epresent[ing] the United States in legal matters generally." When the Attorney General's office is vacant, as it currently is, "the Deputy Attorney General may exercise all the duties of that office." For all relevant purposes, Yates is the Attorney General.

The Attorney General (and here that means the Acting Attorney General) has the clear authority to determine which presidential orders the Department will defend in court, and how, although her determinations are subject to presidential reversal. So unless and until Trump orders Yates to defend the EO or fires her for insubordination, this is Yates' call to make. Yates is right, in other words, that "[a]s the Acting Attorney General, it is my ultimate responsibility to determine the position of the Department of Justice in these actions." Yates is also right that in deciding whether and how to defend presidential action in court, her role is different from the Office of Legal Counsel (OLC), which (as she correctly says) reviews EOs only for the narrow issue of whether the EO "is lawful on its face and properly drafted."

So far so good. But the reasons that Yates then gives for deciding not to defend the EO in court are labored and, to me, unconvincing. Most importantly, *Yates does not say that she has concluded that the EO is unlawful. Nor does she say that defending the EO in court would be unreasonable.*

Instead, Yates gives four reasons for refusing to defend the EO. Here they are, with my quick reactions.

First, Yates says that OLC did not take into account "statements made by an administration or its surrogates close in time to the issuance of an Executive Order that may bear on the order's purpose." I assume Yates is referring here to statements such as the one by Rudy Giuliani, who recently claimed that Trump wanted a "Muslim ban" and sought "the right way to do it legally." I am sure OLC didn't take such statements into account, since they would not be relevant to review for form and legality. I can imagine these and similar statements properly informing the Attorney General's view of the legality of the EO, if she believed that these statements amounted to the EO being motivated by invidious discrimination (though even if she concluded that, the relevance of such discrimination in the context of the immigration issues here is tricky). But Yates does not say she has concluded that, and it is pretty clear from the context of her letter that she has not ruled out that there are reasonable arguments in support of the EO.

Second, she says that OLC did not "address whether any policy choice embodied in an Executive Order is wise or just." True, that is not OLC's job. But nor is it the Attorney General's—at least not if the President has decided that the policy choice is wise and just. The Attorney General can personally advise the President about an EO's wisdom and justness. And the Attorney General can decide to resign if she thinks the President is pursuing a policy so unwise and unjust as to be morally indefensible. But an Attorney General does not typically (I cannot think of a counterexample offhand) refuse to defend an Executive Order in court because she disagrees with the policy basis for the EO.

Third, Yates says her "responsibility is to ensure that the position of the Department of Justice is not only legally defensible, but is informed by our best view of what the law is after consideration of all the facts." This is *not* the standard that the Attorney General and DOJ typically use in deciding whether to defend presidential action in court. (Some have suggested that this is the standard that OLC should use in deciding whether presidential action *outside of judicial review* is lawful, though that position is contested.) Rather, the longstanding DOJ view is that DOJ will defend a presidential action in court if there are reasonable arguments in its favor, regardless of whether DOJ has concluded that the arguments are persuasive, which is an issue ultimately for courts to decide. DOJ very often—typically—defends presidential action in court if there is a reasonable legal basis for the action, even if it is not supported by the "best view" of the law. Indeed, that happened a lot in the Obama administration, as it does in all administrations.

Fourth, Yates says she is responsible "for ensuring that the positions we take in court remain consistent with this institution's solemn obligation to always seek justice and stand for what is right." This sounds like a restatement of the policy choice point above. The Attorney General has discretion to make some DOJ decisions based on what she thinks is just and right. But in the context of deciding whether to defend a presidential EO, the question for Yates is reasonable legality, not what is just and right. If Yates thought the EO, independent of its legality, had crossed a red line of justice and rightness—whatever those terms mean—she should have counseled the President on that point and resigned if he disagreed.

Yates states at the end of her letter that she is "not convinced that the defense of the Executive Order is consistent with these responsibilities nor am I convinced that the Executive Order is lawful." This statement summarizes the two major points above. First, she believes the standard for defending the EO is "best view of the law," not reasonable legality, and she is not convinced the EO is consistent with the best view of the law. But as noted above, the typical standard for the Attorney General to defend an EO of the President is not whether she is convinced of its legality. Rather, the standard is something closer to the idea that she should defend the EO unless she is convinced of its illegality—i.e. she defends if there is a reasonable argument for its legality. Second, Yates believes that defending the EO is inconsistent with her responsibilities to interject a policy analysis about the wisdom and justness of the EO independent of the President. For reasons stated above, I do not believe that either of these arguments are persuasive given her role. Nor are they consistent with what I understand the duties and responsibilities of the Attorney General to be.

Yates is obviously in an extraordinarily difficult position as Acting Attorney General for a President whose policy goals she does not share. She is clearly repulsed by the EO, and wants no part in its enforcement. (One of the many elements of poor governance by the Trump administration was to issue the controversial and poorly thought-through EO when Barack Obama's Deputy Attorney General is serving as Acting Attorney General.) But if Yates feels this way, she should have resigned (though if Yates goes, there may be no statutory officer in DOJ who can approve FISA orders.) Instead, she wrote a letter that appears to depart sharply from the usual criteria that an Attorney General would apply in deciding whether to defend an EO in court. As such, the letter seems like an act of insubordination that invites the President to fire her. Which he did.

GOVERNMENT LAWYERS IN THE TRUMP ADMINISTRATION

W. Bradley Wendel
69 Hastings L. J. 275 (2017)

My view is that the attorney's obligation is to advise the President on the legality of the proposed executive order and to take care not to allow her judgments concerning its legality to be influenced by political or ethical disagreement with its objectives. True, [the relevant ethics rules] permits the attorney to "refer not only to law but to . . . moral, economic, social, and political factors" that may bear on the client's decision. The attorney may give this advice, but should not be surprised when it is ignored. The President has other advisors to consider social and political factors, and the President is a moral agent who is responsible for the decisions he makes. If the order turns out to be a catastrophe, blame properly belongs to the President. If the attorney's moral disagreement with the President's objectives can be characterized as fundamental, the attorney may resign. If there is a delegation of authority to an attorney to exercise discretion, moral considerations may come into play. For example, the Attorney General may make discretionary decisions concerning enforcement priorities. However, the Attorney General is also subject to the direction of the President, and if the President insists on pursuing some objective, the Attorney General should determine whether that objective is lawful, and if so, provide assistance to the President in carrying it out.

First, the Justice Department does have an obligation to seek justice and stand for what is right, but the content of those values is not self-evident. Acting Attorney General Yates has her views on what is in the public interest; President Trump and his political advisor Steven Bannon have another. In the moral division of labor that characterizes the service conception of attorney-client relationship, it is for elected political officials to make the judgment call concerning issues of justice and what is right. If Yates's letter stated that she refused to enforce the order because it was unlawful because it was motived by invidious discrimination, her stance would have been ethically proper, and her firing by Trump would have more closely resembled the firing of Archibald Cox in the Saturday Night Massacre.* But she chose in her letter to attack the order as unjust, not to question its legality.

Second, a government attorney, even acting in a non-litigation capacity, does not have an obligation to seek the *best* view of the law unless her client asks for this advice. Instead, the attorney's ethical responsibility is to ensure that a proposed course of action is legally permissible. In this

---

* [Eds.: The Saturday Night Massacre was a series of events on the evening of October 20, 1973, during the Watergate scandal. President Richard Nixon ordered Attorney General Elliot Richardson to fire independent prosecutor Archibald Cox. Richardson refused and resigned. Nixon then ordered Deputy Attorney General William Ruckelshaus to fire Cox, but he also refused and resigned. Solicitor General Robert Bork, who was third in line, followed Nixon's orders and fired Cox.]

case the executive order may even be approaching the line of unlawfulness. President Trump cannot un-ring the bell of Islamophobia he so vigorously sounded during the campaign, and statements by advisors like Rudy Giuliani and Michael Flynn have heightened suspicion that the facially neutral executive order is motivated by discriminatory animus. If Yates believed the history of the executive order would render it unlawful, she should have given that advice. It appeared from her letter, however, that she believed the order to be lawful—perhaps only barely so—but inconsistent with her best view (or the Department's best view) of the law. . . As a matter of agency law and the rules of professional conduct, where there are two competing visions of the public good available to a lawyer, the responsibility for selecting between them is the client's. If the proposed course of action is lawful, the lawyer's duty as an advisor is complete, and the client may go ahead and execute on the planned action.

NOTES ON THE MUSLIM BAN AND YATES FIRING

1. ***The Attorney General's Role?*** How does Yates characterize her duties as Acting Attorney General, and how does her characterization differ from the understanding of the role advanced by Goldsmith? How does it differ from the more general characterization of the lawyer's role advanced by Wendel? Which of these positions do you find most persuasive?

2. ***Semantic Quibbling?*** National security scholar and former OLC lawyer Marty Lederman argued that those who criticized Yates for her emphasis on the "best" view of the law and the department's obligation to do what is just and right were nit-picking. He said that she really meant to suggest that the Trump administration had a discriminatory motive in enacting the ban, but that she had not wanted to say so outright.[25] Is that interpretation of her memo supported by language in it indicating that she was not "convinced that the Executive Order is lawful"?

3. ***Mutual Mistrust and the Yates Controversy.*** In an interview several months after Trump fired her, Yates explained that she first learned about the executive order from her deputy, who had read about it online, just hours after Yates met with White House Counsel Don McGahn to discuss security concerns relating to Michael Flynn, Trump's designated national security advisor. McGahn did not mention the executive order to her during that meeting. Yates later learned that lawyers in the Office of Legal Counsel had reviewed the executive order and had been instructed not to share it with Yates.[26] How might this history relate to how Yates handled the situation?

4. ***Why Didn't Yates Resign?*** Several days after learning about the executive order, Yates met with political appointees and senior staff to discuss whether the order was constitutional. She later told a reporter that she left the meeting deeply skeptical about the argument advanced by some officials in the

---

[25] Marty Lederman, *Sally Yates Did the Right Thing,* JUST SECURITY, Jan. 31, 2017.

[26] Ryan Lizza, *Why Sally Yates Stood Up to Trump,* NEW YORKER, May 29, 2017.

room that the order had nothing to do with religion. According to Yates, she went back to her office to weigh her options and decided that she should either resign or refuse to defend the order. In explaining why she chose the latter option, she said this:

> Resignation would have protected my own personal integrity, because I wouldn't have been part of this, but I believed, and I still think, that I had an obligation to also protect the integrity of the Department of Justice. And that meant that D.O.J. doesn't go into court on something as fundamental as religious freedom, making an argument about something that I was not convinced was grounded in truth. . . In fact, I thought, based on all the evidence I had, that it was based on religion. And then I thought back to Jim Crow laws, or literacy tests. Those didn't say that the purpose was to prevent African-Americans from voting. But that's what the purpose was. . . This is a defining, founding principle of our country: religious freedom. How can the Department of Justice go in and defend something that so significantly undermines that, when we're not convinced it's true?[27]

Does this explanation suggest something about what Yates meant in her memo by the "best" view of the law? If it indicates that she thought that the order was illegal based on what she thought about how the law applied to the facts, would that provide sufficient justification for refusing to defend the order rather than resigning in protest, as Goldsmith and Wendel suggest she should have done instead if she had deep moral objections to the order?

D. SUMMARY

In this chapter we considered two issues: (1) Who is the client of the government lawyer? (2) How should the government lawyer approach her counseling duties? The size and complexity of government and the often diffuse nature of authority and electoral accountability often make it challenging for government lawyers to identify the client and to provide advice that serves the client's interest.

---

[27] *Id.*

SUBPART C

INDIVIDUAL AND SMALL BUSINESS CLIENTS

■ ■ ■

In this section, we examine the sectors of the legal profession that serve primarily individuals and small businesses. Most of these lawyers work in solo and small firm practices. Within solo and small firm practice, however, there are wide variations in lawyers' social backgrounds, the types of clients they represent and the work they do, and how they find clients and manage their practice. We begin our examination of these sectors with an overview of solo and small firm practice in Chapter 12. In In Chapter 13, we explore the plaintiffs' bar, with particular focus on the variety, status hierarchies, and referral networks within the sector of the profession that represents plaintiffs, individuals, and small businesses. In Chapter 14, we study boutique firms, many of which resemble large law firms, in that they represent large organizational clients, but resemble small firms in their size, personnel practices, and specialization in particular subject areas.

CHAPTER 12

SOLO AND SMALL FIRM PRACTICE

■ ■ ■

A. INTRODUCTION

The largest single sector of law practice consists of lawyers who practice alone or in small firms. There are significant differences among solo and small firm practitioners in different regions and different practice types. Some small firm practitioners represent large organizational clients, but many do not. This chapter focuses primarily on solo and small firm lawyers who represent individuals and small businesses; Chapter 14 examines the sector of small firm practice commonly known as "boutique" practice in which lawyers identify themselves as engaging in a similar quality and sophistication of practice as at large firms.

We begin with a sample of scholarly and journalistic descriptions of solo and small firm practice. The first part of the chapter illustrates the huge variety among types of solo and small firm practice, with particular attention to the differences in the way that these lawyers enter the practice, find clients, and manage their work lives. We also note the differences between rural, suburban, and urban practice, and different subject matter specialties. We will then examine some of the major ethical issues that are most salient to solo and small firm practitioners, many of which stem from cash flow problems that plague many small businesses. We will explore reasons why solo and small firm lawyers are more likely to face bar discipline than are lawyers in large firms, and we consider what, if anything, should be done about it.

B. PORTRAITS OF SOLO AND SMALL FIRM PRACTICE

Solo practitioners constituted three-fifths of the bar in 1948. Now they are 50 percent of lawyers in private practice, or about 38 percent of the bar. They are the largest single practice setting among American lawyers.[1] Small firms (five or fewer lawyers) account for another 10 percent of the profession, bringing solo and small firm practice to over half of lawyers in private practice and about 40 percent of the bar. Solo and small firm practice reflects the diversity of the American profession, but immigrants and people from modest socioeconomic backgrounds long predominated, in

---

[1] THE LAWYER STATISTICAL REPORT, AMERICAN BAR FOUNDATION (2012).

part because of the considerable barriers to entry to large firm, corporate, and government legal practice. The early-twentieth century waves of immigration from Ireland and Southern and Eastern Europe triggered a nativist alarm, especially among well-to-do whites in the urban areas where immigrants settled. The elite bar, composed primarily of Protestant corporate lawyers, attempted to curb the business-getting conduct of ethnic urban solo and small firm lawyers who practiced in areas such as personal injury and criminal law. The elites wrote ethics rules that proscribed client-getting activities such as solicitation and regulated contingent fee practices. In this and other ways, the organized bar "conveyed the impression that these ethnic lawyers—who struggled for clients—were less ethical than other lawyers."[2] Understanding this background sheds light on ways in which the rules of professional conduct have reflected social power and generated conflict within the profession over conceptions of professionalism.

In this segment, we explore the reality behind these stereotypes about solo and small firm practice. The first excerpt is from the leading study of the practice setting, a 1996 book based on lengthy interviews with solo and small firm lawyers in the greater New York City area. It portrays some of the distinctive qualities of the metropolitan solo and small firm practice sector.

THE BUSINESS OF PRACTICING LAW: THE WORK LIVES OF SOLO AND SMALL-FIRM ATTORNEYS

Carroll Seron (Temple University Press, 1996)[3]

Getting Started. There were two fairly typical career trajectories. One group began by working for the government. An equally notable group began as associates or employees of solo or small-firm practitioners. Less typical was the small group who began their careers in major Wall Street firms.

Attorneys described three fairly distinct though not mutually exclusive strategies of coping with the initiation rites of professionalization. Some cultivated an informal network of attorneys and court officials on whom they could call to ask questions, copy legal forms, or clarify court procedures. Some learned by watching other lawyers and then trying out what they saw. A minority of attorneys learned through mentors.

The desire for autonomy runs throughout the work lives of these attorneys. [They] knew that they did *not* want to work in a large firm. [One] "didn't want to be a cog in a wheel," and [another] thought "corporate law

---

[2] Leslie Levin, *The Ethical World of Solo and Small Law Firm Practitioners*, 41 HOUSTON L. REV. 309 (2004).

[3]

seemed awfully dull!" A small group of women reported that they modified their expectations about work because of children or other family obligations.

Getting Clients. Most of these attorneys overwhelmingly agree that, with time, the single most important source of new clients is referrals from former clients. Most pointed out that referrals from professional colleagues—other lawyers, real estate agents, accountants or bankers—are another important source of business.

[F]riends and family are a big but "unfortunate" source of business because "they're a pain; they feel they can call you any time and it's very hard to be candid." It can also be difficult to bill friends who "always call you up for advice. It is always cheap!" One group of men, however, have turned family and friends into a positive client-getting resource. These men reported that work has come through local sports activities, high school friends who now own business, or special interest clubs.

Non-advertising newspaper coverage may be a source of business. [A] Manhattan lawyer had some cases with substantial verdicts, and the local paper had written them up. [One lawyer reported getting] her name known in the community through her efforts on "public service type of things." For instance, she said, "I recently spoke at the YWCA. I was asked to speak on a panel, and that was covered really heavily by the press. I've had several shows that I've been involved in that have run on cable and several things on the radio."

[Many] feel that television advertising crosses the social divide between professional and unprofessional solicitation. [One] asked, "Can you really take anything seriously that you see on TV?" Some pointed out that they do not advertise on television because of what their colleagues will think or because of potential damage to their reputation.

[Other lawyers described slight variations in their marketing practices. One with a] practice focusing on immigration was asked to write a weekly column on current immigration issues for the largest Korean newspaper in the United States. [Anticipating major change in federal immigration law enacted in 1986], he accepted the invitation and has been writing the column ever since. [He also does television and radio programs frequently], speaking for fifteen minutes and then taking calls on the air. His television and radio style is "like a type of documentary." He also produces "a lot of brochures," which he hands out when he does lectures.

Organizing Practices. Most of these attorneys [characterized the majority of their practices as] "routine in the sense that they involve things I've done before," and observ[ed] that their professional practices do not entail very much legal research. Rather, it is the "people side" of the law that complicates their work and makes each case different.

For partners in small, traditional law firms, friendship—if not family—is the concept that captures the essential dynamic of their organization. The majority of these partnerships are between men of approximately the same age, many of whom met at other firms or in school, or shared office space and decided to start a firm together. Typically, partners explain, their agreement is verbal. By contrast, an associate in a small firm is an employee—somewhat marginal, isolated, or cut off from the partners. A partnership "track"—the essential building block of the corporate law firm—does not exist in most small-firm practices. Although associates *may* become partners, there are no cues, no time frames, no ground rules, no clear expectations. Associates also reported that they are not quite sure how or if they are formally evaluated.

The process of hiring associates reveals the embeddedness of small firms in a local community. Most typically, partners reported, they look for attorneys with some work experience; they try to avoid hiring a recent law school graduate unless the individual worked for them while in school. They also prefer someone from the immediate area; the rationale is that they have watched the person function in court or in the local district attorney's office; they "know" his or her reputation.

[A] managing attorney at a local Jacoby and Meyers office [said], in weighing the relative importance of entrepreneurial and legal skills, the former is "more important" because the latter can "always be bought." [Another lawyer] explained that working with clients is "all communication and salesmanship." [Other lawyers said] that qualities such as the "personal touch," "communication," and a willingness to cultivate a "bedside manner" are their most important professional skills in working with clients. "I haven't yet had a client who, you know, was looking for Clarence Darrow. I think they obviously want adequate and competent representation. But they *also* need people who are good listeners."

NOTES ON SERON

1. ***Variations in the Demographics of Solo and Small Firm Practice.*** Because of the geographic focus of Seron's study, and the years in which it was conducted, the lawyers whom she interviewed were predominantly (but not exclusively) white, and many were immigrants or children of immigrants from Eastern and Southern Europe. If the study were replicated in greater New York City or other areas today, it would find the population of lawyers to be different. What impact, if any, do you think that might have on the findings? If the study were conducted in the area in which you live now or have lived in the past, what do you imagine it might find?

2. ***The Path to Solo or Small Firm Practice.*** What are the reasons given by lawyers in Seron's study for choosing solo or small firm practice?

3. ***Marketing.*** Should any of the marketing practices used by solo and small firm lawyers in Professor Seron's study be prohibited? If so, why?

4. ***The Influence of the Internet.*** Seron did her interviews before the internet transformed communication. How do you think the Internet has affected solo and small firm lawyers' methods of networking, finding mentors, getting clients, and organizing their practices?

* * *

In the following study, based on interviews with 71 lawyers specializing in immigration law in New York City in 2006, Leslie Levin explores some of the characteristics of a relatively new type of urban practice.

SPECIALTY BARS AS A SITE OF PROFESSIONALISM: THE IMMIGRATION BAR EXAMPLE

Leslie Levin

8 University of St. Thomas Law Journal 194 (2011)

There appear to be some significant commonalities among members of the New York City immigration bar. One-third of the lawyers in the study are immigrants and almost one-third of the U.S.-born lawyers have at least one foreign-born parent. Some others had a strong connection with the immigrant experience. Most of the lawyers in the study did not attend elite law schools. Many are drawn to the work because of a desire to help others. A solo lawyer who was born in India explained:

> I am in this legal profession not only because there's the power, prestige and money in this profession, but I get an opportunity to serve people in the community also—immigration is one area where you can serve—you can really serve needy people, all right? In all other areas like say real estate, it's basically financial gain to your clients, but in immigration law area it's a lifelong gain to your client—that's one reason.

Immigration is comprised of several sub-specialties. Business immigration lawyers perform the work that must be done for organizations to sponsor a foreign national to enter and work legally in the United States. Most immigration lawyers who do not focus primarily on business immigration do at least some family-based immigration work. Family-based immigration lawyers represent foreign nationals who seek legal status based on their familial relationship to someone who is already legally residing in the United States. Some immigration lawyers also handle asylum claims or deportation defense work, the latter of which involves removal proceedings brought against individuals based on criminal convictions or against persons who lack authorization to be in the United States.

Many immigration lawyers work in solo and small firms (two to five lawyers). Even business immigration lawyers who work in this setting may represent large corporate clients. Immigration lawyers also work in larger boutique immigration firms, typically of less than twenty lawyers, although the largest immigration firm, Fragomen LLP, [has hundreds of] lawyers world-wide. A small number of large corporate law firms employ a few business immigration lawyers, primarily as a way to service their existing corporate clients.

Business immigration lawyers often work from offices in midtown Manhattan or in White Plains, New York. A few work from home. Since they do not go to immigration court or routinely attend hearings, proximity to federal buildings is not essential. They may work in relative isolation from other immigration lawyers. In contrast, the offices of many lawyers who do other types of immigration work are clustered in a few office buildings on lower Broadway in Manhattan, close to 26 Federal Plaza, where the immigration courts, the United States Citizenship and Immigration Services' (USCIS) New York City district office, and most of the other immigration enforcement offices are located. Alternatively, those who have family-based or asylum practices work near the immigrant communities they service.

The nature of immigration practice may help create an environment conducive to a strong feeling of community among immigration lawyers. Immigration lawyers, unlike many other lawyers, do not negotiate or litigate against one another. Instead, their opponent is the Government, which may stand in the way of their clients' efforts to legally live or work in the United States. These lawyers are competitors for business, but the competition does not negate the feeling of community. One experienced lawyer explained why:

> [W]e're not generally in an adversarial situation with each other. I mean, there is competitiveness . . . I would like that big client; they would like that big client. Some are more cutthroat than others, in terms of that. But we're non-adversarial . . . [W]e're not in court on opposite sides of the table, and I guess because we are helping. [T]he main focus of my practice is business immigration, and you know, that's less helping than when—when I'm representing a French banker, it's less helping and nurturing than [when] I'm helping a housekeeper from Jamaica come here and make a better life for her children, which I do, too. And then the cases that are even more are when you're dealing with humanitarian issues, and helping issues. So that's still the roots of it.

More than two-thirds of the lawyers in the study had taken no immigration law course or clinic during law school. (Almost all who had done so had graduated from law school within the past dozen years.) Only 40% of the lawyers reported that they received some systematic training in the workplace in how to practice immigration law. As a result, many immigration lawyers in the study had to teach themselves how to practice immigration law. Several lawyers reported that early in their careers, they relied on mentors, materials, or seminars [provided by the American Immigration Lawyers Association (AILA), which is the largest immigration lawyers' specialty bar] to learn how to practice immigration law. This was especially likely if the lawyer worked in an office with no other experienced immigration lawyers. One solo lawyer who was relatively new to immigration practice explained his learning process: "I sort of did it on my own, and took some seminars . . . And then I keep reading a lot. AILA has a lot of publications, also, that are like tips, particular to how you handle Immigration officers, and what to do, or not to do—things like that."

It is no accident that new lawyers turn to AILA to learn how to practice law. AILA deliberately seeks to train new immigration lawyers.

Not all immigration lawyers are good lawyers. In fact, some lawyers in the sample were openly critical of many of the lawyers who practice immigration law—including other AILA members. But in the view of many of the interviewed lawyers, a lawyer cannot even begin to be a good immigration lawyer unless he or she belongs to AILA. As one noted, "AILA represents, [I] . . . wouldn't say all of the immigration lawyers, but probably most good immigration lawyers belong to AILA." Closely connected to the conception of being a "good lawyer" is staying up to date with the law.

The fact that solo and small firm practitioners predominate in the immigration field may also create the conditions for a successful and collegial specialty bar. Generally speaking, lawyers in larger firms may rely heavily on office colleagues for information and for their understanding of professional norms. But many immigration lawyers are the only ones in their firms or office-sharing arrangements who practice immigration law. For such lawyers, AILA helps to provide collegial support not otherwise readily available. Indeed, membership in AILA seemed especially important for lawyers who worked on their own.

Although many immigration lawyers believe that their bar is unique, it shares certain similarities with other practice specialties in which solo and small firm lawyers predominate. Notably, personal injury lawyers generally do not oppose one another in court, and they share a common enemy: insurance companies. Personal injury lawyers also belong to a very collegial specialty bar association, the American Association for Justice, in which there is a great deal of information sharing. Criminal defense lawyers, like immigration lawyers, work in a system they consider unfair and they share a common opponent: the Government. Criminal defense attorneys also have a well-established specialty bar, the [National

Association of Criminal Defense Lawyers (NACDL)], which provides services similar to AILA.

* * *

The following vignettes round out Seron's and Levin's portraits of solo and small firm practice by showing different paths which lawyers have recently taken into the practice setting and how lawyers in these practices today describe the rewards and challenges of their work. Unlike the Seron and Levin studies, most of these vignettes are drawn from news stories and are accounts of the experience of just a few lawyers.

Solo and Small Practice After Big Firm Practice. Some solo practitioners graduate from elite law schools and/or practice in elite large firms before leaving to find more autonomy and closer connections to their clients than they can find in a large firm representing large corporate clients. Those who continue to represent large organizational clients while in solo or small firm practice are covered in Chapter 14 on boutique practice. The following vignettes illustrate the phenomenon of those who choose a solo or small firm practice serving individuals and small businesses.

> When Clair Harrington finished a three-year stint as a clerk for the Virginia Supreme Court, she had a plum job waiting for her at a big New York City law firm. But Harrington—who graduated high in her class at St. John's University School of Law—told the firm, Cahill Gordon & Reindel, that she wasn't interested. Instead, she joined Meyer, Goergen & Marrs, a firm of fewer than 10 lawyers in Richmond, Va.
>
> Harrington had spent a law school summer working for the 250-lawyer New York firm. She knew what to expect and decided she wanted something else. Though the salary was smaller, she says, the quality of life of a small firm in a small city made the choice easy. "A really common complaint I heard from associates that summer was that they had three or four years' experience, and they still weren't even allowed to take their own depositions, much less appear in court," says Harrington.
>
> At the Richmond firm, Harrington started out in litigation, and she was handling her own trials within three months. Eventually, she moved to the transactional side and found her niche in small-business lending. She was asked to become a partner after four years.
>
> Harrington also likes having greater autonomy to handle her caseload. "I don't have to report to multiple tiers of managers, each with their own agenda. I like not being micromanaged," she says.

> Harrington says she has noticed that certain personalities seem drawn to smaller firms: entrepreneurial types and those who prefer control of their work environment over a large salary. "It's about the relationship between effort and benefit. In a smaller firm, that relationship is much more obvious."[4]

Family-Friendly Solo Practice. As Seron's study showed, many lawyers choose solo practice because they believe it will give them greater control over their hours than they could have at a large firm. Some lawyers like the idea of solo practice, especially running a solo practice out of their home, so that they can be more available to their children.

> "Both physically and psychologically, the comfort of being in my own space helps my productivity," says [Danielle G.] Van Ess, 34, now the mother of three girls. [Van Ess does estate planning, adoptions, and residential real estate work.] "I can change the heat, make coffee at any time and tend to my baby privately. I always hear people complaining about how they spilled coffee on their clothes on the way to work and are uncomfortable all day. If that happens to me, I can just run upstairs."
>
> Isolation is [a] consideration for home-based workers, and [home-based solo practitioners say] finding ways to engage with the outside world is essential. Scheduling lunch appointments with colleagues and using public spaces (like a courthouse or law school library) to perform research are two of their strategies for staying connected.
>
> [T]he home-based office was a no-brainer financially for Van Ess, who used the money she would have spent on rent for technology and to hire a team of virtual assistants. But her decision to work from home was also rooted in the psychological benefit that the cozy setting provides for her clients, many of whom are initially intimidated by the idea of seeking legal advice.
>
> It works, Van Ess says, because she thinks of clients as guests, noting that many hug her on the way out. And when she goes to her clients' homes to conduct closings or to execute final documents, they get to return her gesture of hospitality. "It becomes very friendly instead of a sterile, buttoned-up kind of meeting," she says.[5]

---

[4] Margaret Graham Tebo, *Living Large at a Smaller Size: Top-Tier Law Grads and Big-Firm Hot Shots Take Their Smarts to Smaller Practices*, ABA J., Jan. 2007, at 26.

[5] Becky Beaupre Gillespie & Hollee Schwartz Temple, *Making the Home Work: It Takes More Than Space to Find Home Office Success* ABA J., July 2010, at 30.

There may be a connection between the type of clients Van Ess represents and her decision to locate her practice in her home and to describe her clients as guests.

New Social Sites. Solo practitioners have long shared office space and administrative support with other solos. In urban areas with co-working spaces, some use co-working space for client meetings and for a sense of workplace community. Lawyers' duty of confidentiality requires more private meeting areas and printing facilities than some co-working spaces allow, so businesses in major urban areas have sprung up to offer co-working space tailored to the needs of lawyers. Some facilitate sharing expertise and continuing education programs required by bar licensing rules.[6] Online social networks and other technologies also facilitate lawyers' exchange of expertise and other cooperative work arrangements.

Rural Solo Practice. Most studies of the legal profession in the last half-century have focused on urban or suburban lawyers. While this is unremarkable for many reasons, including the increasing urbanization of the United States, small town lawyers still exist. Their practices are in many ways similar to any other solo or small firm practice, but the leading study of the rural bar, published by Donald Landon in 1990, found a number of differences between the urban or metropolitan and rural bars.[7] Landon found the rural bar in Missouri that he studied was relatively homogeneous racially, ethnically, and religiously because the rural communities he studied were homogeneous. He observed a close consensus on values among the lawyers and zealous partisanship in advocacy to be muted because the social context discouraged rural lawyers from some of the zealous and conflictual advocacy that is tolerated or encouraged in larger urban areas.[8] He also found the rural Missouri bar to be minimally stratified, with many lawyers' practices sharing a similar mix of clients. According to Landon, the status hierarchy was not based on who the lawyer represented, because lawyers represented a similar mix of clients, but rather on how lucrative the lawyer's practice was. The stigma that urban large firm lawyers attach to solo and small firm practitioners and to their entrepreneurial client-getting efforts did not exist; there were no large firms in small towns and *all* lawyers needed to be entrepreneurial in the same ways. Whereas "[t]he city entrepreneur adapts to the urban setting by a heavy reliance on brokers for business" "the rural entrepreneur relies on reputation."[9] The small town lawyers in Landon's study were less likely

---

[6] Katie Thisdell, Co-Working Spaces for Lawyers Grow in Popularity, NAT'L JURIST, May 17, 2017.

[7] DONALD D. LANDON, COUNTRY LAWYERS: THE IMPACT OF CONTEXT ON PROFESSIONAL PRACTICE (1990).

[8] *Id.* at 146.

[9] *Id.* at 149.

to specialize, as there were not enough clients in a single classification to enable a practice limited to a particular subject area.

The types of matters that predominate differ from one rural area to another; lawyers in a resort community will have different clients and types of cases than lawyers in a farming community.

There is some evidence that rural communities lack sufficient lawyers.[10] For example, South Dakota has 66 counties, 64 of which have courthouses. The South Dakota Chief Justice believed that the administration of justice faced a dire situation as the lone lawyer in many rural counties retired. There were no lawyers in a few counties and only one or two in twenty more, even though over half of South Dakotans live and work in rural areas.[11] In 2013, South Dakota established Project Rural Justice modeled on successful programs to recruit doctors, veterinarians, and various health care professionals to set up practice in rural areas. Project Rural Justice provides a modest stipend to lawyers admitted in North Dakota who will set up practice in qualifying rural counties. Nineteen lawyers have set up practices. The program is funded through 2022 to allow 32 counties to request a lawyer, and the state legislature recently authorized expanding it to 48. Participating lawyers agree to practice in the rural county for five years in exchange for about $60,000 payable over the five years. Thus far, news reports say, only one lawyer has dropped out.[12] Those who stayed have general practices. A news report described two:

> Amanda Work grew up in West Virginia, and during law school she realized she didn't want to start her profession in a large metropolitan area.
>
> When Work heard about Project Rural Practice, she applied and was placed at Swier Law Firm working in Winner. It's her fourth year in the program and she has no plans to move or change jobs after the initial pilot program ends sometime next year. In addition to her legal work, she is also involved in the community, sitting on several committee boards and is president of the local chamber of commerce. Winner has a population of fewer than 3,000 people, but Work said she always has clients.
>
> "I pretty much take on any case that walks in the door—from family law to criminal defense," Work said. "As a rural attorney,

---

[10] Ethan Bronner, *No Lawyer for Miles So One Rural State Offers to Pay*, N.Y. TIMES, Apr. 8, 2013.

[11] David Gilbertson, *Reflections on the Rural Practice of Law in South Dakota: Past, Present, and Future*, 59 S.D. L. REV. 433 (2014).

[12] Libby Leyden, *Program to Establish Attorneys in Rural SD Thriving After Five Years*, WEST FARGO PIONEER, Oct. 6, 2017.

you help the community locally . . . and more attorneys are likely to move into the area knowing there is already an attorney there."

Similar to Work, Jake Fisher, the program's first official participant, has no plans to move once his five years are finished. Fisher went to school at Parkston High School and his family owns a farm between Parkston and Corsica. When he heard about the program after completing law school in Minneapolis, he decided it was time to return to his roots.

"Frankly I think the program ended up being a fairly big motivator in bringing me back to South Dakota," Fisher said.

Since moving to Corsica, Fisher has worked on agricultural, family, estate planning, and public defense cases. He is one of four or five attorneys practicing full time in Douglas County but said he is "constantly busy." Fisher said as a rural attorney he must become an expert on several areas of law. "It can take a lot of extra work to research and prepare because I am not doing the same thing every day," Fisher said.[13]

Rural practice requires the solo practitioner to be a generalist, to invest time in getting to know everyone in the local community, to be able to practice without mentoring, and to be willing to take the risk of practicing in an environment that is vulnerable to economic downturns.[14] The economic risk of a rural solo practice is illustrated by a news report that began by recounting a plaintive advertisement placed in the *Journal of the Kansas Bar Association* by a realtor in tiny Sedan, Kansas: "We, the people of Sedan, Kan., have a dire need for an attorney. Chautauqua County has one remaining attorney, who is looking forward to retirement." A few months later, Sedan found itself with a new lawyer, a woman who had a law office in another small town and thought she might open an office in Sedan. The story continues:

> Upon opening her Sedan office, McElroy placed a newspaper ad, giving her location as, simply, "between the Norgan's Sedan barber shop and Tom McCann's restaurant." She planned to charge clients $125 an hour but, given the recession, she decided to charge $80. Typical of a small-town practice, many Sedan residents stopped by McElroy's office just to talk.
>
> Rural attorneys discover that they enjoy helping neighbors, owning their own cases and, for some, watching their practices flow with farming seasons.

---

[13] Id.

[14] Bruce Cameron, BECOMING A RURAL LAWYER (2013); Lorelei Laird, *In Rural America, There are Job Opportunities and a Need for Lawyers*, ABA J., Oct. 2014.

But after opening her Sedan office, McElroy only managed to pick up a handful of clients. "I think it's the economy," she says. "If people had more resources, I think they would have contacted me. I just couldn't hold out." McElroy closed her office in Sedan. She still has her Coffeyville office and is retooling her business model to make it work financially. "I also travel to Elk County, which is pretty small. Really, most areas around here are small," she says. "Most attorneys in the area, of which there are not many, travel to other counties to represent people. That is what I do."[15]

NOTES ON PATHS TO SOLO OR SMALL FIRM PRACTICE

1. ***Getting Started, Getting Clients, and Organizing the Practice.*** The Seron excerpt focused on three aspects of solo and small firm practice: getting started, getting clients, and organizing the practice. How do the lawyers in these excerpts approach these three fundamental aspects of law practice?

2. ***Rewards and Challenges of Solo and Small Firm Practice.*** These studies and vignettes identify a number of features of solo or small firm practice that you may find appealing and some that may seem daunting. What are the major rewards and challenges of the practices? Which accounts of the practice do you find most plausible and which ones do you suspect may not reflect the realities of such practices in the area in which you live today?

3. ***The Economic Challenges of Small Businesses.*** Most of the lawyers in these accounts identified autonomy and work-life balance as the attractions of solo practice. And, yet, they also identified the struggle to get clients and the razor-thin profit margins as the most significant challenges of the practice. Is there a tension between these two visions of solo practice? As we examine the following materials on ethical issues in solo and small firm practice, consider whether the financial pressures facing small law practices, which are of course shared with other small businesses, present unique challenges for lawyers because the ethical obligations they owe their clients may be more stringent than the ethical obligations other small business owners owe their clients.

C. ETHICAL ISSUES IN SOLO AND SMALL FIRM PRACTICE

Lawyers in solo and small firm practice are thought by some to be less competent and less ethical than lawyers in the large organizational client hemisphere. That perception may partly reflect pure animus of elites against the ethnic groups who tended to dominate the small firm sector in urban areas in the early and mid-twentieth century. It may also reflect a

---

15 Leslie A. Gordon, *Green Achers: The Lure of BigLaw and Big Cities May Stir Some. But for a Certain Solo Breed, the Small Town is the Place to Be*, ABA J., Nov. 2009, at 42.

tendency of urbanites to dismiss rural areas as less sophisticated. But that perception may also have some basis in phenomena other than ethnic or regional bias. Jerome Carlin's classic study of solo practitioners found that the pressures of running a marginal practice did lead to ethical violations.[16] Lawyers in solo and very small firm practice are more likely than lawyers in large firms or government to be the subject of bar discipline. Is that because they commit more ethical violations? If so, are the ethical violations of solo lawyers attributable to personal traits of the lawyers or to the economic pressures of running a small business or other factors?

Many complaints filed against solos and small firm lawyers allege neglect of client matters and failure to communicate with clients. Another rule that is enormously important for all lawyers but that some lawyers facing cash flow problems find challenging is Model Rule 1.15, which requires lawyers to maintain client funds in an account separate from the lawyer's or law firm's own accounts.

In the materials that follow, we explore the ethical issues most salient in solo and small firm practice. In the process, we address some of the questions about the reasons for the disparity in bar discipline based on practice sector.

THE ETHICAL WORLD OF SOLO AND SMALL LAW FIRM PRACTITIONERS

Leslie C. Levin
41 Houston Law Review 309 (2004)

Solo and small firm lawyers are disciplined at a far greater rate than other lawyers. For example, in California, 78% of disciplinary cases prosecuted and completed in 2000–2001 were against solo practitioners, even though they represented only 23% of the lawyers practicing in that state. Similarly, 34% of Texas lawyers are solo practitioners, yet they receive 67% of all public sanctions. When Texas lawyers who practice in firms of two to five lawyers are added with solo practitioners, they make up 59% of all practicing lawyers yet they receive over 98% of all public discipline. Much of the discipline imposed on lawyers is for failure to communicate with clients and neglect of client matters.

Of course, the fact that solo and small firm practitioners receive a disproportionate amount of discipline does not, in itself, prove that these lawyers are less ethical than their colleagues who work in other practice settings. Individual clients with personal plight problems may be more likely than corporate clients to file discipline complaints against their lawyers. This may occur because individuals of moderate means have fewer mechanisms for redress when their lawyers engage in wrongdoing than do

[16] JEROME E. CARLIN, LAWYERS ON THEIR OWN: THE SOLO PRACTITIONER IN AN URBAN SETTING (1994 rev. ed., originally published 1962), Chapter 4.

corporate clients. In addition, individuals are more likely to be emotionally invested in their personal plight matters or more adversely affected by their outcomes. It may be easier for under-financed discipline systems to successfully prosecute cases against solo or small firm practitioners—who have fewer resources to defend against these complaints—than it is to pursue large firm lawyers who may be able to hide behind the conduct of others. Finally, bias within the disciplinary system may account for a disproportionate amount of discipline being imposed on solo and small firm practitioners.

The discipline statistics provide only part of the picture, because many ethical issues arise in practice that are undetected by clients—who are the primary source of disciplinary complaints—or by the discipline system. In some cases, lawyers themselves do not know that bar rules have been violated. Even when complaints are made to disciplinary bodies, many violations of ethical rules are diverted outside the discipline system or are routinely underenforced. In order to get a better sense of the ethical world of these lawyers, it is therefore necessary to look beyond the statistics and more broadly into their practices and ethical decision-making.

In an effort to learn more about the ethical world and ethical decision-making of solo and small firm practitioners, I asked forty-one lawyers in the New York City metropolitan area about their professional development, office practices, and work experiences. I wanted to explore how lawyers who work on their own—or in very small practice settings—learn professional norms and go about resolving ethical questions.

The lawyers' practices ranged from the traditional solo or small firm "personal plight" practice to sophisticated transactional or corporate litigation practices. Most of the lawyers in the sample practiced in the areas of family law, personal injury, real estate, commercial work, workers' compensation, and trusts and estates. However, some of the other areas of practice included banking, criminal law, common carrier law, education law, intellectual property, and securities. Six lawyers in this group predominantly represented large corporations, sophisticated investors, or governmental entities such as school districts.

Although the lawyers practiced in a variety of physical settings, had significantly different types of clientele, and very different areas of expertise, many of them agreed that the tremendous pressure to bring in clients, along with cash flow, are the biggest challenges of working in a solo or small firm practice.

Specialization. Forty years ago, most lawyers practiced in solo and small firm practices, and it was not unusual for those lawyers to maintain general practices in which they did real estate closings, personal injury cases, wills, and small corporate transactions. As the practice of law has become more complex and technology has increased the speed at which law is practiced, it has become both easier and harder for solo and small firm practitioners to keep up with changes in the law and to perform their work in a competent fashion. As a threshold matter, the ability of these lawyers to provide competent representation is affected by decisions they make about the number of areas in which they practice law, the number and types of clients they take on, their willingness to reach out to colleagues for assistance, and their diligence in staying abreast of changes in the law.

While some lawyers reported that when they started out in practice they did "everything," a number of them eventually made decisions about how many substantive areas of law they could handle competently, and most decided to limit their practices to a few substantive areas.

[O]ne third of the solo and small firm lawyers I interviewed were true general practitioners who regularly practiced in four or more areas. Most of them were male and worked outside of Manhattan. One important motivation for not limiting their work to a single practice area appears to be economic. Some lawyers who do not specialize are also motivated by the desire to provide "cradle to grave" service to their clients who rely on them heavily for advice.

The comments of a few of the lawyers I interviewed indicated that the pull to provide a range of legal services can be especially strong when the lawyer is rooted in the ethnic community or when the lawyer feels that she is a trusted family lawyer.

Advice Networks. For lawyers in solo and small firm practices, part of the key to performing competently is their ability to draw on the knowledge and judgment of other lawyers. Many of the lawyers I interviewed reported that they routinely reached out with questions that arose in practice, not only to other attorneys with whom they were formally affiliated, but also to suite mates and to attorneys outside their offices. Many lawyers reported having a group of attorneys—ranging in size from three to twelve lawyers—to whom they would reach out with questions. The group of attorneys to whom a lawyer reaches out when the lawyer has a question in practice is referred to here as the lawyer's advice network.

These lawyers rely on advice networks early in their careers to learn how to practice law, and they typically look first to lawyers with whom they are formally affiliated, to suite mates and to lawyer friends. As they become more experienced, many of them still rely on those networks for questions of judgment, when they want to learn about a judge or an adversary, or when they face legal questions they have not previously confronted.

Staying Up-to-Date on the Law. Most of the solo and small firm lawyers I interviewed believed that they were able to stay up-to-date on the law in the areas in which they practiced. More than half of them reported reading the *New York Law Journal*, the local daily legal newspaper, on a regular basis. The lawyers who specialized also often read a variety of trade and specialized legal materials because they felt it was essential to their representation of their clients. General practitioners relied heavily on written materials distributed by bar associations and on CLE courses, which are mandatory in New York, to stay current on the law in the areas in which they practiced.

Perception and Frequency of Ethical Challenges. Lawyers face ethical issues—in the broadest sense of the term—on a daily basis. Yet when asked about the "ethical issues" they encountered in their practice, the lawyers I interviewed rarely paused to ask what was meant by this deliberately ambiguous term. The lawyers' responses suggested that they usually interpreted the question to mean compliance with formal rules of professional conduct; only a handful of them interpreted it to include broader moral questions of right and wrong. More significantly, many of the lawyers I interviewed did not appear to think much about the ethical issues they encountered in their day-to-day work lives.

Of course, the reports by lawyers that they did not encounter many ethical issues in their practices does not mean that they did not actually confront ethical issues with some frequency. While a small number of the lawyers recognized that they constantly face ethical issues such as whether they represent their clients adequately, the responses of many of the lawyers I interviewed suggested that they simply did not think very much about legal ethics or that they did not consider the issues they confronted in moral or ethical terms.

The "Bad" Client. The lawyers identified a wide array of ethical issues they encountered, but one of the most common ethical challenges encountered by solo and small firm practitioners was the problem of a client who wished to engage in some form of fraud. One attorney stated, "I've had clients ask me to change documents, change dates, change amounts, and I have had people ask me to do that. And you gotta be like, whoa." As another lawyer explained, "It's definitely clients who want to do stuff."

Some lawyers who frequently encountered clients who wished to engage in unethical conduct attributed this phenomenon to the nature of their practice specialty rather than to the size of their practice. For example, a lawyer who specialized in estate planning noted that many of his clients were in cash businesses and therefore "I'm constantly confronted with what my client is going to report." He observed, "Basically, my clients are hiring me to do things that are unethical." For this reason, "If you want to be a lawyer and you want to practice [tax] law, sometimes you have to bend the law."

Matrimonial lawyers reported that clients often sought to underreport their income on financial disclosure statements; real estate and commercial lawyers said that money "under the table" in purchase and sale transactions was common; and personal injury lawyers reported clients who faked the cause of their injury or who would ask about staying out of work longer than necessary to improve their chances of recovering a larger amount of money. These situations present some of the most serious ethical challenges for lawyers, as well as some of the greatest personal risks, because of the potential civil or criminal liability if they help their clients engage in fraud.

[S]ome solo and small firm lawyers reported that they had declined to represent certain clients for ethical reasons. The ability to turn away business is, however, a luxury reserved for lawyers who have developed economically successful law practices. As one successful estates lawyer explained, “Once you've been at this game for a while, I guess once you've amassed a couple of dollars, it's a lot easier to say no to a client than to take it on.”

Office Management Problems. One common view of solo and small firm lawyers is that they often face difficulties arising from poor law office management, ranging from taking on too many matters, to poor filing and calendaring systems, to an inadequate understanding of the economics of law practice. These problems can directly contribute to neglect of client matters and failure to communicate with clients, which are among the most common reasons for lawyer discipline. Contrary to the conventional view, however, most of the lawyers I spoke with reported that they had control over their caseloads and calendaring and filing systems. Only a small number indicated that these were recurrent difficulties in their practices. [L]ife events can sometimes cause even a well-run practice to become temporarily unmanageable for lawyers, especially when they are working on their own. One of the solo practitioners I interviewed described how serious surgery had made it extremely difficult for him to keep his practice going while he was recovering, especially because he had no secretary. Another solo attorney described how a client had threatened to file a grievance against her because she had failed to promptly handle a client matter after the unexpected death of the lawyer's husband. In these cases the lack of a partner, associate, or paralegal made the task of handling client matters diligently virtually impossible for periods of time, even for the most conscientious lawyers.

The office arrangements and affiliations described by the lawyers I interviewed presented potential—yet mostly unrecognized—conflict of interest problems. Most of the lawyers I interviewed had no formal system for checking conflicts of interest among their clients, relying on an “in your head” method when new clients sought representation.

Resolving Ethical Problems in Practice. [T]he lawyers I interviewed learned informal bar norms through their communities of practice, starting with observations of other lawyers and conversations within their law offices. Indeed, their office-sharing arrangements often create rich social environments from which they learn a great deal during their early years in practice.

Although many of the early lessons are acquired through listening and passive observation, when new lawyers confronted serious ethical issues such as client fraud, some of them talked about reaching out to mentors or advice networks for guidance. For example, one lawyer told the story of running down the hall to consult with her partner, who was also her father-in-law, when she suspected that a long-time firm client had manufactured a personal injury claim. A solo practitioner explained that he was about to call a lawyer in his advice network to talk about a client who wanted to testify falsely at an upcoming criminal trial. Not surprisingly, sometimes the advice the lawyers received conformed with formal bar rules and sometimes it did not.

It appears that the conclusions that these lawyers reach the first few times they confront a particular ethical problem may provide a template of sorts that is used throughout their legal careers absent an extraordinary event, such as a disciplinary complaint, that may cause them to reconsider their practices. For example, some older lawyers described a stock response to ethical issues that was developed by watching a mentor or employer during their early years in practice. One lawyer described his response to what he said was the weekly problem of workers' compensation clients who were interested in defrauding insurance carriers: "My policy, which I inherited from my father, is basically to throw them out immediately, and I do. They always manage to find someone that will represent them but we won't."

Although it is possible that the lawyers' own personal morality also affects their responses to this issue, at least some of the lawyers I interviewed indicated that their personal morality did not play much of a role in their responses to this problem. Indeed, one young lawyer who self-described herself as a "good person" and who claimed, "if something doesn't feel right, I'm not going to do it," routinely looked the other way when cash was passed under the table in real estate transactions.

Psychological Processes and Ethical Decision-Making. [T]he lawyers I interviewed rarely spoke of lessons learned in law school when they described their ethical decision-making. Instead, they seemed to form their conclusions about how to resolve certain ethical questions during their early years in practice. Colleagues and mentors often affected their decision-making when first confronted with ethical issues. Once these lawyers become more experienced, they do not seem to reconsider ethical questions they have previously addressed.

Lessons from social psychology help explain these observations. The psychological pressure on individuals to conform to the behavior of a group can be powerful. Although solo and small firm practitioners view themselves as "independent," these lawyers often operate within—and are influenced by—a rich social environment comprised of suite mates and members of their advice networks. Social psychologists have found that a group is more effective at inducing conformity if (1) it consists of experts; (2) the members are important to the individual; or (3) the members are comparable to the actor in some way. Certainly within collegial office-sharing arrangements or tightly-knit legal communities or practice specialties, many young lawyers would view the other lawyers with whom they come in contact as experts, as "important" colleagues, mentors, sources of referrals, or, at a minimum, as comparable to the young lawyer in some ways. Therefore, it would not be surprising that the psychological pressure to conform to certain types of behaviors would be powerful in this context.

The Perception of Formal Rules and Discipline. The lawyers I interviewed view certain formal bar rules and the lawyer discipline system with open skepticism. Historically, solo and small firm lawyers have felt that some of the formal rules were written to limit their business-getting opportunities and they may be, to some degree, correct. These lawyers also harbor a concern that solo and small firm attorneys are unfairly targeted for discipline more often than lawyers who practice in other settings.

When skepticism about formal rules is coupled with concerns about the fairness of the discipline system, the likelihood of lawyer compliance with formal rules is further reduced. [S]ome of the lawyers I interviewed believe that bias arises not only in the disproportionate prosecution of solo and small firm practitioners, but also in the types of matters prosecuted and in the discipline actually imposed. Under-enforcement of formal bar rules that are clear and specific may also contribute to this perception. A few of the lawyers I interviewed questioned why prosecutors rarely face lawyer discipline or why large firm lawyers are rarely disciplined for clearly impermissible conduct. Of course, discipline may be imposed on these lawyers more often than other lawyers realize because the discipline may be private. But when the perception persists that the rules are not enforced—or that they are selectively enforced—this can lead to disrespect of formal bar rules and cynicism about the efficacy and purpose of the discipline system.

NOTES ON LEVIN

1. ***What Accounts for the Disparity in Rates of Discipline?*** Why do you think lawyers in solo and small firm practice are disciplined at much higher rates than lawyers in other types of practice?

2. ***Are Solo Practitioners Disciplined Too Much or Large Firm Lawyers Too Little, or Neither?*** How would we know whether the problem in the disparity of rates of discipline, if there is one, is that solo practitioners

are disciplined too much or that the bar hasn't done enough to regulate incompetent or unscrupulous lawyers in other practice settings? What is the relationship between ethics rules and bar regulatory processes, on the one hand, and the social structure and politics of the American legal profession, on the other?

3. ***Cash Flow Problems.*** Solo and small firm lawyers who are strapped for cash may be tempted to borrow from client accounts to make ends meet. That is strictly forbidden by state ethics rules. (Large well-established firms are rarely so short of cash, or so cut off from the ability to borrow from a bank, that they feel tempted to borrow money from client accounts in order to pay their staff or their rent.) What might be done to improve compliance with state ethics rules requiring lawyers to keep client funds segregated from lawyers' personal funds and from law firm funds?

4. ***Ethical Norms and the First Job.*** Seron and Levin identified the first job out of law school as being very important in teaching skills and norms. Do you think the first job is more or less significant for small firm and solo practitioners as compared to other lawyers? Is the phenomenon something that the bar should focus on in its efforts to ensure that lawyers are competent and ethical?

5. ***Should the Bar Prohibit Solo Practice? Should It Regulate It Differently?*** Professor Richard Abel, an eminent scholar of the legal profession, has proposed that lawyers be prohibited from practicing entirely solo. That is, every lawyer should be required to affiliate with at least one other lawyer in order to protect both the lawyers and their clients from the sort of problems identified by Seron and Levin. What do you think of that proposal? Do Levin and the note above about the growth of lawyer co-working spaces and on-line services and lawyer networks suggest that informal affiliation is already occurring? Many solo practitioners are also providing services through web-based services like LegalZoom, Rocket Lawyer, and many other companies that offer both online automated assistance completing legal documents and the opportunity, for a flat fee, to consult by phone or live chat with lawyers affiliated with the business. (These services are discussed in more detail in Chapter 19 on unauthorized practice.) How might the bar build on the informal affiliations described by Seron and Levin, the co-working phenomenon, and the growth of online legal services and lawyer networks to protect lawyers and clients from the hazards of truly solo practice?

D. SUMMARY

In this chapter, we studied the nature of solo and small firm practice and some of the major ethical challenges lawyers face in this practice setting. Urban, suburban, and rural solo and small firm practice differ, and the ethnic and religious heterogeneity that has long characterized the sector in urban areas is less in some rural areas. We examined the ethical decision-making of solo and small firm practitioners and identified the ethical violations for which they are most likely to be disciplined. We considered the reasons why they are more likely to face bar discipline than are lawyers in large firms. We concluded by considering proposals to improve ethics rules compliance in this sector.

CHAPTER 13

PLAINTIFFS' PRACTICE

■ ■ ■

A. INTRODUCTION

The sector of the bar that specializes in representing plaintiffs is varied and also stratified, with some types of practices being more profitable and prestigious than others. The demographics and stratification of this sector have implications for the regulation of lawyers and for a number of contemporary debates about the desirability of changing the law governing torts, class actions, and attorneys' fees.

While large corporations occasionally sue each other and are represented by large firms as plaintiffs, they are frequently sued by employees, consumers, and other individuals or small businesses. Litigators at large firms are more likely to represent defendants, and litigators at small firms often specialize in representing plaintiffs. There are major differences in sophistication, complexity, remuneration, and business generation among practices specializing in representing plaintiffs. This chapter begins with a look at how plaintiffs' lawyers' professional identity is shaped in relation to their position on substantive law, the way they find clients and organize their practices, and their perception of how the public views the law. The chapter then examines the referral networks among lawyers who represent plaintiffs. Finally, the chapter examines how lawyers in this sector are paid, including through contingency fee agreements and statutes authorizing the court to order the losing defendant to pay a prevailing plaintiff's attorneys' fees.

B. THE STRUCTURE OF THE PLAINTIFFS' BAR AND STRATIFICATION WITHIN IT

As we saw in Chapter 2, class, race and ethnic divisions are quite visible within the American legal profession and have been for many years. Until the mid-twentieth century, corporate firms would not hire Jews or people of color, and some would not hire Catholics. As a result, well into the twentieth century, urban plaintiffs' lawyers, like many lawyers in solo and small firm practice, were predominantly from working class families and often were Catholics or Jews from immigrant families. Even today, lawyers serving large corporations tend to have attended elite universities, which draw disproportionately from privileged communities, while lawyers serving individuals and small businesses are more likely to come from working class and lower middle class backgrounds and to have attended state university law schools or local law schools.

The way that socioeconomic class and ethnicity have affected the careers of lawyers and contributed to the particular patterns of stratification in the bar generally, and among plaintiffs' lawyers, is the subject of the excerpt that follows. Although the article is relatively recent, the world of urban lawyers generally has changed since the events described in the study. Large law firms have abandoned their refusal to hire Catholics, Jews, and people of color, which has opened career opportunities. In addition, immigration from all parts of the world is changing the demographics of the bar.

PHILIP CORBOY AND THE CONSTRUCTION OF THE PLAINTIFFS' PERSONAL INJURY BAR

Sara Parikh & Bryant Garth
30 Law & Social Inquiry 269 (2005)

Philip Corboy has been at the top of the personal injury bar in Chicago for most of the period after World War II. Corboy personifies the characteristics of elite personal injury lawyers in Chicago today. The elite tend to be Catholic or Jewish males who come from modest backgrounds and attend local law schools. They are at the top of a referral chain that channels the biggest cases to them and their firms, and they reinforce their position through their ability and willingness to bring high-risk cases to juries.

In the period after World War II, the legal profession appeared to a young lawyer like Corboy to be dominated by and for the corporate bar, which recruited almost exclusively from a WASP establishment legitimated with degrees from Ivy League schools. Corporate lawyers controlled the bar associations and played civic roles that reinforced their professional status. Catholics or Jews or the graduates of local law schools, doubly penalized for their working-class or immigrant backgrounds, had limited access to the corporate elite. Lacking this access, they typically followed a different track.

[In an interview, Corboy recounted that his grandparents immigrated from Ireland; his parents graduated only from high school. After military service, Corboy graduated from Loyola Law School of Chicago as valedictorian in 1948, but found that Chicago firms refused to even interview young men like him. He said the] corporate bar "did not come on campus. They did not interview. I don't know how you got [a job with them], because I didn't get one. I think they chose people who were from prestige law schools who were on the law review and all that. The same way they do today." [Corboy explained that his uncle got him a job interview at the

City of Chicago Corporation Counsel's office, where he got his first job as a lawyer.]

Legal careers within the political machine provided an alternative track to the one available to the corporate bar. The predominantly Irish Catholic political system in Chicago produced politicians, U.S. attorneys, municipal corporation counsel, state's attorneys, and public defenders, and there were places in the judiciary to reward those who provided service in the other positions. The products of the system, as Corboy himself noted, were "shaped" and "matured" by the "pristine political system." He added, "When I started the practice of law, all judges came through the political system." The judiciary's background meant that they "understood people. That understanding of people made them very, very good judges." The Chicago plaintiffs' bar has its roots in this local political environment.

James Dooley was another Irish Catholic graduate of Loyola. Dooley was building a reputation in the emerging field of personal injury. At the time, according to Corboy, there were "two types of lawyers that handled personal injury cases. Those who acquire business and are either called litigation lawyers or they're just called personal injury lawyers; they don't try cases." Then there were those like Dooley, who "tried cases." [Corboy went to work for Dooley.]

Dooley did not recruit from the corporate bar or the elite schools. Those with elite credentials still thought of personal injury lawyers as ambulance chasers with poor standards of professional ethics. Personal injury lawyers did not occupy prominent positions in professional organizations or have a reputation for trial craft. Dooley, Corboy could see, was working to distance himself and others like him who "tried cases" from the ambulance chasers and case processors.

The Dooley strategy was to gain respect for their craft as attorneys who tried cases. While a law practice focused on advice and negotiation had the highest prestige in the corporate bar at the time, the quest for professional respectability among personal injury lawyers militated in favor of investment in pure law—litigation—that would separate these lawyers from the taint of ambulance chasing and case processing. Dooley's activities also included an extensive appellate practice seeking to expand tort law on behalf of plaintiffs. Dooley invested in scholarship, authoring a three-volume treatise, Modern Tort Law (1977). Dooley in these ways built his reputation for trial and doctrinal expertise and not incidentally helped promote liberalization in tort law. He continued to practice as a leading plaintiffs' lawyer until he was elected to the Illinois Supreme Court in 1976.

Under Dooley's tutelage, Corboy invested heavily in the practice of trying cases. Corboy learned the importance both of trial craft and of the organizations that would celebrate it. Corboy also learned from Dooley how to prosper without the overt taint of ambulance chasing. Dooley followed a professional strategy to get business—through referrals from other lawyers. With this experience under his belt, Corboy left Dooley's firm in 1952 to start his own practice. At the time, it was standard practice for a young personal injury attorney to learn the trade under an established player, then leave to build his own practice.

Having seen how Dooley got business, when he went out on his own, he networked aggressively with other lawyers to generate business.

The referral system ensures that the higher value cases will, as a general rule, work their way up through the hierarchy of the plaintiffs' bar, thereby reinforcing the stratification in the profession and the dominance of the prevailing elite. [P]ersonal injury lawyers work hard to develop and maintain these referral relationships, and having a referral-based business is a sign of prestige in the personal injury bar. Corboy reflected that "I think there is a feeling of accomplishment when another lawyer recognizes your specialty . . . I like getting business from lawyers who think I'm competent." Another high-end plaintiffs' lawyer commented: "Having a good, strong referral base means that you don't have to do the other things that most attorneys desiring respect would want to avoid: advertising, chasing, having to work really hard to get cases."

The 1960s were watershed years for the plaintiffs' bar. They were able to improve their reputation with a combination of trial craft and professional bar activity, and they improved their economic position through legislative lobbying and legal arguments made to judges like themselves. The timing was right. They were in tune with the spirit of the socially activist state and indeed relatively moderate as a group in relation to the civil rights struggles and antiwar efforts.

Elite plaintiff and defense lawyers helped to define the rules that governed their growing field. Certainly there were differences in perspective, but there was a shared sense that the law and practice of personal injury was developing in a positive fashion. The growing success in the courtroom fed further success in the appellate courts.

The attack on the plaintiffs' bar did not begin with corporate America. As litigation picked up for a number of reasons, attention began to focus more on the personal injury sector. The major challenge began through the writings of two academics, Robert Keeton and Jeffrey O'Connell, who promoted no-fault automobile insurance as an efficient way to bring compensation to accident victims. Liberal Democrats led by Michael Dukakis in Massachusetts, along with a few insurance companies, also lined up behind no-fault. The relatively liberal impetus for this activity underscores the fact that plaintiffs' lawyers—despite their proximity in background to the Chicago Democratic Party—had operated by emphasizing professionalism, especially skill in litigation and bar service—and a consensus in favor of compensation for victims. Their political connections remained quite local as well, and they had not invested much in the legal academy. They now confronted a group of policy and academic professionals who sought to take them out of the picture at a time when personal injury lawyers depended largely on automobile accidents.

In addition to the no-fault automobile insurance movement, the medical community also mobilized against the tort system in the 1970s. In 1976, the Illinois legislature passed the Medical Malpractice Reform Act, which, among other things, imposed a $500,000 cap on compensatory damages in medical malpractice disputes. [L]eading Illinois plaintiffs' lawyers used a litigation strategy to challenge the new legislation. The Illinois Supreme Court again sided with the plaintiffs, invalidating the statute as unconstitutional.

In the face of no-fault and other emerging tort reform movements, accordingly, plaintiffs' lawyers made a concerted effort to establish ties to state legislators. The elite plaintiffs' lawyers in this way became major and sustained players in politics as a result of no-fault and its aftermath. They also became linked more directly to the Democratic Party. In the fight against no-fault, itself the product of academics and liberal politicians, some Republican defense lawyers also played important roles. Yet this plaintiff-defense alliance was short-lived. The plaintiffs' bar ultimately invested not in a bipartisan professional strategy above politics but rather in the Democratic relationships that were already built into their careers and their personal histories. They sought to protect their clients and their practices increasingly through the Democratic Party at the local and national level. They shifted from a concentration on professional respectability to one that combined efforts to build professional status with intense political partisanship.

Today, in fact, the very close ties to the Democratic Party are as much a part of the identity of the plaintiffs' bar as their commitment to professional bar activity, trial craft, and the referral system that channels the largest cases to the elite of the subprofession.

Plaintiffs' lawyers today do not have to reach out to establish contacts; they are sought after for their financial resources, for input on judicial candidates, and the like. In the words of Corboy, "Two senators called yesterday. One was from the State of Illinois. He was asking me my opinion of people who have been recommended for federal judgeships. There was another who wanted money from the State of Massachusetts." Another elite plaintiffs' lawyer noted, "I mean it's relentless. Relentless. And, you know, people think that plaintiffs' lawyers are just rolling in money. They call us every day. People running for Congress. People running for state rep. And nationally. Not just the president. You know, the attorney general in Iowa. The plaintiffs' bar, we get hit a lot." Professional responsibility within this subprofession, in short, now includes an obligation to give generously to the Democratic Party—which now embraces the plaintiffs' bar as well. To make the obvious point seen in national politics today, there are very strong personal and policy divisions now between the Republicans and the Democrats on the question of tort reform—an issue that energizes each side's stock of major contributors.

While Dooley had limited his activities to the plaintiffs' bar, Corboy became active in general bar associations as well, particularly the Chicago Bar Association. Corboy and others could see that they needed to gain recognition in the general bar associations long dominated by the corporate bar.

Corboy also followed the professional model of the corporate bar by building a philanthropic presence in the community. By the 1980s Corboy was already well known as a local philanthropist, with scholarship and fellowship programs at high schools and colleges across the city.

The brand of professionalism embraced by the personal injury bar also highlights the modest personal characteristics (working-class background) of the successful plaintiffs' lawyer rather than the prestige of his or her degrees. Plaintiffs' lawyers draw upon their modest beginnings in their public rhetoric and in their appeal to juries. Stories of working-class men who now serve the underdog are ubiquitous in the rhetoric and self-concept of plaintiffs' lawyers. This rhetoric, along with their personal histories, distinguishes plaintiffs' lawyers from their corporate counterparts. It is part of their unique brand of professionalism.

Perhaps most illustrative of how far the plaintiffs' bar has come in just 50 years is its prominence in the national scene. One example is how the plaintiffs' bar quickly mobilized in response to the terrorist attacks of September 11, 2001. Shortly after the attacks, Congress pondered granting immunity to the airlines in order to protect the industry. In the process, Congress sought counsel from the plaintiffs' bar, who argued on behalf of the September 11 Victim Compensation Fund in lieu of lawsuits against the airlines. ATLA leaders called for a moratorium on lawsuits resulting from the attacks, and most plaintiffs' lawyers demonstrated restraint. The ABA then created a Task Force on Terrorism and the Law that, among other things, reviewed and advised the government on the development and administration of the September 11 Victim Compensation Fund. The mobilization and cooperation of the plaintiffs' bar was critical to the voluntary moratorium on lawsuits and the success of the fund. The plaintiffs' bar is sufficiently cohesive to hold in check those who might be tempted to take advantage of the disaster to reap financial gain but jeopardize the hard-earned respectability of this subprofession.

David Wilkins's study of black Chicago lawyers reveals striking parallels between the development of the plaintiffs' bar in the second half of the 20th century, and the evolution of the black bar in that same time period. For example, originally excluded from mainstream professional associations that were dominated by the white Protestant corporate elite, both plaintiffs' lawyers and black lawyers responded by establishing their own professional associations. Early on, both groups essentially operated in "parallel worlds" alongside mainstream professional associations that were dominated by the corporate elite. Eventually, both groups began to make headway into mainstream professional associations. Today, general bar associations are no longer the exclusive domains of the corporate elite. Instead, many formerly excluded groups—including plaintiffs' lawyers, black lawyers, and women lawyers—now play an active role in these associations and are represented in the leadership of these organizations.

In both groups, we also see a heavy reliance on social networks, within a relatively small subgroup, for career building and for advancing the interests of the collective. As the plaintiffs' bar relies heavily on referral networks for securing business, social networks among black Chicago lawyers are an important source of business and career advancement. Wilkins found that black lawyers in Chicago took advantage of their ties to rising [black] political power to further their individual careers and their collective advancement. [T]he history of the plaintiffs' bar, like the history of the black bar, is a story about the central role that social networks and local political power play in the making of a subprofession.

Despite a powerful desire for status in the mainstream legal profession, these plaintiffs' lawyers have not sought to draw on the credentials and powerful professional networks that come from elite law schools. In fact, the plaintiffs' bar thrives in part because it has managed to resist some of the hierarchies embedded more generally in the profession. The plaintiffs' bar has made a virtue out of its own relative marginality. Rather than deny their working-class heritage and lack of connection to the elite law schools, they celebrate their differences. In doing so, they position themselves as uniquely qualified to serve their "disadvantaged" clients, creating both a market niche and a professional niche that at once defines and protects their place in the system.

While the unique professional ideology of the plaintiffs' bar solidifies and protects their market niche, the focus of Chicago plaintiffs' lawyers on local law schools, working-class backgrounds, and local philanthropy perpetuates the relatively lower status of the plaintiffs' bar and reinforces the dominant position of the corporate bar. [D]espite increasing numbers of bar presidents and ever more impressive philanthropy, the plaintiffs' bar cannot come close to matching the prestige of the corporate bar—which, after all, defined the rules.

NOTES ON PARIKH & GARTH

1. ***Social Class and Stratification of the Bar.*** Note the relationship between socioeconomic background, religion, ethnicity, and practice setting described in this excerpt. In what ways did Corboy's social background affect where Corboy went to law school and what his job opportunities were? To what extent do you observe similar phenomena in your law school experience or that of your friends?

2. ***Legal Education and Stratification of the Bar.*** How did legal education contribute to the stratification within the profession described in the Corboy article? Until the 1960s, elite colleges and universities maintained quotas on the number of Jews they would admit, typically capping enrollment at about 10 percent, and they refused to admit or only reluctantly admitted other racial, religious, and ethnic groups. To what extent do you think that America's education system might continue to affect the social composition of the legal profession?

3. ***Then and Now?*** If a study were to be done today of the urban bar in the largest metropolitan area near you, what do you imagine it would show regarding stratification? Being Catholic or Jewish is much less likely to predict career trajectory today than in the 1940s and 1950s when Corboy began his career. In their 1995 study of the Chicago bar, John Heinz and his co-authors found that religion and ethnicity played a much smaller part in the social structure of the bar than they did in the mid-1970s. On this point, it may be worth noting that all but one of the justices on the U.S. Supreme Court are Catholic or Jewish. The Heinz *et al.* research suggests that the axes of stratification in the Chicago bar have shifted from religion and ethnicity to gender and minority status.[1]

* * *

Regional Variation. How would the story of solo and small firm and plaintiffs' practice, and of stratification, differ if scholars had studied the West? Professors Carroll Seron and Richard Abel discussed this issue at the West Coast Law & Society meeting in 2011. The following is an edited synthesis of notes of their comments (used with permission of Professors Abel and Seron):

> Immigration patterns differ radically. In the East Coast and Mid-West, the dominant waves were eastern and southern European immigrants in the late nineteenth and early twentieth

---

[1] JOHN HEINZ, ROBERT NELSON, REBECCA SANDEFUR AND EDWARD LAUMANN, URBAN LAWYERS: THE NEW SOCIAL STRUCTURE OF THE BAR (2005). Other studies of solo and small firm lawyers and plaintiffs' lawyers have also found a predominance of white men, but many such studies were conducted in the Northeast and the Upper Midwest. *See* Herbert Kritzer, *The Fracturing Legal Profession: The Case of Plaintiffs' Personal Injury Lawyers*, 8 INT'L J. LEGAL PROF. 225 (2001) (Wisconsin); Jerry Van Hoy, *Markets and Contingency: How Client Markets Influence the Work of Plaintiffs' Personal Injury Lawyers*, 6 INT'L J. LEGAL PROF. 345 (1999) (Indiana); Sara Parikh, *How the Spider Catches the Fly: Referral Networks in the Plaintiffs' Personal Injury Bar*, 5 N.Y.L.SCH. L. REV.243 (2006/07) (Chicago).

centuries; the great northern migration of African Americans in the mid-twentieth century; and recent migrations from everywhere. On the West Coast the significant migrations were internal (from the East and mid-West), from Asia, and from Mexico and Central America. These migrations affect the demographics of both the legal profession and its clients. Most immigrant groups have established their own professional associations. Sentiment about immigration is stronger in the West and Southwest.

To be sure, the urban centers of the West and Southwest developed their own entrenched elites, but they were always much more fluid and porous than the Northeast. How did the fluidity of status and class in the West shape the development of the profession? Is it only a story of institutionalization of eastern firms? What role did the different types of economy play? In the west, ranching and agriculture played a bigger role. LA became a center of the film and TV industry and many Jewish lawyers succeeded in it. While Jews were outsiders in some LA circles, they also had the space to develop their own, relatively important base of power—and, influence. In thinking about the structure of the legal profession in the West and Southwest, it evolves in a place where people came to get away from the entrenched hierarchies that they could not break into in the East or elsewhere in the world. To be sure, they met new and perhaps different forms of hierarchy, but they were also more fluid. There are reasons to believe that the particular stories vary by area, and that the story in Los Angeles was different from that in San Francisco or Portland or Phoenix.

In thinking about solo and small-firm practice in the West and Southwest, I would think that its history would show one of ethnic enclaves, particularly within the individual-client hemisphere. But, is this sustained over generations, or is it an entry point? Does the West and Southwest actually lay the foundation for immigrants' leveraging law as a site for social mobility?

Without romanticizing the West, perhaps its wedge of fluidity and its attraction to outsiders is a "model." Much scholarly research on the legal profession finds the cup half full—there's always a residual where the WASPs enjoy privileges even in this more fluid, heterogeneous profession. But, the other way to think about this is that the cup is getting smaller and smaller—with fewer and fewer sites where this closed, homogeneous elite can go it alone. I'm not suggesting that we live in a world without elites, or inequalities—far from it; rather, we may be a bit too hung up on documenting the vestiges rather than the main events—the collaborations, mergers, and negotiations across elites to form new synergies and sites of power and influence.

One study that addresses an aspect of the void identified by Professors Seron and Abel is a survey of all Latino lawyers in Los Angeles County conducted in 2000 by Professor Cruz Reynoso. The survey found a smaller percentage of Latinos in solo practice in Los Angeles (35%) than the percentage of lawyers in solo practice statewide (53% of all private practitioners) or nationwide (47%), but that the percentage of Los Angeles Latinos in firms of 2–5 lawyers or 6–10 lawyers was roughly similar to that of lawyers nationwide and statewide. As with studies of lawyers in the East and Midwest, the survey found that law school was a path of upward mobility for many Los Angeles Latinos: 92% of the Latino lawyers surveyed were the first in their immediate family to go to law school, 78% were the first in their extended family, and half were the first in their immediate family to attend college. Just over half of survey respondents reported having attended a first tier law school, and another third reported having attended a second tier school.[2]

One study of 460 Texas plaintiffs' lawyers based on a survey conducted in 2006 found many similarities between plaintiffs' bars in Texas and Chicago. Although the authors did not discuss the ethnicity of the lawyers in their sample, they did observe generally that the Texas plaintiffs' bar resembles the plaintiffs' bar in other regions, and many scholars have noted that plaintiffs' lawyers are largely white, male, and educated at local or regional law schools. The authors continued:

> [P]laintiffs' lawyers constitute a distinct practice community in Texas and elsewhere. [T]hese lawyers are specialists. [O]ver one-third of the respondents are board certified in personal injury trial law and/or civil trial law. In contrast, only 4% of all Texas lawyers are certified in personal injury trial law and/or civil trial law.
>
> For most of our respondents, automobile accident cases account for the largest percentage of their caseloads, followed by medical malpractice, commercial litigation, and products liability. Most do not handle high-value cases—the typical case value is modest ($38,000 in 2006 dollars). In addition, the size of their practices is small. Thirty-seven percent of our respondents are solo practitioners, and another 48% work in firms of 2 to 5 lawyers. This means that 85% work in very small firms or as solos. The comparable figure for Texas lawyers generally is 60%. With the exception of the visible lawyers with high-volume or mass tort

---

[2] Cruz Reynoso, *A Survey of Latino Lawyers in Los Angeles County—Their Professional Lives and Opinions*, 38 UC DAVIS L. REV. 1563, 1593, 1626 (2005).

practices, Texas plaintiffs' lawyers also tend to have small staffs. This would be expected for practices relying on the contingency fee, which must keep overhead as low as possible.

[T]he predominant source of clients is some form of referral. [J]ust under three-quarters of their caseloads comes from referrals. Referrals from other lawyers are much more important for plaintiffs' lawyers than for lawyers generally, and this may reflect their status as specialists and their willingness to pay referral fees to the lawyers who refer cases to them. Referrals from clients are the most important source of business for lawyers generally, and they are the second-most important for plaintiffs' lawyers.

Three elements appear important in understanding the community's normative values. First is the commitment to public service or the public good—as the plaintiffs' lawyers define it. Related is the idea of actually trying cases. Last is the nature and substance of the solicitation techniques used. [T]he remarks of a younger lawyer in Houston [are illustrative of the commitment to the public good as these lawyers perceive it]: "Amongst plaintiffs' lawyers . . . you have true believers who are doing this because they really care, they love people, they want to work for people, they want to help people and that's why they got into this business in the first place. It wasn't just making money."[3]

Referral Networks and Referral Fees. Studies of the plaintiffs' bar note the significance of referrals to the operation of a plaintiffs' practice. Although at one point, elites in the organized bar considered it unseemly for one lawyer to pay another to refer a matter, contemporary state ethics rules explicitly allow it so long as the referral fee is reasonable and the client consents.

The justification typically offered for allowing referral fees is that it provides an incentive for lawyers to recognize their own limited expertise and to refer cases to lawyers whom they believe most capable of providing successful representation.

In her study of referral networks, Sara Parikh found that these networks are highly organized and are more likely to transfer cases from low-end, neighborhood practices that tap into ethnic or occupational niches to high-end personal injury lawyers than the reverse or than laterally within a sector. She also found that referral relationships reinforce and reproduce stratification within the profession, with high-end lawyers securing more high-value cases and low-end lawyers securing more low-

[3] Stephen Daniels & Joanne Martin, *Plaintiffs' Lawyers and the Tension Between Professional Norms and the Need to Generate Business*, in LAWYERS IN PRACTICE: ETHICAL DECISION MAKING IN CONTEXT 112–114 (Leslie C. Levin & Lynn Mather eds., 2012).

value cases through the referral networks.[4] Parikh's study concluded that this referral network may be beneficial for lawyers as well as clients:

> Referring attorneys would benefit by securing fees in cases they referred out; recipients would benefit from the additional business; and consumers would benefit because they would be more likely to end up in qualified hands.
>
> [M]ost individual consumers are unaware of the different types of expertise within the legal profession. When a personal legal matter arises, individual consumers often turn to a lawyer they know who may or may not practice the kind of law specific to the case. Attorneys serving individual clients are frequently faced with cases that are outside of their expertise. The risk is that the attorney will take cases that he is unqualified to handle. Fee-splitting was designed to discourage this. The institutionalization of referral fees was thought to benefit the client, whose case would be more likely to end up in the hands of an attorney capable of managing the case. Most personal injury attorneys believe that the fee-splitting system does serve the client's best interest.[5]

The Role of Substantive Law in Defining Professional Identity. The Parikh & Garth article on the Chicago plaintiffs' bar notes the significance of so-called "tort reform" in constructing the identity of lawyers in that practice segment. (Tort is the area of law that allows people to sue to recover damages for injury to persons or property.) Views about tort policy became a significant feature of the professional identity of plaintiffs' lawyers. One empirical study of plaintiffs' lawyers in Texas found that changes in tort law that limit damages has not only had "a profound effect on the cultural environment surrounding civil litigation," but also has dramatically changed the nature of the practice sector in Texas:

> Among the lawyers we interviewed, there is a widely shared conclusion that the impact of the reformers' public relations campaigns has fallen the heaviest on the typical plaintiffs' lawyers, the ones handling "bread and butter" cases (simple cases of lower value), rather than the lawyers handling larger, more complex matters.
>
> "Bread and butter" practices tend to be built upon the frequently occurring, lower-value car wreck cases. Such lawyers depend on a reasonable return on these cases, including non-economic damages, for cash flow and for survival. Many lawyers say they are not getting a good return on these cases, especially when it comes to non-economic damages. "The cases aren't . . .

---

[4] Sara Parikh, *How the Spider Catches the Fly: Referral Networks in the Plaintiffs' Personal Injury Bar*, 5 N.Y. L. SCH. L. REV. 243, 252 (2006/07).

[5] *Id.* at 261, 265.

don't settle for what they used to," said one lawyer in a frequently heard complaint. A Fort Worth lawyer whose practice relies heavily on car wreck cases summarized the situation bluntly: "Without cash flow coming in you can't pay your bills and you can't fund your cases . . . we are in a brutal process of some [lawyers] being weeded out—and I may be one of them."

What have "bread and butter" lawyers done in reaction to what they see as an altered, harsher environment? Some lawyers, in response to the altered environment, have simply gone out of business or substantially re-oriented their practices away from a primary concern with plaintiffs' cases taken on a contingency fee basis. Downsizing is more common, and similar to lawyers leaving the practice area, it diminishes the available supply of legal services for potential litigants. Greater attention to screening is the third reaction to the altered environment by "bread and butter" lawyers. Since juries and insurance companies are tougher, a number of lawyers commented that they need to be more careful in the cases they choose. Lawyers are less willing to take cases with relatively low damages and primarily soft tissue injury.

[M]any lawyers also said they must now pay more attention to who they will take as a client. In the survey, "bread and butter" lawyers were asked if they would take the hypothetical $3,000 soft tissue case described earlier if the client is unemployed; 53.5 percent said they would take the client today, while 71.3 percent would have taken the client five years ago. If the client had been a personal injury plaintiff in the past, 47.0 percent would take the client today, while 68.2 percent would have taken the client five years ago. If the client has a criminal record, 38.1 percent would take the client today, while 57.4 percent would have taken the client five years ago.[6]

NOTES ON THE COMMUNITIES OF PLAINTIFFS' PRACTICE

1. ***Local and Specialty Bar Associations.*** Parikh and Garth note the importance of involvement in organized bar association activities in Corboy's career and in the self-conception of elite plaintiffs' lawyers, and the study of the Texas plaintiffs' bar echoes this finding. A number of studies of bar associations, including the ABA, state and local bar associations (like the Associated Bar of the City of New York), and specialty bar associations like ATLA have documented their importance in the professional socialization of

---

[6] Stephen Daniels & Joanne Martin, "The Impact That It Has Had Is Between People's Ears: Tort Reform, Mass Culture, and Plaintiffs' Lawyers, 50 DEPAUL L. REV. 453 (2000).

lawyers.[7] Why is membership in a local bar association and, especially, a specialty bar like ATLA (in the Corboy excerpt) so significant in the lives of these lawyers? Local and specialty bars, unlike the ABA or the state bar, do not have the influence (in the case of the ABA) or the power (in the case of the state bar) to propose or adopt regulations governing the profession, although they sometimes adopt their own specialized standards of practice and encourage their members to abide by them.[8]

2. ***Choosing Sides.*** Plaintiffs' lawyers specializing in tort are not unique in practicing consistently on one side of a particular type of dispute. In labor and employment, civil rights, some aspects of securities, consumer protection, environmental law, and other fields, lawyers also tend to specialize in representing either plaintiffs or defendants but not both. How do such lawyers develop a professional identity in relationship to the kinds of clients they represent and their views about desirable social and legal policy? In other practice areas, lawyers may switch from one "side" to another intermittently or frequently. For example, some lawyers represent both plaintiffs and defendants in intellectual property infringement cases. Do you think it is good or bad for society (or lawyers) that lawyers in some fields do not switch sides?

C. CONTINGENCY FEES AND FEE-SHIFTING STATUTES

Major differences among practice settings exist in how and how much lawyers get paid. Apart from the realities of who has money to pay lawyers, the law of attorneys' fees has a great impact on the practices of lawyers. The American Rule, as it is known, is that each side in litigation pays its own fees. In England, and those countries following the English Rule, the loser pays the winner's attorneys' fees in litigation. Under the American Rule, in the absence of any legal right to recover attorneys' fees, lawyers and clients have developed the contingent fee agreement as a way to enable plaintiffs to vindicate their legal rights.

Contingency Fees. Plaintiffs' lawyers are typically paid on contingency: that is, they get paid only if they recover money at trial or through settlement. They must count on winning or settling a case and taking a percentage of the recovery (often 25% if the matter settles before trial; 30–40% if the matter is tried to a jury; and 40–50% if the matter must be litigated through an appeal). Lawyers in private practice who represent large entities, like corporations, the government, and insurance companies, have typically been compensated on an hourly basis. They typically have

---

[7] *See*, e.g., Robert L. Nelson & David M. Trubek, *Arenas of Professionalism: The Professional Ideologies of Lawyers in Context*, in LAWYERS' IDEALS/LAWYERS' PRACTICES: TRANSFORMATIONS IN THE AMERICAN LEGAL PROFESSION 179, 185 (Robert L. Nelson et al. eds., 1992); Jack King, *Origins of the Organized Criminal Defense Bar: The National Association of Criminal Defense Lawyers—Part One*, THE CHAMPION, May/June 2008.

[8] *See, e.g.*, THE AMERICAN ACADEMY OF MATRIMONIAL LAWYERS, BOUNDS OF ADVOCACY: AMERICAN ACADEMY OF MATRIMONIAL LAWYERS STANDARDS OF PRACTICE (2000).

counted on their clients having money to pay them, and when they litigate they usually have expected to be paid regardless of the outcome. However, the sharp divide between the ways plaintiffs' and defense counsel are compensated has broken down recently, as in-house counsel have begun insisting upon fixed-fee or "value-based" billing agreements, and sometimes even a "reverse contingency fee." A "reverse contingency fee" agreement is one in which the firm is paid more for better results; it is a "reverse" contingency fee in the sense that the less the defendant has to pay to the adversary the more it will pay to the lawyer.

Contingent fees are considered improper in some countries, reflecting a view that litigation is an evil that should not be incentivized through fee arrangements. In the United States, by contrast, many regard litigation as a mechanism to vindicate important rights and contingent fees as a way to achieve that.

Statutory Fee Shifting. The American Rule makes litigation unaffordable for any person who does not have the money to hire a lawyer unless the possible recovery in litigation is enough to cover the costs, and sometimes even meritorious cases do not offer the promise of sufficient recovery. For example, intentional discrimination in employment, education, voting, and housing is unlawful, but the economic damages, if they are calculable at all, are often too small to cover the cost of litigation. To address this problem, Congress and many legislatures have enacted fee-shifting statutes covering several categories of cases in which the likely recovery in a meritorious case may not be enough to cover the costs. Fee-shifting statutes are particularly common in civil rights cases, including employment, education, voting, and housing discrimination, as well as in cases of police abuse. Fee shifting provisions also exist in environmental protection and consumer protection statutes. The purposes of such statutes are both to provide an incentive to private persons to enforce the public policy reflected in the law (individual plaintiffs play the role of "private attorneys general") and to protect the poor and vulnerable from violations of their rights by enabling them to find lawyers to take their cases.

Litigation Finance. A new industry has emerged at the intersection of law and finance: businesses that lend money to lawyers and litigants to finance litigation in return for a share of the recovery. Plaintiff-side litigation finance has the same effect as a contingency fee agreement—enabling a litigant who otherwise lacks capital to bring a case—but it shifts the risk from the lawyer to a third party financier. Some see it as a way to enable litigants with little money to bring a complex and expensive litigation without worrying that a better-funded adversary will squelch meritorious claims simply by grinding them into the ground in the discovery and pretrial process. Others see it as an unethical practice that stirs up litigation and that endangers loyalty to client by making the lawyer dependent on the litigation finance company. Defense-side litigation finance operates like after-the-event insurance: the defendant and the financier agree on a target outcome (such as a settlement below a certain sum) and the litigation financier agrees to indemnify the defendant for the cost of a settlement or judgment above the target, thus shifting the risk of an unexpectedly large sum to the financier.

D. SUMMARY

In this chapter, we studied the plaintiffs' bar. We considered similarities within the plaintiffs' bar across regions of the country and the possible regional and practice specialty variations among some sectors of the individual and small business client hemisphere. We saw how referral networks, contingency fee agreements, and fee-shifting statutes are very important to clients and lawyers in these practice sectors.

CHAPTER 14

BOUTIQUES

■ ■ ■

A. INTRODUCTION

Boutiques are small law firms that represent large organizational clients, offer highly specialized services, and/or attract elite lawyers. Boutiques fit both in the world of small firms and in the world of large firms because many boutiques are small firms that compete with large firms for work from corporate clients. When boutiques serve large entities, they challenge the generalization that lawyers in small firms serve primarily individual clients and small businesses. When they attract lawyers with elite credentials, they defy the notion that those lawyers tend to work in large firms or in corporate counsel offices when they work in private practice. Thus, boutiques straddle the divide between what Heinz and Laumann once termed the two hemispheres of the bar. The bulk of this chapter explores how and why boutiques form and how they structure their business.

B. WHAT IS A BOUTIQUE?

Lawyers do not agree on the definition of a boutique law firm and, in particular, on how boutiques differ from small firms. In one of the rare scholarly treatments of this practice setting, two scholars have defined boutiques as small, specialized firms that intentionally "cultivate their comparative advantage in selected specialties and suppress any push to more general coverage in order to maintain their attractiveness for referral work."[1] For purposes of the following discussion, we define a boutique as a small law firm that provides highly specialized services and emphasizes its elite practice.[2]

Some boutiques represent some of the same large corporations that big firms represent, and they succeed in competing with large firms for business because they offer highly specialized services and competitive rates. Common areas of specialization include intellectual property, tax, employment, environmental, immigration, bankruptcy, and civil or criminal trial or appellate work. Although many boutiques cater primarily

---

[1] MARC GALANTER & THOMAS PALAY, TOURNAMENT OF LAWYERS: THE TRANSFORMATION OF THE BIG LAW FIRM 125 (1991).

[2] Black's Law Dictionary defines "boutique": "[a] small specialty business; esp., a small law firm specializing in one particular aspect of law practice."

to clients in the corporate hemisphere, some also serve individuals and small business clients. Some boutiques represent only individuals or nonprofit organizations (civil rights boutiques fit this description). Some boutiques focus on criminal and civil litigation, which may include such a broad area of subject matters that it stretches the notion of specialization.[3] Conversely, not every small firm that specializes in a field of practice calls itself a boutique. Small firms that specialize in areas of practice associated primarily with individual client service, such as small real estate transactions, family law, or plaintiffs' personal injury, rarely claim to be boutiques. Although boutique generally connotes small, there is no consensus among lawyers about how small a firm must be in order to be defined as a boutique. Some large firms with hundreds of lawyers and multiple offices that specialize by subject area (typically in tax, immigration, or intellectual property) call themselves boutiques and others do not.[4]

To sociologists of the profession, one of the most intriguing aspects of boutiques is that they tend to regard themselves, and to be regarded by others, as elite firms. Firms that claim the term boutique tend to use boutique synonymously with "elite" to describe themselves, and appear to do so to because of the social status associated with the eliteness claimed by large corporate firms.[5] Many of them trumpet their lawyers' credentials and previous experience in large firms and other prestigious practice sectors.[6]

The following readings present information, mainly drawn from the legal press, about how boutiques form, how they attract clients and lawyers, and why they thrive or fail. The readings explain how the creation and survival of boutiques are influenced by conflicts of interest, client pressures on billing, and lawyers' concerns about life-style issues in large firms. There is no substantial scholarly literature on boutiques. (You may notice that, unlike academic sociological studies, popular or legal press articles are based on unsystematic interviews and may be less empirically rigorous, more impressionistic, and thus less thorough or reliable.) The legal press emphasizes that boutiques were especially well-positioned to benefit from the restructuring of the legal services market generated by the recession of 2008–2012 because they typically charge lower rates than large firms, and they face fewer disqualifying conflicts of interest. Boutiques attract highly qualified lawyers who wish to develop and offer specialized expertise without working in large bureaucratically organized

---

3 *Harlee & Bald, P.A.: A litigation boutique law firm*, SARASOTA MAGAZINE (June 22, 2003).

4 *See, e.g.*, Larry Smith, *Tax Boutiques Maintain Independence As New Challenges Loom*, OF COUNSEL (Apr. 5, 1993), p.1.

5 *See, e.g.*, PIERRE BOURDIEU, DISTINCTION: A SOCIAL CRITIQUE OF THE JUDGMENT OF TASTE (Richard Nice, trans., 1984).

6 *See* Bryant G. Garth & Joyce S. Sterling, *Diversity, Hierarchy, and Fit in Legal Careers: Insights From Fifteen Years of Qualitative Interviews*, 31 GEO. J. LEGAL ETHICS 123, 168 (2018).

institutions. They also draw lawyers who are willing to sacrifice financial compensation for "life-style" benefits, such as flexible work arrangements. Some boutique firms are structured to allow lawyers to mesh client service with political activism.

C. THE FORMATION AND SURVIVAL OF BOUTIQUES

One factor contributing to the emergence and prosperity of boutique firms is conflicts of interest. Conflicts of interest rules complicate the ability of large firm practitioners to accept work because the rules prohibit a lawyer from representing a client whose interests are adverse to any other client represented by that lawyer or even by another lawyer in the same firm. Large firms with multiple offices spread across many cities represent large corporations with multiple subsidiaries, and when (for example) the transactional lawyers in New York represent a large corporation, that firm's intellectual property lawyers in California or international commercial arbitration lawyers in Dubai are prohibited from handling matters for adversaries of the same company without client consent. It may be more profitable for the California lawyers to set up shop in a smaller, boutique firm so that they can accept the work that clients are trying to send. As an article in the legal press put it, without the conflict problems, "the clients can hire the same people they would have chosen to hire at a larger firm, at a potentially lower rate. The draw: substantial savings, same people."[7] When a large law firm has a conflict of interest prohibiting it from representing a valued client, it may prefer to refer the matter to a boutique rather than to another large firm because the boutique will be less likely (because less able) to attempt to recruit the client to give all its legal work to the firm.[8]

Cost is another reason why lawyers leave large firms to start boutique practices and why large corporate clients hire boutique firms. Boutiques generally operate with lower overhead costs because they have smaller and less expensive offices and smaller administrative staffs. Boutiques, therefore, can charge less. When they can provide the same quality legal service at lower cost, corporate in-house counsel, who are expected to control legal costs while producing good results for the corporation, find them an appealing choice. As one news account explains:

> Boutiques can be unique service providers in that they typically have a specific expertise or focus in niche areas that enable them to offer specialized services to clients, along with a personal touch.

---

[7] Debra Tsuchiyama Baker & David P. Young, *Unique Times for Boutiques*, 47 HOUSTON LAWYER 4 (Mar/Apr 2010).

[8] Larry Smith, *Orange County Debacle Raises Key Business Issues for Law Firms*, OF COUNSEL, July 17, 1995.

> IP boutiques were one of the first to become highly competitive among sophisticated consumers of legal services, competing with firms that were larger in headcount and geographic desirability. The complexities of intellectual property law and the attorneys' day-to-day focus on that subject matter gave those boutiques a competitive edge in their field. Similarly, attorneys practicing in environmental boutiques, immigration boutiques, and other specialty areas often focus their attention on the complexities of specific regulations and develop skill sets in areas that may not be available in many firms. In addition, because the focused practitioners have chosen a boutique for their practice, they may be able to offer their specialized services for a more competitive rate and innovative or flexible fee structure as they are not burdened by the overhead that comes with multiple offices, non-billing service staff such as recruiters and marketers, and other fixed costs that must be passed on to the client.[9]

With lower fixed costs, boutiques have more flexibility when it comes to billing arrangements. They can take on small matters at lower billing rates, which has advantages for lawyers who provide specialized representation to small clients unable to afford large firm fees. Lower billing rates also help junior lawyers who would like to develop their trial or other skills in small-dollar cases and would like to bring in their own business but are unlikely to be able to recruit Fortune 100 companies as clients. The freedom to charge a lower hourly rate or a flat rate may enable boutiques to recruit very talented lawyers. For example, lawyers who want to try cases may find boutique litigation firms the most realistic opportunity to get into the courtroom and actually try cases before a jury, which is a relatively rare occurrence for lawyers at large law firms. The billing rates of large firms make litigation through trial economically irrational for all but so-called "bet the company" cases. When tens or hundreds of millions of dollars are at stake in litigation, clients may settle rather than gamble on a jury verdict. And when such high-dollar cases do go to trial, a client will typically allow only the most seasoned trial lawyer to stand up in court. Particularly for young lawyers who need to try cases to gain experience, a boutique may be the only path (other than going into government work) to gaining that experience. Boutiques also are able to complete conflicts checks and negotiate fee arrangements quickly, which can help in the effort to retain a client who needs immediate legal assistance.[10]

---

[9] Debra Tsuchiyama Baker & David P. Young, *Unique Times for Boutiques*, 47 HOUSTON LAWYER 4 (Mar/Apr 2010).

[10] Heather Chambers, *Boutique Law Offices Appear More Charming*, SAN DIEGO BUS. J., Jan. 18, 2010.

Some boutiques appear to benefit from the diversification of the bar and globalization, and market themselves to clients and to prospective lawyers as valuing cultural, linguistic, and ethnic or racial diversity. For example, in a study drawn from qualitative interviews with lawyers in the AJD study, Professors Bryant Garth and Joyce Sterling described the example of a Spanish-speaking Latinx lawyer who felt he did not fit in the white male culture of the large law firm where he first worked. He found a rewarding practice at a boutique firm that formed to market the ethnic, cultural, and linguistic diversity of its lawyers to clients that wanted to hire a minority-owned law firm that offers the linguistic and cultural fluency of immigrant lawyers to global clients.[11]

Some boutiques formed because lawyers sought more autonomy than they could find at large firms. These boutiques, like many others, market the elite credentials and large firm experience of their lawyers, but manage through keeping costs down to offer competitive billing rates and sophisticated work. The partners may earn less than their counterparts in large firms but prefer the flexibility.[12] One example of this type of boutique is a firm specializing in white collar criminal defense that hires former Assistant U.S. Attorneys and markets their expertise in federal criminal trial practice to corporate and high-net-worth individual clients. One news story reported the founding of at least ten such firms between 2012 and 2017.[13]

Intellectual property boutiques formed in the 1980s and 1990s with the explosion of the technology and internet sectors of the economy. They could compete with large firms for clients who needed lawyers with technical backgrounds because intellectual property is a large and lucrative practice area and law firms with the right intellectual property expertise did not need to offer a full range of legal services in order to attract large corporate clients.[14] Patent prosecution and patent litigation were so specialized that IP boutiques could succeed without needing a broad array of expertise. Large law firms began to grow their IP practices by some combination of lateral hiring or merger with an IP boutique, but some IP boutiques survive either because of their expertise or because some clients do not need a large firm's full array of legal services and prefer the billing structure that boutiques offer.[15] Commentators thought that IP boutiques' reliance on patent prosecution would render them vulnerable to

---

[11] Bryant Garth & Joyce Sterling, *Diversity, Hierarchy, and Fit in Legal Careers: Insights from Fifteen Years of Interviews*, 31 GEO. J. LEG. ETHICS 123, 168 (2018).

[12] *See* Renee Beasley Jones, *Enterprise: Law, Boutique Also Means Unique*, SAN DIEGO BUS. J., Nov. 25, 2002.

[13] Elizabeth Olson, *A New Route for U.S. Prosecutors: Hanging Out Their Own Shingle*, N.Y. TIMES, Oct. 3, 2017.

[14] Larry Smith, *IP Update: Outside, Inside Counsel in Tug of War as Profitability Soars*, OF COUNSEL, Mar. 18, 1991 (describing the growth in the amount of and profitability of IP work in the late 1980s and the competition between boutiques and large firms to attract clients).

[15] Olivia Clarke, *The IP World: A Place for Firms of All Sizes*, CHICAGO LAWYER, May 2008.

outsourcing to India, and so some boutiques focused increasingly on patent litigation but were vulnerable to competition from top litigation practices in large law firms.[16] The example of IP boutiques illustrates a common theme in the scant literature on boutique practice: specialization means that boutiques are at greater risk of changes in the market for legal services than are large law firms with diverse practices, and therefore boutiques must be especially attentive to changes in the market.[17]

The increasing availability of high-end boutique practitioners has changed the way corporate clients structure their legal teams. One article in the legal press explains how in complex or unusual cases, a general counsel might choose to pair firms to obtain the necessary expertise. "For instance, environmental regulatory specialists may not have a significant record of courtroom trial experience and may not be familiar with the client's litigation style or risk tolerance. Another litigation boutique that has the requisite trial experience may lack the needed regulatory expertise." By hiring both firms, the general counsel gets the necessary expertise without the high cost of a general service large corporate firm.[18]

Many successful boutique firms confront the question whether to remain small and specialized or to grow to whatever size the business will support. News accounts of Boies, Schiller Flexner, which started as a boutique but grew rapidly, capture a number of the phenomena contributing to the founding and success of boutiques.[19] The firm was founded in 1997, when Boies left his equity partnership at the large New York law firm, Cravath, Swaine & Moore. He left because Cravath's biggest client at the time, Time Warner Inc., parent of the Atlanta Braves, objected to Boies's representation of the New York Yankees in a suit against Major League Baseball. Schiller had been a partner at a Washington, D.C. boutique which later merged with a large New York firm, and Schiller and Boies had been co-counsel on a case in the late 1980s. According to a news account,

> Boies set up an office in Armonk, New York, and Schiller opened one in Washington, D.C. Their initial budget was around $4 million. It was the perfect size. Or at least Boies thought so. He figured that he could avoid administrative headaches and take only the cases that interested him.

---

16 *Id.*

17 Jorge Goldstein & Michael Ray, *The State of the IP Boutique: Part 2*, LAW360.COM, Apr. 4, 2017.

18 Debra Tsuchiyama Baker & David P. Young, *Unique Times for Boutiques*, 47 HOUSTON LAW. 4 (Mar/Apr 2010).

19 Andrew Longstreth, *Don't Bet Against the House: Big Wins on Contingency Cases Push Boies Schiller into the Am Law 100*, AM. LAW. (May 2009), p. 124.

> But the firm proved to be a magnet for business. Clients like the Yankees, E.I. du Pont de Nemours and Company, Philip Morris International, Inc., and CBS Corporation, and new ones like Napster, Inc., and Calvin Klein, Inc., kept calling. Along the way, there was also that small government case against Microsoft Corporation and an election dispute between George W. Bush and Al Gore.[20]

The firm grew from 50 lawyers in 1999 to become a large, nationwide general service law firm.

> When they started out, Boies and Schiller had a business plan that called for 40 percent of the firm's time to be devoted to repeat clients; about 30 percent for one-off engagements; and about 30 percent allotted for plaintiffs' class action suits, where the firm could reap 30 percent of a settlement or verdict. The firm never ended up devoting that much time to pure contingency fee cases, but the fees reaped from them have generally increased over the years.
>
> Both Schiller and Boies had developed a taste for plaintiffs' work before they started their firm. While at Cravath, Boies had represented the government against financier Michael Milken on partial contingency, and Schiller had taken on a company called Mc-Caw Cellular Communications, Inc., in a class action breach-of-contract suit. Having their own shop allowed them to be more aggressive in filing class actions. "The idea was that we wouldn't have to be as highly leveraged if we were able to achieve some premiums over the hourly rate through contingency cases and some of those one-shot matters," says partner William Isaacson, who came with Schiller from Kaye Scholer.

Boies Schiller Flexner is unusual for large firms in representing plaintiffs in large class actions. Large firm clients often consider it a positional conflict if their lawyers represent plaintiffs in this type of suit, in which corporations are almost invariably defendants. But, "[s]eeing a case from a plaintiff's side, the Boies, Schiller lawyers argue, informs their work as defense lawyers. They can better size up a case from the start and know what costs will be involved."[21]

* * *

The survival of a boutique, like any other law firm, depends on the continuing ability of the firm to attract and retain clients. That, in turn, can depend on three factors. First there is the question of how they continue to compete with other firms for business. Second there is the

---

20 *Id.*

21 *Id.*

temptation to merge with a larger firm. Third is the question faced by all small firms: whether the firm can groom both the legal skills and the business development abilities of younger lawyers so that the firm survives the retirement of the core group of founding partners whose reputations made the firm a viable entity in the first place. As large law firms began to abandon the exclusive reliance on hourly billing in favor of various value-based billing arrangements, the boutiques lost that competitive edge and had to find others. Similarly, many boutiques initially enjoyed a competitive edge because of their specialized expertise in, for example, tax or intellectual property, but large law firms then began to build their own departments with comparable expertise. Many boutiques then had to consider whether to merge with a larger firm or to find new subpractice areas to keep a step ahead of their large firm competitors. Boutiques still compete well on cost because of their lower overhead and leaner staffing.

These questions about the durability of the boutique business model have not been extensively studied. However, one interview-based study of businesses that lend money to law firms to finance litigation suggests a way that the recent development of litigation finance as an organized business specialty may address some of the instability of the boutique business model.

THE LAW OF INTEREST VERSUS THE INTEREST OF LAW, OR ON LENDING TO LAW FIRMS

Radek Goral
29 Geo. J. Leg. Ethics 253 (2016)

Litigation firms sometimes face what may be called the inelasticity problem: a mismatch between the workload of a law firm and the inelastic resources it employs in connection with that workload—labor (the amount of work the people working for the firm can do within a unit of time) and capital (the amount of operating and financial costs the firm can assume). The input-output mismatch in a law firm may result from temporary difficulties with originating new business; limited skill in financial budgeting; or its business model. For example, "boutiques," which handle few large cases at a time, not only have irregular cash flows, but also experience significant volatility in the intensity of work required by their caseload. Since litigators do not control dockets of the cases they handle, they run the risk that a number of big disputes with uncertain timelines may stay dormant for a stretch of time only to reach an active stage all at the same time. As a result, litigators face periodic and unpredictable "spikes" in lawyer time and money they must expend.

The unpredictability of the litigation business forces many litigation firms into a structural inefficiency: they continue to incur a fixed cost of peak-level production capacity which they are unable to adjust in a short term; at the same time, that capacity remains underutilized off-peak. On the other hand, by setting a budget too low a firm may find itself on the other side of the same problem: having bitten off more than it can chew and lacking adequate resources to develop potentially profitable cases.

The solution to the inelasticity problem seems obvious: match the supply of transient litigation overcapacity with the demand for it. For example, a struggling law firm could "rent" itself to another law firm in return for immediate cash (participation agreement), and sometimes, also a share in the future proceeds from the shared case, if any (co-counsel agreement). Potentially, the arrangement may serve well both cooperating law firms—the cash-heavy partner is able to handle more cases than it could have managed on its own while the cash-poor firm benefits from improved liquidity and participates in additional cases without bearing the cost of acquiring them. In addition, participation agreements tend to create ongoing relationship, helping both firms to make budgets in reliance on an extra capacity and a supplemental stream of cash, respectively.

The inelasticity problem can also be addressed by arranging for a transfer of "assets" between law firms, which, after a fashion, is the inverse of a participation agreement. Here, a more liquid law firm would take over some of the cases—together with the accompanying costs—which the backlogged firm cannot cope with. Both firms would then be able to share fees from the transferred cases, with the "selling" firm likely receiving some immediate cash payment, formally a referral fee, from the "buying" firm. The caseload transfer could help the overextended partner by providing more cash and less overhead in the present. In return, the transferor would need to give up some of its potential future earnings. The transferee would gain by obtaining preselected cases in progress, usually at a distressed-asset price.

Another response to the inelasticity of law-firm inputs involves a law-firm joint-venture, where several law firms take on an additional case, sharing its costs and profits. The arrangement allows firms to increase their workload incrementally, by adding to its portfolio what essentially is a fraction of a case. Collaborating law firms can also mix and match their resources in a way that accounts for their respective advantages and time schedules. A wholesale variant of a legal joint-venture is a merger between law firms. Sometimes, it is intended as a true union combining two or more partnerships; at other times—a special-purpose law firm is created to pool resources and allocate interests in a limited portfolio of cases.

Irrespective of the nature of the firm-to-firm deal, however, a major challenge remains: compatible firms need to find each other. But an organized market for spare legal capacity simply does not exist, and the culture of the American legal profession does not encourage lawyers to reach out to potential business partners. Lawyers in need of work are not very likely to advertise their troubles among peers. And approaching another lawyer with the needed set of skills requires information about that lawyer: the quality, quantity, and price of her work, as well as the probable delivery time.

Enter law-firm funders.

A law-firm funder has insider knowledge about a dispersed group of litigation partnerships, because she is (or was, not long ago) engaged in their day-to-day operations as a financial adviser or credit monitor. The continuous information feed about a pool of law firms transforms funders from passive outsiders into informed insiders in the legal community. And they use their information advantage to broker deals among the firms they consider part of the network. Some merely make sporadic, opportunistic introductions; others consciously organize systematic network structures.

One funder-side source described several firm-to-firm transactions his company brought about. For instance, an East Coast law firm entered into a participation agreement with a firm from the South East that specialized in a particular type of toxic-tort litigation. To a fundee from the Southwest representing a number of clients with securities-litigation matters, the funder recommended a partner from New York, and the two would repeatedly cooperate as co-counsel to those clients. The financier matched aggregators specializing in consumer-protection cases, which then formed a joint-venture, sharing costs of advertising and client acquisition in a mass-action campaign. A small East Coast borrower with a wage-and-hour class action on its hands was introduced to a much larger class-actions practice from California, which assumed the financial and organizational burden of prosecuting the case; the "feeder firm" received cash and retained a stake in the attorneys' fees to be awarded to the class counsel. The funder also helped put together a consortium of plaintiff law firms from several states to represent a group of Texas plaintiffs signed by a local law firm in an environmental-tort suit against a multibillion defendant.

Funders see two primary benefits of their matchmaking endeavors. First, building a network helps acquire new funding business. The second benefit is more important: by matching lawyers with complementary resources, a third-party funder protects their investment and the value of unearned, contingent attorney's fees in the event that a borrowing lawyer stops working on her cases, leaving behind an illiquid inventory of unfinished business which is of little value to a lender unless brought to fruition by somebody else.

[A] funder becomes a bridge among disjoint legal cliques, a matchmaker facilitating relations within a web spun with money. In many circumstances, a funder's network benefits the attorneys within its span. Being introduced by a trusted intermediary to another lawyer may help build confidence and suggests that the potential partner is likely to play by similar rules. Indeed, interview data indicates that lawyers see the matchmaking efforts by a third-party as potentially useful to them. However, attorneys should be also aware that the central role of a funder in the market she makes is a source of precious information. The concern that the "network power" could in fact be abused is not without substance. Such possibility clearly does exist, particularly when the interests of a funder no longer align with those of a fundee. For example, if a funded law firm runs into financial difficulties, a financier might be inclined to "strongly encourage" a fire-sale transfer of collateral to (or a merger with) another firm at terms which the struggling firm could reasonably perceive as less-than-fair.

* * *

As to the question of how boutiques have responded to large law firms' development of comparable specialized expertise in boutiques' niche practice areas, the answer seems to be that some boutiques become even more specialized on particular aspects of a niche practice. The specialization refers not only to knowledge of substantive law and procedure but also to interpersonal business relationships with important people in the sector (such as people working at the IRS or the Treasury Department, in the case of tax practice).[22]

Boutiques typically have higher ratios of partners to associates than large firms do, and their clients often expect a level of attention from senior lawyers that is rare in large firms. Boutiques that make the opposite move, by seeking to become full-service firms, risk alienating referral sources. In short, fundamental cultural and economic differences can present barriers to mergers between boutiques and large firms, at least so long as the boutique can continue to attract clients.[23]

NOTES ON BOUTIQUES

1. ***The Attractions and Drawbacks of Boutiques.*** What are the attractions of boutique firms for lawyers? For clients? What are the disadvantages of boutique firms for lawyers and for clients?

2. ***Are Boutiques More Suited to Some Practice Areas than Others?*** What types of law practice or legal specialty are most conducive to the boutique firm structure?

3. ***Understanding Why Boutiques Are and Are Not Viable.*** What common threads can you identify in why some boutiques thrive and why some either merge into another firm or go out of business? How are these phenomena similar to what occurs at other small firms? How do they differ?

---

[22] Larry Smith, *Tax Boutiques Maintain Independence as New Challenges Loom,* OF COUNSEL, April 5, 1993.

[23] *Id.*

D. SUMMARY

The notion that the private practice of law is divided into two worlds—one in which large law firms represent large organizational clients and the other in which small firms represent individuals and small businesses—remains a powerful heuristic for understanding the work lives of the three-quarters of American lawyers who are in private practice. Like every generalization, however, it has exceptions, and boutique law firms are one interesting, if somewhat ill-defined, exception. Many boutique law firms represent large corporate clients doing the sort of sophisticated intellectual property, tax, transactional, and litigation work performed by large law firms. In this chapter we considered why boutiques form, why they sometimes compete successfully in both the market to provide legal services and the market to hire lawyers, and why some consider boutiques particularly well-suited to thrive in the business environment that has challenged large law firms in the first decades of the twenty-first century.

SUBPART D

LAWYERS AND THE PRACTICE OF DISPUTE RESOLUTION

■ ■ ■

In this section, we examine lawyers in the practice of dispute resolution. In this sector, lawyers work as dispute resolvers rather than as advocates or counselors. This chapter examines two types of work lawyers perform as third-party neutral dispute resolvers: mediation and arbitration. Mediation is a form of dispute resolution in which the mediator has no power to impose a solution, but only facilitates the parties' negotiations with the goal of helping them agree to a solution. In arbitration, by contrast, the third party has the power to decide the dispute.

Lawyers work as mediators and arbitrators in large and small firms and in government; some combine mediation with client representation and others practice only mediation or arbitration or other forms of alternative dispute resolution.

CHAPTER 15

LAWYERS AS THIRD-PARTY NEUTRALS: MEDIATION AND ARBITRATION

■ ■ ■

A. INTRODUCTION

In this chapter we examine the role that lawyers play when they act as third party neutrals who facilitate the resolution of disputes rather than as advocates representing one party to a transaction or a dispute. After surveying the variety of types of ADR, and the sources of regulation of lawyers' work as third party neutrals, we study two of the principal forms of ADR: mediation and arbitration.

Alternative dispute resolution (ADR) is a term that refers loosely to any form of dispute resolution other than a decision by a court. ADR is very common in every sort of legal practice. ADR includes processes of varying degrees of formality, including the following:

Organizational Dispute Resolution. An organization (such as a corporation's human resources department or an online retailer like Amazon.com or service provider like Paypal.com) may allow or require community members, employees, or consumers to present disputes to a third party and receive some form of assistance in resolution. In some organizations, if the informal dispute resolution system does not produce agreement, the parties will be required to resolve it through arbitration. (The next time you visit a website, click on the Terms of Service link and see what dispute resolution system you have "agreed to" by visiting the page.) Some large organizations employ an ombudsperson to investigate and resolve disputes or problems within the organization. For example, an employee who believes that someone within an organization is engaged in unethical or illegal behavior can report the problem to the ombudsperson who is empowered to investigate and, depending on the organization, to issue a report or to resolve the complaint.

Mediation. Parties to a dispute or negotiating a transaction choose a third person as a mediator to assist them in negotiating a resolution. The mediator has no power to impose a solution, but only facilitates the parties' negotiations with the goal of helping them agree to a solution. Mediation can be very casual (any third party, not necessarily a lawyer, can help the parties negotiate a solution) or very formal (a lawyer trained as a mediator convenes and structures a meeting or series of meetings that results in a formal, written agreement). While mediators often emphasize voluntary participation as a cornerstone of mediation philosophy, in fact, participation in mediation is not always voluntary. Most states have enacted laws requiring or strongly encouraging mediation (often known as court-annexed mediation) as part of the pretrial process in certain kinds of cases (often in family law), and sometimes mediation is required by courts as a part of the pretrial process in any civil case.

Arbitration. Parties to a dispute choose (or may be assigned) a third person or panel of people to decide their dispute. Arbitration is used to resolve disputes that would otherwise be litigated. Parties to commercial contracts, especially international contracts, have long agreed to arbitrate disputes arising under their agreements. Unions and the companies that employ unionized workers have long used arbitration to resolve all disputes arising out of their collective bargaining agreements. Since 1990, large employers have often required all employees to agree as a condition of employment to arbitrate all disputes arising out of the employment relationship, and many health care practices require all patients to agree to arbitrate all disputes. Arbitration is also used to resolve negotiating disputes, as when parties agree to present their negotiating positions to a third person to choose whose terms will be part of the contract. (This is called "interest arbitration" and is the way that salary disputes are resolved for professional baseball players.)

Private Adjudication. Parties to a dispute agree to litigate their dispute before a judge hired and paid by them, rather than assigned and paid for by the government. Typically, private adjudication is very similar in process to adjudication in a court, and the judge is often a retired judge. The difference is that the parties do not use the court building or resources and therefore do not have to wait for a trial date, and the parties can adopt the rules of procedure that they wish. Unlike arbitration, however, the judge's decision is appealable.

Mini-Trial or Summary Jury Trial. Parties to litigation agree to present all or part of their case to a mock jury or to a neutral third party acting as a judge to render a decision. The process is not binding on the parties, but rather is to give them an idea of how an actual judge or jury would respond to the parties' evidence and arguments. The parties then use that information in settlement negotiations or to prepare a trial strategy.

Collaborative Courts. Some states (notably California) have developed "collaborative courts," also known as "problem-solving courts," to handle certain kinds of matters. Collaborative courts have a dedicated calendar and judge for specific types of offenders. California's 58 counties had a combined total of more than 420 collaborative courts in 2017 for adults and juveniles to address drug addiction, mental health, homelessness, domestic violence, DUIs, truancy, and veterans' needs. Collaborative courts combine judicial supervision with rehabilitation services and treatment in a multidisciplinary, nonadversarial team approach that seeks to address offenders' complex social problems rather than to rely on criminal conviction and fines or incarceration.

B. WHAT ROLES DO LAWYERS PLAY IN ADR?

Three Roles of Third Party Neutrals:

Facilitator—The neutral assists the parties to negotiate. She helps them articulate their needs (or interests or demands); she suggests alternatives and encourages them to see the dispute in a new light or from the other side's point of view; and she attempts to reduce the risk that anger or intransigence will prevent the parties from reaching a mutually satisfactory agreement.

Evaluator—The neutral offers his assessment of the case. In some types of mediation, the parties expect the mediator to offer his own analysis of their arguments or positions or his own assessment of how a judge or jury is likely to perceive them.

Decisionmaker—The neutral is employed to decide the matter. This is what arbitrators and private judges do.

Lawyers work as third-party neutrals, and they represent clients in ADR proceedings. Employment as a third-party neutral has emerged since the 1980s as an appealing career, or career phase, for many lawyers. The U.S. Bureau of Labor Statistics estimated that 7,800 people were employed full time as mediators, arbitrators and conciliators in the U.S. in 2016, and projected growth in the field.[1] In addition, there is a cadre of international commercial arbitrators who are retained by multinational corporations to resolve disputes over oil, construction projects, and other high value matters that the lawyers for at least one of the parties would prefer not be resolved in national courts.[2]

Some lawyers are employed in-house by corporations or organizations that maintain large internal dispute resolution programs. Some work as solo practitioners offering their service as a mediator or arbitrator. Some are employed by or contract with private organizations that offer ADR services: JAMS (www.jamsadr.com) and AAA (www.adr.org) are two of the best known such organizations in the private sector. JAMS and AAA offer

---

[1] Bureau of Labor Statistics, U.S. Department of Labor, *Occupational Outlook Handbook,* Arbitrators, Mediators, and Conciliators, https://www.bls.gov/ooh/legal/arbitrators-mediators-and-conciliators.htm.

[2] Yves Dezalay & Bryant G. Garth, DEALING IN VIRTUE: INTERNATIONAL COMMERCIAL ARBITRATION AND THE CONSTRUCTION OF A TRANSNATIONAL LEGAL ORDER (1996)

the services of neutrals as well as rules of procedure for different kinds of ADR. For a fee (or, in qualifying cases through their foundations, pro bono) JAMS and AAA offer a package of services to resolve disputes through arbitration, mediation, or some other ADR process. Each of them employs or has as affiliates hundreds of lawyers and retired judges across (and outside) the U.S. with training and experience as arbitrators and mediators. Each of them offers various rules of procedure for conducting different kinds of ADR, ranging from specialized rules for arbitrating employment or insurance or commercial contract disputes, to simple and relatively inexpensive online mediations for small-dollar disputes (or disputes in which the disputants are able or willing to spend only a few hundred dollars for mediation). In the federal government, the Federal Mediation and Conciliation Service (www.fmcs.gov) employs trained mediators to facilitate resolution of a variety of disputes, mainly but not exclusively in the labor-management area, and it maintains a referral list of arbitrators.

International commercial arbitration is a separate field, with its own procedural rules promulgated by the International Chamber of Commerce and other organizations. As with domestic arbitration, it has its own specialized field of practitioners and its own rules of procedure and ethics governing both arbitrators and lawyers for the disputants. Professors Dezalay and Garth explained in their classic sociological study of international commercial arbitration, "There is a kind of 'international arbitration community'—quite often referred to as a 'club'—connected by personal and professional relations cemented by conferences, journals, and actual arbitrations."[3] International commercial arbitration in its contemporary form emerged from dealings among senior European law professors (whose elite credentials and aura of neutrality made them seem trustworthy to multinational firms), a younger group of professional arbitrators (who successfully marketed their expertise in international dispute resolution), the International Chamber of Commerce (an organization they promoted to train arbitrators, to manage arbitrations, and to legitimate the private resolution of international disputes), and the large Anglo-American law firms which dominated the international market for business law.[4] Eventually, there emerged a set of rules governing the ethics of arbitrators and lawyers practicing international arbitration.[5]

Lawyers involved in ADR, both as third party neutrals and as those who represent clients in ADR, strenuously debate the proper mix of these

---

[3] Yves Dezalay & Bryant Garth, *Merchants of Law as Moral Entrepreneurs: Constructing International Justice from the Competition for Transnational Business Disputes*, 29 LAW & SOC'Y REV. 27, 31 (1995).

[4] *Id.* at 36–39.

[5] CATHERINE A. ROGERS, ETHICS IN INTERNATIONAL ARBITRATION (2014).

roles generally, and their merits in addressing particular kinds of disputes. Some of these debates are considered below.

C. HOW IS THE LEGAL PRACTICE OF ADR REGULATED?

The plethora of organizations providing ADR services or requiring or encouraging the use of ADR and the wide range of different types of ADR make it impossible to describe succinctly the regulation of the lawyer's roles in it. And because some types of ADR are performed by lawyers as well as nonlawyers (e.g., family therapists conduct mediation, and managers serve as company ombudspersons), different sources of professional regulation apply to those performing the same service. The following are some of the sources of regulation of ADR.

The Law Governing Lawyers. When lawyers represent clients in ADR, regardless of the type, the same rules and norms that govern their conduct in any other setting apply, including the Model Rules, malpractice liability, and the norms of their practice setting. In addition, many dispute resolution service providers, such as AAA and JAMS, have rules of procedure that regulate the behavior of parties and their representatives, just as courts have rules of procedure to govern lawyers' conduct of cases.

Some Rules of Professional Conduct Apply Only to Lawyers Representing Clients. Lawyers working as third party neutrals are governed by the rules of professional conduct adopted by the state in which they practice, just as are lawyers practicing in any other sector of the profession. However, some rules of professional conduct may apply only to lawyers representing clients. In general, state legal ethics rules do not speak to the specific ethical or other issues that are unique to practice as a third party neutral.

Rules of Court. Virtually every state that requires mediation or arbitration annexed to court adjudication has promulgated rules of conduct governing those who serve as mediators, arbitrators, or other third-party neutrals under those systems.[6]

ADR Service Providers Promulgate Their Own Rules. Many dispute resolution service providers (like JAMS and AAA) have adopted their own requirements of conduct for third party neutrals providing services under their auspices.

Codes of Conduct of Professional Associations of Mediators and Arbitrators. Because the Model Rules of Professional Conduct have almost nothing specific to say about the conduct of lawyers working as third party neutrals, the ABA, the National Arbitration Association, and other

---

[6] Rules governing mediation in all 50 states are compiled in the appendix to SARAH R. COLE *ET AL.*, MEDIATION: LAW, POLICY & PRACTICE (2011–2012).

professional organizations of third party neutrals have promulgated various codes of conduct applicable to particular types of third party neutral practice.

The Uniform Mediation Act and Other State Law. In addition to codes of conduct, some organizations have promulgated model rules of procedure or model laws that contain provisions governing the conduct of third party neutrals. For example, the National Conference of Commissioners on Uniform State Laws has promulgated a Uniform Mediation Act. Ten states and the District of Columbia have enacted the Uniform Mediation Act.[7] Some states have enacted legislation empowering courts to promulgate codes of conduct for mediators and arbitrators and have made compliance with such codes mandatory for third party neutrals.[8]

Employment Contracts. Third party neutrals are typically hired by contract with the parties. As in any other professional-client relationship, the client(s) can insist on certain contract terms.

Market and Peer Group Controls. Most mediators and arbitrators are chosen on a case-by-case basis by parties or their lawyers. To attract future clients, third party neutrals must be perceived as providing a valuable service. Those who work as solo practitioners or in small firms must market their services and develop a reputation through word-of-mouth or client referral. Those who work as employees of organizations or as contractors who are part of a referral network must conform to the demands and expectations of the organization.

The labor market for third party neutrals affects the conditions of work for them, but may also powerfully affect the results of the process for those who rely on them. Arbitrators, mediators, private judges, or any other third party neutral who routinely works for one party may come to depend on that party for their livelihood. We consider this possible source of bias in some detail below.

D. MEDIATION

Mediation takes a wide variety of forms. Mediators sometimes facilitate business transactions, and often resolve disputes either before the parties have framed them as a possible law suit or after both have retained counsel and filed suit. Mediation is required by courts in some civil cases in an effort to encourage settlement. Mediation is required by statute in some kinds of disputes (such as labor-management disputes in

---

[7] *See* www.uniformlaws.org for the current status of enactment.

[8] *See, e.g.*, Cal. Code Civ. Pro. § 1281.85 (requiring arbitrators to adhere to Ethics Standards for Neutral Arbitrators); www.courts.ca.gov/documents/ethics_standards_neutral_arbitrators.pdf.

the railroad and airline industries and in some employment discrimination suits).

Mediation is facilitated negotiation governed by the principle of *party self-determination*. The parties themselves decide what their dispute is about, what their needs or interests are, and whether or how to resolve the dispute through mediation. The mediator is a neutral facilitator who helps the parties agree by helping them understand the other side's point of view; the mediator does not take sides or decide the dispute.

Mediation is thought to be an antidote to destructive strategic behavior in negotiation by reducing opportunities to engage in it. Mediation does so in several ways: (1) It recognizes the full range of party interests, values, and priorities (not just money or the governing law); (2) It manages emotional and relational issues in a "safe" place where the parties can discuss their feelings, gain respect, offer and accept apologies, and share information; (3) It reduces the potential for conflicting interests between lawyer and client by encouraging the client to be involved in the statement of priorities and resolution of the dispute; (4) Mediation reduces the risks associated with honest disclosure of information so as to enable both sides to gain mutually optimal settlements that would not be possible if neither side trusted the other enough to disclose information that would lead to a settlement; (5) It improves communication and preparation by both lawyers and clients by forcing them to focus on the dispute and carve out time in their busy schedules to resolve it; (6) It reduces cognitive barriers to settlement by forcing parties to see the matter from the perspective of others.[9] After describing the mediation process and the role of the mediator, we will consider the circumstances in which mediation can address the problems of self-interested, strategic, and potentially destructive behavior that can occur in unfacilitated negotiation, and when it cannot.

Mediation can take many forms, and can last anywhere from a few hours to many days, but a typical mediation might go something like this. Mediators generally prefer that the parties be present, not just their lawyers. Indeed, some mediation experts insist that without parties there, it's not really mediation because it's not party self-determination. In some cases neither side is represented by counsel. Mediators often resist having only one party be represented by counsel, and law in some states regulates when counsel can and cannot be present in mediation.[10] Court-annexed settlement mediations generally deem it crucial that each party have at least one person present who has full settlement authority. Many court

---

[9] *See* COLE, *ET AL.*, MEDIATION: LAW, POLICY & PRACTICE at 51–60; Russell B. Korobkin, *Psychological Impediments to Mediation Success: Theory and Practice*, 21 OHIO ST. J. DISP. RES. 281 (2006).

[10] *See, e.g.*, Cal. Fam. Code § 3182(a) (mediator may exclude attorney from participating); Wis. Stat. § 767.405(10) (permitting mediator to include counsel).

programs and provider organizations require that the attorneys provide to the mediator in advance a short confidential mediation statement. The statement summarizes the issues involved (legal and otherwise) and indicates what the attorney and client are looking for.

At the beginning of the mediation session, the mediator generally provides an explanation of the mediation process, and the parties agree to the procedures and the extent of confidentiality of mediation communications. The mediator generally asks each or all parties—both the clients and their attorneys—to take turns providing a brief overview of the dispute and what they want to say about it. Mediators encourage the parties to speak in addition to their attorneys. By having the parties present during the mediation, the parties obtain a better understanding of the other parties' interests and positions. Mediators insist that this process creates a better understanding between the parties.

The mediator often suggests an individual caucus with each party separately. Whatever is said during the caucus is confidential, and is not repeated to the other side, unless consent is obtained, although the mediator is free to use the information provided in an effort to nudge the parties toward agreement. After a caucus with all sides, the mediator generally meets with everyone together again. Often the mediator will encourage brainstorming of ideas for resolution and discussion of several options for resolution.

During this discussion, the mediator may be more or less aggressive in suggesting options and possible outcomes, and in assessing each party's statements. In evaluative mediation, the parties expect the mediator to offer her perspective on the parties' statements or asserted desires. (In mediation, it's often frowned upon to refer to the parties' positions; parties have perceptions, concerns, and interests, but they are not supposed to have positions or make arguments.). In facilitative or transformative mediation, the parties' expectations about whether the mediator will state her own assessment may be less clear. Facilitative mediation aids the parties to reach their own agreement, and transformative mediation aspires to help parties transform their relationship (and, perhaps, themselves). Mediators debate when one or another of these approaches is more appropriate. Whatever mediators think, attorneys who represent parties in mediation, at least in some cases, often want evaluation.[11] Yet in some states and in some mediation programs, mediators are strongly

---

[11] ABA SECTION OF DISPUTE RESOLUTION, TASK FORCE ON IMPROVING MEDIATION QUALITY, FINAL REPORT 2006–2008, available at www.abanet.org/dispute.

discouraged from evaluating a case or offering their opinions on it, even when specifically requested to do so by a party or an attorney.[12]

The role of mediators as evaluators and the proper mix of party discussion in joint session and separate caucuses are hot topics among mediators, as is the role of lawyer representatives in mediation. Some scholars lament that the increasingly widespread use of court-annexed mediation has fundamentally changed the nature of mediation, and not for the better.[13] In essence, the critique is that the mediator has become more like a settlement facilitator.[14]

Whatever mix of party- and lawyer-control and individual and joint sessions, eventually the parties decide whether they have reached agreement or if they need more time. Ideally, the mediation ends (whether after one session lasting a few hours, or multiple sessions over days or weeks), when an agreement is reached. The mediator usually requires the agreement to be reduced to writing and signed by all parties. Sometimes the mediator will draft all or portions of the agreement, but sometimes the mediator will avoid doing so.

Many mediators speak in rather glowing terms about the mediation process and about their role in it. Surveys of mediators and lawyers who represent clients in mediation have found that the mediators are more likely than the lawyers to value what some call the "softer" side of the process—articulating feelings, believing one has been heard, healing or preserving relationships, and the like.[15] Some speak in lofty terms about the skilled mediator's capacity to bring happiness to unhappy people, to transform relationships, to bring peace to families and communities, to promote moral growth, and to promote democracy and justice by empowering individuals to resolve their own disputes, to create their own norms to govern their relationships.[16] Mediators typically contrast their perspective on mediation as a process—it is more likely than negotiation or adjudication to produce creative solutions to problems and to expand

---

[12] In North Carolina, for example, the Standards of Conduct for all mediators certified by the state Dispute Resolution Commission or who are conducting court-annexed mediation provide:

> A mediator shall not impose his/her opinion about the merits of the dispute or about the acceptability of any proposed option for settlement. A mediator should resist giving his/her opinions about the dispute and options for settlement even when he/she is requested to do so by a party or attorney.

North Carolina Supreme Court, Standards of Professional Conduct for Mediators, Preamble § V(C) (2014), *available at* https://www.nccourts.gov/assets/documents/publications/StandardsConduct.pdf?e2dD2UQUqwN6Ypo3wEFy3CtHORzZzp8r.

[13] Nancy A. Welsh, *Making Deals in Court-Connected Mediation: What's Justice Got to Do With It?*, 79 WASH. U. L.Q. 787, 789–793 (2001).

[14] James J. Alfini, *Mediation as a Calling: Addressing the Disconnect Between Mediation Ethics and the Practices of Lawyer Mediators*. 49 S. TEX. L. REV. 829, 834 (2008).

[15] ABA TASK FORCE ON MEDIATION QUALITY, at 8.

[16] Sara Cobb, *Creating Sacred Space: Toward a Second-Generation Dispute Resolution Practice*, 28 FORDHAM URB. L. J. 1017, 1017 (2001).

rather than just divide the settlement pie—with lawyers' tendency to focus only on the results—whether the mediation produced a good settlement for the client, and whether the client is happy with the results.

Some criticisms of mediation are similar to criticisms of other forms of dispute resolution, including litigation. In short, the criticism is that mediation rarely succeeds in its most transformative aspirations. It suppresses conflict rather than defusing or resolving it, and it produces compromise in cases in which there should be none.[17] An important critique of mediation in cases in which there has been domestic violence asserts that mediation sacrifices the right to be free from violence to the "interests" or "needs" of batterers to explain away violence as simply anger or overreaction to the victims' poor housekeeping or unwillingness to do what they want.[18] How we assess the success of the mediation as a process or in its results might depend on the underlying facts.

NOTES ON MEDIATION

1. ***Enthusiasm About Mediation.*** All lawyers are prone to a certain amount of hyperbole about the importance of their role, but the tone and the substance of the praise of mediation are particularly glowing. Why do many find it such an appealing form of practice?

2. ***How Strictly Should Mediation Be Regulated?*** A longstanding debate about mediation concerns whether or how strictly law should regulate who may be a mediator. In some states, one critic complained, "there are stiffer requirements to become a hair stylist than there are to become a mediator."[19] Enacting legislation to establish qualification, licensing and disciplinary standards for mediators as for other professions can be controversial because, as the former executive director of the Society of Professionals in Dispute Resolution said, "There are many paths to competence, such as life skills and on-the-job experience, as well as professional training. . . . Just because [people have] a professional degree doesn't mean that they're going to be good mediators."[20]

As with every other aspect of the regulation of the legal profession, there is a tension between stiff regulation in an effort to ensure quality and allowing greater access to the practice. Greater regulation of the qualifications of mediators will also operate as a barrier to entry to the occupation. This tension has remained acute over the decades, as illustrated in the Final Report of the ABA Section of Dispute Resolution Task Force on Improving Mediation Quality, which recognized the importance of mediator knowledge and skill but

---

[17] An early and still influential critique of ADR exploring these ideas is Owen Fiss, *Against Settlement*, 93 YALE L.J. 1073 (1984).

[18] *See* Trina Grillo, *The Mediation Alternative: Process Dangers for Women*, 100 YALE L.J. 1545 (1991).

[19] Richard C. Reuben, *The Lawyer Turns Peacemaker*, ABA J. (August 1996), at 54.

[20] *Id.*

took no position on how mediators ought to be trained, and no position on mediator credentialing or regulation.

3. ***Disparities of Bargaining Power.*** Mediation is supposed to address the disparities of bargaining power that plague negotiation and litigation by stripping away the advantages possessed by those who can afford to hire the best lawyers and spend the most money preparing for a negotiation or litigation. The parties themselves come to the mediation and, when it works as intended, speak honestly about their wants, needs, and fears. The advantage the law may give one side in terms of substantive rights—the shadow of the law—is supposed to fade away and the parties meet as equals to brainstorm creative mutually beneficial approaches to their dispute.

There is a tension between party self-determination and disparities of bargaining power. A mediator determined to let the parties work out their own resolution, and to stay strictly neutral about what happens, risks allowing a party with greater bargaining power to exploit the less-powerful party. In some types of mediations, mediators insist they should not attempt to balance disparities of bargaining power or even to consider it as a relevant factor. An example of this is mediation of negotiating disputes in unionized industries. If the labor or product market conditions are such that either the union or the employer is in a position to force the other side to accept major concessions, mediators say they are not in a position to intervene. On the other hand, in marital dissolution mediations in which one spouse has power and the other does not, many mediators say they should attempt to keep disparities of bargaining power from affecting the resolution.

E. ARBITRATION

Arbitration is a process in which disputants agree to have a third party or parties resolve their dispute. It has a long and uncontroversial history of use by sophisticated contracting parties, such as large companies doing business across national borders, who seek an expert to resolve their disputes free from the possible bias of one contracting party's national courts and to obtain a judgment that may be more easily enforceable in courts around the world than a court judgment.[21] It is also the preferred method of dispute resolution under collective bargaining agreements in unionized workplaces because neither unions nor employers have trusted courts to quickly, cheaply, and sensibly resolve disputes arising under their agreements.

---

[21] Indeed, international commercial arbitration is a growth area for American lawyers as "a growing number of companies involved in international projects are choosing to arbitrate big-money disputes." Because millions or billions of dollars are at stake in many international arbitrations, large law firms have found it a lucrative practice area. Elizabeth Olson, *Growth in Global Disputes Brings Big Paychecks for Law Firms*, N.Y. TIMES, Aug. 27, 2013, B1. One lawyer at a large firm estimated the annual revenues generated by the firm's international arbitration practice had increased tenfold between 1997 and 2002. Martha Neil, *Small World, Big Business*, ABA J. (Sept. 2002), p. 28.

Since the mid-1980s, a widespread and highly controversial use of arbitration has emerged in consumer and individual employment contracts. Unlike commercial or union arbitration agreements, which are bilateral agreements freely negotiated by sophisticated contracting parties engaged in ongoing relationships, arbitration agreements imposed on consumers and individual employees are drafted by sophisticated company lawyers and imposed on consumers and employees without negotiation. Some of these agreements, predictably, are one-sided, favoring the corporation in matters of substance, procedure and remedies. Although consumer and employment law plaintiffs and their lawyers have challenged the enforceability of provisions in arbitration agreements imposing defense-friendly procedures and remedies, the Supreme Court has rejected all challenges. Most of the challenges have concerned prohibitions on class actions. Consumers and employees have argued that without the class action procedure, individual claims are of such small dollar value that no lawyer would be willing to take the case. In *AT & T v. Concepcion*, 563 U.S. 333 (2011), the Court held that states cannot prevent enforcement of class action waivers in mandatory pre-dispute arbitration agreements even where the amount at stake in an individual claim is so small that no individual consumer would find it economically rational to arbitrate. The Court extended that rule to arbitration agreements governing complex statutory claims even though the procedural restrictions of arbitration might make it impossible to vindicate the statutory right. *American Express Co. v. Italian Colors Restaurant,* 570 U.S. 228 (2013). Finally, the Court rejected a federal labor agency rule that a substantive statutory right to advocate collectively for improved working conditions trumped the federal policy favoring individual arbitration and upheld a class action waiver in an arbitration agreement. *Epic Systems Corp. v. Lewis,* 138 S. Ct. 1612 (2018). Although critics of these cases have argued that companies use arbitration as a liability avoidance device rather than as a dispute resolution mechanism, that argument has consistently persuaded only four justices.

Arbitration can be almost as formal as adjudication in court. In some arbitrations, especially those that resolve statutory or other claims not limited to those based solely on the contract between the parties, the parties can obtain pretrial discovery of the facts, make motions to dismiss or for summary judgment, conduct hearings in which the rules of evidence apply, and appeal adverse rulings to an appellate panel or to a court. In such arbitrations, the arbitrator(s) are likely to be lawyers or retired judges, and are expected to act exactly as a judge would in following the law and writing an opinion finding facts and making determinations of law. Many companies require that all their employees waive their right to go to court on all statutory, tort, contract, and other common law claims arising out of employment. These employment arbitrations have become more like private trials in order that the arbitration agreement not be deemed to operate as a waiver of substantive statutory or common law legal rights.

Arbitration can also be quite informal: there may be no in-person hearing, the arbitrator is not expected to decide the case based on external law, the rules of evidence do not apply, and the arbitrator is not expected to issue a written decision other than a simple statement of who wins.

The role of the arbitrator thus varies widely depending on the type of arbitration. Just as party-determination is the most important tenet of mediation, the primacy of the contract is the most important tenet of arbitration. The contract defines and limits the power of the arbitrator. Arbitrators are typically chosen for some combination of their judgment and their expertise. While there has been little controversy over the selection of arbitrators in commercial and labor-management arbitration where the contracts are the product of bilateral negotiation and there are sophisticated repeat players on both sides, the selection of arbitrators for consumer and individual employee arbitration has generated criticism. This issue is addressed below.

In some cases the parties agree on a single arbitrator, while in others each party chooses an arbitrator and the two arbitrators together choose a third. Arbitration usually has some characteristics of a trial. The parties may write pre- or post-arbitration briefs framing the legal and factual issues and stating their position on each. The parties make opening statements and then offer evidence through the introduction of documents and the testimony of witnesses. Each side can cross-examine the other's witnesses. The parties make closing arguments. The arbitrator(s) usually do not decide the issue on the spot but instead take some number of days (with the maximum often dictated by the contract), to issue an award (or decision). Sometimes the arbitrator's award will simply state the conclusion: whether the claimant or respondent wins and if the claimant wins, what the remedy will be. Sometimes the award will state reasons. The contract that provides for arbitration will determine whether the arbitrator's award will be confidential (as is typically required in consumer and individual employment arbitration agreements drafted unilaterally by companies) or will be reported in the compendia of arbitration decisions (as is typically the case in unionized labor-management collective bargaining agreements and some international commercial contracts).

Like mediators, arbitrators are regulated by a wide variety of organizations. Although arbitrators are not separately licensed, many aspire to enhance their marketability by joining membership organizations like the National Association of Arbitrators, which imposes conditions on members such as that they only conduct arbitrations that meet the minimum fairness standards known as the "due process protocols." As with mediators, there may be a tension between the desire to ensure that arbitrators have particular sorts of education, training, and experience and the desire to ensure a diverse pool of arbitrators. In *Smith v. American Arbitration Association*, 233 F.3d 502 (7th Cir. 2000), a woman involved in an arbitration sued the arbitration provider because there was only one woman in AAA's entire pool of arbitrators, and that one woman had been struck by the other party in the arbitration. The court rejected the contention that the all-male pool violated the equal protection rights of litigants compelled to arbitrate because arbitration is a private system that does not implicate the state action necessary to trigger equal protection scrutiny.

One of the most challenging issues for lawyers working as arbitrators is whether arbitration processes are fair to those who use them. When an arbitration process is designed and negotiated by two parties of equal sophistication and bargaining power, as in commercial or labor-management arbitration, there may be only small risk that the process would be systematically unfair to one side. Some lawyers complain, indeed, about too much even-handedness: "My experience is that arbitrators usually just want to 'split the baby' in order to make both parties happy—or at least to try to avoid alienating either party to remain on 'the list' for future business."[22] When an arbitration process is designed by a sophisticated party and imposed without negotiation in an adhesion contract on another, there is a risk of systematic unfairness to the party that does not design the process. That risk may be exacerbated if the party that created the system uses it repeatedly against individuals who use it only once.

A major concern about the fairness of arbitration concerns this so-called repeat player effect. It is summarized as follows:

> Unlike judges, arbitrators get paid only when selected to arbitrate a dispute. This economic reality of arbitration has given rise to fears of "repeat-arbitrator bias"-the view that arbitrators will decide cases in favor of the repeat player, which is the party more likely to be in a position to appoint the arbitrator to serve again. In consumer arbitration, consumers are unlikely to be repeat players (although their attorneys may be). Thus, the fear is that arbitrators will tend to favor businesses in the hopes of being selected for future cases more frequently. More broadly, commentators have expressed concerns about what might be called "repeat-player bias" (rather than repeat-arbitrator bias)—bias that results from businesses structuring the dispute resolution process in their favor.

[22] Richard C. Reuben, *The Lawyer Turns Peacemaker*, ABA J. (August 1996), at 54 (quoting a risk manager for a city).

> Several factors may reduce the likelihood or consequences of repeat-arbitrator or repeat-player bias. First, arbitration providers, as well as individual arbitrators, may seek to maintain a reputation for fair and unbiased decision making. Such reputational constraints may reduce the risk that repeat-arbitrator or repeat-player bias will occur. Second, even if arbitrators and arbitration providers have an incentive to make decisions that businesses want, it is not necessarily the case that those decisions will be unfavorable to consumers.[23]

The authors of that study found some evidence of a repeat player effect in its sample of 301 consumer arbitrations, but found it was probably due to better case screening by the repeat player rather than to arbitrator bias. A larger study of arbitration in employment cases found strong evidence of a repeat player effect,[24] and another study found a repeat player effect even when controlling for better screening:

> Both repeat employers and repeat employer-arbitrator pairs are associated with lower employee win rates. Further, the average monetary amount awarded to successful plaintiffs is reduced in cases involving repeat employer arbitrator pairs and continues to decline with each subsequent pairing. We also find that repeat employers and repeat employer-arbitrator pairings show no significant differences in settlement behaviors relative to their one-shot counterparts. This is important because differences in settlement behavior between the two groups could produce a selection effect in which stronger cases are more likely to be settled, producing a weaker set of cases that reach the hearing and award stage, which would in turn result in a depressed employee win rate. The lack of significant differences in settlement behaviors in our results enhances our confidence that the differences in employee win rates that we find between one-shot and repeat players is not simply a function of differences in settlement behaviors in the two groups.[25]

Importantly, the study also found that when plaintiffs were not represented by counsel (which, as noted, is common in small-dollar employment and consumer arbitrations), employees fare even worse in terms of settling, winning, and monetary recovery.[26] However, not every

---

[23] Christopher R. Drahozal & Samantha Zyontz, *An Empirical Study of AAA Consumer Arbitrations*, 25 OHIO J. DISPUTE RESOLUTION 843, 857–860 (2010).

[24] Alexander J.S. Colvin, *An Empirical Study of Employment Arbitration: Case Outcomes and Processes*, 8 J. EMPIRICAL LEG. STUD. 1 (2011).

[25] Alexander J.D. Colvin & Mark D. Gough, *The Individual Employment Rights Arbitration in the United States: Actors and Outcomes*, 68 ILR REV: J. WORK & POL'Y 1019, 1035–36 (2015).

[26] *Id.* at 1036–37. Earlier studies using different data also found a repeat player effect. Alexander J.S. Colvin, *Empirical Research on Employment Arbitration: Clarity Amidst the Sound and Fury?* 11 EMPLOYEE RTS. & EMP. POL'Y J. 405 (2007).

study has concluded that arbitration is, on balance, worse for employee and consumer plaintiffs. One study defending mandatory arbitration asserted that any assessment of arbitration as compared to litigation should analyze how cases are resolved before a final determination as well as how arbitrators and courts ultimately decide those that reach a final decision. This study contends that comparing pre-decision resolutions shows that arbitration has considerable advantages as compared to litigation, in terms of the speed and affordability of the process.[27]

A study of securities arbitration attempted to discern whether arbitrators may be influenced by the fact that many of them do not work full-time as arbitrators. Many work part-time as arbitrators and part-time as lawyers representing parties in the securities industry. The study found that what the lawyer did for a living besides work as an arbitrator had an effect. Attorney-arbitrators who had represented brokerage firms in other securities cases were significantly less generous to plaintiffs in arbitration awards. Attorneys who represent investors in arbitration proceedings were not more generous when they serve as arbitrators, nor were arbitrators who represent both investors and brokerage houses.[28]

F. SUMMARY

In this chapter we examined the roles of lawyers as mediators who facilitate the resolution of disputes and as arbitrators who are empowered by contracts to decide disputes. We considered the strengths and limitations of the principal sources of regulation of lawyers' work as third party neutrals. The rules of procedure of ADR service providers regulate the behavior of parties and their representatives, and courts have rules of procedure to govern lawyers' conduct in court-annexed ADR. Third party neutrals are typically hired by contract with the parties. As in any other professional-client relationship, the client(s) can insist on certain contract terms. Any third party neutral who routinely works for one party may come to depend on that party for their livelihood, which can present difficult ethical issues for the third-party neutral and can have a significant impact on the results of matters they handle.

---

[27] David Sherwyn, Samuel Estreicher & Michael Heise, *Assessing the Case for Employment Arbitration: A New Path for Empirical Research*, 57 STAN. L. REV. 1557 (2005).

[28] Stephen J. Choi, Jill E. Fisch & A.C. Pritchard, *Attorneys As Arbitrators*, 39 J. LEGAL STUDIES 109, 111–12 (2010).

SUBPART E

PUBLIC INTEREST PRACTICE

■ ■ ■

We turn now to the last unit in our survey of the various types of practice settings in which American lawyers work—"public interest practice." As we'll see, the term "public interest law" is used in a variety of different ways, not all of them consistent with one another. For purposes of organizing the following discussion, we use "public interest practice" to refer to organizations and nonprofit groups receiving government or philanthropic subsidies whose purpose is either to serve people who cannot otherwise afford legal services or to pursue some vision of the public good.

We begin this unit with an examination of lawyers who work in legal services programs designed to address the legal needs of poor people (Chapter 16). The next chapter (Chapter 17) considers lawyers who work for nonprofit organizations that seek to serve some vision of the public good.

CHAPTER 16

LEGAL SERVICES

■ ■ ■

A. INTRODUCTION

The U.S. Constitution provides a right to appointed counsel in criminal cases in which the defendant faces the possibility of incarceration because, as the Supreme Court explained, the principle that "every defendant stands equal before the law cannot be realized if the poor man charged with a crime has to face his accusers without a lawyer to assist him." *Gideon v. Wainwright*, 372 U.S. 335, 344 (1963). The constitutional right to counsel in criminal cases obligated every state to set up a system of lawyers to provide criminal defense to indigent persons, thus making indigent criminal defense a recognized practice setting.

In contrast, there is no constitutional right to counsel in civil cases. The Supreme Court held in *Lassiter v. Department of Social Services,* 452 U.S. 18 (1981), that a state did not violate the constitutional guarantee of due process when it imposed what many would consider the most grievous possible harm on a civil litigant—taking a child away from his mother—without providing a lawyer to represent her in the proceeding to terminate parental rights. Because there is no constitutional right to counsel in civil cases, the ability of poor people to obtain legal representation depends on an assortment of state and federal statutes and private charity. The organization and funding of legal services to the poor in civil cases varies from one area of law to another, one city to another, and one state to another.

Early programs to provide legal assistance to the poor began in the late nineteenth century with funding from private charity and local governments. Like many forms of poor relief, these efforts were aimed at undercutting support for socialism and anarchism, to create social stability, not social change. Legal aid societies were terribly underfunded compared to the need.[1] By one estimate, in 1963, all the civil legal services programs in the U.S. combined had only 400 lawyers nationwide and a

[1] An influential 1919 Reginald Heber Smith study, *Justice and the Poor*, and studies conducted by the American Bar Association and others over the course of the mid-twentieth century, documented the need for legal services. EARL JOHNSON, JR., JUSTICE AND REFORM: THE FORMATIVE YEARS OF THE AMERICAN LEGAL SERVICE PROGRAM (1974); REGINALD HEBER SMITH, JUSTICE AND THE POOR (1919, repr. ed. 1972).

budget that was less than two-tenths of one percent of the nation's total annual expenditure on legal services.[2]

The War on Poverty launched by the Johnson Administration in 1964 led to a substantial infusion of federal money and attention to the need for legal services for the poor. In 1965, the Office of Economic Opportunity (OEO) began providing federal funds to civil legal services programs and attracted talented, ambitious young lawyers to OEO-funded legal aid programs. The social and legal change agenda of these legal services lawyers reflected the progressive agendas of the civil rights and welfare rights movements. Civil legal services to the poor became a way for idealistic lawyers to promote social change by trying to empower impoverished communities and eradicate pervasive inequality.

With the election of Richard Nixon in 1968, the conservative backlash against the social movements of the 1960s found a powerful ally in government. The Nixon Administration tried to eliminate the OEO funding of legal services for the poor, but Congress ended up institutionalizing it in 1974 by creating the Legal Services Corporation (LSC) as a private, non-profit corporation to administer federal funding for legal aid to the poor. Because the Legal Services Corporation was essentially born from an effort to kill anything like it, the statute that created it contained restrictions on what the federal funds could be used for. It prohibited LSC-funded attorneys from lobbying and political organizing or from handling what were then particularly controversial matters, including school desegregation cases, cases challenging the military draft, and cases protecting abortion rights. Nevertheless, the Legal Services Corporation expanded civil legal assistance for the poor from a primarily urban phenomenon to a nationwide program with offices scattered across every state.

Meanwhile, philanthropic organizations, most notably the Ford Foundation, began to provide significant funding for legal services as part of a broader effort to address poverty and social injustice. Legal services organizations established with foundation funding in the late 1960s and early 1970s provided legal representation on a range of issues, including workplace discrimination, welfare rights, affordable housing, consumer protection, and environmental justice. Later, the agenda broadened to include immigrant rights, wage theft, homelessness, and HIV/AIDS, among other issues. Although the Ford Foundation ceased being a significant funder of legal services to the poor by the 1980s, many of the organizations founded in the 1960s and 1970s survived based on some

---

2 JOHNSON, JUSTICE AND REFORM, at 6–9.

mixture of philanthropy, federal, state, local, and bar association funding, and attorneys' fees awarded under fee-shifting statutes.[3]

Today, civil legal assistance is provided by a number of different programs. Legal aid offices, organized civil pro bono programs, judicare programs (which offer publicly-funded legal services for low-income persons with certain types of problems), and law school clinical programs all provide representation. Other programs provide only information; these include telephone hotlines delivering specific legal advice or general legal information; courthouse lawyer-for-a-day programs; staffed assistance centers or computer kiosks in courthouses that assist *pro se* civil litigants; and court websites that provide court forms and/or information about using the courts.[4] The Legal Services Corporation is the largest single funder, but overall more funds come from other sources, including state and local governments, the private bar, private foundations, and IOLTA programs (which are explained below). Moreover, every state and most localities have organized pro bono programs run by bar associations, legal aid organizations, or independent nonprofits.[5]

The need for subsidized legal services in civil cases for those who cannot afford lawyers far outstrips the supply of lawyers who provide such service. Unlike public defender offices, which are constitutionally required to provide representation to all eligible criminal defendants, legal services offices can and do turn away huge numbers of eligible people who seek representation. Perhaps the single most significant challenge facing lawyers practicing in this sector of the profession, as well as one of the most significant challenges facing courts and other institutions that administer the law, is managing the dearth of legal representation for those in need. There is a debate over the extent of the unmet legal needs of poor and moderate income people, but whatever the nature of and reasons for the problem, legal services lawyers experience a shortage of time and resources.

B. FUNDING OF LEGAL SERVICES

Lawyers who work full time providing legal services for the poor are funded by four principal sources: (1) the Legal Services Corporation provides federal funds to legal services offices; (2) governments and bar associations provide funds for particular types of legal services as parts of other social welfare programs (such as to address homelessness, domestic

---

[3] For a recent, comprehensive history of civil legal aid in the United States, see EARL JOHNSON JR., TO ESTABLISH JUSTICE FOR ALL: THE PAST AND FUTURE OF CIVIL LEGAL AID IN THE UNITED STATES (2014).

[4] Rebecca Sandefur & Aaron Smyth, *Access Across America: First Report of the Civil Justice Infrastructure Mapping Project* (Oct. 11, 2011), at 11.

[5] Alan W. Houseman, *The Future of Civil Legal Aid: A National Perspective*, 10 U. D.C. L. REV. 35 (2007).

violence, problems of veterans, elderly or disabled people, and public health issues); (3) states provide funding through the Interest on Lawyer Trust Accounts (IOLTA) program; (4) private philanthropy funds some offices, or provides funding to support a lawyer in an office. In addition, law school clinical programs are an important source of legal services, and many legal services offices operate networks of lawyers in private practice who provide pro bono legal service. This patchwork of funding has been attacked by the left as being inadequate and by those who oppose the aims of legal services programs as being unduly political. The following excerpt describes some of the principal sources of funding, and recent challenges to their continued existence.

TAKING OUT THE ADVERSARY: THE ASSAULT ON PROGRESSIVE PUBLIC-INTEREST LAWYERS

David Luban
91 California Law Review 209 (2003)

The 1996 Legal Services Corporation Restrictions. The single biggest source of funding for poor people's lawyers is the Legal Services Corporation.* [T]his budget fund[s] [about] one underpaid legal-services lawyer per 10,000 poor people.

Restrictions on the use of LSC funding have always existed. From the beginning of the program, Congress prohibited LSC recipients from using their federal funds on volatile political issues like abortion, school desegregation, and the military draft. LSC lawyers could still advocate on these issues provided they did not use federal funds to do so.

In 1996, however, Congress enacted restrictions on legal-services lawyers that went much further. Not only do they prohibit LSC recipients from taking on certain issues, but they also forbid them from representing entire classes of clients. These include whole classes of aliens, many of whom are legal. The new regulations likewise prohibit the representation of all incarcerated people, including those not convicted of a crime, and those whose cases have nothing to do with why they are in jail, as, for example, in parental-rights lawsuits. The restrictions also prevent LSC attorneys from using specific procedural devices or arguments. They cannot attempt to influence rulemaking or lawmaking, participate in class actions, request attorney's fees under applicable statutes, challenge any welfare reform, or defend anyone charged with a drug offense in a public-housing eviction proceeding. Furthermore, LSC grant recipients must file statements revealing the identity of their clients and stating the facts of the case, and these statements must be made available "to any Federal

* [Eds.: The budget for the Legal Services Corporation in fiscal year 2017 was $385 million. Data on funding levels for the LSC since its founding may be found at http://www.lsc.gov/congress/funding/funding-history.]

department or agency that is auditing or monitoring the activities of the Corporation or of the recipient."

Perhaps the most devastating regulation, however, is Congress's prohibition on LSC recipients using their nonfederal funds for these prohibited activities. This requirement had a drastic effect. A legal-aid office could no longer accept an LSC grant if it did any prohibited legal work. This provision forced legal-services providers to split into separate organizations with separate offices, one receiving federal funds and abiding by the restrictions, the other maintaining its freedom of action at the cost of its LSC grant. The result was bifurcated organizations substantially weaker than the initial organization. Some organizations had to purchase duplicate computer systems and hire duplicate staff. Some locales could afford only a restricted office, so that clients with the "wrong" cases were forced to travel hundreds of miles to find counsel or, more realistically, do without. In hundreds of ongoing cases, restricted LSC lawyers had to withdraw.

Opponents of progressive lawyers quickly took advantage of the regulations. For example, when the restrictions went into effect, New York legal-services lawyer David Udell was helping to monitor an already-settled class action against a federal agency. The LSC threatened that if he continued to participate in the case, it would defund every legal-services lawyer in New York City and fire every employee. The LSC backed down when Udell filed a constitutional challenge to the restrictions, in the form of a motion to withdraw conditional on the restrictions being upheld. But later, when Udell informed the monitoring court that the defendant had violated the settlement, "[t]he defendant's counsel (a lawyer in the federal programs branch of the Department of Justice) reported my action to LSC. LSC then declared that my letter to the court was 'adversarial' and ordered me off the case on pain of defunding all legal services programs in New York City, even though the merits of the underlying case had been resolved years earlier." Again, Udell backed the Corporation down through legal action, and the LSC contented itself with merely docking his pay for going to court against it. Udell fared less well in another class action, when the LSC ordered him out but the judge ordered him to stay in the case while at the same time refusing to prevent LSC from taking disciplinary action against Udell or other legal-services lawyers in New York. Udell had no recourse but to work on a part-time basis and handle the class action, during his off hours, for no pay. Although this example makes the LSC seem like the heavy, the LSC was only doing what Congress wanted it to do.

The Challenges to IOLTA Programs. IOLTA programs provide the second biggest source of funds for legal-aid lawyers, after the LSC. Lawyers are required to maintain trust accounts for client money that they hold. When the amount is large, or held for a significant time period, attorneys open an interest-bearing savings account in the client's behalf, but when the amount of money the lawyer holds for clients is small, or the money is held for a short period of time only, the administrative cost of getting the interest to clients would devour the interest and might actually cost the client money. In such cases, the attorney deposits client funds in a demand account, that is, an account from which funds may be obtained on demand. Until 1980, banking law prohibited interest payments on demand accounts. In 1980, Congress amended the law to permit interest-bearing demand accounts, but only for "funds in which the entire beneficial interest is held by one or more individuals or by an organization which is operated primarily for religious, philanthropic, charitable, educational, political, or other similar purposes and which is not operated for profit." States responded to the new law by creating IOLTA programs: nonprofit foundations to fund low-income legal services, financed by the interest on lawyer's demand trust accounts. Lawyers participating in IOLTA programs pool client funds that are too small or held for too short a time to generate collectible interest for the client in an IOLTA account, where the interest goes to the nonprofit foundation funding low-income legal services. Client funds that are capable of generating collectible interest for the client—that is, interest that would not be devoured by the transaction costs of getting it to the client—must still be deposited into a separate savings account for the client, not into the IOLTA account.

The idea was ingenious. The clients could not get the interest on small or short-term lawyer-held funds because transaction costs would gobble it up. Because no one else could get the interest either, it all went to the banks by default. As one Texas judge quipped, IOLTA takes from the banks and gives to the poor. IOLTA programs generated more than $125 million a year for indigent legal services in 2001. Almost all were enacted by the states' highest courts under their rulemaking authority. All fifty states and the District of Columbia have IOLTA plans, and half of them are mandatory.

[Professor Luban explained in some detail that IOLTA faced constitutional challenges from conservative activists who objected to using interest on trust fund accounts to fund legal services programs. The Supreme Court upheld the IOLTA system against the argument that the use of interest constituted an unconstitutional taking of private property, reasoning that absent the program no one would receive the interest anyway. *Brown v. Legal Foundation of Washington*, 538 U.S. 216 (2003).]

Law School Clinics and the Battle of New Orleans. Civil and criminal litigation clinics form the backbone of clinical education in the United States, and they typically provide one-client-at-a-time, more-or-less routine, direct client representation. Clinical education also includes street-law programs, entrepreneurial clinics with business clients, and externships. While nothing in principle prevents conservatives from starting clinics devoted to issues they favor, for example, crime victims' rights or small business deregulation clinics, it has rarely come to pass, although the [Washington Legal Foundation (WLF)] started an Economic Freedom Law Clinic at George Mason Law School, which takes a "pro-free enterprise, limited government, and economic freedom perspective." The perception of a leftward tilt makes law school clinics a natural target for adversaries of progressive public-interest law.

The principal lightning rod has been environmental-law clinics, which sometimes take anti-development stances that put them at odds with business interests. [The article recounts efforts in the 1980s, 1990s and 2000s, to eliminate environmental law clinics at the University of Oregon, the University of West Virginia, the University of Wyoming, the University of Pittsburgh, and Tulane University. Some of the efforts succeeded.]

* * *

The 1996 Restrictions on Legal Services Corporation Funding. The efforts to eliminate LSC and federal funding for legal services for the poor recurred over the years. After 1979, the LSC never again achieved a level of funding (measured in real dollars) that it had in the 1970s. In real dollars, the LSC budget in 2009 was less than half of what it was in 1979. Although each effort to entirely eliminate the program failed, many of them succeeded in adding to the list of matters that LSC-funded lawyers cannot handle.

As noted by Professor Luban, the largest set of restrictions was enacted in 1996 when Congress enacted the Omnibus Consolidated Rescissions and Appropriations Act (OCRAA), P.L. 104–134 (1996). Section 504 of that statute contains a long list of restrictions on whom LSC funding recipients can represent. The statute prohibits any person or entity that receives LSC funds from representing unauthorized immigrants, or prison inmates, from filing class action litigation, from seeking legal change through lobbying a legislature or administrative agency, from conducting or participating in trainings "for the purpose of advocating a particular public policy or encouraging political activity," from participating in litigation relating to abortion, or from participating in litigation, lobbying, or rulemaking seeking "to reform a federal or state welfare system." The statute requires regular audits of all LSC-funded offices to ensure compliance with the restrictions.

The 1996 OCRAA restrictions not only prohibited the use of LSC funds to engage in prohibited activities, but also prohibited any entity that received such funds to use *other funds* to support the activity. As a consequence, any office receiving LSC funds either had to cease the activity or give up all LSC funds. Many legal services offices that received LSC funds decided to split into two entirely separate organizations: one continued as an LSC-funded organization and gave up all matters prohibited by the restrictions; the other would rely on private philanthropy, IOLTA funds, and attorneys' fees and would handle matters that LSC prohibits.

The restrictions were challenged. The one that was struck down prohibited recipients of LSC funds from challenging the validity of existing law. The Supreme Court found it unconstitutional because it prevented lawyers from discharging their obligation to courts to provide a fully-informed analysis of the validity of a law. *Legal Services Corp. v. Velazquez*, 531 U.S. 533 (2001). The Supreme Court did not rule on the validity of any other provision of the LSC funding restrictions. Should the goals and policies of legal services programs be set by lawyers, clients, or governmental actors (including, but not limited to, when government is the source of funding)? In particular, should Congress or legal services lawyers decide on priorities? Does your answer depend on the nature of the issue involved?

C. THE WORK OF LEGAL SERVICES LAWYERS

In the remaining two sections of this chapter, we examine the work of poverty lawyers through the lens of the dominant problem many face: a scarcity of resources relative to the number of people who need and qualify for subsidized legal services. We examine how the inadequate number of lawyers relative to the need for legal services affects the work lives of legal services lawyers. We explore how they envision their work and assess their success, the techniques they adopt to address scarcity, and critical perspectives on whether legal services programs ameliorate the problems that lawyers aspire to solve.

Given the scarce resources, how should offices handle client intake? Should resources be focused on particular issues (e.g. housing) to the exclusion of others (e.g. domestic violence)? Should prospective clients with complex matters be turned away because their cases will take too many resources, or should those with simple matters be turned away because they are more likely to work them out on their own?

The dearth of resources in the face of the never-ending stream of problems creates a variety of quotidian problems for legal services lawyers as well. Forming an effective lawyer-client relationship across linguistic, cultural, and socioeconomic differences is challenging in any circumstance. The difficulties are exacerbated by the need to define the scope of the representation when a single client faces a multitude of legal problems (for example, domestic violence, consumer debt, and impending eviction) and the lawyer may be able or willing to handle only some.

A number of studies based on in-depth interviews with legal services lawyers explore how legal services lawyers adapt to the challenges of their work. In the first study, an ethnography of Chicago legal aid lawyers published in 1982, the scholar Jack Katz found:

> However important as a political or moral issue, poverty is presented to legal assistance offices in a stream of individual problems. So long as he or she is poor, a person's civil conduct will rarely affect the interests of more than a small circle of others.
>
> There is typically no elaborate social network attending problems when they are presented to legal assistance lawyers. The poor seek out lawyers for assistance with personal troubles which are often in or near a crisis state: having been denied public aid, having received an eviction notice, having had utilities shut off, having had a violent domestic argument. In such a practice, it is unusually difficult to treat problems as of far-reaching significance.
>
> Poor clients may insist their problems are of unsurpassed importance, and their lawyers may agree; but the latter will not be urged to that opinion by adverse parties and opposing counsel. Typical adversaries for legal assistance lawyers include other poor people, as for example, in domestic relations conflicts; small real estate owners, as in disputes between tenants and resident landlords; and the lower echelons of workers in public-aid bureaucracies, retail stores, and debt-collection agencies. A poor person usually will have a great deal to lose from litigation but not enough to make it worthwhile for an adversary to expend substantial legal resources to take it from him.
>
> Because poverty is taken as a reason for routine treatment by adversaries, opposing counsel, and even courts, it is reasonable for the poor themselves, who live constantly in this environment, not to expect more than summary service from legal assistance lawyers. The statement by clients "I only came here because I couldn't afford a real lawyer" has become a stock and somewhat bitter joke among legal assistance lawyers.[6]

An ethnography of Chicago legal aid lawyers published in 2011 found no change in many of the same phenomena that Katz found in 1982.[7] One thing, however, had changed: lawyers were less convinced of their ability to do something significant about the problems their clients faced because of the 1996 LSC restrictions on filing impact litigation or engaging in lobbying or other systematic approaches to address the structural causes of the problems of poverty.

---

[6] JACK KATZ, POOR PEOPLE'S LAWYERS IN TRANSITION (1982).

[7] Marina Zaloznaya & Laura Beth Nielsen, *Mechanisms and Consequences of Professional Marginality: The Case of Poverty Lawyers Revisited*, 36 LAW & SOC. INQUIRY 919 (2011).

[Our] findings differ significantly from Katz's conclusions about lawyers' motivations. Katz's lawyers tolerated difficulties at work because of their access to litigation. Present-day legal aid lawyers, limited to individual cases, lack the ability to construct their feelings of professional significance around impact litigation.

For legal aid lawyers today, the realization that they will not be able to effect the change they had envisioned is often connected to turning down large numbers of qualified clients. Rejecting clients is particularly taxing for these lawyers because legal aid offices tend to be the client's last resort.

The interviewees reported that sustaining empathetic attitudes toward their clients was challenging within the constraints of their practice. Many newcomers discover that their dedication to social justice does not translate into actual compassion for their clients, who at times fail to measure up to their idea of a perfect client. Because most attorneys have middle-class backgrounds and only indirect knowledge of the poor, many find it hard to remain understanding and appreciative of their clients who may not have a middle-class sensibility when it comes to keeping appointments or following up with lawyers' requests.

At the same time, our interviewees agreed that too much empathy can also be debilitating for lawyers. Several shared stories about their colleagues who got so caught up in caring for their clients that they could no longer do their best as attorneys.

What do present-day legal aid attorneys do to maintain positive professional identities and mitigate their marginalization in a context in which impact litigation is no longer accessible? About half of the attorneys who had been in practice for more than three years made their peace with the routine character of their work by finding other benefits in legal aid practice. The emphasis on lifestyle advantages associated with working in legal aid, such as not having to bill hours, spending time at home with families, and maintaining hobbies. These respondents saw their positive impact on individuals' lives an added benefit of the job.

More than half of long-term lawyers, however, held onto the idea of making a positive difference in a world riddled with inequalities. [They frame] the importance of legal aid in terms of helping specific individuals rather than bringing about abstract socioeconomic justice. Their stories were ones of initial disappointment and eventual realization that their work was just as, if not more, important than effecting large-scale change through litigation.[8]

Another in-depth study of legal services lawyers and their clients found that both lawyers and clients derive deep satisfaction from their professional work and interaction. One lawyer said, "I mean, am I changing the world? No. But the revolution still isn't happening and at some basic level this office, legal aid programs, and myself personally make a difference in people's lives. I love this job, this is a great job. And we do make a difference, both individually and on issues that affect our client population. And *but for* the work we did, things would be considerably worse for our clients." A client in the same study said, "I guess without legal service I wouldn't be sitting here. So I'm really grateful for that. That was like a load of pressure—you can't imagine—off of me. I couldn't deal with anything else until, you know, until that assurance. I needed a lawyer, somebody to represent me or to speak for me."[9]

NOTES ON THE WORK OF LEGAL SERVICES LAWYERS

1. ***What Is the Role of the Poverty Lawyer?*** Notice the extent to which the studies above reflect a range of opinions on whether the role of a lawyer for the poor should be more in the nature of social work or legal work, community organizer or service provider, reformer or revolutionary. How do you imagine the aspirations and disappointments of legal services lawyers are reflected in their evolving conception of their role?

2. ***Would Changes in the Structure and Funding of Legal Services Make a Difference?*** To what extent do you believe that the challenges of legal services practice are inherent in the nature of a poverty law practice, and to what extent do you believe that changes in the structure and funding of legal services could ameliorate them?

3. ***Is It Poverty or Is It Law?*** Some challenges encountered by legal services lawyers are also encountered by those in other professions whose job it is to work with people whose problems may be caused or exacerbated by poverty. Those professions include teachers, social workers, health care practitioners, and clergy. Are there aspects of being a lawyer, as opposed to a teacher, social worker, health care provider, or clergy, that make it more difficult to find satisfaction in working in poor communities? What could lawyers learn from other professions about these issues?

* * *

The scarcity of funds to support civil legal assistance for the poor has spawned a number of powerful critiques of the work of legal services lawyers. One concerns the process by which legal services lawyers decide

---

[8] *Id.*

[9] COREY S. SHDAIMAH, NEGOTIATING JUSTICE: PROGRESSIVE LAWYERING, LOW-INCOME CLIENTS, AND THE QUEST FOR SOCIAL CHANGE 45–46, 67 (2009).

whom to represent and whom to turn away, and what representation to provide for those clients whom the lawyer does undertake to represent. At the broadest level, some have argued that, by choice or by circumstances, legal services lawyers have become fundamentally conservative, putting band-aids on festering social wounds. They settle for results that are inadequate even to ameliorate client problems, let alone solve them. They are isolated from client communities, and therefore lack a guiding vision and expertise about how to conduct client matters and address client needs. They miss opportunities to work with nonlawyers in a multidisciplinary way to solve social problems. They are not properly accountable to their clients because the clients are not paying their fees or sufficiently involved in decision-making about the work.

Lawyers and community organizers have explored a number of ways to be effective in their shared effort to address social problems. The following essay is by a lawyer with practice experience as both a legal services lawyer and a lawyer for other organizations.

LAW AND ORGANIZING FROM THE PERSPECTIVE OF ORGANIZERS: FINDING A SHARED THEORY OF SOCIAL CHANGE

Betty Hung
1 Los Angeles Public Interest Law Journal 4 (2009)

[L]egal strategies, when pursued in combination with and in support of grassroots organizing campaigns, are more effective than legal strategies alone in both empowering communities and achieving social justice goals. In practice, however, tensions between lawyers and organizers persist and, at times, hinder campaigns for social justice. Rather than building the power of marginalized communities, lawyers tend to create dependency on lawyers and legal strategies without altering structural inequalities and the status quo.

The key to effective partnerships in social justice movements is a shared theory of social change based on the primacy of affected community members. Community members—not lawyers or organizers—should lead and be at the center of efforts seeking to improve their lives. Organizers and lawyers can and should find common ground as facilitators, supporters, and allies of affected community members.

According to organizers, the decision to involve lawyers in their organizing campaigns is contextual and based on strategic considerations, namely whether legal strategies can help to advance a campaign. [O]rganizers uniformly [say] that they view legal strategies, including litigation, legal community education, and legislative advocacy, as just one of multiple components that comprise a campaign.

The key strategic questions that organizers consider in deliberating whether to involve lawyers include: Will legal tactics put *pressure* on the organizing targets? Will legal tactics help to enhance the *legitimacy* of the grievances against the target? Will lawyers and legal tactics provide *support for organizers* by defending them from attacks, providing them with legal guidance, or helping to build trust and credibility with members? Will lawyers and legal tactics provide *support for members* by defending them from attacks, educating them about their legal rights, or providing support through direct legal services? Will legal tactics generate *publicity* and *public support* that will put pressure on the targets and cultivate allies, alliances, and support for the campaign? Will legal support help to *institutionalize* and *enforce* hard fought victories?

[Organizers are dismayed that] lawyers—even those who profess to value the primary role of community organizing in social justice struggles—privilege litigation and other legal strategies at the expense of organizing. They also [say] lawyers often do not communicate effectively with clients or organizers about the status of legal advocacy. Organizers commented that members who have pending cases often complain that attorneys do not keep them updated about their cases and/or that they did not understand fully what the attorneys told them. The members, who sometimes are intimidated by the attorneys, will then ask the organizers, whom they trust, to explain what is going on with their cases. All too often, however, organizers feel that the lawyers have not apprised them of the status of the case. When organizers ask the attorneys, often on behalf of the members/clients, for updates on the legal advocacy, they are told that attorney-client privilege prevents disclosure of such information. The result is that organizers and members both feel disempowered.

In essence, affected community members—not lawyers or organizers—should be in the lead and at the center of campaigns for social justice. In my experience, two additional factors are essential to achieve authentic relationships of trust and solidarity. First, there must be an understanding and appreciation of the particular experiences, skills, and knowledge that each person—whether an organizer, lawyer, or community member—brings to the table. It entails recognition that multiple strategies—organizing, legal, research, media, alliance building—are necessary to challenge existing institutions and power structures and to shift power to the hands of those who are marginalized. Organizing, like lawyering, is a skilled profession and craft and should be valued. Most importantly, community members themselves are the "experts" on the conditions in which they live and work and, with their first hand knowledge and experience, possess wisdom and insight into what type of social transformation is necessary and the best means to get there. In offering and honoring their respective knowledge, experience, and skills, community members, organizers, and lawyers can establish relationships based on equality and mutual respect.

Second, there is a human dimension to movement building that is integral to developing trust. In my years of working with garment workers, immigrant youth, taxi drivers, and car wash workers, a fundamental lesson I have learned is to approach and respect community members first and foremost as human beings and partners in a shared struggle for social change. People are not simply "clients" or "members" to be organized, but rather individuals with their own histories and hopes for achieving a measure of justice. Trust is built when community members feel that a relationship with lawyers or organizers is not about expediency or utilitarianism in achieving campaign goals, but is based on true solidarity and friendship.

NOTES ON HUNG

1. ***What Should Poverty Lawyers Aspire to Do?*** Are you persuaded by Hung's account of the nature of a social movement lawyer's practice? Are you persuaded by her critique of how lawyers are trained to think about problems?

2. ***Who Should Decide?*** What are the advantages and disadvantages of relying on the judgments of legal services lawyers in determining what will most benefit the client population? Does your answer to this question, informed by Hung's arguments, suggest you might revise your answer to the question we considered above about whether Congress, legal services program boards of directors, individual legal services lawyers, or clients should decide how to allocate scarce resources? How would a client-directed process of priority setting be implemented?

3. ***Can an LSC-Funded Lawyer Be an Effective Organizer?*** If an LSC-funded lawyer were convinced by Hung's arguments, would the OCRAA restrictions pose an obstacle to implementing their suggestions?

* * *

A distinctive innovation in legal services practice has been to re-imagine the nature of the attorney-client relationship to enable lawyers to help clients without investing much time or other resources. Many legal aid programs throughout the country operate self-help programs independently or in conjunction with courts. These websites and kiosks with touch-screen computers provide pro se litigants and others needing legal assistance with pleadings and access to other legal services, such as help with filing for the Earned Income Tax Credit. The programs are explained by the former head of the Legal Services Corporation:

> Some programs provide only access to information about the law, legal rights, and the legal process. Other programs actually provide individualized legal advice and often provide also legal

> assistance in drafting documents and advice about how to pursue cases.
>
> A critical part of expanding access has focused on a range of limited legal assistance initiatives to provide less than extended representation to clients who either do not need such extended representation in order to solve their legal problems or live in areas without access to lawyers or entities available to provide extended representation. Many legal aid programs now operate legal hotlines, which enable low-income persons who believe they have a legal problem to speak by telephone to a skilled attorney or paralegal and receive advice and brief service. Legal hotlines may provide answers to clients' legal questions, analysis of clients' legal problems, and advice on solving those problems so that the client can resolve the problem with the information from phone consultation.[10]

Is the emphasis on self-help a necessary evil of scarce resources or, instead, a step toward enabling clients to achieve self-reliance? Should the goal of every legal aid lawyer be to provide the most thorough and comprehensive service possible? Should legal services lawyers aspire to provide the same "no stone left unturned" standard of service that corporate clients demand (and pay for) from their lawyers?

D. THE IMPACT OF LEGAL SERVICES PROGRAMS

The political controversy about legal aid to the poor, combined with the constant threat of drastic cuts in government and private funding, have produced a longstanding debate over the impact and value of subsidized legal services. Moreover, the need to triage cases and turn away thousands or tens of thousands of eligible prospective clients every year has prompted legal services lawyers to think about how to allocate their scarce time and resources.

A fundamental premise of free legal services to poor people is that legal assistance will leave the client better off than if the client had no lawyer. Although the Supreme Court in *Lassiter* rejected the contention that a lawyer is necessary to ensure due process of law in civil cases, lawyers tend to believe they make a real difference. In a world of scarce resources, however, it is important to think about where having a lawyer makes the most difference. The following excerpt surveys the substantial empirical literature on the effect of legal representation on outcomes in litigated disputes across a wide array of subject areas.

---

[10] Alan W. Houseman, *The Future of Civil Legal Aid: A National Perspective*, 10 UNIV. D.C. L. REV. 35 (2007).

DO LAWYERS MATTER? THE EFFECT OF LEGAL REPRESENTATION IN CIVIL DISPUTES

Emily S. Taylor Poppe & Jeffrey J. Rachlinski
43 Pepperdine Law Review 881 (2016)

Juvenile Cases. Most studies of juvenile court find that representation is not associated with more favorable outcomes for juveniles. Not only do these studies provide scant evidence that representation benefits clients, but numerous studies have found that juveniles with legal representation are *more likely to experience worse outcomes*. Juveniles who face more serious charges are more likely to obtain representation than those who do not. Hence, even if lawyers benefit their clients, represented juveniles are apt to do worse in the aggregate than unrepresented juveniles. Even accounting for this bias among the observational studies, however, our review suggests that representation is unhelpful at best, and perhaps harmful.

These results are hard to explain. Many scholars emphasize that the association between representation and bad outcomes for juveniles might actually reflect greater rates of representation among more serious cases, a possibility that is particularly probable given judges' role in appointing counsel. Even where the law requires the mandatory appointment of legal counsel—which should alleviate some of these selection concerns—scholars find significant judicial non-compliance and large variation in rates of representation. [However], even the results of [a] randomized study, which should be free of these concerns, are mixed. Indeed, these studies support the proposition that the effect of legal representation varies not only by case, but also by court.

Housing. Concerns about the value of representation in housing court inspired much of the current concern with the value of lawyers. A recent randomized experiment on summary eviction cases heard primarily in a Massachusetts Housing Court found no evidence that litigants benefit from an offer of full representation. The study's findings stand in sharp contrast to every other study conducted in this area of law. Two other studies have used random assignment to study the value of representation in this context. In one, the same Harvard researchers [who found no evidence that litigants benefit from representation in Massachusetts Housing Court] analyzed the effect of randomized offers of full representation in eviction cases heard in a Massachusetts District Court. They found that tenants who were offered full legal representation were less likely to lose possession, less likely to have a judgment or writ of execution entered against them, and required to pay less, on average, than those in the limited-assistance control group. The most striking results come from a study of Philadelphia's Housing Court. This study estimates that tenants with legal representation were *nineteen times* more likely to win than tenants without legal representation.

Administrative Hearings/Government Benefits. [I]ndividuals appearing before administrative agencies allocating various benefits fare better when they are represented. Unemployment claims, disability claims, and welfare benefit claims might be similar to housing disputes in that those with strong claims might be more apt to seek representation. [Authors of one study] concluded that while they randomized offers of representation among those in their sample, the sample as whole was not representative of the population. Rather, those individuals who sought out legal representation differed—either in terms of their case or some personal characteristic—that made their cases more likely to be successful.

In asylum cases, the situation may differ. Given the enormously high stakes, one might expect that claimants would do everything they can to remain in the country. The ability of these individuals to seek legal counsel, however, may vary greatly depending on their detention status and whether they are seeking asylum affirmatively or in defense to a proposed removal. Given the tremendous shortfall in representation in asylum cases, it seems unlikely that lawyers would select those cases that have little chance of success. Thus, if there is a trend toward lawyers representing "better" cases, then the finding that lawyers achieve more favorable outcomes in administrative hearings might be driven in part by this screening process.

Employment Law. Employment cases are difficult for employees. Numerous studies document chronically low success rates by employees in employment discrimination cases. Even when employees succeed, they lose far more often on appeal than employers or other kinds of individual plaintiffs. Attorneys invariably represent employers, whereas employees often are not represented. Does legal representation improve the outlook for employee plaintiffs? Studies of the effect of legal representation in federal employment discrimination suggest employees fare better when represented. One study analyzed a sample of dispositive pre-trial motions in federal district court cases of alleged racial discrimination and concluded that unrepresented plaintiffs were nearly half as likely as represented plaintiffs to win. A companion review of a smaller sample of case filings also documents less favorable outcomes for unrepresented plaintiffs who were less likely to obtain a settlement, more likely to have their cases dismissed, and more likely to lose at the pre-trial stage. Analyzing a broad sample of employment discrimination cases filed in federal court, [one study] found that the cases of unrepresented plaintiffs are more likely to be dismissed, less likely to be settled early, and more likely to lose on motions for summary judgment than the cases of plaintiffs who are represented during the litigation.

[Studies of employment cases resolved in mandatory arbitration proceedings reached mixed results.] One study of American Arbitration Association (AAA) employment dispute arbitrations found that 50% of represented employees won compared to 48% of unrepresented employees. Three more recent studies, however, have uncovered disparities in outcomes between cases involving representation and those without. [One] analysis of a large, national sample of mandatory employment arbitrations found that the odds of settlement were 62.5% lower for unrepresented employees than for those with representation, the odds of winning were 45.6% lower, [and] on average, unrepresented employees received damage awards that were 47% lower than those of represented employees.

Family Law. Both large scale studies of court records and smaller survey analyses have found evidence that legal representation matters in divorces, custody issues, and domestic violence cases. A project analyzing a random sample of 10% of all divorce and custody cases filed in Maryland in 1999 found that legal representation for a plaintiff was associated with an increase in the odds of an award of alimony or support. The study also found that legal representation for the defendant was associated with a lower average spousal support or alimony award, although representation for the plaintiff did not have a statistically significant relationship with the award amount.

Studies focused on domestic violence have also documented a positive link between legal representation and client outcomes. An analysis of domestic violence cases in Dane County, Wisconsin found that represented petitioners obtained temporary restraining orders in 69% of cases, compared to a success rate of only 55% for unrepresented petitioners. Similarly, a survey of women seeking assistance in confronting domestic violence found that 83% of the women who were represented in seeking a protective order were successful, compared to a success rate of 32% among unrepresented women.

Small Claims. Small claims court might be an unlikely venue for lawyers to display any advantage. The setting is supposed to be informal. If Judge Judy is to be believed, small claims court is the place for common sense, not legal jargon. Most of the studies that have considered legal representation have concluded that legal representation is beneficial and that representation is most helpful when the opposing party is unrepresented. A study of Manhattan small claims litigants, for example, found that plaintiffs were more likely to report a higher rate of recovery when they were represented and the opposing party was unrepresented and more likely to report the lowest rate of recovery when they were unrepresented and the opposing party did have legal counsel. The study also offered evidence of lawyers' involvement in out-of-court settlements, finding that plaintiffs with representation who failed to appear were more likely to report having reached a settlement than those without legal counsel, although they were most likely to report having reached a settlement when they were represented but their opponents were not.

Research also suggests that the role of legal counsel might vary by party. A study of New Mexico small claims cases found that representation was associated with more favorable monetary outcomes for claimants but with less favorable outcomes for respondents in adjudicated cases. A study combining small claims cases from multiple jurisdictions, however, found evidence of a stronger positive relationship between representation and case outcome for defendants than for plaintiffs. The authors of that study surmised that this result may reflect the availability of court assistance for plaintiffs in filing a claim and preparing for trial, while unrepresented defendants were unlikely to come to court until trial.

[Empirical studies on the effect of legal representation in tax, bankruptcy, and personal injury tort cases show that having legal representation benefits the taxpayer, debtor, or personal injury plaintiff. When represented by counsel, these litigants are more likely to have a favorable recovery and the size of the financial benefit is larger.]

Endogeneity is unlikely to account for the observed benefits of representation across the many different areas of law. In some cases, endogeneity might be the best explanation for the observed effect of representation. In family law, parties who actively want custody of their children are apt to both be more likely to present as better parents and to seek attorneys to defend what they view as a critical interest. Likewise, in torts cases, parties with more at stake are more apt to be able to obtain attorneys. And as we noted above, endogeneity can make attorneys look like they are doing harm in juvenile cases because children who face more serious charges are more apt to be represented.

It is not clear, however, why litigants in small claims court and those who are seeking government benefits (where the stakes are all small) do better with attorneys. Nor is it quite as obvious why asylum-seekers—who all have a great deal at stake—are better off if represented (although in this area, attorneys might be selecting cases more carefully). Endogeneity also cannot easily account for the finding that parties obtain a greater percentage of their debt discharged in bankruptcy or that parties appearing before the IRS obtain a greater percentage of taxes reduced.

[Moreover], several of the studies look beyond outcomes to identify what lawyers actually do for litigants. Except for two juvenile courts studies, all of the studies that observe attorneys show them to raise more arguments and ask more questions than unrepresented parties. Lawyers offer more than just in-court advocacy; lawyers also prepare pleadings, ensure compliance with procedural requirements, and offer advice that helps their clients better understand the matter at hand.

NOTES ON THE IMPACT OF LEGAL ASSISTANCE

1. ***What Explains the Different Findings?*** Why do you suppose that lawyers helped clients in almost every matter except juvenile justice? Why do the authors suggest that variations among judges as to when to appoint counsel to represent a juvenile might explain the difference?

2. ***What Do Lawyers Do?*** Many of the studies surveyed in the Taylor Poppe & Rachlinski article did not directly answer the question of what specifically the lawyers did that produced the positive results. However, the lawyers interviewed in a Harvard study of the impact of lawyers in housing cases identified four tasks that lawyers do that typically make a difference. Lawyers (1) determine what rent is owed; (2) negotiate a reasonable time period for payment when money is owed; (3) negotiate or litigate when, e.g., the housing agency has not issued the full amount of arrears, has issued them to the wrong landlord, or when the client qualifies for a special grant to cover rent; and (4) obtain abatements of rent when repairs were not completed in a timely manner.[11] One of the studies found that legal representation seemed to generate a bigger benefit in bankruptcy matters after a statutory change that made consumer bankruptcy matters more procedurally complex. This suggests that where a legal process or legal rules are complex, it may matter whether the litigant is represented.

3. ***Policy Implications.*** What are the policy implications of these studies? If reducing complexity of law and procedure reduces the need for lawyers, should courts and advocates for the poor aim to reduce complexity? If screening cases at the intake stage leads to better results for those litigants who proceed past the intake stage, what should legal services lawyers do? What other policies would you recommend in light of these studies?

E. SUMMARY

In this chapter, we studied the nature, regulation, and funding of civil legal services programs, with particular emphasis on the limits imposed by Congress through the Legal Services Corporation on what law offices that receive LSC funding can do and who they can represent. We examined the work of legal services lawyers, and a variety of philosophies lawyers have about how to provide the best quality legal service and to empower clients to address the legal problems they face. We considered the ways in which legal services work is affected by the pervasive problem of too many prospective clients relative to the available legal resources, and we surveyed some of the approaches legal aid lawyers have adopted to deal with the shortage of resources and to provide adequate representation to underserved clients. Lastly, we considered empirical studies of the impact of subsidized legal services.

---

[11] D. James Greiner, et al., *The Limits of Unbundled Legal Assistance: A Randomized Study in a Massachusetts District Court and Prospects for the Future*, 126 HARV. L. REV. 901 (2013).

CHAPTER 17

PUBLIC INTEREST LAW

■ ■ ■

A. INTRODUCTION

This chapter examines lawyers who work in what are commonly called public interest law organizations. As we'll see throughout the following materials, the definition of public interest law has been the subject of a good deal of controversy over several decades, and the term continues to be used in a variety of ways that are not entirely consistent. We explore these definitional issues and why they matter. We consider how and why this form of practice emerged, how it relates to larger political struggles over social change and the roles of lawyers in such efforts, and the connection between this form of practice and access to justice. We compare the term "public interest lawyer" with a related and overlapping concept of "cause lawyer" and explore the relationship between cause lawyering and conventional practice. We also examine issues of accountability frequently faced by lawyers in public interest practice.

B. WHAT IS PUBLIC INTEREST LAW?

The term public interest law is used in many different ways. As one scholar has noted, "Today, people use the term 'public interest' law as a gloss for a wide range of sometimes contradictory lawyering categories":

> Some people define "public interest" law as lawyering for the poor. Some define it as "cause" lawyering. Others think of it as lawyering specifically with a left wing or politically progressive agenda. Still others define the term as encompassing jobs in the public and nonprofit sectors. This last definition equates "public interest" law with law practiced in organizational forms in which lawyers do not take fees for their legal services from their clients.[1]

In the materials that follow, we will try to distinguish among these various definitions of public interest law and explain how definitional issues relate to fundamental questions about the roles of lawyers in society and the moral content of lawyers' work.

---

[1] Susan D. Carle, *Re-Valuing Lawyering for Middle-Income Clients,* 70 FORDHAM L. REV. 719, 729–30 (2001).

The following excerpt sketches the early history of the term's use and some criticisms of the concept's premises:

DEFINING PUBLIC INTEREST LAWYERING

Alan Chen & Scott Cummings
Public Interest Lawyering: A Contemporary Perspective (2012)

For at least the last century, lawyers have sought to deploy their legal skill to advance the interests of individual clients or social groups deemed less powerful: legal aid lawyers from the early twentieth century who dispensed free legal services to aid the urban poor; so-called "country lawyers" who provided professional charity in order to help their less fortunate neighbors; and activist lawyers who defended war protesters, labor organizers, and racial minorities suffering discrimination.

Yet it was not until the 1960s that the term "public interest law" was coined in a self-conscious effort to describe a nascent movement to use legal advocacy, primarily litigation, to advance a liberal political agenda associated primarily with the protection and expansion of rights for racial minorities, the poor, women, and other disadvantaged groups, while also providing collective goods, like a clean environment. At the outset of the U.S. public interest law movement, its definition was sometimes couched in the language of market failure. In a classic study from the 1970s, public interest law was defined as "activity that (1) is undertaken by an organization in the voluntary sector; (2) provides fuller representation of underrepresented interests (would produce external benefits if successful); and (3) involves the use of law instruments, primarily litigation." The study drew upon economic analysis to elaborate the concept of "external benefits," which was grounded in efficiency—putting productive resources "to their most 'valuable' uses"—and equity—ensuring that the distribution of the resulting goods and services was fair. The central claim was that public interest law was activity that "if it is successful, will bring about significant external gross benefits to some persons; that is, the activity provides more complete representation for some interest that is underrepresented in the sense that the interest has not been fully transmitted through either the private market or governmental channels."[2]

It was this notion of "underrepresentation" that informed other definitional efforts. For Gordon Harrison and Sanford Jaffe, the Ford Foundation program officers who designed and executed the foundation's initial PIL [Public Interest Law] funding initiative (and one of the first to use the term), public interest law was "the representation of the

[2] Burton A. Weisbrod, *Conceptual Perspective on the Public Interest: An Economic Analysis*, *in* PUBLIC INTEREST LAW: AN ECONOMIC AND INSTITUTIONAL ANALYSIS 10–12, 22 (Burton A. Weisbrod, Joel F. Handler & Neil K. Komesar et al. eds., 1978).

underrepresented in American society."[3] This included both the provision of lawyers to "poor or otherwise deprived individuals who are unable to hire counsel," as well as legal actions in the defense of "broad collective interests"—such as on behalf of "consumer protection and environmental quality"—"for the benefit of large classes of people" who could not individually afford the cost of mounting lawsuits and who could not easily organize collectively to advance their political interests. Nan Aron, writing about public interest law at the end of the 1980s, articulated a similar position:

> Public interest law is the name given to efforts to *provide legal representation to interests that historically have been unrepresented or underrepresented* in the legal process. Philosophically, public interest law rests on the assumption that many significant segments of society are not adequately represented in the courts, Congress, or the administrative agencies because they are either too poor or too diffuse to obtain legal representation in the marketplace.[4]

The classic definition, rooted in underrepresentation, came under attack from two directions. Beginning in the 1970s, and gaining momentum in the 1980s, the emergent conservative movement took issue with both the efficiency and equity rationales for public interest law. In terms of efficiency, conservatives argued that it was not obvious that regulation benefitted society at large, rather than simply making distributional choices. Thus, environmental regulation could have the effect of reducing jobs, or consumer regulation might increase prices. Without aggregating individual preferences for a clean environment and jobs, for consumer safety and low prices, it was not clear *ex ante* what the optimal social welfare function was. The concept of equity was indeterminate as well. What qualified as an underrepresented group? Conservatives argued that the concept of underrepresentation was politically contingent and changed over time. Whether or not one agreed with the conservative framing, it highlighted a fundamental tension in equity conceptions of public interest law: on contested issues of public policy, one group's benefit could be construed as another's burden.

As conservatives challenged the meaning of public interest law from the right, critics on the left challenged its practice—and offered new theories to supplant what many viewed as the outmoded and politically ineffective model of litigation-centered reform embodied in the conventional definition of public interest law. Beginning in the 1980s, new theories emerged with an impressive array of new labels: community

---

[3] Gordon Harrison & Sanford M. Jaffe, *Public Interest Law Firms: New Voices for New Constituencies*, 58 A.B.A. J. 459, 459 (1972).

[4] NAN ARON, LIBERTY AND JUSTICE FOR ALL: PUBLIC INTEREST LAW IN THE 1980S AND BEYOND 3 (1989) (emphasis added).

lawyering, critical lawyering, facilitative lawyering, political lawyering, progressive lawyering, rebellious lawyering, third dimensional lawyering, law and organizing, and legal pragmatism—to name some of the most prominent. Although these theories varied considerably, they shared the concern that rights-based efforts, by themselves, were inadequate to the task of radical social transformation. All of these efforts rested upon a liberal discomfort with lawyer-led strategies that undercut genuine participatory democracy and risked inflicting a double-marginalization on clients: disempowered by society and then by the very lawyers who purported to act on their behalf. This critique of "lawyer domination" was the foundation for the most powerful left critique of public interest law—one that corresponded to the right-wing attack on public interest law as democratically unaccountable.

Despite all the critiques of its political and conceptual coherence, the use of "public interest" as a rubric for a distinctive, equality-enhancing form of lawyering has shown great resilience. Although it is unavoidably contested, public interest law remains the term-of-choice for U.S. practitioners, and has taken root in emerging democracies around the world.

NOTES ON CHEN & CUMMINGS

1. ***What Is the Public Interest?*** Is a public interest lawyer one who represents the public's interest? Would it be possible for everyone to agree on what types of lawyers' work benefit the public as a whole? Do questions about what serves the public interest inevitably generate conflict among competing visions of the public good? If a public interest lawyer is not a lawyer who advocates for the public good, what is she?

2. ***The Underrepresentation Rationale.*** Most definitions of public interest law incorporate the idea of serving interests that are underrepresented in the private market for legal services or in the political process. What exactly does it mean to be underrepresented? The Chen & Cummings excerpt identifies two ways in which a group or cause might be underrepresented: 1) because they are too poor to afford counsel, or 2) because they are too diffuse to organize effectively to pursue their collective interests. People who do not have enough money to hire lawyers clearly meet the first part of this definition. What types of interests and groups qualify under the second part? This rationale sometimes has been invoked to cover consumer and environmental advocacy within the definition of public interest law. Does it matter that these two groups cut across socio-economic lines and include some wealthy people?

3. ***Does It Matter Why Interests Are Underrepresented?*** Do lawyers who represent groups that find it difficult to find representation because their views or conduct are abhorrent—such as Nazis, pedophiles, terrorists, and serial killers—fall within a definition of public interest law that turns on

underrepresentation?[2] If not why not? Does your answer depend on the type of work performed for the client?

4. ***Can Public Interest Lawyers Oppose One Another?*** Is it problematic that "underrepresented" interests might sometimes come into conflict with one another? When that happens, are both sets of opposing advocates still public interest lawyers?

5. ***"Private Public Interest Law"?*** Can a lawyer who collects fees for her services be a public interest lawyer? If not, why not? If so, under what circumstances? Notice that the Weisbrod definition quoted at the beginning of the Chen & Cummings excerpt specifies that public interest law is by definition in the "voluntary" (nonprofit) sector. However, not all definitions of public interest law include that criterion. Some lawyers in private practice claim that their firms prioritize service to underrepresented constituencies over profitability and therefore deserve the public interest law label. Such firms, sometimes called "private public interest law firms," generally rely on fees awarded pursuant to fee-shifting statutes rather than charitable donations to keep their practices afloat.[3]

6. ***Are Some Plaintiffs' Lawyers Public Interest Lawyers?*** Some plaintiffs' lawyers challenge corporate practices on behalf of large, disorganized and diffuse groups of accident victims, consumers, and investors who could not individually afford the cost of pursuing lawsuits. The clients in these lawsuits therefore appear to fit the second part of the concept of underrepresentation described in the Chen & Cummings excerpt. Moreover, the plaintiffs' lawyers in these lawsuits typically view themselves as advocates for the little guy. But contingency fee arrangements and fee shifting statutes sometimes make it possible for entrepreneurial plaintiffs' lawyers to earn very large fees for such work in the private sector. Are these lawyers public interest lawyers? If not, why not?

7. ***Strategies.*** Much of the literature on the roles of lawyers in social change movements concentrates primarily on the roles of litigators, who advocate for clients in the courts and agencies. But the tactical repertoire of these lawyers is much broader. It includes transactional work for nonprofit groups, community organizing, policy advocacy, public education, and media strategies.

* * *

The following excerpt explains how advocates associated with conservative and libertarian causes adapted the form and rhetoric of public interest law to advance their own public policy objectives, many of which

---

[2] This question comes from ALAN K. CHEN & SCOTT L. CUMMINGS, PUBLIC INTEREST LAWYERING: A CONTEMPORARY PERSPECTIVE 14 (2013).

[3] For a discussion of this model, see Scott Cummings & Ann Southworth, *Between Profit and Principle: The Private Public Interest Law Firm,* in PRIVATE LAWYERS AND THE PUBLIC INTEREST: THE EVOLVING ROLE OF PRO BONO IN THE LEGAL PROFESSION (Robert Granfield & Lynn Mather, eds., 2009).

the founders of the public interest law movement in the late 1960s and early 1970s would have opposed. The article explores how lawyers of the political left and right now battle one another in the courts, legislatures, and media—while all claiming to do so under the banner of public interest law.

CONSERVATIVE LAWYERS AND THE CONTEST OVER THE MEANING OF "PUBLIC INTEREST LAW"

Ann Southworth
52 U.C.L.A. Law Review 1223 (2005)

The term "public interest law" first appeared in the late 1960s and initially was associated almost exclusively with liberal causes. Since then, however, conservative and libertarian legal advocacy groups have multiplied, and the idea that these organizations and their lawyers might be similar in important respects to those of the liberal public interest law movement has gained currency. Conservative and libertarian lawyers have created a vibrant, highly differentiated field of conservative legal advocacy organizations modeled on liberal public interest law firms (PILFs) and have generated substantial competition among legal advocacy groups of the left and right over the meaning of "public interest law."

The creation of conservative PILFs was just one part of a larger phenomenon of conservative institution building that began around the time of Barry Goldwater's failed 1964 presidential bid. That campaign was the first political expression of a rising conservative movement that had intellectual roots in the work of traditionalists, classical liberal economists, and anticommunists. Despite substantial contradictions among these intellectual currents, they came together in opposition to the liberal establishment. This powerful coalition of religious conservatives, libertarians, business interests, and nationalists united behind the task of building a conservative infrastructure—a "counter-establishment"—to help win hearts and minds for conservative ideas.

The conservative public interest law movement was a direct response to the creation of public interest law organizations in the late 1960s and 1970s and to the legal and social changes these groups helped produce. The success of these organizations presented an obvious counterstrategy for conservatives: to beat liberals at their own game by creating public interest law groups to speak for competing values and constituencies. They adopted the organizational form and rhetoric of public interest law to serve sometimes conflicting causes of the conservative movement.

The organizational counterattack began with business-oriented groups [in the 1970s]. Christian evangelicals, whose ambivalence about engaging with secular law delayed their participation in legal rights advocacy, took up the challenge soon thereafter.

The field of conservative public interest law is now quite well developed, with distinct constituencies of conservatives represented by different organizations and lawyers. Where there once were a few regional conservative organizations representing the business perspective on regulatory matters, there now are dozens of groups, including some libertarian organizations that attempt to distance themselves from large business interests. The views of Christian evangelicals are now advocated by many groups representing particular interests, differentiated along theological lines and by issue. There now are specialized legal advocacy groups focusing on affirmative action, home schooling, pornography, property rights, school vouchers, tort reform, and gun ownership. Organizations also distinguish themselves from one another according to the types of strategies pursued—for example, direct representation versus amicus participation, grassroots activism versus insider networking, and research targeted at Congress and the media versus scholarly publications directed primarily at professors and judges. Conservative and libertarian PILFs sometimes oppose one another and occasionally even form alliances with liberal PILFs.

During the past three decades, as conservatives have deployed an organizational model born of liberal legal activism to pursue different social and political goals, they have unsettled conventions and assumptions about public interest practice, increased competition in the courts, agencies, and legislatures, and gained the upper hand in public policy debates. In the late 1960s, the public interest law movement was almost synonymous with left legal activism. Today dozens of conservative and libertarian organizations call themselves "public interest law" groups. In accordance with the prescription [of one conservative strategist during the early 1980s], conservative and libertarian groups have "challenged the moral monopoly . . . enjoyed by traditional public interest lawyers and their allies"* and stripped the term "public interest law" of its exclusively left-oriented connotations.

This competition between PILFs of the left and right has made public policy formation more complicated and antagonistic and has contributed to acrimony over judicial nominations. It also has laid bare an essential truth about public interest law—that advocates for [nonprofit] law reform organizations, all viewing themselves as public interest lawyers, may disagree fundamentally about what the public interest requires.

NOTES ON SOUTHWORTH

1. ***Do Conservative Groups Fit the Definition of Public Interest Law?*** Is Southworth correct to characterize religious conservative and

* [Eds.: *See* Michael Horowitz, The Public Interest Law Movement: An Analysis with Special Reference to the Role and Practices of Conservative Public Interest Law Firms 1, 3 (n.d.) (unpublished memorandum) (on file with author).]

libertarian organizations as public interest law groups for causes of the political right? If not, how would you distinguish them from organizations that you do think qualify as public interest law groups?

2. ***Subsequent Research on the Use of "Public Interest Law" in Supreme Court Briefs.*** In a follow-up study of discourse around public interest law, Southworth examined how various organizations use the phrase "public interest law" or "public interest legal" to describe themselves in U.S. Supreme Court briefs. She found that from 1970 through 2011, 1281 briefs were submitted by organizations that called themselves "public interest law/legal" organizations. Of those 1281 briefs, 812—almost two-thirds—were filed by groups that pursued conservative and libertarian missions.[4]

Does that finding suggest that conservative and libertarian groups think it's important to be regarded as public interest law groups by the Court and other potential audiences for their briefs, including, perhaps, their own members and supporters? If so, why?

3. ***Does the Label Matter?*** Southworth describes this struggle over use of the phrase "public interest law" as a "frame contest" with significant consequences:

> The contest over the meaning of public interest law is symbolically important because the phrase conveys approval; the organizations, activities, and lawyers associated with the term are understood to enhance access to justice, or to advance some other vision of the public good. This struggle over discourse also carries direct and practical implications because financial benefits—such as law school scholarship eligibility, summer funding, loan forgiveness, and pro bono credit—sometimes turn on the definition of public interest law. Thus, how the phrase is used and defined is integrally related to the allocation of some types of legitimacy and resources within the American legal profession. Moreover, this contest over framing may have significant consequences for judicial decision making and public policy formation to the extent that public interest law organizations and lawyers exercise special influence tied to their perceived status as champions of underrepresented constituencies . . .
>
> The phrase "public interest law" may once have been understood to apply to a relatively small number of organizations and lawyers serving a limited set of constituencies, but [it] is now used to describe a much larger set of groups, advocates, and policy agendas. These "public interest law/legal" organizations take opposing sides of nearly every divisive social and economic issue of our time; they advocate for gun control as well as gun rights, for environmental protection and property rights, for stronger protections for organized labor and for

---

[4] Ann Southworth, *What is Public Interest Law? Empirical Perspectives on an Old Question*, 62 DEPAUL L. REV. 493 (2013).

the "right to work," for pro-choice and pro-life positions, and for diversity initiatives and the end of affirmative action. All of these groups claim the special professional legitimacy that the "public interest law" label confers.

In the article's conclusion, Southworth suggests that the term "public interest law," as it is used in briefs, the press, and popular discourse, may "obscure[ ] more than it reveals about the relative disadvantage of the clients represented and how policies pursued under its banner relate to the public good."[5] Do you agree or disagree? Why?

C. WHAT IS A CAUSE LAWYER?

The next excerpt explains why some scholars have rejected the term public interest lawyer in favor of "cause lawyer"—a concept that focuses less on the notion of the underrepresentation of the interests served and more on the lawyer's motivation. This excerpt also examines what some people find attractive about cause lawyering and how it differs from conventional practice.

PROFESSIONAL AND POLITICAL PERSPECTIVES

Stuart A. Scheingold & Austin Sarat
Something to Believe In (2004)[6]

At gatherings of lawyers, talk of alienation and anxiety about their work is frequently present. Worries about increased commercialism, complaints about the costs of their work to family, and stories about the strains of having to provide services to clients whose goals are incompatible with the lawyer's personal moral commitments abound.

But alienation and anxiety about the nature of lawyering work do not affect all lawyers equally. For those whose idea and practice of lawyering involves service to a cause, many of the symptoms of alienation and anxiety are absent. This is not to suggest that such lawyers have no worries about their work. That is surely not the case. It is to suggest, however, that what William Simon says about lawyering in general—namely that "no social role encourages such ambitious moral aspirations as the lawyer's, and no social role so consistently disappoints the aspirations it encourages"—is markedly less true of those lawyers whose practices are devoted to the realization of their own moral aspirations.

Moral and political commitment, the defining attributes of cause lawyers are, for most of their peers, relegated to the margins of their professional lives. Conventional or client lawyering involves the

[5] Ann Southworth, *What is Public Interest Law? Empirical Perspectives on an Old Question*, 62 DEPAUL L. REV. 493, 516 (2013).

[6]

deployment of a set of technical skills on behalf of ends determined by the client, not the lawyer. Lawyering, in this conception, is neither a domain for moral or political advocacy nor a place to express the lawyer's beliefs about the way society should be organized, disputes resolved, and values expressed.

For cause lawyers, such objectives move from the margins to the center of their professional lives. Lawyering is for them attractive precisely because it is a deeply moral or political activity, a kind of work that encourages pursuit of their vision of the right, the good, or the just. Cause lawyers have *something to believe* in and bring their beliefs to bear in their work lives. In this sense, they are neither alienated from their work nor anxious about the separation of role from person.

On the Definition of Cause Lawyering. Scholarship on cause lawyering is plagued by definitional and conceptual challenges. Indeed it is not possible to provide a single cross-culturally valid definition of cause lawyering. At its core, cause lawyering is about using legal skills to pursue ends and ideals that transcend client service—be those ideals social, cultural, political, economic or, indeed, legal. Yet cause lawyers are associated with many different causes, function with varying resources and degrees of legitimacy, deploy a wide variety of strategies, and seek extraordinarily diverse goals.

Included under the umbrella of cause lawyering are such polar ideological opposites as poverty and property rights lawyers, feminist and right-to-life lawyers, as well as such disparate pursuits as human rights, environmental, civil liberties, and critical lawyering. Cause lawyering is found in the full range of professional venues: large and small private firms, salaried practice in national and transnational nongovernmental organizations, and government and privately funded lawyering. For better or for worse, this tremendous variation is the hallmark of cause lawyering. Indeed, the term *cause lawyering* conveys a core of meaning which is valid within a wide range of historical and cultural contexts while at the same time being sufficiently inclusive to accommodate a variety of forms.

Definitionally, cause lawyering is associated with both intent and behavior. Serving a cause by accident does not, in our judgment, qualify as cause lawyering. On the other hand, there is evidence that the accidental can be transformed into the intentional when a lawyer's ideals are awakened by service undertaken for other reasons. Thus, clinical activities in law school, which may be undertaken solely to escape the classroom and gain practical experience, can lead students to cause lawyering because they put students in touch with the problems of marginalized elements of the population. In other words, commitment to a cause can just as easily be a consequence of representation undertaken for different reasons as the other way around. Nor does cause lawyering preclude mixed motives.

Still, whether pure or impure, whether before or after the fact, we deem political or moral commitment an essential and distinguishing feature of cause lawyering. Lawyers are drawn to causes by a search for something in which to believe or as an outlet to express their already formed beliefs. Although cause lawyering is in general a low status and poorly paid professional activity, it does provide what conventional legal ethics deny—the opportunity to harmonize personal conviction and professional life.

What we call cause lawyering is often referred to as public interest lawyering within the legal profession and among academics. However, we prefer *cause lawyering* because it is an inclusive term. It conveys a determination to take sides in political and moral struggle without making distinctions between worthy and unworthy causes. Conversely, to talk about public interest lawyering is to take on irresolvable disputes about what is, or is not, in the public interest. Whether the pursuit of any particular cause advances the public interest is very much in the eye of the beholder.

Invocations of the public interest have a long history in the literature of reform. Muckrakers from time immemorial have railed against the special interests in the name of the public and its interest. But what is the public interest and how is it defined?

The public interest is a notoriously slippery concept, which generally does little or no analytic work. According to one scholar, "The public interest may be described as the aggregate of common interests, including the common interest in seeing that there is fair play among private interests. The public interest is not the mere sum of the special interests, and it is certainly not the sum of the organized special interests. Nor is it an automatic consequence of the struggle of the special interests." In this conception, discovering the public interest is a "value neutral technical process."

Unfortunately, as David Truman long ago observed, such appeals "do not describe any actual or possible political situation within a complex modern nation. We do not need to account for a totally inclusive interest, because one does not exist." The public interest neither identifies any interest, nor can it point the way toward policy or reform. Instead, the primary function of the concept in our language is to convey approval or commendation. It serves as a symbol to legitimize the acts of any group that can successfully identify itself with it in the public mind. For cause lawyers, the way to justice is the way of politics, a way that names and defends interests with particularity and acknowledges the conflicts and costs which the pursuit of those interests necessarily entails. This assertive engagement in the contentious issues of public life is one way in which lawyering provides something to believe in.

[B]oth cause lawyers and conventional practitioners see themselves as divided by, and united in, a professional project which provides a public good. This ethical discourse over the nature of legal professionalism and its contribution to society is captured in the contrasting answers of conventional and cause lawyers to one deceptively simple ethical question. Should lawyering be driven primarily by client service, or are lawyers entitled, even obligated, to serve objectives that transcend service to clients?

Cause lawyers identify explicitly, and without apologies, with the latter possibility. In so doing, they distinguish themselves from, and put themselves ethically at odds with, the vast majority of lawyers, who see their primary professional responsibility as providing high-quality service to individuals and organizations without being substantively committed to the ends of those clients. Of course, cause lawyers also serve their clients but tend to see client service as a means to their moral and political ends. Accordingly, conventional practitioners are likely to view cause lawyering as ethically suspect at best. In sharp contrast, cause lawyers believe that they are responding to higher ethical standards. Cause lawyering thus stands in an ambiguous relationship to the professional project of the organized bar.

Cause Lawyers and the Legal Profession. It is important to acknowledge that both cause and conventional lawyers have ideals, that conventional lawyers are not simply cynical maximizers of their own wealth and status, and that cause lawyers are not simply altruistic and self-abnegating. However, the ideals of conventional and cause lawyering are dramatically different.

Conventional lawyers are not supposed to have any qualms about switching sides or representing clients whose values and behavior are reprehensible to them. The prevailing codes of professional ethics expressly allow lawyers to represent clients without endorsing their views or goals. The rules allow the sale of legal expertise without requiring a lawyer to take into account any of the moral or political implications of their representation. Indeed, to do so is a point of professional pride and a demonstration of professional responsibility. British barristers are, thus, readily prepared to both prosecute and defend in criminal cases—in accordance with the "cab-rank" rule. Similarly, the noted American "litigator" David Boies probably considers it a hallmark of his professionalism to have successfully represented IBM in an antitrust suit brought by the U.S. Justice Department and subsequently to have represented the Justice Department in an antitrust suit brought against Microsoft. More broadly, politically liberal U.S. lawyers, including Boies, think nothing of working on behalf of corporations, on the one hand, and serving liberal causes or serving in Democratic administrations on the other. Conventional practitioners would see anyone who characterizes this flexibility as inconsistent or cynical as confusing professional ethics with personal morality.

Cause lawyers reject this way of thinking about the professional project. They expressly seek clients with whom they agree and causes in which they believe. Not only are they eager to take sides in social conflict and to identify themselves with the sides they take, but they are determined to construct their legal practice around this taking of sides.

Cause lawyers tend to transform the nature of legal advocacy, becoming advocates not only, or primarily, for their clients but for causes and, one might say, for their own beliefs. In thus reversing the priorities of the organized legal profession and in staking out the moral high ground, cause lawyers challenge their professional community.

Convergence Between Conventional and Cause Lawyering. At first glance, it might therefore seem that cause and conventional lawyers inhabit entirely different and mutually antagonistic professional worlds. Yet there are points of convergence and overlap that blur the widely acknowledged distinctions between them. Many so-called conventional lawyers tend to represent primarily, perhaps exclusively, those with whom they agree. This certainly seems to be the case with many, perhaps most, lawyers who represent corporations. Consider also personal injury lawyers in the United States. They are divided between a plaintiffs' bar and a defense bar. The plaintiffs' bar represents almost exclusively individuals or classes of individuals who have been injured—whether as consumers, workers, victims of police abuse, or the like. Conversely, the defense bar represents only the targets of such suits—typically business corporations and insurance companies. Thus, these and many other conventional practitioners certainly fail to convey the requisite sense of neutrality called for by the ideology of advocacy. However, many of these conventional practitioners would deny what cause lawyers proudly proclaim—that they are self-consciously choosing sides in basic social conflicts.

Consider also that many cause lawyers use conventional legal practices to finance low-fee or no-fee representation of causes in which they believe. Similarly, lawyers in conventional corporate practice frequently set aside a portion of their time to provide pro bono advocacy for a variety of causes to which they are committed. Although cause and conventional lawyers are marching to distinctly different ethical drummers, there is often substantial convergence and overlap in the ways that they practice law.

In addition, there is a long-standing tradition, going back at least to de Tocqueville, of viewing conventional legal practice as a bulwark of civil society and liberal democracy. Accordingly, the profession has regularly represented itself as providing a public good in return, some have argued, for an official entitlement to monopolize the provision of legal services. To our way of thinking, it is not important whether this broader vision of professional responsibility is attributable to a strategic quid pro quo or to taking seriously the conception of the legal profession as a foundational social institution. Either way, conventional lawyers in general and the organized profession in particular clearly take comfort from a belief that the whole of their enterprise of client representation is somehow bigger and more beneficent than the sum of its parts.

This widely proclaimed conception of lawyering as a higher calling leads to convergence between some types of conventional practice and cause lawyering. Nonetheless, we argue that there is a meaningful distinction—albeit with some contestable conceptual terrain at the point of convergence. To think of law as a higher calling leads almost inevitably to some receptivity to cause lawyering among conventional practitioners. The extent of convergence and receptivity depends not only on the way in which cause lawyering is practiced [but also on] how conventional lawyers interpret their own higher calling.

NOTES ON SCHEINGOLD & SARAT

1. ***Public Interest Lawyer v. Cause Lawyer.*** Why do Scheingold & Sarat find the concepts of public interest law and public interest lawyering problematic? Why do they prefer the concept of cause lawyering? How do they define the term?

2. ***Cause Lawyer v. Conventional Lawyer.*** How is a cause lawyer different from a "conventional" lawyer? What do Scheingold & Sarat mean by insisting that "political or moral commitment is an essential and distinguishing feature of cause lawyering"?

3. ***Convergence and Overlap.*** Do cause lawyering and conventional lawyering sometimes converge and overlap in practice? If corporate lawyers and plaintiffs' lawyers generally agree with and are comfortable representing their clients, are they really conventional lawyers? If cause lawyers take some cases that they do not find particularly compelling in order to finance their work on causes about which they care much more, are they nevertheless cause lawyers? Are lawyers in private practice who do significant amounts of pro bono work for causes they believe in better described as conventional lawyers or part-time cause lawyers? Is a lawyer who works in a nonprofit organization but does not feel particularly committed to the organization's mission a cause lawyer or a conventional lawyer? What, if anything, matters about the answers to these questions?

4. ***Lawyer Alienation.*** Scheingold & Sarat assert that cause lawyers rarely express alienation from their work and that they differ from conventional lawyers in this regard. If Scheingold & Sarat are correct, what accounts for this? Based on what you have read about the many sectors of legal practice thus far, why do some lawyers feel alienated from their work and why do Scheingold and Sarat believe cause lawyers do not? Under what

circumstances do you think conventional lawyers are likely to feel alienated, or not?

D. ISSUES OF ACCOUNTABILITY IN PUBLIC INTEREST PRACTICE

When lawyers seek to serve causes or constituencies in addition to individual clients, questions arise about how the people whom the lawyers purport to represent can ensure that the lawyers are responsive to their needs and preferences. Issues about lawyer power vis-à-vis clients can be worrisome when clients are poor and/or vulnerable in other respects. But they also can be problematic when the represented constituency or cause is disorganized and/or diffuse. Concerns about the accountability of public interest lawyers have been raised by critics on both sides of the political spectrum. They implicate conflicts of interest (involving tensions among the priorities of lawyers, clients, and causes), and as well as the allocation of decision-making authority between lawyers and clients.

The first excerpt in this section considers the responsibilities of lawyers who handle class actions for injunctive relief on behalf of large plaintiff classes. The second excerpt examines the responsibilities of lawyers who pursue precedents that would benefit large categories of people but whose actual client is an individual with interests that diverge from the cause that the litigation advances. The third excerpt considers variation in problems of accountability in collective representation and the responsibilities of lawyers who represent groups.

Institutional Reform Class Actions. The following excerpt, Derrick Bell's classic "Serving Two Masters," raises questions about the conduct of civil rights lawyers in connection with the campaign to achieve racial equity in public schools. At the start of the campaign, the lawyers and most parents of children in the schools that were the subject of the litigation shared the view that integration was the key to improving educational opportunity for their children. Over time, however, many parents became doubtful that complete integration—and the racial tension, long bus rides, and white flight associated with school integration—was the best approach. NAACP lawyers opposed compromise desegregation plans that community leaders and school officials had negotiated to settle class action lawsuits in several cities because the plans concentrated on improving predominantly black schools rather than bussing white students into black schools to achieve full integration. Bell criticized the lawyers who opposed those compromise plans. He argued that the lawyers' commitment to maximum desegregation led them to disregard the wishes of parents who questioned the price of pursuing full integration and who placed a higher priority on securing better educational opportunities for their children.

The class action device used in the NAACP's school desegregation campaign is a procedural mechanism for litigating on behalf of large groups of people who have suffered common injury. Rule 23 of the Federal Rules of Civil Procedure allows representatives to sue on behalf of all members of a class if: "(1) the class is so numerous that joinder of all members is impracticable; (2) there are questions of law or fact common to the class; (3) the claims or defenses of the representative parties are typical of the claims or defenses of the class; and (4) the representative parties will fairly and adequately protect the interests of the class." Rule 23(a). There are several types of class actions, including suits for damages (common in personal injury and consumer litigation brought by lawyers in the private plaintiffs' bar) and institutional reform class actions (sometimes pursued by public interest lawyers, such as the NAACP lawyers considered in Bell's article). A court order approving or "certifying" a class action determines that the criteria for proceeding as a class have been met and that the lawyer representing the class fairly and adequately represents the interests of class members. A judgment in a class action will bind all members of the class and very likely prevent them from pursuing individual claims on the same subject. That raises the question whether it is fair to allow lawyers for the class and the class representatives to define the goals and tactics of the class. Attorneys' fees may sometimes be awarded to class counsel, which raises the possibility that lawyers will be motivated by their own pecuniary interests rather than the interest of serving the class members.

Professional responsibility issues relating to class action litigation are so numerous that they are the subject of entire textbooks and law school classes, and we will not try to canvass all those issues here. Bell's article highlights two issues that sometimes arise in institutional reform class actions: conflicts of interest among members of a plaintiff class (in this case, conflicts between the interests of parents who wanted complete integration and those who preferred to focus on improving predominantly black schools) and conflicts between class lawyers' ideological commitments and their clients' preferences.

Under the ethics rules in most states, a lawyer is prohibited from representing a client if one of two types of conflicts of interest exists: 1) if the client's interests are "directly adverse" to those of another client, or 2) if there is a "significant risk" that a representation will be "materially limited" by a lawyer's obligation to another client or the lawyer's own interests. If either of these types of conflicts exists, the lawyer may proceed only with informed consent. ABA Model Rule 1.7. In class actions, conflicts of interest can be particularly problematic because, by definition, large numbers of people nominally represented by class counsel are not before the court and therefore are not in a position to monitor the lawyer's actions on their behalf. Although class actions do not receive any special attention in the ethics rules, a good deal of commentary suggests that a lawyer for a class has especially strong duties to identify conflicts of interest within a represented class, to apprise the judge of conflicts that arise during the course of the representation, and to assist in taking corrective measures, including supporting the appointment of another lawyer to represent dissenting members of a class. But the lawyer has strong disincentives to identify and remedy conflicts where doing so threatens to derail litigation in which the lawyer and his employer have invested a good deal of time and resources, where the appointment of additional counsel is likely to complicate negotiations, and where opposing counsel may take advantage of the surfacing of such conflicts to argue that the class should be "decertified" and that no attorneys' fees should be awarded to class counsel.

Bell argues that those kinds of disincentives arose in the school desegregation litigation. He asserts that civil rights lawyers' "single-minded commitment" to maximum integration led them to disregard both conflicts among the parents they represented and conflicts between the lawyers' commitment to full integration and their obligations to the plaintiff class.

SERVING TWO MASTERS: INTEGRATION IDEALS AND CLIENT INTERESTS IN SCHOOL DESEGREGATION LITIGATION

Derrick A. Bell Jr.
85 Yale Law Journal 470 (1976)

How should the term "client" be defined in school desegregation cases that are litigated for decades, determine critically important constitutional rights for thousands of minority children, and usually involve major restructuring of a public school system? How should civil rights attorneys represent the often diverse interests of clients and class in school suits? Do they owe any special obligation to class members who emphasize educational quality and who probably cannot obtain counsel to advocate their divergent views? Do the political, organizational, and even philosophical complexities of school desegregation litigation justify a higher standard of professional responsibility on the part of civil rights lawyers to their clients, or more diligent oversight of the lawyer-client relationship by the bench and bar?

This article will review the development of school desegregation litigation and the unique lawyer-client relationship that has evolved out of it. It will not be the first such inquiry. During the era of "massive resistance," southern states charged that this relationship violated professional canons of conduct. A majority of the Supreme Court rejected those challenges, creating in the process constitutional protection for conduct that, under other circumstances, would contravene basic precepts of professional behavior.*

Lawyer-Client Conflicts: Sources and Rationale. Having convinced themselves that *Brown* stands for desegregation and not education, the established civil rights organizations steadfastly refuse to recognize reverses in the school desegregation campaign. Why have [civil rights lawyers] been so unwilling to recognize the increasing futility of "total desegregation," and, more important, the increasing number of defections within the black community?

[Here Bell argues that civil rights lawyers have seen school integration as a major test of the country's continued commitment to civil rights progress and therefore have been reluctant to consider any retreat from that goal. He also argues that civil rights attorneys have been responsive to the supporters of the organizations that employ them—primarily middle class blacks and whites who believe strongly in integration.]

Client-Counsel Merger. The position of the established civil rights groups obviates any need to determine whether a continued policy of maximum racial balance conforms with the wishes of even a minority of the class. This position represents an extraordinary view of the lawyer's role. Not only does it assume a perpetual retainer authorizing a lifelong effort to obtain racially balanced schools; it also fails to reflect any significant change in representational policy from a decade ago, when virtually all blacks assumed that integration was the best means of achieving a quality education for black children, to the present time, when many black parents are disenchanted with the educational results of integration.

This malady may afflict many idealistic lawyers who seek, through the class action device, to bring about judicial intervention affecting large segments of the community. The class action provides the vehicle for bringing about a major advance toward an idealistic goal. At the same time, prosecuting and winning the big case provides strong reinforcement of the attorney's sense of his or her abilities and professionalism. The psychological motivations which influence the lawyer in taking on "a fiercer dragon" through the class action may also underlie the tendency to direct the suit toward the goals of the lawyer rather than the client.

The questions of legal ethics raised by the lawyer-client relationship in civil rights litigation are not new. The Supreme Court's 1963 treatment of these questions in *NAACP v. Button*, however, needs to be examined in

* [Eds.: This refers to the Supreme Court's decision in *NAACP v. Button*, 371 U.S. 415 (1963), which held that the First Amendment prohibits states from preventing the NAACP from soliciting clients for its national litigation campaigns. Some southern states had argued that soliciting clients for these purposes constituted unprofessional conduct.]

light of the emergence of lawyer-client conflicts which are far more serious than the premature speculations of a segregationist legislature.

The Court deemed NAACP's litigation activities "a form of political expression" protected by the First Amendment. Justice Brennan conceded that Virginia had a valid interest in regulating the traditionally illegal practices of barratry, maintenance, and champerty, but noted that the malicious intent which constituted the essence of these common law offenses was absent here. He also reasoned that because the NAACP's efforts served the public rather than a private interest, and because no monetary stakes were involved, "there is no danger that the attorney will desert or subvert the paramount interests of his client to enrich himself or an outside sponsor."

Joined by Justices Clark and Stewart, Justice Harlan expressed the view that the Virginia statute was valid. In support of his conclusion, Harlan carefully reviewed the record and found that NAACP policy required what he considered serious departures from ethical professional conduct [including the requirement that NAACP attorneys follow policy directives from the national board of directors, and retainer agreements signed by prospective litigants that did not contain the names of attorneys retained; Justice Harlan also observed that some of the named plaintiffs had no personal dealings with the lawyers handling their cases.]

Idealism, though perhaps rarer than greed, is harder to control. Justice Harlan accurately prophesied the excesses of derailed benevolence, but a retreat from the group representational concepts set out in *Button* would be a disaster, not an improvement. State legislatures are less likely than the ABA to draft standards that effectively guide practitioners and protect clients. Even well-intentioned and carefully drawn standards might hinder rather than facilitate the always difficult task of achieving social change through legal action.

Client involvement in school litigation is more likely to increase if civil rights lawyers themselves come to realize that the special status accorded them by the courts and the bar demands in return an extraordinary display of ethical sensitivity and self-restraint. The "divided allegiance" between client and employer which Justice Harlan feared would interfere with the civil rights lawyer's "full compliance with his basic professional obligation" has developed in a far more idealistic and thus a far more dangerous form. For it is more the civil rights lawyers' commitment to an integrated society than any policy directives or pressures from their employers which leads to their assumptions of client acceptance and their condemnations of all dissent.

NOTES ON BELL

1. ***What Conflicts?*** What conflicts of interest does Bell identify in the school desegregation litigation? Are some of them conflicts among members of the plaintiff class? Are some of them conflicts between clients (members of the class) and the cause that the public interest organization that employs the lawyer seeks to advance (desegregation)? Which of these types of conflicts are implicated in Bell's assertion that "[i]dealism, though perhaps rarer than greed, is harder to control"? What exactly does he think can be dangerous about lawyer idealism?

2. ***Ethical Sensitivity and Self-Restraint.*** Notice that Bell does not advocate restricting class action litigation or changing the ethics rules. Instead, he urges judges to carefully monitor class actions to ensure that the interests of class members are adequately protected, and he calls on civil rights lawyers to exercise "ethical sensitivity and self-restraint." What would the latter part of Bell's prescription mean in practice? Would it require lawyers to regularly canvass the views and preferences of members of a plaintiff class? How might lawyers go about discerning the interests and preferences of the members of a large plaintiff class? Would it sometimes require lawyers to acknowledge dissent within the plaintiff class and support the appointment of separate counsel to represent dissenting class members, even if those steps might jeopardize the litigation strategy?

* * *

Law Reform on Behalf of Individual Clients. Some types of law reform pursued by public interest lawyers proceed on behalf of individual clients rather than classes of affected people. The following excerpt considers the responsibilities of lawyers in reform litigation on behalf of individual clients whose interests diverge from those of the cause. The lawyer and client at the heart of the controversy analyzed in this article are not particularly famous, but the litigation that brought them together—*Roe v. Wade*—certainly is.

OF CAUSES AND CLIENTS: TWO TALES OF *ROE V. WADE*

Kevin C. McMunigal
47 Hastings Law Journal 779 (1996)

Consider the following situation. It is the late 1960s and criminal statutes prohibiting abortion are common throughout the country. A lawyer wants to challenge the constitutionality of one such statute and interviews a pregnant woman to be the plaintiff in the case. The lawyer is bright, idealistic, and committed to the cause of women's reproductive choice. Having had an illegal abortion herself, she is working without pay and determined to change the law limiting access to abortion. The would-be plaintiff is unsophisticated, nearly destitute, and neither aware of nor committed to any cause. Having once before given a child up for adoption, she is desperate to abort her current pregnancy. Finding a plaintiff has not been easy, and the lawyer feels this woman meets her criteria: she is pregnant, wants an abortion, and is too poor to travel to a state where abortion is legal.

There is one complication: the young woman says she was raped. This allegation confronts the lawyer with a strategic choice. The criminal statute in question has no rape exemption, so she could rely on the rape allegation and argue that the statute is unconstitutional because of its failure to exempt rape victims. Or she could ignore the rape allegation in favor of a broad challenge to the statute's general prohibition of abortion.

Which strategy is the lawyer to choose? The narrower strategy probably has a greater chance for success, at least in the abstract. Of all aspects of the criminalization of abortion, banning abortion in rape cases is perhaps the least popular and most difficult to defend. Thus, it may be the statute's most vulnerable point. Higher likelihood of success on the merits may also speed resolution of the case and increase the availability of injunctive relief in the trial court. Because the prospective plaintiff is already pregnant, she must prevail and probably also obtain injunctive relief in the trial court in a matter of months to have any hope of aborting her pregnancy.

The lawyer, though, has concerns about the rape allegation. The woman states that she failed to report the rape and there were no corroborating witnesses. Weakness on the rape allegation might undermine the entire case. In addition, the broad strategy would advance the cause of reproductive choice more significantly than the rape strategy, appealing to the lawyer's sense of responsibility to a broad female constituency dedicated to expanding abortion rights and to women in the future who will seek to abort pregnancies not resulting from rape.

May the lawyer agree to represent the woman but reject using the rape allegation? If so, on what ground? Suspected falsity? Inadequate proof? Because it would be in the woman's best interest or because the broader challenge would better serve the abortion rights cause?

We rarely have access to detailed accounts of public interest litigation from both the lawyer's and the client's perspectives. Two recent books on *Roe v. Wade*, however, give us both the lawyer's and the client's stories of that case. Sarah Weddington, the most celebrated of the *Roe* lawyers, provides a lawyer's account. Norma McCorvey, the individual plaintiff fictitiously named "Jane Roe," writes from a client's perspective.

As the autobiographical portions of their books indicate, Weddington and McCorvey brought to the *Roe* case some common experiences and interests. Each knew first-hand what it was like to experience an unplanned pregnancy and to be desperate for an abortion but unable to obtain one because of the Texas criminal ban on abortion. Weddington and

McCorvey each had an interest in having the Texas abortion statute abrogated and each needed the other to accomplish this end. Unlike some lawyers and clients in public interest practice, no barriers of sex or race divided them.

But their experiences and interests also diverged significantly. Weddington was well educated, politically aware and committed, while McCorvey was poorly educated, and neither politically aware nor committed. Weddington was interested in making history, changing the law to "somehow, someday free women from the horrors of illegal abortion." McCorvey, by contrast, was simply "at the end of [her] rope," interested in terminating the pregnancy that was the source of her current dilemma.

In more abstract terms, their relationship reflected a tension between McCorvey's present individual interest in obtaining an abortion and the future collective interests of other women in greater access to abortion. In a legal system in which individual cases both resolve present disputes and generate future legal norms, any case may be subject to such a tension between the present individual interests of parties affected by the case as a dispute resolution mechanism and the future collective interests of those affected by the case as a precedent. In *Roe*, this tension was particularly acute. McCorvey was desperate and had no one other than her lawyer to look out for her interests. At the same time, the case also held the potential to dramatically advance the emotionally charged collective interests animating the abortion rights cause, to undo in one bold stroke a century of restrictive abortion legislation.

How, then, did this mix of similar and dissimilar interests play itself out in the *Roe* case?

The Rape Allegation. McCorvey in her first meeting with Weddington claimed that her pregnancy resulted from rape. More than ten years later, McCorvey would admit in an interview with Carl Rowan that this claim was false. But in 1970 and for years thereafter, McCorvey maintained that she had been raped. Weddington chose not to use the allegation.

When Weddington met McCorvey in 1970, abortion rights activists in the United States were pursuing two distinct strategies in attacking the criminal prohibition of abortion. The nature of each is critical to appreciating Weddington's response to McCorvey's rape claim. A reform strategy sought to liberalize the law of abortion by decriminalizing certain categories of abortion, such as those of pregnancies resulting from rape or incest, but otherwise left the criminal ban on abortion intact. An abolition strategy sought complete repeal of criminal abortion laws, including liberalized statutes such as those advocated by the reform strategy. Exemplified by the American Law Institute's Model Penal Code abortion provision, the reform strategy had succeeded in a number of states and was gaining momentum at the time Weddington met McCorvey in early 1970.

The abolition strategy, by contrast, supported by groups such as the National Organization for Women, had met with little success in state legislatures in the late 1960s. In 1973, the abolitionist strategy ultimately prevailed in *Roe*, which invalidated restrictive abortion statutes, and in its companion case, *Doe v. Bolton*, which invalidated liberalized abortion statutes.

McCorvey's rape claim, then, had strategic significance because it raised the possibility for Weddington of choosing either a reform or an abolition strategy in pursuing *Roe*. Weddington was clearly cognizant of both strategies. In 1970, both reform and abolition strategies were being actively pursued by abortion reformers around the United States. Indeed, Weddington describes herself as "moderating a conflict among pro-choice forces" in Texas in 1970 about whether to back reform or abolition legislation, describing the dispute between reform and abolition strategies as a "conflict between what was possible and what was ideal."

How should Weddington have handled this choice? Was she required to reject the rape allegation because of suspected falsity? If Weddington had known McCorvey was lying, she would have been required to reject the allegation. Because she did not know McCorvey was lying, she was not barred on that ground from using the allegation. Neither suspected falsity nor lack of corroboration required Weddington to reject McCorvey's rape claim.

What decision was best for McCorvey? A reform strategy relying on the rape allegation probably had the better chance of success, as Weddington's own description of reform legislation as representing the "possible" and abolition the "ideal" suggests. Higher likelihood of success on the merits would have increased the chances of a speedier resolution and obtaining injunctive relief, both significant for McCorvey's chances for obtaining an abortion since she was already pregnant. But there were also significant risks associated with use of the rape allegation. If proof of the rape allegation was weak and its truth suspect, it might provide the opposing side a point of vulnerability for attacking and undermining the plaintiff's entire case. In other words, lack of credibility on that one issue might result in loss of credibility and sympathy on other factual and legal issues. It also might raise a contested factual issue which could delay resolution of the case and thus decrease McCorvey's chances for obtaining an abortion.

What decision on the rape allegation was best for the abortion rights cause? This is not an easy question to answer. The advantages and disadvantages of both the reform and abolition strategies were widely debated at the time by abortion reformers. Some favored an incremental approach of attempting to liberalize abortions laws, while others favored the more ambitious strategy of seeking complete abolition. The suspected falsity of the rape claim weighed against its use. If it was later exposed as false, it could cause a public relations nightmare for the abortion rights cause.

Weddington and her co-counsel Linda Coffee, who was present at Weddington's first meeting with McCorvey, opted not to rely on McCorvey's rape claim. They chose instead an abolition strategy. Weddington offers the following justification for the decision not to rely on the rape claim:

> As the conversation continued, Jane Roe asked if it would help if she had been raped. We said no; the Texas law had no exception for rape. It was just as illegal for a doctor to do an abortion for someone who had been raped as it was in any other situation. I did ask, "Were there any witnesses? Was there a police report? Is there any way that we could prove a rape occurred?" Her answer in each instance was no.
>
> Neither Linda nor I questioned her further about how she had gotten pregnant. I was not going to allege something in the complaint that I could not back up with proof. Also, we did not want the Texas law changed only to allow abortion in cases of rape. We wanted a decision that abortion was covered by the right of privacy. After all, the women coming to the referral project were there as a result of a wide variety of circumstances. Our principles were not based on how conception occurred.

Though rejection of McCorvey's rape claim may well have been appropriate, this justification is problematic for several reasons. Weddington fails to confront directly the strategic significance of the decision being made or even to mention the possibility of a reform strategy. Nor does she mention the interests of her client, McCorvey, or how Weddington's decision about the rape allegation and choice of strategy might affect her client's interests.

The third justification offered by Weddington for rejecting the rape raises several problems. First, to whom is Weddington referring when she uses the words "we" and "our"? She might simply mean the lawyers, herself and [her co-counsel] Linda Coffee. Or she might be referring to the lawyers' broader constituency, supporters of the abortion rights cause, such as the abortion referral project volunteers who first suggested bringing a test case to challenge the Texas abortion statute. In either case, the assumption underlying this reference to the desires and principles of the lawyers or their constituency as a justification for rejection of the rape allegation is at odds with basic conflict of interest norms governing lawyers. Neither the interests of the lawyer nor the interests of third parties are permitted to influence the judgment of a lawyer in representing a client. Rather, only the interests of the client are to guide the lawyer.

McCorvey appears not to have been informed by Weddington about her decision not to use the rape allegation and consequently agonized for years over her false claim of rape. It seems that whatever might have been in McCorvey's best interest at the time the case was filed, McCorvey, in retrospect, seems relieved that the rape allegation was never used.

Two Tales of Roe v. Wade. For Weddington, the story of *Roe v. Wade* is first and foremost a story of law reform in the service of the collective interests of women. In this story, the idea of service to an individual client has no particular significance. Weddington at the end of her book, for example, states that "the story of *Roe* is the story of the women of this country and their continuing efforts to push back the barriers that have limited their decisions and circumscribed their freedoms" Significantly, McCorvey as an individual is not mentioned. Rather, the protagonists of Weddington's story are women as a group, and the story's drama arises from the conflict between two large interest groups—the abortion rights cause and the anti-abortion movement.

[Surprisingly,] McCorvey in her book ultimately describes the process of being reshaped through the *Roe* case as an experience of empowerment and liberation, rather than one of disempowerment and subjugation. She states at the end of her book, for example, "without Jane Roe, without a cause to fight for and a purpose for living, the original Norma would never have survived." However, McCorvey's realignment on the abortion issue and her baptism by the national director of Operation Rescue, the militant anti-abortion group, roughly a year after publishing her book, make the transformatory experience she describes in that book look more like another example of her tendency to allow others to dominate her.

A recurring problem in the regulation of lawyers is how to deal with incentives that tempt a lawyer to behave improperly. Concern with this problem is common in any agency relationship. Legal and ethical rules governing lawyers often focus on risks to a client from economic incentives that may affect her lawyer, while ignoring risks from noneconomic incentives such as the lawyer's ideals. [T]he Model Rules, reflecting the pecuniary-nonpecuniary distinction found in the Supreme Court's solicitation cases, prohibit a lawyer from soliciting a potential client in person "when a significant motive for the lawyer's doing so is the lawyer's pecuniary gain." Here, again, financial motives are viewed as dangerous, rendering such solicitation "fraught with the possibility of undue influence, intimidation, and overreaching." Nonpecuniary motives such as idealism, by contrast, are seen as benign. Accordingly, public interest lawyers driven by ideals rather than dollars are exempted by the Model Rules from the personal solicitation prohibition on the ground that "[t]here is far less likelihood that a lawyer would engage in abusive practices against an individual where the lawyer is motivated by considerations other than the lawyer's pecuniary gain."[123]

Weddington's and McCorvey's stories prompt us to examine closely the assumptions that underlie this view. They provide a powerful illustration of how a lawyer's ideals may be a potent threat to a client's interests and support Derrick Bell's observation that "[i]dealism, though perhaps rarer than greed, is harder to control."[124]

NOTES ON MCMUNIGAL

1. ***Who Speaks for Causes and Constituencies?*** When lawyers seek to represent causes or constituencies as well as individuals and organizations, who "speaks" for the causes or constituencies? If the lawyer herself decides what is in the interests of the cause or constituency, what steps can she take to ensure that her judgments about the interests and preferences of the client are consistent with her client's interests and preferences?

2. ***Is It Permissible to Consider the Impact of Precedent?*** Was it necessarily wrong for Weddington to consider the interests of women who would be affected by the precedent in *Roe v. Wade?* If not, how might she have better reconciled her clear duty to protect McCorvey's interests with her desire to advance to cause of abortion rights?

E. SUMMARY

This chapter examined lawyers who work in "public interest law" organizations. It addressed definitional controversies surrounding this type of practice and related questions about what makes this sector distinctive, attractive, and sometimes controversial. We explored how public interest practice has grown over the past several decades and how persistent disagreement among advocates of the political left and right about what exactly "counts" as public interest law relates to the white hat status that public interest law enjoys in the courts and other arenas in which law and public policy are made. We examined a concept of the "cause lawyer" and its relationship to public interest law and conventional lawyering.

This chapter has also examined issues of accountability that arise when the intended beneficiaries of the lawyer's work are large constituencies, plaintiff classes, and groups rather than individual clients.

---

123 Model Rule 7.3, comment [4]. [Eds.: This language is now in paragraph 5 of the comment and varies slightly.]

124 Derrick A. Bell, Jr. *Serving Two Masters: Integration Ideals and Client Interests in School Desegregation Litigation*, 85 YALE L. J. 470, 504 (1976).

PART III

CHALLENGES AND OPPORTUNITIES FOR THE PROFESSION IN THE 21ST CENTURY

■ ■ ■

The third and final Part of this book steps back—from questions about the various practice contexts in which lawyers work (the focus of Part II)—to explore big-picture questions about problems and opportunities for the American legal profession as a whole. The purpose of this Part is to prepare you to develop informed views on an interesting set of policy questions with major implications for lawyers and the public.

We begin with three chapters on access to legal services: the market for legal services, unauthorized practice and innovation in legal services delivery, and pro bono. We then address the consequences of the nationalization and globalization of the legal services market, as well as some legal and practical challenges posed by multi-disciplinary and transnational practice. We next consider legal education and bar admission and discipline. The two final chapters review the literature on lawyer satisfaction and well-being, and the future of the legal profession.

CHAPTER 18

THE MARKET FOR LEGAL SERVICES

■ ■ ■

A. INTRODUCTION

This chapter is the first of three that consider issues of access to legal services. In Chapter 16, we examined legal assistance programs, where lawyers serve some of those who cannot afford to hire lawyers. That chapter also briefly reviewed available research on the legal needs of ordinary Americans. But we have not previously considered the larger questions of how the market for legal services operates, how well it works for various types of clients, who is permitted to provide legal services, and the organized bar's positions on these issues. The next several chapters explore those topics.

The ideal of equality before the law, or equality under law, is a fundamental political commitment and legitimating principle of the American system of government, reflected in the inscription over the main entrance to the United States Supreme Court building: "Equal Justice Under Law." Our legal system is complex, and navigating the system and gaining access to the machinery of law often requires assistance from someone with legal training. Therefore, whether people find equal justice under law may turn on the availability of affordable legal services.

Discussions about access to legal services are often intertwined with controversies over whether existing legal rules and procedures are too complex and whether our society relies excessively on law, lawyers, and litigation. These are topics of hot debate in American political life, and they reflect hard trade-offs. For now, we sidestep questions about the role of the courts in our society, the relationship between law and other mechanisms of social control, and whether the complexity of our legal system is a vice or virtue. Our focus here is on the availability and distribution of legal services and their implications for the justice system.

This chapter examines how the market for legal services operates. Much as lawyers may like to think of themselves as a profession that functions apart from markets, legal services in this country are distributed almost entirely through market mechanisms. Moreover, the market for legal services profoundly affects how our legal system and economy function, and it is shaped fundamentally by rules governing who can provide legal services and under what conditions. Understanding how this market works and its effects on the civil justice system is critical to debates about whether lawyers should continue to hold almost exclusive regulatory control over the provision of legal services.

The profession is quite protective of its control over the provision of legal services. It limits entry into the profession through legal education requirements and bar admissions standards. The profession also restricts competition through prohibitions on the unauthorized practice of law and on sharing fees with nonlawyers. The profession's efforts to control the market for legal services have generally been more effective with respect to the domestic market for services to individuals and small businesses than to the global market for services to large corporations. This chapter focuses primarily on the domestic market.

The first excerpt in this chapter, by law professor and economist Gillian Hadfield, identifies uncompetitive features of the American market for legal services. Hadfield argues that lawyers' market power drives up the cost of legal services and makes them unaffordable for most individual consumers. We then consider the views of sociologist Rebecca Sandefur, who challenges the premise that cost is a major impediment to ordinary Americans' use of lawyers and suggests alternative explanations for why people often do not "take their problems to law." The third excerpt, also by Hadfield, notes that issues of access are not just about obtaining legal services to manage crises after the fact; also implicated are ex ante (before-the-fact) legal services—e.g., advice and assistance on loan agreements, insurance coverage, employment options, health care, and legal issues relating to family relationships. Her article raises troubling questions about whether lawyer control over the provision of legal services impedes ordinary households' access to the assistance they need to navigate the "law-thick" world in which we live.

B. THE COST OF LEGAL SERVICES

THE PRICE OF LAW: HOW THE MARKET FOR LAWYERS DISTORTS THE JUSTICE SYSTEM

Gillian K. Hadfield
98 Michigan Law Review 953 (2000)

Why do lawyers cost so much? Conventional popular culture has one suggestion: lawyers are an avaricious lot who will bleed you dry. Conventional economics has another: legal training is expensive. And conventional professional wisdom has another: lawyers enjoy a state-granted monopoly over which they control entry for the purposes of protecting the public. None of these is particularly compelling. While each seems to hold some grain of truth, each also raises more questions than it answers. How is it that the profession has come to be dominated by vice?

Why is law so complicated that legal training is so expensive? Is the public better off with inexpensive low quality legal advice or high quality legal advice it cannot afford?

[In this article] I catalogue features of the market for lawyers and legal services that can be expected to cause the market to deviate from the conditions of perfect competition.

Complexity: The Cost of Complex Reasoning and Process. Lawyers are expensive, in the first instance, when what they do is complex and requires sophisticated and careful reasoning and the exercise of thoughtful judgment.

This account of the high price of lawyers appears quite benign, the product of competitive market forces: price equals cost. And indeed the fact of legal complexity and the cost of legal training plainly are a basis for legal expense in many cases. There are a few pieces of the complexity argument that we need to examine more closely, however, in order to see the problem with a straightforward claim that the cost of lawyers is simply the result of competitive market mechanisms and hence, in a sense, just a fact of economic life.

The hours required to resolve a legal matter are not fixed by abstract and immutable principles of justice. They are determined by procedures and reasoning requirements established and implemented by members of the profession (lawyers and judges and legislators) in an antagonistic, interactive process. From an economic point of view it then makes sense to ask whether the amount of time required to resolve a matter—essentially the complexity of the relevant law and procedure—is optimal: is the value obtained by an increase in complexity justified by the cost of increased lawyer time? This question has to be asked not only of a particular case, but, more importantly, of the system as a whole.

Credence Goods: The Role of Uncertainty. Economists refer to a good as a credence good if it is provided by an expert who also determines the buyer's needs. Buyers of credence goods are unable to assess how much of the good or service they need; nor can they assess whether or not the service was performed or how well. This puts buyers at risk of opportunistic behavior on the part of sellers: they may be sold too much of a service or billed for services not performed or performed poorly.

Legal services are credence goods. The sheer complexity of law makes it difficult for clients to judge the service they are receiving. Law is not merely complex. It is so complex that it is also highly ambiguous and unpredictable.

The process of resolving anything other than a routine legal matter involves many cumulative effects resulting from a cascade of judgments, large and small—what evidence to produce, how to craft pleadings or contractual language, what tone of voice to adopt in testimony or argument or negotiation, how cooperative or combative to be in response to other parties, how quickly to push for a decision, how much to spend on research or outside experts, and so on.

As a result of this sensitivity to detail and differences, law is also highly unpredictable. This makes it extremely difficult for anyone, including other lawyers, to judge whether the time spent on a case was honestly and carefully determined—whether the work performed on a case was the result of care and skill. As a consequence, the market for legal services is even more fundamentally disrupted than is ordinarily the case for credence goods. There is no way for ordinary competitive mechanisms to operate effectively when it is difficult to assess and therefore compare the services offered by competing providers.

Winner-Take-All. It might seem that the difficulty of attributing legal outcomes to the quality of lawyering and so differentiating among lawyers would lead to a situation in which clients, recognizing the difficulties, are willing to pay only small premiums for lawyers they believe to be "better." If that were the case, high prices could be undercut by lawyers clients believed to be slightly less good but considerably cheaper. But the market for lawyers does not work this way.

The impact of a lawyer on a legal outcome is a function not of the absolute quality of the lawyer, but of the lawyer's quality relative to the lawyers on the other side. Having a lawyer who is marginally better pays off disproportionately. Conversely, entrusting your case to a lawyer who is likely to be outperformed, even if only slightly, can cost you the case. As a result, the difference in value between a lawyer who is good and one who is marginally better can be very large. Clients are therefore (rationally) willing to pay a lot for a little.

Monopoly. The commonly recognized source of [lawyers'] monopoly power is artificial barriers to entry to the practice of law: state prohibition of the practice of law by nonlawyers and limitations on the number of people admitted to law schools and the bar. [Another] less recognized but probably more important source of the power to extract rents* is the state's monopoly on coercive dispute resolution—only dispute resolution through the public courts can force the other party to the table.

In light of its monopoly over coercive dispute resolution, the unified and importantly homogeneous nature of the legal profession takes on tremendous importance. The profession defines and reproduces itself. It establishes entry requirements that homogenize the reasoning processes and to some extent the values of its members—judges, lawyers, even many legislators. [D]ramatic responses to the perceptions, needs, and constraints

* [Eds.: Economic rents are the additional profits that the monopolist can extract on account of its market position.]

of those who require dispute resolution services are unlikely to come from within the profession.

NOTES ON THE PRICE OF LAW

1. ***Imperfect Competition in the Legal Services Market.*** In what ways, and to what extent, according to Hadfield, do structural attributes of the U.S. market for legal services cause it to deviate from conditions of perfect competition?

2. ***Credence Goods.*** What is a credence good and why does Hadfield think that legal services fall within the definition? Do you think she is right?

3. ***Complexity and Monopoly.*** How do the complexity of law and the legal profession's monopoly affect the cost of legal services? Are you persuaded by Hadfield's account on these points? To the extent that these features of our system are undesirable, what reforms might address the problem and what would be the disadvantages of such reforms?

4. ***Legal Training.*** In a section of the article not included here, Hadfield draws attention to the fact that all lawyers in the U.S. are trained and licensed under a single model: three years of general law school education followed by a bar exam. How might this aspect of our legal system—its reliance on one unified set of educational and licensing requirements for lawyers serving all types of clients—bear on the cost of legal services? Would you favor disaggregating the legal profession into different tracks with different training requirements for lawyers serving different types of clients? What would be the advantages and disadvantages of such a change?

5. ***Is the Market Truly Uncompetitive?*** Is it possible to square Hadfield's claims about uncompetitive aspects of the market for legal services with the experience of lawyers, many of whom report feeling enormous competitive pressure in their daily work? In a recent book, Hadfield addresses this point:

> Lawyers don't like it when I say that theirs is not a competitive business. Many lawyers feel under intense competitive pressure. But that's not the type of competition I'm talking about. Even if individual lawyers [must compete for business], there are few market pressures on the profession itself. If the profession is producing law that is too complex, too costly, and not of high value, if the rules the profession imposes on practice prevent innovators from bringing better ideas to market, the users of law cannot vote with their feet and move to another way of doing law.
>
> The real monopoly problem is not that individual lawyers and law firms don't have competitors. It is that the system lacks competitors. Even if individual lawyers lose clients, the legal profession doesn't lose customers. Anyone who comes up with a better way to train lawyers can't siphon students off from ABA-approved schools without being approved by the ABA. A professional

> organization that devises a set of professional qualification and practice rules that does a better job at achieving quality at lower prices than the existing legal professions can't bid customers away. So those delivering the current system don't live under the pressure to innovate to produce a better product.[1]

Does this clarification make it possible to believe that two seemingly conflicting propositions might both be true: that many lawyers are struggling financially *and* that the legal services market may be less competitive than it should be?

Consider a 2018 report prepared by William Henderson for the State Bar of California on the state of the legal services market.[2] The report concludes that ethics rules, which are the primary mechanism for regulating the legal services market, stand in the way of innovations that would help address unmet legal needs. Henderson notes that individuals are struggling to afford legal services and often are going without them. Some individuals and small businesses turn to legal publishers such as LegalZoom and Rocket Lawyer, which provide access to tech-enabled forms, contributing to "a consumer DIY [Do It Yourself] culture."[3] The report also highlights the deteriorating economic prospects of lawyers serving individual clients. It cites data from the U.S. Bureau of Labor Statistics showing that the price of legal services has risen steadily while the proportion of income that U.S. consumers allocate to legal services has declined by almost 50 percent over the past three decades. Data from the U.S. Census Bureau's Economic Census show that from 2007 to 2012, the total amount spent on legal services for individual clients declined by nearly $7 billion. Building a financially successful law practice in this sector is very difficult; it requires business judgment and managerial ability as well as capital for technology and marketing. Henderson argues that ethics rules relating to nonlawyer ownership and the unauthorized practice of law create problems for both consumers and lawyers: "[A]s a sizable portion of the public struggles to afford a lawyer and a sizable portion of the bar struggles to find sufficient fee-paying client work, legal regulators need to seriously evaluate whether the consumer protection benefits of these ethics rules are worth the cost."[4]

C. OTHER INFLUENCES ON ORDINARY AMERICANS' USE OF LEGAL SERVICES

Hadfield's economic analysis in "The Price of Law" considers how imperfect competition in the market for legal services affects the cost of those services. In her account, the cost of legal services is a major barrier to access to legal services for all but corporations and very wealthy

---

1 Gillian K. Hadfield, RULES FOR A FLAT WORLD: WHY HUMANS INVENTED LAW AND HOW TO REINVENT IT FOR A COMPLEX GLOBAL ECONOMY 234–35 (2017).

2 *See* William D. Henderson, LEGAL MARKET LANDSCAPE REPORT: COMMISSIONED BY THE STATE BAR OF CALIFORNIA 16–18 (2018).

3 *Id.* at 19.

4 *Id.*

individuals. The following article questions Hadfield's assumption that cost is the primary impediment to ordinary Americans' use of lawyers.

MONEY ISN'T EVERYTHING: UNDERSTANDING MODERATE INCOME HOUSEHOLDS' USE OF LAWYERS' SERVICES

Rebecca L. Sandefur
Middle Income Access to Justice (eds. Michael Trebilcock, Anthony Duggan, Lorne Sossin & Michael Trebilcock, University of Toronto Press 2012)

Public Experience with Civil Justice Problems in the United States. In contemporary market democracies, law reaches deeply into many aspects of daily life. Civil justice problems are common and widespread. Though such problems come in many different forms that affect different aspects of people's lives and concern different kinds of relationships, they share a certain important quality: they are problems that have civil legal aspects, raise civil legal issues and have consequences shaped by civil law, even though the people who experience them may never think of them as "legal" and may never attempt to use law to try to resolve them.

For many people living in market democracies, such troubles emerge at the intersection of civil law and everyday adversity. For example, conservative estimates suggest that more than 100 million Americans are currently living in households that are experiencing at least one civil justice problem involving key areas of contemporary life such as livelihood, shelter, employment, health care, the intergenerational conservation of property, intimate relationships, and the care and support of dependent children and adults. [M]ost of these justice problems never make it to law: they are not taken to lawyers for advice or representation, nor do people pursue them in court.

A predominant account of why Americans do not take their problems to law features cost—not the cost of the civil justice system itself, which Americans have in a sense already paid for with their taxes, but the direct costs of using the system, particularly the cost of lawyers' services.

The Cost of Lawyers' Services. A quick glance at the disparity between the average lawyer's earnings and the average American's earnings reveals some of the basis for the perception that lawyers' services are priced out of the reach of many ordinary people. In 2009, the median annual earnings of American lawyers were $113,240. Compare that with median income for an American household in the same year, $49,777, and one sees that a single lawyer, on average, earns more than twice as much in a year as an entire American household, many of which include more than one earner. Lawyers do make a lot of money, at least on average and in relative terms.

However, when we examine not lawyers' earnings but what people pay lawyers, we learn quickly that we do not know a great deal about the costs of personal legal services—the kind that might be purchased by middle income folks when they face a divorce, or need to settle an estate, or have a problem with their employer, or experience identity theft, for example. No major contemporary survey asks Americans how much they paid for lawyers' services to handle a specific justice problem; nor do any of the recent social scientific surveys of lawyers ask attorneys or firms how much they charged for a case or consultation or body of work.

The information that does exist about what lawyers charge and what people pay for common legal services is thin, but it suggests that the costs of legal services vary greatly, from sums that would be affordable out-of-pocket for many moderate income households to sums that are potentially ruinous. A small body of work examines lawyers who work on contingent fee arrangements in tort cases, such as medical malpractice and auto accidents. Much of this work explores how lawyers secure clients, select cases, and allocate their work effort. When it explores lawyers' fees, the typical finding is that the effective hourly rates charged by contingent fee attorneys are, on average, modest: the mean effective hourly rate lawyers received for contingent fee service circa 1980 was $47 per hour. These studies are informative, but they tend to focus more on lawyers than on consumers. They also provide information about only one group of justice problems. Some common justice problems, like divorce and child support, may not be served through contingent fee arrangements.* Other justice problems involve stakes that are too small to support contingent fee legal services, or appear to attorneys to have too low a likelihood of success to justify the costs of pursuing a case. In general, contingent fees are not practical for contractual work in which no money changes hands, such as writing a will or renegotiating the terms of a lease, or for preventative legal advice.

Information more to the point comes from a smattering of sources that survey lawyers about what they charge for specific services or ask consumers about what they actually paid. [A] survey, conducted in 1987 and 1988, inquired into lawyers' typical charges for specific legal services as part of their applications to participate in a group legal services plan. The quantities reported are the average full retail cost that lawyers reported in the survey, which I am terming a "Rack rate" in recognition of the fact that many clients will pay less.

The second source of cost information, which I am terming the Anecdata Cost, comes from a website, Cost Helper, that receives cost estimates for selected services from consumers and providers who visit the site. This information is "anecdata" because it is a sample of convenience, reflecting the reports of people who happened to post to the website. Anecdata give us a glimpse of some people's experiences, but give us no information about how representative those experiences are. Nevertheless,

* [Eds.: ABA Model Rule 1.5(d) provides that a lawyer may not enter into a contingent fee arrangement in divorce and criminal defense matters.]

CostHelper is a contemporary source, and produces estimates that are on par with the inflation-adjusted estimates based on the 1987–88 survey of attorneys.

[S]ome kinds of basic, transactional legal services appear to be relatively affordable. Based on the attorney survey, real estate settlements cost in at a Rack Rate of around $1,000, depending on one's assumptions about inflation. Anecdata suggest that residential contract review may cost a couple of hundred dollars. A simple will has an average Rack Rate cost of $139 to $201, depending on assumptions about inflation, and an Anecdata Cost range of $150 to $600 or more. To put these amounts in perspective, in 2009 American households spent an average of about $2,600 on eating out in restaurants, and an additional about $2,700 on various forms of entertainment. Given these expenditures, we can surmise that many households probably could have afforded the costs of, for example, a simple will. On the other hand, some kinds of personal legal services are more expensive. The notable example is divorce. Especially when substantial litigation is involved, as in the case of contested divorces, legal services can be quite costly, running into the tens of thousands of dollars. To put the costs of contested divorce into perspective, consider that, for what an American might pay in legal fees for a contested divorce, he or she could alternatively buy a new car.

Taken together, the available data reveal that some legal services, in particular contested divorces, may cost tens of thousands of dollars. Other legal work, such as writing a simple will or settling the sale of a house, may cost as little as a few hundred dollars.

The little we know about the costs of legal services to ordinary Americans suggests that these costs vary from affordable to expensive. What we know about consumer satisfaction with legal fees suggests that when Americans purchase lawyers' services, they are often content with what they had to pay. Taken together, these two findings suggest that other factors besides money must be at play when people who are facing justice problems consider what to do about them. Indeed, when we turn to people's own accounts of why they do not turn to lawyers for their justice problems, cost plays a role, but it is not the predominant reason that people report for not taking their civil justice problems to lawyers.

The Social Construction of Legality. Among the most important reasons that people do not take their problems to lawyers is the fact that they do not think of those problems as legal. The legal nature of any given civil justice problem is not a self-evident fact, but is socially constructed. When confronted with a specific situation, the characterization of that situation as a legal problem reflects both how people think about and what people do about their own troubles, as well as the interactions they have with the friends, neighbors, family members and service providers to whom they may bring their troubles.

When Americans are asked not about their use of law, but simply about their experiences with justice problems, it becomes quickly evident that they often do not think of their justice problems in legal terms. In some of my own recent work, I invited randomly selected low- and moderate-income Americans living in two middle-sized cities in the U.S. Midwest to attend focus group meetings where they could discuss their experiences with "challenges facing American families today." The groups were income stratified, so that people discussed these challenges in a context where other participants faced similar general economic circumstances and were eligible for similar kinds of charitable and public services.

People face many different kinds of problems and challenges; my interest was in those that might have civil legal aspects. Therefore, to help focus the participants' thinking on common justice problems, they were handed a card that listed some common kinds of challenges, all of which can involve civil justice problems. In the meetings, the first exercise was to go around the room and invite each participant to tell a story about his or her own experiences with a problem like the kinds listed on the card. [A]lmost all of the problems they described were civil justice problems in the sense that they had justiciable, or legally actionable, aspects.

One quality common to many participants' accounts of their experiences with civil justice problems was alegality: people described their experiences with problems that had clear legal aspects, raised obvious legal issues, and often had routes to remedy provided by formal law, but they did so in terms that made no reference to law, lawyers or courts.

There are clear legal aspects in the situation [one] person described. [S]he wanted to make a claim for the death benefits to which her child would be entitled under the federal Social Security program, a publicly subsidized life insurance program that pays survivors' benefits to the minor children of decedents who had been employed in eligible occupations and made tax contributions into the system before death. In order to secure these benefits, petitioners must go through a formal process that requires properly filling out specific forms and submitting documents in support of the application. In this case, a successful application would require providing evidence establishing the paternity of the child. It appears that this person's initial application was denied, which means that, in order to pursue her claim, she would have had to file a formal appeal asking for a reconsideration of her file, leading perhaps eventually to an administrative hearing.

But despite law being "all over" her situation, she never mentions law, lawyers or attorneys in her account. On the other hand, among the most common words in her account is "help." This focus on help, but not specifically legal help, was also a common quality of people's stories about their experiences with their civil justice problems. People wanted help with their problems, but it was often not legal help that they described wishing for or turning to.

The pattern of alegality that I found in my study of public experience with civil justice problems is consistent with findings from studies of rights consciousness. The work seeks evidence of how people understand their legal rights when confronted with different kinds of situations that are formally governed by those rights. What I am terming alegality, the absence of thinking in terms of law or rights, turns out to appear in people's experiences with a wide variety of kinds of justice problems, including those involving family relationships, personal injury, invasions of privacy, street harassment, and employment and working conditions.

A pattern of pervasive alegality is consistent with behaviors of people who report in response to their justice problems in U.S. surveys. Among moderate income households in the 1992 ABA survey, law "was not considered at all" for the majority—60 percent—of civil justice problems experienced.

If we take people's behavior as indicative of what is shaping their thinking, we can infer an important factor that shapes the social construction of legality: the institutions of remedy that are available to people facing civil justice problems. Institutions of remedy provide ways of understanding civil justice problems, tools for handling them, and established, regularized routes to their resolution. Law is one such institution of remedy, but people regularly handle their problems in other ways, for instance by turning to other kinds of third parties for assistance. For some civil justice problems in the U.S. context, however, there are few alternative routes to resolution besides law. Divorce is a prime example of this. While one can quit a job without going to court, it is not possible to formally dissolve a marriage or authoritatively assign custody of dependent children without a legal process. It is not surprising, therefore, that the category of civil justice problem most likely to involve lawyers is—family and domestic matters. In the 1992 ABA survey of moderate income households, 63% of justice problems involving family and domestic matters involved consultation with a lawyer, by comparison with 28% of civil justice problems overall.

One way to try to change how people think about their justice problems would be through campaigns of public legal education, in an effort to encourage people to think of certain kind of problems as legal problems and to go to attorneys for advice about them. An alternative or complementary strategy might be to ask people about the kinds of help they would like with their own justice problems and then develop services that meet people's own perceived needs—even if those services turn out not to be traditional legal services. In the U.S. context, it is likely that providing some of the kinds of services that the public might envision as helpful would require changes in the regulation of lawyers' monopoly.

Policies that would address only the costs of legal services also do nothing to assist middle income people with another problem they face when they want to use lawyers, the problem of selecting a specific provider. Even in a context like the United States, where lawyer advertising has long been permitted and where bar-sponsored lawyer referral services have existed in many communities, members of the public seeking attorneys appear to eschew these impersonal sources in favor of information that comes with a personal warrant, whether from their own experience or the recommendation of someone they know. Expanding access to matching institutions that provide some kind of warrant of quality for providers, such as group legal services plans with performance assessments of serving attorneys, might be one mechanism that would assist people in selecting attorneys.

NOTES ON SANDEFUR

1. ***Why Don't Americans Take Their Problems to Law?*** According to Sandefur, what factors influence whether moderate income people use lawyers? In what ways does her account of the significance of the cost of legal services differ from Hadfield's?

2. ***Why Worry?*** Should we be concerned by Sandefur's finding that many Americans do not view their civil justice problems as legal problems and that they often do not turn to law to resolve those problems? If so, why?

3. ***Revisiting Lawyers' Monopoly on the Provision of Legal Services.*** Do you agree with Sandefur that responding effectively to Americans' perceived needs with respect to civil justice problems might involve abandoning lawyers' monopoly on the provision of legal services?

4. ***The Problem of Finding a Lawyer.*** Sandefur notes that middle-income people often have trouble finding a lawyer, in part because they lack reliable information about the quality of alternative providers. But lawyer rating services, employing a variety of methodologies, have proliferated during the past several decades. The most popular of the rating services catering to ordinary American consumers is Avvo, which rates lawyers on a scale of 1 to 10 and provides profiles and client reviews.

5. ***Reconciling Sandefur and Hadfield.*** Do Sandefur and Hadfield disagree fundamentally about the relationship between the cost of legal services and access to justice, or do they disagree mainly about emphasis?

D. EX ANTE LEGAL SERVICES

Discussions about access to legal services tend to focus clients' needs for representation during crisis situations—for example, providing criminal defense, preventing the client's eviction from housing, or seeking compensation for personal injury. The following excerpt explores a broader array of services that bear on whether ordinary Americans are able to organize their personal relationships and market interactions in ways that take full account of the law. It explores how ex ante (before the fact) advice can help ordinary citizens manage their lives in accordance with law and legality.

HIGHER DEMAND, LOWER SUPPLY? A COMPARATIVE ASSESSMENT OF THE LEGAL RESOURCE LANDSCAPE FOR ORDINARY AMERICANS

Gillian K. Hadfield
37 Fordham Urban Law Journal 129 (2010)

The vitality of a market democracy premised on the rule of law depends on more than minimal provision for those in desperate need at poverty levels of income. And it depends on more than the quality and cost of services available to corporate and other large entities. It depends on the success with which law manages to serve in fact—not merely on the books—as the fundamental organizing principle of the institutions and relationships of the ordinary citizen. Is law routinely available, for example, to consult before deciding how to choose between market options, or to evaluate how one has been treated in a relationship governed by legal principles? Or is law merely alive in moments of crisis? We know that even in those moments of crisis—the impending loss of a relationship with one's child, the loss of one's home to foreclosure, bankruptcy in the face of impossible medical bills, or grievous injury in an accident—our legal system is not committed (as it is somewhat half-heartedly committed in the case of a felony charge) to ensuring that an individual is fully able to participate in the systems that will manage this crisis. But what of the everyday life that falls short of crisis, that sets the path on which a crisis may occur or may be averted?

We live in an everyday world that is, in fact, flooded with law—how our children are supposed to be treated in school, what lenders are supposed to tell us when they sell us a mortgage, when our employers can and cannot change our conditions of work or pay, what is fair play in consumer markets, and so on. Every time we sign a document, click a box that says "I Agree," enter a retail shop, or get on a local bus we navigate a world that is defined by legal obligations and rights and, importantly, one that assumes that the ordinary citizen who moves in this world is doing so as a functioning, choosing, legal agent. Should that citizen end up in a crisis that requires more active use or response to the legal system—filing or responding to a lawsuit or enforcement action—she will inevitably be treated as if she functioned with this kind of legal agency on the path that brought her to this point: bound by the contracts she "agreed" to or the risks she was given "notice" of or the legal consequences of the actions she took in caring for her children.

We know that in the corporate client world, this is how the relationship with the legal system operates. Most corporate work is before-the-fact, everyday advice on what contracts to sign, which regulations apply, how conduct is likely to be interpreted by enforcement authorities or, in the event of litigation, what the options are for modifying the extent of legal liability, how to manage a dispute before it becomes a lawsuit, and so on. But for ordinary citizens in the U.S. there is almost no functioning legal system in this ex ante sphere. This has implications not only for the probability of a crisis down the road that the legal system will have to address—with or without legal services made available to the individual in crisis—but, fundamentally, for the extent to which it is realistic to look at our elaborate legal and regulatory structures as effective organizing principles for everyday relationships. That can have implications far beyond the consequences for a single individual, reaching into the efficacy of our legal systems and the rule of law as a whole.

Empirically, we lack any real data on the quantity or quality of legal services available to ordinary individuals, although casually most of us in the profession know that the bulk of civil legal services, and especially ex ante advisory services, are ultimately provided to corporations rather than ordinary folks. Indeed, we could say that the utter lack of attention to the size and vitality of the legal markets serving ordinary individuals in the conduct of their everyday lives in a law-thick world is itself testament to how the profession has defined these markets out of existence. We can look—and in what follows I will try to give some sense of what we will find—but for the most part there is nothing there.

To give some sense of just what is missing, after reviewing the few existing—and well-worn—legal needs studies, I provide some tidbits of data that might shed some light on the size of the U.S. legal markets serving non-corporate clients. The methodology here is to look for the macro indicators of the extent to which resources across the economy as a whole are devoted to providing legal inputs to ordinary citizens for civil matters. In doing so, I hope to broaden the focus beyond the existing studies which focus largely on the poor in particular moments of legal crisis and dispute. The goal is to try to get a handle on the health of the legal markets serving ordinary citizens as a whole. The paucity and unreliability of the data, however, make this an exercise in questions, not answers.

In 1993, the ABA conducted a study, published in 1994, assessing the legal needs of the poor (defined as those living at or below 125% of the poverty line), and of those with moderate income (those with incomes falling in the middle 60% of the income distribution). The study defined "legal needs" as problems or disputes that households had encountered, such as sub-standard housing, job loss, or divorce, and that could be addressed through the civil legal system. With few exceptions (review of documents for a real estate transaction, for example) the focus of the study was on ex post dispute resolution and the nature of the legal assistance that might be offered.

The study found that approximately 50% of households (47% of poor households and 52% of moderate-income households) were experiencing one or more legal needs at the time of the survey. Of those with legal needs, 37% of the poor sought assistance from a third-party for resolution of the problem, 29% from a specifically legal third party such as a lawyer (21%) or other from a non-legal third party (8%). Among moderate-income households, assistance from a third-party was sought with 51% of problems, 39% from a specifically legal source (lawyers 28%, other legal/judicial 12%).

Although the ABA opted not to update the 1994 Legal Needs studies, the Legal Services Corporation ("LSC") in 2005 published a study drawing on nine state surveys, assessing the incidence of legal needs among the poor and the experience in LSC-funded programs with unmet demand for legal aid and the number of legal aid lawyers. If anything, these studies suggest the situation is worse. LSC-funded programs reported that, as a result of resource limitations, they were only able to serve half of the poor who sought assistance.

The legal needs surveys give us a close-to-the-ground look at the legal problems encountered by ordinary Americans, albeit with a heavy focus on poor Americans. As we have seen, these surveys suggest that "law" plays a very small role in the everyday handling of potentially justiciable problems in the U.S. Put differently, the vast majority of the legal problems faced by (particularly poor) Americans fall outside of the "rule of law," with high proportions of people simply accepting a result determined not by law but by the play of markets, power, organizations, wealth, politics, and other dynamics in our complex society.

In this section, I review some indicators—incomplete at best—of the overall extent to which the U.S. devotes resources at a macro level to the delivery of legality. I hope to move the emphasis away from the provision of legal support to the poor in ex post crisis and towards the systemic everyday use of law in fact by ordinary citizens throughout the income spectrum.

Of the roughly $277 billion spent on legal services [in the U.S.], approximately 31% is consumed by individuals as part of personal consumption expenditures ($85.6 billion in 2005). Another 1% ($2.8 billion) can be attributed to services provided by legal aid lawyers and public defenders. Some share, but it is not possible to easily say how much, of the expenditure on government lawyers other than legal aid and public defenders may be attributable to providing services to individual Americans; in some sense, one could classify all of those expenditures (approximately $22 billion or 8%) as being on behalf of ordinary citizens. This suggests that at most 40% of legal services are serving the needs of individual citizens as opposed to corporations and businesses.

These figures comport with data from the only U.S. study addressing the allocation of legal effort across different types of matters and clients. The Chicago Lawyers' Survey, first conducted in 1975 and updated in 1995, estimated that Chicago lawyers devoted 29% of total effort to services for individual or small business clients with an additional 6% serving organizations such as unions, environmental plaintiffs, state administrative agencies or municipalities for a total of 35%; this is a decrease from 45% in 1975.

In the abstract and in isolation it is difficult to say whether this share of legal services devoted to ordinary citizens' interests is enough. Of course, the ordinary citizen benefits from the operation of well-regulated and efficient markets and thus from the availability of legal services to corporate entities as well. To put further perspective on these numbers, I have therefore calculated what the personal share of the legal services market represents in terms of available legal effort and how this has changed over the last few decades.

In 1990, total expenditures by households on legal services were $62.2 billion in 2000 dollars. At that time, the average hourly rate for lawyers in small firms (less than 20 lawyers, where we find most of the lawyers providing services to individuals) was roughly (very roughly!) $157 in 2000 dollars. Based on the total U.S. population for that year, this implies an average of 1.6 hours per person for the year or 4.15 hours per average household. Conducting the same calculation for 2005 (total expenditures of $67.4 billion in 2000 dollars, an average hourly rate of $182 for small-firm lawyers) yields an average of 1.3 hours per person or 3.34 hours per household, a decline of 20%. As a rough calculation, using the ABA 1994 Legal Needs estimates of numbers of problems per household in a given year (1.0) and a straight average of the number of problems per household reported by the state surveys (2.0) for 2005 this suggests that in 1990 American households were able on average to draw on approximately 4 hours of legal time to address a legal problem and in 2005 they were able to draw on 1 hour and 40 minutes of legal time to address a problem.

These are startlingly low numbers, and they reflect only the corner of the legal landscape that involves a crisis such as a dispute over employment, a foreclosure, a denial of health care, or the risk of injury to or a diminished relationship with a child. They exclude the demand for legal assistance before problems arise, such as legal advice in assessing a complex mortgage offer, employment options, insurance coverage, or the potential for conduct to influence custody of a child. Suppose that for every dispute-related need there is an ex ante advice-related need (as appears to be the case for large corporations), meaning that there are twice as many legal needs as those measured by studies asking only about dispute-related needs. This would then imply that the average household is able to draw on less than an hour's worth of legal advice or assistance in dealing with the points at which their everyday lives intersect with the legal system.

The access problems in the U.S. legal system are largely conceptualized by the profession as problems of the ethical commitments of individual lawyers to assist the poor and the failure of federal and state bodies to provide adequate levels of funding to legal aid agencies and the courts. The first conceptualization fails, I believe, to come to grips with the dimensions of the problem, which cannot be solved with an increase in pro bono efforts, as welcome as such an increase would be. Pro bono currently accounts for at most 1–2% of legal effort in the country; even if every lawyer in the country did 100 more hours a year of pro bono work, this would amount to an extra thirty minutes per U.S. person a year, or about an hour per dispute-related (potentially litigation-related) problem per household. This does not even begin to address the realistic demands that ordinary households have for ex ante assistance with navigating the law-thick world in which they live, some of which could indeed reduce the need for ex post legal representation in litigation and crisis. The problem is not a problem of the ethical commitment of lawyers to help the poor. Nor is an increase in public legal aid likely to make a substantial impact. The cost of even that extra hour per dispute-related problem per household would be on the order of $20 billion annually at a market rate of $200 per hour. That would entail a twenty-fold increase in current U.S. levels of public and private (charitable) legal aid funding. Again, more legal aid funding would be welcome and is clearly called for, but it cannot make a serious dent in the nature of the problem.

The problem we face in the American legal system is not a problem of how to increase pro bono or legal aid (although we should do that too), which are ultimately mere drops in the bucket on the order of a few percentage points of total legal effort and resources. Rather, the problem is one of urgent need for structural reform in the regulatory and policy/funding system responsible for the critical infrastructure of market democracy, particularly one that draws as heavily as the American system does on law and legalism to structure economic, political, and social relationships.

NOTES ON EX ANTE LEGAL SERVICES

1. ***Are Ex Ante Services Important?*** Why do ordinary Americans need access to ex ante legal advice and planning services? What is the relationship,

if any, between access to such services and the operation of American democracy and the rule of law?

2. ***Self-Regulation.*** Hadfield is highly critical of the bar's control over the regulation of lawyers and the delivery of legal services in this country. Recall the discussion in Chapter 2 about the reasons that the legal profession offers to justify self-regulation—that the specialized knowledge that lawyers possess means that they should be governed only by others trained and immersed in the same activity and that they can be trusted to transcend their own self-interest in order to protect the interests of both clients and the public good. Is Hadfield's cynicism about self-regulation justified or misplaced?

In a part of Hadfield's article not included above, she asserts that the problem with giving the legal profession exclusive control over the regulation of legal services is that the bar is politically unaccountable and thus far has been unwilling to take responsibility for ensuring that our legal system gives ordinary Americans access to assistance with their everyday legal needs:

> Those concerned with access to justice have long emphasized how the extreme approach to unauthorized practice of law in the United States drastically curtails the potential for ordinary folks to obtain assistance with their law-related needs and problems. The regulatory problem, however, goes beyond a straightforward restriction on supply. The more fundamental problem with the existing regulatory structure is traceable to the fact that the American legal profession is a politically unaccountable regulator.
>
> Because the bar, together with the state judiciaries, asserts exclusive policy authority in this field but is not in fact a politically accountable policymaking body, there is effectively no mechanism for policy change. There is nowhere to address policy proposals and no process for influencing policy adoption. The process is a wholly closed shop. That this does not seem an extraordinary way for an advanced market democracy to make economic and social policy is itself a consequence of the framing that results from the bar's assertion of authority. The bar bases its role on its expertise in the attorney-client relationship—and it styles its regulatory functions as the promulgation and enforcement of ethical standards. There are indeed ethical demands on lawyers and their professional bodies. But this defines out of the frame the fundamentally economic character of the market regulation the bar and judiciary control.

Does Hadfield's argument sound similar to critiques of the profession canvassed in Chapter 2? Recall that some critics of the legal profession say that lawyers use claims of distinctive knowledge and ethical commitments to justify exclusionary policies and to pursue advantages for themselves at the expense of competitors and the larger public.

3. ***What Would Change?*** If the organized bar were more directly politically accountable to the American public, what changes do you think

would result? Keep this question in mind as we turn to our next topic—unauthorized practice and innovation in the delivery of legal services.

E. SUMMARY

This chapter examined the market for legal services. It considered how structural features of the market affect the cost of legal services and how factors other than cost influence the likelihood that ordinary Americans will seek lawyers' assistance with their problems. We considered the mechanisms by which citizens find lawyers (or do not) during times of crisis. But we also explored a type of legal services not typically contemplated in most discussions of access to justice issues—ex ante advice to help ordinary citizens align their social, political, and economic arrangements with law so as to avoid trouble. This chapter raised questions about whether the market for legal services meets the needs of ordinary Americans, and, if not, what responses might be called for. We explore those options in the following two chapters.

CHAPTER 19

UNAUTHORIZED PRACTICE AND NON-LAWYER INVOLVEMENT IN THE PROVISION OF LEGAL SERVICES

■ ■ ■

A. INTRODUCTION

Many types of work that are arguably legal in nature can be performed only by a lawyer in the United States. Individuals are allowed to handle their own legal problems; for example, they can write their own contracts, represent themselves in civil and criminal cases (appear "pro se"), and write their own wills. But nonlawyers cannot provide legal assistance to others. Lawyers enjoy a monopoly on the provision of legal services. This monopoly is protected through unauthorized practice restrictions—prohibitions on the provision of legal services by anyone not licensed to practice law. Indeed, practicing law without a license is a crime in most states. In addition, nonlawyers are prohibited from participating in the financing, ownership, or management of a business engaged in the practice of law. This chapter examines what it means to "practice law" and the impact of statutes that prohibit nonlawyers from engaging in the practice of law. It considers whether and under what circumstances restrictions on unauthorized practice are justified in order to protect the legal system and consumers. We next review innovations in the delivery of legal services designed to expand access through means other than the two primary strategies supported by the organized bar—increased funding for legal services for the poor and greater support for private bar pro bono. Some of those innovations involve participation by non-lawyers and thereby violate current rules restricting who may provide legal services and what form legal practice can take. Finally, we consider the wisdom of allowing business models that might make it possible to deliver legal services more efficiently and cheaply but would require outside nonlawyer investment.

B. WHAT IS THE UNAUTHORIZED PRACTICE OF LAW?

Until the Great Depression, the practice of law was thought to be appearing in court on behalf of another person, and so nonlawyers could provide services in connection with business transactions, real estate acquisition, and other out-of-court situations. But in the 1930s, the bar began taking a much more aggressive stance toward defining services that only lawyers should be allowed to provide and in policing the boundaries of "the practice of law." Bar associations negotiated agreements with other service providers to distinguish tasks that would be limited to lawyers only and those that competitors could offer without being charged with unauthorized practice. In the 1970s, fears about antitrust liability led the bar to abandon these agreements with other occupational competitors, but unauthorized practice restrictions remain in place in all states.

The ABA does not offer a uniform definition of the practice of law for purposes of identifying the parameters of unauthorized practice. In 2002, the ABA Board of Governors established a Task Force on the Model Definition of the Practice of Law to examine the issue. The Task Force proposed that every state and territory adopt a definition of the practice of law and that its definition should include "the basic premise that the practice of law is the application of legal principles and judgment to the circumstances or objectives of another person or entity." It further proposed that each state should "determine who may provide services that are included within the state's or territory's definition of the practice of law and under what circumstances, based upon the potential harm and benefit to the public." The proposal generated a good deal of negative commentary, including a joint statement from the Department of Justice and the Federal Trade Commission on the proposal's anticompetitive effects. The Task Force then decided to leave it to states to adopt their own definitions, but it advised that such definitions should follow the broad outlines of the ABA's proposal.

There remains a good deal of variation in how states define the practice of law, but the definitions are generally quite broad and vague. Georgia's, for example, includes "the giving of any legal advice."[1] Nebraska defines the practice of law as "the application of legal principles and judgment with regard to the circumstances or objectives of another entity or person which require the knowledge, judgment, and skill of a person trained as a lawyer."[2] In Florida, the definition is the "traditional tasks of

---

[1] Code of Georgia Annotated Title 15. Courts Chapter 19. Attorneys Article 3. Regulation of Practice of Law, § 5–19–50.

[2] The statute goes on to say that the practice of law includes, but is not limited to, the following: "(A) Giving advice or counsel to another entity or person as to the legal rights of that entity or person or the legal rights of others for compensation, direct or indirect, where a relationship of trust or reliance exists between the party giving such advice or counsel and the party to whom it is given; (B) Selection, drafting, or completion, for another entity or person, of legal documents which affect the legal rights of the entity or person; (C) Representation of another entity or person in a court, in a formal administrative adjudicative proceeding or other formal dispute resolution process, or in an administrative adjudicative proceeding in which legal pleadings are filed or a record is established as the basis for judicial review; (D) Negotiation of legal rights or responsibilities on behalf of another entity or person; (E) Holding oneself out to another as being entitled to practice law as defined herein." Nebraska Court Rules, Section 3–1001.

the lawyer" such as "the giving of legal advice, preparing and submitting claims, representing clients in proceedings," and giving "counsel to others as to their rights and obligations under the law and the preparation of legal instruments, including contracts, by which legal rights are either obtained, secured or given away."[3] Similarly, Iowa case law provides that the practice of law "includes, but is not limited to, representing another before the courts; giving of legal advice and counsel to others relating to their rights and obligations under the law; and preparation or approval of the use of legal instruments by which legal rights of others are either obtained, secured or transferred even if such matters never become the subject of a court proceeding."[4] In California, a statute makes unauthorized practice of law a crime but does not define the practice of law.[5] Cases define it broadly to include giving legal advice and preparing legal instruments.[6]

Under some of these expansive (and sometimes circular) definitions, a great deal of everyday conduct by other occupational groups and ordinary citizens seems to run afoul of unauthorized practice restrictions. Are police officers practicing law when they give Miranda warnings? Are credit counselors engaging in the practice of law when they help consumers negotiate payment plans with their creditors? Are realtors practicing law when they explain the terms of an agreement to sell a house or explain the nature of a mortgage? Are tenants' associations engaging in the practice of law when they inform renters of their legal rights and responsibilities? Do these statutes reach everyday citizens trying to help each other navigate our law-rich world—for example, a parent advising his or her child on the consequences of signing a contract? Among the major sources of controversy in the prohibition of unauthorized practice are the following:

Non-Lawyer Service Providers. Unauthorized practice of law statutes have been applied to a broad range of non-lawyer service providers. Most commonly, the statutes have been used to close down the operations of secretaries and paralegals who charge fees to help people fill out forms. For example, in *Florida Bar v. Brumbaugh*, the court enjoined a former legal secretary from helping couples fill out necessary forms to obtain amicable no-fault divorces.[7] She had served hundreds of customers without complaint, and the bar presented no evidence that her services were less competent than those provided by licensed lawyers. It found that she could legally sell forms and type up instruments completed by clients but that she could not correct any errors in the selection or preparation of

---

3 *Florida Bar v. Rapoport*, 845 So.2d 874, 877 (2003); *State ex rel. The Florida Bar v. Sperry*, 140 So.2d 587, 591 (1962), vacated on other grounds, 373 U.S. 379 (1963).

4 *Committee on Professional Ethics & Conduct v. Baker*, 492 N.W.2d 695, 701 (Iowa 1992); Iowa Code of Prof'l Responsibility EC 3–5.

5 Cal. Bus. & Prof. Code §§ 6125–6126.

6 *See, e.g., Birbrower, Montalbano, Condon & Frank v. Superior Court*, 17 Cal. 4th 119, 128 (1998).

7 *Florida Bar v. Brumbaugh*, 355 So. 2d 1186 (Fla. 1978).

legal forms or provide any assistance in filling them out. In a similar case, the Florida Supreme Court ordered jail time for a former legal secretary who violated a court order enjoining her from helping couples obtain simple no-fault divorces.[8] The defendant never served jail time for practicing without a license, but only because Florida's governor intervened. More recently, the Kentucky Supreme Court imposed a $5,000 fine against a woman who continued to prepare documents in uncontested divorce cases after receiving a warning letter from the Kentucky Bar Association. She was also ordered to pay costs and fees incurred by the bar association in bringing the action.[9] Similarly, the Supreme Court of Delaware found that special education consultants who represented parents in administrative hearings in which parents attempted to require schools to provide services for students with special education needs under the Individuals with Disabilities Education Act (IDEA) were engaged in the unauthorized practice of law.[10] On the other hand, simply the sale of legal forms from a website is not unauthorized practice so long as the person does not advise on the use of the forms.[11]

Interactive Websites. The internet has dramatically expanded the possibility of connecting people who need limited legal assistance and information with those possessing legal knowledge. Innovative companies attempting to make that connection have encountered a wide range of legal issues relating to unauthorized practice (and to outside finance of law practices, an issue we consider below). The tech-enabled provision of legal guidance and assistance completing legal forms began with software. A case in Texas involved Parsons Technology, a company that published and sold a computer software program called Quicken Family Lawyer, which provided various types of legal forms (e.g., employment agreements, real estate leases, premarital agreements, and will forms) along with instructions about how to fill them out. The program included a disclaimer indicating that users of the forms should understand that their particular circumstances should be taken into account in determining whether any particular form would meet their needs, and therefore that it might be advisable to seek the assistance of a lawyer. When the Texas Unauthorized Practice of Law Committee sued to enjoin the sale of the software in Texas, Parsons argued that its product did not violate the Texas unauthorized practice of law statute because it involved no personal contact. In *Unauthorized Practice of Law Committee v. Parsons Technology, Inc.*, a federal district court found that Parsons had violated the statute and also rejected Parsons' argument that the statute was unconstitutionally vague. The Texas legislature thereafter amended that state's unauthorized

---

8 *Florida v. Furman*, 451 So.2d 808 (Fla. 1984).

9 *Kentucky Bar Association v. Tarpinian*, 337 S.W.3d 627 (Ky. 2011).

10 *In re Arons*, 756 A.2d 867 (Del. 2000).

11 *State ex rel. Comm'n on Unauthorized Practice of Law v. Hansen*, 286 Neb. 69 (2013).

practice statute to provide that the practice of law does not include "computer software, or similar products . . . [that] clearly and conspicuously state that . . . [they] are not a substitute for the advice of an attorney." Thereafter, the Fifth Circuit vacated the injunction against the distribution of Quicken Family Lawyer.[12]

As the internet enabled even easier access to interactive software, the challenges to the sale of such services grew. *In re Reynoso*, 477 F.3d 1117 (9th Cir. 2007), held that Frankfort Digital Services, the seller of web-based software that prepares bankruptcy petitions, had engaged in the unauthorized practice of law. One of the websites, the Ziinet Bankruptcy Engine, stated that "Ziinet is an expert system and knows the law. Unlike most bankruptcy programs which are little more than customized word processors the Ziinet engine is an *expert* system. It knows bankruptcy laws right down to those applicable to the state in which you live. Now you no longer need to spend weeks studying bankruptcy laws." The site stated that its services were comparable to those of a "top-notch bankruptcy lawyer." It also offered access to a "Bankruptcy Vault" that included information about "stealth techniques" and "loopholes" that would enable customers to hide a bankruptcy from credit bureaus and help them retain property. The court held that Frankfort violated California's unauthorized practice statute because it went well beyond providing secretarial services and instead held itself out as holding legal expertise.

LegalZoom, a popular online legal information business established in 2000, has tangled repeatedly with state bar organizations and lawyers over whether the company is violating unauthorized practice rules. LegalZoom provides interactive guidance and legal document generation for creating a business structure, a will, a living trust, a power of attorney, a demand letter, a nondisclosure agreement, and many other documents. It also provides guidance and forms for filing for divorce or bankruptcy, and registering a trademark, patent, or copyright. LegalZoom has faced and, thus far, survived unauthorized practice complaints from many state bars and litigation from lawyers who believe it is engaged in unfair business practices by providing legal services without complying with bar admission requirements.[13] In 2015, LegalZoom filed a lawsuit against the North Carolina bar, seeking $10.5 million in antitrust damages. The parties settled the suit several months later. Under the settlement agreement, LegalZoom must employ North Carolina lawyers to vet its documents and must inform consumers that its on-line templates are no substitute for in-person advice from an attorney. The settlement agreement also provided

---

[12] *Unauthorized Practice of Law Committee v. Parsons Technology, Inc.*, 179 F.3d 956 (5th Cir. 1999). *See also N.C. State Bar v. Liengard, Inc.*, 2014 NCBC Lexis 11 (2014) (a website offering lien filing service engaged in unauthorized practice when online software printed forms populated with information provided by consumer).

[13] *E.g., LegalZoom.com, Inc. v. McIllwain*, 2013 Ark. 370 (2013); *Medlock v. LegalZoom.com, Inc.*, 2013 S.C. Lexis 362.

that the state bar would support legislation clarifying the definition of unauthorized practice and permitting the operation of interactive legal-help websites that abide by the terms of the settlement agreement.[14] In 2016, the North Carolina legislature enacted a law saying that the practice of law does not include software that generates a legal document based on a user's responses to legal questions.[15]

In an effort to respond to the criticisms in earlier cases that software is no substitute for consultation with a lawyer, LegalZoom and its many competitors supplement the online interactive document preparation service with opportunities to consult attorneys from their online database of participating lawyers.[16]

Although LegalZoom, and other web-based legal services businesses, such as Rocket Lawyer, Nolo, and Law Depot, have skirmished with bar authorities and private plaintiffs in many states,[17] the businesses survive. LegalZoom, for example, currently does business in all 50 states and the District of Columbia, and in the U.K.[18]

C. DO UNAUTHORIZED PRACTICE RESTRICTIONS PROTECT THE PUBLIC?

The bar has long maintained that unauthorized practice restrictions protect consumers against the harm that unqualified and unscrupulous service providers might cause. But many critics of the profession charge that current unauthorized practice restrictions serve primarily to protect the profession's occupational interests and that regulations less restrictive than outright bans on nonlawyer services would better protect consumers. Some say that concerns about protecting individuals from incompetent or unscrupulous service by nonlawyer providers could be met through a combination of registration and certification requirements to ensure adequate training, mandatory malpractice insurance, and minimum

---

[14] See Terry Carter, *LegalZoom Resolves $10.5M Antitrust Suit Against North Carolina State Bar*, ABA J., Oct. 23, 2015.

[15] *See* Jason Tashea, *Nonlawyers at LegalZoom performed legal work on trademark applications, UPL suit alleges*, www.abajournal.com, Dec. 20, 2017.

[16] *See* Amit Chowdury, *How LegalZoom Provides Businesses with Affordable Legal Assistance,* FORBES, Oct. 9, 2017; David Gialanella, *Avvo, LegalZoom, Rocket Lawyer Declared Off-Limits*, N.J. L.J. (June 21, 2017) (reporting on New Jersey Supreme Court bar committees' opinion that Avvo facilitates impermissible fee-splitting and LegalZoom and Rocket Lawyer operate legal services plans that are required to register with the New Jersey bar regulatory authorities).

[17] *See* Thomas Spahn, *Commentary: Battle Over Divorce Forms: Defining the Contours of Unauthorized Practice of Law*, LAWYERS WEEKLY USA, July 17, 2012; Janson v. LegalZoom.com, Inc., 802 F.Supp.2d 1053 (W.D. Mo. 2011); Connecticut Bar Ass'n Unauthorized Practice of Law Comm. Informal Op. 2008–01 (2008); Pennsylvania Bar Ass'n Unauthorized Practice of Law Comm. Formal Op. 2010–01 (2010).

[18] *See* Martha Neil, *LegalZoom Gets OK to Operate in the UK*, ABA J., Jan. 8, 2015.

ethical standards.[19] These scholars note that other countries allow nonlawyers to provide advice and services that in the United States only lawyers can provide, that consumers favor relaxing the restrictions on unauthorized law practice, and that there is little evidence that ethical and competent service cannot be provided by nonlawyers.

In opposition to the ABA's proposed Model Definition of the Practice of Law, the Department of Justice (DOJ) and the Federal Trade Commission (FTC) (which together enforce federal competition law) submitted comments urging the ABA not to adopt the proposed definition because it was "overbroad and could restrain competition between lawyers and non-lawyers to provide similar services to American consumers":

> [W]e urge the Task Force to consider carefully what specific harms the Model Definition is designed to address, whether the Definition is appropriately tailored to addressing those harms, and whether the elimination of any such harms would outweigh the reduction in lawyer-non-lawyer competition that could occur if any state adopted the proposed Model Definition. [T]he proposed Model Definition [does not] provide a clear articulation of the harms the Definition seeks to address. [It] notes only in general terms that "The primary consideration in defining the practice of law is the protection of the public."
>
> The DOJ and the FTC recognize that there are circumstances requiring the knowledge and skill of a person trained in the law, and acknowledge the legitimacy of the Task Force's efforts to protect consumers in such situations. Nonetheless, the DOJ and the FTC believe that consumers generally benefit from lawyer-non-lawyer competition in the provision of certain services.

Some consumer advocates offered similar objections. One argued that the ABA's proposed model definition of the practice of law "poses a major threat to the rights of millions of American consumers who choose to handle their routine legal tasks with the help of non-lawyer resources, such as document preparers, independent paralegals, title agents, independent insurance adjusters, even self-help books and software. The ABA proposal would largely stymie much-needed efforts to increase accessibility to our civil justice system through the expansion of such non-lawyer services."[20] A consumer advocacy group argued that the concept of unauthorized practice should be limited to fraudulent practice—holding oneself out as a lawyer when one is not.

---

[19] *See* DEBORAH L. RHODE, ACCESS TO JUSTICE 87–91 (2004); Deborah L. Rhode, *Access to Justice: Connecting Principles to Practice*, 17 GEO. J. LEGAL ETHICS 369 (2004).

[20] *See* James C. Turner, *Lawyer vs. Non-lawyer: ABA Chose Wrong Side in Drafting Unauthorized Practice Rule*, LEGAL TIMES, Feb. 3, 2003.

Some proponents of expanded access to nonlawyer services argue in favor of allowing the development of various types of legal services providers to serve consumers with varied types of needs. Reform advocates often draw comparisons to developments in medicine, where pressure to reduce costs and expand coverage has led to extensive diversification and experimentation. According to this view, paralegals operating independently from lawyers could provide some types of routine legal services, much as nurse practitioners provide a cost-effective alternative to doctors for some types of basic medical care. Legislatures in several states, including California and Arizona, have taken small steps in this direction by making it legal for nonlawyers to prepare certain types of legal documents.[21] In 2012, the Washington Supreme Court approved a rule allowing licensed legal technicians to help civil litigants navigate the court system—helping them select and complete forms, inform clients of procedures and deadlines, review and explain pleadings, and identify additional required documents.[22] In 2018, the Utah Supreme Court approved rules creating a new role of "licensed paralegal practitioners," who will be permitted to provide limited assistance to clients without lawyer supervision in some family law, forcible entry and detainer, and debt collection matters. Some advocates of regulatory reform would also liberalize lawyers' ethics rules to allow for the creation of high volume, low-cost options that either do not currently exist, or that operate under the shadow of threatened legal action by the bar because lawyers do not control all aspects of the services.

The following excerpt surveys the research on whether prohibitions on nonlawyers providing some legal services in fact protects consumers.

THE MONOPOLY MYTH AND OTHER TALES ABOUT THE SUPERIORITY OF LAWYERS

Leslie C. Levin

82 Fordham Law Review 2611 (2014)

The conventional wisdom—and the vast majority of studies—indicate that individuals who are represented by lawyers obtain better outcomes in civil proceedings than those who are not. For example, 21 percent of asylum seekers who were represented by counsel obtained relief as compared to 1 percent who were not represented by counsel. Lawyer representation in social security disability appeals increases the represented party's chances of success. Individuals represented by counsel in small claims courts enjoy

[21] In California, document preparers must be registered and bonded, while in Arizona they must be certified. *See* California Business and Professions Code Section 6400–6401.6; Arizona Code of Judicial Administration Section 7–208.

[22] Washington Courts, "Supreme Court Adopts Rule Authorizing Non-Lawyers to Assist in Certain Legal Matters," June 15, 2012, available at http://www.courts.wa.gov/newsinfo/?fa=news info.internetdetail&newsid=2136.

better outcomes. Represented parties obtain significantly better financial results in cases tried before the Tax Court than unrepresented parties.

[I]t is instructive to consider the studies that explore whether lawyers obtain better outcomes than nonlawyer representatives. Taken together, the studies suggest there is little evidence to support the legal profession's claims of superiority as compared to nonlawyer representatives in certain legal contexts.

In the most systematic of the U.S. studies, Herbert Kritzer looked at nonlawyer representation in four types of civil proceedings.[61] Kritzer concluded that the "presence or absence of formal legal training is less important than substantial experience with the setting." Three types of expertise were important: knowledge about the substantive law, an understanding of the procedures, and familiarity with the regular players in the process. Similar findings about nonlawyer representatives have emerged from the United Kingdom. [One 2003 study] found that nonlawyers performed to higher standards than lawyers when providing representation in the areas of welfare benefits work, housing, and debt matters.[72] Client surveys indicated that clients were somewhat more satisfied with nonlawyer representatives, although nonlawyers did less well with handling the initial client appointment.

[T]he bar also justifies its monopoly of the legal services market with the argument that lawyers are more trustworthy (i.e., ethical) than nonlawyers. Lawyers bolster their claim with references to their legal training, their ethical code, the character and fitness inquiry, the lawyer discipline system, and the threat of malpractice liability.

As an empirical matter, the bar's claim that lawyers are *more* trustworthy than nonlawyer legal services providers is exceedingly difficult to test. Much misconduct by lawyers and nonlawyer providers is undetected and unreported, so the true extent is unknown. Even a comparison of complaints against lawyers and nonlawyers is difficult as the complaints can be made in different fora, and the ease of filing a complaint against lawyers and nonlawyer providers of legal services differs considerably. [However,] lawyers' decisionmaking processes have not been shown to be different than the decisionmaking processes of other individuals. [Levin concludes that there is no evidence that lawyers are more trustworthy and speculates that they may be less so.]

---

[61] HERBERT M. KRITZER, LEGAL ADVOCACY: LAWYERS AND NONLAWYERS AT WORK (1998).

[72] Richard Moorhead et al., *Contesting Professionalism: Legal Aid and Nonlawyers in England and Wales*, 37 Law. & Soc'y Rev. 765 (2003).

HOW TO REGULATE LEGAL SERVICES TO PROMOTE ACCESS, INNOVATION, AND THE QUALITY OF LAWYERING

Gillian K. Hadfield & Deborah L. Rhode
67 Hastings Law Journal 1191 (2016)

The U.K. approach [to regulating lawyers], in contrast [to the American approach], carves out specific activities for licensed lawyers, and leaves the residual open for competition from alternative nonlawyer providers. A second major difference is that the category of [persons authorized to practice law] in the United Kingdom includes multiple legal professions and licenses. [T]here are nine different professional licenses or designations for those performing [legal services for which a license is required]: solicitor, barrister, legal executive, notary, licensed conveyancer, patent attorney, trademark attorney, costs lawyer, and chartered accountant. Professionals practicing under these licenses have nonexclusive authorization to perform particular reserved activities and hence there is interprofessional competition.

Regulation of each of these professions is carried out by a different approved regulator. Approval and oversight of these front-line regulators is carried out by the Legal Services Board ("LSB"), an independent administrative body that is accountable to Parliament and operates out of the Ministry of Justice. The Legal Services Act requires the LSB to have a lay chair and a majority of lay members.

[A] legal practitioner who wishes to conduct litigation, for example, can choose from which professional body authorized to regulate that particular activity she wants to secure a license. This means that not only are existing practitioners engaged in interprofessional competition across dimensions such as cost and quality, so too are the front-line regulators in competition in the design and implementation of their regulatory requirements.

The U.K. approach foregoes none of the traditional framework of professional regulation. It preserves all of the profession's long-held duties. And it preserves the capacity of the professional body to revoke individual lawyers' authorization to practice regardless of practice setting. The U.K. approach substantially relaxes or eliminates the traditional restrictions on the business models within which lawyers can practice and the financial and managerial relationships they can enter into with nonlawyers without sacrificing the professional values that have so worried American judges and bar associations.

[The U.K. experienced growth in legal employment and revenues after the 2007 regulatory reform and the competition among different professions. The U.K. has more flat fee pricing than the U.S., which the authors assert benefits consumers. And there is no evidence of an increase in malpractice.]

NOTES ON THE CONSUMER PROTECTION RATIONALE FOR UNAUTHORIZED PRACTICE RESTRICTIONS

1. ***Consumer Beware?*** Should consumers be allowed to take the risk of hiring a person who has not attended law school to perform services that are arguably "legal"? Or should the state protect consumers from making unwise decisions—at least in some circumstances? Under what conditions would you allow consumers to take the risk of hiring a nonlawyer to perform legal services?

2. ***Does the Type of Service Matter?*** Does your answer to the previous question depend upon whether the client wishes to use the services for in-court representation, for advising, or for transactional services? In a criminal matter, where the state arguably has an especially large stake in ensuring the fairness of the process, or in a civil matter? Does your answer depend on the complexity of the matter or the stakes involved? Does it matter whether the client can afford an attorney, or whether the state is prepared to provide free or subsidized counsel?

3. ***Where Lawyers Excel.*** A study of 5,000 unemployment insurance appeal hearings and the lawyers and nonlawyer advocates who handled them found that judges play a crucial role in shaping nonlawyer legal expertise and that, although experienced nonlawyers are effective representatives in many cases, they are not equipped to challenge judges on contested issues of law, nor to advance novel legal claims in court or advocate for law reform on a broad scale.[23] What light might this shed on how to incorporate both lawyers and nonlawyers into an area of practice to gain the benefits of broader access to justice without losing the role that lawyers apparently play in advocating for legal change?

4. ***Regulatory Alternatives to Flat Bans.*** What measures, short of complete bans on lay competition, might answer potential concerns about unethical or incompetent service by nonlawyers? What barriers do you see in implementing a system of effective training, certification, and oversight of nonlawyer representation? Should such training and oversight be done by law schools and the bar or by other educational and regulatory institutions?

* * *

Deregulation. Some critics have argued for more radical proposals that would not only allow for greater competition between lawyers and nonlawyers for out-of-court and relatively routine legal services, but also eliminate occupational licensing in law altogether. Consider the following argument in favor of completely deregulating legal services.[24]

---

[23] Anna E. Carpenter, *et al.*, *Trial and Error: Lawyers and Nonlawyer Advocates*, 42 L. & SOC. INQ. 1023 (2017).

[24] Clifford Winston and Robert Crandall, *Time to Deregulate the Practice of Law*, WALL ST. J., Aug. 22, 2011, A13.

FIRST THING WE DO, LET'S DEREGULATE ALL THE LAWYERS

Clifford Winston, Robert Crandall, & Vikram Maheshri (Brookings Institution Press 2011)

Lawyers are among the 20 percent of the U.S. labor force that is required to obtain a government license to practice a profession—a requirement that may not be justified because some legal services could be competently provided by persons who have not had a formal legal education and who have not passed a state bar examination to obtain a license.

An underlying argument supporting occupational licensing in law is that a minimum level of intellectual ability or talent is required to be a competent practitioner; a licensing requirement therefore serves as a screening device to identify and weed out people who do not meet this standard of competence. However, the screening device also serves to prevent laypeople who could compete effectively with licensed lawyers from doing so legally. Further, some talented people are undoubtedly discouraged from entering the legal profession because they chafe at the expense and opportunity costs of a three-year course of study.

We recognize that specific legal training may be essential for providing certain legal services and that some unlicensed and untrained lawyers may not be able to perform certain complex legal services adequately, such as complex contracts and appellate litigation. But clients requiring more complex services are more likely to be sophisticated and therefore better able to determine a lawyer's quality without relying solely on an attorney's educational or bar examination history. Thus, given that substantial earnings premiums have been widespread and commonplace in the legal profession for decades, it is likely that eliminating the licensing requirement would allow a greater number of qualified participants to spur competition in the legal services market and reduce legal fees, creating substantial economic welfare gains.

Given the increasing ease with which information is transferred, we have good reason to believe that potential clients could privately assess—at least qualitatively—an attorney's quality level. Information culled from the Internet (along with other sources) about a lawyer's track record, level of experience, education, and certification status could serve to educate potential customers quickly and efficiently about that lawyer's credibility and competence. As in most other service industries, potential clients would likely be cautious about hiring someone to perform legal services who cannot provide assessments based on previous work or evidence of certification.

Even if lawyers had no licensure requirements, certification schemes could be used to help consumers find lawyers with certain desirable or unusual capabilities. For example, the National Board of Legal Specialty

Certification provides certification for trial, civil, criminal, family, and Social Security disability lawyers. Of course, individuals claiming particular certification would be subject to general business laws that could result in their being charged with fraud if they were unable to prove certification claims. Over time, consumers would then determine whether one's education, examinations passed, and certification are in fact signals of greater ability and better service, and reward those accomplishments or ignore them accordingly. [Some researchers] have actually found in England and Wales that non-lawyers provided better legal service in civil matters such as welfare benefits, debt, housing, and employment than solo and small-firm practitioners provided.

Current licensure requirements may create only the perception of quality and increase the demand for credentialed lawyers even in situations where the credential does not add social value. [L]icensure may even create a false sense of security if consumers assume that state bar requirements and licensure mandates ensure a certain level of quality that does not really exist.

[T]he benefits from deregulating entry into the legal profession far outweigh any costs. By eliminating mandatory occupational licensing of lawyers in the United States and by forcing law firms to compete with suppliers of legal services that utilize alternative organizational forms, we would expect that competition in legal services would sharply increase, resulting in significantly greater variation in the price and quality of those services. Low-cost lawyers and non-lawyers would advertise their services, engage in aggressive price competition, and create a low-cost market centered on offering basic legal services that do not require extensive training to provide. Other lawyers (and law firms) would undoubtedly attempt to differentiate their services as "high quality" and try to maintain high prices, but most of those lawyers and their law firms would be forced to compete more intensely for clients.

NOTES ON DEREGULATION

1. ***A Good Idea?*** Would you favor deregulating the legal profession? What would be the potential costs and risks of such an approach? Would those costs and risks be likely to vary by the types of clients served? Would it be feasible to deregulate the practice of certain types of law, or at least to lower the regulatory barriers to entry to certain types of practice?

2. ***Can Consumers Adequately Evaluate Legal Services?*** The authors claim that the increasing access to information via the Internet enables prospective consumers of legal services to adequately assess the quality of those services. Is it possible to square that claim the argument that lawyers' services are credence goods? If not, which argument do you find more convincing?

3. ***Consequences for Vulnerable Populations.*** Consider the argument that unlicensed purveyors of legal services sometimes victimize unsophisticated consumers in immigrant communities. Would the kinds of voluntary certification systems and consumer research that Winston, Crandall & Maheshri predict will flourish in a deregulated legal services sector adequately protect such consumers?

D. INNOVATIONS IN THE PROVISION OF LEGAL SERVICES TO INDIVIDUAL CLIENTS

A variety of efforts are now underway to improve access to affordable legal services for ordinary Americans. We have already seen the use of technology, especially web-based tools. Other efforts include simplifying judicial processes to make them easier for consumers to navigate and improving assistance to pro se litigants; allowing lawyers to offer "unbundled" (less than full) services; and encouraging innovations in employer-provided and privately marketed legal insurance programs.

The following excerpt explores such developments and the bar's position on these initiatives:

LEGAL SERVICES FOR ALL: IS THE PROFESSION READY?

Jeanne Charn
42 Loyola of Los Angeles Law Review 1021 (2009)

Private Bar Innovations. The solo and small-firm bar is the main legal resource for middle-income people and serves two to three times more poor people than the not-for-profit, government-funded legal services offices. Forty years ago, resistance and even hostility to government-funded legal aid was the norm in this sector of the bar. In the intervening years, experience has persuaded most solo and small-firm lawyers that legal aid does not draw from their client base. Rather it helps those whom the market cannot serve. As a result, not only has resistance declined, but many solo and small-firm lawyers are now strong supporters of subsidized legal services.

These lawyers practice in challenging, highly competitive markets. Their efficiency and effectiveness in meeting the needs of low-and middle-income clients is critically important to the access agenda because subsidies are not needed when the market can provide good quality, affordable service. Fortunately, service innovations that attract new clients, increase client choice, and control costs are flourishing. Examples include a lawyer who offers "will parties" modeled after Tupperware parties, with price per simple will decreasing as attendees increase. A solo practitioner in North Carolina operates a virtual law office. She provides mainly transactional services to households and small businesses entirely online.

More broad-based changes are under way as well. Discrete task representation, also known as "unbundled legal services," has gained a great deal of attention, including attention in bar ethics opinions, where the trend is clearly in the direction of acceptance and accommodation. Discrete task representation breaks down lawyer services into tasks that a client can purchase a la carte. Services may be provided at a fixed price or at hourly rates. This flexibility gives clients a great deal of control over costs and greater knowledge about what they are purchasing. Both attorneys and clients report high satisfaction with services provided on these terms.

Collaborative lawyers seek to save clients money and emotional turmoil by offering clients the opportunity to commit up front to solve disputes through negotiation, mediation, or other interest-based, non-adversarial means. Clients who choose collaborative lawyers typically agree that litigation is off the table and that if they are unable to reach a resolution, the collaborative lawyer cannot represent either party in subsequent litigation. Family law disputes are particularly amenable to collaborative lawyering, but firms are experimenting with the approach in employment cases and some transactional matters. The ABA supports collaborative lawyering and has addressed its particular features in light of its model ethics rules.

Court Innovations. A revolution is under way in state trial courts dealing with housing, consumer, family, and similar everyday problems of low-and middle-income households. These courts have huge volumes of unrepresented litigants. Prior practice was to urge unrepresented parties to "get a lawyer." In the past decade, however, lower trial courts in state after state have fundamentally altered their processes, staffing, and self-conceptions to facilitate and, in many instances, welcome litigants without lawyers. Courts have developed and funded self-help centers to aid unrepresented parties, hired or recruited pro bono "lawyers of the day" to offer on-site advice to people appearing without counsel, simplified forms and posted them on court Web sites, and changed calendars to better accommodate the schedules of people who work.

Legal Services Innovations. Many LSC grantees and other not-for-profits have embraced hotlines and other sources of limited assistance. For example, LSC has initiated and sustained a competitive Technology Initiative Grants program that fosters new uses of technology in service delivery. Impressive inventories of service innovations are available on the Web sites of LSC, NLADA (National Legal Aid & Defender Association), and the ABA Standing Committee on Legal Aid and Indigent Defendants.

The Legal Aid Society of Orange County ("LASOC") is one of the most innovative providers of legal services in the country. The program's Web site identifies an array of services that include "a hotline intake system, self-help clinics, workshops, on-line court forms," and in-depth representation. Client eligibility is determined via the program hotline, the main access point for those seeking help. In addition, the program offers services that do not require eligibility screening, including a "Small Claims Advisory Program, Legal Resolutions, and LASOC's Lawyer Referral Service."

The LASOC has full-time computer programmers on staff to update its highly effective I-CAN! online forms and Earned Income Tax Credit ("EITC") electronic filing software that allows users anywhere in the country to file for the EITC while at the same time filing their state and federal income tax returns. LASOC innovations are disseminated by LSC and have been adopted by many legal services providers.

NOTES ON CHARN

1. ***Will the Organized Bar Support Innovation?*** Charn identifies a number of reasons to be optimistic about of the willingness and ability of the bench and bar to expand access to legal services by providing innovative ways to deliver legal services other than through a traditional full-service lawyer-client relationship. On the other hand, some of the excerpts that precede Charn's excerpt offer reasons to be skeptical about the bar's support for innovation, and the title of Charn's article suggests her own doubts. Why do you think the bench and some segments of the bar have embraced (or at least tolerated) the reforms that Charn identifies while other segments of the bar have continued to insist on broad prohibitions on unauthorized practice?

2. ***Far Enough?*** Do the developments that Charn identifies in her article go far enough in addressing the need for legal services and the problems caused by the restrictions on unauthorized practice?

3. ***A Bigger Role for For-Profit Enterprises?*** Does Charn underestimate the role that large-scale for-profit businesses, including web-based enterprises, could play in making legal services more readily available to ordinary Americans? Or does she perhaps implicitly underestimate the willingness of the bar to experiment with such changes?

4. ***Law School Clinics.*** Several law schools have started clinics to provide legal information short of full-scale representation. Through the Access to Legal Information (LawHelp) Project at Albany Law School, students act as online LawHelp operators providing "know your rights" materials and referrals to free or low cost legal services to New Yorkers through an instant messaging live chat program. Legal Aid at Work, a San Francisco nonprofit focusing on employment law, runs clinics statewide at which volunteer lawyers supervise students who provide information and referrals to people who visit the clinics seeking employment law advice. A project called Volunteer Legal Assistance for Artists at Arizona State University Law School provides free online legal information for artists, arts managers, curators, and venue owners.

5. ***Apps?*** A number of smartphone apps have been developed to provide legal information. Ask a Lawyer: Legal Help allows users to get preliminary legal advice by chatting with a lawyer for free. Citizenship Works assists immigrants with the naturalization process. Disastr provides disaster relief assistance information, including how to access food stamps, health care, and help dealing with insurance. DOL Timesheet is an app developed by the U.S. Department of Labor to help people check the correctness of information on their paystubs. Stop & Frisk Watch helps New York civilians record police interactions with the public.[25]

The machine learning that causes some to fear for the future employment prospects of lawyers may have potential to improve access to justice. A chatbot, DoNotPay.com, apparently successfully contested 160,000 parking tickets in London and New York in 21 months, and its developer has proposed new possible uses for machine learning in law, including seeking compensation for delayed flights.[26] But critics question the accuracy of some of the advice provided on this and other such services.[27]

E. OUTSIDE OWNERSHIP OF LEGAL SERVICES PROVIDERS

Should Walmart and Target be allowed to hire lawyers to offer legal services in their stores, in much the same way as some of their stores currently hire nurses, pharmacists, ophthalmologists, and doctors to provide medical services in on-site clinics? Should law firms be allowed to seek outside investors in order to increase the size and efficiency of their operations?

Innovations such as these would require changes in the regulation of U.S. legal services markets by allowing non-lawyer ownership, or partial ownership, of organizations that provide legal services. England, Australia and Canada now allow such arrangements, but they are forbidden in the U.S. Most jurisdictions have enacted a version of the ABA Model Rule 5.4, which provides that "a lawyer or law firm shall not share legal fees with a non-lawyer" except in certain limited circumstances; that a lawyer "shall not form a partnership with a non-lawyer if any of the activities of the partnership consist of the practice of law"; and that "a lawyer shall not practice with or in the form of a professional corporation or association authorized to practice law for a profit, if a non-lawyer owns any interest therein. . . ." These restrictions are premised on the idea that allowing a lawyer to practice or share fees with nonlawyers threatens the lawyer's

---

[25] *See* Jason Tashea, *Tech Is Not the Only Answer to Legal Aid Issues,* ABA J., June 13, 2018 (discussing what tech can and cannot do to provide access to justice).

[26] Samuel Gibbs, *Chatbot Lawyer Overturns 160,000 Parking Tickets in London and New York,* THE GUARDIAN, June 28, 2016.

[27] *See* Steph Wilkins, *DoNotPay Is the Latest Legal Tech Darling, But Some Are Saying Do Not Click,* ABOVE THE LAW, Oct. 12, 2018, https://abovethelaw.com/legal-innovation-center/2018/10/12/donotpay-is-the-latest-legal-tech-darling-but-some-are-saying-do-not-click/.

ability to exercise professional independence. The only U.S. jurisdiction that allows any non-lawyer participation in the ownership of a for-profit entity providing legal services is the District of Columbia, which for over twenty years has permitted such non-lawyer participation provided that the non-lawyers are employees of the firm, the firm provides exclusively legal services, and the non-lawyers agree to be bound by lawyers' ethical obligations.[28] In 2009, the ABA created a commission (known as the Ethics 20/20 Commission) to identify and offer solutions for a growing number of ethics issues arising from globalization and rapid changes in technology. One of the issues that the Commission initially identified as worthy of study was the possibility of permitting limited non-lawyer ownership of law firms. It considered several proposals that would have limited the percentage of non-lawyer ownership and required non-lawyer owners to comply with the Rules of Professional Conduct. A discussion paper on alternative practice structures circulated by the Commission cited evidence of substantial market demand for "legal services that firms with nonlawyer partners are well-positioned to provide." It offered as examples "firms that focus their practice on land use planning with engineers and architects; law firms with intellectual property practices with scientists and engineers; family law firms with social workers and financial planners on the client service team; and personal injury law firms with nurses and investigators participating in the evaluation of cases and assisting in the evaluation of evidence and development of strategy." The report also noted that there have been no disciplinary cases involving interference with lawyers' professional judgment by nonlawyers with ownership interests in District of Columbia firms and that "[t]here is simply no evidence that the perceived risk of interference has materialized."[29] Nevertheless, in April 2012, the Commission abandoned the proposal without issuing a report.

The current prohibitions have come under fire from organizations that aspire to develop business models premised on high volume and low costs, but challenges to them have failed. In 2011, for example, the law firm of Jacoby & Meyers filed a lawsuit seeking to overturn the ban on non-lawyer ownership of law firms in New York. The firm argued that the ethics rule against outside ownership is unconstitutional and perpetuates economic inequality because smaller firms do not have the same access to capital markets that large firms do. In 2017, the Second Circuit Court of Appeal rejected the claim, stating (without elaboration) that the prohibition on outside investment "preclude[s] the creation of incentives for attorneys to violate ethical norms, such as those requiring attorneys to put their clients' interest foremost," and therefore serves the government's "well-established interest in regulating attorney conduct and in maintaining ethical behavior

[28] D.C. Rules of Professional Conduct, Rule 5.4.

[29] ABA Commission on Ethics 20/20, *Discussion Paper on Alternative Practice Structures*, Dec. 2, 2011, p. 2.

and independence among members of the legal profession."[30] Can you supply the reasoning that the Court of Appeals did not to explain how the prohibition on outside investment actually serves that interest?

Economist Gillian Hadfield has argued that the proposal considered by the Ethics 20/20 Commission (and ultimately abandoned by it) did not go far enough. She asserts that a much more fundamental loosening of restrictions on the permissible forms of practice is necessary to support the kinds of radical innovation required to bring ordinary Americans the legal help they need. According to Hadfield, the legal profession is due for the kind of major restructuring that medicine has undergone in recent decades, including "larger scale organizations and more creative financial and management relationships between those who provide legal expertise—lawyers—and those who provide many of the other components that go into ultimately delivering legal assistance to people."[31]

Meanwhile, the U.K. Parliament's passage of the Legal Services Act of 2007 has begun to significantly change how legal services are delivered and regulated in the U.K. The act allows law firms to seek outside investment and for companies that are not law firms to offer legal services. Proponents of the law assert that greater competition will drive down prices, create new means for delivering legal services, and improve access to the law. The first major retailer to enter the market was the Co-Operative Group supermarket chain, which operates a national network of supermarkets, banks, funeral services and pharmacies. In 2012, it announced plans to hire 3,000 lawyers to provide consumer legal services.[32] The first U.S. firm to take advantage of changes under the Legal Services Act was Jacoby & Meyers, which in 2013 announced plans to expand to Europe through a joint venture with a London-based firm, MJ Hudson.[33]

In 2007, the Australian law firm of Slater & Gordon was listed on the Australian Stock Exchange. The firm seeks to serve "everyday people" in areas such as personal injury, medical malpractice, employment, workers' compensation, family law, wills, real estate, and class actions.[34] Scholars who have studied Australia's and the UK's experience have found that the firms that took advantage of outside investment and ownership were not predominantly large firms seeking to raise capital. Rather, they were small firms that sought the benefits of non-lawyer management or co-ownership by the spouse of a lawyer. There are differences between the U.K., which

[30] Jacoby & Meyers LLP, Presiding Justices of the First, Second, Third & Fourth Departments, Appellate Div. of Supreme Court of State of New York, 852 F.3d 178 (2d Cir. 2017).

[31] Gillian Hadfield, *The Cost of Law: Promoting Access to Justice Through the (Un)Corporate Practice of Law*, INT'L REV. LAW & ECON. (2013).

[32] *See* Owen Bowcott, *Co-op to Hire 3,000 Lawyers in Challenge to High Street Solicitors*, THE GUARDIAN, May 28, 2012.

[33] Ashley Post, *Jacoby & Meyers to Expand in Europe*, INSIDE COUNSEL, Aug. 14, 2013.

[34] Martha Neil, *Australia's Publicly Traded Slater & Gordon Raising $64M to Buy More UK Personal Injury Firms*, A.B.A J., May 7, 2013.

has seen significant outside investment in law firms, and Australia, which has not.[35]

NOTES ON OUTSIDE OWNERSHIP OF LEGAL SERVICES PROVIDERS

1. ***Would Americans Buy Legal Services from Walmart?*** One journalist has described a vision of what loosened restrictions might mean for U.S. consumers: "Imagine an afternoon trip to a Wal-Mart: You pick up socks, a flat-screen television and a microwave meal. After checking out, you stop in the photo studio at the front of the store for a family portrait, and then shift one booth over to a lawyer, who drafts your will or real estate contract."[36]

Do you think that American consumers would be willing to buy basic legal services through a retailer such as Walmart or Target? More generally, what effects do you think a liberalized rule on outside ownership of the providers of legal services would have on the delivery of legal services to ordinary Americans?

2. ***A Threat to Professional Values?*** Opponents of proposals to allow nonlawyers to invest in law firms argue that nonlawyer owners could influence lawyers' judgments or otherwise erode the profession's ethical obligations of client loyalty and confidentiality. Supporters of the rule change argue that lawyers in law firms already are subject to pressure to focus on profitability and that allowing non-lawyer participation in organizations that provide legal services would not change that fact. Moreover, they argue that nonlawyers in organizations that provide legal services could be required to obey the ethical rules that apply to lawyers, thereby ameliorating concerns about how nonlawyer investment might dilute lawyers' commitments to core professional values. Which set of arguments do you find more convincing?

F. SUMMARY

The chapter explored what it means to "practice law" and considered the vast reach of statutes that prohibit nonlawyers from engaging in the unauthorized practice of law. We addressed the policies that underlie those restrictions and whether and to what extent the restrictions further those purposes. We explored various proposed innovations in service delivery models for ordinary consumers and how some of these approaches conflict with current rules restricting who may provide legal services and what form legal practice can take. Finally, we considered whether corporations should be allowed to offer legal services, much as they now provide banking, real estate, accounting, and even medical services. Such

---

[35] Laurel S. Terry, *The Power of Lawyer Regulators to Increase Client & Public Protection Through Adoption of a Proactive Regulation System*, 20 LEWIS & CLARK L. REV. 717 (2016); Nick Robinson, *When Lawyers Don't Get All the Profits: Non-Lawyer Ownership, Access, and Professionalism*, 29 GEO. J. LEG. ETHICS 1 (2016).

[36] John Eligon, *Selling Pieces of Law Firms*, N.Y.TIMES, Oct. 29, 2011.

enterprises run afoul of ethics rules that prohibit lawyers from sharing legal fees with nonlawyers and forming enterprises with them to deliver legal services.

CHAPTER 20

PRO BONO

■ ■ ■

A. INTRODUCTION

The American legal profession has a longstanding tradition of providing free or reduced price legal services *pro bono publico* ("for the public good"), or "pro bono," to poor people, nonprofit organizations, civic groups, neighbors, friends, relatives, or clients who have fallen on hard times. Two rationales are commonly cited in support of this practice, which many lawyers believe is an ethical obligation. One is that lawyers, as officers of the court, have a special responsibility for the administration of justice. Second, the profession's monopoly on the delivery of legal services is thought to entail a responsibility to distribute some of the monopoly profits to those unable to afford lawyers' services. Some people also note that pro bono service educates lawyers about the legal needs of the poor and thus makes them better informed about the ways in which the administration of justice falls short.[1]

The ethics rules in most states recognize pro bono service as a professional obligation but not a mandatory duty.

As we'll see, lawyers' understanding and practice of pro bono—what it means, what form it should take, whether it should be required, etc.—vary by practice setting and lawyer characteristics. The first part of this chapter explores the role that pro bono plays in meeting the needs of people of limited means. It then addresses how pro bono is defined in different practice sectors, the extent to which various types of lawyers engage in it, and how lawyers' differing interests within the profession affect debates about how much pro bono lawyers should be expected to perform. Finally, we consider proposals to make pro bono mandatory.

B. PRO BONO'S ROLE IN PROVIDING ACCESS TO LEGAL SERVICES

The first two excerpts in this chapter examine the role that pro bono plays in responding to unmet legal needs in this country. The first excerpt considers how pro bono has come to be institutionalized in large law firms and the benefits and limitations of this model of pro bono service. The

1 *See* GEOFFREY C. HAZARD, JR., ET AL, THE LAW AND ETHICS OF LAWYERING 982 (2010).

second excerpt considers how reliance on pro bono as a major component of civil legal assistance for the poor makes that system vulnerable—how the market for legal services can affect the type, quality, and amount of pro bono legal services available to individuals and groups.

THE POLITICS OF PRO BONO

Scott L. Cummings
52 UCLA Law Review 1 (2004)

[In the late 1990s], a radical change [was] taking place in how pro bono services were being dispensed. Whereas pro bono had traditionally been provided informally—frequently by solo and small firm practitioners who conferred free services as a matter of individual largesse—by the end of the 1990s pro bono was regimented and organized, distributed through a network of structures designed to facilitate the mass provision of free services by law firm volunteers acting out of professional duty.

This transformation was apparent at multiple levels. The American Bar Association (ABA) campaigned to make "pro bono a priority," revising the ethical rules on pro bono service, challenging the nation's biggest law firms to step up their pro bono commitments, and supporting the development of a pro bono infrastructure in nonprofit groups, law firms, and law schools. Local bar associations, public interest organizations, and legal services groups expanded programs designed to link unrepresented clients with pro bono volunteers. Big law firms, in turn, augmented their own pro bono systems, creating new pro bono positions, developing innovative projects, and sending their associates to staff public interest organizations and poverty law clinics. Private foundations turned their attention to funding pro bono programs, new ranking systems emerged to track pro bono performance, and states experimented with pro bono reporting requirements. As pro bono infiltrated corporate legal departments and business law practice groups, penetrated small-town communities, and shot across national borders, its transformation could not be ignored. Once confined to the margins of professional practice, pro bono had become radically institutionalized, emerging as the dominant model of delivering free legal services.

Pro bono's institutionalization has depended critically on the rise of the big corporate law firm. Although small-scale practitioners have been important actors in the pro bono system, it has been big firms that have provided the resources and prestige to promote pro bono as a central professional goal. At one level, the big firm's organizational structure provides very practical advantages over smaller practice sites in delivering pro bono services. Since the pro bono model seeks to deploy large numbers of lawyers to provide free services, it relies heavily on the big firm as a mass supplier of pro bono personnel. In addition, because big firms are highly leveraged, they can generally absorb the costs associated with pro bono more readily than their smaller counterparts, which cannot afford to forgo significant amounts of billable work. Finally, big firms have the administrative capacity to coordinate large-scale pro bono efforts that small firms cannot match.

Yet the relationship between pro bono and big firms has not been one-sided, with pro bono programs merely the lucky recipients of big-firm largesse. Pro bono has also provided critical organizational benefits to big firms themselves. Law firms, like other organizational structures, adapt to the demands of their environments in order to gain economic resources. A key resource for big firms is talented lawyers. As part of the intense market competition to attract elite law school graduates, many of whom care deeply about pro bono opportunities, big firms have therefore designed pro bono programs to complement broader recruitment and retention plans.

The first wave of institutionalization occurred in the late 1960s, as rapid law firm growth increased demand for new associates at a time when the lure of exciting new opportunities within the public interest field was drawing the attention of elite law students away from commercial work. There was a widespread perception that elite graduates would not opt for big firms unless they developed programs that provided opportunities to engage in pro bono. As a result, the number of formalized pro bono programs expanded. Some firms assigned partners and committees to screen and coordinate pro bono cases, while others provided attorneys to staff legal services clinics. Particularly in the Washington, D.C. area, the ethos of public service was translated into a number of innovative pro bono programs. A few firms, notably Hogan & Hartson, established full-fledged public interest departments with dedicated staff devoted full-time to pro bono work. Other firms, like Covington & Burling, participated in "release-time" programs which provided full-time lawyers and support staff to maintain a local legal services office. Taking this model one step further, Baltimore-based Piper & Marbury established a branch office in a low-income community to provide pro bono services. Thus, at the height of the federal legal services era, pro bono emerged as an institutionally viable, if still underdeveloped, feature of big-firm practice.

It was not until the 1990s that pro bono became deeply embedded within the large law firm structure. Pro bono's assimilation to big-firm practice came at a time of heightened anxiety about the direction of the profession, which was undergoing a dramatic economic expansion. Indeed, the biggest and most profitable law firms grew even bigger and more profitable during the 1990s.

This growth corresponded to several changes in the internal structure of big firms. The rising volume of business meant that firms needed to hire aggressively. To lure new associates in an environment where increasing numbers of lawyers were defecting to take positions in start-up businesses, investment banks, and venture capital companies, firms significantly raised starting salaries. In order to pay for six-figure starting salaries, law firms raised billable rates and ratcheted up billable-hours expectations for firm associates. Whereas one survey placed the average yearly billable hours of associates in all firms at just over 1800 in the mid-1990s, by 1999, another survey reported that the average had climbed to over 2000.

At the height of the boom, these changes appeared to be taking their toll on big-firm pro bono. In 2000, a front-page article in the *New York Times* reported that law firms were "cutting back on free services for poor," noting that only eighteen of 100 firms surveyed in 1999 had met the ABA guideline of fifty hours of pro bono per attorney. *AmLaw*'s headline in its 2000 survey was "Eight Minutes," which was the number of minutes per day that the average attorney spent on pro bono work. The *National Law Journal* reported that pro bono work in big law firms declined from 2.6 percent of billable hours in 1999 to 2.5 percent in 2000, emphasizing that "based on a 2,000-billable-hour year and a billable rate of $175, the drop represents a thousand pro bono hours at a firm of 300 lawyers, the median number of attorneys at the 250 largest U.S. firms." In addition to decreasing numbers, there was evidence that some firms were also pulling back from pro bono in other ways. For example, San Francisco's Pillsbury Madison & Sutro revised its pro bono policy in response to associate pay increases. Under the newly instituted policy, the first twenty hours of pro bono work did not count toward an associate's required minimum of 1950 billable hours. Many other top firms followed suit, changing their policies to give less credit to pro bono work.

Yet this period of economic growth and competitive pressure, which made pro bono more difficult to perform, also had the effect of deepening its institutional structure within big firms, which moved to shore up their public image and gain a competitive edge in the recruiting wars. As the National Association for Law Placement (NALP)—which distributes a Directory of Legal Employers that is widely read by prospective firm associates—and law schools began publishing information about law firm pro bono activity, firms were forced to take seriously the importance of pro bono as a recruitment device. As a result, big firms began tracking their own pro bono activity, factoring pro bono into firm budgets, and marketing pro bono as part of their recruitment efforts.

The advent of pro bono reporting in the legal trade press accelerated this trend. The *American Lawyer* began reporting data on the pro bono activity of AmLaw 100 firms in 1992, which transformed the way big firms viewed their pro bono programs. Whereas previous discussions of pro bono mostly relied on impressionistic evidence, now fluctuations in pro bono among the elite firms could be tracked on a yearly basis. More importantly, firms were actually ranked based on pro bono performance, which meant not just that recruits could compare pro bono among firms with more precision, but also that firms could make up for weaknesses in other areas by scoring high on pro bono.

The "Law Firm Pro Bono Challenge," launched in 1993 by the ABA-sponsored Law Firm Pro Bono Project, raised the stakes by calling on big firms to contribute 3 to 5 percent of their billable hours to pro bono, and publicizing which firms succeeded in meeting the Challenge and which failed. The Challenge was designed to promote pro bono programs in large firms, requiring signatories to demonstrate their "institutional obligation to encourage and support" pro bono by "promulgating and maintaining a clearly articulated and understood firm policy" and using their "best efforts" to ensure compliance with the 3 to 5 percent goal. In its first two years, there were over 170 signatories to the Challenge, which included many of the nation's elite firms. By requiring specific pro bono commitments and tracking compliance, the Challenge established another public benchmark that became a means to evaluate the relative merits of different firms on the basis of pro bono activity.

The combination of these developments prompted many large firms to augment their pro bono programs as a way to appeal to interested law students, improve their rankings, and facilitate compliance with the Challenge. Firms increased their reliance on pro bono committees, hired full-time coordinators to expand pro bono dockets, formalized pro bono policies, and undertook large-scale pro bono projects. They also cemented relationships with legal services and public interest groups, launched new externship programs, and publicized pro bono achievements on web sites and in annual reports.

[P]rivate lawyers do a tremendous service representing individual poor clients in routine matters and lending their institutional resources to support the reform agendas of public interest groups. Their volunteer work ranges from the mundane to the transformative and includes matters of intense personal interest and immense social import. But the central dilemma of pro bono remains: A system that depends on private lawyers is ultimately beholden to their interests. This means not just that private lawyers will avoid categories of cases that threaten client interests, but also that they will take on pro bono cases for institutional reasons that are disconnected from the interests of the poor and underserved. This is most apparent in the use of pro bono for law firm associate training.

There are other drawbacks to the pro bono system. Pro bono lawyers do not invest heavily in gaining substantive expertise, getting to know the broader public interest field, or understanding the long-range goals of client groups. Particularly in contrast to the way big-firm lawyers seek to understand and vigorously advance the goals of their client community, the partiality and narrowness of pro bono representation is striking. And the disparity of the resources devoted to billable versus pro bono work—which, even at the most generous firm, rarely constitutes more than 5 percent of total hours—underscores the vast inequality in legal services that persists.

The story of pro bono is still being written. As trends of privatization, volunteerism, and globalization press forward, one can expect pro bono to be a growth industry in the years to come, not simply shaping the American system of free legal services, but informing the discussion about equal access to justice around the world. Questions about pro bono's effectiveness as a model for meeting the legal needs of poor and underserved groups will therefore take center stage. It is important that the advantages of pro bono—its decentralized structure, collaborative relationships, pragmatic alliances, and flexible approaches—receive full attention. Yet these advantages must be carefully weighed against the systemic challenges that pro bono poses: its refusal to take on corporate practice and its dilettantish approach to advancing the interests of marginalized groups. Instead of professional platitudes about the virtues of volunteerism, robust debate is therefore in order—debate that includes a full airing of both the promise and perils of pro bono, and provides a rigorous account of what equal access to justice looks like in practice. To avoid this debate invites the uncritical expansion of pro bono as a stop-gap measure rather than a thoughtful response to the dilemma of unequal legal representation. More fundamentally, the failure to confront pro bono's limitations risks privileging professional interests over concerns of social justice—promoting the image of equal access without the reality.

NOTES ON CUMMINGS

1. ***Trends.*** What trends have fostered the development and "institutionalization" of big firm pro bono?

2. ***What Role Does Pro Bono Play?*** In what ways has big firm pro bono contributed toward answering the problem of unequal access to justice in this country? What are the drawbacks of relying on large firm pro bono as a means for addressing this need? According to Cummings, how do the pro bono services that large firms provide compare with those supplied by small firms?

3. ***Benefits for Firms.*** What benefits do large law firms derive through pro bono service, according to Cummings?

LAWYERS' PRO BONO SERVICE AND AMERICAN-STYLE CIVIL LEGAL ASSISTANCE

Rebecca Sandefur
41 Law & Society Review 79 (2007)

A large, and perhaps increasing, share of the civil legal assistance available to indigent Americans reflects lawyers' work in organized civil pro bono programs. Reliance on lawyers' pro bono work renders the stock of legal assistance vulnerable to those factors affecting pro bono participation. Empirical analysis of state-to-state differences in lawyers' participation in organized civil pro bono programs reveals that this activity is sensitive to conditions in legal services markets.

Pro Bono and Professionalism. Legal aid scholars have long expressed concerns that strong connections to the market can corrupt or disable lawyers' charity as a means of facilitating the poor's use of law. Most often recognized have been positional conflicts of interest, which emerge from a lawyer's service to classes of clients whose interests may be opposed, such as landlords and tenants, unions and employers, or merchants and consumers.

Positional conflicts are likely to have their most pronounced effects on the distribution of pro bono effort across different types of legal work. In particular, lawyers appear hesitant to take on pro bono cases that place their firms in positions of conflict between the interests of classes of existing and potential paying clients and classes of pro bono clients. For example, a lawyer in a firm that does legal work for one major banking company may be presented with a potential pro bono client who is a consumer with a complaint against a different major banking company. The concern is that the lawyer, if he or she took the pro bono case, would not give zealous representation and incisive advice for fear of antagonizing the paying client, the bank.

Reliance on charity in a market context may also affect the sheer amount of available assistance, through market conditions' effect on the amount of pro bono performed. Two dynamics, one internal to the organizations in which lawyers work and one characterizing lawyers' relationship with other occupations, illustrate how this can occur. Most simply, lawyers must be able to afford to do pro bono. Work that is billed to a client for less than the cost of performing it must be cross-subsidized by other work if the firm or the lawyer is to survive in business. Lawyers choose which cases to take and which to decline based, at least in part, on the other actualized and potential sources of revenue in their "portfolio" of work, trying to balance risk and potential payoffs. Individual lawyers and law firms likely make at least implicit and informal, if not explicit and highly rationalized, calculations about how much pro bono work they can afford to do.

More subtly, pro bono participation may reflect strategies of market closure and the dynamics of competition between law and other occupations. As in other professions, lawyers act collectively through professional associations and other means to try to ensure that they can make a good living, both by encouraging demand for their services and by restricting the supply of those services. One important way in which they achieve the latter goal is by protecting legal work from encroaching occupations. Pro bono service can be understood as an important element of boundary maintenance.

When lawyers fail to assist indigent clients with their justiciable problems, other occupations—document preparers, estate planners, financial advisors, social workers—can step in to provide services at fee levels (including no fee) that poor people can afford. Historically, competing occupations have sometimes defended their activities by arguing that the high cost of lawyers' services puts civil justice beyond the budget of many ordinary Americans. In response to these concerns, state legislatures have both entertained the possibility of legalizing currently unauthorized practice and have actually done so by recognizing non-attorney providers of limited services in areas of historically legal practice. These legislative actions infringe upon lawyers' powers of self-regulation by taking away some of their authority to define what they do as the practice of law.

Market Conditions. In the analyses here, I focus on those ways in which the market context may affect the amount, rather than the type, of pro bono service provided.

Some lawyers and state professions can more easily afford to provide free services to indigent people because they can subsidize the free services with income from paid work. By this logic, states in which the profession takes in more receipts per lawyer should exhibit higher rates of pro bono service than states in which lawyers bring in less money; one might term this the *cross-subsidy* hypothesis. Cross-subsidy can operate both at the individual level, as individual members of firms or solo practitioners make decisions about how much pro bono work they will do, and at the organizational level, through the presence of "organizational slack." Organizational slack comprises spare resources of funds, technology, skill, and personnel that can be reserved until pressure of work requires them or can be deployed in other activities, such as pro bono service. At the level of states, higher revenues to the legal profession may reflect not only a brisk market for legal services, but also the greater presence of the kinds of legal organizations that perform the most lucrative legal work and accumulate substantial organizational slack, large law firms.

The second way in which conditions in the markets for legal services may affect the amount of pro bono service is through jurisdictional conflicts. If lawyers' pro bono service reflects, in part, an attempt to maintain jurisdictional closure, we would expect states where the legal profession feels that some historically legal work is under threat from other occupations to exhibit higher levels of pro bono service than states in which the profession does not feel under threat; one might term this the *interoccupational competition* hypothesis.

[Sandefur then explained her methods for analyzing the relationship between pro bono service, average per lawyer revenues, and perceived threat of encroachment by other occupations.]

Analysis of the available data suggests that conditions in state legal services markets bear strong relationships to pro bono participation. Higher revenues per lawyer are associated with greater participation in organized civil pro bono programs, as is the perception that the state's legal profession is under threat from unauthorized practice by other occupations. Lawyers' participation in this public service activity appears highly sensitive to the dynamics of legal services markets.

NOTES ON SANDEFUR

1. ***Market Conditions and Pro Bono.*** As Sandefur observes, pro bono has become an essential part of "American style legal assistance." How do conditions in the market for legal services affect pro bono service?

2. ***Positional Conflicts.*** Both the Cummings and Sandefur excerpts refer to how conflicts of interests and business considerations sometimes interfere with law firms' willingness to provide pro bono. Here Cummings explains in more detail how conflicts of interest, and especially "positional conflicts," limit what types of pro bono work large firms pursue:

> Decisions about pro bono are always filtered through the lens of how they will affect the interests of commercial clients. As a threshold matter, pro bono requests are subject to the same screening process that applies to fee-generating cases. Under the Model Rules of Professional Conduct, a private lawyer is generally not permitted to take on a pro bono matter that is directly adverse to another client or materially limits the lawyer's ability to represent another client. In specific cases, these conflict rules can operate to preclude pro bono representation.
>
> Even when actual conflicts do not bar pro bono representation, the specter of so-called positional conflicts presents an additional hurdle. Positional conflicts arise when a lawyer advances an argument on behalf of one client that is directly contrary to, or has a detrimental impact on, the position advanced on behalf of a second client in a different case or matter. Existing ethical rules generally permit representation despite the existence of positional conflicts, stating that a conflict exists only "if there is a significant risk that a lawyer's action on behalf of one client will materially limit the lawyer's effectiveness in representing another client in a different case." [Rule 1.7 comment [24]] This creates a fairly high standard for refusing oppositional work.
>
> Large commercial law firms in theory treat positional conflicts the same in the pro bono and billable context. However, despite the latitude for accepting oppositional cases under the ethical rules,

positional conflicts pose unique barriers for pro bono cases. One reason is that pro bono cases frequently involve claims asserted against businesses, which constitute the economic lifeblood of the big commercial firm. Particularly as corporate clients become more aggressive about ensuring that law firms do not switch sides on important business matters, law firms are reluctant to accept pro bono cases that even appear to adopt antagonistic positions. Moreover, when a positional conflict does emerge, law firms are generally unwilling to sacrifice fee-generating cases for those undertaken for free. Firms therefore tend to take an expansive view of positional conflicts in the pro bono context, making cautious case selection decisions that screen out potentially troublesome pro bono work.[2]

One consequence of law firms declining to take pro bono cases presenting positional conflicts is that the lawyers with the greatest expertise in particular areas—such as employment, consumer credit, or land use law—are the ones least likely to bring their expertise to bear on pro bono projects. This has consequences not only for pro bono clients, who lose the benefit of lawyer expertise, but also for lawyers who would like to use their expertise on pro bono matters as well as for paying clients.

C. WHO DOES PRO BONO, HOW MUCH, AND WHY?

There is plenty of anecdotal evidence that lawyers who participate in pro bono work generally derive satisfaction from doing it. Lawyers' motivations for doing pro bono work vary. Some say that that family background, personal experiences, or volunteer service before law school have shaped their commitment to public service or particular causes. Some report that pro bono provides a welcome diversion from commercial concerns. Some welcome the opportunity to handle a small matter that makes an appreciable and immediate difference for an individual client that is hard to see in the large and complex matters they handle for corporate clients. Some cite professional benefits, including the opportunity to develop new skills and areas of expertise and to build ties in the community.

The following excerpts from two empirical studies—one quantitative and the other qualitative—shed additional light on why lawyers engage in pro bono service and how it relates to their career aspirations and daily practices. These studies also lend perspective to questions about the characteristics of lawyers who participate in pro bono and variations in how lawyers define the concept.

---

[2] Scott L. Cummings, *The Politics of Pro Bono*, 52 U.C.L.A. L. REV. 1, 116–118 (2004).

PRO BONO AS AN ELITE STRATEGY IN EARLY LAWYER CAREERS

Ronit Dinovitzer & Bryant G. Garth
Private Lawyers and the Public Interest: The Evolving Role of Pro Bono in the Legal Profession (Robert Granfield & Lynn Mather eds. 2009)[3]

Pierre Bourdieu's 1998 lecture entitled "Is a Disinterested Act Possible?" provides a useful starting point to situate pro bono activity within the patterns of behavior of actors in the legal field. In contrast to the legal profession's largely promotional and selfless view of pro bono, Bourdieu indicates that actors may invest in such "disinterested" activity while doing so "in accordance with their interests." Activity in a particular field may be *at the same time* interested (as opposed to disinterested) *and* altruistic. Within a Bourdieusian framework, then, one does not merely counterpose altruism to selfishness. Indeed, participation in some realms of social life *requires* actors to engage in what are apparently gratuitous, unprofitable, and altruistic acts, and an actor who has internalized the rules of the game of the field will spontaneously orient his or her strategies according to these underlying stakes and principles.

[W]e wish to draw on this theoretical perspective to better understand pro bono work in the legal field. First, the legal field tends to be structured in order to reward those who work to sustain the legitimacy of the field as a whole. That means that pro bono generally helps to legitimate a system whereby the overwhelming amount of resources work to sustain corporate power and clients with substantial economic means. Second, we posit that there is a division of labor within the legal field such that elites take the lead in promoting the ideals of the profession while also reaping the profits that come from those ideals. They and their law firms, for example, compete to gain recognition for pro bono activity and public service. Third, the rank and file of the profession typically do not have quite the same orientation to those ideals, because ordinary practitioners have to survive and make a living. They need in the first place to build a demand for their services. They are judged within the profession as a whole, however, according to a definition of pro bono that makes more sense in legitimating legal services to large corporate entities. Fourth, the division of labor within the legal field tends to reinforce social advantage and disadvantage. The strategy of investment in professional virtues is relatively more available to those who are socialized in the virtues of *noblesse oblige* and are in a position to implement the strategy. Elite status is confirmed in part because of the enactment of legal virtue—and the apparent distance it provides from the pure commerce of providing legal services.

[3] By permission of Oxford University Press, USA.

THE *AFTER THE JD* STUDY

This [paper] relies on the first wave of data from the *After the JD* (AJD) study, a national longitudinal survey of law graduates. The study is based on a sample representative of the national population of lawyers who were admitted to the bar in 2000 and who graduated from law school between June 1998 and July 2000.

Analysis. We begin by offering an overview of the patterns of pro bono work in the AJD sample. Table 6.1 outlines the distribution of pro bono by practice settings. It is not surprising to find that across the profession, lawyers working in legal services and nonprofits report the highest average hours of pro bono work (261 hours and 80 hours [per year], respectively), though the data suggest that some of these respondents count their regular work hours as pro bono work. Among those working in private law firms, the highest number of pro bono hours—as expected—is found among those working in the largest firms of over 251 lawyers, with about 70 percent of these lawyers engaging in some pro bono work. In these largest corporate law firms, lawyers performed an average of 73 hours of pro bono work in a 12-month period, which is a full 26 hours more than the amount of pro bono work in the settings with the next highest averages (firms of 101–250 lawyers and solo practice). In private law firms we find that pro bono hours decline as firm size declines, though it flattens out among the smaller and larger firms of between 2 and 100 lawyers. Another constituency that reports fairly high levels of pro bono is solo practitioners, with almost 80 percent of these lawyers reporting that they do some pro bono work, and with the average solo practitioner engaging in 47 hours of pro bono service over 12 months.

TABLE 6.1 PRO BONO HOURS BY PRACTICE SETTING

Pro Bono Hours (excluding zero)			Any or No Pro Bono	
	Mean	Median	Some pro bono	No pro bono
Solo	46.58	30	79.60%	20.40%
Private firm 2–20	30.29	20	56.00%	44.00%
Private firm 21–100	29.39	16	47.10%	52.90%
Private firm 101–250	47.29	25	62.50%	37.50%
Private firm 251+	73.27	40	69.80%	30.20%
Government	20.21	10	16.90%	83.10%
Legal services or PD	261.15	20	23.10%	76.90%
Public interest	28.51	20	21.30%	78.70%
Nonprofit or education	80.18	30	41.40%	58.60%
Business	21.32	20	50.50%	49.50%
Other	10	10	46.90%	53.10%

[T]here is a strong relationship between law school eliteness and the settings within which lawyers work, with graduates of the country's most elite law schools obtaining positions in large corporate law firms. As indicated in Table 6.2, the average hours of pro bono peak at 90 hours for graduates of top-ten schools and decline to a low of 31 hours for the *U.S. News* category of tier three graduates; the anomaly is that graduates of *U.S. News* fourth tier law schools engage in more pro bono work than their counterparts from schools ranked 41st to 100th. It may be that graduates of the fourth tier are more committed to pro bono work and will find ways to engage in public service even if their work settings do not explicitly promote or reward it. Alternatively, some may argue that this anomaly may be the result of market forces; fourth tier graduates may be relying on pro bono to account for unpaid client bills or to build up their client base, or perhaps they are not getting as much responsibility and client work as they would like in law firm settings.

The patterns of pro bono work by gender and race reveal some expected and some surprising patterns (Table 6.2): African American respondents engage in the most pro bono work per year (66 hours) and Hispanics (for no apparent reason) the least (37 hours), whereas women on average engage in about 4 more hours of pro bono work per year than men (48 vs. 44 hours). Because practice settings are such strong determinants of participation in pro bono work, we also stratified the race and gender results by practice settings. The data indicate that Black lawyers on average engage in more pro bono service, but only in particular settings; in larger law firms (and especially in the largest law firms), Black lawyers engage in more pro bono work than other lawyers (106 hours in firms of over 251 lawyers compared to 72 hours for white lawyers in these firms), but in small and solo practice the averages are much more similar. Stratifying by firm size also demonstrates that Hispanic lawyers report some of the highest pro bono hours in the largest law firms (76 hours), but that Hispanic respondents working outside of the largest firms report lower pro bono hours than the average lawyer. Thus the earlier finding of lower pro bono hours among Hispanic respondents seems to be due, in large part, to the settings within which they work. The data for women are much more consistent, with women reporting higher hours compared to men in all settings except for solo practice.

TABLE 6.2 PRO BONO HOURS BY LAW SCHOOL TIER, RACE, AND GENDER

	Pro Bono Hours		Any or No Pro Bono	
	Mean	Median	Worked some pro bono	Worked no pro bono
LAW SCHOOL TIER				
Ranked 1–10	89.58	50	71.00%	29.00%
Ranked 11–20	59·33	40	68.30%	31.70%
Ranked 21–40	45.71	20	57.80%	42.20%
Ranked 41–100	37.17	20	60.60%	39.40%
Tier 3	31.42	20	55.40%	44.60%
Tier 4	41.3	20	54.70%	45.30%
RACE				
Black	65·7	30	71.40%	28.60%
Hispanic	36.91	20	50.30%	49.70%
Asian	51.06	30	51.90%	48.10%
White	45.22	20	61.00%	39.00%
GENDER				
Female	48.25	25	60·70%	39.30%
Male	43.58	20	59.80%	40.20%

The patterns we identify above highlight stratification in pro bono service, with graduates of more elite law schools and corporate lawyers in the largest firms more likely to engage in pro bono work. These patterns are closely related to, and in part derive from, different orientations and dispositions toward engaging in pro bono work. As we show in Table 6.3, lawyers who perform the most pro bono work report that pro bono opportunities were an extremely important factor in their job choice: these lawyers report an average of 98.5 pro bono hours per year. In contrast, lawyers who rated pro bono as not at all important in their choice of first job reported an average of 34.5 pro bono hours. We also find that engaging in pro bono activities during law school is related to the number of pro bono hours lawyers perform once they are in the job market, with prior pro bono experience resulting in about 14 more hours of pro bono service per year. Finally, we analyze the patterns of pro bono based on respondents' ratings of their desire to help individuals as a goal in their decision to attend law school. The results in Table 6.3 indicate that although the average pro bono hours are almost identical regardless of their desire to help individuals, 67 percent of respondents who indicated a desire to help individuals engaged in some pro bono work compared to 52.5 percent of those whose desire to help individuals was rated as irrelevant.

TABLE 6.3 PRO BONO HOURS BY IMPORTANCE OF PRO BONO HOURS TO JOB CHOICE, ENGAGEMENT IN PRO BONO DURING LAW SCHOOL, AND DESIRE TO HELP INDIVIDUALS

	Pro Bono Hours (excluding zero)	Percent Reporting any Pro Bono
	Mean	
Pro bono not at all important in job choice	34.49	51.4%
Pro bono extremely important in job choice	98.53	93.1%
Did not engage in pro bono work in law school	40.32	55.4%
Performed pro bono work while in law school	54.2	71.3%
Desire to help individuals as a lawyer rated as "irrelevant"	48.04	52.5%
Desire to help individuals as a lawyer rated as "very important"	48.73	67.14%

Discussion and Conclusions. Our work is situated within a viewpoint that posits a division of labor within the legal field, with elites more likely than the rank and file of the profession both to promote the ideals of the profession and to reap the profits that come from those ideals; the elites are more likely to compete to gain recognition for pro bono activity and public service, and they are rewarded for it.

Our results provide support for this characterization of the legal profession. We find that although lawyers in large law firms engage in more pro bono work, not all large-firm lawyers equally perform this altruistic work. Indeed, our results suggest that elite law school graduates working in the largest corporate law firms engage in significantly more pro bono work than their peers—and this holds when controlling for a full range of factors including the incentives that law firms offer (e.g., counting pro bono work as billable time), work hours, and social background. We also find that engaging in pro bono work is related to lawyers' orientations toward legal practice. We find that individuals who rate pro bono work as an extremely important feature of their job engage in more pro bono hours, and we also demonstrate that elite law graduates are more likely than others to express this disposition.

Our work also explored the contention that there is a value to disinterestedness by investigating the relationship between pro bono work and job satisfaction. Again, our results suggest that engaging in pro bono work brings with it important symbolic and tangible capital for new lawyers. We find that engaging in some pro bono work versus none increases all forms of job satisfaction, but that increasing pro bono hours either decreases or has no effect on job satisfaction; this combination suggests that pro bono provides a symbolic form of capital that is divorced from how much pro bono work one actually does. The data also suggest that pro bono work likely functions in a more concrete way to increase lawyer satisfaction by offering new lawyers substantively interesting work and opportunities to engage with clients—features that are otherwise largely absent from their private law settings.

Our analysis is of course incomplete in some respects. [D]espite documenting the value of disinterestedness, we must clearly also acknowledge that pro bono work provides a good in and of itself, regardless of the secondary value that it might bring to the lawyers who provide it. Therefore, we are not arguing that pro bono work is all "shuck" simply because there is an interest in disinterestedness. What we are positing is that it is important to recognize the value of pro bono so that we can better understand positions of power within the legal profession and how that professional hierarchy is structured and maintained.

NOTES ON DINOVITZER & GARTH

1. ***Eliteness and Pro Bono Ideals.*** What is the relationship that the authors posit between eliteness in the legal profession and pro bono ideals? Does their theory seem plausible to you? Do their preliminary findings support it?

2. ***Pro Bono in Law School and Beyond.*** What do you think explains the relationship between students' pro bono participation in law school and their pro bono participation once in practice?

PRO BONO AND LOW BONO IN THE SOLO AND SMALL FIRM CONTEXT

Leslie C. Levin

Private Lawyers and the Public Interest: The Evolving Role of Pro Bono in the Legal Profession (Robert Granfield & Lynn Mather eds. 2009)[4]

Lawyers in solo and small (2–5 lawyer) firms, who comprise more than 60 percent of all private practitioners, contribute more time and in greater numbers to the pro bono legal representation of persons of limited means than any other group of lawyers. [But] solo and small firms differ significantly from larger firm settings with respect to the ways in which pro bono work is found and performed, the motivations and incentives for performing it, the types of work performed, and the supports available for this work.

Just a few examples of the differences suffice to make this point. In large law firms, pro bono has been thoroughly institutionalized. A lawyer or administrator runs the law firm's pro bono program. Matters are often selected that can be appropriately handled by junior attorneys and that will not create conflicts with corporate clients. Pro bono work performed by large firms is typically performed entirely for free and is supplied to entirely different clients than those ordinarily serviced by the firm. Firm lawyers may be given time off to work exclusively on pro bono matters while still receiving full compensation. They may devote enormous resources to a single case. Large law firms view their pro bono programs as critically important to recruitment of new associates and firm marketing. Consequently, some large firm lawyers feel direct pressure from their colleagues or their clients to perform pro bono work.

In contrast, lawyers in solo and small firms do not have the support staff or associates that are available to large firm lawyers to help them with pro bono work. Some of the pro bono work performed by solo and small-firm practitioners is received from referrals by organized pro bono programs designed to provide free legal services to the poor, but more often it comes through friends, family and existing clients. Because their compensation is very directly tied to what they earn on an hourly or flat-fee basis, every hour these practitioners spend performing pro bono work directly affects their monthly take-home income. Many consider themselves to be doing pro bono when they perform "low bono" work, which involves the provision of legal services at reduced rates to individuals, including regular clients, who cannot otherwise pay. Thus, the very meaning of pro bono in the solo and small firm context is different than in the large firm setting. Moreover, the firm cultures of solo and small firms, and the motivations of lawyers in such firms for taking pro bono cases, are often very different from those in large-firm practices. Pro bono is rarely important for small firm recruiting and may actually be discouraged by firm partners due to economic concerns.

It would be a mistake, however, to think of solo and small firm lawyers as a monolithic group, even in the context of pro bono. They vary considerably in the types of clients they represent, in their level of administrative support, and in their economic success. Some are essentially cause lawyers who deliberately choose to represent underserved populations. Other lawyers build practices serving middle class and wealthier clients in personal plight areas such as family, landlord-tenant or criminal law, which are areas in which underserved populations also need legal assistance. Still others represent organizations and work in the same practice areas found in large law firms. Solo and small firm lawyers do, however, share common concerns about bringing in new business and being able to service their clients' matters diligently and competently. Cash flow is also a constant concern, and can make it difficult for these lawyers to hire as much administrative support as they need. These concerns can raise special challenges when these lawyers contemplate taking on pro bono work.

Exploration of the different mechanisms through which solo and small firm lawyers deliver pro bono services can help to provide a deeper understanding of the meaning of "pro bono" in this practice setting.

Occasional Planned No-Fee Pro Bono. Lawyers in solo and small-firm practice, like large-firm lawyers, participate in formal bar, court or legal services pro bono programs in which individuals of limited means are referred to volunteer attorneys who provide their services free of charge. Some of the planned pro bono work also comes to solo and small firm lawyers through friends and family, or from individuals who simply walk in the door "and tug at your heartstrings." This may be especially common in rural areas, where lawyers personally know many of the people in the community.

Formal Reduced Fee Programs. Solo and small firm attorneys also provide reduced-fee services through formal programs designed to assist individuals of limited means. Reduced-fee programs take two forms. In the first, the lawyer receives the reduced fee from the government or a legal services organization and the lawyer provides legal representation without cost to the client. In the second, which is often run by a bar association, legal services organization, or other non-profit organization, the lawyer receives the reduced fee directly from the client. These programs are grouped together because they both result in lawyers being paid a reduced fee through a formal program that is designed to benefit low income clients.

Perhaps the best-known example of a reduced-fee program in which the government pays the lawyer is court-appointed counsel for indigent clients in criminal cases. A few jurisdictions have also institutionalized judicare programs, which pay private attorneys a low hourly fee to provide legal services to low income individuals in civil cases.

Low Bono Law Practices. A third way in which solo and small firm lawyers deliver legal services to persons of limited means is through law practices that are consciously positioned to service low-income individuals. During the last dozen years, law schools and other groups have worked with solo and small-firm practitioners to organize and support "low bono" law firm practices that provide discounted fee work to clients and take on other cases that may produce revenue through fee-shifting statutes. For example, the Law School Consortium Project is a network of 16 law schools that helps solo and small-firm attorneys who are interested in serving low- and middle-income communities and in finding an economically viable way in which to do so. It created the Community Legal Resource Network, which includes about 800 solo and small-firm practitioners and provides support for these lawyers through mentoring, listservs, and discounted support services, such as electronic research and insurance.

Unplanned Pro Bono: Nonpayers Who Become Pro Bono Clients. When a lawyer has a client who can no longer afford to pay her fees, the lawyer may find herself providing free or reduced-fee legal work, but not always for those who are indigent and not in an entirely voluntary sense. In some cases, the lawyer may feel a desire or a moral commitment to continue to represent the client. In other cases, the lawyer may not feel such a desire or commitment, but cannot readily withdraw from representing a client, especially when litigation is ongoing. Social relations within small communities may also make withdrawal difficult. Ethical obligations to handle client matters competently may require lawyers to continue to perform some legal work, even when it becomes apparent that the client will be unable to pay.

Solo and small-firm lawyers who perform free or reduced-fee work under these circumstances sometimes view it as pro bono work, although it is not recognized as such under ABA Model Rule 6.1(a), which only includes work undertaken without expectation of a fee. Not surprisingly, even though there may be some altruism involved in the continuing willingness to represent the client for little or no compensation, this type of work is often viewed as a failure of the lawyer's business management skills.

NOTE ON LEVIN

Parallel Universes. In what ways is pro bono in solo and small firms different from pro bono in large firms? In particular, what are the differences in the types of work performed, the motivations and incentives for doing the work, and the supports available?

D. MANDATORY PRO BONO

As noted above, the ethics rules in most states do not require lawyers to engage in pro bono representation. Over the years, some advocates of pro bono have argued that lawyers should be required to engage in pro bono as a condition for retaining their licenses to practice. Proponents of mandatory pro bono argue that lawyers, as trustees of the legal system and beneficiaries of a monopoly in the legal services market, owe the public such services. They further argue that imposing a mandatory requirement would inject sorely needed resources into legal assistance programs, and that it would help bring the legal profession's rhetoric into better alignment with its actual practices.[5] Some opponents assert that lawyers should not be required to provide their assistance involuntarily because the needs of the poor are a societal problem that society as a whole should find ways to

---

[5] *See* DEBORAH L. RHODE, ACCESS TO JUSTICE 145–84 (2004).

address. Other opponents argue that mandatory pro bono would not meet its intended purposes because the political compromises that would be necessary to secure bar approval would likely broaden the scope of activities qualifying as pro bono so much that the resulting services would do little to address the needs of the indigent.[6] Some argue that requiring lawyers who are unfamiliar with the problems of the poor to provide legal services to them is likely to result in the provision of low quality services.

NOTES ON MANDATORY PRO BONO

1. ***A Good Idea?*** Should all American lawyers engage in pro bono service? Should pro bono be mandatory—a condition of licensure? Do your answers depend on how pro bono is defined?

2. ***Common Criticisms.*** As noted above, critics of mandatory pro bono tend to suggest that while in principle lawyers are obliged to do pro bono, imposing a mandatory duty on them would be unfair, counterproductive, or impractical. Do you find these criticisms convincing?

3. ***Divisions by Practice Type.*** In a portion of the Levin piece not included in the excerpt above, she notes that solo and small-firm lawyers have strongly opposed mandatory pro bono and have seen it "as something that the elite of the bar was attempting to foist upon them." She also observed that the opposition was likely exacerbated by the fact that most mandatory pro bono proposals define pro bono as free legal services to individuals of limited means—and as not including the types of reduced-fee services that solo and small-firm practitioners often provide to their clients who are unable to pay.[7]

4. ***New York's Rule.*** New York recently adopted a new rule requiring recent law school graduates who apply for admission to the New York bar to demonstrate that they have performed 50 hours of pro bono service.[8] Qualifying pro bono work includes work performed in the service of low-income or disadvantaged individuals who cannot afford counsel, or involves the use of legal skills for an organization that qualifies as a tax-exempt charitable organization under the Internal Revenue Code, or for the benefit of the court system or government agencies or legislative bodies. A student's receipt of academic credit through law school clinics or externships does not disqualify the work.[9]

---

[6] *See* Esther Lardent, *Mandatory Pro Bono in Civil Cases: The Wrong Answer to the Right Question*, 49 MD. L. REV. 78, 100–101 (1990).

[7] Leslie C. Levin, *Pro Bono and Low Bono in the Solo and Small Law Firm Context,* in PRIVATE LAWYERS AND THE PUBLIC INTEREST: THE EVOLVING ROLE OF PRO BONO IN THE LEGAL PROFESSION (Robert Granfield & Lynn Mather eds. 2009).

[8] *See* Anne Barnard, *Top Judge Makes Free Legal Work Mandatory for Joining State Bar*, N.Y. TIMES, May 2, 2012.

[9] *See* New York State Bar Admission Pro Bono Requirement FAQs, Aug. 26, 2013, available at http://www.nycourts.gov/attorneys/probono/FAQsBarAdmission.pdf.

Do you support such a requirement? Should other states adopt it? What are the arguments for and against imposing such a requirement on new bar applicants but not existing members of the bar?

A California State Bar task force recently recommended adoption of a requirement of 50 hours of pro bono service prior to admission, or in the first year of practice, starting in 2016. But Governor Jerry Brown vetoed it, saying that while he supports law students and lawyers providing pro bono legal services, he did not believe that a state mandate could be justified given the high cost of legal education.[10]

5. ***Reporting Hours.*** Some states, including Florida, Illinois, Indiana, Maryland, Nevada, and New Mexico, require the reporting of pro bono hours but do not impose mandatory pro bono.

E. SUMMARY

This chapter explored the concept of *pro bono publico* and its role in meeting unmet legal needs. It considered the benefits and limitations of reliance on large firm pro bono as a means of delivering legal services to poor and otherwise vulnerable individuals, and it investigated how and why lawyers in solo and small firm practices tend to define pro bono differently than lawyers in large firms. We also examined how lawyers' various understandings of pro bono relate to their career aspirations and daily practices. Finally, we addressed whether pro bono should be mandatory—a condition of licensure.

[10] David Siders, *Pro Bono Rule for New California Lawyers? Not So Fast, Jerry Brown Says,* SACRAMENTO BEE, Aug. 29, 2016.

CHAPTER 21

PRACTICING ACROSS BORDERS AND BOUNDARIES

■ ■ ■

A. INTRODUCTION

Not so long ago, American lawyers served primarily local clients on local matters in local courts. It was unusual for lawyers to form partnerships with lawyers practicing outside the state where they lived and were licensed. Today, however, it is common for lawyers to serve clients on matters that span state and national borders and to have partners who practice halfway around the globe. Moreover, many large firm lawyers in the U.S. compete with foreign lawyers in an increasingly global legal services market. Pressure by corporate clients to unbundle legal services and to provide them "a la carte" has created new opportunities for various types of competing service providers. Those competitors include foreign lawyers, non-lawyer service providers (such as accountants), and entities that combine legal and other types of expertise into "multi-disciplinary practices" (MDPs)—a form of practice that is prohibited in most U.S. jurisdictions. Technology has facilitated cooperation and competition among lawyers and other service providers across state and national borders, as work can easily and instantaneously be transported via the Internet. Even cause lawyers are teaming up with one another across national borders to tackle social justice issues.

These changes in the geographic scope of lawyers' services, the types of service providers with whom lawyers compete in global markets, and the role of technology, have raised a host of practical and regulatory issues, which are the primary focus of this chapter. We first consider the issue of multijurisdictional practice—the question of whether and to what extent a lawyer may serve clients in a U.S. jurisdiction other than the one in which she is licensed and, when that occurs, which jurisdictions have authority to regulate and what law applies. We then examine the phenomena of unbundling, outsourcing, and multidisciplinary practice. Finally, we consider circumstances in which U.S. lawyers, especially those serving corporate clients, compete in a global legal services market and interact with foreign-educated lawyers.

B. MULTIJURISDICTIONAL PRACTICE

Admission to the bar in one state does not permit a lawyer to practice law in another. Rather, American lawyers are subject to state-based admission and disciplinary processes. About half the states have reciprocity statutes allowing nonresidents to be admitted to the state's bar without having to pass the bar examination if the applicant's state also does so. But many states, including California, require all lawyers to take the state bar examination in order to practice there.

Unauthorized practice restrictions in every state prohibit non-lawyers from practicing law without a license. But those restrictions generally do not distinguish between lawyers and non-lawyers; a lawyer practicing law in a jurisdiction in which she is not licensed violates unauthorized practice restrictions, just as those without any legal training do. Restrictions on out-of-state practice by lawyers licensed in another state are typically justified on the ground that competence to practice in one jurisdiction does not necessarily guarantee competence in another.

Lawyers admitted in one jurisdiction are sometimes allowed to participate in a specific litigation in another jurisdiction in which they are not licensed by permission of a court. A lawyer seeks permission by filing a motion to appear *pro hac vice* and to provide advice to the client in connection with that matter. Such motions are usually brought by a lawyer already admitted to the court for purposes of bringing a lawyer with special competence into the case.

There are no mechanisms comparable to *pro hac vice* motions to allow for lawyers who provide counseling and transactional services to move across state lines for limited purposes. Moreover, most transactional work takes place in settings that never come to the attention of the bar. As a consequence, while there is no process by which lawyers may obtain permission to provide transactional or counseling services in a jurisdiction to which they are not admitted, there is also no formal court or bar oversight of whether lawyers are doing so. (As we will see, however, a disgruntled client can raise the issue of unauthorized practice by refusing to pay the lawyer's bill or filing a complaint with the bar.) Some critics of restrictive reciprocity standards argue that the ready availability of information about the law of every state undercuts justifications for limiting transactional practice to in-state lawyers based in arguments about local competence.[1]

The current ethics rule on multijurisdictional practice in most states prohibits lawyers from establishing an office or other "systematic and continuous presence" in a jurisdiction in which the lawyer is not licensed

[1] *See* Restatement Section 3 cmt. E ("Modern communications, including ready electronic communication to much of the law of every state, makes concern about a competent analysis of a distant state's law unfounded.").

or "hold out to the public or otherwise represent that the lawyer is admitted to practice in that jurisdiction." However, the rule allows a lawyer to provide legal services "on a temporary basis" in a jurisdiction under certain conditions. Model Rule 5.5. The system of state-by-state licensure based on geography turns on the sometimes perplexing question of whether a lawyer is providing legal services *in* a jurisdiction.

The Katrina Rule. In 2007, in response to unauthorized practice issues arising from the dislocation of lawyers and clients after Hurricane Katrina, when many lawyers moved from Louisiana and Mississippi to neighboring states, and lawyers came from other states to help those in hard-hit areas, the ABA adopted the so-called "Katrina Rule." That rule authorizes out-of-state lawyers to provide pro bono services in a state in which there has been a disaster and allows lawyers from that state to conduct their home state practices in jurisdictions that have adopted the Katrina rule. As of the date this edition went to press, 18 states had adopted the rule.

Virtual Law Firms. What does the current state-based regulatory system mean for lawyers who provide virtual legal services online without brick and mortar offices? Are such practices even permitted? Virtual law firms deliver legal services to clients directly over the Internet and communicate with firm members and co-counsel through secure online interfaces. VLP Law Group, one of the first of these firms, was founded in 2008 by a group of senior lawyers who saw life-style and scheduling advantages in pooling their resources in a single firm while working remotely. VLP's 50-plus lawyers do not work in traditional law offices; most of them work from home or on-site at clients' locations. The firm claims that its smart use of technology and low overhead enable it to provide sophisticated, focused services to clients at competitive rates.[2] Another virtual firm, Axiom Law, does not call itself a law firm (perhaps because doing so would raise questions about the legality of the model) but rather a "global leading alternative legal services provider."[3] It recruits experienced lawyers from major law firms, assembling teams of lawyers to handle discrete client matters for in-house counsel. The firm currently employs more than 13,000 lawyers in seventeen offices in New York, San Francisco, Chicago, Houston, Los Angeles, Washington, D.C., Boston, Atlanta, Toronto, London, Belfast, Frankfurt, Zurich, Hong Kong, and Singapore.[4] The claim that the organization is essentially a temp agency rather than a law firm allows it to raise capital in ways not permitted by

---

[2] VLP Law Group LLP, "Flexible, Value-Driven Approach," https://www.vlplawgroup.com/about/.

[3] Axiom Law, "A New Era of Legal Services," https://www.axiomlaw.com/about-us/our-story.

[4] *See* Axiom Law, "Where to Find Us," at https://www.axiomlaw.com/about-us/global-reach.

law firms—that is, by allowing non-lawyers to participate in Axiom's ownership and management.[5]

If the lawyers who participate in these enterprises are located in different jurisdictions, and the firm itself does not have any physical location apart from the location of its lawyers, it is unclear whether they must comply with the ethics rules in all the jurisdictions in which their lawyers are located and all places where their clients reside. Lawyers who seek to establish and maintain virtual firms face considerable uncertainty about the applicable rules and regulations.[6]

NOTES ON MULTIJURISDICTIONAL PRACTICE

1. ***What Is "Practicing in" a Jurisdiction?*** In an age of geographic mobility and instant communication, what does it mean to "practice law in" a jurisdiction? Does a regulatory system that turns on geographic location make any sense? Would we be better off with a licensing regime modeled on the licensure of automobile drivers, who may freely cross state boundaries so long as they are duly licensed in one state?

2. ***National Standards.*** Would you support proposals to replace the current state-by-state bar admissions process with a uniform national system? Why or why not? Alternatively, should we maintain state-by-state licensing for lawyers who practice in tribunals (for whom some understanding of local rules and practice may be essential), but leave lawyers who handle primarily advising and transactional work to compete freely with one another in a national market? Who would benefit and who would lose under each of these alternatives to the current system?

C. UNBUNDLING AND OUTSOURCING

This section explores recent trends toward disaggregating legal services and outsourcing some of their components to lawyers and non-lawyers trained in other jurisdictions or abroad. As you read these materials, consider the advantages and disadvantages of these developments for consumers and providers of legal services. Please also consider how lawyers and legal educators in the U.S. should adapt to the forces that are driving these trends.

---

[5] *See* Stephen Gillers, *A Profession, If You Can Keep It: How Information Technology and Fading Borders Are Reshaping the Law Marketplace and What We Should Do About It*, 63 HASTINGS L. J. 953 (2012).

[6] *See* Stephanie L. Kimbro, *Regulatory Barriers to the Growth of Multijurisdictional Virtual Law Firms and Potential First Steps To Their Removal*, 13 N.C. J. L. & TECH. ON. 165 (2012).

OUTSOURCING AND THE GLOBALIZING LEGAL PROFESSION

Jayanth K. Krishnan
48 William & Mary Law Review 2189 (2007)

It is difficult to say precisely when American law firms first began outsourcing legal work abroad. News accounts report that over a decade ago the Dallas litigation firm of Bickel & Brewer established a subsidiary in Hyderabad, India, named Imaging and Abstract International, "to scan, abstract and index documents." Throughout the next several years other American firms, as well as some British law firms, turned to cheaper labor markets to handle legal services.

India has received a large amount of attention by those engaged in American legal outsourcing. [There are] three primary business models of U.S. legal outsourcing to India.

The first model involves American corporations outsourcing their legal work to their subsidiaries, a practice which began in earnest in 2001. Among the first of the U.S. companies to start this trend was General Electric. By establishing an in-house legal office in India, staffed by Indian lawyers to handle issues relating to its plastics and consumer finance divisions, GE reportedly has saved over two million dollars.

A second way that legal outsourcing has developed involves American businesses directly hiring Indian law firms. Nishith Desai Associates (NDA) is one of India's best-known tax planning and business law firms. With offices in Mumbai, Bangalore, and now California and Singapore, NDA boasts a client list of over two dozen large, American-based corporations. Rather than relying on lawyers from the United States, these corporations outsource both litigation-related and transactional matters to this Indian firm.

Numerous Silicon Valley law firms have also been directly hiring Indians to write patent applications in order to satisfy the demands of cost-conscious clients. As one well-known San Francisco intellectual property lawyer stated, "I had reservations [about hiring foreign workers], and still do, about holding ourselves out to be the Wal-Mart of patent prosecution . . . [but] [t]he client is happy, and the patents are good, and we're profitable, so it's working out."

Aside from corporations establishing subsidiaries or directly hiring Indian law firms, third party niche vendors are becoming the most significant players in the legal outsourcing field. Sometimes referred to as legal processing outsourcing (LPO) companies, these third-party vendors serve as intermediaries between the American corporation or American law firm looking to outsource and Indians eager to do the work.

The low cost of labor, the surge in information technology, favorable macroeconomic policies, [and] the high quality of workers with advanced educations [make] India [a] fertile ground for American legal outsourcers.

SUPPLY CHAINS AND POROUS BOUNDARIES: THE DISAGGREGATION OF LEGAL SERVICES

Milton C. Regan, Jr. & Palmer T. Heenan
78 Fordham Law Review 2137 (2010)

An announcement on June 18, 2009, by global mining company Rio Tinto sent a powerful message to law firms that the world is changing. The company declared that it had entered into an agreement with legal process outsourcing (LPO) company CPA Global to perform legal work on a scale that would reduce Rio Tinto's annual legal expenses by an estimated twenty percent, or tens of millions of dollars. This work currently was being done by lawyers in the company's legal department. Traditionally, if a company's inside lawyers did not handle legal work, the company engaged an outside law firm to do much of it. Rio Tinto's managing attorney, Leah Cooper, however, explained that the company no longer wanted to pursue that option: "For a long time," she said, "we've been asking law firms to provide us with ways to better control and predict our costs, but at best they offered a discount or a cap in fees . . . . In the end, we decided to take the initiative ourselves."

Rio Tinto's contract with CPA Global represents an initiative in which inside counsel is attempting to manage legal costs by expanding competition for corporate legal work beyond law firms. CPA Global will be doing millions of dollars' worth of work that law firm associates otherwise would be doing. Rio Tinto's standard for using CPA lawyers poses a direct threat to firms: "If you had a junior associate sitting next to you, would you hand the assignment to that junior associate? If the answer is 'yes,' it can probably go to India." The competitive threat to law firms does not end there, however. Rio Tinto is not satisfied with limiting CPA Global to routine work; it wants the LPO increasingly to assume responsibility for more complex matters. As CPA does so, this will mean even less business for outside law firms. Rio Tinto stresses that it will still hire law firms for their "strategic expertise." As time goes on, and LPOs gain more sophisticated expertise, however, that may begin to encompass a smaller and smaller portion of work, which could spell trouble for many of today's large law firms.

To compete in this world, law firms will have to begin considering how they might engage in the same disaggregation process as their clients. That is, they will need to break work down into discrete units and determine who is the most cost-efficient provider of each component. In some cases, that provider may be outside the firm, and the firm will need to engage in outsourcing. Law firms thus might increasingly face the same decision that their corporate clients regularly confront: whether to produce all the goods or services they need inside the firm or contract to obtain them from third parties in the market.

Legal services traditionally have been regarded as relatively "bundled," in the sense that they consist of tightly linked elements that cannot be easily separated. The underlying premise of this assumption is that someone with a distinct sense of legal judgment is necessary to understand how the various elements of a matter are linked together. The corollary is that persons without this perspective are likely to miss legally significant features of information.

Law firms, however, have been decomposing their work within the firm for quite some time. They delegate responsibility for discrete aspects of a case or a transaction to a variety of people, both lawyers and non-lawyers, in what we might think of as a supply chain.

Ideally, this division of labor reflects an effort to direct work to the least costly person who can perform it and to maximize use of the distinct set of skills that each person can deploy. Furthermore, the allocation of responsibility has shifted over time, as junior partners now do what senior partners used to, senior associates do work formerly done by junior partners, junior associates complete the tasks that used to be done by senior associates, paralegals take on responsibilities formerly borne by junior associates, and technology substitutes for some tasks paralegals used to do. Law firms also increasingly have begun to use contract lawyers as part of these teams. They have looked, in other words, to workers outside the firm so that they can use even lower-cost personnel to perform services, both to reduce costs to clients and to avoid high fixed overhead in the face of fluctuating demand.

The emergence of LPOs in recent years provides further evidence that such decomposition is feasible. Consider, for instance, the range of different activities in which CPA Global engages. It includes preparing summonses and complaints, interrogatories and requests for production of documents, motions, witness kits, timelines of events and exhibits, deposition summaries in various formats, memoranda of law, legal briefs, letters to third parties presenting a legal position, multijurisdictional surveys of laws, and annotated summaries of cases. Its document review and management services include analysis and identification of documents for due diligence purposes, materiality in litigation, and privilege in response to discovery requests. Contract management includes drafting, revising, summarizing, and analyzing contracts.

Pangea3, another major LPO, performs a similar range of tasks, which includes merger and acquisition due diligence reports on companies' potential or existing liabilities; drafting contracts such as nondisclosure agreements, vendor contracts, supply agreements, software license agreements, telecommunications service agreements, office leases, and internet, advertising, and media agreements; and litigation document organization and review.

Assuming that some decomposition of services is feasible, law firms must then determine which tasks are most suitable for completion by persons inside and outside the firm. That is, which resources are integral to the firm's performance of its core functions and which are not? In general terms, the basic function of law firms is to provide legal services, with specific firms defining their core functions in different ways depending upon the types of practices on which they focus. Law firms confront a threshold challenge, however: it is not entirely clear exactly what constitutes legal services. The organized bar has been notoriously unsuccessful in defining the practice of law in order to exclude non-lawyers from engaging in what lawyers traditionally have done. Other occupations increasingly are furnishing services that formerly were provided only by lawyers, such as tax advice, estate planning, organizing responses to requests for production of documents, litigation case assessment, and legal compliance monitoring. Legal process outsourcing companies are becoming involved in an expanding range of activities, which include legal research, contract analysis, preparation of questions for depositions and trial, and creation of legal documents.

The San Diego County Bar Association, for instance, has held that a firm in India was not practicing law in California when it took responsibility for conducting legal research, developing case strategy, preparing deposition outlines, and drafting correspondence, pleadings, and motions in an intellectual property dispute in San Diego Superior Court. The Bar Association noted that "when the client asked how the attorneys developed the theory on which summary judgment was granted, and had done the work so inexpensively, the attorney told him that virtually all of the work was done by India-based Legalworks." As long as the two-lawyer California law firm that engaged Legalworks retained control over the case and reviewed the draft work performed by the contractor, the Indian company was deemed to be assisting a California lawyer in practicing law in the state, not engaging in the practice of law itself.

The difficulty in defining law firm core functions raises a fundamental question: Why would a client engage a law firm rather than contract directly with LPOs or other specialized suppliers to obtain the services it needs? What do law firms offer that a client cannot obtain from a collection of providers who furnish particular types of services?

Law firms will need to articulate reasons why clients should turn to them rather than other professionals for such assistance. On a more general level, the continuing advance of disaggregation would create even more ambiguity about what skills distinguish lawyers from other occupations.

This trend reflects the maturation of the legal services sector into a highly competitive industry driven more forcefully than ever by pressures for efficiency. How law firms, clients, and organizations connected with this industry respond could shape not only the future of law firms, but of the legal profession itself.

* * *

More recent research on unbundling and outsourcing found that the variety and types of legal work outsourced to India is growing. Most of this work is still in areas that can be broken into pieces and replicated, such as document support, litigation support, and patent drafting, but some more skilled work, such as appellate brief writing and drafting contracts, is also being outsourced. And while India receives a very large share of outsourced business, LPOs are also operating in other places, such as South Africa, Latin America, and the Philippines.[7]

NOTES ON UNBUNDLING AND OUTSOURCING

1. ***Drivers of Outsourcing.*** What factors explain the growth in outsourcing of legal services from the U.S. to India and other low-cost countries? Note that some of the same outsourcing companies that have been sending work to India also have recently begun to hire lawyers in lower-cost areas of the U.S., such as Texas, West Virginia, North Dakota, and Kansas. A 2011 *N.Y. Times* story reported that Pangea3 had hired hundreds of American lawyers in Carrollton, Texas. The story also noted that many of Pangea3's competitors were also hiring steadily in depressed regions of the U.S.[8]

2. ***Unbundling.*** What economic forces are causing law firms to unbundle legal services? How does the challenge of identifying skills that differentiate lawyers from other types of service providers relate to the trends described in the Regan & Heenan excerpt?

3. ***Outsourcing and Unauthorized Practice.*** In 2008, the ABA issued an opinion finding that LPO does not constitute unauthorized practice if a U.S. qualified lawyer is supervising the outsourced work.[9] The California Bar has similarly opined that legal work is assistance rather than unauthorized practice if it is adequately supervised or reviewed by a lawyer admitted in California and if the California lawyer retains control of the case

---

[7] Vikramaditya Khanna, *The Evolving Global Supply Chain for Legal Services: India's Role as a Critical Link,* in THE INDIAN LEGAL PROFESSION IN THE AGE OF GLOBALIZATION (David Wilkins, Vikramaditya Khanna & David Trubek eds. 2017).

[8] *See* Heather Timmons, *Where Lawyers Find Work*, N.Y. TIMES, June 3, 2011, B1.

[9] ABA Formal Opinion 08–451, Lawyer's Obligations When Outsourcing Legal and Nonlegal Support Services (August 5, 2008).

or matter. How should the bar decide how much supervision or control is enough?

4. ***The Growth of LPO.*** Legal process outsourcing has continued to grow since these articles were published. The two LPO service providers identified in the Regan and Heenan article, CPA Global and Pangea3, now compete with Integreon, UnitedLex Corp. Elevate Services, Inc., and others. Industry analysts estimate that the LPO market will exceed $40 billion by 2024.[10] Legal process outsourcing is just one aspect of dramatic recent changes in the structure of legal services. We will consider more of those changes in the book's final chapter.

5. ***Client Consent.*** Should law firms that outsource work to foreign lawyers or to lawyers working in other U.S. jurisdictions be required to notify clients of the outsourcing arrangements and obtain their consent? The ABA's 2008 opinion provides that outsourcing may be permissible as long as the in-state lawyer makes appropriate disclosures to the client regarding the use of lawyers or non-lawyers outside of the lawyer's firm, and gains client consent if those to whom work will be outsourced will have access to confidential information.[11] Does the ABA opinion take the right approach?[12]

6. ***Professional Prestige in the Indian Outsourcing Industry.*** Swethaa Ballakrishnen's research shows a notable rise in prestige accorded to jobs in the Indian legal process outsourcing industry since its introduction just a few years ago. Ballakrishnen explains that, while much of the work is routine, its connection to leading brand name Western companies and its status as international work has afforded it a kind of "halo" prestige. Employees of these outsourcing firms also find advantages in Western work environments (large U.S.-law-firm-style offices in high-prestige business district spaces), in Western business cultures (with clear work trajectories and more transparent promotion policies than those of the typical family-run legal offices in India), and in interaction with foreign-trained lawyers. In short, she finds that "working for an LPO firm ha[s] become a real legal career option for many who would have never coveted the position before: a viable alternative to domestic legal jobs."[13]

---

[10] Global Market Insights, Inc., *Legal Process Outsourcing Market to Hit $40 billion by 2024*, May 8, 2017, https://globenewswire.com/news-release/2017/05/08/979979/0/en/Legal-Process-Outsourcing-Market-to-hit-40bn-by-2024-Global-Market-Insights-Inc.html.

[11] ABA Formal Opinion 08–451, Lawyer's Obligations When Outsourcing Legal and Nonlegal Support Services (August 5, 2008).

[12] In 2012, the ABA adopted a resolution adding new commentary to Model Rules 1.1, 5.3, and 5.5 to clarify how these rules operate within the context of outsourcing arrangements. ABA Resolution 105(c).

[13] Swethaa Ballakrishnen, *'I Love My American Job': Professional Prestige in the Indian Outsourcing Industry and Global Consequences of an Expanding Legal Profession*, 19 INT'L J. LEGAL PROF. 379 (2012).

D. MULTIDISCIPLINARY PRACTICE

Most U.S. jurisdictions forbid lawyers to join forces with other service providers, such as accountants, engineers, social workers, business consultants, and economists, to address clients' complex needs through multidisciplinary practices ("MDPs"). Most jurisdictions follow some version of an ethics rule which provides that "a lawyer or law firm shall not share legal fees with a non-lawyer" except in certain limited circumstances. Model Rule 5.4. These restrictions are premised on the idea that allowing a lawyer to practice or share fees with non-lawyers threatens the lawyer's ability to exercise professional independence because the lawyer may be tempted to recommend the MDP's services to clients even if those services are of lower quality than available alternatives. Critics of MDPs also argue that these institutions are unlikely to honor other ethical rules that lawyers must obey (such as rules on conflicts of interests and confidentiality) and that they will exert pressure on lawyers to bend to MDPs' business imperatives. They also argue that mixing legal services with other types of services is likely to jeopardize application of the attorney-client privilege, which covers only communications between lawyers and clients (and their agents).

Large accounting firms have long employed lawyers as full-time employees to serve their clients, but they have taken the position that these lawyers are providing tax advice, not legal advice. (Accountants are authorized to provide tax advice and to advocate regarding tax matters before the Internal Revenue Service.) The distinction between tax advice and legal advice is indistinct in practice. But accounting firms have successfully maintained that this distinction allows them to escape the reach of unauthorized practice restrictions and rules prohibiting lawyers from sharing fees with nonlawyers and entering into law practice with them.

In the 1990s, major international accounting firms appeared to be well-positioned to become significant players in the global legal services industry. However, accounting scandals arising out of the 2001 financial crisis led to regulatory reforms that limited the ability of the big accounting firms to provide non-auditing services to their audit clients. These developments temporarily prevented accounting firms from becoming major players in law, but, as explained in the following excerpts, they are making a comeback.

THE RISE, TRANSFORMATION, AND POTENTIAL FUTURE OF THE BIG 4: ACCOUNTANCY NETWORKS IN THE GLOBAL LEGAL SERVICES MARKET

David B. Wilkins & Maria J. Esteban Ferrer
The CLS Blue Sky Blog, Sept. 26, 2017

Throughout the 1990s, the Big 5 accounting firms made a concerted effort to enter the legal services market. By the close of the twentieth century, legal networks directly owned or closely affiliated with the Big 5 were major players in many markets around the world, and were threatening to enter those like the United States from which they were still barred. However, after the wave of accounting scandals arising out of the 2001 financial crises—scandals that brought down Arthur Andersen and ushered in regulatory reforms in the United States and other major economies that appeared to place severe restrictions on the ability of the now Big 4's ability to offer non-auditing services to their audit clients—most observers concluded that the accounting firms' legal networks were effectively dead. As a result, both practitioners and academics stopped paying attention to what these firms were doing in law.

Our research, however, points to a quite different conclusion. [A]s Mark Twain might say, that the reports of the death of the Big 4's legal ambitions have been greatly exaggerated.

Hiding in Plain Sight. In the immediate aftermath of the Sarbanes-Oxley Act, the Big 4 appeared to confirm that they had abandoned their efforts to become important players in the market for legal services, publicly declaring that they were unwinding their legal networks. Notwithstanding these public pronouncements and some initial actions to disband their legal arms, however, over the last decade the Big 4 have quietly rebuilt their legal networks to the point where they are now larger than they were in 2002. [B]y May 2016, PwC had established legal practices in 85 countries worldwide and KPMG in 53 countries, while Deloitte and EY each had legal practices in 73 countries. Taken together, a total of 106 countries are currently hosting at least one of the Big 4's legal practices, giving them a significant presence in every important legal market in the world

Nor are the legal services delivered by these networks confined to tax. Although tax-related advisory services remain an important cornerstone, the Big 4 legal networks are now delivering services in a broad range of legal fields, including premium practices such as finance and M&A, and fast-growing ones such as compliance and employment law. The success of this strategy is evident from the growth in size, profitability, and prestige of the Big 4's legal networks in recent years. In France, Spain, Italy, and Russia, for example, law firm rankings now put the Big 4's legal practices in the top 10 in terms of revenue. In Germany and the UK, the Big 4 are showing double-digit annual revenue growth. The Big 4's progress in emerging markets is even more impressive. In 2015, for example, EY Law's network firm in China—EY Chen & Co.—was ranked in the top third for "Eminent Performance" in capital-market related legal services. That same year, PDS Legal—EY's law network firm in India—was ranked among the top-10 advisors in completed M&A deals.

To support this expansion, the Big 4 have returned to the kind of lateral recruiting of star lawyers not seen since the 1990s, luring top lawyers away from leading law firms such as Freshfields Bruckhaus Deringer, Linklaters, and King & Wood Mallesons. As impressive as this lateral hiring spree is, however, the fact that the global leaders of the Big 4's legal networks have all grown up inside these organizations underscores their strong commitment to integrating these practices into the broader culture and practices of their global multidisciplinary network.

Finally, and most important, beginning in January 2014 PwC, KPMG, and EY have all filed applications to launch an "Alternative Business Structure" (ABS) that will allow them to provide legal services in the UK under the new law that allows for organizations not exclusively owned and controlled by lawyers to deliver legal services. Significantly, two of the three—EY and KPMG—have now been granted a license to become a "multidisciplinary professional service firm," under which they are now entitled to provide a mix of legal and non-legal services to clients.

More than a decade after they were proclaimed dead by most pundits—the Big 4's increasingly integrated and expansive legal networks are alive and well in the global market for legal services.

How Did this Happen? Looking back, we believe that four interrelated factors have allowed the Big 4 accounting firms to expand their legal offerings notwithstanding efforts to prevent them from doing so. First, while Sarbanes-Oxley and other related statutes severely restrict the Big 4's ability to sell non-audit services, these laws do not prohibit them from the legal market altogether. While accounting firms are barred from selling legal and other non-audit services to their audit clients, nothing prevents them from marketing such services to non-audit clients, which they all now aggressively do. Second, combined with this important gap in the regulation of auditor independence, as the UK reforms cited above underscore, the regulation of the legal profession has become increasingly open to entities not owned or controlled solely by lawyers providing legal services. The General Agreement on Trade in Services (GATS) with its emphasis on encouraging the free flow of professional services has only reinforced this trend. As a result, the kind of multidisciplinary practice championed by the Big 4 is now expressly legal in many major legal markets, most importantly in the UK. At the same time, the Big 4 have been able to exploit loopholes in the regulation of the legal profession in emerging economies where this regulatory framework is far less developed than it is in the West to establish their legal practices.

This last development underscores the third factor that has allowed the Big 4 to reemerge as important players in law: globalization. As multinational companies have rapidly expanded their operations around the globe, they have increasingly looked for professional service firms that can provide these sophisticated entities with consistent services—including legal services—across their entire platform. Given their extensive experience in marshaling global resources, the Big 4 are in an ideal position to meet this need. This is particularly true in the rapidly growing emerging markets in Asia, Latin America, and Africa, where few law firms can credibly claim to provide comprehensive service—and those that claim to have this capacity often do so through a set of loosely affiliated offices. Although the Big 4 were the first to pioneer th[e] Verein structure, the accountancy networks have taken concerted steps over the last two decades to move away from this structure in favor of one that emphasizes greater integration of their multidisciplinary practices. This evolution of the Big 4's business model constitutes the fourth—and potentially the most important—reason for their reemergence as significant players in the market for legal services, one that could hold the key to their long-term success this time around.

It has taken decades for the Big 4 to elaborate their MDP structure into a robust organizational model. [T]his evolution [has been] from a "nascent MDP model" in the 1980s, where the Big 4 first began to build up their legal capacity to sell to their existing audit clients, to the fully "integrated solutions model" they purport to use today, which is designed to leverage their strong capabilities in information technology, process management, and their global reach to provide "globally integrated business solutions" to global clients—with legal services bundled as part of the global solution.

To be sure, the promise of fully integrated business solutions may still be more rhetoric than reality. Nevertheless, it is a promise that is likely to appeal to companies who have been seeking lawyers who "understand the company's business" in the years following the global financial crisis. Similarly, the Big 4's promise of providing a better model of professional development is also likely to appeal to many young lawyers who have become disenchanted with what they perceive as the oppressive environment of many large law firms. But the greatest force propelling the Big 4's integrated solutions model may be their embrace of technology. Deloitte's investments over the past several years in this area are illustrative of this trend. In 2014, Deloitte purchased ATD Legal, one of the few providers of managed document review services in Canada. In 2016, they followed with a purchase of Conduit Law, a provider of outsourced lawyers ranked by the Financial Times as one of the "Most Innovative

North American Law Firms." Most recently, Deloitte formed a strategic alliance with Kira Systems, which has been described by the company's chief executive, Noah Waisberg, as "the largest professional services AI [artificial intelligence] deployment anywhere, period." PwC's recently announced partnership with General Electric provides one example of what a managed legal services future might look like. In 2017, PwC signed an agreement with GE to provide integrated, enterprise managed tax services on a global basis for a five-year period. As part of the deal, PwC agreed to hire more than 600 members of GE's tax team, including many lawyers. PwC announced that these individuals will not only service GE, but will also be available for other clients. To be sure, most of the tax work that PwC will be doing for GE would not be considered premium by the tax departments of most top law firms. But as the global head of one of the Big 4's legal arms underscored, their goal is not to concentrate on "bet the company" cases, as most large law firms obsessively do, but instead on "run the company" cases. Such a strategy will give the Big 4 a seat at the table as companies strive to rein in the cost of providing legal and other related services in the new global age of more for less.

The Future? Whether these and other similar moves by the Big 4 will enable these newly energized players to significantly disrupt the market for corporate legal services remains to be seen. Important obstacles ranging from potential conflicts of interest, to regulatory backlash, to internal resistance in companies to relying too heavily on a single professional service provider could yet again derail the Big 4's ambitious plans. For now, we simply conclude by urging that academics and practitioners pay greater attention to how these important players are attempting to redraw the boundaries of professional services, and to how law firms, clients, and regulators respond to the potentially disruptive, but still largely unexplored, changes that the Big 4 are bringing to the global legal services market.

* * *

The ABA has more than once considered and rejected proposals to permit MDPs. The ABA Commission on Multidisciplinary Practice, established in 1998, proposed allowing some limited forms of MDPs. But in 2000 the ABA House of Delegates soundly defeated that proposal and instead urged states to reaffirm their commitment to enforce unauthorized practice restrictions and prohibitions on fee sharing. The Ethics 20/20 Commission considered a proposal to permit alternative practice structures, but it abandoned the proposal in 2012.

The United Kingdom and Australia now allow multidisciplinary practice arrangements. In the 2007 UK Legal Services Act, the United Kingdom authorized lawyers to engage in multidisciplinary practice and to work in law firms owned by non-lawyers. In 2012, the United Kingdom

Solicitors Regulation Authority began issuing licenses for "alternative business structures" (ABSs). These are organizations that are more flexible than traditional law firms in the following respects: lawyers and non-lawyers can share the management and control of the business; the entity can allow external investment and ownership; and the organization can offer multiple services to clients, including legal services, from within the same entity. The Solicitors Regulation Authority already has issued hundreds of licenses to alternative business structures.[14] While many of the ABSs were existing law firms that converted to the ABS status, the removal of restrictions on the ownership of law firms has also enabled many new entrants into the market, including multi-disciplinary practices, supermarkets, and union-owned firms providing legal and other types of services for union members.[15]

NOTES ON MULTIDISCIPLINARY PRACTICE

1. ***A Good Idea?*** Would you favor allowing nonlawyers to invest in legal businesses and permitting the creation of MDPs? Why or why not? Are you persuaded by critics who warn that lawyers employed in firms partially owned by nonlawyers will be less likely than lawyers in private law firms to obey rules of professional conduct? Some scholars have concluded that the experimentation promoted by the UK Legal Services Act has produced benefits for consumers in terms of innovation and reduced cost.[16]

2. ***Global Competition.*** Do you agree with those who argue that the U.S. legal profession's strict limitations on fee sharing and permissible forms of practice put U.S. firms at a serious competitive disadvantage in the global market for legal services?

E. TRANSNATIONAL PRACTICE

Many American lawyers seek to serve foreign clients or to handle disputes and problems that have international implications. Similarly, foreign lawyers seek opportunities to practice within the United States and/or to give advice about U.S. law abroad.

In the corporate legal services market, global competition is commonplace. The global legal services market was valued at nearly $849 billion in 2017.[17] The United States International Trade Commission has

---

[14] *See* Centre for Strategy & Evaluation Services, *Impact Evaluation of SRA's Regulatory Reform Programme: A Final Report for the Solicitors Regulation Authority* 11, https://www.sra.org.uk/sra/how-we-work/reports/abs-evaluation.page.

[15] *Id.* at 13–16.

[16] *See* GILLIAN K. HADFIELD, RULES FOR A FLAT WORLD 241–45 (2017); Judith A. McMorrow, *UK Alternative Business Structures for Legal Practice: Emerging Models and Lessons for the U.S.*, 47 GEO. J. INT'L L. 665 (2016).

[17] The Business Research Company, *Legal Services Global Market Opportunities and Strategies to 2021,* https://www.thebusinessresearchcompany.com/report/legal-services-market.

estimated that the U.S. exported $9.0 billion in legal services in 2015.[18] Of the world's 100 highest grossing firms, 77 have more of their lawyers in the U.S. than anywhere else, and 12 have the greatest share of their lawyers in the U.K.[19]

As global firms pursue clients and business opportunities around the world, they sometimes encounter restrictive policies toward foreign lawyers. U.S. trained lawyers who want to provide legal services overseas often face rules that sharply limit the practice of foreign firms. Some jurisdictions, such as Korea, Singapore, Malaysia and India, have recently liberalized access to their legal services markets by foreign lawyers, but bar associations in other countries, such as Brazil and Vietnam, have called for more restrictions on foreign law firms.[20] Similarly, while most states in the U.S. allow lawyers who have been trained abroad to practice as "foreign legal consultants" in the U.S. and to advise about the laws of their home country, non-U.S. lawyers still are subject to state-by-state regulation that restricts their access to the U.S. market.

Global law firms—firms with offices and lawyers stationed around the world—may be better positioned than domestic firms to take advantage of trends toward globalization of the economy. Corporate law firms have grown quickly since the 1980s. One such firm, U.S.-based Baker & McKenzie, has seventy-seven offices in forty-seven countries, including Indonesia, Malaysia, Vietnam, Bahrain, Kazakhstan, and Azerbaijan.[21] Similarly, U.K.-based Clifford Chance has 33 offices in 22 countries, including Romania, United Arab Emirates, and Morocco.[22] The notion that global law firms might hold advantages in competing for lucrative corporate legal work has fueled some international law firm mergers, as firms have tried to build a global presence across key markets, including emerging markets. In 2012, for example, China's King & Wood merged with Australia's Mallesons Stephen Jaques into the firm of King & Wood Mallesons,[23] and in 2013, King & Wood Mallesons merged with SJ Berwin, a U.K. firm with a strong European and Middle East practice, to form a

---

18 UNITED STATES INTERNATIONAL TRADE COMMISSION, RECENT TRENDS IN U.S. SERVICES TRADE, 2017 ANNUAL REPORT 105 (2017).

19 *The 2018 Global 100*, AM. LAW., Sept. 2018, https://www.law.com/americanlawyer/2018/09/24/the-2018-global-100-ranked-by-revenue/.

20 *See* Luciana Gross Cunha, Daniela Monteiro Gabbay, Jose Garcez Ghirardi, David M. Trubek and David Wilkins, THE BRAZILIAN LEGAL PROFESSION IN THE AGE OF GLOBALIZATION 25 (2018); Elizabeth Broomhall, *Foreign Law Firms in Vietnam Face Pushback from Local Practices*, LegalWeek, Dec. 6, 2012 http://www.legalweek.com/sites/legalweek/2012/12/06/foreign-law-firms-in-vietnam-face-pushback-from-local-practices/.

21 Baker & McKenzie, *Passionately Global*, http://www.bakermckenzie.com/.

22 Clifford Chance, *People and Locations*, https://www.cliffordchance.com/people_and_places.html.

23 Hildebrandt Consulting LLC, *2013 Client Advisory*, available at http://hildebrandtconsult.com/uploads/Citi_Hildebrandt_2013_Client_Advisory.pdf.

2700-lawyer firm.[24] The U.K.'s Norton Rose merged with Australian, Canadian and South African firms before joining with U.S.-based Fulbright & Jaworski to form Norton Rose & Fulbright, a 3800-lawyer firm.[25] In 2015, Dentons merged with Dacheng Law Offices of China, to form a firm with 6,500 lawyers in more than 50 countries.[26] In 2017, Dentons expanded its global footprint by acquiring firms in Scotland, the Netherlands, Mexico, Peru, Uganda, Myanmar, and Uzbekistan,[27] and in 2018 its partners voted to combine with firms in Kenya, Mauritius, Indonesia, Malaysia, the Cayman Islands, and Barbados.[28] The firm now employs approximately 7,800 lawyers. Many recent mergers take the form of loose organizational structures called vereins, in which the merged entities remain financially independent.[29]

Law firms that do not have offices abroad nevertheless often participate in international legal networks.[30] The largest of these networks, Lex Mundi, has 21,000 lawyer members and 160-member firms in more than 100 countries.[31]

British solicitor firms, especially the so-called "Magic Circle" firms based in London, drove the initial competition for work associated with the global business expansion into the developing world. U.S. firms followed, initially emphasizing nonlocal law but more recently competing for both local and transnational business.[32] U.S.-based global law firms employ not only U.S. trained and licensed lawyers but also many host-educated lawyers, who bring deep knowledge of and relationship with clients, professional and regulatory actors, and the legal framework.[33]

Lawyers in emerging markets who want to practice in international contexts sometimes seek advanced degrees in the U.S. as a way to signal

---

[24] Elizabeth Broomhall, *SJ Berwin-King & Wood Mallesons Merger Gets Green Light Creating $1 Billion Global Giant*, LEGALWEEK.COM, July 31, 2013.

[25] Brian Baxter, *Report: Law Firm Mergers Poised for Record Year in 2013*, THE AM LAW DAILY, July 8, 2013, available at https://www.law.com/americanlawyer/almID/1202609982829/.

[26] Neil Gough, *Dentons to Merge with Dacheng of China to Create World's Largest Law Firm*, N.Y. TIMES, Jan. 27, 2015, https://dealbook.nytimes.com/2015/01/27/dentons-to-merge-with-dacheng-of-china-to-create-worlds-largest-law-firm/.

[27] Elizabeth Olson, *2017 Record Year for Law Firm Mergers,* BLOOMBERG LAW, Jan. 3, 2018, https://biglawbusiness.com/2017-record-year-for-law-firm-mergers/.

[28] Dentons Votes to Combine With Seven Elite Firms in Africa, the Caribbean and South East Asia, https://www.dentons.com/en/whats-different-about-dentons/connecting-you-to-talented-lawyers-around-the-globe/news/2018/april/dentons-votes-to-combine-with-seven-elite-firms-in-africa-the-caribbean-and-south-east-asia.

[29] Chris Johnson, *Vereins: The New Structure for Global Firms*, AM. LAWYER, Mar. 7, 2013.

[30] *See* STEPHEN MCGARRY, PROFESSIONAL SERVICES NETWORKS: THE FUTURE OF THE ACCOUNTING AND LEGAL PROFESSIONS (2015).

[31] *About Lex Mundi*, https://www.lexmundi.com/lexmundi/About_Lex_Mundi.asp.

[32] James Faulconbridge and Daniel Muzio, *Global Professional Service Firms and the Challenge of Institutional Complexity,* 53 J. MANAGEMENT STUD. 89 (2016).

[33] Carole Silver, *The Variable Value of U.S. Legal Education in the Global Legal Services Market,* 24 GEO. J. LEGAL ETHICS 1 (2011).

language ability and international experience.[34] Although the largest segment of international students studying law in the U.S. are enrolled in LL.M. programs,[35] the number of international students in mainstream JD programs has increased substantially in the last decade.[36]

Transnational practice on behalf of large corporate clients receives more attention than cross-border practice for individual and small business clients, but the latter is common. The United States Census Bureau reported that virtually every state in the U.S. experienced a substantial increase in its foreign-born population between 1990 and 2000, and that all but five jurisdictions had at least a 30% increase during that period. Foreign-born residents often have family law, inheritance, or business relationships with their country of origin, and lawyers sometimes facilitate those interactions.[37] Thus, even within the individual client hemisphere, transnational practice has become a reality for many lawyers. The *After the JD* study found that seven years after entering the bar, 41% of the surveyed lawyers had performed at least some work that involved clients from outside the U.S. or cross-border matters in the past year. Although lawyers in large firms and corporate legal departments were the most likely to report doing international legal work (67 and 65% respectively), 61% of legal services lawyers and public defenders also reported that they had done some such work in the past year.[38]

Even public interest law is becoming more transnational. An American-born concept once largely confined to the United States has evolved into a more globalized set of institutions and practices.[39] For example, American lawyers have sued multinational corporations in the U.S. and other courts for human rights abuses. Public interest organizations have also worked with local grassroots groups to research, document, and expose legal and human rights violations and to seek redress from governments and corporations, often working in transnational fora governed by so-called soft law norms (quasi-legal international norms that lack legally binding force), as well as in domestic tribunals. Canvassing the rich emerging literature on these trends would take us far afield from the primary focus of this chapter—the practical and regulatory challenges of globalization for the American legal profession. Suffice it to say for our purposes that activist lawyers interested in

---

[34] *Id.*

[35] See Carole Silver, *States Side Story: "I Like to be in America:" Career Paths of International LLM Students*, 80 FORDHAM L. REV. 2383 (2012).

[36] Carole Silver and Swethaa Ballakrishnen, *Sticky Floors, Springboards, Stairways & Slow Escalators: Mobility Pathways and Preferences of International Students in U.S. Law Schools,* 3 U.C. IRVINE J. INT'L, TRANSNT'L & COMP. L. 101 (2018).

[37] ABA SECTION OF LEGAL EDUCATION AND ADMISSIONS TO THE BAR, REPORT OF THE SPECIAL COMMITTEE ON INTERNATIONAL ISSUES 8 (JULY 2009).

[38] AFTER THE JD II: RESULTS FROM A NATIONAL STUDY OF LEGAL CAREERS 35 (2009).

[39] *See* Scott L. Cummings and Louise G. Trubek, *Globalizing Public Interest Law,* 13 U.C.L.A. J. INT'L L. & FOR. AFF. 1 (2008).

promoting social justice in the global arena are crossing national borders, both literally and virtually, as never before.

As noted in the Wilkins and Ferrer excerpt above, legal services are covered by a variety of international trade agreements, which seek to lower trade barriers by overriding national laws that restrict the import of goods and services. Indeed, the United States is subject to fifteen bilateral and regional trade agreements that apply to legal services.[40] The potential impact of these agreements on the United States legal services market and lawyer regulation is just beginning to receive attention. International trade agreements may be implicated whenever a U.S. lawyer regulation affects foreign lawyers. For example, state rules that severely restrict admission and/or temporary practice by foreign lawyers might be deemed an illegitimate restraint on free trade in services under some of these agreements.[41] Similarly, transnational trade agreements, such as the General Agreement on Trade in Services, have imposed pressure on emerging economies, including India and Brazil, to open their markets to foreign lawyers and law firms.[42]

International trade agreements have also promoted conversations about lawyer regulation, differences in the legal ethics rules applicable to lawyers engaged in transnational practice, and the potential benefits of harmonizing those rules,[43] as well as the difficulty of doing so given different understandings of basic ethical issues among lawyers in various countries.[44]

NOTES ON TRANSNATIONAL PRACTICE

1. ***Implications for Lawyer Regulation.*** What are the implications of transnational practice for lawyer regulation? Would it be useful to have more uniform standards for admission and practice across national boundaries?

2. ***Is Uniformity Attainable or Advisable?*** What are the impediments to achieving uniformity in the regulation of lawyers across national borders? What would be the costs?

F. SUMMARY

This chapter has explored ways in which law practice has globalized over the past several decades, as U.S. lawyers seek to compete in markets

---

[40] *See* Laurel S. Terry, *From GATS to APEC: The Impact of Trade Agreements on Legal Services*, 43 AKRON L. REV. 875, 877 (2010).

[41] *Id.*

[42] Bryant G. Garth, *Corporate Lawyers in Emerging Markets*, 12 ANNU. REV. L. SOC. SCI. 441 (2016).

[43] *See* Laurel S. Terry, *The Impact of Global Developments on U.S. Legal Ethics During the Past Thirty Years*, 30 GEO. J. LEGAL ETHICS 365 (2017).

[44] *See* Carrie Menkel-Meadow, *Ethical Ordering in Transnational Legal Practice? A Review of Catherine A. Rogers's Ethics in International Arbitration*, 29 GEO. J. LEGAL ETHICS 207 (2016).

that do not observe state and national boundaries. These changes have placed considerable strain on the American system of state-by-state licensing. The current ethics rules generally prohibit lawyers from practicing law in states where they are not licensed but allow lawyers some flexibility to provide services to clients there on a temporary basis. We considered whether the current regulatory scheme strikes the right balance between ensuring adequate regulatory oversight over lawyers and permitting them freedom to compete with one another and with non-U.S. based providers and giving clients choice in the selection of legal service providers. We also examined trends toward disaggregating legal services and outsourcing some of their components, as well as the resurgence of the Big 4 accountancy networks as competitors in the global legal services industry. We explored proposals that would allow U.S. lawyers to join with other service providers in multidisciplinary practices, concerns that have thus far led to the defeat of such proposals, and ways in which these arrangements are occurring even in the face of regulatory obstacles. Finally, we examined how transnational practice has become a reality for many American lawyers—not just for those serving corporate clients but for those serving individuals as well.

CHAPTER 22

LEGAL EDUCATION

■ ■ ■

A. INTRODUCTION

This chapter surveys some of the most important issues about contemporary legal education. The chapter begins with a history of legal education and critiques of legal education. The chapter surveys the content of legal education, with particular focus on the contemporary mix of doctrinal, skills, clinical and interdisciplinary instruction. The chapter then examines contemporary debates over the content, pedagogy, length, and cost of legal education and considers some of the most significant proposals for reform. As you read the materials that follow, note the ways various interest groups in the organized bar influence the structure and content of legal education.

B. THE HISTORY OF LEGAL EDUCATION

Until the early twentieth century, many lawyers did not attend law school and had no college degree; most states did not even require lawyers to have graduated from high school. Although some lawyers attended law school, law schools were not affiliated with universities but instead were stand-alone proprietary schools. The majority of lawyers learned law the same way anyone learned a skill or a trade: by working as an apprentice under the supervision of one already practicing the trade. This was known as "reading the law," and it is still permitted in a few states (including California) as an alternative to attending law school, although the requirements of study and supervision have become much stricter.

One of the principal goals of the American Bar Association from its founding in 1878 was to enhance the stature and quality of the bar by requiring all lawyers to graduate from law school. In 1900, the American Bar Association Section on Legal Education created the Association of American Law Schools (AALS) to help improve and standardize legal education, a function the AALS still performs today. In 1921, the ABA adopted its first set of Standards for Legal Education and, shortly thereafter, issued its first list of law schools that met its standards. This was the beginning of the ABA's role as an accrediting agency for law schools, and its power increased over time as many states adopted rules allowing only graduates of ABA-accredited schools to be admitted to practice.

Although critics of contemporary American legal education charge it has changed too little in the last 100 years, legal education today differs radically from the haphazard and largely inadequate training that most aspiring lawyers received before 1870. The distinctive features of today's legal education—3 years of university-based graduate education delivered by a full-time professoriate teaching a curriculum focused on legal doctrine, with a sprinkling of theory, social science, and humanities—are the product of reforms adopted between 1870 and 1930. The emphasis on teaching skills was the product of reforms adopted since 1970.

1. FOUNDATIONS OF CONTEMPORARY LEGAL EDUCATION

LAW SCHOOL: LEGAL EDUCATION IN AMERICA FROM THE 1850S TO THE 1980S

Robert B. Stevens (University of North Carolina Press, 1983)[1]

Such success as American legal education had had before the Civil War had been achieved through proprietary schools [which were not affiliated with universities]. [In 1870, at the beginning of the deanship of Christopher Columbus Langdell, Harvard Law School] had no relation to Harvard College. During Langdell's deanship, which lasted until 1895, Harvard not only became the preeminent law school in the country, but institutionalized legal training was established as *de rigueur* for leaders of the profession. In addition to the development of a system of teaching that emphasized the analysis of appellate cases, it was Langdell's goal to turn the legal profession into a university-educated one—and not at the undergraduate level but at a level that required a three-year post-baccalaureate degree.

Harvard's innovations concerned not only its student body but also its faculty. James Barr Ames [appointed in 1873 as assistant professor of law] was the first of a new breed of academic lawyer, a law graduate with limited experience of practice who was appointed for his scholarly and teaching potential. Ames, a recent Harvard Law graduate who had scarcely practiced law, was exactly the type of professor Langdell demanded: "A teacher of law should be a person who accompanies his pupils on a road which is new to them, but with which he is well acquainted from having often traveled it before. What qualifies a person, therefore, to teach law, is not experience in the work of a lawyer's office, not experience in dealing

[1] Copyright © 1983 by the University of North Carolina Press. Used by permission of the publisher.

with men, not experience in the trial or argument of cases, not experience, in short, in using law, but experience in learning law."

The case method proved to be a brilliant and effective vehicle for the "imaginative activity" of the law. Generations of law students were to be weaned on determining relevant facts, making arguments to a law professor masquerading as a court, and justifying or destroying judicial opinions in terms of legal "rightness" and, later, in terms of the nonlegal desirability of some principle or another. Practitioners had always had some doubts about the case method, both intellectually and politically. Even John Chipman Gray [a noted nineteenth-century legal scholar] was forced to admit that "given a dunce for a teacher, and a dunce for a student, the study of cases would not be the surest mode to get into the Bar."

It was in this context that the 1891 report of the ABA Committee on Legal Education attacked the heart of the Harvard system. The report argued that the ideal work of the lawyer was to be done by knowing the rules and keeping clients out of court. Teaching decisions without systematically instilling rules led to the "great evil" manifested by young lawyers who were all too willing to litigate, did not restrain their clients, cited cases on both sides in their briefs, and left all responsibility to the court. As it turned out, the ABA meetings of 1891 and 1892 were the last serious doubts the legal establishment expressed about the case method. The fashionability of the Langdell system grew with remarkable rapidity. [In the 1890s, as graduates of Harvard Law School or faculty who had taught there took teaching jobs at law schools across the country, the case method was adopted at most university-affiliated law schools.]

The case method system held a trump card—finance. The method enabled the establishment of the large class. Although numbers fluctuated, Langdell in general managed Harvard with one professor for every 75 students; the case method combined with the Socratic method enabled classes to expand to the size of the largest lecture hall.

Part-time law schools opened up a whole new sector of the legal education market. The first of these was established in the 1860s for students who had full-time jobs. [I]n the late 1880s part-time law schools began to spring up in the cities with heavy immigrant populations. [I]mmigrant groups early saw the importance of both education and of law in America as well as the need and advantage of being a lawyer.

[Through the expansion of the number of law schools, it became] increasingly possible for white males, even poor immigrants, to qualify for the legal profession. The portals were far narrower for blacks and women. Although blacks seem to have entered the legal profession in this country sooner than women, their success was more limited. Already facing social ostracism, they fought white middle-class prejudice against blacks practicing law. The career of John Mercer Langston was exceptional. The son of a Virginia planter and a half-black, half-Indian slave, he entered Oberlin, one of four colleges in the country then admitting blacks, in 1849. He eventually went on to be the first dean of Howard Law School, which opened in 1868, and later acted as president of Howard University. Howard's Law School ought to have increased the number of black lawyers quickly, and for a while it did flourish because of the absence of admission requirements, a two-year program, and a reasonable supply of government clerks to fill its evening program. Then it fell on harder times. In 1877, the District [of Columbia, where Howard is located] moved to require three years of training for lawyers. In 1879, Congress announced that none of its appropriation might be used for Howard's professional schools. Census figures show that although black lawyers nationwide, at one point, outnumbered women lawyers, reaching 431 in 1890, the Jim Crow system took its toll. By 1900, their number was only 728, below that for women.

Despite the intimidation from the Supreme Court [which held in *Bradwell v. Illinois*, 83 U.S. 130 (1873), that states could exclude women from the practice of law], women fought for their right to be lawyers. As early as 1869 the University of Iowa admitted women law students. Michigan soon followed Iowa's lead and in 1872 Boston University Law School admitted women. In 1878 two women successfully sued to be admitted to the first class at Hastings Law School. The elite law schools, however, remained hostile. A Yale Law School alumnus opined in 1872, "In theory I am in favor of their studying law and practicing law, provided they are ugly." Overall, the census reported five women lawyers in the United States in 1870. As of 1880, it listed 75 and, by 1900, there were 1,010.

At its first meeting in 1879, the ABA Committee on Legal Education and Admissions to the Bar began the crusade for an expansive program of standardization. In 1896, the ABA approved the requirement of a high school diploma and two years of law study for bar admission. By 1897, the period of study required was lengthened to three years, with the hope that state legislatures would not only approve but also restrict the method of study to that of attending law school. In 1908, the association was discussing a requirement of two years of college before law school, although its official requirement was still a high school diploma (and would remain so until 1921).

By 1916, the AALS was prepared to debate a resolution not to recognize any night [law school courses] after 1920. It was in that debate that Eugene Gilmore, a law professor at Wisconsin, later to be president of the University of Iowa, announced: "the universities can turn out all the lawyers the country needs; we don't have to sit up nights to find ways for the poor boy to come to the Bar." The leaders of the bar shared the then current assumptions about the ethnic superiority of native white Americans. In 1909, the ABA adopted a requirement that lawyers had to be American citizens. A New York delegate defended the college requirement of prelaw training: it was "absolutely necessary" to have lawyers "able to read, write and talk the English language—not Bohemian, not Gaelic, not Yiddish, but English." In 1922, the Yale Board of Admissions was deeply concerned about "the Jewish problem." Dean Swan of the Yale Law School suggested to the state bar in 1923 that students with foreign parents should be required to remain longer in college than native-born Americans before being admitted to law school. At a Yale faculty meeting in the same year, Swan argued against using grades as the basis of limiting enrollment to the law school, because such a development would admit students of "foreign" rather than "old American" parentage, and Yale would become a school with an "inferior student body ethically and socially."

In 1923, the ABA issued its first list of approved schools. In 1924, the AALS established a requirement of one full-time teacher for each 100 students, tightened the definition of part-time education, and [revised requirements first set in1912 regarding the number of books a law library must contain.] ABA standards were met by only about half the country's law schools. [I]n 1927, of the 48 states and the District of Columbia, 32 still had no formal legal requirement for prelaw studies, and 11 required merely high school graduation or its equivalent. In 1927, none required attendance at law school.

[Over the course of the 1930s, states began to require two or three years of prelegal college education.] Increasingly, the states required law school training and required that training to be in ABA schools; and, increasingly, the students went to those schools.

NOTES ON LEGAL EDUCATION BEFORE 1940

1. ***Why Require Graduation from Law School as a Condition of Admission to the Bar?*** Today, about half the states (not including California and New York) restrict bar admission to graduates of law schools that are accredited by the American Bar Association. A tiny number of states (including California and New York) do not require law school graduation, but instead allow candidates for admission to "read the law" under the tutelage of a lawyer. Why did the ABA urge attendance at law school almost to the exclusion of apprenticeship in a law office as a way of training lawyers? Why require ABA accreditation? Which of the reasons motivating the ABA to accredit law schools in the early twentieth century remain valid today?

2. ***The Case Method.*** What do you think of the reasons why the case method and the Socratic method were adopted in law schools and rapidly became the norm?

3. ***Part-Time Law School.*** The ABA waged a long campaign against part-time law schools, including night schools, in the early twentieth century. Are there any legitimate reasons to restrict admission to the bar to those who study law full time? What is the connection between the elite bar's opposition

to part-time law schools and its opposition to proprietary law schools? What echoes of the debate over university based "academic" study of law as opposed to trade-school based "practical" study of law can you see in legal education today?

4. ***Should Law Be a Graduate Degree?*** The United States is unusual in making law entirely a graduate degree; this was a result of the ABA's long campaign to reform legal education. Many countries are transforming law from an undergraduate to a graduate degree. What are the arguments for law being a graduate or undergraduate degree?

5. ***Why a Full-Time Law Faculty and Well-Stocked Library?*** Why did the ABA and the AALS insist on a minimum number of full-time law faculty and a minimum number of volumes in the law library? What are the costs and benefits of these requirements? What are the tensions between law professors being members of university faculty and law professors being members of the profession, in terms of teaching and scholarship?

2. THE HISTORY OF CRITIQUES OF LEGAL EDUCATION

Although the appellate case method dominated elite legal education through the 1960s, it had critics beyond those in the practicing bar who thought it trained lawyers to litigate rather than to advise clients how to avoid litigation. Another major criticism was leveled in the 1930s by the Legal Realists, who insisted that study of appellate cases did not effectively train lawyers to understand law as social policy and was intellectually impoverished because it neglected the insights of the social sciences. Legal Realism was a major challenge to the Harvard-Langdell model of legal education. Although Legal Realism was a broad critique of law as well as legal education, it had more influence in changing legal education than it did in changing the way that lawyers practice or judges decide cases. As legal historian Laura Kalman explained:

> The realists' success in using the social sciences in the classroom was [slight]. On the one hand, the realists and almost everyone afterward changed the titles of their casebooks "from 'Cases on X' to 'Cases and Materials on Y.' " On the other, there was widespread agreement that with but few exceptions, realist casebooks made ineffective use of the social sciences and did not significantly depart from their precursors. They ensured that social science would be kept at its proper distance: "law and," with the "and" functioning to marginalize social science.
>
> In the end, realism changed the lives of teachers more than students. It made many elite law professors wonder whether they should move closer to the university. But that created a sense of unease. Torn between campus and the profession, [the law professor] was a victim of "intellectual schizophrenia," which had

> him "devoutly believing that he can be, at one and the same time, an authentic academic and a trainer of" practitioners. [T]he law teacher must continue training potential lawyers to pick apart cases. Since a good lawyer was supposed to be a jack-of-all trades, a good law teacher must fill whatever hole in the core curriculum arose, no matter how much time preparation consumed.[2]

The push to integrate the study of legal doctrine with the study of social sciences and the humanities continued throughout the twentieth century and had a significant long-term impact. Many law schools offer courses on law and economics, sociology, anthropology, history, philosophy, and literature. A substantial number of law professors have a PhD as well as a JD. In the 1980s, the formal study of law and economics became especially influential and pervasive at many law schools, particularly as the Olin Foundation gave large gifts to many law schools to hire faculty trained in economics and to support research on the economic analysis of law. Law and economics as a school of thought penetrated policymaking in the administrative, legislative, and judicial branches of government.

Besides the Legal Realists' attack in the 1930s on the intellectual poverty of the case method, a second strand of criticism of the structure and content of legal education gained traction in the progressive activism of the 1960s. Law student activists across the country lambasted the tension and tedium of the classroom, the failure of professors to provide meaningful feedback, the overwhelming importance of grades, and a curriculum that was focused on the legal issues of concern to business rather than on the problems of the poor. They also challenged the denial of admission to women and people of color and the absence of student involvement in important law school governance decisions, including faculty hiring, curriculum, and admissions.[3]

Student activists demanded and, in many cases, achieved changes in law school policies in the 1960s and 1970s. Schools changed admissions policies to allow women and people of color to matriculate in greater numbers. They allowed some student involvement in setting academic policy. Selection for law review was not based on first-year grades alone. Some courses were graded on something other than just a single final examination. Schools offered more courses to train students in skills like writing, negotiation, interviewing. They established law school clinics to enable students to develop practical legal skills and to provide legal services to poor people.

Criticism of the elitism, hierarchy, dearth of real-world training, and corporate focus of legal education, especially at elite law schools, continued

---

[2] LAURA KALMAN, YALE LAW SCHOOL AND THE SIXTIES: REVOLT AND REVERBERATIONS (2005).

[3] *Id.* at 11, 28.

through the 1970s and the 1980s and merged with criticism of American law more generally. The most influential strains of criticism were Critical Legal Studies (CLS) and, slightly later, Critical Race Studies (CRS). These intellectual movements encompassed widespread critiques of law and politics as well as legal education. Critical Race Studies (CRS), which remains influential in legal education, identifies ways in which law enables racial subordination and makes systematic racial inequalities seem normal or inevitable rather than the product of deliberate legal policies.

CLS produced a pithy indictment of legal education authored by Duncan Kennedy, a professor at Harvard Law School, who originally published the critique in 1983 as a pamphlet addressed to first year law students. In *Legal Education and the Reproduction of Hierarchy: A Polemic Against the System*, Kennedy excoriated law schools for squelching the public service aspirations of entering first year law students and channeling them into large firm corporate practice. He also criticized law schools for fomenting competition among law students, and for the content and pedagogy of the curriculum:

> The classroom is hierarchical with a vengeance, the teacher receiving a high degree of deference and arousing fears that remind one of high school rather than college. [Class discussion] is a demand for a pseudo-participation in which you struggle desperately, in front of a large audience, to read a mind determined to elude you.
>
> The actual intellectual content of the law seems to consist of learning rules, what they are and why they have to be the way they are, while rooting for the occasional judge who seems willing to make them marginally more humane. The basic experience is of a double surrender: to a passivizing classroom experience and to a passive attitude toward the content of the legal system.
>
> Law students learn skills, to do a list of simple but important things. They learn to retain large numbers of rules organized into categorical systems. They learn "issue spotting," which means identifying the ways in which the rules are ambiguous, in conflict, or have a gap when applied to particular fact situations. They learn elementary case analysis. And they learn a list of balanced, formulaic, pro/con policy arguments that lawyers use in arguing that a given rule should apply to a situation, in spite of a gap, conflict or ambiguity, or that a given case should be extended or narrowed. These are arguments like "the need for certainty," and "the need for flexibility;" "the need to promote competition," and the "need to encourage production by letting producers keep the rewards of their labor."

The intellectual core of the ideology is the distinction between law and policy. Teachers convince students that legal reasoning exists, and is different from policy analysis, by bullying them into accepting as valid in particular cases arguments about legal correctness that are circular, question-begging, incoherent, or so vague as to be meaningless.

[The first year curriculum of] contracts, torts, property, criminal law and civil procedure [teaches students] the ground-rules of late nineteenth century laissez-faire capitalism. Teachers teach them as though they had an inner logic, as an exercise in legal reasoning with policy playing a relatively minor role.

This whole body of implicit messages is nonsense. Legal reasoning is not distinct, *as a method for reaching correct results*, from ethical and political discourse in general (i.e., from policy analysis). There is never a "correct legal solution" that is other than the correct ethical and political solution to that legal problem.

Law schools channel their students into jobs in the hierarchy of the bar according to their own standing in the hierarchy of schools. Students confronted with the choice of what to do after they graduate experience themselves as largely helpless: they have no "real" alternatives to taking a job in one of the conventional firms that hires from their school. Partly, faculties generate this sense of student helplessness by propagating myths about the character of the different kinds of practice. They extol the forms that are accessible to their students; they subtly denigrate or express envy about the jobs that will be beyond their students' reach; they dismiss as ethically and socially suspect the jobs their students won't have to take.

The actual capacities of lawyers have real social value; they are difficult to acquire; and one can't practice law effectively without them. But they are nowhere near as inaccessible as they are made to seem by the mystique of legal education. By mystifying them, law schools make it seem necessary to restrict them to a small group, presumed to be super-talented. That, in turn, makes it seem necessary to divide the labor in the joint enterprise of providing legal services so that most of the participants (secretaries, paralegals, office assistants, court clerks, janitors, marshals, and so on) are firmly and permanently excluded from doing the things that are most challenging and rewarding within the overall activity. Once they have devalued everyone else on "professional" grounds, it also seems natural for those who have gone to law school to specialize in the most desirable tasks, while controlling the whole show and reaping the lion's share of the rewards.

Beginning in the late 1970s, a different set of criticisms of legal education came from the conservative movement, which claimed that law schools were bastions of liberal legal orthodoxy. In the early 1980s, the Federalist Society for Law and Public Policy was founded by law students at Yale and the University of Chicago and sponsored by conservative and libertarian faculty, including Robert Bork and the late U.S. Supreme Court Justice Antonin Scalia. The founders sought to create a forum for conservative law students to debate, make connections with conservative lawyers and judges, and "proclaim the virtues of individual freedom and of limited government."[4]

C. CONTENT AND PEDAGOGY

The curricula at most law schools are strikingly similar in content and pedagogy. The number of classroom hours and a few elements of the content of the curriculum are dictated by the American Bar Association as part of the accreditation process and by the bar in each state as a requirement for admission to the bar. The bulk of the curriculum is determined by the judgment of each faculty about what lawyers should know and, at some schools, by the content of the state bar examination. The vast majority of law schools offer first-year courses in civil procedure, contracts, torts, property, criminal law, constitutional law, and legal research and writing. The upper-level curriculum typically consists of a mix of courses teaching legal doctrine in a wide variety of subject matters in the lecture-discussion format of the first year, smaller courses offering advanced treatments of doctrine and comparative, theoretical, or interdisciplinary perspectives on law, and an array of courses teaching skills. The ABA imposes an upper level writing requirement and a professional responsibility course. Eighty-five percent of law schools surveyed by the ABA in 2010 regularly offered in-house live-client clinical opportunities, 30 percent offered off-site, live-client opportunities,[5] and the number and variety of experiential learning opportunities has grown since.

Some critics have long suggested that the curriculum at many law schools better prepares students for corporate practice than for service to individuals and small business clients. The emphasis on appellate opinions and legal memo and brief writing is said not to reflect the work that

---

[4] *Preface,* 6 Harv. J.L. & Pub. Pol'y, at iii, iii–iv (1982). For more on the founding and current operations of the Federalist Society, see AMANDA HOLLIS-BRUSKY, IDEAS WITH CONSEQUENCES: THE FEDERALIST SOCIETY AND THE CONSERVATIVE COUNTERREVOLUTION (2015); ANN SOUTHWORTH, LAWYERS OF THE RIGHT: PROFESSIONALIZING THE CONSERVATIVE COALITION 116–117, 131–141 (2008); STEVEN TELES, THE RISE OF THE CONSERVATIVE LAW MOVEMENT: THE BATTLE FOR CONTROL OF THE LAW 135–151 (2008).

[5] ABA SECTION OF LEGAL EDUCATION AND ADMISSIONS TO THE BAR, A SURVEY OF LAW SCHOOL CURRICULA: 2002–2010 (2012).

lawyers typically do for individual clients and not to train lawyers to meet the legal needs as to which there is the largest unmet demand, such as divorces, landlord-tenant matters, immigration issues, and personal bankruptcy.[6] Critics also urge law schools to train students in marketing and law office management so they can launch or work in solo or small practices.[7] In response, many schools have adopted courses and clinics to prepare students to practice in a wider array of settings representing the full range of clients.

If law schools tend to focus on preparing students for service to large organizations rather than to individuals and small businesses, that phenomenon may be driven in part by the perspectives of faculty, who are overwhelmingly graduates of elite law schools.[8] This is one of a number of aspects of legal education in which the role of faculty as scholars at research universities is sometimes in tension with their role in training students for the practice of law.

Another concern about the law school curriculum is that inadequate attention is paid to identity formation and career planning. Common critiques (many with no clear ideological position) suggest that law schools focus too much on channeling students into available private-sector jobs and too little on helping students understand the range of career options, how to manage a nontraditional law practice, and how to maintain general well-being. Recent scholarship, for example, suggests that a failure to educate students about the full range of career options in the first year results in students (at least at elite schools) choosing large firm practice rather than the public interest practice they aspired to before law school; one consequence of the so-called public interest drift was that students developed an alienated sense of professional self as a way of managing the dissonance between their social justice aspirations and their professional path.[9] Others suggest that the law school curriculum may be partly to blame for allegedly high levels of unhappiness among lawyers by failing to inculcate in students an awareness of how to manage stress and manage a law practice.

A major debate over legal education concerns the relative emphasis on "academic" or "doctrinal" courses (typically taught in a discussion format) and "skills" or "clinical" courses. This debate dates back to the nineteenth

---

[6] Deborah L. Rhode, *Legal Education: Rethinking the Problem, Reimagining the Reforms*, 40 PEPPERDINE L. REV. 437, 447–48 (2013).

[7] *See* William Hornsby, *Challenging the Academy to a Dual (Perspective): The Need to Embrace Lawyering for Personal Legal Services*, 70 MD. L. REV. 420, 437 (2011); Randolph J. Jonakait, *The Two Hemispheres of Legal Education and the Rise and Fall of Local Law Schools*, 51 N.Y.L. SCH. 864, 889–96 2006/07.

[8] *See* Brian Leiter, *Where U.S. Law Faculty Went to Law School*, http://leiterlawschool.typepad.com/leiter/2008/01/where-us-law-fa.html (last visited May 22, 2018.

[9] John Bliss, *From Idealists to Hired Guns? An Empirical Analysis of "Public Interest Drift" in Law School*, 15 U.C. DAVIS L. REV. 1973 (2018).

century and the efforts of elite schools and the ABA to improve the stature (and, they thought, the quality) of the bar by increasing the academic rigor of legal education and downplaying the traditional emphasis on learning through apprenticeship. Recently, however, the debate on experiential education has been framed in terms of whether law students get their money's worth if they do not learn everything that lawyers really do.

Although the ABA waged a long campaign to emphasize doctrinal teaching in the late-nineteenth and early-twentieth centuries, recently the ABA and other influential commentators on legal education have urged greater emphasis on teaching skills and ethics through actual or simulated experiential or clinical instruction and skills training. Two of the most influential proposals for reform in legal education were the ABA's MacCrate Report of 1992 and the Carnegie Report of 2007.[10] Both faulted excessive reliance on the case method and lecture-discussion classroom instruction on doctrine. The Carnegie Report identified what it termed "two major limitations on legal education." First, "[m]ost law schools give only casual attention to teaching students how to use legal thinking in the complexity of actual law practice." Second, "[l]aw schools fail to complement the focus on skill in legal analyses with effective support for developing ethical and social skills. Students need opportunities to learn about, reflect on and practice the responsibilities of legal professionals. Despite progress in making legal ethics a part of the curriculum, law schools rarely pay consistent attention to the social and cultural contexts of legal institutions and the varied forms of legal practice."

Both the Carnegie Report and the MacCrate Report called for greater emphasis on clinical education. Clinical and some other faculty and deans, with some but not unqualified support of the AALS, embraced the MacCrate Report and issued calls for every law school to provide faculty-supervised direct client representation clinical experiences. Yet adopting such clinical experiences for every law student is very expensive, which creates a tension with the goal of making legal education affordable (an issue we consider below). Moreover, as a matter of pedagogy, some faculty believe that simulated exercises are better for students, because they allow instruction in a wider range of skills, and are better for clients, who should not run the risk of having students learn at their expense.

Many critics of legal education have urged law schools to emulate the model of medical education in which the first two years are classroom instruction and the third and fourth years are spent rotating through various real-world practice settings. Unlike medical schools, which are

---

[10] SECTION ON LEGAL EDUCATION AND ADMISSION TO THE BAR, LEGAL EDUCATION AND PROFESSIONAL DEVELOPMENT—AN EDUCATIONAL CONTINUUM: REPORT OF THE TASK FORCE ON LAW SCHOOLS AND THE PROFESSION, NARROWING THE GAP (1992) (known as the MacCrate Report, after one of its authors); WILLIAM M. SULLIVAN, ET AL., EDUCATING LAWYERS: PREPARATION FOR THE PROFESSION OF LAW (Carnegie Foundation 2007) (known as the Carnegie Report).

affiliated with or run hospitals and outpatient medical clinics, law schools do not operate substantial legal services offices and would therefore depend on persons other than faculty to train students in real-world practice settings. Moreover, medical care is funded by an elaborate mix of private and public funding. In contrast, there is almost no public funding for legal services, and there is thus no obvious way to compensate lawyers whose job it is to train fledgling lawyers.

NOTES ON THE LAW SCHOOL CURRICULUM

1. ***The Evolution of Classroom and Experiential Instruction.*** The Stevens excerpt on legal education before the 1960s and the MacCrate Report reveal that the views of ABA leaders have evolved over the course of a century as to what skills, knowledge, and aptitudes law school should cultivate. What are those changes and what accounts for them?

2. ***What Should Be Emphasized?*** There is a long history to the debate over whether legal education should emphasize vocational education or academic graduate training, and to some extent the debate presents a false dichotomy, as legal education can include both vocational and academic components. Nevertheless, when resources are finite, priorities must be identified. How would you approach that issue?

3. ***The Role of Cost.*** In light of the Stevens excerpt recounting the financial advantages of classroom lecture-discussion, a response to the MacCrate Report that involves a dramatic increase in resources for clinical education would require the money to come from somewhere. Given that a significant increase in the cost of legal education to finance more clinical teaching is unlikely, what would you recommend to the law faculty at your university about how to reallocate resources to implement your preferred vision of legal education?

D. THE GLOBALIZATION OF LEGAL EDUCATION

One of the most dramatic recent changes in American higher education is the increase in the number of international students. Although, as explained in the excerpt below, the number of international students in most U.S. law schools remains small in comparison to the number studying other subjects in U.S. colleges and universities, still the increase has been dramatic and the influence of such students is noteworthy.

STICKY FLOORS, SPRINGBOARDS, STAIRWAYS & SLOW ESCALATORS: MOBILITY PATHWAYS AND PREFERENCES OF INTERNATIONAL STUDENTS IN U.S. LAW SCHOOLS

Carole Silver & Swethaa S. Ballakrishnen

3 U.C. Irvine Journal of International, Transnational, and Comparative Law 39 (2018)

[A]s of the 2016–2017 academic year, the number of international students in the United States alone is more than one million, with 68% of all these students originating from Asia. [E]ngineering and business account for the top and largest share of international student enrollment. In contrast, international legal education remains a small sliver of this international transfusion, accounting for just over 1% of all international students in U.S. higher education.

[T]he LLM degree (which is the standard master's training in law that approximately three-quarters of law schools in the United States offer for international students) has changed the way legal training is perceived by suppliers and consumers of this education. From the U.S. law school's perspective, in addition to the obvious commercial advantage,[13] the inclusion of international students signals an internationalization of the school's educational atmosphere and experience. On the other hand, from the perspective of the incoming students, changes in the world market for legal services have created a new environment in which an international legal education has practical value and demand.

The percentage of international students in mainstream JD programs not only has increased substantially in the last decade but also has surpassed other domestic minority groups in certain instances. [Eds.: here the authors cite data showing that international JD students comprised a larger proportion of the student body than Blacks, Asians or Latinos at 13%, 14% and 8% of ABA-approved law schools, respectively, in 2016.]

[E]nrollment in post-JD programs approximately doubled between the mid-1990s and the mid-2000s. Importantly, during this phase of global legal education, the signal of the LLM was to convey a readiness for interaction beyond home country borders, and it served as a mechanism to distinguish its holder from others at home whose experience was limited to the local context.

[T]oday nearly 80% of all law schools offer at least one post-JD degree program for international law graduates, a figure that has approximately doubled over the last ten years. The number of students enrolled in post-JD programs more than doubled between 2004 and 2016 to just below 10,000 students.

---

[13] LLM programs are financially important for U.S. law schools because the schools can charge full tuition without worrying about the credentials of the students for the purpose of national rankings (e.g., U.S. News & World Report).

But international students have not been contained in non-JD programs. There has been growth over the last five years or so in the proportion of international students enrolling in U.S. JD programs, too. LLM graduates were stymied by the refusal of most U.S. jurisdictions to recognize the degree as leading to bar eligibility. This caused problems for graduates who wanted to work in states other than New York and California (the two major jurisdictions where the LLM could satisfy the U.S. legal education conditions for bar admission), and motivated them to pursue a JD.

[W]hile bar eligibility was important, many [of this study's survey] respondents found the jump from an LLM to a JD useful even beyond this functional issue. [S]tudents have described the LLM as a "field test" for the JD. A Chinese student who did an LLM first and then transferred into the JD program at her law school explained that she initially hedged her bets in her decision about which degree to pursue: "[Y]ou know, like JD is really a big commitment either in terms of time or money. So I think it's a good thing for me to do LLM and see if I really like. If I don't like it, I can just go back." [T]he decision to pursue the JD was [also] seen as a way to distinguish oneself in a market that had begun to saddle the LLM with a distinct, unshakeable international tag. For other students, the path to the JD was more direct, usually following a home country undergraduate degree in a field other than law. A student explained her thinking about whether to earn her law degree in the United States or Hong Kong: "I received my undergrad in kind of the best university in Hong Kong and I know how this education is like. And also if I receive a JD degree in the States I can always go back to Hong Kong if I want, because they really welcome American JD. So, and if I'm lucky enough, I can stay in the U.S. So, pursuing a JD degree in the U.S. gives me more choices, and also I think that U.S. has the best legal education so that's why I want to come here." Finally, there were international students whose first degree was earned in the United States. For these students, applying for a U.S. JD felt like an extension of their undergraduate degree.

From the perspective of sending countries, the enthusiasm for global legal education may reflect a fluidity regarding the characteristics, experiences and skills associated with power, status and access. During this period, the number of students from Europe has remained relatively constant, but their proportion in the group of all international students has dropped by half. This is due in large part to the rise of Asian and, to a lesser extent and recently of Middle Eastern students. But equally important is that the way students from Asia are participating has shifted, at least in law, from a marginal role institutionally to one that may more deeply puncture existing hierarchies.

NOTES ON THE GLOBALIZATION OF LEGAL EDUCATION

1. ***Legal Education and Bar Admission.*** The District of Columbia Bar considered, but has yet to adopt, a rule making it the first U.S. jurisdiction to allow foreign-educated lawyers who are not admitted to any other U.S. bar to satisfy the requirement of U.S. legal education by taking courses through distance learning. The distance-learning courses would have to be offered by an ABA-accredited law school and would have to satisfy the ABA accreditation requirements for distance learning.[11] What do you see as the advantages and disadvantages of such a rule?

2. ***Visa Challenges.*** Some law schools with substantial LLM programs worry that stringent Trump Administration restrictions on visas may tarnish the United States' reputation as a premier global venue for legal education, and make it ever harder for foreign citizens to obtain visas to study and work in the U.S. as lawyers. What role should U.S. law schools play in educating lawyers from around the world?

E. CONTEMPORARY DEBATES OVER LEGAL EDUCATION

1. RANKINGS AND STRATIFICATION

ABA accreditation requirements and ferocious competition to succeed in the *U.S. News* rankings have had a significant effect on legal education. A book-length social science study of law school rankings concluded that they affect where students choose to apply to law school and which law school they attend. Rankings have reduced deans' discretion and changed the way they relate to peers, alumni, and legal employers and how they are evaluated by university administration. Rankings shape how career services offices counsel students about jobs, and shift resources away from counseling and network building and toward tracking students for purposes of reporting to *U.S. News.* Additionally, rankings influence employers' decisions about whom to interview and hire.[12] While rankings offer a form of transparency and accountability, they do not just measure what law schools do; they change it. Critics insist the change is not for the better, asserting that rankings discourage experimentation and divert law schools from meeting law students' diverse expectations.[13]

Some accreditation requirements, such as those that require support for faculty scholarship, may serve the needs of some types of students more than others. Relatedly, the *U.S. News*' emphasis on the academic

---

[11] Sarah Kellogg, *Breaking Down Barriers for Foreign Lawyers*, WASH. LAWYER 35 (Sept. 2017).

[12] WENDY NELSON ESPELAND & MICHAEL SAUDER, ENGINES OF ANXIETY: ACADEMIC RANKINGS, REPUTATION, AND ACCOUNTABILITY (2016).

[13] Deborah L. Rhode, *Legal Education: Rethinking the Problem, Reimagining the Reforms*, 40 PEPPERDINE L. REV. 437, 447–48 (2013).

reputations of faculty and the school's reputation with lawyers and judges troubles some. The emphasis on faculty scholarship is unpopular with those who believe students do not benefit from attending a great research institution. And the method used to measure law schools' reputations with the bench and bar rests entirely on a survey that goes to unnamed legal professionals, and the response rate to the survey is exceedingly low.[14] The rankings race also leads law schools to shift scholarship money from students most in need to those with the highest LSAT scores and undergraduate GPAs, because those scores also figure prominently in the rankings.[15] Critics argue that all of these factors tend to work against students who aspire to serve low and moderate income clients because they drive up the cost of tuition and reduce the availability of need-based financial aid. On the other hand, the rankings may benefit students in some ways. *U.S. News* ranks schools based in part on the percentage of the graduating class that has employment in a job requiring a JD, which encourages schools to help their graduates find jobs at graduation. The ranking formula also encourages schools to maintain a low student-faculty ratio (recall Harvard's was 75 to 1 in the nineteenth century; elite schools now maintain a 12–1 student-faculty ratio).

2. COST

Few issues in contemporary legal education have garnered more public attention than its cost, especially since 2009, as the recession dimmed job prospects.[16] To understand the many issues associated with the cost of legal education, consider the elements of a law school budget. Education is a labor-intensive process, which means that at most schools the largest single category of expenditure is faculty and staff salaries and benefits, which consumes at least two-thirds of the budget. The remaining third of the annual budget is spent on the library collection and information technology, operations, and scholarships.

Only a few schools have endowments and receive charitable giving in amounts large enough to free them from dependence on tuition. At one point, state universities received public funding to subsidize low tuition for students enrolled in all degree programs, but many states ceased significant subsidies for their public law schools in the 1990s. Tuition at elite state university law schools approaches tuition at private universities, although many state law schools remain committed to a lower-cost model of legal education.

---

14 STEVEN HARPER, THE LAWYER BUBBLE: A PROFESSION IN CRISIS 17–18 (2013).

15 *See* William D. Henderson & Andrew P. Morris, *Student Quality as Measured by LSAT Scores: Migration Patterns in the U.S. News Rankings Era*, 81 IND. L.J. 183 (2006).

16 David Segal, *Is Law School a Losing Game?* N.Y. TIMES (Jan. 8, 2011); David Segal, *Law School Economics: Ka-Ching!* N.Y. TIMES (July 16, 2011).

Even at state universities that still enjoy public funding for legal education, and at virtually all other schools, the major source of revenue is tuition. Not every student pays the full tuition. Many law schools offer scholarships to recruit students with particular credentials, including high undergraduate GPA or LSAT scores or other indicators of talent or promise for professional success. Critics assert that law schools offer too few need-based scholarships and too many "merit-based" scholarships in order to attract students with high grades and LSAT scores to boost their *U.S. News* ranking and academic profile. These critics argue that students with less sought-after credentials pay full tuition (typically with money financed by loans) while students with valued credentials pay less than the full tuition, with the result that some students subsidize the legal education of others. If financial aid were strictly need-based, the wealthier students would subsidize the education of poorer students; if it is largely merit-based, the students with less valued credentials subsidize the education of those with more valued credentials.

Those students without wealth sufficient to afford tuition borrow money. Hence, most law schools are quite dependent on the availability of student loans. Law students are eligible in most cases to borrow the full cost of tuition and living expenses in some combination of federally subsidized and unsubsidized loans, depending on financial need. Educational loan programs were a reform effort of the 1960s intended to make elite college and graduate and professional education financially accessible to all students. Defenders of readily available student loans argue that they enable any student with the academic qualifications to attend even the most elite and expensive university. Critics argue that liberal loan programs have fueled a rapid increase in the cost of elite and nonelite education and have made students and schools insensitive to whether the benefits of education are justified by the cost.

As the amount of debt incurred by students rose, some began to worry that graduates who did not obtain high-paying large law firm jobs would be unable to pay their debt and would be deterred from choosing jobs most suited to their interests or to social needs and perhaps even from enrolling in law school at all. Some federal student loans are eligible for the Income Based Repayment (IBR) program in which borrowers with lower incomes after law school pay less than the ordinary monthly repayment amount.[17] The IBR amount is capped at 10 to 15 percent of the borrower's "discretionary income," a term of art defined in the program. After 25 years of payment on the reduced IBR schedule, the remaining balance may be forgiven. In addition, under the federal IBR program, after 10 uninterrupted years of employment in qualifying public service employment and steady repayment under the IBR, debtors in qualified

---

[17] U.S. Department of Education, Federal Student Aid, *Income Driven Plans*, https://studentaid.ed.gov/sa/repay-loans/understand/plans/income-driven (visited July 23, 2018).

public service employment may have the balance of their debt forgiven. Some law schools have created loan repayment assistance programs (LRAPs) which subsidize the loan payments of alumni who take qualifying low-income public interest jobs.[18] The IBR and most LRAP programs cover all of a borrower's educational debt, not just law school debt. Those schools that maintain LRAP programs to cover the educational debt not covered by the federal IBR program typically fund such programs out of their operating budgets, which effectively means that the charitable contributions of alumni and the tuition payments of current students subsidize the educational costs of past students who have taken public interest jobs. LRAP programs tend to be more generous at schools with substantial numbers of alumni in highly-paid law firm and corporate jobs.

One of the most influential contemporary criticisms of American legal education focuses on the high cost of full-time law faculties.

FAILING LAW SCHOOLS

Brian Tamanaha (University of Chicago Press, 2012)[19]

Law faculties have been growing for some time now owing to a combination of factors: to handle larger numbers of students, to make up for reduced teaching loads, to add more scholars, to add clinical and legal writing teachers, and to lower faculty-student ratios (a factor on *U.S. News* rankings). AALS tallied 7,421 full-time law faculty in 1990–91. The number has increased every year since, reaching 10,965 in 2008–09. Student-faculty ratios have plummeted as a result. At the largest law schools, the ratio was cut almost in half, from 27.3 students per faculty in 1989–90, to 15.3 in 2009–10; at midsized schools over this period it dropped from 25 to 14.4.

Although it is frequently suggested that this reduction is beneficial to students, and it does result in more seminars with smaller enrollments, the reality is that students do not necessarily gain more interaction with professors from having more of them around. Student face time takes away from scholarship, which is what professors are rewarded for.

Law professors *do not* teach in legal studies departments but in law schools. That is why persistent complaints arise about the excessive academic orientation of the faculty. Law professors—and the PhDs on law faculties—are paid substantially more than they would earn had they worked in legal studies departments. Students matriculate to gain entry to the practice of law and expect to learn the skills that will enable them to

[18] *Clarifying Common Questions About Using Loan Repayment Assistance Programs (LRAPs) in Enrollment Management*, Higher Ed Industry News, Dec. 19, 2018, https://ardeoeducation.org/4-misconceptions-about-loan-repayment-assistance-programs-lraps-as-an-strategic-enrollment-management-tool/ (visited September 9, 2019).

[19]

succeed as lawyers. It is questionable whether a professor with little or no practice experience is ideally suited to train students for legal practice.

Law schools are financially trapped by what they have become: top-heavy institutions with scholars teaching few classes (writing a lot) and clinicians teaching few students. The perpetual "more" of recent decades—creating more time for writing, hiring more scholars and more skills-training teachers, and spreading more money around—severely constrains law schools going forward.

Taking the entire span from 1985 through 2009, resident tuition at public law schools increased by a staggering 820 percent—from $2,006 to $18,472 (nonresident tuition increased by 543 percent, from $4,724 to $30,413)—while tuition at private law schools went up by 375 percent—from $7,526 to $35,743. These increases far outstripped the rate of inflation.

Student debt has ballooned in conjunction with tuition. The average combined debt (undergraduate and law school) of law school graduates in the mid-1980s was $15,676. The average debt of law graduates was $47,000 in 1999. In 2010, average law school debt alone was $68,827 for graduates from public schools and $106,249 at private schools. Average college debt for graduates of the class of 2010 was $25,250.

Students from elite law schools have a solid chance of securing corporate law jobs that pay a salary sufficient to comfortably manage $120,000 debt. Top-fifteen law schools send 30–60 percent or more of their graduates to NLJ 250 firms each year. But the percentage of graduates securing these positions rapidly falls the further down the law school ranking one goes.

Starting pay for new law graduates falls into a distinctive pattern called a bimodal distribution, with two earnings clusters separated by a large gap of about $100,000. For the class of 2010, nearly half of law graduates earned between $40,000 and $65,000. Among those who reported their salaries, nearly 20 percent of law graduates earned around $160,000. [A]bout one-third of law graduates in the past decade have not obtained jobs as lawyers, and this is disproportionately the case at the lowest-ranked law schools.

Law schools have raised their tuition to obscene levels because they can. Elite law schools charge $10,000 to $15,000 higher than nonelite schools do because demand for their credentials is greater. But even nonelite schools can charge hefty tuition because demand for law degrees is strong enough to support it.

Taken in isolation, what [elite] schools have done can be justified. Yale and Harvard distribute financial aid on an exclusively need basis, which in effect makes the students from higher socioeconomic classes help defray the costs of those from lower (in contrast to the reverse-Robin Hood merit scholarship arrangement at virtually all other law schools in which the bottom half of the class subsidizes the top.)

The wisdom of the members of the bar who a century ago argued on behalf of a differentiated system of legal education—wanting to allow research-oriented law schools to coexist alongside law schools that focus on training good lawyers at a reasonable cost—has been confirmed by subsequent events. Unfortunately, they lost the battle to elite legal educators who imposed their standard on all. The research brand of law schools became the model imposed and enforced through AALS and ABA standards.

Affordability and elite status are mutually exclusive under current circumstances. [A law school that aspired to be] an excellent law school that trains top quality lawyers at an *affordable price* would [adopt a different model].

What might that [look] like? For starters, [it] would have to sell the vision of affordable excellence, recruiting top faculty who were willing to accept less pay (more in line with professors in other departments) to make that vision a reality; professors would have practice experience as well as [be] excellent scholars; they would teach two classes a semester, leaving ample time to write; the entering class would be capped at two hundred students; the third year would entail externships in excellent public-service work settings; tuition would be set below $20,000; there would be no merit scholarships; [the endowment would be used for] need-based scholarships, supplemented by fund raising. [If such a school existed at an elite university], quality students would [enroll]. And graduates would leave law school with manageable debt levels that would enable them to eschew the corporate law route if they so desired. This would have been the ideal law school for the twenty-first century. The only problematic element in an otherwise realistic plan would [be] recruiting enough top professors who would teach four courses and accept lower pay.

NOTES ON THE COST OF LEGAL EDUCATION

1. ***Can Law Schools That Cut Costs Compete for Faculty and Students?*** Professor Tamanaha suggests that the ideal law school would pay faculty and staff substantially less than is current practice, have a smaller faculty who teach more classes and more students, and would recruit good students by charging lower tuition. If, as is the case, labor costs are two-thirds of the cost of operating a law school, the main way in which the cost of law school could be reduced would be a drastic cut in salaries and benefits. A 50 percent cut in faculty salaries and benefits will reduce the budget (and, therefore, tuition) by about a third. Do you think that a law school could cut faculty and staff salaries by half, increase teaching loads, and still recruit top faculty? If not, would it nevertheless be better for students if a school followed

his model? Would some students choose to attend such a school if it were one-third less expensive than other schools to which they were admitted?

2. ***Law School Debt and Law Graduates' Salaries.*** Tamanaha cites statistics on the correlation between the cost of tuition and law graduates' salaries in their first positions after law school, and he suggests that only those who begin in corporate law firms will be able to manage their debt. But many law graduates who begin their careers in large law firms leave after just a few years, and some lawyers who begin in small and medium firms move into large firms. Data from the *After the JD* study show that the salaries of lawyers in all practice settings except solo practice rose substantially between three and seven years after graduation and between seven and twelve years out; many of these lawyers are doing quite well financially.[20] These findings may suggest that Tamanaha's focus on the match between debt and law school rank and first jobs following graduation may yield misleading conclusions about whether law school is a good investment for those who cannot gain admission to elite schools.

3. ***Rates of Repayment of Educational Debt.*** The *After the JD* study has gathered data about debt, including all educational debt—not just law school loans. By twelve years after law school, 47.4 percent of respondents reported no remaining educational debt. Those in large law firms were most likely to have no debt remaining, but respondents working in federal government settings, certain public interest jobs, and business were almost as likely as those in large firms to have no remaining debt.[21]

The *After the JD* study also finds uneven patterns of debt load and debt repayment by racial/ethnic identity. At Wave 3, only 23.3% of African-Americans and 30.4 % of Hispanic law graduates reported no remaining debt, as compared to 60.1% of Asians and 48% of whites. And of those with educational debt, African-American and Hispanic respondents reported more debt than whites and Asians. At Wave 3, African-Americans still had a median of $57,000 in educational debt, compared with $50,000 for whites, $75,000 for Hispanics, and $37,000 for Asians.[22]

4. ***What Is the Purpose of an LRAP Program?*** As noted above, LRAP programs are a form of subsidy from students and alumni who take high-paying jobs to those who do not, and from students with little educational debt to those with large debt. They tend to be generous only at schools in which a significant percentage of the graduating class take jobs at the high end of the bimodal income distribution. Why do law schools that can adopt such programs have them? What is the purpose of an LRAP? Given that purpose, should undergraduate debt be covered?

---

20 The American Bar Foundation and the NALP Foundation for Law Career Research and Education, *After the JD III: Third Results from a National Study of Legal Careers* Table 5.1 (2014).

21 *Id.* at 80.

22 *Id.* at Table 10.1.

3. SHOULD LAW SCHOOL BE TWO YEARS OR THREE?

As noted above, the ABA adopted a new set of accreditation requirements in 1921 to address anxieties about the character and competence of lawyers who were graduating from part-time law schools in the early 1900s. Among the new standards was a mandate that law students must complete three years of full-time study or devote the equivalent number of hours to study through part-time schooling.[23] Most university-affiliated law schools already had adopted a three-year requirement, but it was inconsistent with many of the programs that served working people.[24] In acrimonious ABA meetings that preceded adoption of the three-year requirement, advocates for increased admissions standards railed against the threat posed by uneducated foreigners, while advocates for night law schools argued against restrictions that would inhibit mobility for students from working-class families.

In adopting the three-year requirement, the ABA rejected recommendations of a Carnegie Commission report authored by Alfred Z. Reed (the Reed Report), which concluded that differences in law schools' educational programs were inevitable and reflected the fact that different types of law schools served "radically different types of practitioners."[25] It asserted that full-time university-affiliated law schools were necessary to provide the rigorous and broad legal education required for the lawyers who would become society's leaders, while two-year and part-time programs were adequate for most practitioners and would ensure that law schools "shall be kept accessible to Lincoln's plain people."[26] The ABA rejected the Reed Report's reasoning and recommendations, instead adopting unitary standards for all lawyers.

Proposals to abandon the three-year requirement have surfaced periodically since the 1920s. In 1971, a study by legal educators concluded that the third year of law school was unnecessary as long as certain essential courses were included in the two-year option. The study recommended that law school be available to those who had completed three years of undergraduate study and that the third year of law school should be eliminated as a requirement but made available for those who wanted to specialize.[27] The Carnegie Commission issued a similar recommendation the following year.

---

[23] REPORT OF THE SPECIAL COMMITTEE TO THE SECTION OF LEGAL EDUCATION AND ADMISSIONS TO THE BAR OF THE AMERICAN BAR ASSOCIATION, ANNUAL REPORT OF THE ABA 679, 687–88 (1921).

[24] JEROLD S. AUERBACH, UNEQUAL JUSTICE 118–19 (1976).

[25] *Id.* at 111 (quoting the Reed report).

[26] ALFRED Z. REED, TRAINING FOR THE PUBLIC PROFESSION OF THE LAW 290 (1921).

[27] The Carrington Report, reprinted as app. A in HERBERT L. PACKER AND THOMAS EHRLICH, NEW DIRECTIONS IN LEGAL EDUCATION 93 (1972).

Calls to reexamine the three-year requirement have reemerged recently in connection with critiques of the high costs of legal education. Advocates of rule change have argued that allowing law students to sit for the bar exam after two years of law school rather than three would enable more students to afford to pursue careers in service to low or moderate-income Americans, while three-year programs would continue to attract students who believe that the additional training and specialization would give them sharper skills and better preparation for the real-world challenges of practice and the job market.[28]

In *Failing Law Schools,* the book excerpted above, Professor Tamanaha outlines the argument in favor of two-year law school programs:

> The bar's position a century ago made consummate sense: two years of book learning followed by a one-year apprenticeship, then admission to the bar. The Carrington Report of four decades ago, which proposed three years of an undergraduate education followed by two years of law school, was also sensible.
>
> The essential change could be achieved in a stroke. The current ABA-imposed minimum of 1,120 classroom hours can be reduced by a third, instead mandating 747 hours of instruction.
>
> Some degree programs will be two years, others will remain at three, with clinical components; some will be heavily doctrinal, others will be skills oriented. One-year degrees (the current LLM) will be widely available for an additional year of specialization in a chosen subject. Schools will offer two-year and three-year program options for students, incentivizing schools to create a third year that adds significant value.
>
> Differentiation across the market for legal education—currently suppressed by ABA standards—would arise. The law school parallel—in program and pricing—of vocational colleges and community colleges will come into existence, many of two-year duration. Prospective students will be able to pick the legal education program they want at a price they can afford. A law graduate who wishes to engage in a local practice need not acquire, or pay for, the same education as a graduate aiming for corporate legal practice. This is not the race to the bottom prophesied by AALS. It simply recognized that every law school need not be a Ritz-Carleton [sic]. A Holiday Inn-type law school would provide a fine education for many, adequate for the type of legal practice they will undertake.[29]

---

[28] *See* Samuel Estreicher, *The Roosevelt-Cardozo Way: The Case for Bar Eligibility After Two Years of Law School,* 15 N.Y.U. J. L & PUB. POL'Y 599 (2012).

[29] BRIAN Z. TAMANAHA, FAILING LAW SCHOOLS 173–174 (2012).

NOTES ON TWO YEARS VERSUS THREE YEARS

1. ***Competence.*** Some critics of proposals to allow students to sit for the bar after two years of law school argue that it would glut the market with attorneys who do not have the skills and training that they need to practice competently. Are they right? Are proposals to reduce law school to two years in tension with the demand that law schools produce practice-ready graduates?

2. ***Must We Choose?*** Do we need to choose between a two-year and a three-year model, or could these different types of legal education programs co-exist? Tamanaha suggests that we should let students choose what type of training they will receive. What are the advantages and disadvantages of insisting on a unitary standard?

3. ***A Third Year Apprenticeship?*** Tamanaha argues that even if law schools do not change to a two-year model, they should devote the third year to apprenticeships:

> Law schools can place students on a wholesale basis in already-existing practice settings (law firms, governments legal offices, courthouses, etc.), as many law schools already do through "externship" programs. A more ambitious program would involve the participation by law schools, in partnership with government-funded agencies, with the delivery of legal services to the middle class and poor at low cost. Under currently existing "hybrid" programs, a clinical professor has an office at the practice setting and works with the students on location. If understaffed legal services offices were offered the full-time assistance of the third-year class of local law schools, that would help fill unmet legal needs while the students get useful training. Privately financed, privately run versions of low-cost legal services are also possible, in conjunction with law schools, in areas like immigration services, tax services, employment problems, and a variety of other common tasks on which third year students can hone their practice skills.
>
> Whichever the external setting, students would work as lawyers at an office earning basic wages (which would require a rule change in order to implement)—reviving a form of apprenticeship. Think of the lawyer equivalent of residency programs for graduates out of medical school. Law school staff and attorneys in the office would maintain oversight and provide advice, but students would handle much of the work themselves. Many third-year students already work part-time in law offices—this would amount to an institutionalized version of that. The responsibility of the law school would be to secure placement opportunities in practice settings while running a supplemental education component on the side. Tuition for the third year can be reduced to a level commensurate with the extent of the outplacement and supervision services provided by the school.

What practical or other obstacles do you see to adoption of the third-year apprenticeship model? How could the obstacles be overcome?

4. ***President Obama Joins the Debate.*** During the summer of 2013, in a question-and-answer session on higher education, President Obama endorsed cutting the classroom component of law school from three to two years and having students devote the final year of law school to work experience.[30] His comment generated strong responses. Yale Law School's Bruce Ackerman, for example, asserted that the third year is "not an expensive frill but a crucial resource in training lawyers for 21st-century challenges." He argued that legal decisions rest on economics, statistics, psychology, and other social sciences, and that law schools must prepare students to handle relevant insights from those other disciplines. President Obama's "cost-cutting" measure, Ackerman insisted, would "impoverish American public life" and "push legal education back more than 75 years":

> The predictable outcome will be massive professional retreat. Increasingly, lawyers will become secondary figures who prepare the way for "experts" to present the crucial arguments before administrative agencies, courts and legislatures. Decision-makers with two-year law degrees will proceed to rubber-stamp the expert testimony that seems most impressive because they aren't prepared to test it in a serious way.[31]

Do you agree with Professor Ackerman's predictions? How do you suppose former President (and former University of Chicago Law School Senior Lecturer) Obama would respond?

4. TOO MANY LAWYERS? TOO MANY LAW SCHOOLS?

Some say that the U.S. already has plenty of lawyers and that too many law graduates have recently flooded a saturated market.[32] Others cite evidence of unmet legal needs of low-income and moderate-income individuals and argue that the problem is not too many lawyers but rather that legal education is not producing legal services providers with the right kind of training at the right price.[33]

The assertion that the U.S. has too many lawyers grew especially prevalent during and after the recession of 2009–2013, when the number of legal jobs seemed to be plummeting. As Steven Harper wrote in the *Chronicle of Higher Education,* "[t]hat loud pop you're hearing is the bursting of the law bubble—firms, schools, and disillusioned lawyers

[30] *See* Peter Lattman, *Obama Says Law School Should Be Two, Not Three, Years*, N.Y.TIMES, Aug. 23, 2013.

[31] Bruce Ackerman, *Why Legal Education Should Last for Three Years*, WASH. POST, Sept. 6, 2013.

[32] *See*, e.g., Eric Posner, *The Real Problem with Law Schools: They Train Too Many Lawyers*, SLATE, Apr. 2, 2013.

[33] *See* Deborah Rhode, *Legal Education: Rethinking the Problem, Reimaging the Reforms*, 40 PEPPERDINE L. REV. 437, 445 (2013).

paying for decades of greed and grandiosity. Like the dot-com, real-estate, and financial bubbles that preceded it, the law bubble is bursting painfully." Harper focused on the mismatch between the number of law school graduates and the number of available law jobs as defined by the U.S. Department of Labor Statistics. He argued: "For full time, long-term jobs that require passing the bar, only a dozen law schools out of 200 reported employment rates exceeding 80 percent nine months after graduation. Considering the investment in money, time, and brainpower that law school requires (not to mention the promises that law schools make to prospective students), something's gotta give, and maybe it finally has."[34]

The number of law graduates who obtain full-time jobs practicing law shortly after graduation is one measure of the value of a legal education, but it is not the only one. The excerpt below rejects the notion that law schools should restrict access to legal training and expertise, and it also questions what counts as a law job.

DOING GOOD INSTEAD OF DOING WELL? WHAT LAWYERS COULD BE DOING IN A WORLD OF "TOO MANY" LAWYERS

Carrie Menkel-Meadow (Oñati Socio-Legal Series 2013)

For some time now I have found the question, "are there too many lawyers" somewhat off putting, if not downright offensive. Who is asking that question to suggest that we restrict access to a legal education and/or to the legal profession itself? There are a lot of people wanting to study law. Whether that study of law immediately results in employment in a high-paying large law firm or should result in any particular form of employment is a different question. Law is a general first degree in much of the world, so might it be in the United States. But even if it is an expensive graduate degree, as long as there is truthful disclosure of employment data and people can make informed choices about what they want to study, I can see the value of a law degree far exceeding immediate employment pay-offs. Other commentators have suggested that if we simply stop thinking of law as a special "profession," but simply as a field of expertise, subject to the same vagaries of any other employment, with some specialized knowledge (and some ethical rules), the practice of law might more honestly face up to its modern economic challenges and begin to adapt, respond and perhaps innovate, as other fields of work have had to do.

[L]aw study may be an entry "portal" into a large number of other kinds of work—business, politics (either as a candidate or in the new profession of political consulting), policy work, government (non or quasi-legal work), NGO advocacy in both legal and non-legal settings,

---

[34] Steven J. Harper, *Pop Goes the Law*, CHRONICLE OF HIGHER EDUCATION (March 11, 2013).

community, labor or other interest group organizing work, creative work (start-ups of many kinds, including scientific, educational, economic and entertainment), real estate work, education (teaching others about the law, whether lay people or other law students), deal making and social entrepreneurship, and peace work (whether legal mediation or non-legal international or domestic), which is hardly exclusive of all the possible jobs and tasks that someone with a law degree might perform. With some knowledge of the law all of these jobs and others we cannot even imagine at the moment are likely to be performed with a better sense of justice, equity, logic and rule-based accountability.

[I]f there are "too" many or just "many" lawyers, maybe some reallocation might actually provide for some better distribution of lawyers to those who are currently underserved. Or, the many lawyers might "re-deploy" their legal skills in different, more socially useful ways. If the legal profession were subject to regular market forces, an oversupply of lawyers should lead to a lowering of price and to reallocation of services. [P]erhaps if "too" many lawyers are trained in the same way there might be some competition or reconfiguration of how legal education is delivered. [S]ome schools are offering more diversified legal education with the hope of making more "practice-ready" lawyers or training lawyers to do different things. Perhaps it is time to return to the ill-fated Reed Report on legal education and recognize that American legal education might be diversified, sectored and specialized. Some might study law to practice, others to train their minds in "legal thought" (logic, order, both inductive and deductive reasoning), others as an overlay on some other field (science, economics, business), and others just to become educated citizens of their countries or the world. [Finally], some might use law study to change the way we think about the world. Entrepreneurial (socially, legally and economically) new lawyers might just adapt, reconfigure and reconceive the work that lawyers do and see that there is more that people with legal education can do, not just for personal gain, but for the global society in which we live. With other ways to practice law (more conflict resolution, more diversity of the individual and organizational client base, with different forms of practice, and more sites and locations of legal issues, some policy based, some law-making, some transactional, some dispute resolving), there should be both more and different work for those who call themselves lawyers. The question then might be, not "are there too many lawyers?," but are lawyers being socially productive and what are they doing? There is no one "right" way to practice law, as there most certainly is no one way to achieve social justice.

Somewhat related to the question whether there are too many lawyers is the question whether there are too many law schools. Between 1970 and 2010, growth in the demand for legal education prompted the establishment of many law schools. When law school applications dropped (by about 38%) after 2009, many law schools struggled to admit enough qualified students. Predictably, bar pass numbers sank as the cohort of students with weak grades and LSATs struggled on bar exams. The graduates' poor record of finding employment and passing the bar prompted the ABA to threaten or revoke accreditation of many schools, and at least half a dozen schools closed after 2015.* Litigation ensued, as critics asserted that some law schools admitted students who lacked the academic preparation to pass the bar examination. The ABA was under considerable pressure to take action against schools whose admissions criteria were too lax and who were said to exploit students by admitting them, encouraging them to take out loans, and then flunking out those whom the schools feared would fail the bar and jeopardize the schools' bar pass statistics. But loss of ABA accreditation was a blow to students who could pass the bar and find employment but who could not gain admission to a more selective school.*

NOTES ON THE "TOO MANY LAWYERS" QUESTION

1. ***What Is a Law Job?*** How should we measure whether law schools are producing the right number of lawyers? Some use Department of Labor Statistics data on positions requiring a JD as a measure. The *U.S. News* formula for rankings treats jobs requiring a JD differently than other jobs when calculating the employment rate of law graduates. Is it possible that having a JD improves one's prospects for getting or performing well in a job even if the position does not require a JD? Recall Lawrence Friedman's observation in Chapter 2 that American lawyers prospered throughout the 19th century because "the profession was exceedingly nimble at finding new kinds of work and new ways to do it." Is trying to identifying the right number of lawyers a useful exercise? If so, how does one specify what constitutes a law job?

2. ***What to Make of the Rise and Fall in Law School Applications?*** Critics cited recession-era declines in the numbers of LSAT test-takers and law school applicants as evidence that many fewer people are finding law school an attractive choice. After several years of decline, the number of LSAT takers and law school applicants rose substantially for the 2018 entering class.[35] The growth was attributed both to a strong economy and to a "Trump bump," that is, news stories emphasizing the importance of lawyers and judges to the rule

* [Eds.: Indeed, several law schools have closed. See Karen Sloan, *RIP, Law Schools. A Look at Closed Campuses: Six Law Campuses Have Shuttered or Soon Will Close Up Shop, and More Are Likely to Follow Suit*, www.law.com (Mar. 26, 2018).]

* [Eds.: For a discussion of the controversy over law schools admitting students who fail to find law jobs after graduation, see David Frakt, *Admissions, Accreditation and the ABA: An Analysis of Recent Law School Lawsuits* (May 23, 2018), http://www.thefacultylounge.org/2018/05/admissions-accreditation-and-the-aba-an-analysis-of-recent-law-school-lawsuits-.html#more.]

[35] *See* Ilana Kowarski, *Less Competitive Law School Admissions a Boon for Applicants*, www.usnews.com (Aug. 8, 2017); Ilana Kowarski, *Law School Applications Increased This Year*, www.usnews.com (Jan. 29, 2018).

of law and democracy. What light does this shed on whether we have too many lawyers?

3. ***Access to the Profession.*** One professor and former law school dean worries that crisis rhetoric about the profession will dissuade students who cannot gain admission to elite law schools from attending law school at all. He argues that the result may be that they miss the opportunity to make a worthwhile investment that would pay large dividends over the course of a career and that the profession will lose the diversity that comes from admitting students from less privileged backgrounds.[36] The closure of law schools that serve students with marginal academic credentials compounds the problem, as it reduces the opportunity to learn the law unless a student has the academic predictors of success on the bar examination. Which should worry us more—that some students will assume substantially more educational debt than they can handle or that they will forgo a career that requires expensive training but may yield long-term individual and societal benefits?

5. LAW SCHOOL ADMISSIONS

A major contemporary debate about legal education concerns admission criteria. Critics of admissions policies argue that heavy reliance on undergraduate grades and LSAT scores has a disparate impact on the basis of race and socioeconomic class and may not accurately screen for all the qualities that make for professional competence. Defenders of reliance on undergraduate GPA (UGPA) and LSAT scores emphasize the correlation between them and first-year law school grades, the correlation between UGPA and overall law school performance, and the correlation between first-year law school grades and bar passage. They posit that grades and test scores measure skills and aptitudes that lawyers need.[37] In doctrinal terms, the issue is whether consideration of race in admissions constitutes unlawful race discrimination, and the use of race remains controversial and legally vulnerable even in those states that have not banned it outright for public universities. *Grutter v. Bollinger,* 539 U.S. 306 (2003) (upholding the use of race as a factor in law school admissions decisions); *Fisher v. University of Texas,* 136 S. Ct. 2198 (2016) (holding a race-conscious undergraduate admissions program to be lawful under equal protection clause).

---

[36] *See* Bryant Garth, *Crises, Crisis Rhetoric, and Competition in Legal Education: A Sociological Perspective on the (Latest) Crisis of the Legal Profession and Legal Education,* STAN. L. & POL'Y REV. 503 (2013).

[37] The literature on law school admissions policies is substantial. One qualified defense of the reliance on grades and test scores is an empirical study of every graduating class at the law school at Brigham Young University. It found that the correlation between LSAT and first-year law school grades is stronger than the correlation between undergraduate GPA and first year law school grades; the correlation between undergraduate GPA and law school GPA is stronger than the correlation between LSAT and law school GPA, but overall concluded that the undergraduate grades and GPA are not strong predictors of academic success in law school. David A. Thomas, *Predicting Law School Academic Performance from LSAT Scores and Undergraduate Grade Point Averages: A Comprehensive Study,* 35 ARIZ. ST. L. J. 1007 (2003).

Two professors at UC Berkeley conducted a large-scale empirical study to determine whether measurable qualities other than UGPA and LSAT might be more effective in predicting lawyer effectiveness. Professors Marjorie M. Shultz and Sheldon Zedeck surveyed and interviewed hundreds of lawyers, clients, judges, and law professors to identify 26 factors that are important to lawyer effectiveness.[38] The authors then devised and validated instruments to measure these professional performance factors and developed new tests that correlated with the large majority of the 26 factors conducive to lawyering effectiveness. The authors collected measures of prior academic achievement for 1,148 lawyers. The authors then asked supervisors, peers, and participants themselves to evaluate participants' professional performance on the effectiveness factor scales. The authors compared the evaluations of professional performance with the data on the participants' academic achievement and with their scores on the authors' tests. The authors found their tests predicted lawyer performance better than the LSAT, UGPA, or Index (which is a composite of UGPA and LSAT). By contrast, most of the 26 factors identified by attorneys as important to lawyer performance were not well predicted by the LSAT, UGPA, or Index score. In addition, unlike the LSAT, the authors' measures showed few racial or gender subgroup differences. The authors suggested a law school might use performance-predictive measures like those they studied in addition to or in lieu of UGPA and LSAT.

Later studies seemed to confirm the Shultz-Zedeck findings that other measures of likely professional competence predict success better than the UGPA and LSAT.[39] The desire to open the application process to students who had taken other standardized tests that also predicted success in law school prompted several schools to accept a GRE score in lieu of an LSAT score.[40] As controversy swirled over schools' use of the GRE, the ABA Section on Legal Education and Admissions to the Bar voted to eliminate the requirement that law schools use the LSAT in admissions, but the ABA will still consider, in its periodic accreditation process, whether law schools' admissions standards ensure likelihood of success in law school.[41] The ABA decision may allow law schools to experiment with alternative measures of likely success, though the emphasis *U.S. News* rankings give to the

---

[38] Marjorie M. Shultz & Sheldon Zedeck, *Predicting Lawyer Effectiveness: Broadening the Basis for Law School Admissions Decisions*, 36 LAW & SOC. INQUIRY 620 (2011).

[39] *See* Alli Gerkman & Logan Cornett, Foundations for Practice: The Whole Lawyer and the Character Quotient (July 2016), http://iaals.du.edu/sites/default/files/documents/publications/foundations_for_practice_whole_lawyer_character_quotient.pdf; Susan Case, Summary of the National Council of Bar Examiners Job Survey Results 3 (Jan. 2013); Neil W. Hamilton, *Law Firm Competency Models and Student Professional Success: Building on a Foundation of Professional Formation/Professionalism*, 11 U. ST. THOMAS L.J. 6, 15–18 (2013) (study of Minnesota law firm attorneys).

[40] Karen Sloan, *University of Arizona Law School's Use of GRE Scores Creates LSAT Trouble*, NAT'L L.J. (May 2, 2016).

[41] Scott Jaschik, *ABA Panel Moves to End LSAT Requirement*, INSIDE HIGHER ED (May 14, 2018).

LSAT/UGPA index may dissuade schools from abandoning reliance on standardized tests until a critical mass of peer schools decide to change admissions processes.

NOTES ON LAW SCHOOL ADMISSIONS

1. ***Should Law Schools Adopt New Criteria for Admission?*** The Shultz and Zedeck study suggests that law schools should modify their admissions criteria in order to screen for additional aptitudes or forms of intelligence that law school admissions criteria currently do not systematically consider. Are you persuaded?

2. ***What Might Happen if One Did?*** If a law school decided in principle to abandon reliance on LSAT/UGPA, what difficulties do you foresee in the implementation of a proposal like the Shultz and Zedeck one? How might those obstacles be overcome?

F. PROPOSALS FOR REFORM

In 2013, the ABA Task Force on the Future of Legal Education issued a report recommending substantial changes in the American legal education system. Among its primary observations, conclusions, and recommendations were these:

- A fundamental tension underlies the current problems in legal education. On the one hand, lawyers play a central role in the "effective functioning of ordered society" and therefore society "has a deep interest in the competence of lawyers, in their availability to serve society and clients, and their values." On the other hand, unlike medical training, which is subsidized by state and federal governments, lawyer training is delivered primarily through private markets. Therefore, it should be responsive to the preferences of law students, who have a legitimate interest in ensuring that they receive an education that will equip them to make a living and repay their loans.
- The system through which law school education is funded should be revamped: "Schools announce standard tuition rates, and then chase students with high LSAT scores by offering substantial discounts without much regard to financial need. Other students receive little if any benefit from discounting and must rely mainly on borrowing to finance their education. The net result is that students whose credentials (and likely job prospects) are the weakest incur large debt to sustain the school budget and enable higher credentialed students to attend at little cost." The Task Force recommended that a commission be established to

recommend reforms regarding law school pricing and financing.

- Legal education is too standardized, and some ABA accreditation requirements add expense without ensuring commensurate value. Several of the accreditation standards should be revised or repealed, including those governing the proportion of courses that must be taught by full-time faculty, tenure and security of employment for faculty, the amount of required instruction time, and physical facilities. The ABA should expand opportunities for law schools to vary from accreditation requirements in order to pursue experiments in legal education.
- Law schools should devote more attention to skills training and experiential learning.
- State supreme courts and regulators of lawyers and law practice should consider reducing the amount of law study required for eligibility to sit for the bar examination or to be admitted to practice.
- States should create additional frameworks for licensing providers of legal services, such as licensing limited practitioners or authorizing bar admission for people whose bar preparation is not in the traditional three year classroom mold.[42]

The ABA Commission on the Future of Legal Education continues to study three topics: (1) the skills lawyers need now and in the future and how law schools can better provide them and be "more agile to the pace of change"; (2) what law schools can do to increase access to justice; and (3) whether or how well state licensure requirements, especially bar examinations, correlate to entry-level competence for attorneys.[43]

Although the Task Force and the Commission emphasize innovations in legal education focusing on reducing cost while increasing practice readiness, other ABA proposals for reform may discourage such innovations. In particular, the ABA issued a Guidance Memo stating that a school would be in compliance with the accreditation standard for the school's graduates bar passage only if 75 percent of its graduates within the five recent calendar years who sat for the bar examination passed it. This standard would result in substantial numbers of schools losing ABA accreditation in states like California that have low pass rates. (The

---

[42] *See* Working Paper, American Bar Association Task Force on the Future of Legal Education (2013).

[43] American Bar Association, Commission on the Future of Legal Education, https://www.americanbar.org/groups/leadership/office_of_the_president/futureoflegaleducation.html (July 23, 2018).

California bar examination pass rate for all takers from ABA-approved California law schools has ranged from a low of 45.9% (February 2016) to a high of 69.5% (July 2013).[44] The minimum passing score on each administration of the bar examination is set by the state bar.

NOTES ON PROPOSALS FOR REFORM

1. ***Are You in Favor?*** Would you support some or all of the changes proposed by the ABA Task Force, the Commission, or the Guidance Memo? Which of them do you think are likely to gain sufficient support to have a reasonable possibility of eventual adoption? What obstacles stand in the way of the successful adoption of whatever recommendations you support?

2. ***Resistance from Some Law Professors.*** Some law faculty were not pleased with the Task Force's recommendation to diminish the role of full-time faculty and change the tenure rule. More than 500 law professors signed a letter objecting to the elimination of tenure as an accreditation requirement.[45] The letter argued that the elimination of the requirement would threaten academic freedom, discourage dissenting voices in legal education, and impede efforts to recruit and retain minority law professors.[46]

3. ***Legal Education Reform by the States.*** One state has adopted and a few have considered changes in legal education to ensure that law graduates are competent to practice law before they are admitted to the bar. New York adopted a "skills competency requirement" requiring J.D. students to follow one of five specified "pathways" for demonstrating competency—e.g., taking 15 units of approved experiential coursework, completing a supervised post-graduate apprenticeship, or practicing for at least one year in another jurisdiction.[47] A State Bar of California Task Force recommended a pre-bar admission competency training requirement that could be fulfilled either by taking 15 units of practice-based, experiential course work designed to develop practice competency or 15 units of a bar-approved externship, clerkship, or apprenticeship any time during or after completion of law school. It also recommended an additional competency training requirement of 50 hours of pro bono service.[48] The State Bar took no action on the proposal, and in 2016 the California governor vetoed legislation requiring 50 hours of pro bono service before obtaining admission to the bar; the governor cited the high cost of legal education and said it was unfair to burden law students with mandatory pro bono work.

---

[44] www.calbar.ca.gov/admissions/law-school-regulation/exam-statistics.

[45] *See* Mark Hansen, *500 Law Profs Urge ABA Legal Ed Council to Keep Faculty Tenure as an Accreditation Requirement*, ABA J., Oct. 22, 2013.

[46] Letter to Judge Oliver, Council Chairperson, Section on Legal Education and Admissions to the Bar, Oct. 8, 2013.

[47] https://www.nybarexam.org/skills/skills.htm.

[48] State Bar of California, Task Force on Admissions Regulation Reform: Phase II Final Report (September 25, 2014); Calif. Gov. Vetoes Pro Bono Requirement for Bar Entry, www.law360.com/articles/834658/calif-gov-vetoes-pro-bono-requirement-for-bar-entry.

G. SUMMARY

This chapter showed that the content and style of teaching in American law schools was the product of a series of reform efforts beginning at Harvard Law School in the 1870s and continuing with a sustained effort of the ABA and elites in the organized bar through the 1930s. Among students, the bench, the bar, and even the public, some have questioned the content and methods of classroom instruction, the balance of doctrinal and skills education, and the cost of and access to legal education. The reforms that resulted from the criticisms of the past have, in turn, been the subject of controversy today. The full-time faculty composed of gifted scholar-teachers with relatively little law practice experience was considered necessary to the intellectual and social credibility of law as a profession. Today critics insist the faculty are too expensive and too removed from practice. The 3-year requirement for a JD degree was the result of a long campaign to increase the quality and social standing of the bar. Today, critics say it makes law school too expensive. The larger number of experiential and skills courses in law schools was likewise the product of a longstanding reform effort aimed at improving the practice readiness of law graduates. It, too, makes law school expensive.

The hierarchy among law schools has its roots in the late-nineteenth century efforts of university-affiliated law schools to distinguish themselves from proprietary schools. Today the distinctions among schools are at the heart of debates over the cost of legal education, how law schools can best serve their students, and whether legal education adequately trains students to serve the right sort of clients. On these, as well as the other most hotly-contested contemporary issues—the cost of law school, the role of debt in financing higher education, and admissions criteria—current practices have their roots in earlier reform efforts that attempted to improve the quality of education and increase the stature of the bar, to make high-quality education affordable to those without family money, and to ensure that law graduates reflect the racial, ethnic, socioeconomic, and cultural diversity of the American population.

CHAPTER 23

BAR ADMISSION AND DISCIPLINE

■ ■ ■

A. INTRODUCTION

A distinctive feature of the legal profession, one cherished by lawyers, is the power of self-regulation. Lawyers, through the bar association of each state and with the permission of the state legislature and high court, determine the criteria and administer the processes for granting and revoking licenses to practice law. The power to admit to practice, to discipline, and to disbar (and to collect dues to fund these operations) are the only coercive powers of the organized bar; all else the bar does is voluntary.

The bar's control over admission to practice affects many aspects of law schools, ranging from admissions criteria to curriculum. Once a lawyer is admitted to practice, the norms of the institutions within which lawyers practice, peer pressure, and client expectations may be more significant than the bar's influence for most lawyers most of the time. But while the threat of bar discipline may not concern most lawyers in their daily practices, the bar's standards influence the norms of the institutions in which lawyers work. Bar rules guide law office practices on conflicts of interest, confidentiality of client information, and client funds. Bar disciplinary rules also affect the law of malpractice, which in turn prompts malpractice insurers to impose conditions on issuing policies, which affects law office management. Courts, not the state bar, create and enforce malpractice law, but they often look to the disciplinary rules in defining lawyers' standards of conduct. Finally, the bar's standards and processes for admission and discipline are significant for the profession's legitimacy and its ongoing efforts to protect the prerogatives of self-regulation.

This chapter first covers the requirements for admission to the bar, especially the bar exam and the Multistate Professional Responsibility Exam, and demonstrating good moral character. The chapter then briefly examines the bar discipline system by which a lawyer can be banned, temporarily or permanently, from the practice of law.

B. ADMISSION TO THE BAR

Today's requirements for admission to practice were not established until the 1930s. Until the early twentieth century, many lawyers had no college degree, and most states did not even require lawyers to have graduated from high school. Most lawyers learned law the same way anyone learned a skill or a trade: by working as an apprentice under the supervision of one already practicing the trade. Today a small number of states (including California) still permit bar admission by this "reading the law," with strict requirements of study and supervision.

Bar admissions standards were not always used, or intended, solely to protect consumers from corrupt or demonstrably incompetent lawyers. They were also used to ensure that the right sort of people (as defined by those running the universities and the organized bar) became lawyers. Today, however, bars insist that the admission standards are focused solely on protecting clients from incompetent and unethical practitioners.

1. BAR EXAMINATION

Bar examinations were rare until the late nineteenth century. States (either through a court or through individual lawyers appointed by the court) typically administered a short oral examination. The oral examinations did not ask a standard set of questions; both the questions and the grades were left to the discretion of the examiner. In the middle and late nineteenth century, states began using written bar examinations, and by the early twentieth century most states required lawyers to pass a written bar exam.

Between the late 1880s and the early 1920s, the ABA waged a successful campaign to persuade states to require the bar examination. All states except Wisconsin and New Hampshire now require candidates not admitted in another jurisdiction to pass the bar examination, and almost all states also require the Multistate Professional Responsibility Examination (MPRE).[1] Graduates of Wisconsin's two law schools (at the University of Wisconsin at Madison and at Marquette University in Milwaukee) and graduates of an honors program at the University of New Hampshire law school enjoy the "diploma privilege"; the JD diploma from an in-state school entitles them to join the state bar without sitting for the bar exam. If they choose to practice outside the state in which they attended law school, they must take the bar exam.

The bar exam consists of multiple elements. In most states, it includes one day (six hours) of multiple choice questions known as the Multistate Bar Exam (MBE), which is the same test across the country. The MBE tests knowledge of certain subjects of federal law (such as constitutional law, evidence, and civil and criminal procedure) as well as general common law doctrine (such as contracts, torts, property, and criminal law) not specific to any particular state. Every state requires completion of a second day of

[1] The National Conference of Bar Examiners maintains a website explaining the examination requirements of each state: www.ncbex.org.

examination, and some require a third day. The additional day(s) of examination consist of various types of essay questions. Thirty-four states (as of this writing; that number will likely grow) plus the District of Columbia and the Virgin Islands use the Uniform Bar Exam (UBE), which consists of the MBE plus the nationally uniform Multistate Essay Exam (MEE) to test knowledge of substantive law, and the Multistate Performance Test (MPT), which requires examinees to write a contract, a client letter, or an analytic or persuasive memorandum, to test the "ability to use fundamental lawyering skills in a realistic situation and complete a task that a beginning lawyer should be able to accomplish."[2] Some states require additional essay questions to test knowledge of substantive and procedural law that is unique to the state (such as family law, state evidence and civil procedure, oil and gas law, and so forth).

The Multistate Professional Responsibility Examination (MPRE) is a two-hour, 60-question multiple choice test on the rules of legal and judicial ethics that, in most states, can be taken any time after the first year of law school. The MPRE was first administered in 1980 and spread rapidly in the decade thereafter.[3]

The UBE facilitates the ability of lawyers to move from state to state or to practice in more than one state. Although each state that adopts the UBE sets its own minimum passing score, and not all states adopt the same minimum, candidates whose scores are above the minimum can be admitted to practice in multiple states so long as they pass the character and fitness requirement and, in some states, a test of state-specific law.

Although court challenges to the bar examination have almost uniformly failed, debate continues about whether the bar exam is an effective screening device and about how to make it more effective. The materials that follow focus on the major issues.

a. Does the Bar Exam Measure Competence?

There are two principal criticisms of the bar exam as a measure of competence. The first focuses on the substance of what is tested. The criticism is that a one-size-fits-all test of wide array of subjects is a poor fit for the specialized nature of today's law practice; in other words, it tests both too much and too little. Knowledge of the minutia of future interests in real property, for example, will never be used by lawyers specializing in criminal law. Conversely, the relatively superficial level at which knowledge of criminal law and criminal procedure are tested on the bar exam do not measure whether a law graduate is competent to begin prosecuting or defending felonies.

---

[2] http://www.ncbex.org/exams/mpt/.

[3] *See* Paul T. Hayden, *Putting Ethics to the (Nationally Standardized) Test: The Origins of the MPRE*, 71 FORDHAM L. REV. 1299 (2003).

The second common criticism of the bar exam is that it does not measure competence at the skills that lawyers need. Answering a series of multiple choice questions or writing a short essay spotting the issues in a hypothetical set of facts does not indicate whether a lawyer can negotiate and write a contract, interview or cross-examine a witness, draft a complaint, formulate a discovery plan, persuade a client or a witness to be candid, design an efficient strategy to solve a legal problem, woo a prospective client, or run a successful law office. As the MacCrate Report said, "the traditional bar exam does nothing to encourage law schools to teach and law students to acquire many of the fundamental lawyering skills. [T]he examination influences law schools, in developing their curricula, to overemphasize courses in the substantive areas of law covered by the examination at the expense of courses in the area of lawyering skills."[4] This criticism is similar to the criticism made of law schools for relying heavily on the LSAT in the admissions process: both the LSAT and the bar exam measure certain cognitive skills that do not necessarily correlate with or predict lawyer competence.

Criticism of the MPRE as a device for measuring ethical competence is similar. The MPRE tests knowledge of rules rather than judgment. It encourages law schools to teach to the standardized test; it does not help students cultivate the habits and attributes of ethical lawyers. The MPRE may even undermine the teaching of professional ethics by encouraging aspiring lawyers to treat professional responsibility as a set of technical rules, rather than a matter of professional identity and values, judgment, problem-solving, and introspection.[5]

b. Is the Bar Exam Sufficiently Job-Related to Justify Its Disparate Impact?

A common criticism of the LSAT, the bar exam, and even the MPRE is that they, like many standardized pencil-and-paper tests, disparately affect people of certain races and socioeconomic backgrounds.[6] Controversy about the racial and socioeconomic impact of the bar exam is affected by the fact that, unlike the organizations that administer the SAT, LSAT and other high-stakes standardized admissions tests, many state bars do not report aggregate data of bar exam pass rates by race, ethnicity, or other demographic factors. One state that does report bar passage statistics by

---

[4] MacCrate Report at 278.

[5] California debated this. *Bar Gets Tougher on Ethics Exam*, CAL. BAR J., Jan. 2006, at 1.

[6] William C. Kidder, *The Bar Examination and the Dream Deferred: A Critical Analysis of the MBE, Social Closure and Racial and Ethnic Stratification*, 29 LAW & SOC. INQUIRY 547 (2004); Kristin Booth Glen, *When and Where We Enter: Rethinking Admission to the Legal Profession*, 102 COLUM. L. REV. 1696 (2002); LINDA F. WIGHTMAN, LAW SCHOOL ADMISSION COUNCIL NATIONAL LONGITUDINAL BAR PASSAGE STUDY (1998).

race and ethnicity (California) indicates that a higher percentage of white bar exam takers pass than do other racial/ethnic groups.[7]

Assessing whether the bar exam's discriminatory impact is justified by its effect in ensuring competence is complicated by the fact that bar examiners are not transparent in explaining their reasoning for setting the minimum passing score. Analysis of efforts to raise passing scores in Florida, Illinois, Minnesota, New York, Ohio, Pennsylvania, and Texas noted that many of the states that attempted to raise the passing score have relatively large numbers of lawyers. "Several common themes emerged in the bar exam controversies: (1) each proposal drew heated opposition from law schools and civil rights organizations; (2) in each case, concerns were raised about the potential disparate impact on students of color; (3) the methods used to study and set the new passing standard were called into question; and (4) there was major debate about the relationship between the bar exam and competency to practice law, including skepticism about what truly motivated bar examiners to recommend raising the bar."[8]

Critics point out that the selection of a minimum passing score is somewhat arbitrary, and that bar exam graders do not consistently apply a uniform set of standards in grading answers, such that two graders might disagree about whether a particular question or examination merits a passing score.[9] In 2014, when bar pass rates dropped abruptly, 80 law school deans asked jointly for details about how the test questions were scored; the controversy was stoked by the insistence of officials of the National Conference of Bar Examiners that the drop was due to a drop in the academic ability of test-takers rather than a change in the testing and grading.[10] The controversy simmered down, but it erupts periodically when bar pass rates fall. Individual efforts to challenge the minimum passing score have failed. In one case, a disappointed bar applicant alleged that the Arizona Board of Bar Examiner's practice of setting the passing score after the exams were graded was an illegal anticompetitive effort to restrict the number of licensed lawyers. The Supreme Court rejected the contention, reasoning: "By its very nature, grading examinations does not necessarily separate the competent from the incompetent or—except very roughly—

[7] On the July 2017 California Bar Exam, the pass rates of first-time takers who graduated from ABA-approved California schools were 75.1% for Whites, 48.9% for Blacks, 57.1% for Hispanics, 69.7% for Asians, and 64.7% for the category "Other Minorities." http://www.calbar.ca.gov/Portals/0/documents/admissions/Statistics/JUL2017STATS.122617.pdf. These pass rates are roughly similar to those reported for the previous July administrations of the exam.

[8] Kidder, *The Bar Examination and the Dream Deferred*, 29 LAW & SOC. INQUIRY at 547–548.

[9] Andrea Curcio, *A Better Bar: Why and How the Existing Bar Should Change*, 81 NEB. L. REV. 363 (2002); DEBORAH L. RHODE, IN THE INTERESTS OF JUSTICE: REFORMING THE LEGAL PROFESSION 51–52 (2000); Michael J. Thomas, *The American Lawyer's Next Hurdle: The State-Based Bar Examination System*, 24 J. LEGAL PROF. 235 (2000).

[10] Elizabeth Olson, Bar Exam, the Standard to Become a Lawyer, Comes Under Fire, N.Y. TIMES, Mar. 19, 2015.

identify those qualified to practice and those not qualified. At best, a bar examination can identify those applicants who are more qualified to practice than those less qualified." *Hoover v. Ronwin,* 466 U.S. 558, 578 n.31 (1984).

Bar examinations have also been criticized for their effect on law school curricula and on how people prepare for the bar. Conventional methods of preparation for the bar exam are asserted to be both unproductive and unfair. Some law schools (typically those whose graduates pass the bar exam at a relatively low rate) encourage or require their students to take a course on every subject tested on the bar exam, or encourage or require their faculty to use assessment devices that mimic the bar exam (such as closed book, time-pressured, essay and multiple choice exams). Critics insist that these practices deprive law students of opportunities to learn skills or professionally useful knowledge in law school and have the same racially disparate impact that other high-stakes tests have. Another criticism of bar exam preparation focuses on the prevalence of expensive commercial bar review courses after an expensive legal education. In addition, as any recent bar exam taker will tell you in excruciating detail, spending six to eight weeks doing nothing but cramming for the bar exam is often a mind-numbing and anxiety-inducing rite of passage that is available only to those with enough resources to devote to full-time study and it may have no useful purpose other than simply gaining admission to the bar.

Alternatives to the bar exam have been proposed that would measure competence through observed demonstration of practice skills in a real-world setting. Thus far, no state has adopted such an alternative.

NOTES ON BAR EXAMINATIONS

1. ***The Purpose of Examinations.*** What is the purpose of the bar exam and the MPRE? Do they serve their purposes? Would another type of device serve the same purposes?

2. ***What Should Be Tested?*** What subjects should be tested on the bar exam or the MPRE?

3. ***In the Real World.*** What are the practical obstacles to replacing examinations with an alternative measure of competence?

4. ***The Diploma Privilege.*** What are the advantages and disadvantages of a system like Wisconsin's, in which graduates of approved law schools in the state may be admitted to practice without taking the bar exam? Why did the ABA oppose the diploma privilege? Could or should the diploma privilege be implemented in a state like California, which has a large number of law schools of varying degrees of selectivity? One solution to that problem might be to extend the diploma privilege only to graduates of some law schools, or only to some graduates of law schools. Would such a limit be

desirable? If a state were to extend the diploma privilege only to some graduates of a law school, how should it define who is eligible? Grades? Courses taken? Something else?

5. ***Practice-Based Ways to Assess Competence.*** An approach currently implemented only in New Hampshire, which has only one law school, extends the diploma privilege only to some graduates of the law school, and even then requires that candidates must take prescribed courses in substance and skills and complete a series of written exercises that are reviewed by the bar examiners. Similar proposals have been made to allow candidates to demonstrate competence through something like a Public Service Alternative Bar Exam that would measure competence in the ten core skills proposed in the MacCrate Report by having candidates work as lawyers in a court system supervised by law school clinical faculty.[11]

2. MORAL CHARACTER AND FITNESS TO PRACTICE

The third requirement for admission to the bar—beyond getting a JD and passing the bar examination—is demonstrating good moral character and fitness to practice law. Typically, this requirement is satisfied by a candidate filling out a lengthy statement regarding his or her past and providing a list of references. The law school from which the candidate graduated fills out a form indicating that the person has obtained a JD and disclosing whether the law school is aware of anything in the candidate's record that would render him or her unfit to practice law. The bar examiner in the state sends a form to each of the candidate's past employers, as well as to all of the candidate's listed references, asking brief questions about whether the reference is aware of any reason why the candidate should not be admitted to practice.

The moral character questionnaire demands full disclosure, and applicants may be denied admission for failing to make full disclosure. State ethics rules prohibit applicants for admission to the bar from knowingly making a false statement of material fact or failing to disclose a fact necessary to correct a factual misapprehension, or knowingly failing to respond to a lawful demand for information from an admission or disciplinary authority. Some applicants to the bar find the requirement of full disclosure to be offensive, especially when the information not disclosed would not be disqualifying.

A second hurdle for many applicants has to do with which aspects of their past conduct may be grounds for the bar to determine they lack good moral character or fitness for the practice of law. Currently, the Code of Recommended Standards for Bar Examiners, adopted by the ABA, the

---

[11] Kristin Booth Glen, *When and Where We Enter: Rethinking Admission to the Legal Profession*, 102 COLUM. L. REV. 1696, 1720–1722 (2002).

National Conference of Bar Examiners, and the AALS, identify a number of relevant factors.

Moral Character and Fitness

Standard of Character and Fitness. Ethics rules in most states provide that a lawyer should be one whose record of conduct justifies the trust of clients, adversaries, courts, and others with respect to the professional duties owed to them. A record manifesting a significant deficiency in the honesty, trustworthiness, diligence, or reliability of an applicant may constitute a basis for denial of admission.

Relevant Conduct. Ethics rules in most states state that the revelation or discovery of any of the following should be treated as cause for further inquiry before the bar examining authority decides whether the applicant possesses the character and fitness to practice law:

- unlawful conduct
- academic misconduct
- making of false statements, including omissions
- misconduct in employment
- acts involving dishonesty, fraud, deceit, or misrepresentation
- abuse of legal process
- neglect of financial responsibilities
- neglect of professional obligations
- violation of an order of a court
- evidence of mental or emotional instability
- evidence of drug or alcohol dependency
- denial of admission to the bar in another jurisdiction on character and fitness grounds
- disciplinary action by a professional disciplinary agency of any jurisdiction[12]

What bar committees have found disqualifying over the years has varied. There appears to be no consensus about whether conduct is disqualifying because it predicts future behavior as a lawyer, because it creates an appearance to the public that the lawyer (or the bar generally) is not to be trusted, or for some other reason. As to criminal record, some states have admitted to the bar and others have refused to admit

[12] http://www.ncbex.org/assets/media_files/Comp-Guide/CompGuide.pdf.

candidates who graduated from college and law school with a good academic record after having served a lengthy prison sentence for a felony.[13] Likewise, bar authorities have sometimes admitted and sometimes denied admission to candidates who were found or credibly alleged to have plagiarized papers in law school, cheated on law school exams, or otherwise committed academic misconduct. Having been fired from a job for egregious misconduct has been the basis for denial of admission when the bar authorities were not convinced that the person was reformed.[14]

Many states in the 1950s refused to admit candidates to the bar if they were or had been members of the Communist Party or declined to state whether they had been. The Supreme Court overturned these decisions, ruling that party membership without evidence of violent or disloyal conduct was not sufficient to establish unfitness to practice law.[15] More recently, Matthew Hale was denied admission to the Illinois and Montana bars because he was a leader of a white supremacist organization. Hale ran the organization's web site, which made a variety of hateful statements about blacks, Jews, and "other mud races." The Illinois Bar justified its decision on the ground that Hale's views would lead to disciplinable conduct even if simply holding the views themselves is not a basis for denying admission, and the Supreme Court denied review.[16] More recently, other states have struggled with whether to admit avowed white supremacists in cases where the candidate had engaged in protest activities and had a long record of hate speech on social media.[17]

Most state bar admissions committees ask questions about mental health and drug and alcohol abuse. Prior to the 1980s, most states did not inquire about mental health or substance abuse on bar admission applications. States then began to inquire broadly into applicants' mental health and substance abuse at any point in time, typically asking whether the applicant had "ever had" or "been treated for" mental illness or

---

[13] *See In the Matter of Hamm*, 123 P.3d 652 (Ariz. 2005); Elizabeth Olson, *Are Felons Fit to Be Lawyers? Increasingly, Yes*, N.Y. TIMES, Jan. 21, 2018 (profiling two people who had been convicted of felony drug offenses who were admitted to the bar).

[14] Maura Dolan, *Stephen Glass' Fragile Dream*, L.A. TIMES, July 4, 2012, A1. The California Supreme Court ruled unanimously that the candidate could not be admitted to the bar because he had engaged in a pattern of deceit and had failed to prove he had been sufficiently rehabilitated. Maura Dolan, *Stephen Glass, Ex-Journalist Who Fabricated Stories, Can't Be a Lawyer*, L.A. TIMES, Jan. 27, 2014.

[15] *Schware v. Board of Bar Examiners*, 353 U.S. 232 (1957); *Konigsberg v. State Bar of California*, 366 U.S. 36 (1961); *In re Anastaplo*, 366 U.S. 82 (1961). *See* George Anastaplo, *Lawyers, First Principles, and Contemporary Challenges: Explorations*, 19 N. ILL. L. REV. 353 (1999).

[16] *Hale v. Committee of Character and Fitness of the Illinois Bar*, 723 N.E.2d 206 (1999) (denying review of Illinois Supreme Court's character and fitness committee decision), cert. denied, 530 U.S. 1261 (2000). Hale was later convicted of soliciting an undercover FBI agent to kill a federal judge who had ruled against Hale's organization in a trademark dispute over the name of the organization. *United States v. Hale*, 448 F.3d 971 (7th Cir. 2006).

[17] *See* Jessica Schulberg, *Should White Supremacists Be Allowed to Practice Law?* HUFFINGTON POST, Dec. 24, 2017.

substance abuse. After the effective date of the Americans With Disabilities Act of 1990, which prohibits disability discrimination in employment and licensing, states narrowed their inquiries to focus on severe mental health issues, hospitalizations, or conditions that would currently interfere with the practice of law.[18] However, critics assert that many states still ask questions that invite judgments about fitness that are based on stereotyped notions about mental health. The National Council on Bar Examiners in 2014 changed its standard question (one used by many state bars) to inquire whether the applicant has in the past five years exhibited conduct that could call into question the applicant's ability to practice law in a competent, ethical, and professional manner.[19]

3. RETHINKING REQUIREMENTS FOR BAR ADMISSION

The three requirements for admission to the bar—obtaining a JD, passing the bar exam and MPRE, and demonstrating good moral character—are nearly universal among states, but each of them has been criticized. The moral character requirement has also been sharply criticized as biased, arbitrary, and ineffective in protecting clients.[20] Should states abandon the requirement of demonstrating good moral character, or at least sharply narrow the grounds for denial of admission? If they were to do so, should the bar devote the resources it now spends screening the moral character of applicants to more vigorous enforcement of the ethics rules? What other admissions requirements, if any, should states impose?

New York requires that applicants for admission to the bar demonstrate that they have performed 50 hours of law-related pro bono work under the supervision of a law professor or a licensed attorney during law school.[21] Work in a law school clinic for which the student received academic credit satisfies the requirement. Lawyers already admitted to practice in New York, or those admitted elsewhere seeking admission in New York, need not satisfy the pro bono requirement. What are the justifications for requiring applicants to the bar to perform pro bono work? Is it a way to demonstrate competence or is it a way to demonstrate moral

---

18 *See* John Bauer, *The Character of the Questions and the Fitness of the Process*, 49 U.C.L.A. L. REV. 93 (2001) (analyzing whether the open-ended inquiries into mental health violate the Americans With Disabilities Act).

19 *See* Anna Stolley Persky, *State Bars May Probe Applicants' Behavior, But Not Mental Health Status, Says DOJ*, ABA J., June 1, 2014.

20 *See* Leslie Levin, et al., *The Questionable Character of the Bar's Character and Fitness Inquiry*, 40 LAW & SOC. INQ. 51 (2015); Deborah L. Rhode, *Moral Character as a Professional Credential*, 94 YALE L.J. 491 (1984).

21 http://www.nycourts.gov/attorneys/probono/FAQsBarAdmission.pdf; http://www.calbarjournal.com/October2012/TopHeadlines/TH2.aspx.

character? What is the justification for requiring pro bono work only of applicants not admitted elsewhere?

If the pro bono requirement is motivated by the concern that the bar exam does not sufficiently test skills and that an additional requirement is necessary to ensure competence, perhaps requiring 50 hours of pro bono is not enough. Should states require applicants for admission to the bar to have completed a clinic during law school, in order to demonstrate that the prospective lawyer has developed some level of proficiency in representing clients? Should states require applicants to have completed a certain number of skills courses, such as interviewing, counseling, negotiation, drafting, trial practice, or appellate advocacy?

C. DISCIPLINE

Bar associations in every state exercise power, typically delegated by the courts or the legislature or both, to discipline lawyers, including by revoking their license to practice law. Bar disciplinary proceedings are quasi-criminal in nature and, therefore, must comply with the constitutional requirements that those charged be accorded due process of law. Due process includes notice of the charges, the opportunity to present and to confront evidence and witnesses, and the right to make arguments. Lawyers may not be disciplined for invoking the constitutional privilege against self-incrimination.

Lawyer discipline tends to focus on two kinds of transgressions: incompetence and poor moral character. Many of the same policy and legal issues arise in disciplining lawyers on these bases as arise in denying admission, although sometimes the bar will deny admission for conduct that likely would not be the basis of discipline and, occasionally, may impose at least mild discipline for conduct that would not prevent admission.

Bar discipline ranges from a private reprimand that is placed in a file but not reported to the public to various forms of public discipline, including a public reprimand, or temporary or permanent suspension of the license (disbarment). Bars do not have the authority to order lawyers to pay compensation to victims of wrongful conduct. However, bar disciplinary bodies have sometimes negotiated settlements of disciplinary proceedings in which the lawyer(s) pay a fine or perform some form of community or pro bono legal service as a condition of imposition of a lesser punishment than disbarment. For example, President Bill Clinton agreed to a $25,000 fine and a five-year suspension in lieu of disbarment as punishment for lying under oath about his sexual relationship with Monica Lewinsky. Alston & Bird and its client, DuPont company, settled a criminal investigation relating to concealment of documents in a suit over a contaminated fungicide by each paying $2.5 million to various Georgia law schools to endow a chair in professional ethics, $1 million to endow an annual symposium on legal ethics, and $250,000 to support work by the Georgia bar's commission on professionalism.[22]

The discipline system administered by each state's bar includes a mechanism for clients, lawyers, judges, or members of the public to report lawyer misconduct. Each year, bar disciplinary agencies receive approximately 120,000 complaints against lawyers. (There are about 1.3 million lawyers in the U.S.) In 2014, states disciplined a total of about 10,000 lawyers, and disbarred about 900.[23] Bar disciplinary authorities dismiss the vast majority of complaints without investigation or explanation because the bar decides it lacks probable cause to pursue the matter or lacks jurisdiction over the conduct alleged. Less than one percent of investigated complaints result in disbarment. There is a wide variation among states in the frequency with which severe sanctions such as disbarment or a long suspension are imposed.[24]

The most common grounds for discipline are neglect of client matters, misappropriation of client funds, and failure to communicate with clients. The most common complaint against lawyers concerns the fees charged, but lawyers are rarely disciplined for their fees.

Another major controversy over bar discipline has to do with which lawyers are disciplined. Solo practitioners and lawyers in very small firms account for the overwhelming majority of discipline cases, which may reflect a larger number of egregious ethics rules violations as well as the limited resources given to disciplinary agencies to investigate and prove the kinds of violations that may occur at larger law offices.

Trying to understand why lawyers engage in ethical misconduct is a difficult task. Professor Richard Abel wrote two lengthy books on New York and California lawyer discipline and read hundreds of discipline cases during the research.[25] In the cases he chose for close study, the lawyers protested their innocence to the end, even in cases in which it was clear that they had transgressed fundamental rules of ethics and criminal law. They regarded themselves as victims of an unfair system, not as criminals. Among the experienced lawyers he profiled, "[e]thical misconduct is

---

[22] Milo Geyelin, *DuPont and Atlanta Firm Agree to Pay Nearly 13 Million in Benlate Matter,* WALL ST. J., Jan. 4, 1999, at A18.

[23] American Bar Association Center for Professional Responsibility Standing Committee on Professional Discipline, 2014 Survey on Lawyer Discipline Systems, chart III, https://www.americanbar.org/content/dam/aba/administrative/professional_responsibility/2014_sold_final_results.authcheckdam.pdf; Annual Discipline Report of the State of California, http://www.calbar.ca.gov/Portals/0/documents/reports/2015_2014AnnualDisciplineReport.pdf?ver=2017-05-19-134135-803.

[24] *Id.; see generally* DEBORAH L. RHODE, IN THE INTERESTS OF JUSTICE: REFORMING THE LEGAL PROFESSION 159 (2000) (discussing the bar discipline system).

[25] *Id.*; RICHARD L. ABEL, LAWYERS IN THE DOCK: LEARNING FROM ATTORNEY DISCIPLINARY PROCEEDINGS (2008).

learned behavior, it is not the product of ignorance,"[26] and the misconduct reflected "greed more than need. None of the lawyers suffered the kind of poverty we associate with street crime. None was a substance abuser." However, among all lawyers disciplined, substance abuse is often a factor. Abel also found in the cases he studied that the misconduct was habitual; it was not simply a momentary lapse of judgment brought on by personal life stress.[27]

Bar disciplinary agencies have almost always targeted individual lawyers, and have seldom prosecuted law firms either directly, for breaching the ethics rules binding on firms, or vicariously, by holding the firm accountable for the actions of its employees or partners. As one scholar noted, the focus on individuals probably results from the disciplinary system's tie to licensing of individuals and to the development of bar discipline during the long era in which most lawyers practiced solo. Yet, many ethical lapses are encouraged by firm policy (which would be an appropriate case for vicarious liability) or are committed jointly by a number of lawyers in the firm, each of whom will attempt to shift responsibility onto others, such that it would be unfair to pin on one or two people the blame for misconduct committed or encouraged by many.[28]

Many have called for law firms to adopt some form of peer review that has long been the norm in medicine.[29] In hospitals, for example, doctors examine the records of morbidity and mortality for the entire hospital or a segment of it in order to identify problems and fix them prospectively, and some law firms have begun to implement such programs.[30] Law firms already review partners and associates at least annually to set compensation. Peer review to ensure ethics compliance in a law firm might consist of interviewing partners, associates, and clients, as well as examining compliance with firm policies.[31] Management systems can detect common violations, such as neglecting client matters, misappropriating client funds, and engaging in conflicts of interest.[32] Many law firms have adopted such compliance systems as an element of their strategies for managing risk.[33]

---

[26] ABEL, LAWYERS ON TRIAL at 461.

[27] *Id.* at 461–464.

[28] Ted Schneyer, *Professional Discipline for Law Firms?* 77 CORNELL L. REV. 1 (1992).

[29] *See, e.g.,* RICHARD L. ABEL, LAWYERS IN THE DOCK: LEARNING FROM ATTORNEY DISCIPLINARY PROCEEDINGS 525 (2008)

[30] Susan Saab Fortney, *Are Law Firm Partners Islands Unto Themselves? An Empirical Study of Law Firm Peer Review and Culture,* 10 GEO. J. LEGAL ETHICS 271 (1996).

[31] *Id.*

[32] Theodore Schneyer, *On Further Reflection: How "Professional Self-Regulation" Should Provide Compliance with Broad Ethical Duties of law Firm Management,* 53 ARIZ. L. REV. 577 (2011); Elizabeth Chambliss & David B. Wilkins, *The Emerging Role of Ethics Advisors, General Counsel, and Other Compliance Specialists in Large Law Firms,* 44 ARIZ. L. REV. 559 (2002).

[33] Elizabeth Chambliss, *New Sources of Managerial Authority in Law Firms,* 22 GEO. J. LEGAL ETHICS 63 (2009).

NOTES ON BAR DISCIPLINE

1. ***Who Should the Bar Target for Discipline?*** How should bar disciplinary authorities identify priorities, given scarce resources? Should they focus on egregious cases? Easy to prove cases? Cases indicating corruption, as opposed to incompetence? (There is strong evidence that state bars already do the latter, as recent studies of large numbers of New York and California discipline cases show that the overwhelming majority of cases involve unethical conduct rather than simple incompetence.[34])

2. ***Peer Review?*** Why have law firms been slow to adopt a peer review system that is common in medicine? Would it be a good idea to require it?

D. SUMMARY

This chapter examined the almost universal requirements for admission to the bar: obtaining a JD degree, passing the bar examination and the MPRE, and demonstrating good moral character. As to each of these three, the chapter considered the most commonly asserted justifications for the requirement—ensuring the competence and trustworthiness of lawyers and protecting their reputation—and also considered whether the requirement adequately serves the justification and whether alternatives might be preferable on the grounds of efficacy or fairness. Many have called for reconsideration of requirements for admission to practice to increase focus on practical skills rather than knowledge. The chapter also examined bar discipline. We identified the grounds on which lawyers can be disciplined, the principal grounds on which lawyers are in fact disciplined, the disciplinary process, and the penalties imposed. Bar discipline is designed to serve the goals of prevention and deterrence, not compensation of clients or third parties who are harmed by lawyer misfeasance or malfeasance. We considered whether the bar disciplinary system adequately protects clients and whether alternative mechanisms might better ensure competence and trustworthiness.

---

[34] *See* RICHARD L. ABEL, LAWYERS ON TRIAL: UNDERSTANDING ETHICAL MISCONDUCT (2010) (study of California lawyer discipline); RICHARD L. ABEL, LAWYERS IN THE DOCK: LEARNING FROM ATTORNEY DISCIPLINARY PROCEEDINGS (2008) (study of New York lawyer discipline).

CHAPTER 24

LAWYER SATISFACTION AND WELL-BEING

■ ■ ■

A. INTRODUCTION

In the popular and legal press, one commonly hears that lawyers are miserable and that they regret their career choices. Are those claims true? Do lawyers typically regret the decision to attend law school or to enter the profession? What are the sources of satisfaction and dissatisfaction in lawyers' careers? Do they vary by types of practice or job setting? What factors are correlated with broader measures of lawyer well-being? This chapter considers these questions and the best available research on these issues.

The first excerpt, by a law professor and former large firm lawyer, asserts that lawyers generally are unhappy, that lawyers in large law firms are the least happy of all lawyers, and that long hours and an excessive focus on money are at the root of the trouble. The remaining materials in this chapter examine the available evidence on lawyers' career satisfaction and well-being.

B. ARE LAWYERS UNHAPPY?

ON BEING A HAPPY, HEALTHY, AND ETHICAL MEMBER OF AN UNHAPPY, UNHEALTHY, AND UNETHICAL PROFESSION

Patrick J. Schiltz
52 Vanderbilt Law Review 871 (1999)

Dear Law Student:

I have good news and bad news. The bad news is that the profession that you are about to enter is one of the most unhappy and unhealthy on the face of the earth—and, in the view of many, one of the most unethical. The good news is that you can join this profession and still be happy, healthy, and ethical. I am writing to tell you how.

A study of California lawyers by the RAND Institute for Civil Justice found that only half say if they had to do it over, they would become lawyers. On the whole, California lawyers were reported to be " 'profoundly pessimistic' about the state of the legal profession and its future." [A] nationwide poll of attorneys conducted by the National Law Journal found that less than a third of those surveyed were "very satisfied" with their careers.

For almost thirty years, the University of Michigan Law School has been surveying its former students five years after they graduate. Given the stellar reputation of their alma mater, Michigan graduates would presumably have more employment options available than graduates of most other law schools and thus would presumably be among the most satisfied practitioners in America. Yet the annual surveys have discovered surprisingly low levels of career satisfaction in general and a marked decline in career satisfaction over time, at least for lawyers in private practice.

The most comprehensive data on career satisfaction of lawyers were produced by three national surveys conducted under the auspices of the Young Lawyers Division of the American Bar Association ("ABA"). Taken together, the surveys show a substantial decline in the job satisfaction of attorneys. In 1984, 41% of lawyers said that they were "very satisfied" with their jobs; in 1990, only 33% of all lawyers surveyed were "very satisfied," a decline of one-fifth in just six years. At the same time, the number of lawyers who were "very dissatisfied" with their jobs rose from 3% in 1984 to 5% in 1990.*

[C]areer dissatisfaction is not distributed equally throughout the profession. Lawyers in some practice settings are happier than lawyers in others. And lawyers in large law firms are often among the least happy. This appears to be true for both associates and partners.

Explaining the Unhappiness of Lawyers. In every study of the career satisfaction of lawyers of which I am aware, in every book or article about the woes of the legal profession that I have read, and in every conversation about life as a practicing lawyer that I have heard, lawyers complain about the long hours they have to work. Without question, the single biggest complaint among attorneys is increasingly long workdays with decreasing time for personal and family life. Lawyers are complaining with increasing vehemence about living to work, rather than working to live—about being asked not to dedicate, but to sacrifice their lives to the firm.

---

* [Eds.: More recent results of surveys of law graduates have been reported since this article was written. Readers curious about recent survey data on lawyer satisfaction and related topics may wish to consult RONIT DINOVITZER ET AL., AFTER THE JD II: SECOND RESULTS FROM A NATIONAL STUDY OF LEGAL CAREERS 27 (2009); Gabriele Plickert, Joyce Sterling, Robert Nelson, Bryant Garth, David Wilkins & Rebecca Sandefur, *After the JD III: Third Results from a National Study of Legal Careers* (2014); Ronit Dinovitzer & Bryant G. Garth, *Lawyer Satisfaction in the Process of Structuring Legal Careers,* 41 LAW & SOC'Y REV. 1 (2007); John Monahan and Jeffrey Swanson, *Lawyers at Mid-Career: A 20-Year Longitudinal Study of Job Satisfaction,* 6 J. EMPIRICAL LEGAL STUD, 451 (2009); Milan Markovic & Gabriele Plickert, *Attorney Career Dissatisfaction in the New Normal,* available at https://papers.ssrn.com/sol3/papers.cfm?abstract_id=3001391. Some findings from these studies are summarized at the end of this chapter.]

[In the late 1960s], most partners billed between 1200 and 1400 hours per year and most associates between 1400 and 1600 hours. As late as the mid-1980s, even associates in large New York firms were often not expected to bill more than 1800 hours annually. Today, many firms would consider these ranges acceptable only for partners or associates who had died midway through the year.

Workloads, like the job dissatisfaction to which they so closely relate, are not distributed equally throughout the profession. Generally speaking, lawyers in private practice work longer hours than those who work for corporations or for the government.

Why do lawyers work too much? In one sense, the answer is easy: It's the money, stupid. It begins with law students. The vast majority of law students—at least the vast majority of those attending the more prestigious schools (or getting good grades at the less prestigious schools)—want to work in big firms. And the reason they want to work in big firms is that big firms pay the most.

Of course, students deny this. Students—many of whom came to law school intending to do public interest work—don't like to admit that they've "sold out," so they come up with rationalizations, justifications, accounts, and disclaimers for seeking big firm jobs. They insist that the real reason they want to go to a big firm is the training, or the interesting and challenging work, or the chance to work with exceptionally talented colleagues, or the desire to "keep my doors open." They imply that the huge salaries are just an afterthought—mere icing on the cake. Or they reluctantly admit that, yes, they really are after the money, but they have no choice: Because of student loan debt, they must take a job that pays $80,000 per year. $60,000 per year just won't cut it.

Most of this is hogwash. As I will explain below, almost all of the purported non-monetary advantages of big firms either do not exist or are vastly overstated. Moreover, there are few lawyers who could not live comfortably on what most corporations or government agencies pay, whatever their student loan debt. Students are after the money, pure and simple. The hiring partner of any major firm will tell you that if his firm offers first year associates a salary of $69,000, and a competitor down the street offers them $72,000, those who have the choice will flock to the competitor—even if the competitor will require them to bill 200 hours more each year.

As the salaries of first year associates go up, the salaries of senior associates must rise to keep pace. After all, no sixth-year associate wants to be paid less than a first-year associate. And as the salaries of senior associates go up, the salaries of junior partners must rise to keep pace. After all, no junior partner wants to be paid less than a senior associate.

And, of course, as the salaries of junior partners go up, so must the salaries of senior partners.

How do firms pay for this ever-spiraling increase in salaries? In reality, firms have only one option: They have to bill more hours. The market for lawyers' services has become intensely competitive. As the number of lawyers has soared, competition for clients has become ferocious. Clients insist on getting good work at low hourly rates. If clients do not get what they want, they will move their business to one of the thousands of other lawyers who are chomping at the bit to get it. Raising billing rates to pay for spiraling salaries is simply not much of an option for most firms. As a result, firms get the extra money to pay for the spiraling salaries in the only way they can: They bill more hours. Everyone has to work harder to pay for the higher salaries. And when salaries go up again, everyone has to work still harder.

I am leaving out one wrinkle—an important wrinkle that you should know about if you are contemplating joining a large law firm (or a firm that acts like a large law firm). The partners of a big firm have a third option for making more money. This option involves what big firm partners euphemistically refer to as "leverage." I like to call it "the skim." Richard Abel calls it "exploitation."* The person being exploited is you.

Basically, what happens is that big firms buy associates' time wholesale and sell it retail. Here is how it works: As a new associate in a large firm, you will be paid about one-third of what you bring into the firm. If you bill, say, 2000 hours at $100 per hour, you will generate $200,000 in revenue for your firm. About a third of that—$70,000 or so—will be paid to you. Another third will go toward paying the expenses of the firm. And the final third will go into the pockets of the firm's partners. Firms make money off associates. That is why it's in the interests of big firms to hire lots of associates and to make very few of them partners. The more associates there are, the more profits for the partners to split, and the fewer partners there are, the bigger each partner's share.

Money is at the root of virtually everything that lawyers don't like about their profession: the long hours, the commercialization, the tremendous pressure to attract and retain clients, the fiercely competitive marketplace, the lack of collegiality and loyalty among partners, the poor public image of the profession, and even the lack of civility. Almost every one of these problems would be eliminated or at least substantially reduced if lawyers were simply willing to make less money. Thousands of lawyers choose to give up a healthy, happy, well-balanced life for a less healthy, less happy life dominated by work. And they do so merely to be able to

* [Eds.: Richard Abel is prominent sociologist of the legal profession.]

make seven or eight times the national median income instead of five or six times the national median income.

The Ethics of Lawyers. It is hard to practice law ethically. Complying with the formal rules is the easy part. The rules are not very specific, and they don't demand very much. Acting as an ethical lawyer in the broader, non-formalistic sense is far more difficult. I have already given you some idea of why it is hard to practice law in a big firm (or any firm that emulates a big firm) and live a balanced life. But even practicing law ethically in the sense of being honest and fair and compassionate is difficult. To understand why, you need to understand what it is that you will do every day as a lawyer.

Here is the problem: After you start practicing law, nothing is likely to influence you more than the culture or house norms of the agency, department, or firm in which you work. If you are going into private practice—particularly private practice in a big firm—you are going to be immersed in a culture that is hostile to the values you now have. The system does not want you to apply the same values in the workplace that you do outside of work (unless you're rapaciously greedy outside of work); it wants you to replace those values with the system's values. The system is obsessed with money, and it wants you to be, too. The system wants you—it needs you—to play the game.

In a thousand ways, you will absorb big firm culture—a culture of long hours of toil inside the office and short hours of conspicuous consumption outside the office. You will work among lawyers who will talk about money constantly and who will be intensely curious about how much money other lawyers are making.

As the values of an attorney change, so, too, does her ability to practice law ethically. The process that I have described will obviously push a lawyer away from practicing law ethically in the broadest sense—that is, in the sense of leading a balanced life and meeting non-work-related responsibilities. When work becomes all-consuming, it consumes all. However, absorbing the values of big firm culture will also push a lawyer away from practicing law ethically in the narrower sense of being honest and fair and compassionate. In the highly competitive, money obsessed world of big firm practice, most of the new incentives for lawyers, such as attracting and retaining clients, push toward stretching ethical concerns to the limit.

Unethical lawyers do not start out being unethical; they start out just like you—as perfectly decent young men or women who have every intention of practicing law ethically. They do not become unethical overnight; they become unethical just as you will (if you become unethical)—a little bit at a time. And they do not become unethical by shredding incriminating documents or bribing jurors; they become unethical just as you are likely to—by cutting a corner here, by stretching the truth a bit there. [Here Schiltz argues that lawyers begin taking incremental unethical steps that eventually add up to a willingness to engage in serious misconduct—padding hours, cheating in discovery, encouraging witnesses to lie, mischaracterizing precedent in briefs, etc.]

On Being a Happy, Healthy, and Ethical Lawyer. I now want to give you some advice—advice about how you can be a happy, healthy, and ethical member of an unhappy, unhealthy, and unethical profession.

My "big picture" advice is simple: Don't get sucked into the game. Don't let money become the most important thing in your life. Don't fall into the trap of measuring your worth as an attorney—or as a human being—by how much money you make.

If you let your law firm or clients define success for you, they will define it in a way that is in their interest, not yours. It is important for them that your primary motivation be making money and that, no matter how much money you make, your primary motivation continue to be making money. If you end up as an unhappy or unethical attorney, money will most likely be at the root of your problem.

You cannot win the game. If you fall into the trap of measuring your worth by money, you will always feel inadequate. There will always be a firm paying more to its associates than yours. There will always be a firm with higher per-partner profits than yours. There will always be a lawyer at your firm making more money than you. No matter how hard you work, you will never be able to win the game. You will run faster and faster and faster, but there will always be a runner ahead of you, and the finish line will never quite come into view. That is why the game will make your clients and partners so rich and you so unhappy.

Law students and young lawyers have to stop seeing workaholism as "a badge of honor." They have to stop talking with admiration about lawyers who bill 2500 hours per year. Attorneys whose lives are consumed with work—who devote endless hours to making themselves and their clients wealthy, at the expense of just about everything else in their lives—are not heroes. And that is true whether the lawyers are workaholic because they truly enjoy their work or because they crave wealth or because they are terribly insecure. At best, these attorneys are people with questionable priorities. At worst, they are immoral. There are certainly better lawyers after which to pattern your professional life.

NOTES ON SCHILTZ

1. ***Does This Portrait Fit What You Know About Large Firm Practice?*** Are Schiltz's claims about the organizational cultures of big firms consistent with what you learned about these institutions in Chapter 8?

2. ***Students' Motivations and Concerns.*** Schiltz asserts that most law students and aspiring law students are strongly motivated to make money, to accept the highest paying jobs that they can find, and to overestimate the extent to which financial considerations must drive their career choices. Based on your own observations and impressions, does this claim ring true?

3. ***Comparing Other Practice Settings.*** Which of Schiltz's claims about the nature and sources of dissatisfaction would you expect to be true about practice in other settings? Based on what you have read thus far, what do you imagine to be the sources of unhappiness for lawyers in other types of practice?

C. WHAT IS CAREER SATISFACTION; HOW SHOULD WE MEASURE IT?; COMPARATIVE PERSPECTIVES

The next two excerpts critically assess the empirical claims in Schiltz's essay. The first excerpt analyzes the research that Schiltz relies on but draws very different conclusions and puts a finer point on exactly what we mean by career satisfaction and how we should measure it. The second excerpt draws attention to how lawyers compare with other occupational groups in terms of career satisfaction. It also calls into question whether firms are as similar to one another as Schiltz suggests.

CROSS-EXAMINING THE MYTH OF LAWYERS' MISERY

Kathleen E. Hull
52 Vanderbilt Law Review 971 (1999)

At first glance, the evidence on job satisfaction among lawyers may appear mixed, but upon closer inspection it becomes clear that the most valid, well-designed research has produced little if any support for the notion that lawyers are unhappy in their work. The studies cited by Schiltz range from trade journal surveys to more serious scholarly enterprises, and the significance we attach to their findings should be in direct proportion to the validity and reliability of the research techniques employed.

Some of these same studies cited by Schiltz produce findings that fail to support his contention that lawyers are largely unhappy in their work. For example, overall findings from the ABA surveys in 1984 and 1990 do not bolster a claim of widespread dissatisfaction in the profession. In the 1984 survey, 81% of respondents were either "somewhat satisfied" or "very satisfied" with their current job, whereas only 12% were "somewhat dissatisfied" and 3% were "very dissatisfied." In 1990, 76% were either "somewhat satisfied" or "very satisfied," while 14% were "somewhat dissatisfied" and 5% "very dissatisfied." These figures hardly suggest job dissatisfaction of crisis proportions in the law.

Other studies boasting higher response rates and sounder survey techniques provide further confirmation that rumors of lawyers' misery are greatly exaggerated. Chambers' 1989 study of University of Michigan law graduates, which achieved a 71% response rate surveying graduates five years after law school, found that 82% of female graduates and 83% of male graduates were "somewhat" or "quite" satisfied with their careers at the five-year mark. A follow-up survey showed little change in satisfaction levels over time.

Beyond his reliance on studies of dubious data quality and his relative inattention to some studies that produce findings of high satisfaction levels, there is also a conceptual difficulty embedded in Schiltz's discussion of the research on lawyers' satisfaction. Schiltz blends together a number of conceptually distinct findings under the general umbrella of "satisfaction." Asking people whether they hope to be in the same job at some future point in time, or asking them whether they would choose the same occupation if they had it to do over again, produces only indirect evidence at best regarding satisfaction with their current situation. People may hope to change jobs in the future even if they love their current work, possibly because they know a job change will be necessary to keep "moving up" (e.g., from firm practice to a judgeship) or because they hope to renegotiate the tradeoff between work and personal priorities in the future. These kinds of reasons for seeking a change do not necessarily prove that the current job produces unhappiness; they only demonstrate that people like (or sometimes need) change.

Relying on the American Bar Association surveys conducted in 1984 and 1990 and the unpublished Michigan data covering the years 1981 through 1996, Schiltz argues that there has been a "marked" and "substantial" decline in lawyers' job satisfaction in recent years. With regard to the ABA data, he points to the fact that 41% of respondents were "very satisfied" in 1984, compared to only 33% in 1990.

These figures are interesting, but we should not attach undue importance to them for at least two reasons. First, not all of the decline in the "very satisfied" category translated into increases in the proportion of "dissatisfied" or "very dissatisfied" lawyers. In fact, among the overall sample, the proportion who were "dissatisfied" rose modestly from 12% in 1984 to 14% in 1990, and the proportion "very dissatisfied" inched up from 3% in 1984 to 5% in 1990. In other words, only about half of the eight percentage-point decline in the "very satisfied" category is accounted for by increases in dissatisfied respondents. The other half is accounted for by similarly modest growth in the proportion of lawyers who were "satisfied" or merely "neutral."

Second, even given a moderate decline in average satisfaction between the two survey years, we must take into consideration the broader context of these surveys. In particular, this kind of short-term trend in job satisfaction might simply reflect the ups and downs of the legal profession's fortunes over time. Like any industry, the legal services industry experiences periods of boom and bust, often closely linked to the cycles of the larger economy. While the mid-1980s represented a "boom" time for lawyers, by the early 1990s the climate had changed [for the worse].

Other surveys with longitudinal data covering somewhat different time periods show satisfaction levels holding fairly steady across time. In short, there is no consistent body of evidence that lawyers' work satisfaction has been declining in recent years, and the two surveys that suggest such a decline may simply reflect a short-term downturn in the growth in the market for lawyers' services in the U.S.

The assertion that large-firm lawyers are significantly less satisfied than lawyers in other practice settings is central to Schiltz's broader arguments. But how solid is the evidence for this claim?

In data [from a rigorous study of Chicago lawyers], there are no significant differences in satisfaction by practice setting among practicing lawyers. Compared to lawyers in other settings, large-firm lawyers seem neither remarkably happy nor remarkably miserable. Only 39% of large-firm lawyers were "very satisfied," the lowest proportion for any practice setting. By contrast, 60% of public interest lawyers fell into this category, as did 51% of government lawyers, 50% of internal counsel lawyers, 47% of solo practitioners, 46% of small-firm lawyers, and 45% of medium-firm lawyers. But 47% of large-firm attorneys were "satisfied," the highest proportion for any practice setting. And only 2% of large-firm lawyers were "dissatisfied" or "very dissatisfied," compared to 11% of government lawyers, 9% of solo practitioners and small-firm lawyers, 7% of medium-firm lawyers and public interest lawyers, and 5% of internal counsel.

Specifically, large-firm lawyers are significantly more satisfied than other private-practice lawyers with their salaries, their chances for advancement, and the prestige of their organizations. On salary, for example, 73% of large-firm attorneys were either "satisfied" or "very satisfied," compared to 57% of medium and small-firm attorneys and 46% of solo practitioners.

But large-firm lawyers are significantly less satisfied with their control over the amount of work they must do and also with the policies and administration of their firms. Only 56% of large-firm lawyers were "satisfied" or "very satisfied" with control over amount of work, compared to 65% of medium-firm lawyers, 79% of small-firm lawyers and 74% of solo practitioners. Just 43% of large-firm lawyers reported satisfaction with the policies/administration of their firms, similar to the 42% of medium-firm lawyers, but lower than the 68% of small-firm lawyers who liked their firm's policies.

NOTES ON HULL

1. ***What Do the Data Show?*** According to Hull, what are the problems with the data upon which Schiltz relies in asserting that lawyers are unhappy, and what are the problems in how he interprets the available data?

2. ***How to Interpret the Findings.*** How should we characterize the attitudes of lawyers who place themselves higher than the midpoint on the scale but below the "very satisfied" category? The author of a study of University of Michigan law graduates questions whether one should view this as evidence that the lawyer is "satisfied" with her work; he argues that it might instead indicate that the lawyer is ambivalent. He offers this analogy: "Imagine asking a friend about a restaurant where she has recently eaten. She tells you that she was "moderately satisfied" with her meal. Would you call and make a reservation?"[1] Do you find the analogy useful? If not, why not?

3. ***Elements of Career Satisfaction.*** What are the various elements of career satisfaction identified by Hull? How do lawyers in different private practice settings rank in terms of those elements of satisfaction?

THINKING ABOUT THE BUSINESS OF PRACTICING LAW

Michael J. Kelly
52 Vanderbilt Law Review 985 (1999)

The nagging question I have when confronted with all this evidence of discontent is to ask for some evaluative comparison. All the unhappiness data is solely confined to lawyers. If, for example, lawyers were not that much more unhappy than people inside their corporate clients, or physicians struggling with the transformation of the health care industry, would it worry us as much as it does Schiltz? And if we were to postulate that both law and medicine are undergoing significant change, would it not be entirely understandable that young people commencing their careers with expectations of a large degree of autonomy are distressed at the increasing "corporatization" or dominance by the organizations of practice in their professions?

The core of Schiltz's argument with which I most disagree is that large firms are all alike, or, to put it in its more modest, plausible, and compelling form, that big firms and big-firm lawyers are becoming more alike. I cannot disprove Schiltz's claims about the convergence occurring in large law firms. After all, there is evidence and intelligent speculation that supports it. Galanter and Palay's hypothesis, cited by Schiltz, is that in a culture that values autonomy, money is the one measure of the many goods of a practice upon which it is easiest to agree (or the least difficult to avoid) and therefore emerges as the prime focus of most partnership understandings. The vast majority of formulae or weighting systems for compensation in

---

[1] David L. Chambers, *Overstating the Satisfaction of Lawyers,* 39 LAW & SOC. INQ. 1, 5 (2013).

law firms reward those who strengthen the business and deploy to its full potential the firm's leverage by bringing in clients and servicing or retaining important clients.

So why am I so skeptical of the convergence thesis? One response is perhaps only temperamental: I am deeply suspicious of iron laws, particularly when it comes to organizations. Firms are human constructs. The character of an organization is determined by people, not solely by competitive pressures to which people respond. [O]rganizations develop different characters even in a situation of responding to the same economic pressures.

The advice Schiltz gives to law students, whether you agree with his diagnosis of large law firms or not, addresses thoughtfully the huge reality law graduates face—that the law firm is their profession and represents, enforces, and rewards the values that will determine the future of their career. I would encourage someone trying to learn about a firm to ask an interviewer to describe the leader of the firm. Is the leader the rainmaker extraordinaire, the most dominating personality, the most accomplished lawyer, someone with a sense of vision and direction for the firm, or someone with strong management skills? The person who heads the practice, at a time when organizational leadership is so critical to the future of law practice organizations, should speak volumes about the nature, let alone the future, of the firm. A riskier set of questions, probably best left to the time when an offer is in hand, could also be revealing. No firm of any size is likely to be free of conflict. Are people in the firm willing to discuss its internal conflicts, and describe how, if at all, they are resolved? Are people in the firm willing to talk about mistakes the firm has made? Current problems? Whether they do so and how they go about it would tell the questioner much about the self-confidence, character, and transparency (i.e., openness) of the organization.

Law is, and always has been, a business as well as a profession. Lawyers have, for most of American history, made good livings, and many have made fortunes. Once one escapes from the clutches of thinking of "profession" and "business" as dichotomies, and comes to terms with the fact that, whether we like it not, they are joined at the hip in private practice, a refreshing set of possibilities reveals itself. Virtually none of the criticisms or problems posed by Schiltz—imposed workaholic regimens, distorted compensation structures, unhappy professionals used and viewed in totally instrumental ways by management—are unique to large law firms or the private practice of law. [T]here is much to be gained by thinking of these organizations as businesses that may be profitable to their owners but have serious long-term problems. [T]hinking creatively about the business of private law practice could strongly—and realistically—support the enhancement of professional values. A sound business strategy entails a sustained and serious conversation that confronts the threats of drift and opportunism. Understanding the business better and taking creative action to improve the business may ultimately prove the most fruitful approach to developing happy, healthy, and ethical lawyers.

NOTES ON KELLY

1. ***Law v. Medicine and Other Professions/Occupations.*** Do you think that lawyers are more or less satisfied with their careers than doctors, business people, engineers, teachers, professional athletes, car mechanics, or any other occupation? Taking into account the different elements of career satisfaction identified by Hull, what would you expect to be the rewards and sources of dissatisfaction in these other professions and occupations?

2. ***Common Ground and Disagreement.*** What are the points of agreement and disagreement between Schiltz, Hull, and Kelly? How does Kelly's advice to law students differ from Schiltz's?

3. ***Organizational Cultures.*** Notice that Schiltz and Kelly agree that, for better or worse, the cultures of the organizations in which lawyers practice are likely to influence lawyers' lives, including their career satisfaction, much more than the rules of ethics and other activities of the organized bar. What aspects of organizational culture would you expect to be most significant for lawyer satisfaction?

4. ***Variation Among Firms.*** Based on what you have learned thus far about large firms, do you think that Kelly is right to suggest that large firms differ substantially and that lawyers seeking satisfying careers in these institutions need to ask good questions in order to uncover important differences in institutional cultures? Or do you think that whatever variation exists among law firms is too insubstantial to matter?

* * *

More Recent Research on Lawyer Satisfaction. Recent research continues to show high levels of job satisfaction among lawyers. Data from Wave 2 of the *After the JD* Study (*After the JD II*), published in 2009, found that three-quarters of respondents were "extremely" or "moderately" satisfied with their decision to become a lawyer. Moreover, on all but one of 19 measures (the exception was "opportunity for advancement"), respondents reported higher levels of satisfaction in Wave 2 than in Wave 1 of the study. Overall career satisfaction was fairly stable across workplaces, but the sources of satisfaction varied by practice setting. Lawyers in megafirms reported the highest levels of "power track" satisfaction (opportunities for advancement and prestige) but the lowest levels of satisfaction with hours and control over their work. Lawyers in government expressed high levels of satisfaction with balance and control but less satisfaction with the power track. Lawyers in legal services and public interest jobs were most satisfied with the content of their work and the value of their work to society but least satisfied with the power track dimension. Consistent with the results of Wave 1 of the study, black and Hispanic respondents reported the highest levels of career satisfaction in Wave 2; 80 percent of black and Hispanic sample members said that they were moderately or extremely satisfied with their decision to become a lawyer. Overall, women were slightly less satisfied with their career choice than men; 74.1 percent of women were extremely to moderately satisfied with the decision to become a lawyer, as compared with 78.4 percent of men.[2]

A study of University of Virginia Law School graduates, based on survey data gathered in 2007 from the Class of 1990, found that 81.2 percent of respondents were "extremely" or "moderately" satisfied with their decision to become a lawyer, while over 81 percent said that they were satisfied with their job setting. The report found no significant gender differences in respondents' satisfaction with the decision to become a lawyer.[3]

The data collection for the *After the JD II* report and the study of University of Virginia Law School graduates took place before the financial crisis in the autumn of 2008. Some have suggested that the combination of rising law school tuition, increased law school debt, and the 2008 recession, have changed prospects for new law graduates in ways that are likely to have far-reaching implications for lawyer satisfaction. In particular, critics have asserted that graduates of all but elite schools will regret the career choice because they will have difficulty finding jobs in large law firms and will be unable to repay their debt.[4]

But these predictions are not well-supported by the best available data. One article based on the *After the JD II* data cited evidence that more than three-quarters of respondents in the study, irrespective of debt, expressed extreme or moderate satisfaction with the decision to become a lawyer. The authors also noted that while graduates of elite law schools were less likely to have debt seven years after law school than graduates of lower-ranked schools, graduates of lower-ranked law schools paid down their debt at a faster rate than graduates of elite schools. The researchers predicted that data on lawyer satisfaction for the period after the recession were likely to resemble data from the period before the recession.[5]

---

[2] *See* Ronit Dinovitzer et al., After the JD II: Second Results from a National Study of Legal Careers 48–51, 70, 76–77 (2009).

[3] John Monahan and Jeffrey Swanson, *Lawyers at Mid-Career: a 20-Year Longitudinal Study of Job and Life Satisfaction*, 6 J. Empirical Legal Stud. 451 (2009).

[4] *See, e.g.*, David Segal, *For Law Schools, a Price to Play the ABA's Way*, N.Y. Times, Dec. 17, 2011; Brian Z. Tamanaha, Failing Law Schools (2012).

[5] Ronit Dinovitzer, Bryant G. Garth & Joyce Sterling, *Buyers' Remorse? An Empirical Assessment of the Desirability of a Lawyer Career*, 63 J. Legal Ed. 1, 5 (2013).

Results from the third wave of data collection for the *After the JD* study show that the high levels of career satisfaction reflected in earlier phases of this research continued.[6] Thirteen years into their careers, most lawyers (76 percent) reported that they were moderately or extremely satisfied with their decision to become a lawyer—a proportion that is virtually unchanged from prior waves of the survey. The respondents also reported high levels of satisfaction with the balance of personal life and work—5.4 on a 7-point scale, which is slightly higher than at Wave 2.

Overall career satisfaction in Wave 3 was high across workplaces, but lawyers in some practice areas were more satisfied with the decision to become a lawyer than others. The highest overall levels of satisfaction were in the public sector—legal services/public defender and public interest organizations—and in corporate counsel positions. Among lawyers in private practice, those in the largest firms and small firms expressed relatively high levels of career satisfaction, while those in mid-sized firms (101–250 lawyers) reported the lowest levels. As in previous waves of the *After the JD* research, lawyers in various types of practice settings ranked the components of job satisfaction differently. Lawyers in large firms scored well on the power track dimension of their work, but so did lawyers in firms of 2–20 lawyers. Large firms scored relatively poorly on the "job setting" dimension—control over hours worked, work relationships, and work/life balance. Legal services, public defender, and state government jobs scored well on social index and substance of work but lower on the power track dimension. The overall percentages of women and men reporting that they were extremely or moderately satisfied with the decision to become a lawyer were almost identical—76.1 percent for women and 76.2 percent for men. But there were gender differences in satisfaction by area of practice.

A particularly interesting phenomenon noted in the Wave 3 report was the relatively high satisfaction scores for solo practitioners and small firm lawyers. The report observed that 50% of the solos were not solos in Wave 2; many were transitioning from job losses in other sectors, and the category included many women working part time. But solos and small firm lawyers were generally relatively satisfied compared to their peers in other settings across all dimensions of satisfaction.

A recent study of lawyers' career satisfaction and dissatisfaction in the aftermath of the recession, drawing on 2015 survey data from over 11,000 members of the State Bar of Texas, found that only 13.5% of respondents were either very dissatisfied or dissatisfied with their careers.[7] Dissatisfaction was somewhat higher among attorneys who began their

---

6 *See* Gabriele Plickert, Joyce Sterling, Robert Nelson, Bryant Garth, David Wilkins & Rebecca Sandefur, *After the JD III: Third Results from a National Study of Legal Careers* (2014).

7 Milan Markovic & Gabriele Plickert, *Attorney Career Dissatisfaction in the New Normal*, available at https://papers.ssrn.com/sol3/papers.cfm?abstract_id=3001391.

careers after the 2008 recession than among those who began practicing before (17.8% v. 11.5%). Some of this disparity can be explained by other research showing that experienced lawyers generally tend to be more satisfied with their careers than less experienced attorneys.[8] Other possible explanations offered by the authors were that the recession forced more lawyers to begin their careers in non-law related fields and that attorneys who began practicing after the recession were earning less than their predecessors. The study found that lawyers in private practice were more likely to be dissatisfied than lawyers in government or nonprofit/public interest settings. But they also found that lawyers make tradeoffs in terms of income and the inherent satisfaction of the work, so that similar percentages of attorneys in those three practice settings reported being either very satisfied or satisfied with their careers: 65.5% of full-time private practitioners, 68.5% of government lawyers, and 73.9% of lawyers in nonprofit/public interest firms. Among lawyers in private practice, few equity partners and nonequity partners were dissatisfied with their careers, whereas associates, of counsel, and other nonpartner attorneys were more likely to report dissatisfaction.

The authors of the same study of Texas lawyers attempted to explain the "paradox of minority attorney satisfaction"—why African-American and Hispanic lawyers express high levels of satisfaction with their decision to become lawyers despite being underrepresented in the most prestigious sectors of the profession and despite earning less than white attorneys. Like the *After the JD* research, this study found that, after controlling for factors other than race, Black and Hispanic attorneys have significantly higher odds of being satisfied with their decision to attend law school. The survey results suggest that different factors drive the satisfaction of white and non-white attorneys and that "minority lawyers are less concerned with prestige markers such as higher incomes, class rank, and partner status." The authors conclude that "[t]he significant challenges that racial minorities face in the legal profession have not detracted from their professional satisfaction" and that "the secret to their success appears to be that they have not internalized the dominant values of a profession that formerly excluded them."[9]

NOTES ON RECENT RESEARCH

1. ***Common Threads.*** What are the consistent findings and big takeaways of the most recent research on lawyer satisfaction? To the extent that there are discrepancies in the findings, are they explained by what you know about differences in the samples or methods used by the researchers?

---

[8] *See* Ronit Dinovitzer & Bryant Garth, *Lawyer Satisfaction in the Process of Structuring Legal Careers,* 41 LAW & SOC'Y REV. 1, 22 (2007).

[9] Milan Markovic & Gabrielle Plickert, *The Paradox of Minority Attorney Satisfaction,* available at https://ssrn.com/abstract=3205344 (July 2, 2018).

2. ***Tradeoffs.*** The ADJ study asked survey respondents to characterize their levels of satisfaction with a variety of aspects of their jobs, including the income, job security, the value of work to society, opportunities for advancement, relationships with colleagues, intellectual challenge, opportunities to build skills, opportunities for pro bono, level of responsibility, amount of travel, and balance of personal life and work. Is it useful to think of career satisfaction in terms of combinations of, and sometimes tradeoffs among, those components?

Does it seem plausible to you that people might value these various aspects of their jobs differently? A study of graduates of the University of Michigan Law School from the late 1970s found that, even though women lawyers with children bore primary responsibility for the care of children in their households, they nevertheless were more satisfied with their careers and with the balance of their family and professional lives than other women and than men.[10] A follow-up study of Michigan Law graduates surveyed in 1997 through 2006 again found that, despite lower earnings and adjustments made to care for children, women were overall more satisfied than men with their careers. The author concluded that women generally were willing to forego some prestige and income to achieve more satisfying professional lives in other respects, including the value of their work to society and their relationships with co-workers.[11] Does that interpretation of the data seem convincing to you?

3. ***As Compared to Whom?*** How we perceive how we are doing sometimes turns less on objective criteria than on subjective measures. Career expectations are often influenced by our "referents"—those to whom we compare ourselves. One study showed that women have lower career expectations than men because they typically compare themselves with women who hold lower-level positions than the referents identified by men.[12] So, for example, if women lawyers are comparing themselves to stay-at-home mothers or women in lower-status jobs, they are likely to find their career achievements more rewarding than if they are comparing their careers to those of highly successful males. Might this research help explain why women report roughly equal levels of satisfaction with the decision to become a lawyer as men, despite their inferior pay, levels of authority, and opportunities for advancement? Might referents also be relevant to the "paradox of minority attorney satisfaction" identified by authors of the Texas study?

4. ***What Might Be Missing?*** One study of Toronto lawyers found that, while women and men reported similar levels of satisfaction with their careers, women were more likely than men to report feelings of depression or

---

[10] David Chambers, *Accommodation and Satisfaction: Women and Men Lawyers and the Balance of Work and Family*, 2 LAW & SOC. INQ. 251 (1989).

[11] David Chambers, *Satisfaction in the Practice of Law: Findings from a Long-Term Study of Attorneys' Careers*, May 30, 2013, available at https://papers.ssrn.com/sol3/papers.cfm?abstract_id=2274162.

[12] See Donald Gibson and Barbara Lawrence, *Women's and Men's Career Referents: How Gender Composition and Comparison Level Shape Career Expectations*, 21 ORG. SCIENCE 1159 (2010).

despondency.[13] The researchers concluded that women tended to internalize feelings of disappointment deriving from their work rather than to externalize their feelings by expressing job dissatisfaction.[14] The researchers also concluded that women's feelings of despondency were significantly influenced by their lower levels of occupational power and concerns about the consequences of having children on their advancement in the practice of law.[15] They argued that future research on lawyer satisfaction should take into account that women "are more likely to privatize than publicize their professional troubles."[16] Do these findings and conclusions seem plausible to you?

5. ***Reassessing Schiltz.*** After reading Hull's and Kelly's critiques, and the summary of more recent research on lawyer satisfaction, which of Schiltz's claims do you find convincing and which do you doubt?

D. LAWYER WELL-BEING

Some recent research looks beyond lawyer satisfaction with careers to examine broader measures of life satisfaction, substance use, and mental health.

Life Satisfaction. A study by Lawrence Krieger and Kennon Sheldon, published in 2015, examined overall life satisfaction of a sample of over 6,000 lawyers in four states. The report offered data on the correlation between lawyer well-being and various subjective and objective factors, such as work setting, area of practice, income, family and social status, law school achievements, motivations, values, psychological needs, and the level of supervisory support. The authors found that the most powerful predictors of lawyer well-being were autonomy in one's work, relatedness to others (a sense of connection and belonging), competence, and internal motivation for work. They found only modest association between higher earnings and well-being. Overall, their data indicate that "a happy life as a lawyer is much less about grades, affluence, and prestige than about finding work that is interesting, engaging, personally meaningful, and focused on providing needed help to others." The authors concluded that the tendency of law students and young lawyers to place extrinsic values, such as prestige or financial concerns, ahead of intrinsic values, such as their desire to make a difference or serve others, would ultimately undermine their ability find happiness in the profession.

The Krieger and Sheldon study found that lawyer well-being was also significantly correlated with personal life choices, including taking vacation days, having children, being in a marriage or similar relationship,

[13] John Hagan and Fiona Kay, Even Lawyers Get the Blues: Gender, Depression, and Job Satisfaction in Legal Practice, 41 LAW & SOC'Y REV. 51 (2007).

[14] *Id.* at 58.

[15] *Id.* at 62.

[16] *Id.* at 69.

and exercising at least weekly. Demographic characteristics other than age—gender, race, and ethnicity—showed little predictive value for lawyer well-being, but older lawyers were moderately happier than younger lawyers.[17]

A longitudinal study of University of Virginia law graduates found that 67.6 percent of the respondents were very highly satisfied or highly satisfied with their lives, and an additional 18 percent reported average life satisfaction.[18] Respondents' ratings of their health, and being married or in a partnered relationship, were significantly positively related to life satisfaction, while cumulative law school GPA and the number of hours worked during the prior week bore a significantly negative relationship to current life satisfaction. Although salary bore a significantly positive relationship with career satisfaction, it was not significantly correlated with life satisfaction. Being employed in a large private firm was negatively correlated with life satisfaction. There were no significant gender differences in life satisfaction, but women were less satisfied than men with the balance between their work and their personal and family lives, holding constant the number of hours worked, the practice setting, and other variables.

Substance Abuse and Mental Health. A 1990 study involving roughly 1200 lawyers in Washington State found that 18% of the attorneys were problem drinkers, as compared to 10% of the general adult population. The study also found that problematic drinking increased with number of years spent in the profession. In addition, the research showed that 19% of Washington lawyers suffered from elevated levels of depression, as compared with an estimated 3–9% of the general adult population.[19]

No reliable data on lawyers' substance use and mental health emerged again until 2016, with the publication of a study involving a sample of almost 13,000 lawyers in 19 states. The study, based on written surveys, found alcohol use disorders among lawyers at a much higher rate [20.6%] than in the general population [12%]. The rates of problematic drinking in this research were similar to those reported in the 1990 study. But while the earlier study found a positive association between the increased prevalence of problematic drinking and an increased number of years in the profession, the new research found that younger lawyers were more likely than older and more experienced lawyers to report problematic levels of alcohol consumption. Attorneys in the first ten years of practice reported

---

[17] Lawrence S. Krieger & Kennon M. Sheldon, *What Makes Lawyers Happy?: A Data-Driven Prescription to Redefine Professional Success*, 83 GEO. WASH. L. REV. 554 (2015).

[18] John Monahan & Jeffrey Swanson, *Lawyers at Mid-Career: A 20-Year Longitudinal Study of Job and Life Satisfaction*, 6 J. EMP. LEGAL STUD. 451 (2009).

[19] Andrew Benjamin, Elaine Darling & Bruce Sales, The Prevalence of Depression, Alcohol Abuse, and Cocaine Abuse Among United States Lawyers, 13 INT'L J. L. PSYCH. 233 (1990).

the highest rates of problematic use (28.9%), followed by lawyers practicing 10 to 20 years (20.6%), and declining rates thereafter. Lawyers in private firms exhibited higher proportions of problem drinking behavior than lawyers in other practice environments. The study also found significant levels of mental health distress among the lawyers in the study, with 28% struggling with depression, 19% with anxiety, and 23% with stress. Levels of mental health distress declined with lawyers' years in practice; lawyers in the early stages of their careers were more likely to experience mental health problems than those who had been in the profession for 15 years or more. The researchers concluded that pervasive fears about reputational harm discouraged lawyers from seeking treatment.[20]

In 2017, the ABA Task Force on Lawyer Well-Being issued a report calling on the profession to expand educational outreach and programming for lawyers on mental health and substance abuse disorders. The report highlighted the relationship between lawyer well-being, lawyer competence, and the success of the organizations in which lawyers practice, and it cited humanitarian concerns about how untreated substance use and mental health disorders can ruin lives and careers. It recommended a variety of measures to improve lawyer well-being, including efforts to reduce the stigma associated with mental health and substance use disorders; building more robust lawyer assistance programs to help lawyers, judges, and law students who experience substance abuse and mental health problems; and considering how longstanding structures and norms of the profession might be modified to enhance lawyers' sense of control over their lives and to promote healthier lifestyles.[21]

NOTES ON LAWYER WELL-BEING

1. ***Big Takeaways on Life Satisfaction.*** What are the most significant findings of the studies of life satisfaction? Did any of them surprise you?

2. ***Sources of Stress for Younger Lawyers?*** The research does not explain why younger lawyers are experiencing higher levels of substance abuse and mental health disorders than more experienced lawyers. Some have speculated that high levels of student debt, a tough job market, and inhospitable working conditions may be contributing factors.[22] Do those explanations seem plausible to you?

---

[20] Patrick R. Krill, Ryan Johnson and Linda Albert, The Prevalence of Substance Use and Other Mental Health Concerns Among American Attorneys, 10 J. ADDICTION MEDICINE 46 (2016).

[21] National Task Force on Lawyer Well-Being, Creating a Movement to Improve Well-Being in the Legal Profession, August 14, 2017, available at https://www.americanbar.org/content/dam/aba/images/abanews/ThePathToLawyerWellBeingReportRevFINAL.pdf.

[22] Elizabeth Olson, High Rate of Problem Drinking Reported Among Lawyers, N.Y. TIMES, February 4, 2016; Steven J. Harper, The Real Reasons for Big Law's Mental Health Problem: Opinion, AM. LAW, June 2, 2017.

3. ***Sources of Stress in Private Practice.*** The 2016 study found that lawyers in private firms exhibited higher proportions of problem drinking behavior than lawyers in other practice environments. That finding is consistent with recent research finding that two common sources of stress in the legal profession, overwork and work-life conflict, are more prevalent in the private sector. The same study found that these sources of stress increase with firm size.[23]

4. ***A High-Profile Example of Lawyer Distress and Illicit Drug Use.*** In the summer of 2017, a *New York Times* story explored the descent of a Silicon Valley intellectual property lawyer into drug addiction and eventual death from a bacterial infection common to intravenous drug users. The story suggested that drug abuse among high-powered lawyers may be an under-reported and under-recognized phenomenon.[24] In the 2016 study of lawyer substance use and other mental health problems described above, only 3,419 of the almost 13,000 lawyers who completed the survey answered questions about drug use. The study's lead author surmised that lawyers might have been afraid to answer questions about illicit drug use.

5. ***Law Students' Experience.*** A recent study of law students' well-being, based on data from 15 law schools and over 3,300 law students, found that 17% of the students experienced depression, 14% experienced severe anxiety, and 23% reported mild or moderate anxiety. Forty-three percent reported binge drinking at least once in the previous two weeks, and 22% reported binge-drinking two or more times during that period.[25]

Do these findings suggest a general problem in the legal profession and in legal culture that extends beyond particular institutions and workplaces and that begins before aspiring lawyers enter the profession?

Some research suggests that the experience of law school changes law students' orientations in ways that make them more susceptible to mental health and substance use disorders.[26] The Krieger and Sheldon research, for example, found shifts in students' values, from community-oriented values toward extrinsic rewards-based values. The study also found similar changes in law students' motivations for studying law and becoming lawyers, from salutary internal purposes (for interest, enjoyment, and meaning) toward more superficial and external reasons (financial rewards, recognition, or to impress

---

[23] Jonathan Koltai, Scott Schieman, and Ronit Dinovitzer, The Status-Health Paradox: Organizational Context, Stress Exposure, and Well-Being in the Legal Profession, 59 J. HEALTH & SOC. BEHAV. 20 (2018).

[24] Eilene Zimmerman, *The Lawyer, the Addict,* N.Y. TIMES, July 15, 2017.

[25] Jerome M. Organ, David B. Jaffe & Katherine Bender, *Suffering in Silence: The Survey of Student Well-Being and the Reluctance of Law Students to Seek Help for Substance Use and Mental Health Concerns,* 66 J. LEGAL EDUC. 116 (2016).

[26] *See, e.g.,* Matthew Dammeyer & Narina Nunez, *Anxiety and Depression Among Law Students: Current Knowledge and Future Directions,* 23 LAW & HUM. BEHAV. 55 (1999); Kennon M. Sheldon & Lawrence S. Krieger, *Does Legal Education Have Undermining Effects on Law Students? Evaluating Changes in Motivation, Values, and Well-Being,* 22 BEHAV. SCI. & L. 261 (2004).

or please others).[27] The article's authors assert that "[t]he psychological factors seen to erode during law school are the very factors most important for the well-being of lawyers."[28]

If Krieger and Sheldon are correct about psychological changes that law students undergo and the consequences of those changes for students' mental health, what steps can law schools and students take to prevent the erosion of beneficial values and thereby improve law students' well-being? Note that the ABA, state bar associations, and many law schools now sponsor educational programs focusing on law students' mental health.[29]

E. SUMMARY

This chapter explored whether lawyers are satisfied with their careers and with their lives. We began with an essay that boldly asserts that lawyers are unhappy. We then examined what career satisfaction *means* and how one might measure it. The best available empirical research on this topic suggests that career satisfaction varies by practice type and even within practice setting. It also indicates that lawyers experience different types of career satisfaction. These elements of career satisfaction include financial compensation, prestige, relationships with colleagues, levels of responsibility, control over work, intellectual challenge, a sense of the social value of one's work, and diversity of the workplace. Research from the *After the JD* study suggests that dimensions of job satisfaction are not distributed evenly across practice types and that job satisfaction and social background are significantly related.

We also considered research on broader measures of lawyer well-being. Studies show that mental health and substance use disorders are all too common in the legal profession. Research also identifies some factors associated with higher levels of well-being and life satisfaction. Studies suggest that meaningful work and supportive work supervision are more important for lawyer happiness than external indicia of success, and that personal routine and lifestyle choices are at least as powerful predictors of lawyer well-being as income, honors, and credentials.

---

[27] Sheldon & Krieger, 22 BEHAV. SCI. & L. 261, at 270–72

[28] Krieger & Sheldon, 83 GEO. WASH. L. REV. 554, at 560.

[29] *See, e.g.,* Mental Health Resources, https://abaforlawstudents.com/events/initiatives-and-awards/mental-health-resources/; ABA, *Mental Health & Substance Abuse Toolkit for Law Students and Those Who Care About Them,* https://www.americanbar.org/content/dam/aba/administrative/lawyer_assistance/ls_colap_mental_health_toolkit_new.authcheckdam.pdf.

CHAPTER 25

REFLECTIONS ON THE FUTURE OF THE LEGAL PROFESSION

■ ■ ■

A. INTRODUCTION

In this final part of the book, we have examined a number of significant problems and opportunities facing the legal profession. They represent challenges for the society of which the profession is a part, for the profession, and for individual lawyers. In this chapter, we reflect on those challenges and offer a few ideas about navigating the interesting times that lie ahead for the legal profession and those just entering it.

At the broadest level, the profession confronts difficulty in delivering services to all who need them. Inadequate access to legal services for poor and middle-class Americans is a continuing threat to the ideal of equality before the law. If the rule of law is to be maintained in the daily lives of the governed and those who govern, people need access to legal services because legal services are often necessary to make law work in a complex and highly regulated society like ours. Lawyers enjoy considerable power and wealth by virtue of the fact that they have a monopoly on the practice of law and the power of self-regulation. A continuing failure to address access to justice may ultimately threaten both the profession's monopoly and its prerogatives of self-regulation.

Other challenges and changes relating to diversity, globalization, and technology will also shape the profession's future and new lawyers' places in it. Women have entered the U.S. legal profession in large numbers since the 1970s (as they have in many other countries around the world),[1] but there continue to be significant disparities in pay and in women's representation in law firm partnerships and other prestigious positions. The American legal profession has also become more diverse in terms of race, ethnicity, religion, and other demographic characteristics since the 1970s, but it remains significantly less diverse than the general population. Globalization and technology have fundamentally reshaped the legal services market, moving lawyers and legal work across borders and boundaries. We have also seen dramatic changes over the past several

[1] Ethan Michelson, *Women in the Legal Profession, 1970–2010: A Study of the Global Supply of Lawyers*, 20 IND. J. GLOBAL LEGAL STUD. 1071 (2013).

decades in the structure and organization of many forms of law practice, and there is reason to expect more fundamental change ahead.

The first section of this chapter addresses the changing nature of legal services and some predictions about the future. The second section considers how new generations of lawyers might influence the structure and operation of the legal profession and the delivery of legal services. The final section reflects on the changes that new lawyers undergo as they prepare to enter the legal profession and on how they might approach additional challenges in the years to come.

B. THE FUTURE OF LEGAL SERVICES

There is a lively debate underway about how technology and globalization are transforming legal services and what those changes mean for the legal profession's future. As you read about these predictions, consider whether you think they are plausible and, if so, whether they are likely to apply to all types of practice or just to some. Also consider whether your find these predictions attractive or problematic and why.

The most dramatic predictions come from Richard Susskind, British author of several books on the profession, including *The Future of Lawyers,* and the apocalyptically titled *The End of Lawyers*. Susskind says that the legal services industry is undergoing a radical transformation driven by three related factors: 1) the "more for less" challenge—the expectation by clients of all types that lawyers deliver more legal services at less cost; 2) "liberalization," by which he means pressure to allow nonlawyers to compete directly with lawyers to deliver legal services; and 3) the rapid growth of powerful information technologies, which allow increasing amounts of legal work to be handled by advanced computer systems. He summarizes these trends and their implications in *The End of Lawyers*:

> Clients are requiring *more for less*. At the same time, new competitors are emerging. Liberalization of the legal market will bring external funding and a new wave of professional managers and investors who have no nostalgic commitment to traditional business models for law firms. To cap it all, a number of disruptive legal technologies are emerging which will directly challenge and sometimes even replace the traditional work of lawyers.[2]

Susskind asserts that the "more-for-less" challenge affects lawyers serving clients of every type, including not only corporations, but also small businesses and individuals who are unable to afford lawyer services.[3]

---

[2] RICHARD SUSSKIND, THE END OF LAWYERS: RETHINKING THE NATURE OF LEGAL SERVICES (2010).

[3] RICHARD SUSSKIND, TOMORROW'S LAWYERS: AN INTRODUCTION TO YOUR FUTURE 4–5, 32–55, 93–129 (2017).

Susskind argues that these three major drivers of change will produce a world that is very different from the world that lawyers experience today and that lawyers' futures could be either "prosperous or disastrous," depending on their attitudes and preparation for the inevitable changes ahead: "Lawyers who are unwilling to change their working practices and extend their range of services will struggle to survive," while "those who embrace new technologies and novel ways of sourcing legal work are likely to trade successfully for many years, even if they are not occupied with the law jobs that most law schools currently anticipate for their graduates."

Susskind predicts that there will be fewer jobs for traditional lawyers in the future because clients will be unwilling to pay for expensive services that could be undertaken by less expert advisers supported by standard processes and sophisticated systems. Although there will remain "expert trusted advisors," who provide customized services to clients, he warns that the demand for expert trusted advisors will be limited and that lawyers who assume that all their clients' work will require such tailored treatment will do so at their peril. On the other hand, Susskind argues that there will be abundant opportunity for lawyers who are flexible, open-minded and entrepreneurial.

In a series of lectures on the theme of "Legal Careers in the Global Age of More for Less," Harvard Law Professor David Wilkins agrees with Susskind that big change lies ahead. He argues that the globalization of economic activity, the rise of information technology, and the blurring of 19th century categories of knowledge and organization are fundamentally reshaping the market for legal services. He predicts that competition will move away from reputation and credentials and toward valuation assessed according to metrics determined by clients, and that these changes will put substantial pressure on existing modes of practice and regulation. According to Wilkins, lawyers who are not prepared for these challenges will not fare well, as clients insist on receiving "more for less" and as new types of service providers compete on price and efficiency. However, Wilkins also says that demand for legal services will be strong over the long term because clients and policymakers will continue to need lawyers to help them navigate an increasingly complex world.[4]

New Jobs. In *Tomorrow's Lawyers: An Introduction to Your Future,* Susskind describes some new types of jobs he expects to be available for future lawyers. They include: "the legal knowledge engineer," who analyzes, organizes, and distills huge quantities of legal materials and processes to be embedded in computer systems; the "legal technologist," who is trained and experienced in law as well as systems engineering and IT management; the "legal hybrid," a lawyer with training in other

[4] Slides for Wilkins's lectures on this topic are posted on the Harvard Program on the Legal Profession website, http://www.law.harvard.edu/programs/plp/pdf/wilkins_iba_slides.pdf.

disciplines, such as business, engineering, or science; the "legal process analyst," who analyzes legal work, subdivides it into manageable chunks, and identifies the appropriate supplier of each type of service; the "legal project manager," who follows up on the work of the legal process analyst by allocating the work to appropriate providers; the "legal data scientist," an expert in machine learning and predictive analytics as well law; the "R&D worker," who helps to design and develop services and solutions at the heart of new legal businesses; the "ODR practitioner," who works in and advises clients about "on-line dispute resolution," in which experts in resolving disputes conduct their work largely or entirely through the Internet;[5] "legal management consultants," who advise in-house legal departments on management challenges, such as the introduction of information technology; and "legal risk managers," who develop processes, techniques, and systems to help clients identify, assess, quantify, hedge, monitor and control the risks that they confront.[6]

Notice that many of the jobs described by Susskind relate primarily to the needs of corporate clients (especially "legal management consultants" and "legal risk managers"), while others may be more generally applicable to legal businesses and nonprofit organizations that seek to serve individuals and small businesses. None of them seems to bear much relevance for clients in the criminal justice process—on either the prosecution or the defense side.

Different Employers. Just as Susskind predicts that the jobs of tomorrow will be in many ways different from the jobs of today, he also anticipates that many of the employers of young lawyers will not be conventional law firms but rather different types of businesses, some of which already exist. These alternative employers include global accounting firms, such as PwC, Deloitte, EY, and KPMG, major legal publishers such as Thomson Reuters and Reed Elsevier, and legal process outsourcers, such as CPA Global and Pangea3. They include "legal leasing agencies," such as Axiom, Lawyers On Demand, and UnitedLex, which assemble teams of lawyers to work on discrete projects on a temporary basis. Another group of new and emerging alternative employers are what Susskind calls "new-look law firms," by which he means firms that eschew the old business models and pyramidic profit structure in favor of cost-containment, lower fees, and efficient use of technology. Examples of such firms are Riverview Law in the U.K. and Atrium LLP in the U.S. Other important sources for jobs in the future, according to Susskind, will be online legal service

---

[5] An example of such a firm is Cybersettle, an Internet company that uses double-blind bidding to help parties find a middle ground, primarily in connection with personal injury and insurance claims. *See* Robert Ambrogi, *Is there a Future for On-Line Dispute Resolution for Lawyers?*, LawSites, Apr. 11, 2016, https://www.lawsitesblog.com/2016/04/future-online-dispute-resolution.html.

[6] RICHARD SUSSKIND, TOMORROW'S LAWYERS: AN INTRODUCTION TO YOUR FUTURE 133–45 (2d ed. 2017).

providers, including not only large-scale businesses that produce legal documentation for the individual/small business sector, such as LegalZoom and Rocket Lawyer, but also charitable organizations that try to increase access to justice through technology. Legaltech companies, of which there are now over 1,200 worldwide, will create new products and services that disrupt the legal marketplace. Finally, Susskind predicts that legal management consulting businesses, which specialize in legal process analysis, legal project management, and legal risk management, will hire lawyers with expertise and experience in these fields.[7]

The last of these categories deserves additional explanation because it is likely to be the least familiar and because it receives little attention elsewhere in the book. New businesses such as Elevate, UnitedLex, and Counsel on Call design, build, and staff systems for efficiently completing corporate legal work. The work delegated to these companies is often sophisticated and important to businesses but too repetitive to be handled cost-effectively by law firm associates or in-house attorneys.[8] It includes e-discovery, document review, corporate due diligence, internal investigations, contract management, patent valuation and portfolio analysis, and compliance programs.[9]

Corporate law departments increasingly rely on legal operations professionals to work with general counsel to find ways to more efficiently manage legal work and to oversee those operations.[10] (In 2016, legal operations professionals established their own consortium to share best practices, and the organization now has nearly 1,300 members worldwide.) The rise of legal operations reflects and reinforces larger changes in how companies purchase legal services. The pressure to do more with less means more experimentation with alternative staffing models and evolving technology. In 2017, DXC Technology, a technology conglomerate, announced that it would hire UnitedLex to restructure its legal department. Under the five-year agreement, UnitedLex will provide a team of more than 250 senior-level professionals, including lawyers and engineers, to support DXC's global operations. As part of the deal, a substantial number of DXC lawyers will be transferred to UnitedLex but will continue to work with DXC's in-house team.[11] Similarly, in early 2018, General Electric signed a multi-year contract with UnitedLex to expand its use of UnitedLex's legal services on issues ranging from e-discovery and

---

7 *Id.* at 146–57.

8 *See* William D. Henderson, *Efficiency Engines: How Managed Services Are Building Systems for Corporate Legal Work,* ABA J., June 2017; Merry Neitlich, *Legal Departments Lead Industry-Wide Change,* TODAY'S GENERAL COUNSEL, Spr. 2018.

9 *Id.*

10 *See* Hugh A. Simons & Gina Passarella, *The Rise (and Fall?) of In-House Counsel,* AM. LAWYER, Feb. 25, 2018; Caroline Spiezio, *Zero to Hero: Legal Ops Leaders Discuss How to Start an Operations Program from Scratch,* CORPORATE COUNSEL, Apr. 24, 2018.

11 *UnitedLex to Support Bulk of DXC Technology's In-House Department,* CORPORATE COUNSEL, Dec. 5, 2017.

document review to litigation and investigations. GE predicts that the agreement will reduce the amount that GE spends on legal services by 30 percent.[12] In 2017, GE also reached an agreement with PwC to handle all of GE's tax work worldwide for at least five years. As part of the deal, PwC hired about half of GE's tax department—approximately 600 lawyers, accountants, and other employees.[13]

Some law firms are also attempting to find new niches for themselves in this new legal services landscape. For example, in 2015 Dentons created NextLaw Labs, a legal technology venture that consults on legal services innovation. In 2018 Reed Smith created Gravity Stack, a spin-off that licenses the firm's technology projects and seeks to provide managed services to law firms and corporate legal departments.

So what do all these changes in the structure of the legal services "industry" mean for tomorrow's lawyers? Susskind asserts that the new jobs he identifies will present a rich and exciting set of opportunities. He also argues that some of the new employers may offer more vibrant and entrepreneurial environments than conventional firms and be more open to young lawyers' ideas about how legal services might be improved. Do you agree?

NOTES ON NEW LAW JOBS AND EMPLOYERS

1. ***Are the Predictions Plausible?*** Do you think that the trends identified by Susskind and Wilkins are as powerful as they suggest? Are they likely to produce the sweeping changes that Susskind predicts?

2. ***New Jobs for Lawyers.*** Consider the types of new jobs that Susskind envisions for lawyers of the future and the tasks that he predicts will be performed by each. If his predictions come to pass, do you think that the work of these new types of lawyers will be more or less plentiful, remunerative, or satisfying than the work of lawyers today?

Not discussed in the Susskind excerpts above is the increased role of contract attorneys provided through national or regional staffing agencies, such as Kelly Law Registry, and lawyer-to-lawyer marketplaces, such as Hire An Esquire, LawClerk.legal, and Lawyer Exchange. This part of the gig economy for lawyers serves law firms and in-house legal departments whose needs for lawyers fluctuate. Some of the lawyers involved in these marketplaces are employed by the marketplaces, while others are independent contractors. The entities running these marketplaces receive payments, sometimes based on percentages of the lawyer's hourly rates or the volume of

---

[12] Miriam Rozen, *GE Inks Legal Outsourcing Deal with UnitedLex, Eying Big Savings,* AM. LAWYER, March 22, 2018, https://www.law.com/americanlawyer/2018/03/22/ge-inks-legal-outsourcing-deal-with-unitedlex-eying-big-savings/.

[13] *PwC Announces New Global Corporate Tax Services Team,* https://www.pwc.com/us/en/press-releases/2017/global-corporate-tax-services-team.html.

work, or subscription arrangements.[14] One source reported in 2017 that Hire An Esquire charges out attorneys at an average of $70/hour.[15]

3. ***Tomorrow's Employers.*** What are the attractions of working for the major types of new employers that Susskind identifies? What are the downsides?

4. ***Tomorrow's Clients.*** Who are the clients served by the new types of jobs and employers envisioned by Susskind? Compare the kinds of legal work that Susskind describes to the kinds of legal work involved in handling criminal, family law, immigration, employment, consumer, or other matters affecting individuals. Which of the legal services tasks performed by lawyers representing individuals and small businesses could be done by less expert advisers supported by standard processes and sophisticated systems, as Susskind describes? Which of them do not lend themselves to such reconfiguration? Do you foresee a time when the work of government lawyers, criminal lawyers, appellate lawyers, or lawyers who handle discrimination claims, or represent children in dependency proceedings, or victims of police abuse, or lawyers who advise public interest organizations or labor unions, will become systematized in the way that Susskind predicts? Or does too much of representing actual people and their organizations in these types of work require the involvement of a lawyer who is perceived as wise, caring, humane, and trustworthy?

5. ***Implications for Legal Careers.*** Which of the practice types/settings/types of work surveyed in Part II of this book are likely to be most and least affected by the trends identified here? What kinds of lawyers do you expect to be doing what kinds of work in the future?

* * *

Artificial Intelligence and Automation. Artificial intelligence has already begun to change the way lawyers practice law. Predictive coding allows for automating document classification in discovery practice, and new legal research tools combine natural language processing with users' aggregate data to improve search results.[16] Ross Intelligence has developed a computer program built on the IBM Watson platform to facilitate the assembly of sophisticated documents. The documents produced through this platform still require lawyer review but not nearly as much drafting time as conventional methods. Artificial intelligence is also being used to

---

[14] *See* William D. Henderson, Legal Market Landscape Report (2018).

[15] *See* Cathy Reisenwitz & Halden Ingwersen, *Need a Freelance Lawyer? 3 Online Contract Marketplaces Compared,* Capterra Legal Software Blog, Sept. 26, 2017, available at https://blog.capterra.com/need-a-freelance-lawyer-3-online-contract-lawyer-marketplaces-compared/.

[16] Nicole Black, *Legal Research and AI: Looking Toward the Future,* Above the Law, July 27, 2017, https://abovethelaw.com/2017/07/legal-research-and-ai-looking-toward-the-future/?rf=1.

predict litigation outcomes[17] and to analyze and streamline workflows and reduce legal risk.[18]

Will artificial intelligence eventually replace lawyers with robots? Richard Susskind says this about the threat that machines pose to lawyers' employment prospects:

> [A]s our machines become increasingly capable, they will steadily eat into lawyers' jobs. The best and the brightest human professionals will last the longest—those experts who perform tasks that cannot or should not be replaced by machines. But there will not be enough of these tasks to keep armies of traditional lawyers in employment. This is not an imminent threat to lawyers. In the 2020s at least . . ., there will be redeployment and not unemployment for lawyers—lawyers will undertake different work. In career terms during this period, lawyers should plan either to compete with machines (look for legal jobs that are likely to favour human capabilities over artificial intelligence) or to build the machines (aim to be directly involved in the development and delivery of new legal technologies and systems). In the very long term, it is hard to avoid the conclusion that there will be much less need for conventional lawyers.[19]

And in *The Future of Professions,* Susskind and his co-author son Daniel assert that nearly all professions, including lawyers, will soon be displaced by automation.[20]

But others expect artificial intelligence to produce much less dramatic changes in the market for lawyer services. One study puts the risk to lawyers from legal automation significantly below that of most other occupations.[21] Other research, based on interviews with computer scientists, legal technology developers, and practicing lawyers, and also drawing on data about how much lawyer time is currently devoted to various types of legal work, observes that the effects of artificial

---

[17] *See* Debra Cassens Weiss, *AI Predicted Case Outcomes with 79% Accuracy by Analyzing Fact Portrayal,* ABA J., Oct. 25, 2016; *AI Beats Human Lawyers in CaseCrunch Prediction Showdown,* ARTIFICIAL LAWYER, Oct. 2017, https://www.artificiallawyer.com/2017/10/28/ai-beats-human-lawyers-in-casecrunch-prediction-showdown/.

[18] *See* Julie Sobowale, *How Artificial Intelligence is Transforming the Legal Profession,* ABA J., Apr. 1, 2016.

[19] Richard Susskind, *Richard Susskind on Artificial Intelligence,* LEGALTECH NEWS, Oct. 10, 2017.

[20] RICHARD & DANIEL SUSSKIND, THE FUTURE OF PROFESSIONS: HOW TECHNOLOGY WILL TRANSFORM THE WORK OF HUMAN EXPERTS (2015).

[21] Carl Benedikt Frey & Michael A. Osborne, *The Future of Employment: How Susceptible Are Jobs to Computerization?,* Sept. 17, 2013), https://www.oxfordmartin.ox.ac.uk/downloads/academic/The_Future_of_Employment.pdf (finding that "for the work of lawyers to be fully automated, engineering bottlenecks to creative and social intelligence will need to be overcome . . .")

intelligence on lawyers' employment has so far been very modest. This research predicts that the future impact of artificial intelligence on lawyers' employment will vary greatly with types of work. It suggests, for example, that predictive coding technologies are likely to displace a significant amount of lawyer labor currently devoted to document review in discovery practice, and that there are also likely to be moderate effects as to some aspects of legal research and due diligence. But it predicts fewer employment consequences for lawyers when it comes to fact investigation, advising clients, court appearances, and negotiation—tasks that do not lend themselves to automation.[22] Another study of the legal services market asserts that AI technologies so far "are being deployed not to replace lawyers but to help manage the relentless increase in the volume and complexity of information and legal tasks."[23]

In their study of the economic value of a law degree, Michael Simkovic and Frank McIntyre observe that "work that requires complex thought and cannot easily be broken down into simple rules or algorithms is more difficult [than routine work] to automate or outsource."[24] They also note that

> predictions of structural change in the legal industry date back at least to the invention of the typewriter. Yet lawyers have prospered with the introduction and adoption of new technologies and modes of work—computerized and modular legal research through Lexis and Westlaw, word processing, citation software, electronic document storage and filing systems, automated document comparison, electronic document searching, e-mail, photocopying, desktop publishing, standardized legal forms, and will and tax preparation software.[25]

The authors acknowledge that while one can imagine future changes that might decrease the value of a law degree, one can "just as easily list reasons that the value of a law degree will increase," including "any number of potential new regulatory regimes."[26]

Other scholars similarly emphasize how future demand for lawyers might depend on the regulatory environment. Consider this claim about the relationship between legal and cultural change and legal automation:

> Situations involving conflicting rights, unique fact patterns, and open-ended laws will likely remain excessively difficult to

---

[22] *See* Dana Remus & Frank Levy, *Can Robots be Lawyers? Computers, Lawyers, and the Practice of Law*, 30 GEO. J. LEGAL ETHICS 501 (2017).

[23] *See* William D. Henderson, Legal Market Landscape Report 8 (2018).

[24] Michael Simkovic & Frank McIntyre, *The Economic Value of a Law Degree,* 43 J. LEGAL STUD. 249, 275 (2014).

[25] *Id.*

[26] *Id.* at 276.

> automate for an extended period of time. Deregulation may, however, effectively strip many persons of their rights and render once-hard cases simple. Consider, for instance, the trend in contract law to permit individuals to give up their right to join class actions, or even seek recourse in a court, via terms of service agreements that almost no consumer actually reads. A robot could dispose of nearly all cases arising in the wake of such agreements, if the only legal issue critical for the vast majority of consumers was whether they had "agreed." Once the law and fact of consent in such situations are settled, the outcomes are entirely predictable.
>
> On the other hand, disputes that now seem easy, because one party is so clearly correct as a matter of law, may be rendered hard to automate by new rules that give now-disadvantaged parties new rights. For example, a person in the United States cannot sue Google for automatically putting a 20-year-old bankruptcy action against him as the top result in a search for his name. In Europe, however, the opposite is the case: A newly recognized "right to be forgotten" (better named the "right to be delisted") gives persons the chance to challenge the inclusion of certain irrelevant, damaging material from such results. This decision realizes the basic principles behind expungement law in the digital age. It also creates new work for attorneys and policy advisors seeking to balance the public right to know against individual rights of privacy and reputational integrity.[27]

These authors conclude that "legal and cultural change can render once contestable disputes essentially automatable, and can also render once automatically resolved disputes open to new levels of contestation."[28]

In addition to questioning the plausibility of the Susskinds' dire predictions about the future of the professions, many commentators take issue with the Susskinds' perspectives on the desirability of the changes they anticipate and their views about why some professionals might resist the changes that the Susskinds foresee. One critic, Frank Pasquale, writes that the Susskinds emphasize situations in which automated systems have performed relatively well (such as some of LegalZoom's services) and too readily extrapolate from those situations to other types of legal work. He says that the Susskinds underestimate the scope of services that people can perform better than machines and that they are "all too prone to dwelling on harmless or uncontroversial automation while downplaying its more sinister overtones." Pasquale also criticizes the "nasty turn" that the Susskinds' argument takes when it suggests that only self-interest could

[27] Frank Pasquale & Glyn Cashwell, *Four Futures of Legal Automation*, 63 UCLA L. REV. DISC. 28 (2015).

[28] *Id.*

explain why lawyers claim that many aspects of current practice are not automatable:

> Repeatedly questioning the motives and competence of current professionals, the Susskinds insinuate that they resist change simply out of hidebound protectionism or technophobia. The values at stake in the human resolution of disputes—versus their automated dispatch to a computer system—are flattened into a utilitarian calculus of speed and efficiency. To counter critics of automation, they treat "cost-cutting" as an all-purpose trump card. The general public should be grateful for more legal automation, they argue, because human lawyers are too expensive.
>
> This is cavalier, not to mention naive. I would worry about any person who decides to file a tort or contract case against a major corporation using an app. If the claim is frivolous, they could be sanctioned. If the claim is serious, it will probably be outmaneuvered by a (human) defense lawyer. And if corporations don't even need to deploy attorneys to deflect such interventions, but can even automate their own defense, then there's little reason to believe this will constitute some great triumph for justice. Our legal system exacerbates inequality because of uneven access to resources for advocacy, not lack of automation. Digital projects to "democratize the law" rarely include the more sophisticated predictive analytics the Susskinds trumpet; instead, they remain the exclusive preserve of wealthy corporations.

Pasquale concludes that the Susskinds "give us little reason to believe that automation will impede—rather than accelerate—inequalities in legal resources."[29]

Another critic, Harvard Education Professor Howard Gardner, worries about who will create and control the new technologies and whether they and their products "can be depended upon": "As the Romans put it, 'Quis custodiet ipsos custodies?' ('Who will guard the guardians?')"[30] Gardner contrasts these largely unaccountable technologies with the responsibilities of "the true professional," who, though "rare and getting rarer," represents "a remarkable human achievement." He defines "true professionals" as individuals who "devote years to mastering an area and use their expertise to serve others in a disinterested way, over a long period of time, without much attention to personal wealth or prestige or power, and then seek to transmit expertise and exemplary values to younger

[29] Frank Pasquale, *Automating the Professions: Utopian Pipe Dream or Dystopian Nightmare?* LA REV. OF BOOKS, Mar. 15, 2016.

[30] Howard Gardner, *Revisiting the Arguments of Richard and Daniel Susskind,* The Good Project, Apr. 13, 2016, http://thegoodproject.org/revisiting-the-arguments-of-richard-and-daniel-susskind/.

acolytes."[31] Gardner explains why professions and professional ideals matter:

> At their best, the professions arose to meet the most basic and deeply desired human needs and expectations. In much of the world and in much of recent history, professionals have been the chosen means—and the chosen role models—for meeting those needs: aspirations for physical health, mental health, justice, safe buildings, equitable financial institutions, mastery of major scholarly disciplines, and nurturance of the 'better angels' of the inhabitants of the planet. Again, at their best, those who assume the role of professionals represent the competent and humane ways in which individuals carry out these tasks; they serve as models for at least one kind of person to whom we can aspire and one kind of society in which we would want to live.
>
> It took many years and many people to construct the professional landscape in which many of us grew up and took for granted. The disruptive forces in our society—intentionally or simply by virtue of their existence—have the potential to slay, to murder the professions. . . It's high time for those of us who continue to value the professions to reinvigorate and, as necessary, reinvent the professions. We need to acknowledge our complicity in the current undesirable situation, embody the principles and values that have enabled professional practice at its best, and work to ensure that they will be strengthened, not undermined, by the technologies to come, and insofar as possible, in harmony with the ever unpredictable winds of history and culture.[32]

NOTES ON ARTIFICIAL INTELLIGENCE

1. ***Which Kinds of Practice Can Be Automated?*** Consider the various types of law practice described in Part II of this book. Which of those kinds of practice necessarily involve human interaction of the type that is impossible to automate? To whom is Susskind is referring in his prediction that "the best and the brightest human professionals" will last the longest? To the extent that the Susskinds predict the automation of legal work, do you think their predictions are generalizable to all areas of practice or just some?

2. ***Who Will Benefit?*** If the Susskinds' sweeping predictions about the displacement of professionals by technology were to come true, would they be good or bad from the standpoint of lawyers, clients, and/or the public?

---

[31] *Id.*

[32] Howard Gardner, *Is There a Future for the Professions? An Interim Verdict,* The Good Project, Dec. 2, 2015, http://thegoodproject.org/is-there-a-future-for-the-professions-an-interim-verdict/.

3. ***Unauthorized Practice Rules.*** Unauthorized practice of law rules typically distinguish between tasks that can be provided only by lawyers and tasks that lay people can perform competently and ethically. In applying this framework to new technologies, courts have asked whether any given technology is more like a scrivener, who merely records the information supplied by the customer (and thus is not engaging in unauthorized practice), or a service provider, who exercises judgment in the completion of the work (and therefore is engaging in unauthorized practice). Is this a useful framework for analyzing whether artificial intelligence and automation should be allowed to displace lawyer services?

In analyzing how unauthorized practice rules apply to artificial intelligence used by lawyers, state bar associations have relied on rules requiring lawyers' oversight of non-lawyer service providers. Do you think that most lawyers are sufficiently knowledgeable about new technology to oversee it effectively?

4. ***Artificial Intelligence and Justice.*** Do you agree with critics that automation is likely to exacerbate rather than diminish economic and social inequality? If growing automation in legal services is inevitable, what can be done to protect and further the goals of our legal system and the ideal of equal justice under law? What is the role of a "true professional" in responding to new technologies?

C. THE INFLUENCE OF MILLENNIAL LAWYERS

This section considers the influence of the next generation of lawyers on the practice of law and the future of legal services.

THE ELASTIC TOURNAMENT: A SECOND TRANSFORMATION OF THE BIG LAW FIRM

Marc Galanter & William Henderson
60 Stanford Law Review 1867 (2008)

According to many human resource experts, the values and preferences of the next generation of lawyers, dubbed the Millennials, are on collision course with the work norms of large law firms. The typical characterization of Millennial lawyers is that they demand a high level of racial and gender diversity within the firm's workforce, are unwilling to sacrifice life and family for work, believe that work should be fun, exciting, and high paying from day one, and are more than willing to frankly express these views to their employer.

[If demand for corporate legal services continues to rise, there could be] a generational "showdown" between entering associates and partners, [and] it is difficult to predict who will prevail or what a compromise might look like. Nonetheless, we cannot resist the urge to speculate.

The key analytical question is whether law firms' managers have the power (a separate question from inclination) to accede to [millennials'] demands. Unfortunately, we are skeptical.

If the law firms and the Millennials are going to strike a deal, it is important to understand the associates' bargaining position. Employment patterns suggest that compensation, prestige, and outplacement options weigh more heavily with prospective associates than attributes like hours worked or family friendliness. Since better working conditions are already available at less elite firms in the Am Law 200, especially in smaller markets, what [some millennials] appear to be asking for is very high pay, very high prestige, location in a desirable urban market, excellent career options, reasonable promotion prospects, and sensible hours.*

This is not necessarily a deal that the prestigious Wall Street firms need to accept. Rather than reducing their hours, which may prompt partner defections, they can rely on higher salaries and their marquee brand—a good that associates routinely trade on to build their resumes—to coax sufficient Millennials to join the firm. For less profitable firms in the Am Law 200, with ratios of partner profits to associate pay below 4.0, each round of the salary wars prompts extremely difficult decisions. There is a strong perception among law firm partners that it is crucial to match the prevailing rate for associate pay. Yet, unless the pay raise is self-funded through higher billable hour requirements or higher billing rates (something clients will resist), firms toward the bottom of the Am Law 200 will be more likely to lose key rainmaking partners to upstream rivals.

We foresee at least two responses by law firms that could fundamentally transform the structure, economics, and norms of large law firm practice. First, large law firms, particularly less elite firms under pressure from the salary wars, can bypass Millennials from elite law schools by slightly reducing their grade cutoffs for interviewing students from less prestigious regional law schools. There is empirical evidence that this may be a prudent strategy. According to a recent study by Ronit Dinovitzer and Bryant Garth, based on data from the After the JD Project, large law firm associates who graduated from less elite law schools are (a) more satisfied with their careers, and (b) express a lower likelihood of wanting to leave the firm.[259] Because graduates of less elite law schools are less likely to come from families with professional or advantaged backgrounds, Dinovitzer and Garth suggest that large law firm employment delivers a much greater sense of accomplishment and mobility than that experienced by their counterparts from elite law schools. The

* [Eds.: Galanter and Henderson were referring here to the demands of Building a Better Legal Profession, a student group founded in 2006 at Stanford Law School, with chapters established soon thereafter at Harvard, Yale, Columbia, and NYU.]

[259] Ronit Dinovitzer & Bryant Garth, *Lawyer Satisfaction in the Process of Structuring Legal Careers,* 41 LAW & SOC'Y REV. 1, 12–13 & Fig.2 (2007).

second major transformation could be the emergence of a law firm that operates like a corporation, scuttling the promotion-to-partnership tournament and basing its hiring and promotion policies on each lawyer's marginal product. A firm operating on this model—once again, probably a semi-elite firm looking for refuge from the salary wars—would not be "selling" the elite credentials of its lawyers. Rather, it would be developing firm-specific capital by focusing on business processes that deliver high-quality legal services at a cost-effective and predictable price. Lawyers would be employees with salaries lower than their elite Wall Street counterparts; but they would also enjoy sensible hours that permit a better work-family balance—a combination of salary, prestige, and hours that is often found in in-house legal departments. Promotions would not be based on a multiyear tournament but on a lawyer's ability to profitably manage client matters, often taken a flat-fee basis or another nonhourly alternative. Demonstrated management and teamwork skills resulting in successful client engagements would carry more weight than Ivy League credentials. Further, a focus on job performance may be an ideal environment to develop the talents and abilities and women and minority attorneys, who have not fared well in a tracked and seeded promotion-to-partnership tournament.

Although general counsel may favor elite law firms for bet-the-company matters, this new business model could make substantial in-roads for higher volume, price-sensitive corporate work.

NOTES ON GALANTER & HENDERSON

1. ***The Generational Showdown.*** Professors Galanter and Henderson published their analysis of the impact of millennials just before the huge recession hit in 2008. To what extent do you think the existence or outcome of a "generational showdown" between new law graduates and large law firms depends on whether law graduates feel they are facing a buyers' or a sellers' market for associates? If the "generational showdown" were to occur today, what do you predict would result? What compromises do you think the law firms and associates might reach?

2. ***How Do Millennials Really Think and How Will They Influence Practice and the Profession?*** Does Galanter and Henderson's description of the characteristics, values, and preferences of millennial lawyers ring true? If not, how would you revise their description of millennials and how would you modify their hypothesis about the likely impact of lawyers of your generation on the profession generally, or on law firms in particular? Do you think that millennials are likely to make the profession more diverse or to achieve different outcomes in terms of the balance of work, family, and other commitments?

3. ***A Corporate Model for Law Firms.*** Recent events suggest that Galanter and Henderson were correct in predicting that some law firms would

modify or reduce their reliance on the promotion to partner up-or-out tournament in favor of a corporate model in which hiring and promotion practices are based on each lawyer's marginal product. Rimon Law and Potomac Law Group, for example, emphasize low overhead (no fancy offices), efficient use of technology, lean staffing, varied fee arrangements, and relatively flat management structures. While these alternative practice models are not as profitable as major corporate firms and do not offer the same paths to lucrative partnerships, they nevertheless are growing fast and competing successfully with conventional large firms for some types of work.

What might be the advantages and disadvantages of the personnel practices of these new types of firms from the perspective of a new lawyer looking for career opportunities? What are the advantages and disadvantages from the standpoint of clients and the public? Some have argued that these new types of firms are a better fit for the values and expectations and the next generation of lawyers.[33] Do you agree?

4. ***Alternative Fee Arrangements.*** Galanter and Henderson also note the increased prevalence of alternative billing arrangements as a feature of changing law practice. There has been a good deal of discussion in recent years about whether and to what extent hourly billing should and will give way to other fee arrangements. In Chapter 4, we saw that high billable hour expectations drive some associates away from large firms and that women's attrition from these institutions is especially high. As discussed in Chapter 8, high hourly billable expectations pit the attorney's incentive to bill more time against the interest of clients, who must pay those bills. Reliance on billable hours as a proxy for lawyer commitment to the firm encourages lawyers to "pad" client bills by inflating the time spent on client matters.

Although the hourly fee has not disappeared, many clients now insist on alternative fee arrangements, such as hourly fees with caps, fixed fees, contingent fees, and base fees with bonuses tied to results. Even when firms bill on an hourly basis, clients' insistence on budgets with caps means, in effect, that traditional billable hour pricing has become rare.[34]

* * *

The following excerpt offers a different account of the values and aptitudes of millennials and a different set of predictions about the likely outcome of a generational showdown than the one offered by Galanter & Henderson.

---

[33] Michael Moradzadeh, *How One Millennial and His Firm See Law Practice Today,* ABA J., May 23, 2018, available at http://www.abajournal.com/voice/article/how_one_millennial_and_his_firm_see_law_practice_today.

[34] Georgetown Law Center for the Study of the Legal Profession, *2017 Report on the State of the Legal Market,* available at https://static.legalsolutions.thomsonreuters.com/static/pdf/peer-monitor/S042201-Final.pdf.

DECIPHERING THE MILLENNIAL LAWYER

Jordan Furlong
Lawyerist.com, October 24, 2017

In several recent conversations I've had with the managing partners of large, mid-sized, and small law firms, the issue of millennial lawyers kept coming up. [Firm leaders seem to be] perplexed and baffled by [millennial lawyers].

The fundamental problem is that baby boomer lawyers (and to a lesser extent, gen-x lawyers like myself) keep trying to interpret the behavior of millennials through the lens of their own cultural assumptions and practices. That's going to work about as well as using a dictionary to understand software code. Here are corrections to some misconceptions you might have about millennials:

1. **Millennials aren't entitled.** They're preternaturally confident in themselves because they were raised to have the utmost belief in their own abilities. Whether that confidence is justified is mostly beside the point. Millennials speak to their elders with a degree of self-possession and authority that their listeners can find off-putting: "Who are you to talk to me this way?" But that's the way they are. You might as well complain that they walk about on two legs.

2. **Millennials aren't lazy.** They work very hard, in fact—but they won't work stupid. They can figure out pretty quickly if a task is make-work, pointless, or counterproductive, and they'll resist and resent your attempts to make them perform it. You might argue that millennials don't want to pay their dues, but that's not true—they don't want to pay *your* dues. They care not the slightest for how you made it in the world. And they'll have difficulty being polite with you about that.

3. **Millennials aren't disloyal.** They're peripatetic, and that's a word you should get used to hearing. They move on quickly from roles and workplaces, primarily because there's an astoundingly exciting world out there and they want to experience as much of it as they can. Oh, and they've seen their friends laid off from associate positions and watched partners jump laterally from firm to firm, so they won't listen quietly to your lectures on "making a commitment to this firm."

4. **Millennials aren't slackers.** They're ambitious because they crave external praise and internal affirmation and they want to over-achieve to obtain these rewards. They do not subscribe to a linear model of responsibility and advancement: they believe that if you're capable of doing

> something, you should do it, regardless of whether "it's their job" or whether permission to try has been extended. They are very impatient for accomplishments and their subsequent payoffs.

Law firms struggling with their millennial lawyers are all coming up against the same fundamental problem: The millennial personality is a poor match for traditional law firm culture. Law firms are conservative, hierarchical organizations that sell time, value experience, reward seniority, and encourage personal sacrifice. It's hard to overstate how little this interests your average millennial, who is drawn to a workspace that offers open collaboration, occupational creativity, rapid advancement, and personal fulfillment.

The millennial personality is the unstoppable force that's colliding with the immovable object of law firm culture. Which will win? Well, in about five years' time, millennials will constitute the majority of lawyers in virtually every law firm in North America, and the majority of partners within ten. Boomers, whose values produced and underpinned the culture of the traditional law firm are leaving the building. My money is on the unstoppable force.

NOTES ON FURLONG

1. ***Millennial Values Redux.*** Does Furlong's description of millennials' attributes and values seem more or less accurate than Galanter and Henderson's? Does it suggest reasons to be more optimistic about how law firms of all sizes might accommodate millennials and how millennials might influence law practice for the better?

2. ***Beyond the Law Firm.*** Which of Furlong's commentary about millennials' values and priorities apply to practice sectors other than law firms? Do you think that sectors of practice other than law firms are heading for their own generational showdown? If so, what might such a showdown entail?

* * *

Millennials and Legal Tech. In addition to whatever roles they might play in reshaping the structure and operation of law firms, millennials are also leaders in technological innovation in the legal industry and developers of a variety of new products. One recent news story describes the emergence of "a whole new legion of millennial legal technologists looking to shape, shake up, and ultimately disrupt old habits in the practice of law." The article highlights 18 young lawyers who have created innovative services and products, including LawTrades (matching freelance lawyers to assignments via mobile app at guaranteed prices), Ross Intelligence (artificial intelligence apps for legal research), Theory & Principle (consulting for organizations that seek to develop access to justice apps), CARA (AI-driven research assistant), OpenText (e-discovery), Legal.io (legal marketplace tool), Alt Legal (intellectual property management platform), InOutSource (data and technology strategies), FastCase Analytics (data analysis applied to legal research), Headnote (e-billing for solos and small firms), ClearAccessIP (integrated patent management and collaboration software), Legalist (litigation financing platform using AI to assess the merits of potential litigation), Hire and Esquire (legal staffing startup), Evisort (software that analyzes contracts and categorizes content), Sagewise (dispute resolution infrastructure for smart contracts), and DFNDER Project (using technology to tackle wrongful convictions).[35]

To which types of clients are these services and products directed? Do you see any potential for legal tech to do more than it has thus far to address access to justice issues?

D. CHARTING A CAREER

Many of the materials in this book suggest that lawyers will face huge changes and challenges in the years to come. The next two excerpts offer perspectives that might inform how young lawyers approach these changes and challenges. In the first, Richard Susskind urges young lawyers to be benevolent custodians of the law. Borrowing wisdom from Wayne Gretzky, perhaps the greatest hockey player of all time, Susskind also advises young lawyers to "skate where the puck's going, not where it's been." The second set of excerpts, from Mark Twain's *Life on the Mississippi*, arguably have nothing whatsoever to do with the legal profession, but we hope that they may nevertheless prompt reflection on the process of preparing to enter the profession.

TOMORROW'S LAWYERS: AN INTRODUCTION TO YOUR FUTURE

Richard Susskind (Oxford Press 2017)

I implore you, tomorrow's lawyers, to take up the mantle of the benevolent custodians; to be honest with yourselves and with society about those areas of legal endeavor that genuinely must be preserved for lawyers in the interest of clients. But you should work in the law in the interests of society and not of lawyers. Where, in all conscience, legal services can responsibly and reliably be offered by non-lawyers, celebrate access to justice and draw upon your creative and entrepreneurial talents to find

---

[35] Gabrielle Orum Hernandez, *18 Millennials Changing the Face of Legal Tech,* THE RECORDER, March 13, 2018, available at https://www.law.com/therecorder/2018/03/13/18-millennials-changing-the-face-of-legal-tech/?kw=18%20Millennials%20Changing%20the%20Face%20of%20Legal%20Tech.

other ways that your legal knowledge and experience can bring unique value to your clients.

As I often remind lawyers, the law is no more there to provide a living for lawyers than ill health exists to offer livelihood for doctors. It is not the purpose of law to keep lawyers in business. The purpose of law is to help to support society's needs of the law.

Alan Kay, a computer scientist from Silicon Valley, makes a different but related point. He once said that the "the best way to predict the future is to invent it." This is a powerful message for tomorrow's lawyers.

Here is the great excitement for tomorrow's lawyers. As never before, there is an opportunity to be involved in shaping the next generation of legal services. You will find most senior lawyers to be of little guidance in this quest. Your elders will tend to be cautious, protective, conservative, if not reactionary. They will resist change and will often want to hang on to their traditional ways of working, even if they are well past their sell-by date.

In truth, you are on your own. I urge you to forge new paths for the law, our most important social institution.

NOTES ON SUSSKIND

1. ***What Do Custodians of Law Do?*** What does Susskind mean when he exhorts young lawyers to be benevolent custodians? How does Susskind's appeal to young lawyers to become benevolent custodians relate to other topics considered in this course, such as the regulation of the profession, the lawyer's role, the market for legal services, unauthorized practice/nonlawyer services, and pro bono?

2 ***Will Senior Lawyers Help or Stand in the Way?*** Do you accept Susskind's assertion that new lawyers will be "on [their] own" in forging a new future for the profession? Might some of the oldsters offer wisdom, even if they cannot offer new ideas or technical know-how?

LIFE ON THE MISSISSIPPI

Mark Twain (1883)

Now when I had mastered the language of this water and had come to know every trifling feature that bordered the great river as familiarly as I knew the letters of the alphabet, I had made a valuable acquisition. But I had lost something, too. I had lost something which could never be restored to me while I lived. All the grace, the beauty, the poetry had gone out of the majestic river! I still keep in mind a certain wonderful sunset which I witnessed when steamboating was new to me. A broad expanse of the river was turned to blood; in the middle distance the red hue brightened into gold, through which a solitary log came floating, black and conspicuous; in one place a long, slanting mark lay sparkling upon the water; in another the surface was broken by boiling, tumbling rings, that were as many-tinted as an opal; where the ruddy flush was faintest, was a smooth spot that was covered with graceful circles and radiating lines, ever so delicately traced; the shore on our left was densely wooded, and the sombre shadow that fell from this forest was broken in one place by a long, ruffled trail that shone like silver; and high above the forest wall a clean-stemmed dead tree waved a single leafy bough that glowed like a flame in the unobstructed splendor that was flowing from the sun. There were graceful curves, reflected images, woody heights, soft distances; and over the whole scene, far and near, the dissolving lights drifted steadily, enriching it, every passing moment, with new marvels of coloring.

I stood like one bewitched. I drank it in, in a speechless rapture. The world was new to me, and I had never seen anything like this at home. But as I have said, a day came when I began to cease from noting the glories and the charms which the moon and the sun and the twilight wrought upon the river's face; another day came when I ceased altogether to note them. Then, if that sunset scene had been repeated, I should have looked upon it without rapture, and should have commented upon it, inwardly, in this fashion: This sun means that we are going to have wind tomorrow; that floating log means that the river is rising, small thanks to it; that slanting mark on the water refers to a bluff reef which is going to kill somebody's steamboat one of these nights, if it keeps on stretching out like that; those tumbling "boils" show a dissolving bar and a changing channel there; the lines and circles in the slick water over yonder are a warning that that troublesome place is shoaling up dangerously; that silver streak in the shadow of the forest is the "break" from a new snag, and he has located himself in the very best place he could have found to fish for steamboats; that tall dead tree, with a single living branch, is not going to last long, and then how is a body ever going to get through this blind place at night without the friendly old landmark?

No, the romance and the beauty were all gone from the river. All the value any feature of it had for me now was the amount of usefulness it could furnish toward compassing the safe piloting of a steamboat. Since those days, I have pitied doctors from my heart. What does the lovely flush in a beauty's cheek mean to a doctor but a "break" that ripples above some deadly disease? Are not all her visible charms sown thick with what are to him the signs and symbols of hidden decay? Does he ever see her beauty at all, or doesn't he simply view her professionally, and comment upon her unwholesome condition all to himself? And doesn't he sometimes wonder whether he has gained most or lost most by learning his trade?

"I STOOD LIKE ONE BEWITCHED."

In my preceding chapters I have tried, by going into the minutiae of the science of piloting, to carry the reader step by step to a comprehension of what the science consists of; and at the same time I have tried to show him that it is a very curious and wonderful science, too, and very worthy of his attention. If I have seemed to love my subject, it is no surprising thing, for I loved the profession far better than any I have followed since, and I took a measureless pride in it. The reason is plain: a pilot, in those days, was the only unfettered and entirely independent human being that lived in the earth. Kings are but the hampered servants of parliament and people; parliaments sit in chains forged by their constituency; the editor of a newspaper cannot be independent, but must work with one hand tied behind him by party and patrons, and be content to utter only half or two thirds of his mind; no clergyman is a free man and may speak the whole truth, regardless of his parish's opinions; writers of all kinds are manacled servants of the public. We write frankly and fearlessly, but then we "modify" before we print. In truth, every man and woman and child has a master, and worries and frets in servitude; but in the day I write of, the

Mississippi pilot had *none*. The captain could stand upon the hurricane deck, in the pomp of a very brief authority, and give him five or six orders while the vessel backed into the stream, and then that skipper's reign was over. The moment that the boat was under way in the river, she was under the sole and unquestioned control of the pilot. He could do with her exactly as he pleased, run her when and whither he chose, and tie her up to the bank whenever his judgment said that that course was best. His movements were entirely free; he consulted no one, he received commands from nobody, he promptly resented even the merest suggestions. Indeed, the law of the United States forbade him to listen to commands or suggestions, rightly considering that the pilot necessarily knew better how to handle the boat than anybody could tell him.

"VERY BRIEF AUTHORITY."

NOTES ON TWAIN

1. ***What's Gained and Lost?*** Law school is famous for its rigor (though many law students find the tales of its horrors to be a bit overblown). Law school is also famous, for good reason, for changing the way students think. There is good and bad in teaching students to "think like a lawyer" and other

aspects of professional socialization associated with law school. How do the excerpts from Twain's *Life on the Mississippi* speak to the experience of law students—about what students gain and lose in the process of becoming a lawyer and entering the profession?

2. ***Independence.*** How do you think being a lawyer stacks up against being a river pilot in terms of independence or autonomy? What are the sources of constraint on lawyers' autonomy, and whose interests do they serve? How do those sources of constraint vary by type of practice, and how are they likely to change in the future?

3. ***Navigating a Career.*** Does the idea of river piloting work as a metaphor for how law students might be able to use information about the opportunities and challenges ahead to navigate successful and rewarding careers in law?

E. SUMMARY

This chapter has asked you to reflect on the future of the legal profession and what it holds for new lawyers. We considered the job market that millennials will encounter and whether and how young lawyers are likely to influence law firms and other institutions that deliver legal services. We surveyed major drivers of change in the legal services industry, including client demands for more value for lower cost, the liberalization of controls over who can compete with lawyers in the legal services market, and technology. We explored predictions about what types of new positions are likely to be available for young lawyers in the coming years and what types of employers are likely to provide those jobs. We suggested perspectives that might bear on how new lawyers respond to the changing conditions in the legal services industry. Finally, we asked you to reflect on how legal education and socialization into the legal profession sometimes changes law students' outlook on life and how knowledge about this changing profession might help them navigate the choices and challenges that lie ahead.

INDEX

References are to Pages